Improving Knowledge Discovery through the Integration of Data Mining Techniques

Muhammad Usman
Shaheed Zulfikar Ali Bhutto Institute of Science and Technology, Pakistan

A volume in the Advances in Data Mining and
Database Management (ADMDM) Book Series

Information Science REFERENCE
An Imprint of IGI Global

Managing Director:	Lindsay Johnston
Managing Editor:	Austin DeMarco
Director of Intellectual Property & Contracts:	Jan Travers
Acquisitions Editor:	Kayla Wolfe
Production Editor:	Christina Henning
Development Editor:	Caitlyn Martin
Typesetter:	Tucker Knerr
Cover Design:	Jason Mull

Published in the United States of America by
Information Science Reference (an imprint of IGI Global)
701 E. Chocolate Avenue
Hershey PA, USA 17033
Tel: 717-533-8845
Fax: 717-533-8661
E-mail: cust@igi-global.com
Web site: http://www.igi-global.com

Library of Congress Cataloging-in-Publication Data

Improving knowledge discovery through the integration of data mining techniques / Muhammad Usman, editor.
   pages cm
 Includes bibliographical references and index.
 ISBN 978-1-4666-8513-0 (hardcover) -- ISBN 978-1-4666-8514-7 (ebook) 1. Knowledge management. 2. Data mining.
I. Usman, Muhammad, 1986-
   HD30.2.I466 2015
   006.3'12--dc23
                          2015010291

This book is published in the IGI Global book series Advances in Data Mining and Database Management (ADMDM) (ISSN: 2327-1981; eISSN: 2327-199X)

British Cataloguing in Publication Data
A Cataloguing in Publication record for this book is available from the British Library.

All work contributed to this book is new, previously-unpublished material. The views expressed in this book are those of the authors, but not necessarily of the publisher.

For electronic access to this publication, please contact: eresources@igi-global.com.

Advances in Data Mining and Database Management (ADMDM) Book Series

David Taniar
Monash University, Australia

ISSN: 2327-1981
EISSN: 2327-199X

MISSION

With the large amounts of information available to organizations in today's digital world, there is a need for continual research surrounding emerging methods and tools for collecting, analyzing, and storing data.

The **Advances in Data Mining & Database Management (ADMDM)** series aims to bring together research in information retrieval, data analysis, data warehousing, and related areas in order to become an ideal resource for those working and studying in these fields. IT professionals, software engineers, academicians and upper-level students will find titles within the ADMDM book series particularly useful for staying up-to-date on emerging research, theories, and applications in the fields of data mining and database management.

COVERAGE

- Association Rule Learning
- Customer Analytics
- Web mining
- Text Mining
- Decision Support Systems
- Enterprise systems
- Web-based information systems
- Heterogeneous and Distributed Databases
- Predictive analysis
- Profiling Practices

IGI Global is currently accepting manuscripts for publication within this series. To submit a proposal for a volume in this series, please contact our Acquisition Editors at Acquisitions@igi-global.com or visit: http://www.igi-global.com/publish/.

Titles in this Series

For a list of additional titles in this series, please visit: www.igi-global.com

Mobile Technologies for Activity-Travel Data Collection and Analysis
Soora Rasouli (Eindhoven University of Technology, The Netherlands) and Harry Timmermans (Eindhoven University of Technology, The Netherlands)
Information Science Reference • copyright 2014 • 325pp • H/C (ISBN: 9781466661707) • US $225.00 (our price)

Biologically-Inspired Techniques for Knowledge Discovery and Data Mining
Shafiq Alam (University of Auckland, New Zealand) Gillian Dobbie (University of Auckland, New Zealand) Yun Sing Koh (University of Auckland, New Zealand) and Saeed ur Rehman (Unitec Institute of Technology, New Zealand)
Information Science Reference • copyright 2014 • 375pp • H/C (ISBN: 9781466660786) • US $265.00 (our price)

Data Mining and Analysis in the Engineering Field
Vishal Bhatnagar (Ambedkar Institute of Advanced Communication Technologies and Research, India)
Information Science Reference • copyright 2014 • 405pp • H/C (ISBN: 9781466660861) • US $225.00 (our price)

Handbook of Research on Cloud Infrastructures for Big Data Analytics
Pethuru Raj (IBM India Pvt Ltd, India) and Ganesh Chandra Deka (Ministry of Labour and Employment, India)
Information Science Reference • copyright 2014 • 570pp • H/C (ISBN: 9781466658646) • US $345.00 (our price)

Innovative Techniques and Applications of Entity Resolution
Hongzhi Wang (Harbin Institute of Technology, China)
Information Science Reference • copyright 2014 • 398pp • H/C (ISBN: 9781466651982) • US $205.00 (our price)

Innovative Document Summarization Techniques Revolutionizing Knowledge Understanding
Alessandro Fiori (IRCC, Institute for Cancer Research and Treatment, Italy)
Information Science Reference • copyright 2014 • 363pp • H/C (ISBN: 9781466650190) • US $175.00 (our price)

Emerging Methods in Predictive Analytics Risk Management and Decision-Making
William H. Hsu (Kansas State University, USA)
Information Science Reference • copyright 2014 • 425pp • H/C (ISBN: 9781466650633) • US $225.00 (our price)

Data Science and Simulation in Transportation Research
Davy Janssens (Hasselt University, Belgium) Ansar-Ul-Haque Yasar (Hasselt University, Belgium) and Luk Knapen (Hasselt University, Belgium)
Information Science Reference • copyright 2014 • 350pp • H/C (ISBN: 9781466649200) • US $175.00 (our price)

DISSEMINATOR of KNOWLEDGE

www.igi-global.com

701 E. Chocolate Ave., Hershey, PA 17033
Order online at www.igi-global.com or call 717-533-8845 x100
To place a standing order for titles released in this series, contact: cust@igi-global.com
Mon-Fri 8:00 am - 5:00 pm (est) or fax 24 hours a day 717-533-8661

Editorial Advisory Board

Table of Contents

Section 1

Section 2

Section 3

Section 4

Detailed Table of Contents

Section 1

Chapter 1

>*Muhammad Usman, Shaheed Zulfikar Ali Bhutto Institute of Science and Technology,*
>*Pakistan*

In high dimensional environments, the sheer size and volume of data poses a number of challenges in order to generate meaningful and informative data cubes. Data cube construction and exploration is a manual process in which analysts are required to visually explore the complex cube structure in order to find interesting information. Data cube construction and exploration has been dealt separately in the literature and in the past there has been very limited amount of work done which would guide the data warehouse designers and analysts to automatically construct and intelligently explore the data cubes. In the recent years, the combined use of data mining techniques and statistical methods has shown promising results in discovering knowledge from large and complex datasets. In this chapter, we propose a methodology that utilizes hierarchical clustering along with Principal Component Analysis (PCA) to generate informative data cubes at different levels of data abstraction. Moreover, automatically ranked cube navigational paths are provided by our proposed methods to enhance knowledge discovery from large data cubes. The methodology has been validated using real world dataset taken from UCI machine learning repository and the results show that the proposed approach assists in cube design and intelligent exploration of interesting cube regions.

Chapter 2

>*M. Asif Naeem, Auckland University of Technology, New Zealand*
>*Noreen Jamil, University of Auckland, New Zealand*

Stream-based join algorithms are a promising technology for modern real-time data warehouses. A particular category of stream-based joins is a semi-stream join where a single stream is joined with a disk based master data. The join operator typically works under limited main memory and this memory is generally not large enough to hold the whole disk-based master data. Recently, a seminal join algorithm called

MESHJOIN (Mesh Join) has been proposed in the literature to process semi-stream data. MESHJOIN is a candidate for a resource-aware system setup. However, MESHJOIN is not very selective. In particular, MESHJOIN does not consider the characteristics of stream data and its performance is suboptimal for skewed stream data. This chapter presents a novel Cached-based Semi-Stream Join (CSSJ) using a cache module. The algorithm is more appropriate for skewed distributions, and we present results for Zipfian distributions of the type that appear in many applications. We conduct a rigorous experimental study to test our algorithm. Our experiments show that CSSJ outperforms MESHJOIN significantly. We also present the cost model for our CSSJ and validate it with experiments.

Multi-Relational Data Mining or MRDM is a growing research area focuses on discovering hidden patterns and useful knowledge from relational databases. While the vast majority of data mining algorithms and techniques look for patterns in a flat single-table data representation, the sub-domain of MRDM looks for patterns that involve multiple tables (relations) from a relational database. This sub-domain has received an increased research attention during the last two decades due to the wide range of possible applications. As a result of that growing attention, many successful multi-relational data mining algorithms and techniques were presented. This chapter presents a comprehensive review about multi-relational data mining. It discusses the different approaches researchers have followed to explore the relational search space while highlighting some of the most significant challenges facing researchers working in this sub-domain. The chapter also describes number of MRDM systems that have been developed during the last few years and discusses some future research directions in this sub-domain.

Multi-dimensional outlier detection (MOD) over data streams is one of the most significant data stream mining techniques. When multivariate data are streaming in high speed, outliers are to be detected efficiently and accurately. Conventional outlier detection method is based on observing the full dataset and its statistical distribution. The data is assumed stationary. However, this conventional method has an inherent limitation—it always assumes the availability of the entire dataset. In modern applications, especially those that operate in the real time environment, the data arrive in the form of live data feed; they are dynamic and ever evolving in terms of their statistical distribution and concepts. Outlier detection should no longer be done in batches, but in incremental manner. In this chapter, we investigate into this important concept of MOD. In particular, we evaluate the effectiveness of a collection of incremental learning algorithms which are the underlying pattern recognition mechanisms for MOD. Specifically, we combine incremental learning algorithms into three types of MOD - Global Analysis, Cumulative Analysis and Lightweight Analysis with Sliding Window. Different classification algorithms are put under test for performance comparison.

Metaheuristics have lately gained popularity among researchers. Their underlying designs are inspired by biological entities and their behaviors, e.g. schools of fish, colonies of insects, and other land animals etc. They have been used successfully in optimization applications ranging from financial modeling, image processing, resource allocations, job scheduling to bioinformatics. In particular, metaheuristics have been proven in many combinatorial optimization problems. So that it is not necessary to attempt all possible candidate solutions to a problem via exhaustive enumeration and evaluation which is computationally intractable. The aim of this paper is to highlight some recent research related to metaheuristics and to discuss how they can enhance the efficacy of data mining algorithms. An upmost challenge in Data Mining is combinatorial optimization that, often lead to performance degradation and scalability issues. Two case studies are presented, where metaheuristics improve the accuracy of classification and clustering by avoiding local optima.

Artificial immune system (AIS) is a paradigm inspired by processes and metaphors of natural immune system (NIS). There is a rapidly growing interest in AIS approaches to machine learning and especially in the domain of optimization. Of particular interest is the way human body responds to diseases and pathogens as well as adapts to remain immune for long periods after a disease has been combated. In this chapter, we are presenting a novel multilayered natural immune system (NIS) inspired algorithms in the domain of optimization. The proposed algorithm uses natural immune system components such as B-cells, Memory cells and Antibodies; and processes such as negative clonal selection and affinity maturation to find multiple local optimum points. Another benefit this algorithm presents is the presence of immunological memory that is in the form of specific memory cells which keep track of previously explored solutions. The algorithm is evaluated on two well-known numeric functions to demonstrate the applicability.

Chapter 7

In recent years, several artificial immune system (AIS) approaches have been proposed for unsupervised learning. Generally, in these approaches antibodies (or B-cells) are considered as clusters and antigens are data samples or instances. Moreover, antigens are trapped through free-floating antibodies or immunoglobulins. In all these approaches, hypermutation plays an important role. Hypermutation is responsible for producing mutated copies of stimulated antibodies/B-cells to capture similar antigens with higher affinity (similarity) measure and responsible to create diverse pool of solutions. Humoral-Mediated Artificial Immune System (HAIS) is an example of such algorithms. However, there is currently little understanding about the effectiveness of hypermutation operator in AIS approaches. In this chapter, we investigate the role of the hypermutation operator as well as affinity threshold (AT) parameters in order to achieve efficient clustering solutions. We propose a three-step methodology to examine the importance of hypermutation and the AT parameters in AIS approaches to clustering using basic concepts of HAIS algorithm. Here, the role of hypermutation in under-fitting and over-fitting the data will be discussed in the context of measure of entropy.

Chapter 8

Identification of cancer pathways is the central goal in the cancer gene expression data analysis. Data mining refers to the process analyzing huge data in order to find useful pattern. Data classification is the process of identifying common properties among a set of objects and grouping them into different classes. A cellular automaton is a discrete, dynamical system with simple uniformly interconnected cells. Cellular automata are used in data mining for reasons such as all decisions are made locally depend on the state of the cell and the states of neighboring cells. A high-speed, low-cost pattern-classifier, built around a sparse network referred to as cellular automata (ca) is implemented. Lif-stimulated gene regulatory network involved in breast cancer has been simulated using cellular automata to obtain biomarker genes. Our model outputs the desired genes among inputs with highest priority, which are analysed for their functional involvement in relevant oncological functional enrichment analysis. This approach is a novel one to discover cancer biomarkers in cellular spaces.

Section 3

Chapter 9

The amount of data collected across various sources in real life situations is never in its complete form. That is, it is never precise or it never gives definite knowledge. It always contains uncertainty and vagueness. Therefore, most of our traditional tools for formal modelling, reasoning and computing can not handle efficiently. Therefore, it is very challenging to organize this data in formal system which provides information in more relevant, useful, and structured manner. There are many techniques available for knowledge extraction form this high dimensional data. This chapter discusses various rough computing based knowledge extraction techniques to obtain meaningful knowledge from large amount of data. A real life example is provided to show the viability of the proposed research.

Chapter 10

Active faults are sources of earthquakes and one of them is north fault of Tabriz in the northwest of Iran. The activation of faults can harm humans' life and constructions. The analysis of the seismic data in active regions can be helpful in dealing with earthquake hazards and devising prevention strategies. In this chapter, structure of earthquake events along with application of various intelligent data mining algorithms for earthquake prediction are studied. Main focus is on categorizing the seismic data of local regions according to the events' location using clustering algorithms for classification and then using intelligent artificial neural network for cluster prediction. As a result, the target data were clustered to six groups and proposed model with 10 fold cross validation yielded accuracy of 98.3%. Also, as a case study, the tectonic stress on concentration zones of Tabriz fault has been identified and five features of the events were used. Finally, the most important points have been proposed for evaluation of the nonlinear model predictions as future directions.

Chapter 11

Tayyeba Naseer, PMAS Arid Agriculture University, Pakistan
Sohail Asghar, COMSATs Institute of Information Technology, Pakistan

Classification is a supervised learning technique in data mining classify historical data. The decision tree is easy method for inductive inference. The decision tree induction process has three major steps – first complete decision tree is constructed to classify all examples in the training data, the second is pruning this tree to decrease misclassification rate and the third is processing the pruned tree to improve the classification. In this chapter, the empirical comparison of pruning the tree created by C4.5 and the fuzzy C4.5 algorithm. C4.5 and Fuzzy C4.5 decision tree algorithms are implemented using the JAVA language in Eclipse tool. In this chapter, first decision tree is built using C4.5 and Fuzzy C4.5 and five famous pruning techniques is used to evaluate trees and the comparison is achieved between pruning methods for refining the size and accuracy of a decision tree. Cost-complexity pruning produce the smaller tree with minimum increase in error for C4.5 and Fuzzy C4.5 decision trees.

Chapter 12

Mohsin Iqbal, University Institute of Information Technology, Pakistan
Saif Ur Rehman, University Institute of Information Technology, Pakistan
Saira Gillani, Corvinus University of Budapest, Hungary
Sohail Asghar, COMSATS Institute of Information Technology, Pakistan

The key objective of the chapter would be to study the classification accuracy, using feature selection with machine learning algorithms. The dimensionality of the data is reduced by implementing Feature selection and accuracy of the learning algorithm improved. We test how an integrated feature selection could affect the accuracy of three classifiers by performing feature selection methods. The filter effects show that Information Gain (IG), Gain Ratio (GR) and Relief-f, and wrapper effect show that Bagging and Naive Bayes (NB), enabled the classifiers to give the highest escalation in classification accuracy about the average while reducing the volume of unnecessary attributes. The achieved conclusions can advise the machine learning users, which classifier and feature selection methods to use to optimize the classification accuracy, and this can be important, especially at risk-sensitive applying Machine Learning whereas in the one of the aim to reduce costs of collecting, processing and storage of unnecessary data.

Umair Abdullah, Foundation University, Pakistan
Aftab Ahmed, Foundation University, Pakistan
Sohail Asghar, Comsats Institute of Information Technology, Pakistan
Kashif Zafar, National University of Computer and Emerging Sciences, Pakistan

Most of the data mining projects generate information (summarized in the form of graphs and charts) for business executives and decision makers; however it leaves to the choice of decision makers either to use it or disregard it. The manual use of the extracted knowledge limits the effectiveness of data mining technology considerably. This chapter proposes an architecture, in which data mining module is utilized to provide continuous supply of knowledge to a rule based expert system. Proposed approach solves the knowledge acquisition problem of rule based systems and also enhances effective utilization of data mining techniques (i.e. by supplying extracted knowledge to rule based system for automated use). The chapter describes the details of a data mining driven rule based expert system applied in medical billing domain. Main modules of the system along with the final analysis of performance of the system have also been presented.

Tasawar Hussain, Mohammad Ali Jinnah University, Pakistan
Sohail Asghar, COMSATS Institute of Information Technology, Pakistan

The web based applications are maturing and gaining the confidence of their users gradually, however, www still lacks the mechanism to stop the hackers. The implementing the adhesive security measures such as intrusion deduction systems and firewalls, are no more useful breaker for online frauds. The Web Backtracking Technique (WBT) is proposed for fraud detection in online financial applications by applying the hierarchical sessionization technique on the web log file. The web log Hierarchical Sessionization enhances the focused groups of users from web log and paves the path for in-depth visualization for knowledge discovery. User clicks are compared with user profiles for change in previous user click records. Those transactions which do not conform to business rules are stopped from business activities. The WBT analyzes suspicious behavior and will produce reports for security and risk mitigation purposes Furthermore, suspicious transactions are mined for the up-gradation of business rules from hierarchical sessionization. The proposed WBT is validated against the university web log data.

Noureen Zafar, University Institute of Information Technology, Pakistan
Saif Ur Rehma, University Institute of Information Technology, Pakistan
Saira Gillani, Corvinus University of Budapest, Hungary
Sohail Asghar, COMSATS Institute of Information Technology, Pakistan

In this article, segmentation of weeds and crops has been investigated by using supervised learning based on feed forward neural network. The images have been taken from the satellite imaginary for a specified region on the geographical space in Pakistan and perform edge detection by classical image processing scheme. The obtained samples are classified by data mining, based on artificial neural network model based on linear activation function at the input and output layer while threshold ramp function at hidden layer. A scenario based results are obtained at a huge samples of the weeds of the corn field and crop in the form of the mean square error based fitness evaluation function. The given scheme has the perks on the existed schemes as applicability of the designed framework, ease in implementation and less hardware needed for implementation.

Chapter 16

Rizwan Aqeel, University Institute of Information Technology, Pakistan
Saif Ur Rehman, University Institute of Information Technology, Pakistan
Saira Gillani, Corvinus University of Budapest, Hungary
Sohail Asghar, COMSATS Institute of Information Technology, Pakistan

This chapter focuses on an Autonomous Ground Vehicle (AGV), also known as intelligent vehicle, which is a vehicle that can navigate without human supervision. AGV navigation over an unstructured road is a challenging task and is known research problem. This chapter is to detect road area from an unstructured environment by applying a proposed classification model. The Proposed model is sub divided into three stages: (1) - preprocessing has been performed in the initial stage; (2) - road area clustering has been done in the second stage; (3) - Finally, road pixel classification has been achieved. Furthermore, combination of classification as well as clustering is used in achieving our goals. K-means clustering algorithm is used to discover biggest cluster from road scene, second big cluster area has been classified as road or non road by using the well-known technique support vector machine. The Proposed approach is validated from extensive experiments carried out on RGB dataset, which shows that the successful detection of road area and is robust against diverse road conditions such as unstructured nature, different weather and lightening variations.

Foreword

Data of different formats and from multiple sources well beyond traditional databases are being created at alarming rates. This is in part attributed to Web 2.0 and the explosive growth in the number of social media users. However, different segments of our society, such as business, industry, commerce, education, entertainment, government, biomedicine, space exploration, etc., all contribute to the growth of data. This phenomenon presents both challenges and opportunities.

In an age often characterized as overloaded with data, it is more important than ever before to be able to make sense of the data and do something useful with the data. Data mining, and in particular data mining for knowledge discovery has been a scientific discipline within Computer Science for a long time, but recently it is increasingly been tackled as a multidisciplinary issue.

This book represents a timely and important contribution to the field by presenting state-of-the-art research in this important area. In particular, contributing authors describe how knowledge discovery can be improved by integrating data mining techniques. Notable techniques featured in the book include multi-relational data mining, incremental learning, variants of C4.5, artificial immune system, rough computing, metaheuristics, etc. The list is not exhaustive. Together, the book forms a body of knowledge that can have applications to many real world problems. These include farming and food production (separating crops and weeds), healthcare (cancer pathways), finance, hazards aversion (earthquakes).

I am pleased to recommend this book to researchers and practitioners not just in the fields of data mining and knowledge discovery, but also others who work with large amounts of data for science, healthcare, and many other forms of human endeavors.

A.C.M Fong
University of Glasgow, UK

A.C.M. Fong *is Deputy Director of University of Glasgow's Computing Science Program in Singapore. He is a Fellow of IET, Chartered Engineer (CEng, UK) and European Engineer (Eur Ing). He holds four degrees in Electrical Engineering and Computer Science from three universities: Imperial College London, University of Oxford, and University of Auckland. His research in Information and Systems Engineering has led to the publication of two books, ten book sections, and 170 papers in leading journals and conference proceedings. He served/serves on the editorial boards of several international journals, such as Journal of Software, Journal of Advances in IT, and IEEE Transactions on Consumer Electronics.*

Preface

1. INTRODUCTION

A huge amount of data of different formats is continually being collected from multiple sources. This fast growth in data has highlighted the requirement of developing new tools and techniques that can intelligently assist analysts to discover meaningful and useful knowledge. Data mining for knowledge discovery has emerged as a promising discipline in Computer Science in order to automatically extract patterns representing knowledge from large datasets. Recently, knowledge discovery using data mining has been tackled as a multidisciplinary issue.

This book explores the tools and techniques of improving knowledge discovery using diverse data mining methods. It is a timely and important contribution to the field as it covers a wide range of state-of-the-art research in this rapidly growing area. In particular, contributing authors describe how knowledge discovery can be improved by integrating data mining techniques. Notable techniques featured in the book include multi-relational data mining, incremental learning, variants of C4.5, artificial immune system, rough computing, metaheuristics, etc. The list is not exhaustive. Together, the book forms a body of knowledge that can have applications to many real world problems. These include farming and food production (separating crops and weeds), healthcare (cancer pathways), finance, hazards aversion (earthquakes).

This preface introduces the general context, the aims and the rationale of this book with a brief description of each chapter's contents. The motivation for integrating data mining, data warehousing and machine learning in non-conventional application domains for improving the knowledge discovery process is given.

1.1 Knowledge Discovery from Large Datasets

Knowledge discovery from large datasets is the result of an exploratory process involving the application of various algorithmic procedures for manipulating data (Bernstein, Provost et al. 2005). It aims to extract valid, novel, potentially useful, and ultimately understandable patterns from data (Fayyad, Piatetsky-Shapiro et al. 1996). Data mining and data warehousing are two key technologies for discovering knowledge from large datasets. Data mining enables the discovery of hidden trends from large datasets, while data warehousing provides for interactive and exploratory analysis of data through the use of various data aggregation methods.

In the past several years, a wide range of data mining techniques have made significant contributions to the field of knowledge discovery in a number of domains. In the banking sector, these techniques are used for loan payment prediction, customer credit policy analysis, classification of customers for targeted marketing, and the detection of money laundering schemes and other financial crimes. Similarly, in the retail industry, such techniques are used in the analysis of product sales and customer retention. In the telecommunication industry these techniques help in identifying and comparing data traffic, system workload, resource usage, profit and fraudulent pattern analysis (Han and Kamber 2006).

Likewise, data warehousing has contributed extensively as a key technology for complex data analysis, decision support and automatic extraction of knowledge from huge data repositories (Nguyen, Tjoa et al. 2005). It provides analysts with a competitive advantage by providing relevant information to enhance strategic decision making. Moreover, warehousing has reduced costs by tracking trends, patterns, and exceptions over long periods in a consistent and reliable manner. Due to sophisticated analytical powers, these warehouse systems are being used broadly in many sectors such as financial services, consumer goods and retail, manufacturing, education, medical, media, and telecommunication. More recently, there has been an increasing research interest in the knowledge engineering community towards integrating the two technologies (Goil and Choudhary 2001; Liu and Guo 2001; You, Dillon et al. 2001; Zhen and Minyi 2001; Wang, Feng et al. 2002; Ohmori, Naruse et al. 2007; Usman and Pears 2010; Usman and Asghar 2011).

1.2 Integrated Use of Data Mining and Data Warehousing for Improving Knowledge Discovery

Both data mining and data warehousing technologies have essentially the same set of objectives and can potentially benefit from each other's methods to facilitate knowledge discovery. Each technology is mature in its own right, and despite the very clear synergy between these two technologies, they have developed largely independent of each other.

The integrated use of data mining and data warehousing techniques such as Online Analytical Processing (OLAP) has received considerable attention from researchers and practitioners alike, as they are key tools used in knowledge discovery from large data datasets (Han 1998; Sapia, Höfling et al. 1999; Goil and Choudhary 2001; You, Dillon et al. 2001; Zhen and Minyi 2001; Ohmori, Naruse et al. 2007; Zubcoff, Pardillo et al. 2007; Pardillo, Zubcoff et al. 2008). (Usman, Asghar et al. 2009) used a hierarchical clustering technique in conjunction with multidimensional scaling (Cox and Cox 2008) to design schema at different levels of data abstraction. They developed an iterative method that explores the similarities and differences in information contained across consecutive levels in the cluster hierarchy. The presentation of such information at different levels of abstraction provides decision makers with a better understanding of the patterns and trends present in the data. Although, a variety of integrated approaches have been proposed in the literature to mine large datasets for discovering knowledge. However, a number of issues remain unresolved in the previous work (Sarawagi, Agrawal et al. 1998; Sarawagi 2001; Kumar, Gangopadhyay et al. 2008; Ordonez and Zhibo 2009), especially on intelligent data analysis front.

The integrated use of data mining and data warehousing techniques such as Online Analytical Processing (OLAP) has received considerable attention from researchers and practitioners alike, as they are key tools used in knowledge discovery from large data datasets. Although, a variety of integrated approaches have been proposed in the literature to mine large datasets for discovering knowledge. However, a number of issues remain unresolved in the previous work, especially on intelligent data analysis front.

This book aims to discuss and address the difficulties and challenges that of seamless integration of the two core disciplines of knowledge discovery. The editor will seek chapters that address different methods and techniques of integration for enhancing the overall goal of knowledge discovery. Additionally, the book will explore the impact of such techniques in a variety of application domains ranging from government, education, science, agriculture engineering etc.

1.3 Aims and Objectives

The primary objective of this book is to provide insights concerning the integration of data mining and data warehousing for enhancing the knowledge discovery process. This is a front-line and important topic that is of interest in both industry and knowledge engineering research community. The current approaches of knowledge discovery in industry are ad-hoc where data mining and warehousing is dealt separately. There is no standard rule of thumb in integrating these two disciplines. This book reports on the existing gaps in this area and presents the novel approaches to bridge the existing gaps.

1.4 Target Audience and Topics Covered

The target audience of this book includes decision makers, academicians, researchers, advanced-level students, technology developers, and Business Intelligence (BI) professionals will find this text useful in furthering their research exposure to relevant topics in knowledge discovery and assisting in furthering their own research efforts in this field.

This book covers the following topics relating to data mining integration with data warehousing.

- Data mining techniques: clustering, classification, association rules, decision trees, etc.
- Data and knowledge representation
- Knowledge discovery framework and process, including pre- and post-processing
- Integration of data warehousing, OLAP and data mining
- Exploring data analysis, inference of causes, prediction
- Interactive data exploration/visualization and discovery
- Data Mining, Data warehousing and OLAP tools
- Data warehousing applications: corporate, scientific, government, healthcare, bioinformatics.
- Data mining applications: bioinformatics, e-commerce, Web, intrusion/fraud detection, finance, healthcare, marketing, telecommunications, etc.
- Data mining support for designing information systems

I hope this book will highlight the need for growth and research in the area of improving knowledge discovery through the integrated use of data mining techniques. This volume consists of sixteen chapters in four sections.

Chapter 1, "**Integration of Data Mining and Statistical Methods for Intelligent Cube Construction and Exploration**" by *Muhammad Usman, Shaheed Zulfikar Ali Bhutto Institute of Science and Technology, Pakistan,* identified that data cube construction and exploration has been dealt separately in the literature and there is very limited amount of work done in the past which guides the data warehouse designers and analysts to automatically construct and intelligently explore the data cubes. A novel methodology has been proposed that utilizes hierarchical clustering and Principal Component Analysis (PCA) to generate informative data cubes at different levels of data abstraction. Moreover, automatically ranked cube navigational paths are provided by their proposed methodology to enhance knowledge discovery from large data cubes. The methodology has been validated using real world dataset taken from UCI machine learning repository and the results show that the proposed approach assists in cube design and intelligent exploration of interesting cube regions.

Chapter 2, "**Online Processing of End-User Data in Real-Time Data Warehousing**" by *Muhammad Asif Naeem, Auckland University of Technology, New Zealand,* highlights that stream-based join algorithms are a promising technology for modern real-time data warehouses. A particular category of stream-based joins is a semi-stream join where a single stream is joined with a disk based master data. The join operator typically works under limited main memory and this memory is generally not large enough to hold the whole disk-based master data. Recently, a seminal join algorithm called MESHJOIN (Mesh Join) has been proposed in the literature to process semi-stream data. MESHJOIN is a candidate for a resource-aware system setup. However, MESHJOIN is not very selective. In particular, MESH-JOIN does not consider the characteristics of stream data and its performance is suboptimal for skewed stream data. The author presents a novel Cached-based Semi-Stream Join (CSSJ) using a cache module in this chapter. The proposed algorithm is more appropriate for skewed distributions, and the results are presented for *Zipfian* distributions of the type that appear in many applications. Rigorous experimental study has also been conducted to test the proposed algorithm. Experiments show that CSSJ outperforms MESHJOIN significantly.

Chapter 3, "**Multi-Relational Data Mining: A Comprehensive Survey**" by *Ali H. Gazala, Auckland University of Technology, New Zealand* and *Waseem Ahmad, Auckland University of Technology, New Zealand* provides a comprehensive survey on growing are of Multi-Relational Data Mining or MRDM. This area focuses on discovering hidden patterns and useful knowledge from relational databases. While the vast majority of data mining algorithms and techniques look for patterns in a flat single-table data representation, the sub-domain of MRDM looks for patterns that involve multiple tables (relations) from a relational database. This chapter discusses the different approaches researchers have followed to explore the relational search space while highlighting some of the most significant challenges facing researchers working in this sub-domain. The chapter also describes number of MRDM systems that have been developed during the last few years and discusses some future research directions in this sub-domain.

Chapter 4, "**Comparative Study of Incremental Learning Algorithms in Multidimensional Outlier Detection on Data Stream**" by *Simon Fong, University of Macau, Macau SAR* focused on multidimensional outlier detection (MOD) over data streams. MOD is one of the most significant data stream mining techniques and when multivariate data are streaming in high speed, outliers are to be detected efficiently and accurately. They highlighted that the conventional outlier detection method is based on observing the full dataset and its statistical distribution. The data is assumed stationary. However, this conventional method has an inherent limitation—it always assumes the availability of the entire dataset. In modern applications, especially those that operate in the real time environment, the data arrive in the form of live data feed; they are dynamic and ever evolving in terms of their statistical distribution and concepts. Hence, it becomes unrealistic for an outlier detection method to wait for all the data when fresh data are streaming in rapidly and continuously. In this chapter, they evaluate the effectiveness of a collection of incremental learning algorithms which are the underlying pattern recognition mechanisms for MOD. Furthermore, their performance has been tested in processing some real-life samples of real time data feed, for multidimensional outlier detection.

Chapter 5, **"Advances of Applying Meta-heuristics to Data Mining Techniques"** by *Simon Fong, University of Macau, Macau, Jinyan Li, University of Macau, Macau* and *Athanasios V. Vasilakos, Kuwait University, Kuwait* presents the importance of applying Meta-heuristics and their successful use in optimization applications ranging from financial modeling, image processing, resource allocations, job scheduling to bioinformatics. In particular, meta-heuristics have been proven in many combinatorial optimization problems. The aim of this chapter is to highlight some recent research related to meta-heuristics and to discuss how they can enhance the efficacy of data mining algorithms. An upmost challenge in Data Mining is combinatorial optimization that, often lead to performance degradation and scalability issues. Two case studies are presented, where meta-heuristics improve the accuracy of classification and clustering by avoiding local optima.

Chapter 6, **"Artificial Immune Optimization Algorithm"** by *Waseem Ahmad, International College of Auckland, New Zealand* discusses the rapid interest in utilizing Artificial Immune System (AIS) approaches to machine learning, especially in the domain of optimization. Of particular interest is the way the human body responds to diseases and pathogens as well as adapts to remain immune for long periods after a disease has been combated. In this chapter, a novel multilayered natural immune system (NIS) inspired algorithms in the domain of optimization has been presented. The proposed algorithm uses natural immune system components such as B-cells, Memory cells and Antibodies; and processes such as negative clonal selection and affinity maturation to find multiple local optimum points. Another benefit this algorithm is the presence of immunological memory that is in the form of specific memory cells which keep track of previously explored solutions.

Chapter 7, **"The Role of Hyper-Mutation and Affinity Maturation in AIS Approaches to Clustering"** by *Waseem Ahmad, International College of Auckland, New Zealand* and *Ajit Narayan, Auckland University of Technology, New Zealand* presents the importance of hyper-mutation as it is responsible for producing mutated copies of stimulated antibodies to capture similar antigens with higher affinity (similarity) measure. Humoral-Mediated Artificial Immune System (HAIS) is an example of such algorithms. Authors believe that there is currently little understanding about the effectiveness of hyper-mutation operator in AIS approaches. In this chapter, they investigate the role of the hyper-mutation operator as well as affinity threshold (AT) parameters in order to achieve efficient clustering. Furthermore, they propose a three-step methodology to examine the importance of hyper-mutation and the AT parameter in AIS approaches to clustering using basic concepts of HAIS algorithm.

Chapter 8, **"Cancer Pathway Network Analysis Using Cellular Automata"** by *Kalyan Mahata, Government College of Engineering and Leather Technology, India* and *Anasua Sarkar, Government College of Engineering and Leather Technology, India* presents a novel approach to discover cancer biomarkers in cellular spaces. Furthermore, the authors elaborate the central goal of cancer pathway identification in cancer gene expression data analysis. Authors use Cellular Automata in Data Mining for reasons such as all decisions are made locally depend on the state of the cell and the states of neighboring cells. In this chapters, a high-speed, low-cost pattern-classifier, built around a sparse network referred to as Cellular Automata (CA) is implemented. LIF-stimulated gene regulatory network involved in breast cancer has been simulated using cellular automata to obtain biomarker genes. Their proposed model outputs the desired genes among inputs with highest priorities, which are analyzed for their functional involvement in relevant oncological functional enrichment analysis.

Chapter 9, **"Knowledge Extraction from Information Systems through Rough Computing"** by *Debi Prasanna Acharjya, VIT University, India* presents the fact that the amount of data collected across various sources in real life situations is never in its complete form. That is, it is never precise or it never gives definite knowledge. It always contains uncertainty and vagueness. Therefore, most of our traditional tools for formal modeling, reasoning and computing cannot handle efficiently. As a result, it is very challenging to organize this data in formal system which provides information in more relevant, useful, and structured manner. This chapter discusses various rough computing based knowledge extraction techniques to obtain meaningful knowledge from large amount of data. A real life example is provided to show the viability of the proposed research.

Chapter 10, **"Data Mining Techniques on Earthquake Data: Recent Data Mining Approaches"** by *Negar Sadat Soleimani Zakeri, University of Tabriz, Iran* and *Saeid Pashazadeh, University of Tabriz, Iran* explains the importance of analyzing seismic data using data mining techniques. Authors believe that the analysis of the seismic data in active regions can be helpful in dealing with earthquake hazards and devising prevention strategies. In this chapter, the authors obtained the seismic data of local regions according to the location parameters using relevant algorithms and intelligent systems. For this purpose, as a case study, the tectonic stress on concentration zones of Tabriz, Iran fault zones which are the most likely locking places of the fault at the present time, have been identified.

Chapter 11, **"An Empirical Comparison of C4.5 and Fuzzy C4.5 with Pruning Methods"** by *Tayyeba Naseer, UIIT, PMAS Arid Agriculture University, Pakistan* and *Sohail Asghar, COMSATS Institute of Information Technology, Pakistan* focuses on the empirical comparison of pruning the decision tree created by C4.5 and the fuzzy C4.5 algorithm. The first decision tree is constructed using C4.5 and Fuzzy C4.5 and then five famous pruning techniques are applied to trees and the comparison is performed between pruning methods for improving the size and accuracy of a decision tree. Cost-complexity pruning produce the smaller tree with minimum increase in error for C4.5 and Fuzzy C4.5 decision trees.

Chapter 12, **"An Empirical Evaluation of Feature Selection Methods"** by *Mohsin Iqbal, University Institute of Information Technology, PMAS Arid Agriculture University, Pakistan, Saif Ur Rehman, University Institute of Information Technology, PMAS Arid Agriculture University, Pakistan, Saira Gillani, Corvinus University Budapest, Hungary* and *Sohail Asghar, COMSATS Institute of Information Technology, Pakistan* studies the classification accuracy using feature selection with machine learning algorithms. Authors tested how an integrated feature selection could affect the accuracy of three classifiers by performing feature selection methods. The filter effects show that Information Gain (IG), Gain Ratio (GR) and Relief-f, and wrapper effect show that Bagging and Naive Bayes (NB), enabled the classifiers to give the highest escalation in classification accuracy about the average while reducing the volume of unnecessary attributes. The achieved conclusions assist machine learning users, which classifier and feature selection methods to use to optimize the classification accuracy.

Chapter 13, **"Data Mining Driven Rule Based Expert System for Medical Billing Compliance: A Case Study"** by *Umair Abdullah, Foundation University, Pakistan, Aftab Ahmed, Foundation University, Pakistan, Sohail Asghar, COMSATS Institute of Information Technology, Pakistan* and *Kashif Zafar, FAST, National University of Computer and Emerging Sciences, Pakistan* discusses that the 'automated' extraction process of data mining at the end depends upon 'manual' use of the information. Most of the data mining works generate information (summarized in the form graphs and charts) for decision makers; however it leaves to the choice of decision makers either to use it or to disregard the extracted information. The manual use of the mined knowledge limits the utilization of data mining technology considerably. This chapter proposes a framework, in which data mining module is utilized to provide continuous supply of knowledge to a rule based expert system. Their proposed approach solves the knowledge acquisition problem of rule based systems and also enhances effective utilization of data mining techniques by supplying extracted knowledge to rule based system for automated use. The proposed framework highlights the details of rule based expert system and its application in medical billing domain.

Chapter 14, **"A Web Backtracking Technique for Fraud Detection in Financial Applications"** by *Tasawar Hussain, Abasyn University, Pakistan* and *Sohail Asghar, COMSATS Institute of Information Technology, Pakistan* describes that the web log files are the rich source of information and can be analyzed to detect the fraudulent clicks and are helpful to web based businesses for risk management. In this chapter a Web Backtracking Technique (WBT) has been proposed by applying data mining techniques on this web log file. The proposed WBT will analyze suspicious behavior and will produce reports for security and risk mitigation purposes. The proposed research will alarm the suspicious (IP, Time, Country, Browser used, Operating system) transaction through analyzing the user clicks and will stop that particular transaction without affecting the normal web applications.

Chapter 15, **"Segmentation of Crops and Weeds Using Supervised Learning Technique"** by *Noureen Zafar, University Institute of Information Technology, PMAS Arid Agriculture University, Pakistan, Saif Ur Rehman, University Institute of Information Technology, PMAS Arid Agriculture University, Pakistan, Saira Gillani, Corvinus University Budapest, Hungary* and *Sohail Asghar, COMSATS Institute of Information Technology, Pakistan* In this chapter, segmentation of weeds and crops has been investigated by using supervised learning based on feed forward neural network. The images are to be taken from the satellite imaginary for a specified region on the geographical space in Pakistan and perform edge detection by classical image processing scheme. The obtained samples are classified with by data mining based on artificial neural network model based on linear activation function at the input and output layer while threshold ramp function at hidden layer. A scenario based results are obtained at a huge samples of the weeds of the corn field and crop in the form of the mean square error based fitness evaluation function. The given scheme has the perks on the existed schemes as applicability of the designed framework, ease in implementation and less hardware needed for implementation.

Chapter 16, **"A Supervised Learning Model for Perception of AGV in Unstructured Environment"** by *Muhammad Rizwan Aqeel, University Institute of Information Technology, PMAS Arid Agriculture University, Pakistan, Saif Ur Rehman, University Institute of Information Technology, PMAS Arid Agriculture University, Pakistan, Saira Gillani, Corvinus University Budapest, Hungary* and *Sohail Asghar, COMSATS Institute of Information Technology, Pakistan* focuses on an Autonomous Ground Vehicle (AGV), also known as intelligent vehicle, is a vehicle that can navigate without human guidance. AGV has a different system structure design according to their applications. The structure of AGV includes perception and a central element which extracts and determine parameters such as road shape, road type, road size, road estimation, road segmentation, etc. Furthermore, the output of perception parameters can be directly used for controlling and planning phase of AGV. Classification, a well-explored area of data mining, is used to classify the new instance in the known categories. This chapter focuses especially on unstructured environment by presenting a classification model to improve road analysis. As an Editor, I hope this book will provide readers some specific challenge that motivates the development and enhancement of knowledge discovery through the integrated use of data mining techniques. I also hope that this book will serve as an introductory material to the researchers and practitioners interested in this promising area of research.

Muhammad Usman
Shaheed Zulfikar Ali Bhutto Institute of Science and Technology, Pakistan
January 2015

REFERENCES

Bernstein, A., Provost, F., & Hill, S. (2005). Toward intelligent assistance for a data mining process: An ontology-based approach for cost-sensitive classification. *Knowledge and Data Engineering, 17*(4), 503–518. doi:10.1109/TKDE.2005.67

Cox, M. A. A., & Cox, T. F. (2008). Multidimensional scaling. Handbook of data visualization (pp. 315-347).

Fayyad, U., Piatetsky-Shapiro, G., & Smyth, P. (1996). The KDD process for extracting useful knowledge from volumes of data. *Communications of the ACM, 39*(11), 27–34. doi:10.1145/240455.240464

Goil, S., & Choudhary, A. (2001). Parsimony: An infrastructure for parallel multidimensional analysis and data mining. *Journal of Parallel and Distributed Computing, 61*(3), 285–321. doi:10.1006/jpdc.2000.1691

Han, J. (1998). Towards on-line analytical mining in large databases. *SIGMOD Record, 27*(1), 97–107. doi:10.1145/273244.273273

Han, J., & Kamber, M. (2006). *Data mining: concepts and techniques.* Morgan Kaufmann.

Kumar, N., Gangopadhyay, A., Karabatis, G., Bapna, S., & Chen, Z. (2008). *Navigation Rules for Exploring Large Multidimensional Data Cubes. Data Warehousing and Mining: Concepts, Methodologies, Tools, and Applications* (pp. 1334–1354). Hershey: IGI Global. doi:10.4018/978-1-59904-951-9.ch076

Liu, Z., & Guo, M. (2001). A proposal of integrating data mining and on-line analytical processing in data warehouse. *Proceedings of ICII 2001 International Conferences* (Vol 3: 146-151). Beijing, China. doi:10.1109/ICII.2001.983049

Nguyen, T. M., Tjoa, A. M., & Trujillo, J. (2005). *Data warehousing and knowledge discovery: A chronological view of research challenges* (pp. 530–535). doi:10.1007/11546849_52

Ohmori, T., Naruse, M., & Hoshi, M. (2007). A New Data Cube for Integrating Data Mining and OLAP. *Data Engineering Workshop 23rd IEEE International Conference.* doi:10.1109/ICDEW.2007.4401082

Ohmori, T., Naruse, M., & Hoshi, M. (2007). A New Data Cube for Integrating Data Mining and OLAP. *Data Engineering Workshop 23rd IEEE International Conference,* (pp. 896-903). doi:10.1109/ICDEW.2007.4401082

Ordonez, C., & Zhibo, C. (2009). Evaluating Statistical Tests on OLAP Cubes to Compare Degree of Disease. *IEEE Transactions, 13*(5), 756–765. PMID:19273013

Pardillo, J., Zubcoff, J., Mazón, J. N., & Trujillo, J. (2008). Applying MDA to integrate mining techniques into data warehouses: A time series case study. [Las Vegas, USA.]. *Proceedings of MMIS, 08,* 47–53.

Sapia, C., Höfling, G., Müller, M., Hausdorf, C., Stoyan, H., & Grimmer, U. (1999). On supporting the data warehouse design by data mining techniques. *Workshop on Data Mining and Data Warehousing.* Magdeburg, Germany.

Sarawagi, S. (2001). idiff: Informative summarization of differences in multidimensional aggregates. *Data Mining and Knowledge Discovery, 5*(4), 255–276. doi:10.1023/A:1011494927464

Sarawagi, S., Agrawal, R., & Megiddo, N. (1998). *Discovery-driven exploration of OLAP data cubes* (pp. 168–182). Springer Berlin Heidelberg.

Usman, M., & Asghar, S. (2011). An Architecture for Integrated Online Analytical Mining. *Journal of Emerging Technologies in Web Intelligence, 3*(2), 74–99. doi:10.4304/jetwi.3.2.74-99

Usman, M., Asghar, S., & Fong, S. (2009). A Conceptual Model for Combining Enhanced OLAP and Data Mining Systems. *Proceedings of the 5th International Joint Conference* (pp. 1958-1963). doi:10.1109/NCM.2009.354

Usman, M., & Pears, R. (2010). Integration of Data Mining and Data Warehousing: A Practical Methodology. *International Journal of Advancements in Computing Technology, 2*(3), 31–46. doi:10.4156/ijact.vol2.issue3.4

Wang, W., Feng, J., Lu, H., & Yu, J. X. (2002). Condensed cube: An effective approach to reducing data cube size. *Proceedings of the 18th International Conference* (pp. 155-165). doi:10.1109/ICDE.2002.994705

You, J., Dillon, T., & Liu, J. (2001). An integration of data mining and data warehousing for hierarchical multimedia information retrieval. *Proceedings of the International Symposium of Intelligent Multimedia, Video and Speech Processing* (pp. 373-376). Hong Kong, China. doi:10.1109/ISIMP.2001.925411

Zhen, L., & Minyi, G. (2001). A proposal of integrating data mining and on-line analytical processing in data warehouse. *Proceedings of the ICII International Conferences*. Beijing, China.

Zubcoff, J., Pardillo, J., & Trujillo, J. (2007). *Integrating clustering data mining into the multidimensional modeling of data warehouses with UML profiles. Data Warehousing and Knowledge Discovery* (pp. 199–208). Springer Berlin Heidelberg.

Section 1

Chapter 1

Integration of Data Mining and Statistical Methods for Constructing and Exploring Data Cubes

Muhammad Usman
Shaheed Zulfikar Ali Bhutto Institute of Science and Technology, Pakistan

ABSTRACT

In high dimensional environments, the sheer size and volume of data poses a number of challenges in order to generate meaningful and informative data cubes. Data cube construction and exploration is a manual process in which analysts are required to visually explore the complex cube structure in order to find interesting information. Data cube construction and exploration has been dealt separately in the literature and in the past there has been very limited amount of work done which would guide the data warehouse designers and analysts to automatically construct and intelligently explore the data cubes. In the recent years, the combined use of data mining techniques and statistical methods has shown promising results in discovering knowledge from large and complex datasets. In this chapter, we propose a methodology that utilizes hierarchical clustering along with Principal Component Analysis (PCA) to generate informative data cubes at different levels of data abstraction. Moreover, automatically ranked cube navigational paths are provided by our proposed methods to enhance knowledge discovery from large data cubes. The methodology has been validated using real world dataset taken from UCI machine learning repository and the results show that the proposed approach assists in cube design and intelligent exploration of interesting cube regions.

INTRODUCTION

The extensive use of computers and Information technology has made data collection a routine task in a variety of fields, continuously increasing data repositories can contribute significantly towards future decision making only if appropriate knowledge discovery mechanisms are applied on large datasets. Data

DOI: 10.4018/978-1-4666-8513-0.ch001

Mining (DM) and Data warehousing (DW) are the two main constituents of the knowledge discovery process. DM permits targeted mining of large datasets in order to discover hidden trends, patterns and rules while DW provides for the interactive exploration and multi-dimensional analysis of summarized data. The two strands of research share a common set of objectives such as information/knowledge extraction from large datasets, support for decision making and use of background knowledge for additional information extraction, both DM and DW have progressed rapidly in their independent ways.

Yet, there is significant potential value in integrating these disciplines. However, little research has been carried out in the integration of the two disciplines (Usman and Pears 2010). Undeniably, it is a challenging task as the techniques employed in each of the disciplines are quite different from each other. This highlights a crucial problem in integrating these incompatible techniques in a seamless manner to extract valuable knowledge from the rapidly growing data repositories. According to (Han and Kamber 2006) when a DM system works in an environment that requires it to communicate with other information system components such as DW, possible integration schemes include no coupling, loose coupling, semi-tight coupling and tight-coupling. Tight coupling means that the data mining system is smoothly (seamlessly) integrated into data warehouse system. Such smooth integration is highly desirable because it facilitates efficient implementation of data mining algorithms, high system performance and an integrated information processing environment (Han and Kamber 2006). However, implementation of such an integrated system is nontrivial and extensive research is required in this area.

Recently, there has been an increase in adapting DM and advanced statistical techniques such as Cluster Analysis and Principal Component Analysis (PCA) for knowledge discovery (Messaoud, Boussaid et al. 2004). With similar objectives, various methods and techniques, researchers have been attracted towards DW design and multi-dimensional modeling, with increasing attention being paid to the integration of mining techniques with data warehousing for data-driven knowledge discovery. However, little progress has been made so far to integrate the outcomes of data mining techniques with data warehouse to perform analytical operations. The reason for this difficulty is that data mining results need to be modelled in the form of a multidimensional schema to support interactive queries for the exploration of data.

Multidimensional modelling is a complex task, which requires domain knowledge, solid warehouse modelling expertise and deep understanding of data structures and their attributes. Certainly, in real world scenarios, data warehouse designers possess modelling expertise but lack the domain knowledge and detailed understanding of semantic relationships among the data attributes, this lack of knowledge is the prime reason for a poor warehouse design that in turn has a dramatic effect on knowledge discovery and decision making process. Additionally, multi-dimensional modelling techniques require multiple manual actions to discover measures and relevant dimensions from the dataset, such manual discovery actions become a bottleneck in the knowledge discovery process even if the human data warehouse designer tries to resolve these problems, the designer can still end up with generating an incorrect design if he/she doesn't understand the underlying relationships among the data items. In data warehouse, the choice of the attributes that are to be considered as measures and dimensions heavily influences the data warehouse effectiveness.

Data mining techniques such as clustering and pattern visualization can assist the human data warehouse designer in understanding and visualizing complex data structures. Clustering is one of the most widely researched areas in the DM discipline; data miners have traditionally used clustering as a method of segmenting data in order to recognize different groups inherent in large collections of data. However, a difficult barrier in the efficient clustering of data is the presence of mixed numeric and nominal variables which are present in real-world data sets. Numerous algorithms and techniques have been proposed in the literature for the analysis of numeric data but little research has been carried out to tackle the problem of mixed numeric and nominal data analysis. Traditional methodologies have assumed that variables are numeric, but as application areas have grown from the scientific and engineering domains to the biological, engineering, and social domains, one has to deal with features, such as country, colour, shape, type of disease etc. that are nominal valued. In addition to the problem of efficient analysis of mixed data, high cardinality nominal variables with large numbers of distinct values such as product codes, country names, model types are not only difficult to analyze but also require effective visual exploration.

The major objective of this research is to propose a novel methodology for the seamless integration between DM and DW technologies. With this methodology both disciplines can benefit from each other's advances in achieving the objective of knowledge discovery. Furthermore, it is the intention of this research to assist the human data warehouse developer to utilize the DM and visualization output in automatically constructing data cubes. This generated multidimensional schema based on results of clustering and visualization help in data driven exploratory analysis and valuable knowledge discovery. Since the DM output (clusters and natural groupings) can be very large even for reasonably small dataset, the main aim in this research is to allow the user to interact and explore the already computed, yet targeted, DM output in a discovery-driven manner similar to what is offered by Online Analytical Processing (OLAP) techniques. Such integrated systems will serve as the new generation of integrated information and decision support systems in a variety of application domains such as engineering, bio-medicine, banking, telecommunication etc. With the advancement of technology, DM and DW systems will evolve and integrating them together into one decision support system with multiple functionalities will provide a uniform knowledge discovery environment.

A number of data cube construction techniques have been proposed in the literature (Usman et al.,2013; Chun et al., 2001; Cheung et al., 1999; Asghar et al., 2004; Geffner et al., 1999; Niemi et al., 2001; Wang et al., 2002; Joslyn et al., 2008; Madkour et al., 2013; Kumar et al., 2005) where data cubes have been constructed in different ways. For instance, Asghar et al. (2004) has proposed a technique to enhance functionality using self-organizing neural networks. They added intelligence to the construction of OLAP system by integrating Data Mining with OLAP and passed only mined data to the OLAP engine and hence added intelligence in data cube construction. Similarly, range SUM queries (Chun et al., 2001; Cheung et al., 1999; Asghar et al., 2004; Geffner et al., 1999) is another technique of intelligent cube construction where parts of data cubes have been pre-computed and accumulative measures have been saved to intelligently answer user queries. Data cube schema design has been proposed by (Cheung et al., 1999) and materialized only right data cubes in order to save storage cost and query response time has been optimized. To achieve the similar objective, fuzzy OLAP has been proposed in (Kumar et al., 2005) which summarized multi-attributes using clustering method in order to take intelligent decisions based on qualitative data. Cube condensing scheme has been proposed in (Wang et al., 2002) which condensed a number of tuples intelligently into a single without loss of information. Similarly, various data cube exploration techniques have been proposed in the literature (Usman et al., 2013; Sathe & Sarawagi, 2001; Sarawagi, 2001; Leonhardi et al., 2010; Agarwal & Sarawagi, 2000; Kumar et al., 2006). However, data cube construction and exploration has been dealt separately in the literature and there is very limited amount of work done in the past which guides the data warehouse designers and analysts to automatically construct and intelligently explore the data cubes.

In this chapter, we propose a methodology that utilizes hierarchical clustering along with Principal Component Analysis (PCA) to generate informative data cubes at different levels of data abstraction. Moreover, automatically ranked cube navigational paths are provided by our proposed methods to enhance knowledge discovery from large data cubes. The methodology has been validated using real world dataset taken from UCI machine learning repository and the results show that the proposed approach assists in cube design and intelligent exploration of interesting cube regions.

The rest of the paper is organized as follows: Section 2 provides related work. Section 3 elaborates the proposed methodology followed by section 4 in which the implementation details and case study results are presented. Finally, in Section 5 the conclusions have been drawn and possible future work directions are indicated.

RELATED WORK

The purpose of reviewing the related work is to study, analyze and identify the limitations of the various techniques proposed for the construction and exploration of data cubes. We review the various techniques proposed in this literature, in which intelligence was involved either in cube construction or exploration phase. This section has been divided into two sub sections. We first present the intelligent techniques used in data cube construction followed by the techniques adopted by the research for intelligent cube exploration.

A. Intelligent Techniques for Data Cube Construction

Geffner et al. (1999) argues that the analysts are interested in current or most recent information to perform analysis. Range-Sum Query is the technique that has been used to sum the measure attributes over time series data. Finding the total sale of a specific product over last 7 days is an example of finding recent information. Authors suggested developing an algorithm for computing Range-Sum Queries i.e. relative prefix sum, which reduces the update complexity. Although this approach reduces update cost but, it requires another array of same size to keep the information of overlay boxes, which becomes impractical for large size data cubes. Moreover, the assumption that the dimensions of each data cube are of same size is not realistic an approach since the ground reality is that dimensions can be and sometimes are of different sizes, therefore, an intelligent technique is required to construct data cubes for different sizes of dimensions with minimized space complexity and reduced update cost.

Two years later Chun et al. (2001) put forward the problem that data elements do change frequently in a dynamic environment thus increasing query response time due to search and update costs. Chun found out that a data cube in prefix sum approach is dense hence proposed a sparse data cube called dynamic update cube, instead of updating prefix sum cube, changes were saved and managed separately in a tree; therefore reducing update cost by avoiding the direct updates in prefix sum cube. The failing of such algorithm is that it requires a separate tree to be maintained for dynamic updates. Also to answer a range sum query, proposed algorithm performs calculations on both prefix sum cube and dynamic tree thus increasing time complexity.

Cheung et al. (1999) identified that the most important design problem of an OLAP system is the choice of the right data cubes to be materialized, which is an impractical approach to answer all queries since the maintenance and storage costs are involved in construction of data cubes but, a careful and a right combination of cubes can optimize the query response time. They designed an approximation algorithm CMP (Cube Merging and Pruning) to efficiently construct data cube design. But the Merging of data cubes will not result in fewer cubes instead will cause larger cubes resulting in an increased maintenance cost hence slowed response time than original data cubes.

Niemi et al. (2001) research paper shows that data cube construction is complicated and single data cube is sometimes impractical for different queries. The argument here shows a direct relation between a query and data cube which similar to an OLAP cube. We find ourselves presented with a technique that automates cube design intelligently by taking information of data warehouse, constraints, functional dependencies and sample OLAP queries. Initially whole data warehouse is considered as a single fundamental cube on which user perform queries, in response to which system suggests a cube designed intelligently and based on queries posed by end user considering the functional dependencies information, the resulting data cube can be accepted, rejected, interactively modified or even can be reconstructed by providing more queries. Demerit of this argument is that the cube constructed will be based on frequently posed queries with the result that the system would take considerably more time in retrieving answers since only frequently asked queries are fed into the system.

Wang et al. (2002) shows us that data cube computation is a costly operation causing larger sized data cubes which in turn takes more time in construction and exploration Here a condensing scheme is, called Base Single Tuple (BST) condensing, which condenses a number of tuples intelligently into a single tuple without the loss of information, hence proposing a technique for condensed data cube which reduces data cube size and ultimately storage capacity also decreases. Proposed condensed cube is a fully pre-computed data cube and no compression and decompression is involved for information retrieval. It also avoids further aggregate calculations to respond to a query. Limitation that we find with this work is that designing a condensed data cube increases time complexity as all dimensions are required to be pre-computed in a condensed data cube construction, which shows that there is a need for a technique, which could construct a data cube intelligently with a minimum time complexity.

Joslyn et al. (2008) highlighted the challenge faced by Department of Homeland Security (DHS) where multidimensional and multi scale analysis is required to identify the potential threats. Moving from summary to details requires manual transfer of information among multiple tools. They have described Cube Link, their integration and mapping from multidimensional analysis into link analysis. For example, there is a central fact table which contains primary keys of all dimension tables. It holds one row for each and every combination of dimension values in a central table. In this structure measure is a value which contains distinct count of entities of the other dimensions. Limitation of their work is that constructing such semantics base schema result in increased complexity. Furthermore, updating a key value in data tables requires central fact table to be updated which increases update cost and overall complexity of the proposed design.

Madkour et al. (2013) raised the issue of handling of larger data is a challenge and systems must be capable of storing and searching data from multiple specialized data cubes based on semantics. This proposal shows knowledge cubes which are intelligent, semantic base and have capability of storing, analyzing and searching data, where, the user issues a query and the cube aware server finds out the suitable knowledge cube to answer query since it keeps information of different knowledge cubes. Each knowledge cube handles only a specific type of data cube based on semantics of data. For example, separate cubes for temporal and spatial data. The strength of this work is that it proposed a *strawman* design which is an initial draft for discussion related to disadvantages of proposed model for knowledge cubes and highlighted challenges that can arise when implementing knowledge cubes. Knowledge cubes use data management architecture which is based on semantics instead of predefined architecture. The proposed model has not yet been implemented. Construction of separate data cubes for each different types of data based on semantics requires more time and space complexity and construction of such data cubes may have overlapped attributes with redundant data.

According to Kumar et al. (2005) data warehouse should be designed to perform qualitative analysis. Here we observe that it is very difficult for decision makers to convert quantitative results to qualitative terms as different parameters are involved at a time. Accordingly data warehouse must be designed to answer queries such as, whether the sale of a particular product is good, average or poor. They have introduced fuzzy OLAP data cubes and summarized the multi-attributes using clustering method to answer such queries in order to take intelligent decisions, they have also presented different operations that can be performed on fuzzy OLAP data cubes, but the limitation here is that fuzzing (an attribute), requires manual interpretation to set corresponding qualitative value that is based on various other factors involved. e.g., fuzzing a sale attribute (Good, Bad and Average) depends on total population and number of other competitors selling the same product. Conclusion being, that there should be some intelligent and smart way to map qualitative with corresponding quantitative values based on provided different parameters.

B. Intelligent Techniques for Data Cube Exploration

In the previous section, we discussed different techniques where data cube has been constructed intelligently; here we will discuss some of the major techniques that have been proposed for intelligent exploration of data cubes.

Agarwal & Sarawagi, (2000) establishes that the current OLAP systems support hypothesis-driven exploration where analyst manually performs traditional operations such as drill down, roll up and selection on large data cubes. They proposed the discovery driven exploration of data cubes, which identifies anomalies and summarizes the exceptions in advance. Exceptions are the measure values in a cell of data cube that are different than anticipated value calculated based on some statistical formulas. For instance, sudden change in regular pattern has been marked as exception and highlighted with different colors, so, these exceptions help analyst in finding interesting regions of data cube intelligently, however they have considered a value as an exception if it differs from anticipated value which is calculated through computing all aggregates. This increases the computation cost when data cube size gets increased. Furthermore, in certain situations analyst may want to change the automated process for calculating exceptions, which requires customization and that, is not supported by this model. Similarly, Sarawagi, (2001) shows that data cubes are being explored using navigational operators like select, drill-down, roll-up etc, which involve manual intuition. To automate the exploration process, new operator *iDiff* has been proposed, the goal of which is to automate exploration process where analysts spend significant manual efforts like exploring reasons for why a certain aggregated quantity is lower or higher in one cell compared to another, instead of which, analyst could invoke the new operator that in a single step performs all the digging and return the reasons in a compact form that analyst can easily understand. However when measure attributes are increased, it becomes difficult to visualize and analyze all the differences observed by *iDiff* at aggregated levels. So, a technique is required to intelligently visualize the differences based on user interest.

For the same objective of defining new operators, Sathe & Sarawagi, (2001) have introduced 'RELAX' operator that automatically generalizes from a specific problem case. For example, analyst observes a significant drop in sales in a specific region and interested to know whether change was restricted to a particular region or has it affected the other regions as well. Author points out that where manual search was involved in pattern drawing process becomes tedious and imprecise. Solution that arises out of this question is a new operator known as 'RELAX' which summarizes a problem in intelligently and in greater detail. But the lack of any such automatic or intelligent mechanism with which to drill down a particular problem, meaning analysts has to manually find solutions to such problems hence resulting longer periods of time taken in coming to the right solution and in order to achieve that user need additional custom settings.

Kumar et al. (2006) presented an algorithm that discovers hidden surprises more precisely to a lower hierarchical level and overcame the limitations of existing techniques. In this approach, a cube can be further navigated based on detected surprise. The limitation that we find here is that the user has to provide surprise level manually against different dimensions and measures which requires specialized domain knowledge on the part of user.

According to Leonhardi et al. (2010) a fixed set of dimensions (such as time, location, etc.) is usually used to analyze various subsets of a multi-dimensional data set. Only these aggregates are not enough. Combining several dimensions in a multidimensional analysis can only discover important information, for example we have sales data describing when customers bought products in any of 20 product categories. Analyzing each category together with other dimensions is difficult but, customers with similar buying habits can be grouped together and can easily be combined with existing, to discover useful information. The analysis here is that most of the existing approaches allow adding dimensions either statically (at the time warehouse is designed) or dynamically (after warehouse has been deployed), however existing techniques only create global dimensions that are not interactive. But the restraint we find here is that the new dimensions can be added interactively during exploration process by any user and which may overlap and initial design of data cube will not remain the same. On the other hand, if new dimensions are temporary and particular to that user then creating and deleting these dimensions will result in inconsistency and performance degradation. The final analysis here being, to be able to combine dimensions in an intelligent manner and to restrict inconsistencies a more detailed method or a technique is required.

From Usman et al. (2013) we recognize the issue with high dimensional data cubes where analysts cannot determine the important dimensions from domain knowledge with mixed data types. This research shows a knowledge discovery method to construct and explore multidimensional data cubes, a thesis which is similar to ours in a sense that we also propose a model to combine these two areas for an intelligent data cube construction and exploration. A salient feature of this case study is the automatic discovery of interesting regions of information without specialized domain knowledge and a method for an intelligent data cube construction by taking advantages of statistical techniques thus helping in exploring the constructed data cubes. Data cube construction works in two steps; first is to discover important and informative dimensions using hierarchical clustering technique, the second step involves dimension reduction techniques like Multiple Correspondence Analyses (MCA) and Principal Component Analysis (PCA) being applied to identify and rank interesting measures and informative dimensions in data cubes, which in turn helps analysts in discovering important and relevant information from a multidimensional data cube.

PROPOSED METHODOLOGY FOR INTELLIGENT CUBE CONSTRUCTION AND EXPLORATION

We have seen that none of the existing technique has been targeted toward the integration of intelligent data cube construction and exploration except (Usman et al., 2013) where dimension reduction has been done using PCA and MCA separately for numeric and nominal variables. We have proposed a methodology to enhance this work by applying PCA on both nominal and numeric type variables. The main purpose of proposed methodology is to help analysts by providing necessary information to analyze and visualize the large multidimensional data cubes with mixed data types. Figure 1 represents the main steps of our proposed methodology.

In the first step, hierarchical clustering has been performed in order to get data abstractions at different levels. Each cluster contains mixed variables both of numeric and nominal type. In second step extraction has been performed for nominal and numeric variables and in the third step nominal values have been mapped with corresponding numeric values as PCA can only be applied on numeric variables. In step 4, PCA has been applied on each individual cluster in order to get the highly ranked dimensions of that particular cluster. In Step 5 we get the ranked values of nominal and numeric variables to generate a multidimensional schema. In next step, schema has been constructed based on highly ranked dimensions and informative data cubes have been constructed based on multidimensional schema and finally informative regions within a data cube have been explored via ranked paths for intelligent knowledge discovery.

EXPERIMENTAL RESULTS AND ANALYSIS ON REAL-WORLD DATASET

In this section, a case study has been performed on real world Automobile dataset (Schlimmer, 2014) taken from UCI Machine Learning Repository (Asuncion & Newman, 2010). This dataset has 205

Figure 1. Methodology for intelligent data cube construction and exploration

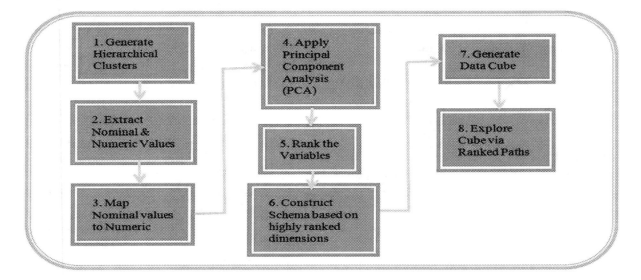

Figure 2. Ranking of Nominal Variables

C1		
Variable Name	**Calculated Value**	**Rank**
ENGINETYPE	0.279615464	1
BODYSTYLE	0.170559357	2
ENGINELOCATIC	0.117087971	3
FUELTYPE	0.092525729	4
ASPIRATION	0.039527753	5

C11		
Variable Name	**Calculated Value**	**Rank**
MAKE	0.13575421	1
ASPIRATION	0.051614703	2
NUMOFCYLINDERS	-0.088921581	3
ENGINELOCATION	-0.109374161	4
ENGINETYPE	-0.121268346	5

C12		
Variable Name	**Calculated Value**	**Rank**
FUELTYPE	0.982082854	1
ASPIRATION	0.982082854	2
FUELSYSTEM	0.982082854	3
ENGINETYPE	0.677640957	4
MAKE	0.264423888	5

Figure 3. Ranking of Numeric Variables

C1		
Variable Name	**Calculated Value**	**Rank**
CURBWEIGHT	0.947664629	1
WIDTH	0.870070194	2
LENGTH	0.842630303	3
ENGINESIZE	0.839400915	4
PRICE	0.839242713	5

C11		
Variable Name	**Calculated Value**	**Rank**
CURBWEIGHT	0.83430942	1
PRICE	0.781389374	2
HORSEPOWER	0.725385286	3
WIDTH	0.68432445	4
ENGINESIZE	0.674032092	5

C12		
Variable Name	**Calculated Value**	**Rank**
COMPRESSIONR	0.967596921	1
CITYMPG	0.951677195	2
HIGHWAYMPG	0.793440194	3
HEIGHT	0.62086169	4
STROKE	0.214611321	5

records with 16 numeric and 10 nominal variables. In first step of proposed methodology, hierarchical clustering has been applied using Hierarchical Clustering Explorer (HCE) tool (Jinwook & Shneiderman, 2002) in order to divide the whole data set into clusters. In our implementation, we have taken the top three clusters named C1, C11 and C12 of the hierarchy to show our results. On each cluster, we have performed PCA to identify the important dimensions and measures. We have listed top 6 numeric and nominal variables in Figures 2 & 3 respectively.

It can be seen that each cluster has unique set of ranked variables. For instance, *ENGINETYPE* is top ranked in cluster C1 but it takes 5th position in cluster C11 which is just one level low in the cluster hierarchy. Similarly, in the numeric variables, PRICE which holds the 5th position in cluster C1 is ranked at 2nd position in cluster C11. Using hierarchical clustering and PCA, we identify and rank important dimensions and measures in each data cluster. In the next step, a multidimensional schema is generated by using the top ranked numerical variables as measure and nominal variables as dimensions. The multidimensional schema serves as the basis for data cube construction. Using these automatically ranked dimensions and measures we intelligently construct the data cubes at different levels of the hierarchy.

Finally, we compare our ranked paths with a similar methodology proposed earlier in (Usman et al., 2013). The results obtained in (Usman et al., 2013) are shown in Figure 4 and the percentage deviation of our proposed approach with the pervious methodology has been compared in Figure 5.

It can be seen that our proposed methodology outperforms the results obtained in (Usman et al., 2013). For instance, Path 1 with the previously proposed methodology gives 87.73%, 44.31% and 96.34% deviations for variable V1, V2 and V3 respectively. On the other hand, with our proposed methodology

Figure 4. Cube Exploration through Ranked Paths using proposed methodology

Ranked Paths	Cluster C1 (Dimensions)	Top 3 Facts		
		Prak-rpm	Comp ration	Height
	All (dimensions)	5103	9.6	54
P1	Fueld_system (1bbl) Make (honda) Engine_type (ohc)	6000	9.4	49.6
	Mean Deviation	897	0.2	4.4
	Other Paths(!dohcv& !hatchback)	5087	9.7	54.1
	Mean Deviation	16	0.1	0.1
	Percentage Deviation	98.22%	50%	97.73%
P2	Fueld_system (1bbl) Make (honda) Engine_type (ohc)	4350	21.5	56.6
	Mean Deviation	753	11.9	2.6
	Other Paths (!rotor& !hatchback)	5292	8.9	52.9
	Mean Deviation	188.8	0.7	1.1
	Percentage Deviation	74.93%	94.12%	57.69%
P3	Fueld_system (1bbl) Make (honda) Engine_type (ohc)	5800	9	53.7
	Mean Deviation	696.8	0.6	0.3
	Other Paths (!l & !wagon)	5133	10	53.5
	Mean Deviation	30	0.4	0.5
	Percentage Deviation	95.69%	33.33%	66.67%

Ranked Paths	Cluster C11 (Dimensions)	Top 3 Facts		
		Wheel base	Length	Symboling
	All (dimensions)	98.7	177.5	0.84
P1	# of Cylinders (six) MAKE (porsche) Engine Type (ohcf)	89.5	169	3
	Mean Deviation	9.2	8.5	2.16
	Other Paths	99.5	177.8	0.84
	Mean Deviation	0.8	0.3	0
	Percentage Deviation	91.3%	96.47%	100%
P2	# of Cylinders (two) MAKE (mazda) Engine Type (rotor)	95.3	169.5	3
	Mean Deviation	3.4	8	2.16
	Other Paths (!isuzu & !std)	99.3	173.4	0.79
	Mean Deviation	0.6	4.1	0.05
	Percentage Deviation	82.35%	48.75%	97.69%
P3	# of Cylinders (eight) MAKE (mercedes-benz) Engine Type (ohcv)	96.6	180	3
	Mean Deviation	2.1	2.5	2.16
	Other Paths	99.3	177.4	0.82
	Mean Deviation	0.6	0.1	0.02
	Percentage Deviation	71.43%	96%	99.07%

Ranked Paths	Cluster C12 (Dimensions)	Top 3 Facts		
		Price	Width	Wheel base
	All (dimensions)	29267.9	69.83	109.4
P1	MAKE (Peugot) Engine Type (l) # of Cylinders (four)	15797	68.4	110.4
	Mean Deviation	13470.9	1.43	1
	Other Paths	33758	70.3	109
	Mean Deviation	4490.1	0.47	0.4
	Percentage Deviation	66.67%	67.13%	60%
P2	MAKE (Porsche) Engine Type (dohcv) # of Cylinders (eight)	37028	72.3	98.4
	Mean Deviation	7760.1	2.47	11
	Other Paths	28859	69.7	110.3
	Mean Deviation	408.9	0.13	0.9
	Percentage Deviation	94.73%	94.74%	91.82%
P3	MAKE (Jaguar) Engine Type (dohc) # of Cylinders (six)	33900	69	113
	Mean Deviation	4632.1	0.83	3.6
	Other Paths	26933	70.1	110.8
	Mean Deviation	2334.9	0.27	1.4
	Percentage Deviation	49.59%	67.47%	61.11%

Figure 5. Comparison of percentage deviation using our proposed methodology and earlier work for Cluster I and Cluster II

%age Deviation Cluster C1	Top 3 Facts			%age Deviation Cluster C1	Top 3 Facts		
Our Proposed Methodology	V1	V2	V3	Earlier Proposed Methodology	V1	V2	V3
Path1	98.22	50	97.73	Path1	87.73	44.31	96.94
Path2	74.93	94.12	57.69	Path2	82.08	78.48	83.65
Path3	95.72	33.33	66.67	Path3	92.79	93.89	95.78

98.22%, 50% and 97.73% mean deviation is achieved which is much higher from the previously proposed methodology. Similarly, it can be seen from Figure 6 that all the ranked paths give better results from the methodology proposed in this paper. It can be concluded that the application of our methodology not only allows the analyst to construct meaningful cubes but also facilitate in the process of intelligent data cube exploration.

CONCLUSION

A number of techniques have been proposed for intelligent knowledge discovery from multidimensional data cubes. In this paper, we have studied different techniques related to intelligent data cube construction and exploration. Some techniques help in the construction of intelligent data cubes while the others are helpful in exploration process. Limitations have been identified and discussed in details against existing techniques and to overcome these limitations, we proposed a model for construction and exploration of intelligent data cubes. Moreover, we implemented the proposed methodology using a real world data set taken from machine learning repository and compared the results with earlier proposed methodology in this regard. We proved that our proposed methodology gives better results as compared to existing techniques. For the future work, we plan to apply and test other statistical techniques for clustering and dimension reduction in order to get more informative regions in complex data cubes.

REFERENCES

Asghar, S., Alahakoon, D., & Hsu, A. (2004). Enhancing OLAP functionality using self-organizing neural networks. *Neural. Parallel & Scientific Computations*, *12*(1), 1–20.

Asuncion, A., & Newman, D. J. (2010). *UCI machine learning repository*. Irvine, CA: University of California, School of Information and Computer Science.

Cheung, D. W., Zhou, B., Kao, B., Lu, H., Lam, T. W., & Ting, H. F. (1999, November). Requirement-based data cube schema design. In *Proceedings of the eighth international conference on Information and knowledge management* (pp. 162-169). New York, USA: ACM.

Chun, S. J., Chung, C. W., Lee, J. H., & Lee, S. L. (2001, September). Dynamic update cube for range-sum queries. *Proceedings of 27th VLDB conference* (pp. 521-530).

Geffner, S., Agrawal, D., El Abbadi, A., & Smith, T. (1999, March). Relative prefix sums: An efficient approach for querying dynamic OLAP data cubes. *Proceedings of 15th International Conference on* (pp. 328-335). IEEE.

Jinwook, S., & Shneiderman, B. (2002). Interactively exploring hierarchical clustering results [gene identification]. *Computer*, *35*(7), 80–86. doi:10.1109/MC.2002.1016905

Joslyn, C., Gillen, D., Burke, J., Critchlow, T., Damante, M., & Fernandes, R. (2008, May). Hybrid Multidimensional Relational and Link Analytical Knowledge Discovery for Law Enforcement. Proceedings of *2008 IEEE Conference* (pp. 161-166). IEEE. doi:10.1109/THS.2008.4534442

Kumar, N., Gangopadhyay, A., Karabatis, G., Bapna, S., & Chen, Z. (2006). Navigation rules for exploring large multidimensional data cubes. [IJDWM]. *International Journal of Data Warehousing and Mining, 2*(4), 27–48. doi:10.4018/jdwm.2006100102

Kumar, P., Krishna, R., & De, K. (2005). Fuzzy OLAP cube for qualitative analysis. *Proceedings of 2005 International Conference on Intelligent Sensing and Information Processing* (pp. 290-295). IEEE. doi:10.1109/ICISIP.2005.1529464

Leonhardi, B., Mitschang, B., Pulido, R., Sieb, C., & Wurst, M. (2010, March). Augmenting olap exploration with dynamic advanced analytics. In *Proceedings of the 13th International Conference on Extending Database Technology* (pp. 687-692).ACM. doi:10.1145/1739041.1739127

Madkour, A., Aref, W. G., & Basalamah, S. (2013, October). Knowledge cubes—A proposal for scalable and semantically-guided management of Big Data. *Proceedings of IEEE International Conference on* (pp. 1-7). IEEE.

Messaoud, R. B., Boussaid, O., & Rabaséda, S. (2004, November). A new OLAP aggregation based on the AHC technique. In *Proceedings of the 7th ACM international workshop on Data warehousing and OLAP* (pp. 65-72). New York, USA. ACM. doi:10.1145/1031763.1031777

Niemi, T., Nummenmaa, J., & Thanisch, P. (2001, November). Constructing OLAP cubes based on queries. In *Proceedings of the 4th ACM international workshop on Data warehousing and OLAP* (pp. 9-15). New York, USA. ACM.

Sarawagi, S. (2001). IDIFF: Informative summarization of differences in multidimensional aggregates. *Data Mining and Knowledge Discovery, 5*(4), 255–276. doi:10.1023/A:1011494927464

Sarawagi, S., Agrawal, R., & Megiddo, N. (1998). *Discovery-driven exploration of OLAP data cubes* (pp. 168–182). Springer Berlin Heidelberg.

Sathe, G., & Sarawagi, S. (2001, September). Intelligent rollups in multidimensional OLAP data. *Proceedings of 27th VLDB conference* (pp. 531-540).

Schlimmer, J. C. (1985). Automobile dataset. Retrieved from http://archive.ics.uci.edu/ml/datasets/Automobile

Usman, M., Asghar, S., & Fong, S. (2010). Integrated Performance and Visualization Enhancement of OLAP Using Growing Self Organizing Neural Networks. *Journal of Advances in Information Technology, 1*(1), 26–37. doi:10.4304/jait.1.1.26-37

Usman, M., & Pears, R. (2010). Integration of Data Mining and Data Warehousing: a practical methodology. *International Journal of advancements in Computing Technology, 2(3),* 31-46.

Usman, M., & Pears, R. (2010, November).A methodology for integrating and exploiting data mining techniques in the design of data warehouses. Proceedings of *6th International Conference on* (pp. 361-367). IEEE.

Usman, M., Pears, R., & Fong, A. C. M. (2013). A data mining approach to knowledge discovery from multidimensional cube structures. *Knowledge-Based Systems, 40*, 36–49. doi:10.1016/j.knosys.2012.11.008

Wang, W., Feng, J., Lu, H., & Yu, J. X. (2002). Condensed cube: An effective approach to reducing data cube size. *Proceedings of 18th International Conference on* (pp. 155-165). IEEE.

Chapter 2
Online Processing of End-User Data in Real-Time Data Warehousing

M. Asif Naeem
Auckland University of Technology, New Zealand.

Noreen Jamil
University of Auckland, New Zealand.

ABSTRACT

Stream-based join algorithms are a promising technology for modern real-time data warehouses. A particular category of stream-based joins is a semi-stream join where a single stream is joined with a disk based master data. The join operator typically works under limited main memory and this memory is generally not large enough to hold the whole disk-based master data. Recently, a seminal join algorithm called MESHJOIN (Mesh Join) has been proposed in the literature to process semi-stream data. MESHJOIN is a candidate for a resource-aware system setup. However, MESHJOIN is not very selective. In particular, MESHJOIN does not consider the characteristics of stream data and its performance is suboptimal for skewed stream data. This chapter presents a novel Cached-based Semi-Stream Join (CSSJ) using a cache module. The algorithm is more appropriate for skewed distributions, and we present results for Zipfian distributions of the type that appear in many applications. We conduct a rigorous experimental study to test our algorithm. Our experiments show that CSSJ outperforms MESHJOIN significantly. We also present the cost model for our CSSJ and validate it with experiments.

INTRODUCTION

Real-time data warehousing plays a prominent role in supporting overall business strategy. By extending data warehouses from static data repositories to active data repositories enables business organizations to better inform their users and to take effective timely decisions. In real-time data warehousing the changes occurring at source level are reflected in data warehouses without any delay. Extraction, Transformation, and Loading (ETL) tools are used to access and manipulate transactional data and then load them into

DOI: 10.4018/978-1-4666-8513-0.ch002

the data warehouse. An important phase in the ETL process is a transformation where the source level changes are mapped into the data warehouse format. Common examples of transformations are units conversion, removal of duplicate tuples, information enrichment, filtering of unnecessary data, sorting of tuples, and translation of source data key.

To explain the transformation phase further we consider an example shown in Figure 1 that implements one of above features, called enrichment. In the example we consider the source updates with attributes *product_id*, *qty*, and *date* that are extracted from data sources. At the transformation layer in addition to key replacement (from source key *product_id* to warehouse key *s_key*) there is some information added, sales price to calculate the total amount, and the vendor information. In the figure these information with attributes name *s_key*, *s_price*, and *vendor* are extracted at run time from master data and are used to enrich the source updates using a join operator.

In traditional data warehousing the source updates are buffered and join is performed off-line. On the other hand, in real-time data warehousing this operation needs to be performed as the updates are received from the data sources. In implementing the online execution of join, it is observed that due to different arrival rate of both inputs, the transactional or stream input is fast and huge in volume while the master or disk input is slow; the algorithm faces some performance issues due to a bottleneck in the stream of updates.

With the availability of large main memory and powerful cloud computing platforms, considerable computing resources can be utilized when executing stream-based joins. However, there are several

Figure 1. An example of content enrichment

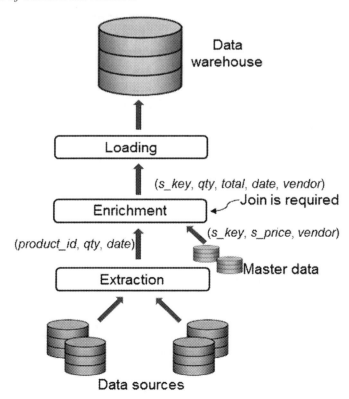

scenarios where approaches that can function with limited main memory are of interest. First, the master data may simply be too large for the resources allocated for a stream join, so that a scalable algorithm is necessary. Second, low-resource consumption approaches may be necessary when mobile and embedded devices are involved. For example, stream joins such as the one discussed here could be used in sensor networks. As a consequence, semi-stream join algorithms that can function with limited main memory are important building blocks for a resource-aware system setup.

In the literature, a seminal semi-stream join algorithm MESHJOIN (N. Polyzotis, Skiadopoulos, Vassiliadis, Simitsis, & Frantzell, 2007; Neoklis Polyzotis, Skiadopoulos, Vassiliadis, Simitsis, & Frantzell, 2008) was proposed for joining a continuous stream data with a disk-based master data, such as the scenario in active data warehouses. The MESHJOIN algorithm is a hash join, where the stream serves as the build input and the disk-based relation serves as the probe input. The algorithm performs a staggered execution of the hash table build in order to load in stream tuples more steadily. Although the MESHJOIN algorithm efficiently amortizes the disk I/O cost over fast input streams, the algorithm makes no assumptions about characteristics of stream data or the organization of the master data. Experiments by the MESHJOIN authors have shown that the algorithm performs worse with skewed data. Therefore, the question remains how much potential for improvement remains untapped due to the algorithm not being consider the characteristics of stream data.

In this paper we focus on one of the most common characteristics, a skewed distribution. Such distributions arise in practice, for example current economic models show that in many markets a select few products are bought with higher frequency (Anderson, 2006). Therefore, in the input stream, the sales transactions related to those products are the most frequent. In MESHJOIN, the algorithm does not consider the frequency of stream tuples.

We propose a robust algorithm called Cache-based Semi-Stream Join (CSSJ). The key feature of CSSJ is that the algorithm introduces a cache module that stores the most used portion of the disk-based relation, which matches the frequent items in the stream, in memory. As a result, this reduces the I/O cost substantially, which improves the performance of the algorithm. CSSJ performs slightly worse than MESHJOIN only in a case when the stream data is completely uniform. This is shown later in our experiments section.

In this work we only consider one-to-many equijoins, as they appear between foreign keys and the referenced primary key in another table. This is obviously a very important class of joins, and they are a natural case of a join between a stream of updates and master data in a data warehousing context (Golab, Johnson, Seidel, & Shkapenyuk, 2009), online auction systems (Arasu, Babu, & Widom, 2002) and supply-chain management (Wu, Diao, & Rizvi, 2006). Consequently, we do not consider joins on categorical attributes in master data, such as gender.

RELATED WORK

In this section we will outline the well-known work that has already been done in this area with a particular focus on those which are closely related to our problem domain. The Symmetric Hash Join (SHJ) algorithm (Wilschut & Apers, 1990) extends the original hash join algorithm in a pipeline fashion. The Double Pipelined Hash Join (Ives, Florescu, Friedman, Levy, & Weld, 1999), XJoin (Urhan & Franklin, 2000) and Early Hash Join (EHJ) (Lawrence, 2005) are further extensions of SHJ for the pipeline execution of join. All these algorithms take both inputs in the form of streams while our focus is to join stream data with archive data.The non-blocking symmetric hash join (SHJ) (Wilschut & Apers, 1990) promotes the proprietary hash join algorithm by generating the join output in a pipeline. In the symmetric hash join there is a separate hash table for each input relation. When the tuple of one input arrives it probes the hash table of the other input, generates a result and stores it in its own hash table. SHJ can produce a result before reading either input relation entirely; however, the algorithm keeps both the hash tables, required for each input, in memory.

The Double Pipelined Hash Join (DPHJ) (Ives et al., 1999) with a two stage join algorithm is an extension of SHJ. The XJoin algorithm (Urhan & Franklin, 2000) is another extension of SHJ. Hash-Merge Join (HMJ) (Mokbel, Lu, & Aref, 2004) is also one based on symmetric join algorithm. It is based on push technology and consists of two phases, hashing and merging.Early Hash Join (EHJ) (Lawrence, 2005) is a further extension of SHJ. EHJ introduces a new biased flushing policy that flushes the partitions of the largest input first. EHJ also simplifies the strategies to determine the duplicate tuples, based on cardinality and therefore no timestamps are required for arrival and departure of input tuples. However, because EHJ is based on pull technology, a reading policy is required for inputs.

MESHJOIN (Mesh Join) (N. Polyzotis et al., 2007; Neoklis Polyzotis et al., 2008) has been designed especially for joining a continuous stream with a disk-based relation, like the scenario in active data warehouses. The MESHJOIN algorithm is a hash join, where the stream serves as the build input and the disk-based relation serves as the probe input. A characteristic of MESHJOIN is that it performs a staggered execution of the hash table build in order to load in stream tuples more steadily. The algorithm makes no assumptions about data distribution and the organization of the master data. The MESHJOIN authors report that the algorithm performs worse with skewed data.R-MESHJOIN (reduced Mesh Join) (Naeem, Dobbie, Weber, & Alam, 2010) clarifies the dependencies among the components of MESHJOIN. As a result, it improves the performance slightly. However, R-MESHJOIN again does not consider the non-uniform characteristic of stream data.

One approach to improve MESHJOIN is a partition-based join algorithm (Chakraborty & Singh, 2009) that can also deal with stream intermittence. It uses a two-level hash table for attempting to join stream tuples as soon as they arrive, and uses a partition-based waiting area for other stream tuples. For the algorithm in (Chakraborty & Singh, 2009), however, the time that a tuple is waiting for execution is not bounded. We are interested in a join approach where there is a time guarantee for when a stream tuple will be joined.Another recent approach, Semi-Streaming Index Join (SSIJ) (Bornea, Deligiannakis, Kotidis, & Vassalos, 2011) joins stream data with disk-based data. SSIJ uses page level cache i.e. stores the entire disk pages in cache while it is possible that all the tuples in these pages may not be frequent in stream. As a result the algorithm can perform suboptimal. Also the algorithm does not include the mathematical cost model.

MESHJOIN AND PROBLEM DEFINITION

In this section we summarize the MESHJOIN algorithm and at the end of the section we describe the observations that we focus on in this paper. MESHJOIN (Mesh Join) (N. Polyzotis et al., 2007; Neoklis Polyzotis et al., 2008) was designed specifically for joining a continuous stream with a disk-based relation, i.e. the scenario in active data warehouses. The MESHJOIN algorithm is a hash join, where the stream serves as the build input and the disk-based relation serves as the probe input. A characteristic of

MESHJOIN is that it performs a staggered execution of the hash table build in order to load in stream tuples more steadily.

In MESHJOIN, the whole relation R is traversed cyclically in an endless loop and every stream tuple is compared with every tuple in R. Therefore every stream tuple stays in memory for the time that is needed to run once through R. At a glance MESHJOIN has a staggered processing pattern, where stream tuples that arrive later start the comparison with R from a later point in R and wait until this point is reached again in the cyclic reading of R.

The usually large relation R has to be stored on disk, and is read into memory through a disk-buffer of size b pages. The relation R is naturally split into k equal parts, where each part is of size b. One traversal of R therefore happens in k steps, in each step a new part of R is loaded into the disk-buffer and replaces the old content.

The crux of MESHJOIN is that with every iteration a new chunk of stream tuples is read into main memory. Each of these chunks will remain in main memory for one full cycle in the continuous traversal of R. The chunks therefore leave main memory in the order that they enter main memory and their time of residence in main memory is overlapping. This leads to the staggered processing pattern of MESHJOIN. In main memory the incoming stream data is organized in a queue, each chunk defining one partition of the queue. At each point in time, each partition has seen a larger number of iterations than the previous, and started at a later position in R (except for the case that the traversal of R resets to the start of R). Figure 2 shows a pictorial representation of the MESHJOIN operation at the moment that a part R_2 of R is read into the disk-buffer but is not yet processed.

Figure 2. MESHJOIN before processing R2

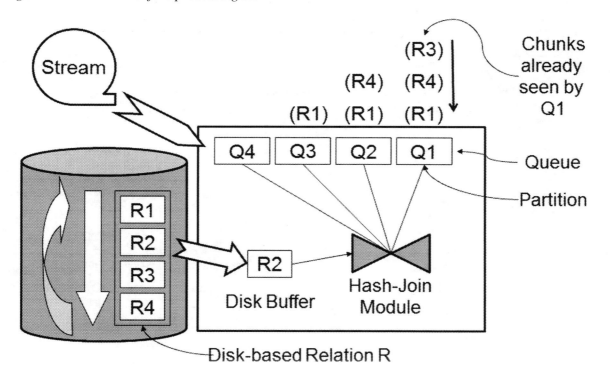

Although MESHJOIN is a seminal algorithm in the field that serves as a benchmark for semi-stream joins, the algorithm makes no assumptions about the data distribution and the organization of the master data. The MESHJOIN authors reported that the algorithm performs worse with skewed data. In summary, the problem that we consider in this paper is to deal with the skew characteristic in the stream data efficiently.

CACHE-BASED SEMI-STREAM JOIN

In this paper, we propose a new algorithm, Cache-based Semi-Stream Join (CSSJ) that overcomes the issues stated in previous section. This section gives a detail overview of the CSSJ algorithm and presents its cost model and tuning.

Execution Architecture

The CSSJ algorithm possesses two complementary hash join phases, somewhat similar to Symmetric Hash Join. One phase uses R as the probe input; the largest part of R will be stored in tertiary memory. We call it the disk-probing phase. The other join phase uses the stream as the probe input, but will deal only with a small part of relation R. We call it stream-probing phase. For each incoming stream tuple, CSSJ first uses the stream-probing phase to find a match for frequent requests quickly, and if no match is found, the stream tuple is forwarded to the disk-probing phase.

Figure 3. Execution architecture of CSSJ

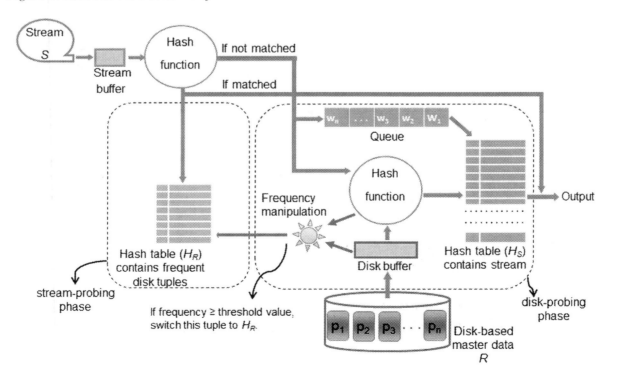

The execution architecture for CSSJ is shown in Figure 3. The largest components of CSSJ with respect to memory size is hash table H_S that stores stream tuples. The other main components of CSSJ are a disk buffer, a queue, a stream buffer, and another hash table H_R. Hash table H_R is cache that contains the most frequently accessed part of R. Relation R and stream S are the external input sources.

CSSJ alternates between the stream-probing and the disk-probing phases. The hash table H_S is used to store only that part of the update stream that does not match tuples in H_R. A stream-probing phase ends if H_S is completely filled or if the stream buffer is empty. Then the disk-probing phase becomes active. In each iteration of the disk-probing phase, the algorithm loads a set of tuples of R into memory to amortize the costly disk access. After loading the disk pages into the disk buffer, the algorithm probes each tuple of the disk buffer in the hash table H_S. If the required tuple is found in H_S, the algorithm generates that tuple as an output. After each iteration the algorithm removes the oldest chunk of stream tuples from H_S. This chunk is found at the top of the queue; its tuples were joined with the whole of R and are thus completely processed now. Later we call them expired stream tuples. As the algorithm reads R sequentially, no index on R is required. After one iteration of disk-probing phase, a sufficient number of stream tuples are deleted from H_S, so the algorithm switches back to the stream-probing phase. One phase of stream-probing with a subsequent phase of disk-probing constitutes one outer iteration of CSSJ.

The stream-probing phase (also called cache module) is used to boost the performance of the algorithm by quickly matching the most frequent master data. An important question is how frequently a master data tuple must be used in order to get into this phase, so that the memory sacrificed for this phase really delivers a performance advantage. In cost model section we give a precise and comprehensive analysis that shows that a remarkably small amount of memory assigned to the stream-probing phase can deliver a substantial performance gain. In fact, CSSJ can be tuned to use a provably optimal distribution of memory between the two phases and for the components within the phases, as described in tuning section. In order to corroborate the theoretical model, we present experimental performance measurements in the experiment section. For determining very frequent tuples in R and loading them into H_R, a frequency detection process is required, which is described in algorithm section.

Algorithm

The pseudo-code for CSSJ is shown in Figure 4. The outer loop of the algorithm is an endless loop, which is common in stream processing algorithms (line 1). The body of the outer loop has two main parts, the stream-probing phase and the disk-probing phase.

Lines 2 to 9 specify the stream-probing phase. In this phase the algorithm reads w stream tuples from the stream buffer (line 1). After that the algorithm probes each tuple t of w in the disk-build hash table H_R, using an inner loop (line 3). In the case of a match, the algorithm generates the join output without storing t in H_S. In the case where t does not match, the algorithm loads t into H_S, while also enqueuing its pointer in the queue Q (lines 4-8).

Lines 10 to 20 specify the disk-probing phase. At the start of this phase, the algorithm reads b tuples from R and loads them into the disk buffer (line 10). In an inner loop, the algorithm looks up all tuples from the disk buffer in hash table H_S. In the case of a match, the algorithm generates that tuple as an output (lines 11 to 13). Since H_S is a multi-hash-map, there can be more than one match; the number of matches is f (line 14).

Lines 15 and 16 are concerned with frequency detection. In line 15 the algorithm tests whether the matching frequency f of the current tuple is larger than a preset threshold. If it is, then this tuple is en-

Figure 4. Pseudo-code for CSSJ

Input: A disk based relation R and a stream of updates S.
Output: $R \bowtie S$
Parameters: w (where $w=w_S+w_N$) tuples of S and b number of tuples of R.
Method:
```
 1: while (true) do
 2:     READ w stream tuples from the stream buffer
 3:     for each tuple t in w do
 4:         if t ∈ H_R then
 5:             OUTPUT t
 6:         else
 7:             ADD stream tuple t into H_S and also place its pointer value into Q
 8:         end if
 9:     end for
10:     READ b number of tuples of R into the disk buffer
11:     for each tuple r in b do
12:         if r ∈ H_S then
13:             OUTPUT r
14:             f ← number of matching tuples found in H_S
15:             if (f ≥ thresholdValue) then
16:                 SWITCH the tuple r into hash table H_R
17:             end if
18:         end if
19:     end for
20:     DELETE the oldest w tuples from H_S along with their corresponding pointers from Q
21: end while
```

---

tered into H_R. If there are no empty slots in H_R, the algorithm overwrites an arbitrary existing tuple in H_R. Finally, the algorithm removes the expired stream tuples (i.e. the ones that have been joined with the whole of R) from H_S, along with their pointer values from the queue (line 20). If the cache is not full, this means the preset threshold is too high; in this case, the threshold can be lowered automatically. Similarly, the threshold can be raised if tuples are evicted from the cache too frequently. This makes the stream-probing phase flexible and able to adapt online to changes in the stream behavior. Necessarily, it will take some time to adapt to changes, similar to the warmup phase. However, this is deemed acceptable for a stream-based join that is supposed to run for a long time.

Cost Model

In this section we develop the cost model for our proposed CSSJ. The main objective for developing our cost model is to interrelate the key parameters of the algorithm, such as input size w, processing cost c_{loop} for these w tuples, the available memory M and the service rate μ. The cost model presented

Table 1. Notations used in cost estimation of CSSJ

Parameter Name	Symbol
Number of stream tuples processed in each iteration through H_R	w_N
Number of stream tuples processed in each iteration through H_S	w_S
Size of disk tuple (bytes)	v_R
Disk buffer size (tuples)	b
Size of H_R (tuples)	h_R
Memory weight for the hash table	α
Memory weight for the queue	1α
Cost to look-up one tuple in the hash table (nano secs)	c_H
Cost to generate the output for one tuple (nano secs)	c_O
Cost to remove one tuple from the hash table and the queue (nano secs)	c_E
Cost to read one stream tuple into the stream buffer (nano secs)	c_S
Cost to append one tuple in the hash table and the queue (nano secs)	c_A
Cost to compare the frequency of one disk tuple with the specified threshold value(nano secs)	c_F
Total cost for one loop iteration (secs)	c_{loop}

here follows the style used for MESHJOIN (N. Polyzotis et al., 2007; Neoklis Polyzotis et al., 2008). Equation 1 represents the total memory used by the algorithm (except the stream buffer), and Equation 2 describes the processing cost for each iteration of the algorithm. The notations we used in our cost model are given in Table 1.

Memory Cost

The major portion of the total memory is assigned to the hash table H_S together with the queue while a comparatively much smaller portion is assigned to H_R and the disk buffer. The memory for each component can be calculated as follows:

Memory for disk buffer $(bytes) = b.v_R$

Memory for H_R $(bytes) = h_R.v_R$

Memory for H_S $(bytes) = \alpha[M - (b+h_R)v_R]$

Memory for the queue $(bytes) = (1 - \alpha)[M - (b+h_R)v_R]$

By aggregating the above, the total memory for CSSJ can be calculated as shown in Equation 1.

$$M = b.v_R + h_R v_R + [M - (b+h_R)v_R] + (1 - \alpha)[M - (b+h_R)v_R] \tag{1}$$

Currently, the memory for the stream buffer in not included because it is small (0.05 MB is sufficient in our experiments).

Processing Cost

In this section we calculate the processing cost for the algorithm. To make it simple we first calculate the processing cost for individual components and then sum these costs to calculate the total processing cost for one iteration.

$c_{I/O}(b)$ = Cost to read b tuples from disk to the disk buffer

$w_N.c_H$ = Cost to look-up w_N tuples in H_R

$b.c_H$ = Cost to look-up disk buffer tuples in H_S

$b.c_F$ = Cost to compare the frequency of all the tuples in disk buffer with the threshold value

$w_N.c_O$ = Cost to generate the output for w_N tuples

$w_S.c_O$ = Cost to generate the output for w_S tuples

$w_N.c_S$ = Cost to read the w_N tuples from the stream buffer

$w_S.c_S$ = Cost to read the w_S tuples from the stream buffer

$w_S.c_A$ = Cost to append w_S tuples into H_S and the queue

$w_S.c_E$ = Cost to delete w_S tuples from H_S and the queue

By aggregating the above costs the total cost of the algorithm for one iteration can be calculated using Equation 2.

$$c_{loop}(secs) = 10^9[c_{I/O}(b) + b(c_H + c_E) + w_S(c_O + c_E + c_S + c_A) + w_N(c_H + c_O + c_S)] \tag{2}$$

The term 10^9 is a unit conversion from nanoseconds to seconds. In c_{loop} seconds the algorithm processes w_N and w_S tuples of the stream S, hence the service rate can be calculated using Equation 3.

$$\mu = \frac{w_N + w_S}{c_{loop}} \tag{3}$$

Tuning

As we have outlined in the introduction, we assume that only limited resources are available for CSSJ. Hence we face a trade-off with respect to memory distribution. Assigning more memory to one component means assigning equally less memory to some other components. Therefore, to utilize the available memory optimally, tuning of the join components is important.

In CSSJ hash table H_R (i.e. stream-probing phase) is an important component for tuning as it exploits the skew in the stream data. Once an optimal memory size is assigned to H_R, the rest of the memory is then assigned to the components of the disk-probing phase. For the disk-probing phase, a big portion of memory is assigned to hash table H_S and a smaller portion is assigned to the queue. The size of the queue is always linear with respect to the size of H_S. The disk buffer also takes up a small amount of memory. Once the disk buffer gets an appropriate amount of memory (that can amortize the disk I/O cost over a fast stream), assigning more memory to it effects the service rate negatively. The stream buffer is a tiny component that usually does not play any role in the tuning process.

We approximated optimal tuning settings using an empirical approach, by considering a sample of parameter values and measuring the service rate. Furthermore, we used the cost model to derive theoretically optimal algorithm parameters, based on calculus of variations.

Empirical Tuning

This section focuses on obtaining samples for the approximate tuning of a stream-probing phase component, hash table H_R, for one memory setting, 0.11 GB (1% of R). We assume the size of R is also fixed, at 100 million tuples (11.18 GB). However, using the same approach this key component can be tuned for different sizes of memory and R.

Since the service rate is a function of h_R, we tested the service rate of the algorithm for a set of values for h_R. The results are shown in Figure 5. From the figure the service rate increases rapidly with increasing h_R. However, after reaching an optimum value the trend changes and the service rate starts decreasing when increasing h_R further. The explanation is that in the beginning when h_R increases, the algorithm exploits the skew in the stream data. After a certain value of h_R, it does not make any significant difference to the stream matching probability due to the characteristics of the skewed distribution. On the other hand, it reduces the memory for the disk-probing phase. The optimal memory settings for h_R (i.e. the size of the stream-probing phase component H_R) can be determined from the results.

Tuning Based on Cost Model

We now show how the cost model can be used to tune CSSJ theoretically. We use the assumption that the stream of updates S has a Zipfian distribution with an exponent of 1. In this Zipfian distribution, the frequency of the second element is half that of the first element. Similarly, the frequency of the third element is 1/3rd that of the first element and this decreasing pattern continues (Anderson, 2006). So as an overall trend, frequency decreases in the tail of the distribution. In this case, the matching probability for stream S in the stream-probing phase can be determined using Equation 4. The denominator is a normalization term to ensure all probabilities sum up to 1.

Figure 5. Tuning of the stream-probing phase component

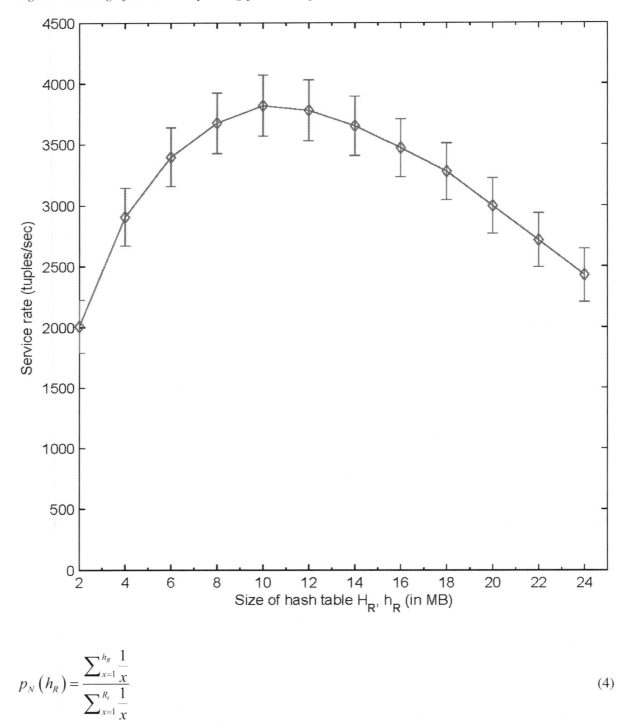

$$p_N\left(h_R\right) = \frac{\sum_{x=1}^{h_R} \frac{1}{x}}{\sum_{x=1}^{R_t} \frac{1}{x}} \qquad (4)$$

We consider the derivative of Equation 4:

$$\frac{dp_N}{dh_R} \approx p_N\left(x+1\right) - p_N\left(x\right)$$ (5)

The service rate produced in the second phase of CSSJ (the disk-probing phase) can be calculated using the following equation.

$$\mu_{dp}\left(M\right) \approx \frac{M-\left(b+h_R\right)v_R}{R_t v_R}$$ (6)

Since we are considering Zipfian distributions with finite skew, there will always be tuples that need to be processed through the disk-probing phase and hence $p_N(h_R) < 1$. The service rate of CSSJ is a function of h_R and can be written as:

$$\mu_{cm}\left(h_R\right) \approx \frac{\mu_{dp}\left(M\right)}{1-p_N\left(h_R\right)}$$ (7)

Now we take the derivative of the above equation using the chain rule.

$$\frac{d\mu_{cm}\left(h_R\right)}{dh_R} \approx \frac{d\mu_{cm}\left(h_R\right)}{dp_N} \times \frac{dp_N}{dh_R}$$ (8)

By using Equations 5, 6, and 7 in Equation 8, we get:

$$\frac{d\mu_{cm}\left(h_R\right)}{dh_R} \approx \frac{M-\left(b+h_R\right)v_R}{R_t v_R\left[1-p_N\left(h_R\right)\right]^2} \times \left[p_N\left(x+1\right) - p_N\left(x\right)\right]$$ (9)

To ensure that the root of the first derivative corresponds to a maximum, we consider the second derivative:

$$\frac{d_2\mu_{cm}}{dh_R^2} \approx \frac{2\left[M-\left(b+h_R\right)v_R\right]}{R_t v_R\left[1-p_N\left(h_R\right)\right]^3} \times \left[\frac{dp_N}{dh_R}\right]^2$$ (10)

From here we can determine the value of h_R at which the value of cm reaches a maximum. Once the optimal memory size for the stream-probing phase component is determined, the rest of the memory is assigned to the disk-probing phase components.

PERFORMANCE EXPERIMENTS

Experimental Setup

Hardware specification: We performed our experiments on a Pentium-core-i5 with 8GB main memory and 500GB hard drive as a secondary storage. We implemented our experiments in Java using the Eclipse IDE. The relation R is stored on disk using a MySQL database.

Measurement Strategy: The performance or service rate of the join is measured by calculating the number of tuples processed in a unit second. In our experiments where it is necessary we calculate the confidence interval by considering 95% accuracy, but sometimes the variation is very small.

Synthetic Data: The stream dataset we used is based on the Zipfian distribution. We test the performance of both the algorithms by varying the skew value from 0 (fully uniform) to 1 (highly skewed). The detailed specifications of our synthetic dataset are shown in Table 2.

TPC-H: We also analyze the performance of both the algorithms using the TPC-H dataset which is a well-known decision support benchmark. We create the datasets using a scale factor of 100. More precisely, we use table *Customer* as our master data table and table *Order* as our stream data table. In table *Order* there is one *foreign key* attribute *custkey* which is *a primary key* in *Customer* table. So the two tables are joined using attribute *custkey*. Our *Customer* table contains 20 million tuples while the size of each tuple is 223 bytes. On the other hand *Order* table also contains the same number of tuples with each tuple of 138 bytes.

Real-Life Data: Finally, we also compare the performance of both the algorithms using a real-life dataset[1]. This dataset basically contains cloud information stored in summarized weather reports format. The same dataset was also used with the original MESHJOIN. The master data table contains 20 million tuples, while the streaming data table contains 6 million tuples. The size of each tuple in both the master data table and the streaming data table is 128 bytes. Both the tables are joined using a common attribute, longitude (LON), and the domain for the join attribute is the interval [0,36000].

Performance Evaluation

In this section we present a series of experimental comparisons between CSSJ and MESHJOIN using synthetic, TPC-H, and real-life data. In our experiments we perform three different analyses. In the first analysis, we compare service rate, produced by each algorithm, with respect to the externally given

Table 2. Data specification

Parameter	Value
Size of disk-based relation R	100 million tuples (11.18GB)
Total allocated memory M	1% of R (0.11GB) to 10% of R (1.12GB)
Size of each disk tuple	120 bytes (similar to MESHJOIN)
Size of each stream tuple	20 bytes (similar to MESHJOIN)
Size of each node in the queue	4 bytes (similar to MESHJOIN)

parameters. In the second analysis, we validate our cost models for each algorithm. Finally, in our last analysis we present time comparisons, both processing and waiting time, for both the algorithms.

External Parameters: We identify three parameters, for which we want to understand the behavior of the algorithms. The three parameters are: the total memory available M, the size of the master data table R, and the skew in the stream data. For the sake of brevity, we restrict the discussion for each parameter to a one dimensional variation, i.e. we vary one parameter at a time.

Analysis by Varying Size of Memory M: In our first experiment we compare the service rate produced by both the algorithms by varying the memory size M from 1% to 10% of R while the size of R is 100 million tuples (11.18GB). We fix the skew value equal to 1 for all settings of M. The results of our experiment are presented in Figure 6(a). From the figure it can be noted that CSSJ performs up to 7 times faster than MESHJOIN in case of 10% memory setting. While in the case of a limited memory environment (1% of R) CSSJ still performs up to 5 times better than MESHJOIN that makes it an adaptive solution for memory constraint applications.

Analysis by Varying Size of R: In this experiment we compare the service rate of CSSJ with MESH-JOIN at different sizes of R under fixed memory size, 1.12GB. We also fix the skew value equal to 1 for all settings of R. The results of our experiment are shown in Figure 6(b). From the figure it can be seen that CSSJ performs up to 3.5 times better than MESHJOIN under all settings of R.

Analysis by Varying Skew Value: In this experiment we compare the service rate of both the algorithms by varying the skew value in the streaming data. To vary the skew, we vary the value of the Zipfian exponent. In our experiments we allow it to range from 0 to 1. At 0 the input stream S is completely uniform while at 1 the stream has a larger skew. We consider the sizes of two other parameters, memory and R, to be fixed. The size of R is 100 million tuples (11.18GB) while the available memory is set to 10% of R (1.12GB).

The results presented in Figure 6(c) show that CSSJ again performs significantly better than MESHJOIN even for only moderately skewed data. Also this improvement becomes more pronounced for increasing skew values in the streaming data. At skew value equal to 1, CSSJ performs about 7 times better than MESHJOIN. Contrarily, as MESHJOIN does not exploit the data skew, its service rates actually decrease slightly for more skewed data, which is consistent to the original MESHJOIN findings. We do not present data for skew value larger than 1, which would imply short tails. However, we predict that for such short tails the trend continues. CSSJ performs slightly worse than MESHJOIN only in a case when the stream data is completely uniform. In this particular case the stream-probing phase does not contribute considerably while on the other hand it reduces memory for the disk-probing phase.

TPC-H and Real-Life Datasets: We also compare the service rate of both the algorithms using TPC-H and real-life datasets. The details of both datasets have already been described in experimental setup section. In both experiments we measure the service rate produced by both the algorithms at different memory settings. The results of our experiments using TPC-H and real-life datasets are shown in Figures 6(d) and 6(e) respectively. From the both figures it can be noted that the service rate in case of CSSJ is remarkably better than MESHJOIN.

In all above experiments the reason of better performance in case of CSSJ is the addition of cache module (stream-probing phase) which processes a big part of stream without an extra I/O cost.

Cost Analysis: The cost models for both the algorithms have been validated by comparing the calculated cost with the measured cost. Figure 6(f) presents the comparisons of both costs for each algorithm.

Figure 6. Performance analysis and cost validation

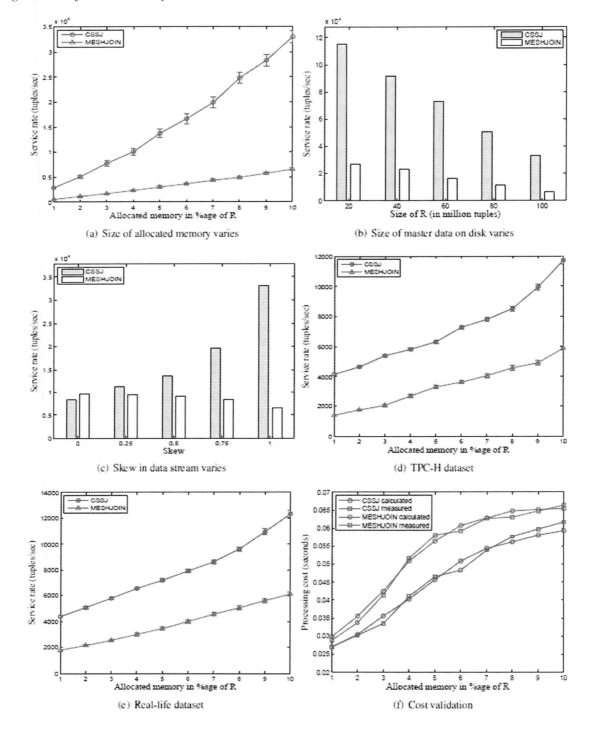

(a) Size of allocated memory varies

(b) Size of master data on disk varies

(c) Skew in data stream varies

(d) TPC-H dataset

(e) Real-life dataset

(f) Cost validation

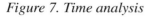

Figure 7. Time analysis

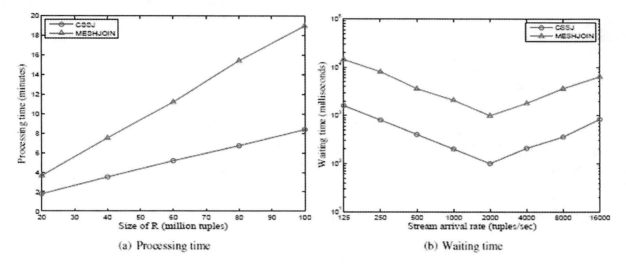

| (a) Processing time | (b) Waiting time |

The results presented in the figure show that for each algorithm the calculated cost closely resembles the measured cost, which proves the correctness of our cost models.

Time Analysis: Another kind of performance parameter besides service rate refers to the time an algorithm takes to process a tuple. In this section, we analyze both processing time and waiting time. Processing time is an average time that every stream tuple spends in join module from loading to matching without including any delay due to a low arrival rate of the stream. Waiting time is the time that every stream tuple spends in the stream buffer before entering into the join module. The waiting times were measured at different stream arrival rates. The experiment, shown in Figure 7(a), presents the comparisons with respect to the processing time. From the figure it is clear that the processing time in case of CSSJ is significantly smaller than MESHJOIN. This difference becomes even more pronounce as we increase the size of R. The plausible reason for this is that in CSSJ a big part of stream data is directly processed through the stream-probing phase without joining it with the whole relation R in memory.

In the experiment shown in Figure 7(b) we compare the waiting time for each of the algorithm. It is obvious from the figure that the waiting time in the case of CSSJ is again significantly smaller than MESHJOIN. The reason behind this is that in the stream-probing phase of CSSJ since there is no constraint to match each stream tuple with the whole of R, each disk invocation is not synchronized with the stream input.

CONCLUSION

In this paper we discuss a new semi-stream join called CSSJ that can be used to join a stream with a disk-based master data table. We compare it with existing MESHJOIN, a seminal algorithm that can be used in the same context. CSSJ is designed to make use of skewed, non-uniformly distributed data as found in real-world applications. In particular we consider a Zipfian distribution of foreign keys in the stream data. Contrary to MESHJOIN, CSSJ stores these most frequently accessed tuples of R permanently in memory saving a significant disk I/O cost and accelerating the performance of the algorithm. We have provided a cost model of the new algorithm and validated it with experiments. We have performed an extensive experimental study showing an improvement of CSSJ over the earlier MESHJOIN algorithm.

REFERENCES

Anderson, C. (2006). *The Long Tail: Why the Future of Business Is Selling Less of More*. Hyperion.

Arasu, A., Babu, S., & Widom, J. (2002). *An Abstract Semantics and Concrete Language for Continuous Queries over Streams and Relations*. Stanford. Retrieved from http://ilpubs.stanford.edu:8090/563/

Bornea, M. A., Deligiannakis, A., Kotidis, Y., & Vassalos, V. (2011). Semi-Streamed Index Join for near-real time execution of ETL transformations. *IEEE 27th International Conference on Data Engineering (ICDE'11)* (pp. 159–170). doi:10.1109/ICDE.2011.5767906

Chakraborty, A., & Singh, A. (2009). A partition-based approach to support streaming updates over persistent data in an active datawarehouse. *IPDPS '09: Proceedings of the 2009 IEEE International Symposium on Parallel & Distributed Processing* (pp. 1–11). Washington, DC, USA: IEEE Computer Society. doi:10.1109/IPDPS.2009.5161064

Golab, L., Johnson, T., Seidel, J. S., & Shkapenyuk, V. (2009). *Stream warehousing with DataDepot*. *SIGMOD '09: Proceedings of the 35th SIGMOD International Conference on Management of Data* (pp. 847–854). Providence, Rhode Island, USA: ACM. doi:http://doi.acm.org/10.1145/1559845.1559934 doi:10.1145/1559845.1559934

Ives, Z. G., Florescu, D., Friedman, M., Levy, A., & Weld, D. S. (1999). An adaptive query execution system for data integration. *SIGMOD Rec., 28*(2), 299–310. doi:http://doi.acm.org/10.1145/304181.304209

Lawrence, R. (2005). Early Hash Join: A configurable algorithm for the efficient and early production of join results. *VLDB '05: Proceedings of the 31st International Conference on Very Large Data Bases* (pp. 841–852). Trondheim, Norway: VLDB Endowment.

Mokbel, M. F., Lu, M., & Aref, W. G. (2004). Hash-Merge Join: A Non-blocking Join Algorithm for Producing Fast and Early Join Results. *ICDE '04: Proceedings of the 20th International Conference on Data Engineering* (p. 251). Washington, DC, USA: IEEE Computer Society. doi:10.1109/ICDE.2004.1320002

Naeem, M. A., Dobbie, G., Weber, G., & Alam, S. (2010). R-MESHJOIN for Near-real-time Data Warehousing. *DOLAP'10: Proceedings of the ACM 13th International Workshop on Data Warehousing and OLAP*. Toronto, Canada: ACM. doi:10.1109/IPDPS.2009.5161064

Polyzotis, N., Skiadopoulos, S., Vassiliadis, P., Simitsis, A., & Frantzell, N. (2008). Meshing Streaming Updates with Persistent Data in an Active Data Warehouse. *IEEE Transactions on Knowledge and Data Engineering, 20*(7), 976–991. doi:10.1109/TKDE.2008.27

Polyzotis, N., Skiadopoulos, S., Vassiliadis, P., Simitsis, A., & Frantzell, N. E. (2007). Supporting Streaming Updates in an Active Data Warehouse. *ICDE 2007: Proceedings of the 23rd International Conference on Data Engineering* (pp. 476–485). Istanbul, Turkey. doi:10.1109/ICDE.2007.367893

Urhan, T., & Franklin, M. J. (2000). XJoin: A reactively-scheduled pipelined join operator. *A Quarterly Bulletin of the Computer Society of the IEEE Technical Committee on Data Engineering, 23*, 2000.

Wilschut, A. N., & Apers, P. M. G. (1990). Pipelining in query execution. *Proceedings of the International Conference on Databases, Parallel Architectures and Their Applications (PARBASE 1990). Miami Beach, FL, USA* (pp. 562–562). Miami, FL, USA: IEEE Computer Society Press. doi:10.1109/PARBSE.1990.77227

Wu, E., Diao, Y., & Rizvi, S. (2006). *High-performance complex event processing over streams. Proceedings of the 2006 ACM SIGMOD International Conference on Management of Data, SIGMOD '06* (pp. 407–418). Chicago, IL, USA: ACM. doi:http://doi.acm.org/10.1145/1142473.1142520 doi:10.1145/1142473.1142520

KEY TERMS AND DEFINITIONS

Data Stream: A data stream is a continuous sequence of items produced in real-time fashion.

Processing Time: Processing time is an average time that every stream tuple spends in join module from loading to matching without including any delay due to a low arrival rate of the stream.

Service Rate: The term service rate means the total number of stream input tuples processed in unit of time.

Stream-Based Join: A stream-based join is an operation to combine the information coming from multiple data sources.

Waiting Time: Waiting time is the time that every stream tuple spends in the stream buffer before entering into the join module.

ENDNOTES

[1]   This dataset is available at: http://cdiac.ornl.gov/ftp/ndp026b/

Chapter 3
Multi-Relational Data Mining
A Comprehensive Survey

Ali H. Gazala
Auckland University of Technology, New Zealand

Waseem Ahmad
Auckland University of Technology, New Zealand

ABSTRACT

Multi-Relational Data Mining or MRDM is a growing research area focuses on discovering hidden patterns and useful knowledge from relational databases. While the vast majority of data mining algorithms and techniques look for patterns in a flat single-table data representation, the sub-domain of MRDM looks for patterns that involve multiple tables (relations) from a relational database. This sub-domain has received an increased research attention during the last two decades due to the wide range of possible applications. As a result of that growing attention, many successful multi-relational data mining algorithms and techniques were presented. This chapter presents a comprehensive review about multi-relational data mining. It discusses the different approaches researchers have followed to explore the relational search space while highlighting some of the most significant challenges facing researchers working in this sub-domain. The chapter also describes number of MRDM systems that have been developed during the last few years and discusses some future research directions in this sub-domain.

1.0 INTRODUCTION

The rapid advance in information and communication technology during the last few decades has allowed generating and processing large amounts of data both affordable and manageable. Today, modern societies depend heavily on tools and machines that generate a large amount of data in various domains including healthcare, finance and social media. The growing demand for a new generation of data analysis algorithms and techniques led the way to raise the field of data mining and knowledge discovery in database (KDD). Data mining is a research field that resides at the intersection of machine learning, artificial intelligence, statistics and database systems. It was described by (Fayyad, 1996) as "the non-trivial process of identifying valid, novel, potentially useful, and ultimately understandable patterns in

DOI: 10.4018/978-1-4666-8513-0.ch003

data". The field of data mining has received a considerable interest during the last years and many new algorithms, techniques and tools have been developed to tackle data mining tasks in different domains.

Most of data generated in the real world is processed in a complex, multi-relational and structured format. In this format, data about objects and individuals is distributed among multiple relations (Tables) using database normalization. Every relation stores a subset of the data that describe some background knowledge about the domain. However, the main stream of data mining algorithms and tools were developed based on the assumption that datasets are pre-processed and stored in a flat single table representation. In this representation, the set of tuples represent individuals or objects while each column represents an attribute. Thus, the sub-domain of MRDM was stimulated by the necessity to analyse and discover valuable knowledge directly from multi-relational databases. Although the objective of MRDM is to develop data mining algorithms capable of extracting hidden patterns from data reside in its natural relational environment, the relational model was initially designed to meet the requirements of the daily business data-processing applications. Therefore, researchers working in MRDM sub-domain have faced significant challenges in terms of data representation and handling the complexity of relational database environment.

The aim of this chapter is to provide the readers with a comprehensive review about MRDM sub-domain. Section 2 presents the different data representation approaches that researchers have followed to develop multi-relational data mining algorithms techniques. Section 3 describes challenges facing MRDM researchers in terms of scalability, efficiency and computational cost while Section 4 highlights future research directions for MRDM and presents a novel object relational data mining framework designed to overcome MRDM challenges.

2.0 MULTI-RELATIONAL DATA MINING

Multi relational data mining sub-domain has emerged to develop novel algorithms and techniques designed to work in relational database environments. During the last two decades, two different approaches have risen to address the challenging task of mining multi-relational structural data; propositionalization and upgrading.

Propositionalization is a process that leads from relational data and background knowledge to a single-table representation (Krogel, 2005). The literature of MRDM suggests two different techniques to achieve propositionalization; joining and aggregation. The joining technique is to use SQL join commands to link all related tables together in a single view, while aggregation technique is to summarize the raw data from multiple relations into a single compact table using SQL grouping commands. Both techniques will generate a universal table that is usually large and contain multiple nulls and redundant values. In addition to that, joining and aggregation techniques cause the loss of important semantic information that is usually represented in relational structure. Although propositionalization techniques are widely used in the domain of KDD, it also has significant drawbacks in terms of data representation and pre-processing cost.

The other approach to mining multi-relational structural data is to upgrade propositional data mining algorithms and techniques to work directly on relational databases. This approach requires the upgraded algorithms to work on a very large search space in compare to the single-table format. In multi-relational environment, upgraded algorithms must consider how unique individuals are represented and how different relationships types are used to link multiple tables. In other words, the computational cost for data mining in the multi-relational environment tends to be larger than classical single-table data mining. Therefore, researchers have tried different methods to overcome these challenges. The focus of this section is to discuss algorithms and techniques that work directly in relational data environment. The research work in this area includes data mining algorithms that are upgraded form the propositional format. It also includes some new techniques that are specifically developed to target relational database environment.

Almost all the research work related to multi-relational data-mining sub domain can fall under one of the following research areas:

- Logic Based Representation
- Graph Based Representation
- Statistical Relational Learning
- Relational Database Model

Figure 1 presents a diagram about the different methods and techniques for multi-relational data mining.

2.1 Inductive Logic Programming

Inductive logic programming or ILP is the earliest and the most established research field that tackled the challenging task of analysing multi-relational data structures. The field was first introduced in 1991 by the work of Stephen Muggleton as an intersection between machine learning and logic programming (De Raedt, 2008). This intersection makes ILP more powerful than traditional techniques that learn from examples, namely, ILP uses an expressive first-order logic framework instead of the traditional-value framework, and facilitate the use of background knowledge (Lavrac & Dzeroski, 1994). Using the logical knowledge base format allows ILP to tackle data analytic tasks that cannot be formulated in classical attribute-value framework. In knowledge base environment, the language of logic programming is used to represent examples, background knowledge and a description hypothesis.

In logic programming language, a relation is called a predicate *p/n* where *p* denotes the name of the predicate and *n* the parameter, which indicates the number of arguments the predicate takes (De Raedt, 2008). Similarly, tuples are represented as set of facts and background knowledge. For example, in a logical knowledgebase about authors and academic citations, the entry *authorOf/2 (lloyd, logic for learning)* represents the fact that lloyd is the author of the publication "logic for learning". Similarly, *reference/2 (logic for learning, foundations of lp)* is a fact stating that "foundations of lp" is in the bibliography of "logic for learning" (De Raedt, 2008). This representation allows ILP systems to provide data analysis features that are extremely difficult to represent in classical propositional data mining environment. During the last two decades, many successful ILP algorithms were presented for different data mining tasks including association, classification and regression (H. Blockeel, 1998; H. Blockeel, Raedt, L.D, 1998; Campbell, Ramsay, & Green, 2001; Dehaspe & Toivonen, 1999; Drever & Whitehead, 1994; Inuzuka & Makino, 2009; Lopes & Zaverucha, 2009; Lyratzopoulos et al., 2012; Menezes & Zaverucha, 2011; Motoyama, Urazawa, Nakano, & Inuzuka, 2007; Nijssen & Kok, 2001; J. R. Quinlan, Cameron-Jones, R. M., 1993; Raedt, 1997).

Association learning is the process in which two or more features become associated with each other (De Raedt, 2008). Association rule is a learning technique designed to discover sets of items that appear together in transactional databases. Apriori (Agrawal, 1997) is one of the earliest and most popular algorithms for discovering frequent itemsets in propositional data mining. The first research work to

Figure 1. Multi-Relational Data Mining Approaches

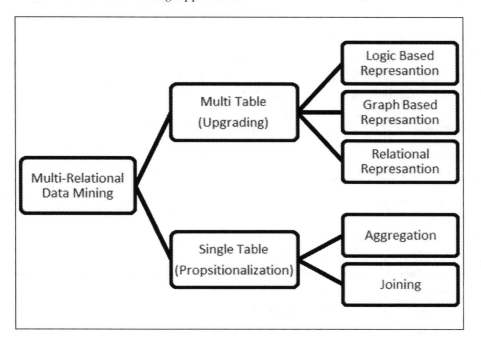

expand Apriori to the multi-relational database environment was in WARMR algorithm (Raedt, 1997). The concept of WARMR is to partition the multi-relational database into multiple disjoint subsets where each subset represents all the records that have the same example ID. The algorithm will then utilizes ILP language to verify associations between multiple tuples using example ID values. WARMR algorithm was applied on several association rules tasks including chemical compounds analysis and natural language processing (Dehaspe & Toivonen, 1999; Drever & Whitehead, 1994).

Even though WARMR algorithm upgraded association rules to the multi-relational environment, its running time was significantly long and expanded to several days on large datasets. Therefore, Nijssen et al (Nijssen & Kok, 2001) presented a novel algorithm called "Faster Association Rules for Multiple Relations" or FARMR designed to accelerate the process of discovering frequent item sets in relational databases. FARMR algorithm suggested some modifications to WARMR'S data representation method. It re-represented the data in format of trie data structure where every path from the root to a node corresponds to an item set. The trie data structure is also used to generate frequent item sets candidates. These modifications allowed FARMR to overcome the expensive computational cost of WARMR algorithm. The performance of FARMR algorithm was tested against WARMR on two datasets. The first dataset is Bongard (Bongard, 1968) contains descriptions of artificial images. Every image consists of several figures that can be included into each other. The task of FARMR was to discover the patterns in the images. The second dataset was binary digit data contains 1000 binary coded numbers. The task was to discover frequent item sets. The results showed that FARMR algorithm presented better performance in terms of running time and number of frequent item sets discovered.

Another group of algorithms (Inuzuka & Makino, 2009; Motoyama et al., 2007) expanded the functionality of WARMR by connecting relational database management systems DBMS with ILP system Prolog. A data mining algorithm that uses Property Items Extracted from Sampled Examples or MAPIX was presented in 2007 by Motoyama et al (Motoyama et al., 2007). The algorithm is designed to extract properties from relational databases using two main steps. It first scans the data set for properties or property items. Then, the algorithm will apply Apriori like procedure on the property itemsets. The extracted properties, called property items are used later to build frequent patterns rules. Another version of MAPIX algorithm called SQLMAPIX was presented in 2009 by Inuzuka et al (Inuzuka & Makino, 2009). SQLMAPIX generate SQL query within the DBMS to search for tuples that satisfy the property itemsets. Both MAPIX and SQLMAPIX utilize Open Database Connectivity ODBC to transfer data between DBMS and the ILP environment. The performance of MAPIX and SQLMAPIX was tested against WARMR algorithm on several benchmark relational datasets ("Bongard Dataset," ; Michie, Muggleton, Page, & Srinivasan; "The mutagenesis dataset," ; "part-of-speech,"). Results showed that the suggested algorithms can overcome the scalability limitation of ILP systems by performing most of the computational expensive tasks within the DBMS (Inuzuka & Makino, 2009; Motoyama et al., 2007).

Another type of association learning tasks is to derive IF-THEN rules from transactional data to predict class values. First Order Inductive Learner or FOIL is one of the earliest and still most popular relational learning algorithms for rules classification (De Raedt, 2008; J. R. Quinlan, Cameron-Jones, R. M., 1993). It utilizes the language of logic programming such as Prolog to represent the database examples and background knowledge. FOIL algorithm will then utilize the language of first order logic to derive classification hypothesis that matches all of the positive examples and none of the negative ones. The scope of FOIL algorithm was limited to relational data represented in ILP format. The work of Bockhorst et al (Lyratzopoulos et al., 2012) presented an extended version of FOIL designed to access data directly from relational structures. The suggested algorithm called FOIL-D express FOIL operations in terms of SQL statements. This feature allowed FOIL-D algorithm to scale up to large datasets that are inaccessible by traditional ILP algorithms. Several other algorithms extended the original work of FOIL (Campbell et al., 2001; De Raedt, 2008).

In addition to the association learning tasks, several other propositional data mining techniques were also upgraded to the relational environment based on ILP settings. The research work (H. Blockeel, 1998; H. Blockeel, Raedt, L.D, 1998; Lopes & Zaverucha, 2009; Menezes & Zaverucha, 2011) upgrade propositional decision tree model to the tasks of multi relational classification and regression. Herdric et al (H. Blockeel, 1998) proposed a novel algorithm called Top-down induction of first order logical decision trees TILDE. The suggested algorithm generates first-order logical decision trees FOLDT. TILDE algorithm is designed to combine features from FOLDTs and propositional classification algorithms such as C4.5 (J. R. Quinlan, 1993). It uses the same heuristics and post-pruning techniques from propositional decision trees. However, TILDE algorithm uses different methods to compute the set of tests to be considered at each node. It employs a classical refinement operator under θ-subsumption. TILDE algorithm was later expanded to the task of relational regression in the work of (H. Blockeel, Raedt, L.D, 1998). The authors proposed an extended algorithm called TILDE-RH that utilizes discretisation techniques to predict numerical values in multi-relational database environment. Both TILDE and TILDE-RH were later expanded to perform on large scale relational databases in (Lopes & Zaverucha, 2009; Menezes & Zaverucha, 2011). The new algorithms HTILDE and HTILDE-RH combine the techniques of TILDE with propositional Very Fast Decision Trees (VFDT).

Inductive logic programming is one of the earliest techniques to upgrade propositional data mining to the multi-relational environment. During the last two decades, many successful ILP algorithms for different learning tasks were presented. However, the work of most ILP systems is usually limited to a small scale datasets due to the data representation and memory specification.

2.2 Graph Based Representation

Graph mining is another research area that was integrated into the sub-domain of MRDM besides the logic-based representation explained previously. The term Graph-based data mining refers to a collection of techniques for mining the relational aspects of graph data (Holder & Cook, 2005). Typically, a graph is visually depicted in diagrammatic form as a set of dots for the vertices, joined by lines or curves called edges (Salisbury, Wallace, & Montgomery, 2010). Graphs data usually represented using two standard methods; adjacency lists and adjacency matrix (Contandriopoulos, Champagne, & Denis, 2014). The adjacency lists are usually used to represent sparse graphs while adjacency matrix is more associated with compact graphs. In graph data mining, unique entities like patients and customers are represented as set of nodes. Each node is connected to the rest of the graph by a number of directed or undirected edges. Edges usually represent different relationships between database entities. The problem of frequent sub-graph discovery is a significant task in graph mining. The first step in this task is to find sub-graphs based on a search strategy. The next step is to find matching ones in the given graph/graphs using sub-graph isomorphism (Jenkinson, Coulter, Bruster, Richards, & Chandola, 2002). The research community of MRDM presented many successful algorithms and techniques based on the graph theory data representation (Holder, Cook, & Djoko, 1994; Inokuchi, Washio, & Motoda, 2000; Kuramochi & Karypis, 2001; Palod, 2004; Pradhan, Chakravarthy, & Telang, 2009; Spyropoulou & Bie, 2011; Yan & Han, 2002).

SUBDUE (Holder et al., 1994) presented by Lawrence et al is one of the earliest algorithms for sub-graph discovery. The algorithm uses the principle of Minimum Description Length or MDL to discover substructures that compress the database and represent structural concepts in the data. The MDL principle states that the best hypothesis for a given dataset is the one that leads to the best compression of the data (Croker et al., 2013). Another approach for frequent sub-graph discovery was presented by Akihiro et al (Inokuchi et al., 2000). The suggested algorithm called Apriori-based Graph Mining or AGM utilize an extended version of market basket analysis to discover association rules among structured data. The algorithm uses adjacency matrix to represent graph data. This representation is generally easier to implement, but there can be a considerable waste of memory if the input graph/graphs is sparse (Jenkinson et al., 2002). The performance of AGM was tested on syntactic, and chemical compounds data (Srinivasan, King, Muggleton, & Sternberg, 1997). The computational time was varying between 40 minutes and 8 days depending on the minimum support threshold. The functionality of AGM was extended by a new algorithm called Frequent Sub-graph Discovery FSG presented by Michihiro et al (Kuramochi & Karypis, 2001). The suggested algorithm applies the same Apriori like search method to discover frequent connected sub-graphs. However, it uses adjacency-list representation instead of adjacency-matrix. This representation saves memory when input transaction graphs are sparse and speeds up computation time. The performance of FSG was tested against AGM algorithm on the same chemical compounds data set presented in (Srinivasan et al., 1997). The results showed that FSG algorithm achieved much faster computational time than AGM even when it was running with low minimum support threshold.

Another algorithm for mining frequent sub substructures was presented by Yan et al (Yan & Han, 2002). The suggested algorithm called graph-based Substructure pattern mining or gSpan extended the functionality of AGM and FSG by applying depth-first strategy. This search strategy allowed gSpan algorithm to minimize the computational cost required to mine the graph data. The performance of gSpan was tested against FSG algorithm using the chemical compounds data set (Srinivasan et al., 1997). The results showed that the running time of gSpan was considerably faster than FSG while the total memory consumption is less than 100M at any point of gSpan running time.

Eirini et al (Spyropoulou & Bie, 2011) preseanted a novel approch to discover interisting patterns in graph datasets. The proposed approch suggest a new syntax called *K-partite* to represeant multi-relational patterns as set of conntected subgraphs. The authors also preseant a novel algorihm called RMiner to discover hidden pattrns from *K-partite* graphs. K-partite is a technique designed to represent multi-relational database in form of graph. It modifies some concepts of entity-relationship (ER) model to generate graphs suitable for pattern discovery tasks. In K-partite graphs, relational databases are re-represented as a collection of entities where each entity has a domain type. Relationships of type many-to-many, one-to-many or one-to-one can be created between any pair of different entity types. In contrast to ER model, tables and attributes are both represented as entities in K-partite graph. Each attribute is treated as an independent entity type and all related attributes are linked together using one of the relationships type mentioned above.

The pattern syntax suggested by (Spyropoulou & Bie, 2011) is designed to discover entities that are related to each other within different domain types. The syntax defines interesting patterns as a connected complete sub-graph (CCS) and maximal CSS (MCCS) in k-partite graph. A sub-graph is considered connected and complete if there is a path between any two nodes that belong to the same entity type. A maximal connected complete sub-graph is a graph where no new nodes can be added without violating the conditions of connectedness of completeness (Spyropoulou & Bie, 2011). RMiner or (Relational Miner) algorithm is designed to search for all CCSs in k-partite graph. All nodes that are connected in CCS are represented using lists. In order to discover related patterns, RMiner algorithm organizes node lists in tree structure search space. After identifying all CSSs in the search space, RMiner algorithm implements a pruning technique to summarize all possible MCCSs. The number of MCCSs discovered is usually large. Therefore, RMiner algorithm utilizes some interestingness measures to rank the discovered patterns.

Another research area in graph-based data mining is generating the graph datasets. Pradhan et al (Pradhan et al., 2009) present a novel algorithm called DB2Graph to transfer transactional relational databases to graph representation. The proposed algorithm utilizes relational database metadata information to build graphical representation of relational databases. It also uses different techniques from graph theory to maintain the semantic of the relational datasets while keeping the size of the generated graphs as small as possible. The generated graph will be used as input data for other graph knowledge discovery algorithms like (Holder & Cook, 2005; Kuramochi & Karypis, 2004; Yan & Han, 2002).

One of the significant challenges in MRDM is the large size of the search space that learning algorithms need to explore. Therefore, the performance of any graph-based data mining algorithm will depend on the size of database graphical representation e.g. number of nodes and vertexes. DB2Graph algorithm extends naïve algorithm (Palod, 2004) to transfer relational database domain to graph representation. The naïve algorithm called RDB2Graph transfers data from relational representation to a forest of sub-graphs based in two steps. It first uses the schema metadata to represent all tuples as connected sub-graphs. Following that, the algorithm will use primary and foreign key values to connect the generated sub-graphs. DB2Graph algorithm interleave the two steps by identifying the relations whose primary and foreign key attribute values are not required to link sub-graphs. The algorithm does that by connecting newly generated sub-graphs to other sub-graphs that have been generated earlier. This step will speed up the connections generation time and minimize the required lookup space. The performance of DB2Graph algorithm was tested against naïve algorithm used in (Palod, 2004) on real world social media data set. The results showed that DB2Graph performed better in terms of running time and the size of space required for lookup data. However, the performance of DB2Graph became closer to naïve algorithm as the number of tuples involved increased.

Graph representation provided many successful algorithms and techniques to perform multi-relational data mining in transactional data. However, data mining algorithms that can apply this representation are limited to the task of frequent pattern and itemsets discover.

2.3 Relational Database Model

The last two sections presented an introductory review about the two forms of data representation used in MRDM; graph-based and logic-based representation. In the last two decades, these two representations were used to develop many successful MRDM algorithms and techniques. However, as the majority of real world data is generated and processed in a multi-relational database environment. The processing cost of transferring relational data to graph-based or logic-based representation is very high and impractical. Therefore, another research direction of MRDM was dedicated toward mining relational databases without re-representing the data in any different format. Since relational data is typically scattered among many tables, the research works in this area distinguish between two types of tables *target* and *non-target* tables. Target tables (also called root tables) contain a unique record for every object included in the database while non-target tables contain descriptive information about the database objects and domain. Researchers presented many successful algorithms and techniques based on the relational model data representation (Appice, 2003; Atramentov, 2003; Chen, Liu, Han, Yin, & He, 2009; Ghionna & Greco, 2011; Goethals, Le Page, & Mampaey, 2010; Goethals & Le, 2008; Jing-Feng, Jing, & Wei-Feng, 2007; A. J. B. Knobbe, Hendrik; Siebes, Arno; Wallen, Daniel M. G. van der, 1999; A. J. H. Knobbe, Eric K. Y., 2005; Koopman & Siebes, 2008; Lee, Tsai, Wu, & Yang, 2008; Leiva, 2002; Seid & Mehrotra, 2004; Siebes, Vreeken, & van Leeuwen, 2006; Wang, Xu, Yu, & She, 2005; Yin, 2004).

One of the earliest frameworks to perform MRDM without the need to re-representing the data was proposed by Knobbe et al (A. J. B. Knobbe, Hendrik; Siebes, Arno; Wallen, Daniel M. G. van der, 1999). The work describes the architecture of a data mining server optimized to work within relational database environment. The main concept of this framework is to build labelled directed graphs (also called selection graph) to represent relational databases without changing the original data structure. This graphical representation is built by calculating a series of predefined statistical primitives to describe the relationship between records in the target and non-target tables. These primitives are direct generalisations of those used in many proposition data mining algorithms. The initial design of selection graph framework was later expanded and improved by the work of Atramentov and Leiva et al (Atramentov, 2003; Leiva, 2002). The research work developed two multi-relational classification algorithms called MRDTL and MRDTL-2 based of selection graph framework. The two algorithms improved the original design of selection graph framework by speeding-up the calculation time required to build a classifier. The authors highlights that some of the calculations that performed during the early stages of search process can be stored and reused at further stages. This modification can minimize the time required to generate the selection graph.

The ability to handle numerical data is an important aspect for both propositional and multi-relational data mining. While there are many techniques to utilize and predict numerical values in propositional data mining, most multi-relational data mining algorithms assume that numerical data are pre-processed into categorical values prior to the data mining tasks. Thus, novel algorithms and techniques to integrate handling numerical values into selection graph framework was presented in (Appice, 2003; A. J. H. Knobbe, Eric K. Y., 2005). The algorithm "MR-SMOTI" developed by Appice et al (Appice, 2003) for regression data mining tasks based on selection graph framework. It builds tree structure models consisting of regression nodes. MR-SMOTI split numerical attributes at each regression node by running a set of regression refinement operators in addition to the pre-defined refinements of multi-relational data mining framework. In 2005 Knobbe et al (A. J. H. Knobbe, Eric K. Y., 2005) introduced dynamic handling mechanism for numerical values within selection graph framework. The mechanism introduces a set of predefined primitives to continuously evaluate numerical data for best threshold values throughout the analysis process. The predefined calculations filter the numerical values generate a reasonable size subset of threshold candidates. This mechanism improves the efficiency of multi-relational data mining algorithms by only considering a small number of numerical values during the classification process.

Although selection graph framework provides a methodology to analyse relational databases without changing its original structure, it still requires searching the entire relational search space. Alternative approach called tuple ID propagation introduced in 2004 by Yin et al (Yin, 2004) to minimalize the cost of searching the entire database. The main idea of this concept is to propagate class labels and tuple IDs from the target table to all non-target tables. This mechanism will eliminate the process of considering the entire relational search space. Several researchers have expanded and applied tuple ID propagation into different domains. Feng et al (Jing-Feng et al., 2007) present an algorithm called RDC that integrates selection graph framework with tuple ID propagation. It builds a relational classifiers based on the definition of selection graph framework used in MRDTL-2 algorithm (Atramentov, 2003). It starts to build the decision tree with a single node representing the target table. Following that, it continues to track foreign key attributes at non-target relations. For each relation, RDC algorithm computes the best splitting attribute using information gain measures. The algorithm also propagates tuple IDs and label class at each relation that join the decision tree.

Lee et al (Lee et al., 2008) utilize tuple ID propagation to solve the problem of mining relational databases with imbalanced number of class labels. In this type of analysis, users are usually interested in a small part of the dataset rather than the entire database. Thus, the authors present a novel decision-tree-based algorithm called Mr.G-Tree to build classification models on imbalanced multi-relational databases. A critical task for this algorithm is to discover accurate classification rules and preserve the delicate distribution of different class labels. Therefore, Mr.G-Tree algorithm applies tuple ID propagation in addition to several mathematical measures to maintain class label distribution between target and non-target relations. Mr.G-Tree algorithm propagates class label and tuple IDs from the target table to all non-target tables. For each non-target relation, the algorithm will add two new columns to store the propagated class label with its associated tuple IDs sets. This mechanism will allow Mr.G-Tree algorithm to build decision tree based classification models that are sensitive to the imbalanced class labels.

The work of Wang et al (Wang et al., 2005) present a new algorithm called Star_DT to build decision tree classifiers for star schema databases using tuple ID propagation. Before building the decision tree, Star_DT algorithm propagate the class label from the root table to all dimensional tables. In each dimensional table, new columns are added to store the count value for each class label. Following that, Star_DT algorithm starts to build the decision tree by selecting the best splitting attribute from the individual tables instead of a joined universal table. This strategy improves the performance of decision tree approach by speeds up the data scan at each node. Ghionna et al (Ghionna & Greco, 2011) examine several methods and techniques to improve the performance of tuple ID propagation for classification tasks. The work also presents a prototype system that integrates all the suggested new techniques to

CrossMine algorithm (Yin, 2004). Two new propagation methods are suggested: Target to Non-Target (**TtoNT_onDBMS**) and Non-Target to Target (**NTtoT_onDBMS**) propagation. These new methods will first filter the involved tuples based on the required class label and then propagate tuple IDs without their associated class label. This will reduce the computing process required by the propagation algorithm.

Dawit et al (Seid & Mehrotra, 2004) presented a novel algorithm called iceberg-cube for association rules discovery in multi-relational database environment. The idea of ice-berg cubes is to transfer transactional data into a prefix tree (trie) structure referred to as multi-relational iceberg cube trie or MICube trie. In trie structure, the target table is represented by the root node while each other node corresponds to an attribute. Each node is created as result of using GROUP-BY function at that attribute in its path from the root node and it stores number of its support counts in the database. The algorithm distinguishes between two types of attributes: *data* attributes and *join* attributes. Join attributes are used to link the database tables using primary and foreign key values while all other attributes are considered to be data attributes. This data representation combines features that used in classical association rules algorithms like WARMR with the notion of target and non-target tables used in classification algorithms like (A. J. B. Knobbe, Hendrik; Siebes, Arno; Wallen, Daniel M. G. van der, 1999). Another multi-relational association discovery algorithm was presented by Arne et al (Koopman & Siebes, 2008). The suggested algorithm called R-Krimp is designed to discover frequent itemsets in relational databases by reducing the size of search space. The idea is to do most of the expensive computational work at the table level and then join small sets of frequent patterns into a local model. The algorithm will first compute projections of each table individually without the costly materialized join. Following that, all frequent item sets from different tables are joined and fed into local model algorithm. This mechanism allowed R-Krimp algorithm to discover relational item sets with much more efficiency than other association rules algorithms. R-Krimp is an extended version to the single table pattern discovery algorithm Krimp (Siebes et al., 2006).

Another approach to extend WARMR algorithm using SQL queries was presented by Bart et al (Goethals & Le, 2008). The authors present an algorithm called Conjunctive Query Generator or Conqueror for mining association rules in multi-relational databases. The proposed algorithm discovers frequent patterns in the database by matching the retrieved tuples from SQL queries. The proposed algorithm will first applies pairs of queries *Q1* and *Q2* on the relational dataset. The first query *Q1* will ask for specific set of tuples that satisfies certain conditions while the second query *Q2* will search for tuples with more specific conditions. If the number of tuples in the output of both queries is almost the same, this could reveal a potentially interesting discovery. Following that, Conqueror algorithm will generate association rules by computing the confidence for tuples set retrieved the two queries. For all queries *Q1* the algorithm finds all queries *Q2* such that $Q2 \subseteq^{\Delta} Q1$. This process will generate association rules with large number of redundancy. Conqueror algorithm applies number of mathematical rules to eliminate the redundancy in the final set of association rules. Another algorithm to discover association rules in relational databases was presented by Bart et al (Goethals et al., 2010). The proposed algorithm called Simple Multi-Relational Frequent Item Sets Generator or SMURFIG uses the concept of relational item sets. In this concept, each two relations are linked together in a middle binary relation using key values. To calculate the support and confidence for frequent patterns, SMURFIG algorithm will first generate a list of all key values for each relation, this list called key ID list. The algorithm will then propagate the values of key ID list to all other entities. This mechanism will remove the need to calculate joins between all database tables and keeps the search space in manageable size.

Finally, Chen et al (Chen et al., 2009) present a novel algorithm called ***SRG-BC*** for multi-relational classification tasks using Bayesian theory. The proposed algorithm utilizes semantic relationship graph or SRG to describe the relational database structure and use it as a guideline for the search process. The SRG graph represents the relational database starting from the target table to all non-target tables. After building the SRG graph, SRG-BC algorithm will implement several optimization strategies to reduce the number of entities and attributes involved in the final datasets. To reduce the number of entities, the algorithm runs a pruning strategy called *Relation Selection* to extract all relations that don't affect the accuracy of the class label in the target relation. SRG-BC algorithm will then apply *features selection* pruning procedure to select attributes that are related to the class label in the target table.

2.4 Other Models

In addition to the three data representation models explained above, few other approaches have recently emerged to develop multi-relational data mining algorithms and techniques (Flach & Lachiche, 1999; Guo & Viktor, 2008; Lachiche & Flach, 2003) . One of the emerging approaches is called Statistical Relational Learning. This approach which also refried to as SRL is a combination of statistical learning that addresses uncertainty in data and relational learning which deals with complex relational structures. A statistical relational model for a given database shows not only the correlations between attributes of each table, but also dependencies among attributes of different tables (Khosravi & Bina, 2010). The authors of (Flach & Lachiche, 1999; Lachiche & Flach, 2003) developed two statistical learning algorithms called 1BC and 1BC2 that apply Bayesian theory to first order data representation. The algorithm 1BC uses dynamic propositionalisation, in the sense that attributes representing as first-order features during the learning process rather than as a pre-processing step while 1BC2 learns from structured data by fitting various parametric distributions over sets and lists to the data. In addition to the statistical relational learning model, another approach called Multi-view Relational Classification or MRC was recently presented by (Guo & Viktor, 2008). The MRC approach learns from multiple views (feature set) of a relational databases, and then integrates the information acquired by individual view learners to construct a final model.

3.0 MULTI-RELATIONAL DATA MINING LIMITATIONS

The previous section presented an overview about the different form of data representation used in MRDM sub-domain. It showed how these forms were used to develop many successful algorithms and techniques for different data mining tasks. However, researchers working have also faced significant challenges to deal with the increased computational cost of exploring the relational database environments. Therefore, many solutions were suggested to improve the performance of MRDM algorithms and to reduce its high computational cost. Nevertheless, these solutions led to an increase in complexity and did not provide a true representation of the relational model. This section highlights the challenges of MRDM in terms of data representation and handling the high computational cost.

Table 1. Multi-Relational Data Mining Algorithms

Algorithm		Year	Function	Data Representation
WARMR		1997	Frequent Itemsets	Logic-Based
FARMR		2001		
MAPIX		2007		
SQLMAPIX		2009		
FOIL		1993	Association Rule	
FS-FOIL		2003		
FOIL-D		2004		
TILDE		1998	Classification	
TILDE-RH		1998		
HTILDE		2009		
HTILDE-RH		2011		
SUBDUE		1994	sub-graph discovery	Graph-Based
AGM		2000		
FSG		2001		
gSpan		2003		
K-partite		2011		
DB2Graph		2009		
Selection Graph		1999	Classification	Relational Database Model
MRDTL		2002		
MRDTL-2		2003		
CrossMine		2004		
RDC		2007		
Star_DT		2005		
Mr.G-Tree		2008		
SRG-BC		2009		
R-Krimp		2008	Frequent Patterns	
Conqueror		2008		
SMURFIG		2010		
MR-SMOTI		2003	Regression	
Iceberg-Cube		2004	Association Rules	
1BC		1999	Classification	Statistical Learning, Multi-View
1BC2		2003		
Mr-SBC		2003		
MRC		2009		

3.1 Data Representation Challenges

Relational databases are the most widely used representation model to store and process real world data. Due to its design purpose, this model is optimized to meet the requirements of the daily business data-processing applications. Therefore, MRDM algorithms and techniques must adapt to the relational database environment to extract useful and hidden knowledge. The challenges facing MRDM algorithms in the relational database environments can be classified into the following:

- Discovering the concept of identity in the relational model
- Handling the relational data temporal dimension

An important task for any MRDM algorithm is to recognize the identities of database objects need to be analysed. In relational database environments, data is usually scattered among many tables. Therefore, the concept of identity will largely depends on the data mining tasks. For instance, in healthcare domain if the data mining task is to estimate the survival time for patients with terminal diseases, then patients will be the unique objects to be analysed and all related medical records must be linked and assessed to each patient accordingly. In a different scenario where the task is to discover the characteristics of a particular disease, then diagnose medical records will be the unique objects to be analysed. Several solutions were suggested for an adequate identity representation. In graph based data mining (Spyropoulou & Bie, 2011), unique entities like patients, customers and so on are represented as set of nodes. Each node is connected to the rest of the graph by number of directed or undirected edges. Edges usually represent relationships between different entities. Another solution to represent unique entities was followed in relational database representation. The algorithms in this representation distinguish between two types of tables; target and non-target tables (A. J. B. Knobbe, Hendrik; Siebes, Arno; Wallen, Daniel M. G. van der, 1999). Target tables contain a unique record for every object included in the database while non-target tables contain descriptive information about the database objects and domain.

Another challenge for MRDM algorithms is to represent the relational data temporal dimension. In relational database environments date and time values are usually embedded in the database semantic. For instance, in a database about healthcare domain each single patient will be linked to multiple records of medical history. The time different between the patients date of birth and his or her recent medical record is usually an important factor for any medical diagnosis. Although date and time data has an important role in discovering patterns in relational databases, most of the work in the sub-domain of MRDM ignores the data temporal dimension. Instead, time and date values usually analysed in a separate sub-domain called temporal data mining. In this sub-domain, temporal data is treated as sequence of events. The goal of temporal data mining is to discover hidden relations between sequences and subsequence's of events (Antunes & Oliveira, 2001). A research area that merges between temporal data mining and MRDM is called "Temporal Relational Data Mining". The work in this area is interested in discovering temporal patterns from relational data structures (Sharan & Neville, 2008). However, temporal relational data mining research area is still in its infancy and most of the proposed solutions do not tackle data representation and computational cost issues in MRDM.

3.2 Computational Cost Challenges

The relational database environments are usually consist of several tables connected with each other using primary of foreign key values. Exploring this large search space and representing the different relationship types between database tables is a non-trivial and costly task. The challenges that facing MRDM algorithms in terms of computational cost can be classified into the following:

- Covering the large search space
- Representing the different relationships between tables

An important challenge for MRDM algorithms is to explore the large search space for relational database environments. Since relational data is scattered among many tables, covering the entire search space can lead to a significant increase in computational cost. Therefore, researchers suggested several techniques to minimize the size of the relational search space. In graph based data mining, the number of vertices and edges determines the space required to represent the search space. Therefore, a novel framework to transfer transactional data into graph representation was presented by Pradhan et al (Pradhan et al., 2009). The suggested framework reduces the required number of edges and vertices while preserving the relational information embedded in the database. In relational database representation, the size of search space is determinant by the number of tables involved. Therefore, the concept of tuple ID propagation was suggested by Yin et al (Yin, 2004) to perform virtual joining between database relations. Another technique called semantic relational graph was presented by Chen et al (Chen et al., 2009) to minimize the number of tables and attributes involved in the data mining task. The suggested graph is designed to avoid undesirable joins between relations and to eliminate unnecessary attributes and tables. The proposed graph then uses the technique of tuple ID propagation to join all the relations in the semantic graph.

MRDM algorithms must also consider the representation of different relationship types between database tables. These relationships are used to connect database tables using primary and foreign key values. Database relationship types include one-to-many; many-to-one and many-to-many. Several solutions were suggested to handle relationship representation. In graph based data mining, representing the relationships one-to-many and many-to-one as set of trees was suggested by Jiménez et al (Jiménez, Berzal, & Cubero, 2012). In relational database representation, summarizing one-to-many relation using SQL aggregation functions was presented by Knobba et al (Sizmur & Redding, 2009). Also, representing many-to-many relationships usually causes a significant inflation in the relational search space size. Therefore, a decision tree classifier for many-to-many relationship that uses propagation technique was presented by Wang et al (Wang et al., 2005).

Although there are significant challenges facing the field of MRDM, researchers have developed many solutions to overcome these challenges. However, most of the suggested work require a considerable computational work and does not provide real world representation for the data. In other words, these solutions add a layer of complexity to the work of MRDM algorithms. The next section present a novel object relational data mining framework designed to perform MRDM tasks based on relational database model.

Figure 2. Multi-Relational Data Representation in Healthcare Domain

Patients						
P.K	Static Attributes				Classification	Regression
Patient ID	Name	DOB	Blood Type	Gender	Hypertension	BP Reading
20	AHH	12 Apr 1984	A	F	No	90
30	ABC	14 Dec 1980	B	M	No	85
40	AUT	15 Mar 1970	O	M	Yes	130

1

0 .. N

Medical Records							
P.K	**F.K**	Dynamic Variables					
Record ID	**Patient ID**	Date	Weight	Smoking	Cloistral	Activity	...
1000	**20**	10 Feb 2005	65	No	180	High	
1001	**20**	18 Mar 2010	68	Yes	185	High	
1002	**30**	07 Sep 2003	88	No	190	Medium	
1003	**40**	09 Oct 1995	85	No	190	High	
1004	**40**	13 Nov 2000	90	No	170	Medium	
1005	**40**	21 Dec 2012	103	Yes	240	Low	
1006	**40**	07 Sep 2013	110	Yes	250	Low	

Example: Figure 2 present multi-relational data representation in healthcare domain. In this representation, each tuple in the (Patients) table is linked to many tuples in (Medical Records) table. The (Hypertension) attribute in (patients) table indicate whether a patient has a high blood pressure or not. The (Patients) table also contain static information that does not change during patients' medical history such as blood type and gender while (Medical Records) table contains all medical information that is related to the current diagnose.

4.0 FUTURE RESEARCH DIRECTIONS IN MRDM

The previous sections presented an extensive review about multi-relational data mining or MRDM sub-domain. The increased number of algorithms and variety of techniques in this sub-domain mean that the demand for better MRDM solutions is in continuing growing. This section suggests a novel framework to upgrade multi-relational data mining to the object-relational database model. The suggested framework employs object oriented programming features to provide better data representation model and reduces the high computational cost of multi-relational data mining algorithms.

Object relational database management system or ORDBMS is a classic relational database management system with an embedded object oriented programming features. The main idea behind ORDBMSs is to add the concept of "Object" to the relational database environment. This feature provides a different perspective to the typical database environment and helps to bridge the gap between relational databases and object oriented programming. In ORDBMS environment, the basic relational tables in addition to object oriented features like inheritance and user defined types are combined together to deliver better data representation perspective. In one layer, the raw data reside in its normal relational tables. While In another layer, the relational data is also represented as set of objects that interact with each other based on their values in the background relational tables. The object-relational data model is thus a powerful model combining the best aspects of two different approaches (Grol et al., 1999). During the last two decades, the research area of ORDBMS has received a considerable attention and many object relational database management systems are currently available like PostgreSQL, INFORMIX and Oracle. By integrating data mining tasks into ORDBMS, the suggested object relational data mining framework or ORDM can overcome the challenges of MRDM by providing better representation, performance and temporal data handling.

In relational database environments, the primary key values are used to ensure that each tuple can be uniquely referenced within a given relation. In object relational databases, however, each object is automatically assigned a unique ID value (OID). This feature allows all records in the relational tables to be instantiated as a unique database objects. The OID value is never reused even if the object is deleted and will never be modified (P, 2001). As each object can be created to represent a real world entity, the search space will work as real-world representation for the background relational data. In other words, the significant pre-processing work to achieve the concept of identity in MRDM can be eliminated in ORDM framework. Therefore, the suggested framework allows MRDM algorithms to have the flexibility to utilize both object and relational representations in the analysis process.

Another feature of ORDBMS is the ability to provide a better representation to the different kinds of relationships between database objects. Instead of utilizing primary and foreign key values to represent relationships between database tables, ORDBMS applies associations or "membership of" relationship between related objects using auto generated OID values. Using an OID value to represent relationships, versus using primary and foreign keys, is thought to result in better performance for object relational databases since joins are not needed to access data in related tables (P, 2001).

The suggested ORDM framework can also reduce the expensive computational cost of exploring the large multi-relational search space. This high cost comes as a result of joining several tables which leads to an inefficient processing time (Bullock, Hassell, Markham, Wall, & Whitehouse, 2009). Several features of ORDBMS can be applied to minimize that cost and improve the performance of MRDM. In ORDBMS related tables can be accessed by using object references instead of table joins. A comparison study between relational databases and ORDBMS found that it is substantially faster to use object reference to access related tables instead of using relational joins (P, 2001). In addition to that, user-defined objects or UDTs can also be applied to reduce MRDM computational cost. The UDTs provides the flexibility to generate database objects based on a small part of the background relational data. These objects are stored in relational tables as column objects, row objects, or nested tables. Therefore, the search space in ORDM framework is generally smaller and requires less computational cost. The above ORDBMS features provide superior built-in solution to the challenge of exploring the large relational

Figure 3. Object Relational Representation

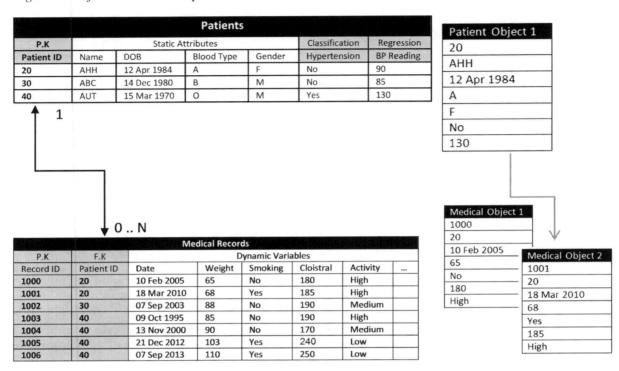

search space. Hence, the suggested ORDM framework eliminates the need for complex search space solutions in MRDM such as ID propagation and join-then mine approaches (Yin, 2004).

In additional to the performance and data representation challenges of MRDM, the suggested ORDM framework can also provide better handling to the data temporal dimension. Since date and time data will be part of each object field values, embedding predefined methods to consider temporal patterns between related objects can provide a more realistic analysis. The suggested ORDM framework utilizes Allen's interval temporal logic (Busby, Burke, Matthews, Cyrta, & Mullins, 2012) to analyze date and time values between related objects. Allen's temporal logic defines potential relations between time intervals using a list of thirteen possible binary relations.

The data representation of ORDM framework provides a real world picture about how different objects can interact with each other. This representation integrates the advantages of relational database model and object oriented programming and therefore, it helps to overcome the limitations of MRDM data representation and improves its performance. Figure 3 demonstrate object relational representation for the healthcare database in example 2.

REFERENCES

Agrawal, R. M., Heikki; Srikant, Ramakrishnan; Toivonen, Hannu; Verkamo, A. Inkeri. (1997). Fast Discovery of Association Rules. *Artificial Intelligence*.

Antunes, C. M., & Oliveira, A. L. (2001). Temporal data mining: Proceedings of the KDD Workshop on Temporal Data Mining

Appice, A., Ceci, M., & Malerba, D. (2003). MR-SMOTI: A Data Mining System for Regression Tasks Tightly-Coupled with a Relational Database. *Proceedings of KDID-2003.*

Atramentov, A. (2003). *Multi-relational decision tree algorithm - implementation and experiments.* Ames, Iowa: Iowa State University.

Blockeel, H. (1998). *Top-Down Induction of First Order Logical Decision Trees.*

Blockeel, H., Raedt, L.D. (1998). TILDE-RT: Top-down induction of First-order logical decision trees. *Artificial Intelligence, 1-2*(101). Bongard Dataset.

Bongard, M. M. (1968). *The Recognition Problem.* DTIC Document.

Bullock, A. D., Hassell, A., Markham, W. A., Wall, D. W., & Whitehouse, A. B. (2009). How ratings vary by staff group in multi-source feedback assessment of junior doctors. *Medical Education, 43*(6), 516–520. doi:10.1111/j.1365-2923.2009.03333.x PMID:19493174

Busby, M., Burke, F., Matthews, R., Cyrta, J., & Mullins, A. (2012). The development of a concise questionnaire designed to measure perceived outcomes on the issues of greatest importance to patients. *British Dental Journal, 212*(8), E11–E11. doi:10.1038/sj.bdj.2012.315 PMID:22516922

Campbell, J., Ramsay, J., & Green, J. (2001). Age, gender, socioeconomic, and ethnic differences in patients' assessments of primary health care. *Quality in Health Care, 10*(2), 90–95. doi:10.1136/qhc.10.2.90 PMID:11389317

Chen, H., Liu, H., Han, J., Yin, X., & He, J. (2009). Exploring optimization of semantic relationship graph for multi-relational Bayesian classification. *Decision Support Systems, 48*(1), 112–121. doi:10.1016/j.dss.2009.07.004

Contandriopoulos, D., Champagne, F., & Denis, J.-L. (2014). The Multiple Causal Pathways Between Performance Measures' Use and Effects. *Medical Care Research and Review, 71*(1), 3–20. doi:10.1177/1077558713496320 PMID:23877955

Croker, J. E., Swancutt, D. R., Roberts, M. J., Abel, G. A., Roland, M., & Campbell, J. L. (2013). Factors affecting patients' trust and confidence in GPs: Evidence from the English national GP patient survey. *BMJ Open, 3*(5), e002762. doi:10.1136/bmjopen-2013-002762 PMID:23793686

De Raedt, L. (2008). *Logical and relational learning.* Springer. doi:10.1007/978-3-540-68856-3

Dehaspe, L., & Toivonen, H. (1999). Discovery of frequent DATALOG patterns. *Data Mining and Knowledge Discovery, 3*(1), 7–36. doi:10.1023/A:1009863704807

Drever, F., & Whitehead, M. (1994). Mortality in regions and local authority districts in the 1990s: Exploring the relationship with deprivation. *Population Trends,* (82): 19–26. PMID:8745102

Fayyad, U. (1996). *Knowledge discovery and data mining: Towards a unifying framework.* Proceedings of 2nd ACM international conference on knowledge discovery and data mining (KDD)

Flach, P., & Lachiche, N. (1999). 1BC: A first-order Bayesian classifier. In *Inductive Logic Programming* (pp. 92–103). Springer. doi:10.1007/3-540-48751-4_10

Ghionna, L., & Greco, G. (2011). Boosting tuple propagation in multi-relational classification. Proceedings of the *15th Symposium on International Database Engineering & Applications*. Lisboa, Portugal. doi:10.1145/2076623.2076637

Goethals, B., Le Page, W., & Mampaey, M. (2010). *Mining interesting sets and rules in relational databases*. ACM.

Goethals, B., & Le, W. (2008, April 24-26). Mining association rules of simple conjunctive queries. *Proceedings of the SIAM International Conference on Data Mining (SDM)*.

Grol, R., Wensing, M., Mainz, J., Ferreira, P., Hearnshaw, H., & Hjortdahl, P. et al. (1999). Patients' priorities with respect to general practice care: An international comparison. *Family Practice*, *16*(1), 4–11. doi:10.1093/fampra/16.1.4 PMID:10321388

Guo, H., & Viktor, H. L. (2008). Multirelational classification: A multiple view approach. *Knowledge and Information Systems*, *17*(3), 287–312. doi:10.1007/s10115-008-0127-5

Holder, L. B., & Cook, D. J. (2005). Graph-based data mining.

Holder, L. B., Cook, D. J., & Djoko, S. (1994). Substucture discovery in the SUBDUE System Symposium conducted at the meeting of the KDD Workshop

Inokuchi, A., Washio, T., & Motoda, H. (2000). An apriori-based algorithm for mining frequent substructures from graph data. In *Principles of Data Mining and Knowledge Discovery* (pp. 13–23). Springer. doi:10.1007/3-540-45372-5_2

Inuzuka, N., & Makino, T. (2009). Implementing Multi-relational Mining with Relational Database Systems. In *Knowledge-Based and Intelligent Information and Engineering Systems* (pp. 672–680). Springer. doi:10.1007/978-3-642-04592-9_83

Jenkinson, C., Coulter, A., Bruster, S., Richards, N., & Chandola, T. (2002). Patients' experiences and satisfaction with health care: Results of a questionnaire study of specific aspects of care. *Quality & Safety in Health Care*, *11*(4), 335–339. doi:10.1136/qhc.11.4.335 PMID:12468693

Jiménez, A., Berzal, F., & Cubero, J.-C. (2012). Using trees to mine multirelational databases. *Data Mining and Knowledge Discovery*, *24*(1), 1–39. doi:10.1007/s10618-011-0218-x

Jing-Feng, G., Jing, L., & Wei-Feng, B. (2007, August 24-27). An Efficient Relational Decision Tree Classification Algorithm Proceedings of the Third International Conference on doi:10.1109/icnc.2007.195

Khosravi, H., & Bina, B. (2010). A survey on statistical relational learning. In *Advances in Artificial Intelligence* (pp. 256–268). Springer. doi:10.1007/978-3-642-13059-5_25

Knobbe, A. J. B., Hendrik; Siebes, Arno; Wallen, Daniel M. G. van der. (1999). *Multi-relational data mining*. Proceedings of Benelearn

Knobbe, A. J. H., & Eric, K. Y. (2005). *Numbers in Multi-Relational Data Mining*. Proceedings of the Principles of Data Mining and Knowledge Discovery (PKDD). doi:10.1007/11564126_56

Koopman, A., & Siebes, A. (2008). Discovering relational item sets efficiently. *Proceedings of SDM*.

Krogel, M.-A. (2005). *On propositionalization for knowledge discovery in relational databases*. Otto-von-Guericke-Universität Magdeburg, Universitätsbibliothek.

Kuramochi, M., & Karypis, G. (2001). Frequent subgraph discovery. Proceedings IEEE International Conference.

Kuramochi, M., & Karypis, G. (2004). An efficient algorithm for discovering frequent subgraphs. Knowledge and Data Engineering. *IEEE Transactions on, 16*(9), 1038–1051.

Lachiche, N., & Flach, P. A. (2003). 1BC2: a true first-order Bayesian classifier. In *Inductive Logic Programming* (pp. 133–148). Springer. doi:10.1007/3-540-36468-4_9

Lavrac, N., & Dzeroski, S. (1994). *Inductive Logic Programming: Techniques and Applications*. New York: Ellis Horwood.

Lee, C.-I., Tsai, C.-J., Wu, T.-Q., & Yang, W.-P. (2008). An approach to mining the multi-relational imbalanced database. *Expert Systems with Applications, 34*(4), 3021–3032. doi:10.1016/j.eswa.2007.05.048

Leiva, H. A. (2002). *A multi-relational decision tree learning algorithm*. Iowa State University.

Lopes, C., & Zaverucha, G. (2009). Htilde: scaling up relational decision trees for very large databases*ACM. Proceedings of the 2009 ACM symposium on Applied Computing*.

Lyratzopoulos, G., Elliott, M., Barbiere, J., Henderson, A., Staetsky, L., & Paddison, C. et al. (2012). Understanding ethnic and other socio-demographic differences in patient experience of primary care: Evidence from the English General Practice Patient Survey. *BMJ Quality & Safety, 21*(1), 21–29. doi:10.1136/bmjqs-2011-000088 PMID:21900695

Menezes, G., & Zaverucha, G. (2011). HTILDE-RT: Scaling up relational regression trees for very large datasets.

Michie, D., Muggleton, S., Page, D., & Srinivasan, A. (n. d.). East - West Train Dataset.

Motoyama, J.-I., Urazawa, S., Nakano, T., & Inuzuka, N. (2007). A mining algorithm using property items extracted from sampled examples. In *Inductive Logic Programming* (pp. 335–350). Springer. doi:10.1007/978-3-540-73847-3_32

Nijssen, S., & Kok, J. (2001). *Faster association rules for multiple relations*. presented at the meeting of the International Joint Conference on Artificial Intelligence

P, N. (2001). *The patient centred dental practice*. London: British Dental Association Books.

Palod, S. (2004). *Transformation of relational database domain into graphs based domain for graph based data mining*. Arlington: University of Texas at Arlington.

Pradhan, S., Chakravarthy, S., & Telang, A. (2009). Modeling Relational Data as Graphs for Mining*Citeseer. Proceedings of the 15th International Conference on Management of Data*. Mysore, India.

Quinlan, J. R. (1993). *C4. 5: programs for machine learning* (Vol. 1). Morgan kaufmann.

Quinlan, J. R., & Cameron-Jones, R. M. (1993). *FOIL: A midterm Report. Proceedings of the European Conf. Machine Learning.* Vienna, Austria.

Raedt, L. D. D., Luc. (1997). Mining association rules in multiple relations. *Proceedings of the Seventh International Workshop on Inductive Logic Programming*

Salisbury, C., Wallace, M., & Montgomery, A. A. (2010). Patients' experience and satisfaction in primary care: Secondary analysis using multilevel modelling. *BMJ (Clinical Research Ed.)*, 341. PMID:20940212

Seid, D. Y., & Mehrotra, S. (2004). *Efficient relationship pattern mining using multi-relational data cubes* [Technical Report UCI-DB 04-05]. Univ. of Calif., Irvine.

Sharan, U., & Neville, J. (2008). Temporal-relational classifiers for prediction in evolving domains*IEEE*. Proceedings of Eighth IEEE International Conference.

Siebes, A., Vreeken, J., & van Leeuwen, M. (2006). Item sets that compress. Symposium conducted at the meeting of the SDM.

Sizmur, S., & Redding, D. (2009). *Core domains for measuring inpatients' experience of care. Europe.* Picker Institute.

Spyropoulou, E., & Bie, T. D. (2011). Interesting Multi-relational Patterns. *Proceedings of the 2011 IEEE 11th International Conference on Data Mining.* doi:10.1109/ICDM.2011.82

Srinivasan, A., King, R. D., Muggleton, S., & Sternberg, M. J. E. (1997). The predictive toxicology evaluation challenge. *Proceedings of the International Joint Conference on Artificial Intelligence.*

Wang, K., Xu, Y., Yu, P. S., & She, R. (2005). *Building decision trees on records linked through key references. Proceedings of the SIAM International Conference on Data Mining.* doi:10.1137/1.9781611972757.64

Yan, X., & Han, J. (2002). gspan: Graph-based substructure pattern mining. *Proceedings. Of 2002 IEEE International Conference.*

Yin, X. H. Jiawei; Yang, Jiong; Yu, Philip S, (2004). CrossMine: Efficient Classification Across Multiple Database Relations. *Proceedings of the International Conference on Data Engineering.*

ADDITIONAL READING

Raedt, L. d. (2008). *Logical and relational learning.* Berlin: Springer. doi:10.1007/978-3-540-68856-3

Džeroski, S. (2005). *Relational data mining* (pp. 869–898). Boston, MA: Springer.

Getoor, L., & Taskar, B. (Eds.). (2007). *Introduction to statistical relational learning.* US: MIT press.

Lavrac, N., & Dzeroski, S. (1994). *Inductive Logic Programming: Techniques and Applications.* New York: Ellis Horwood.

KEY TERMS AND DEFINITIONS

Data: Aggregation: Is a data processing technique to summarize raw data from multiple relations into a single compact table using SQL grouping commands.

Data Joining: Is a data processing technique to use SQL join commands to link all related tables together in a single view.

Data Mining: Is the process of identifying valid, novel, potentially useful, and ultimately understandable information and patterns from raw data.

Knowledge Discovery in Database: Is the process of discovering useful knowledge from a collection of raw data.

Object Relational Database Management System: Is a classic relational database management system with an embedded object oriented programming features. The main idea behind the system is to add the concept of "Object" to the relational database environment.

Propositionalization: Is a process of transferring multiple relational database tables into a single-table representation.

Relational Data Model: Is a data representation model proposed by E.F. Codd in 1970; This model organizes data into one or more tables (or "relations") of rows and columns, with a unique key for each row.

Chapter 4
Comparative Study of Incremental Learning Algorithms in Multidimensional Outlier Detection on Data Stream

Simon Fong
University of Macau, Macau SAR

Dong Han
University of Macau, Macau SAR

Athanasios V. Vasilakos
Lulea University of Technology, Lulea, Sweden

ABSTRACT

Multi-dimensional outlier detection (MOD) over data streams is one of the most significant data stream mining techniques. When multivariate data are streaming in high speed, outliers are to be detected efficiently and accurately. Conventional outlier detection method is based on observing the full dataset and its statistical distribution. The data is assumed stationary. However, this conventional method has an inherent limitation—it always assumes the availability of the entire dataset. In modern applications, especially those that operate in the real time environment, the data arrive in the form of live data feed; they are dynamic and ever evolving in terms of their statistical distribution and concepts. Outlier detection should no longer be done in batches, but in incremental manner. In this chapter, we investigate into this important concept of MOD. In particular, we evaluate the effectiveness of a collection of incremental learning algorithms which are the underlying pattern recognition mechanisms for MOD. Specifically, we combine incremental learning algorithms into three types of MOD - Global Analysis, Cumulative Analysis and Lightweight Analysis with Sliding Window. Different classification algorithms are put under test for performance comparison.

DOI: 10.4018/978-1-4666-8513-0.ch004

1. INTRODUCTION: BACKGROUND OF OUTLIER DETECTION TECHNIQUES

Numerous researchers have attempted to apply different techniques in detecting outlier, which are generally referred to as defined in the following. "An outlier is an observation that deviates so much from other observations as to arouse suspicions that is was generated by a different mechanism" (Hawkins, 1980)."An outlier is an observation (or subset of observations) which appear to be inconsistent with the remainder of the dataset" (Barnet & Lewis, 1994).

Researchers generally focus on the observation of data irregularities, how each data instance relates to the others (the majority), and how such data instances relate to classification performance. Most of these techniques can be grouped into the following three categories: distribution-based, distance-based, and density-based methods.

1.1 Distribution-Based Outlier Detection Methods

These methods are commonly based on statistical analysis. Detection techniques proposed in the literature range from finding extreme values beyond a certain number of standard deviations to complex normality tests. However, most data distribution models are directly applied into the incoming test data; often the data streams are univariate. Thus, these methods that were designed to work on univariate data may be unsuitable for moderately high-dimensional data. Grubbs proposed a method that attempts to remediate the problem by computing the difference between the mean values as Z per attribute. For each particular attribute the testing value is then divided by the standard deviation which is computed from all the attribute values. The Z value is then tested against some significance level ranging from 1% to 5%. No pre-defined parameters are needed for initiating these techniques because they are all derived from the data directly. Nevertheless, the success is largely depending on the availability of exemplars in the data. The more of the available records, the higher the chances of obtaining representative sample statistically would be (Grubbs, 1969).

In the work of (Aggarwal & Yu, 2001), the authors adopted a special outlier detection approach in which the behavior projected by the dataset is examined. If a point is sparse in a lower low-dimensional projection, the data it represents are deemed abnormal and are removed. Brute force, or at best, some form of heuristics, is used to determine the projections. A similar method outlined by (Zhang, Ramakrishnan & Livny, 1996) builds a height-balanced tree containing clustering features on non-leaf nodes and leaf nodes. Leaf nodes with a low density are then considered outliers and are filtered out.

1.2 Distance-Based or Similarity-Based Outlier Detection Methods

Initially introduced by Knorr and Ng (1998), distance-based outlier detection techniques are another type of popular methods. Assume there is an item p in a dataset DS exists $DB(q,dist)$ outlier given the condition that $>q$ out of all the items in DS are distributed a longer distance of $dist$ apart from p. This definition is widely recognized, because it generalizes the use of some statistical outlier test. An extension of the above definition was proposed by Ramaswamy et.al. (2000). There is a rank among all the points according to the outlier score. When there are 2 integers kn and w exist, an item p is considered as an outlier, when there are fewer than w items that have greater values for D^k than $p.D^k$ is defined as the distance between the kth nearest neighbor of the item p and p itself.

In the work of (Arning et al., 1996), the researchers first divided data into many subsets before searching for the subset that would cause the greatest reduction in dissimilarity within the training dataset if removed. The dissimilarity function can be any function returning a low value between similar elements and a high value between dissimilar elements, such as variance.

Another team of researchers (Brighton & Mellish, 2002) applied a k-NN algorithm, which essentially compares test data with neighboring data to determine whether they are outliers by reference to their neighbors. A researcher called P.C. Mahalanobis (1936) introduced as early as 1936, a distance measure that is based on the correlations between variables by which different patterns can be found and analyzed. This measure offers a useful way of determining similarity of an unknown sample set to a known one. It differs from Euclidean distance in that it takes into account the correlations of the data set and is scale-invariant, i.e. not dependent on the scale of measurements. In our paper, we will deploy this method to find outliers.

1.3 Density-Based Outlier Detection Methods

Breunig et al (2000) introduced a method where a numerical indicator called "degree" is assigned to each item showing whether it is an outlier. This indicator is called the local outlier factor (LOF) of an object. The context of "local" in the quantitative measure depends on how secluded the item is located in comparison to the surrounding neighbors. In this algorithm, observations with high LOF values are considered as outliers, whereas observations with low LOF values are probable to be normal with respect to their neighborhood. Low-density neighborhood is indicated by high LOF and consequently high potential of being outlier (Mansur & Sap, 2005). We will adopt this method in this paper to detect outliers.

2. METHODOLOGY OF OUTLIER DETECTION USING MAHALANOBIS DISTANCE (MD)

2.1 Measurement about Distance

For the earliest statistical-based outlier detection, this method is merely applicable for single dimensional datasets, namely, univariate outliers. In such case, "outliers" in a data set could be found by computing the deviation for each number, denoted as either a "Z-score" or "extended Z-score" that tests against some predefined threshold. Z-score usually regarded as the degree of standard deviation in comparison to the statistical mean. Extended Z-score uses instead the median to measure the deviation. In many situations it offers robust detection of outliers than the mean, statistically.

However, in practice, we usually encounter more complex situations with multidimensional records. One method that can be used for identifying bi- or multi-variate outliers is known as Mahalanobis Distance. It measures the distance of particular scores from the centroids of the remaining samples. Formally, the Mahalanobis distance of a vector x which is multi-dimensional is $(x_1, x_2, x_3, ..., x_N)^T$ from a collections of data values with mean $\mu = (\mu_1, \mu_2, \mu_3, ..., \mu_N)^T$ and covariance matrix S is defined as:

$$D_M(x) = \sqrt{(x - u)^T S^{-1} (x - u)}$$

Each x is an observation which needs to be computed the Mahalanobis Distance score from the reference sample. And the u is the mean of the specific reference sample while covariance S is the covariance of the data in reference sample. According to the algorithm of Mahalanobis Distance, the quantity of instances in reference sample must be greater than the quantity of variate, namely, the dimension.

For multivariate data that are normally distributed they can be approximately chi-square distributed with p degrees of freedom (x^2_p). Multivariate outliers can now easily be defined as observations having a large (squared) Mahalanobis distance. For this purpose, a quartile of the chi-squared distribution (e.g., the 97.5% quartile) could be regarded so. After calculating the Mahalanobis Distance for a multivariate instance from the specific data group, we will get a squared Mahalanobis Distance score. If this score exceeds a "critical value", this instance will be considered an outlier. The critical chi-square values for 2 to 10 degrees of freedom (equal to the number of variables under investigation) with corresponding probability level (alpha value) are shown below. When $p<0.05$ we generally refer to this as a significant difference.

For example, the critical value for a bivariate relationship is 13.82. Any Mahalanobis Distances score above that critical value is a bivariate outlier. In our experiment, we will use the Mahalanobis Distance to find the outliers.

2.1 Workflow for Global Analysis Using MD

For the global analysis, we calculate the Mahalanobis Distance for each instance from the whole dataset. This method is somewhat like the traditional measurement. The following diagrams indicate the Global Analysis mechanism for calculating the Mahalanobis Distance of the ith and its next instance. The operation of global analysis using MD is visualized in Figure 1a.

2.2 Workflow for Cumulative Analysis Using MD

With regard to the cumulative analysis, in our experiment, initially we calculate the Mahalanobis Distance of the first 50 records respectively. After that, for the ith record, we treat the top i instances as the reference sample. The following diagrams indicate the Cumulative Analysis mechanism for calculating the Mahalanobis Distance of the ith and its next instance. The operation of cumulative analysis using MD is visualized in Figure 1(b).

2.3 Workflow for Lightweight Analysis with Sliding Window Using MD

As to the lightweight analysis with sliding window, we propose a novel notion which called "sliding window". The sliding window has a fixed size of a certain number of instances; and it moves forward to next instance when we analyze a new record. In our experiment, we set the window size to 50, 100, 200, 300,500 and 1000. Initially we calculate each record's Mahalanobis Distance in the window, respectively. After that, the window slides to the next record, with the corresponding size. For example, if we choose the window size of 50, each record within it will be computed the Mahalanobis Distance from the reference sample (namely, the selected 1 to 50 instances). Then, the window will slide forward by a step of one record. So, the window is formed with the instances of 2 to 51. That is to say, we calculate the 51st instance's Mahalanobis Distance from the reference sample formed by records from 2 to 51. Next, it is supposed to compute the 52nd instance with a reference sample from 3 to 52, and so on. The following

Figure 1. Illustrations of outlier detection that can be done by using MD in three different operation modes.
(a) MD Global Analysis
(b) MD Cumulative Analysis
(c) MD Lightweight Analysis

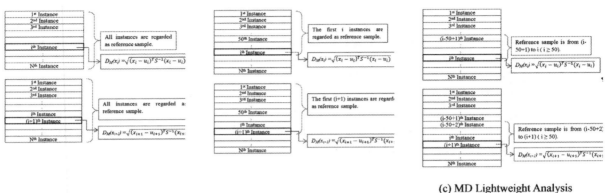

(c) MD Lightweight Analysis

(b) MD Cumulative Analysis

(a) MD Global Analysis

diagrams indicate the method about Lightweight Analysis with window size of 50 for calculating the Mahalanobis Distance of the ith and its next instance. The operation of lightweight analysis using MD is visualized in Figure 1(c).

3. METHODOLOGY OF OUTLIER DETECTION USING LOCAL OUTLIER FACTOR

3.1 Concept of Local Outlier Factor

Outlier ranking is a well-studied research topic. Breunig et al. (2000) have developed the local outlier factor (LOF) system that is usually considered a state-of-the-art outlier ranking method. The main idea of this system is to try to obtain an outlying score for each case by estimating its degree of isolation with respect to its local neighborhood. The method is based on the notion of the local density of the observations. Cases in regions with very low density are considered outliers. The estimates of the density are obtained using the distances between cases. The authors defined a few concepts that drive the algorithm used to calculate the outlying score of each point. These are the (1) concept of core distance of a point p, which is defined as its distance to its kth nearest neighbor, (2) concept of reachability distance between the case $p1$ and p_2, which is given by the maximum of the core distance of $p1$ and the distance between both cases, and (3) local reachability distance of a point, which is inversely proportional to the average reachability distance of its k neighbors. The LOF of a case is calculated as a function of its local reachability distance. In addition, there are 2 parameters that denote the density. One parameter is *MinPts* that controls the minimum number of objects and the other parameter specifying a volume. These 2 parameters determine a density threshold for the clustering algorithms to operate. That is, objects or regions are connected if their neighborhood densities exceed the pre-defined density threshold.

In the work of (Jin et al., 2001), the author summarized the definition of Local Outlier Factor as follows:

Let D be a database. Let p, q, o be some objects in D. Let k be a positive integer. We use $d(p,q)$ to denote the Euclidean distance between objects p and q.

Definition 1. (*k*-distance of *p*)

The k-distance of p, denoted as k-distance(p) is defined as the distance d(p; o) between p and o such that:

(i)   *for at least k objects $o' \in D \setminus \{p\}$* it holds that $d(p, o') \leq d(p, o)$, and

(ii) *for at most k-1 objects $o' \in D \setminus \{p\}$* it holds that $d(p, o') < d(p, o)$.

Intuitively, *k-distance(p)* provides a measure on the sparsity or density around the object *p*. When the *k*-distance of*p* is small, it means that the area around *p* is dense and vice versa.

Definition 2. (*k-distance* neighborhood of *p*)

The k-distance neighborhood of p contains every object whose distance from p is not greater than the k-distance, is denoted as

$N_k(p) = \{q \in D \setminus \{p\} \mid d(p, q) \leq k - distance(p)\}$.

Note that since there may be more than k objects within *k-distance(p)*, the number of objects in $N_k(p)$ may be more than k. Later on, the definition of LOF is introduced, and its value is strongly influenced by the *k*-distance of the objects in its *k*-distance neighborhood.

Definition 3. *(reachability distance of* p *w.r.t object* o*)*

The reachability distance of object p with respect to object o is defined as

$reach - dist_k(p, o) = \max\{k - distance(o), d(p, o)\}$.

Definition 4. (local reachability density of *p*)

The local reachability density of an object p is the inverse of the average reachability distance from the k-nearest-neighbors of p.

$$lrd_k(p) = 1/[\frac{\sum_{o \in N_k(p)} reach - dist_k(p,o)}{|N_{k(p)}(p)|}]$$

Essentially, the local reachability density of an object *p* is an estimation of the density at point *p* by analyzing the *k*-distance of the objects in $N_k(p)$. The local reachability density of *p* is just the reciprocal of the average distance between p and the objects in its k-neighborhood. Based on local reachability density, the local outlier factor can be defined as follows.

Definition 5. (local outlier factor of p)

$$LOF_k(p) = \frac{\sum_{o \in N_k(p)} \frac{lrd_k(o)}{lrd_k(p)}}{|N_k(p)|}$$

LOF is the average of the ratios of the local reachability density of p and those of p's k-nearest-neighbors. Intuitively, p's local outlier factor will be very high is its local reachability density is much lower than those of its neighbors.

In our experiment, we set the inspection effort to 0.1 which means that we regard the top 10% records as outliers according to the outlier score in decreasing sequence.

3.1 Workflow for Global Analysis Using LOF

For the global analysis, we calculate the LOF score for each instance from the whole dataset. The following diagrams indicate the Global Analysis mechanism for calculating the LOF score of the ith and its next instance. The operation of global analysis using LOF is visualized in Figure 2(a).

Figure 2. Illustrations of outlier detection that can be done by using LOF in three different operation modes.
(a) LOF Global Analysis
(b) LOF Cumulative Analysis
(c) LOF Lightweight Analysis

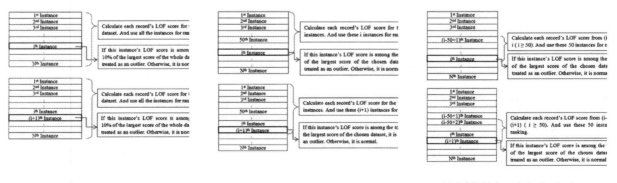

(a) LOF Global Analysis

(b) LOF Cumulative Analysis

(c) LOF Lightweight Analysis

3.2 Workflow for Cumulative Analysis Using LOF

As to the cumulative analysis, in our experiment, at first we calculate the LOF scores of the first 50 records respectively and labeled top 10% of the highest score ones as outliers. After that, for the ith record, calculate the LOF score for all these i records, and then examine this i^{th} one to see whether it is among the top 10% highest score of the present dataset. If yes, then this instance is regard as an outlier. Otherwise, it is normal. The following diagrams indicate the Cumulative Analysis mechanism for calculating the LOF score of the ith and its next instance. The operation of cumulative analysis using LOF is visualized in Figure 2(b).

3.3 Workflow for Lightweight Analysis with Sliding Window Using LOF

The mechanism of lightweight analysis with LOF method to detect outliers is similar to the mechanism of Mahalanobis Distance method which mentioned above. The following diagram in Figure 2(c) indicates the method about Lightweight Analysis using LOF with window size of 50 to estimate an outlier of the ith and its next instance.

4. EXPERIMENT FOR COMPARISON

In this paper, we use a dataset named "household power consumption" from MOA Massive Online Analysis for our experiment. We choose 10,000 instances for analysis in our experiment. As a traditional distance-based method, Euclidean distance should not be omitted. So we also try this classic method in our experiment and use its performance as a benchmark. In the following, we briefly review the basics of estimation theory about the Euclidean distance.

$$D_{Euclidean}(x_i) = \sqrt{((x_i - u_i)^T (x_i - u_i))}$$

where μ_i represents the mean vector of class {I}and x_i represents the sample vector to classify.

We use Global Analysis and Cumulative Analysis as the benchmark respectively and make the comparison with Lightweight Analysis. True Positive Rate (TPR) and False Positive Rate (FPR) are used as the metric. For a comprehensive analysis, we use two standards (hard standard and soft standard) to conduct the experiment with all the methods mentioned above. For the Euclidean distance and Mahalanobis distance, the hard standard is set with the probability of 0.001 and 0.05 of the soft one. With regard to the LOF method, the *minPtsLB* and *minPtsUB* are set to 10 and 40 respectively for hard standard and 50, 80 for soft standard. The following bar charts indicate the result.

In fact, the Cumulative Analysis is closer to the real situation. Imagine that we use the traditional analysis method to detect the outlier. What we need is the whole dataset we got at this very moment, like 1000 instances. Then we conduct the analysis for these 1000 records and get the result. As our paper's assumption, our object is data stream which comes to the database continuously. That means we need to analyze the data continuously. Suppose that after a short while, there are another 200 new datasets coming into the database. For the traditional analysis, we should use all the dataset we currently have, which up to 1200 records. So we do the outlier detection for these 1200 instances. The Cumulative Analysis in our experiment faithfully simulates this situation. But we still implement the Global Analysis as a reference.

The novel method "Lightweight Analysis with Sliding Window" we propose in this paper is real-time, flexible and efficient. What we need to do is to set a window size and the scales for the window to slide with based on actual situation. And the analysis is aimed at the data within the window. Just like the workflow we mentioned above.

4.1 Result of Using Euclidean Distance

We want to test the efficacy of Lightweight Analysis with effects of different window sizes, versus Global Analysis and Cumulative Analysis. This represents a test of outlier detection that is done on the fly (incremental) against using most of the static data points – Global Analysis uses all, and Cumulative Analysis uses all the accumulated data points that have been received up to the current processing time so far.

The results in Figures 3(a) and 3(b) are produced by Lightweight Analysis and they are the accuracies derived from the proportion of outliers being discovered in relative to the benchmarks of Global Analysis (as in Figure 3(a)) and Cumulative Analysis (as in Figure 3(b)) respectively. In each of these Figures, two levels of outlier detections are being used – hard standard and soft standard. From the Figures, we can clearly see that under the hard standard, the TPR is higher than that of soft standard. It is because in the hard standard mode, the Euclidean distance method can only find very few outliers. Once we relax the condition, it detects a lot more outliers, but the accuracy deteriorates considerately.

The following Figures 4(a) and 4(b) are 3-D plots that visualize the data points with color map for cumulative analysis and lightweight analysis with hard and soft standards; the blue points stand for normal instances and the red ones stand for outliers (similarly hereinafter).

The number of outliers found by different measurements may be an interesting statistic. We regard the variable window size of 100 as a small window, size of 500 as medium and size of 1000 as large. The following Figures 5(a) and 5(b) are the comparison of different operation modes using Euclidean Distance; different window sizes are used, in hard and soft standards respectively.

4.2 Result of Using Mahalanobis Distance

The same experiments are repeated but by using Mahalanobis Distance (MD). As we can see in Figures 6(a) and 6(b), the larger the window size, the higher accuracy rate we can get. If we use a looser standard, we not only find more outliers but we also have a slight improvement in the accuracy, which is certainly an advantage of MD over the traditional Euclidean distance method.

More importantly, our proposed Lightweight Analysis method can detect more outliers than the Cumulative Analysis. The reason is that the Lightweight Analysis method focuses on the datasets within the window, which is more sensitive to some regional outliers. However the Cumulative Analysis concentrates on all the current datasets, which evaluates outliers based on the overall average. So our proposed Lightweight Analysis makes a significant improvement against the traditional one.

The number of outliers found by different methods of measurement using MD are shown in Figures 7(a) and 7(b), in hard standard and soft standard respectively as follows.

Figure 3. Accuracy of outlier detection by Lightweight Analysis using Euclidean Distance, wrt Global Analysis.

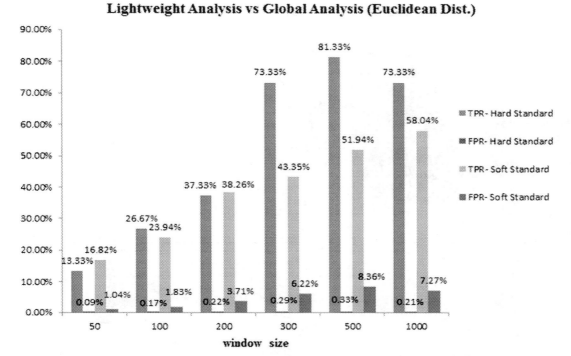

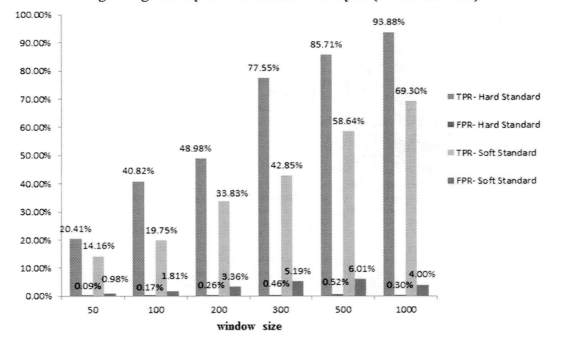

Figure 4. Visualization of outliers detected by hard standard of Lightweight Analysis using Euclidean Distance.

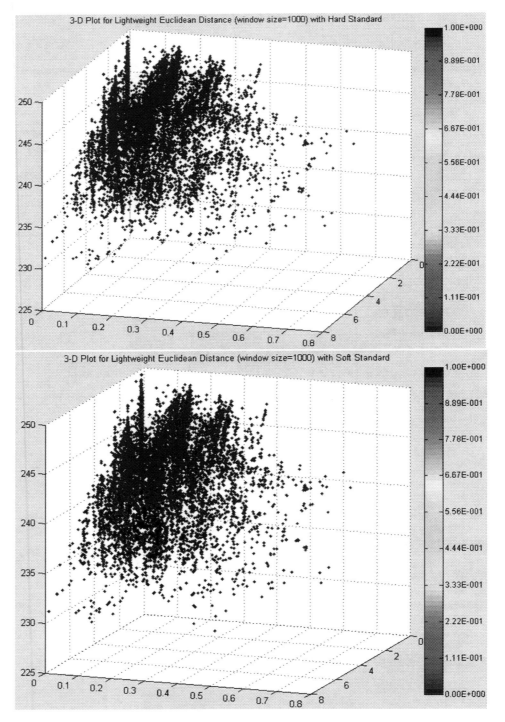

Figure 5. Comparison of different outlier detection operation modes by hard standard using Euclidean Distance.

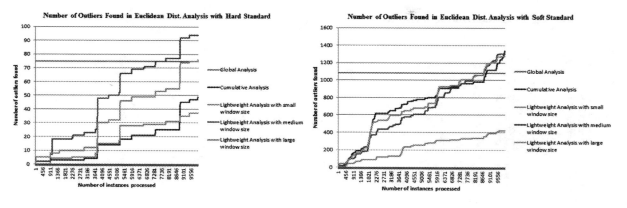

Figure 6. Accuracy of outlier detection by Lightweight Analysis using Mahalanobis Distance, wrt Global/ Cumulative Analysis.

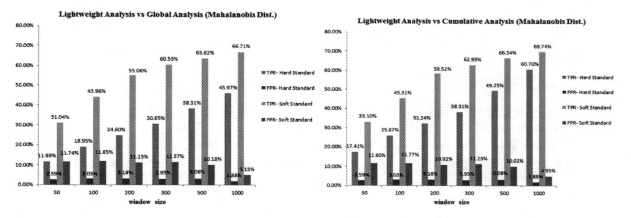

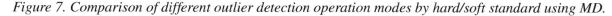

Figure 7. Comparison of different outlier detection operation modes by hard/soft standard using MD.

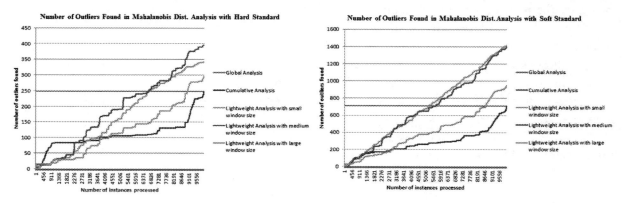

Figure 8. Accuracy of outlier detection by Lightweight Analysis using LOF, wrt Global/ Cumulative Analysis.

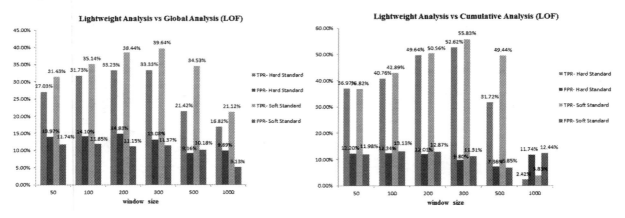

4.3 Result of Using Local Outlier Factor

Again the experiments are repeated by using Local Outlier Factor (LOF) as a distance measurement method. From the comparison charts shown in Figures 8(a) and 7(b), we can see that the window size is no longer the bigger the better. Specifically, after the window size of 300, the accuracy rate is trending downward. So, we may infer that the LOF method has an appropriate or optimal window size. Moreover this method has a higher false positive rate than the Mahalanobis Distance method.

The 3-D plots in Figures 9 (a)-(d) visualize the data with color map for cumulative analysis and lightweight analysis with window size equals to 1000. The purpose is to visually compare how Lightweight Analysis performs wrt to Cumulative Analysis using LOF, because the TPR of Lightweight Analysis wrt to Cumulative Analysis is unusually low when window size is large at 1000, as shown in Figure 7(b).

From the above visualization plots we can see that the Lightweight Analysis has much better performance than the Cumulative Analysis. The Lightweight Analysis method detects a lot more outliers which seem to be real outliers in the dataset. Now we can explain why the TPR in Lightweight Analysis against Cumulative Analysis is usually low in window 1000. Because the latter one did not thoroughly find the outliers but the former one did. In other words, many outliers found in Lightweight Analysis are regarded as normal in Cumulative Analysis thus, leads to a low TPR. This experiment demonstrates that for the LOF method, our proposed Lightweight Analysis performs somewhat better than the traditional one.

Lastly the numbers of outliers found by different methods of measurement are shown in Figures 10(a) for hard standard and 9(b) for soft standards. In both cases, it can be observed that in the context of LOF measurement, the Lightweight Analysis with small window size method is largely producing more outliers. It can find as many outliers as Global Analysis does, after processing about 6000 data points. Lightweight Analysis with small window size started to outperform Cumulative Analysis soon after processing 5900 data points in both hard and soft standards. Lightweight Analysis indeed can find more outliers with small window than large ones using LOF.

A similar phenomenon is observed (c.f. Figure 6(b)) in MD but only in soft standard. In contrast, Lightweight Analysis with small window finds only very few outliers in Euclidean Distance.

Figure 9. Visualization of outliers detected by hard/soft standard of Cumulative Analysis using LOF.

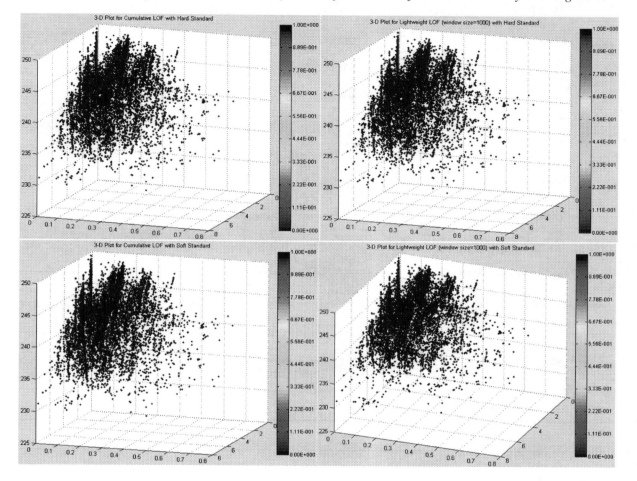

Figure 10. Comparison of different outlier detection operation modes by hard/soft standard using LOF.

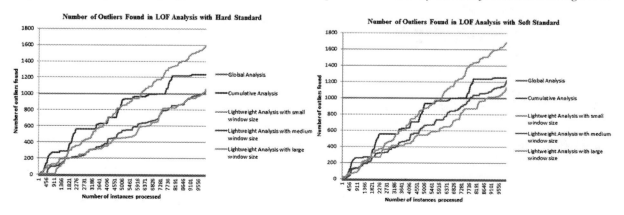

Figure 11. (a&b) The number of correctly classified instances by using outlier detection combined with different classifiers in chart/sequence view. Figure 11(c). The Recall rate achieved by using outlier detection combined with different classifiers.

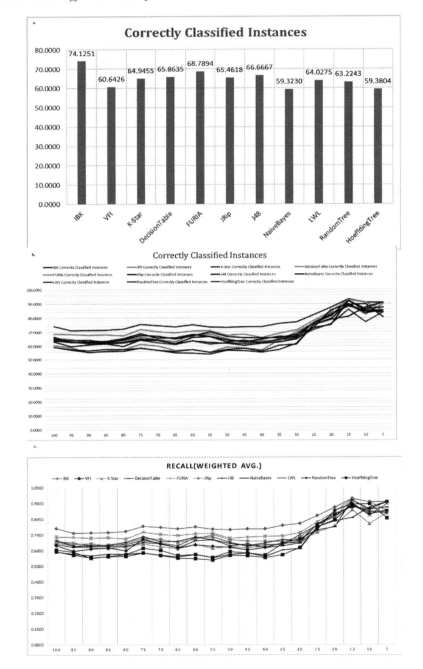

Table 1. Raw data results of Accuracy

Method	100	95	90	85	80	75	70	65	60	55	50	45	40	35	30	25	20	15	10	5
IBK	74.1251	71.1353	71.3193	71.5250	72.2382	75.5164	74.6721	73.7864	75.1434	73.5141	73.2491	73.7245	73.7446	75.9016	77.0554	82.1101	87.3926	93.1034	90.8046	90.8046
VFI	60.6426	59.0580	55.1307	56.3428	57.3888	61.3619	60.0820	56.7520	57.3614	55.4745	59.2423	58.4184	56.9584	64.2623	65.3920	76.6055	83.3811	87.7395	86.2069	90.8046
K-Star	64.9455	63.2246	61.8228	61.5385	62.2669	64.2693	62.4590	61.1650	63.8623	61.4181	62.3421	61.7347	62.6973	64.5902	65.7744	71.5596	75.6447	85.8238	77.0115	83.9080
Decision Table	65.8635	64.8551	63.2887	63.3603	63.7733	66.5647	64.7541	63.1068	68.2600	68.6131	65.2124	62.6276	63.7016	63.6066	69.9809	76.1468	81.3754	89.2720	82.1839	89.6552
FURIA	68.7894	68.5386	67.9414	68.1511	67.4319	71.8439	70.2459	69.5499	70.7457	71.0115	67.7382	68.4949	65.8666	69.0164	71.3193	77.9817	84.5272	92.7203	90.8046	85.0575
JRip	65.4618	64.0700	64.3722	62.9555	64.5624	67.7123	67.1311	65.2251	67.3040	70.0730	66.8197	65.9439	65.8537	65.7377	68.2600	76.1468	81.3754	91.9540	85.0575	85.0575
J48	66.6667	62.8623	63.2250	63.5628	65.4232	68.8600	65.7377	65.9312	68.3556	66.9447	64.4087	63.0102	64.8494	66.8852	66.3480	76.3761	82.2350	88.5050	84.4828	83.9080
Naïve Bayes	59.3230	57.7295	56.7240	57.6923	57.6040	58.4545	56.9672	56.0459	57.4570	55.2659	57.4053	58.2908	56.0976	60.3279	61.1855	75.0000	78.7966	80.8429	87.3563	90.8046
LWL	64.0275	62.9810	62.6514	62.5506	62.8407	65.1875	64.5082	61.6946	66.2524	66.8405	62.9162	64.1582	61.8364	62.7869	64.8184	72.9358	75.0716	91.9540	86.2069	87.3563
Random Tree	63.2243	59.7222	60.9943	61.6734	59.7561	64.6519	64.0984	61.6946	63.6711	62.6694	62.1125	60.3316	61.8364	64.7541	67.3040	73.1651	85.3868	89.6552	83.3333	85.0575
Hoeffding Tree	59.3804	57.1860	55.4493	56.0729	56.1693	58.5310	56.8852	54.9868	54.7801	53.9103	56.8312	56.5051	55.3802	57.2131	61.7591	75.0000	79.3696	89.2720	89.6552	80.4598

Table 2. Raw data results of Recall

Method	100	95	90	85	80	75	70	65	60	55	50	45	40	35	30	25	20	15	10	5
IBK	0.7410	0.7110	0.7130	0.7150	0.7220	0.7550	0.7470	0.7380	0.7510	0.7350	0.7320	0.7370	0.7370	0.7590	0.7710	0.8210	0.8740	0.9310	0.9080	0.9080
VFI	0.6060	0.5910	0.5510	0.5630	0.5740	0.6140	0.6010	0.5680	0.5740	0.5550	0.5920	0.5840	0.5700	0.6430	0.6540	0.7660	0.8340	0.8770	0.8620	0.9080
K-Star	0.6490	0.6320	0.6180	0.6150	0.6230	0.6430	0.6250	0.6120	0.6390	0.6140	0.6230	0.6170	0.6270	0.6460	0.6580	0.7160	0.7560	0.8580	0.7700	0.8390
Decision Table	0.6590	0.6490	0.6330	0.6340	0.6380	0.6660	0.6480	0.6310	0.6830	0.6860	0.6520	0.6260	0.6370	0.6360	0.7000	0.7610	0.8140	0.8930	0.8220	0.8970
FURIA	0.6880	0.6850	0.6790	0.6820	0.6740	0.7180	0.7020	0.6950	0.7070	0.7100	0.6770	0.6850	0.6890	0.6900	0.7130	0.7800	0.8450	0.9270	0.9080	0.8510
JRip	0.6550	0.6410	0.6440	0.6300	0.6460	0.6770	0.6710	0.6520	0.6730	0.7010	0.6680	0.6590	0.6590	0.6570	0.6830	0.7610	0.8140	0.9200	0.8510	0.8510
J48	0.6670	0.6290	0.6320	0.6360	0.6540	0.6890	0.6570	0.6590	0.6840	0.6690	0.6440	0.6300	0.6480	0.6690	0.6630	0.7640	0.8220	0.8850	0.8450	0.8390
Naïve Bayes	0.5930	0.5770	0.5670	0.5770	0.5760	0.5850	0.5700	0.5600	0.5750	0.5530	0.5740	0.5830	0.5610	0.6030	0.6120	0.7500	0.7880	0.8080	0.8740	0.9080
LWL	0.6400	0.6220	0.6270	0.6260	0.6280	0.6520	0.6450	0.6170	0.6630	0.6680	0.6290	0.6420	0.6180	0.6280	0.6480	0.7290	0.7510	0.9200	0.8620	0.8740
RandomTree	0.6320	0.5970	0.6100	0.6170	0.5980	0.6740	0.6410	0.6170	0.6370	0.6270	0.6210	0.6030	0.6180	0.6480	0.6730	0.7320	0.8540	0.8970	0.8330	0.8510
Hoeffding Tree	0.5940	0.5720	0.5540	0.5610	0.5620	0.5850	0.5690	0.5500	0.5480	0.5390	0.5680	0.5650	0.5540	0.5720	0.6180	0.7500	0.7940	0.8930	0.8970	0.8050

4.4 Evaluating the Performance of Different Classifier

In order to test the efficacy of the proposed outlier detection methods, a collection of classifiers which could be embedded as the underlying pattern recognizers are tested. A sequence of multi-variate data are being processed, from which the outliers are detected using our methods and removed. Subsequently the classifiers are used for training up classification models progressively as the data roll along, and testing is done on the fly too for measuring the accuracy and other performance indicators.

In this experiment, the dataset is obtained from a public data archive called UCI; the data is called Gesture Phase Segmentation dataset which is sequential and multi-variate. There are 9900 instances and 50 attributes. Details can be found from the URL (https://archive.ics.uci.edu/ml/datasets/Gesture+Phase+Segmentation). The dataset is comprised by features that are extracted from 7 videos with people gesticulating. The data was recorded for studying the problem of Gesture Phase Segmentation (Madeo et al., 2013). Each video sequence is characterized by two files. One is a raw data file that is consists of the position of different parts of the user, like spine, head, hands and wrists. The other is a processed file that which comprises of the data recorded from the movements of the users' hands and wrists. The movements are measured in terms of velocity and acceleration. The data roll from zero to the last instances as the video data feeds in.

To test the performance of the classifiers, the live sequence of "outlier removal", "train" and then "test" is simulated by a row of partitioned dataset. The data is cut into 20 subsets, the sum of them resembles the full data sequence, i.e. 100%. And it trims progressively from 100% down to 5%, with a portion of 5% being trimmed each time. For outlier detection, Mahalanobis distance measure is used, and accumulative method is used as the outlier detection operation. There are two major performance indicators being used: Accuracy which is defined simply as the number of correctly classified instances over the total instances; and Recall is calculated as #True-Positive/(#True-Positive + #False-Negative). Recall is used here as it reflects the nature of the outlier detection problem: In identifying outlier, we want to identify as many "likely" outliers as we can (that's recall) while not sacrificing the useful information in the data which affects the accuracy.

The performance results are charted in Figures 11(a) and 10(b) respectively for Accuracy and Recall. The detailed figures are tabulated in Tables 1 and 2 for Accuracy and Recall respectively too.

It can be observed from Figures 10(a, b) that the top performers are IBK and FURIA. They managed to achieve the highest accuracy by generating enough quality rules in classification. Similar to Accuracy, the same observation can be made for Recall performance, showing that the performances are consistent with respect to the amount of outliers detected (and subsequently removed). From the line charts, Figure 10(b) and 10(c), it can be seen that when the portion of dataset exceeds 30% the performance for both cases declines, and approach a flat line henceforth.

5. CONCLUSION

This paper proposed a general framework for finding outliers in an incremental fashion. A collection of methods in different operation modes and distance measurements are formulated and experimented. It contributes to outlier detection in data stream mining which is important but a relatively neglected research area.

ACKNOWLEDGMENT

The authors are thankful for the financial support from the research grant "Adaptive OVFDT with Incremental Pruning and ROC Corrective Learning for Data Stream Mining," Grant no. MYRG073(Y3-L2)-FST12-FCC, offered by the University of Macau, FST, and RDAO.

REFERENCES

Aggarwal, C., & Yu, P. (2001). Outlier Detection for High Dimensional Data. *Proc. of the ACM SIGMOD International Conference on Management of Data.*

Arning, A., Agrawal, R., & Raghavan, P. (1996). A Linear Method for Deviation Detection in Large Databases. *Proc. of 1996 Int. Conf. Data Mining and Knowledge Discovery (KDD'96)* (pp. 164–169). Portland, OR.

Breunig, M. M., Kriegel, H. P., Ng, R. T., & Sander, J. (2000). LOF: Identifying density-based local outliers. *Proc. of the 2000 ACM SIGMOD International Conference on Management of Data* (pp. 93-104). Dallas. doi:10.1145/342009.335388

Brighton, H., & Mellish, C. (2002). Advances in Instance Selection for Instance-Based Learning Algorithms. *Data Mining and Knowledge Discovery, 6*(2), 153–172. doi:10.1023/A:1014043630878

Grubbs, F. E. (1969). Procedures for Detecting Outlying Observations in Samples. *Technometrics, 11*(1), 1–21. doi:10.1080/00401706.1969.10490657

Jin, W., Tung, A. K., & Han, J. (2001). Mining top-n local outliers in large databases. *In Proc. of the seventh ACM SIGKDD International Conference on Knowledge Discovery and Data mining* (pp. 293-298). doi:10.1145/502512.502554

Knorr, E. M., & Ng, R. T. (1998). Algorithms for mining distance-based outliers in large datasets. *Proc. 24th Int. Conf. Very Large Data Bases* (pp. 392–403).

Madeo, R. C. B., Lima, C. A. M., & Peres, S. M. (2013). Gesture unit segmentation using support vector machines: segmenting gestures from rest positions. *Proceedings of the 28th Annual ACM Symposium on Applied Computing* (pp.46-52). doi:10.1145/2480362.2480373

Mahalanobis, P. C. (1936). On the generalized distance in statistics. Proc. of the National Institute of Science of India (pp. 49-55).

Mansur, M. O., & Sap, M. N. M. (2005). Outlier detection technique in data mining: a research perspective, *Proceedings of the postgraduate annual research seminar.*

Ramaswamy, S., Rastogi, R., & Shim, K. (2000). Efficient algorithms for mining outliers from large data sets. *Proc. of the 2000* ACM SIGMOD (pp. 427–438). doi:10.1145/342009.335437

Zhang, T., Ramakrishnan, R., & Livny, M. (1996). BIRCH: An Efficient Data Clustering Method for Very Large Databases. *Proc. of the Conference of Management of Data* (ACM SIGMOD '96) (pp. 103-114).

KEY TERMS AND DEFINITIONS

Data Stream: A continuous flow of a long sequence of data which can potentially amount to infinity.

Euclidean Distance: In geometry, it is the distance between two points defined as the square root of the sum of the squares of the differences between the corresponding coordinates of the points.

Incremental Learning: It is a machine learning paradigm where the learning process takes place whenever new example(s) emerge and adjusts what has been learned according to the new example(s).

Mahalanobis Distance: It is a distance measure that accounts for the variance of each variable and the covariance between variables. Geometrically, it does this by transforming the data into standardized uncorrelated data and computing the ordinary Euclidean distance for the transformed data.

Outlier Detection: It is a method used to identify and then remove anomalous observations from data.

Outlier: It is an observation that appears to deviate markedly from other observations in the sample.

Z-Score: A Z-Score is a statistical measurement of a score's relationship to the mean in a group of scores.

Section 2

Chapter 5
Advances of Applying Metaheuristics to Data Mining Techniques

Simon Fong
University of Macau, Macau SAR

Jinyan Li
University of Macau, Macau SAR

Xueyuan Gong
University of Macau, Macau SAR

Athanasios V. Vasilakos
Kuwait University, Kuwait

ABSTRACT

Metaheuristics have lately gained popularity among researchers. Their underlying designs are inspired by biological entities and their behaviors, e.g. schools of fish, colonies of insects, and other land animals etc. They have been used successfully in optimization applications ranging from financial modeling, image processing, resource allocations, job scheduling to bioinformatics. In particular, metaheuristics have been proven in many combinatorial optimization problems. So that it is not necessary to attempt all possible candidate solutions to a problem via exhaustive enumeration and evaluation which is computationally intractable. The aim of this paper is to highlight some recent research related to metaheuristics and to discuss how they can enhance the efficacy of data mining algorithms. An upmost challenge in Data Mining is combinatorial optimization that, often lead to performance degradation and scalability issues. Two case studies are presented, where metaheuristics improve the accuracy of classification and clustering by avoiding local optima.

DOI: 10.4018/978-1-4666-8513-0.ch005

1. INTRODUCTION

With the ever increase in data growth and ease of data collection, data mining has always been a popular computing discipline for business and many other industry domains. Data mining offers insights from the data by analyzing, modeling and detecting outliers or anomalies over the underlying patterns hidden among the data. It is a process of knowledge discovery founded on well-established statistical principles which are deterministic in nature (Fayyad et al., 1996). In general there are two types of learning approaches for uncovering and understanding the representative patterns of the data – one is called supervised learning and the other is unsupervised learning. Supervised learning as the name suggests requires observing through the dataset in order to induce a mathematical model that essentially maps the relations between the variables (attributes) of the data which characterize the whole dataset and the predefined class labels as targets. Unsupervised learning often just let the data to reveal their characteristic patterns, by for examples clustering into groups, visualization, or generating their frequent itemsets or associations. In both types learning, though they are very popular among modern data mining techniques, the process is deterministic and sequential – one can trace from the steps of the process as well as the data that have been so far processed. This typical learning process is by greedy search or divide-and-conquer where the model updates itself whenever new data becomes available.

One drawback about deterministic learning is that often a local optimum is obtained and the learning process ceased, without considering all the combinations of possibilities. The other reason is that it may simply take too long the time to evaluate through all the possible solutions because of the combinatorial limitation such as problems of NP-hard in nature. The limitation introduced by combinatorial property in numerical analysis hinders the efficacy of data mining in producing an intermediate solution of local optimum, or else taking forever to find a globally best solution. Such multidimensional combinatorial problems that constitute to the "curse-of-dimensionality" are often found in data mining problems. The dataset from which a data mining model has to learn from is usually characterized by a very high dimensionality depending on the amount of features or attributes that characterize the data. Measuring the distance between a pair of data points in clustering algorithms, or finding a best fit regression curve in prediction model among a series of data point in a high-dimensional hyper-space is a norm in data mining. Generally the higher the dimension space, the greater the combinatorial explosion on the search space results, making the corresponding model induction extremely difficult and time-consuming. The difficulty lies in the search space of candidate solutions that arise in many combinations expands faster than exponentially, when the size of the problem grows. As a result the increasingly huge search space makes exhaustive search for the best solution infeasible, which cripples the efficacy of the analytical methods far from the globally best.

Having known of this obstacle stemmed mainly from the combinatorial problems, researchers resorted to combinatorial optimization in the hope of breaking through this limitation and improving the data mining performance. Metaheuristics are designed for combinatorial optimization in which an optimal solution is explored over a large search-space. In the context of theoretical optimization and computer algorithms, a metaheuristic is an abstract procedure programmed to manage or control a lower-level search mechanism called heuristic that looks for a sufficiently good solution to an optimization problem. The lower-level search works by searching partially of the whole space but it retains information gained from previous iteration heuristically. This way, without the need of going through the whole search space which is either impossible or too time consuming, metaheuristics is able to work on incomplete information with a known upper bound on the required computation capacity. Metaheuristics are also known as strategies which are generic by taking few assumptions about the optimization problem being solved, therefore they would be usable for a variety of problems like those associated with combinational problems for data mining.

Comparing to deterministic optimization methods, many metaheuristics optimize a solution stochastically, such that the solution obtained at the end is dependent on the values of random variables that are being used at the beginning. The solution is progressively improved by searching through a large set of feasible solutions by replacing the best solution in the memory seen so far with the current solution, if it is better than the best yet solution. In each iteration cycle, the metaheuristic uses its partial search to seek a better solution while at the same time, a higher-level mechanism ensures that the search direction may randomly switch to elsewhere in order to avoid local optima. The solution may keep on being updated as long as new and better solutions happen to be found and the stopping criteria have not met yet. It is known that metaheuristics may not guarantee a globally optimal solution without going through every possible candidate solution, but an on-par solution is always yielded. This way, metaheuristics can often attain acceptable solutions with less computational effort than the deterministic approach making them suitable for combinatorial optimization problems.

The next section reviews some recent advances of applying metaheuristics on different aspects of data mining as related works. Followed by two sections that present two case studies on metaheuristics are being used for classification and clustering respectively, with a potential real-time analysis requirement. The last section concludes the paper.

2. RECENT ADVANCES

Tracing the history of evolutionary algorithms back to the early era of Genetic Algorithm (GA) (Barricelli, 1954) where evolution was simulated by computer, metaheuristics was designed as a search heuristic that routinely generated useful solutions to an optimization problem. Metaheuristics have a heritage of randomized search procedures inspired by the mechanics of natural phenomenon, biology and swarming behaviors of animals or insects. Fister Jr. et al published a comprehensive survey over the metaheuristic algorithms including both the classical and contemporary ones. In particular, Fister Jr. pointed out the taxonomy, stating that bio-inspired is not exactly swarm intelligence based. They have a composite relation nevertheless. SI-based algorithms are referring to the behaviours of biological entities which is a subset of bio-inspired algorithms. Bio-inspired algorithms do not necessarily swarm, for example, the chromosomes in GA mutate instead of swarm. And bio-inspired algorithms are a subset of nature-inspired algorithms which encompass all things in nature covering biology, chemistry, physics and astronomy etc.

Although metaheuristics come in a wide variety of names and inspirations, they have fundamental mechanisms similar to that of GA in regard of evolving a good solution. For instance, metaheuristics start with abounded population of agents that represent possible solutions to a problem at random. Each representative agent is encoded as simple as a binary string or as complex as an embedded computer routine. The initial population may be initially scattered randomly over the search space or strategically according to some domain knowledge or the random seed of the previously known solutions.

The meta-procedure evaluates the agents by some predefined fitness functions to determine how well the solutions that they represent can solve the problem. The agents with the best fitness are retained or gathered for evolving a hopefully better solution in the next generation. Then the metaheuristics move on to generating new agents while retaining the essence of the best solution from the past generations, or relocating the existing ones to other randomized search spaces in the hope of fitness breakthrough. Then new solutions are generated, evaluated, selected and evolved repeatedly until a satisfactory solution is obtained or a preset cycle limit has elapsed.

Such fundamental search concept by metaheuristics has lately been adapted for the use in data mining algorithms. The adaption includes redesigning the logics of data mining algorithms with the aim of searching for an induction model that offers the best results, wrapping the essential codes of data mining mechanism into the metaheuristics search, and preprocessing the input dataset for keeping the optimal subset that leads to the best performing data mining model. Depending on the complexity, different levels of modification are required for coupling data mining algorithms into metaheuristics.

Not meant to be exhaustive, in the following sections below we show the recent advances on how metaheuristics are applied on data mining with respect to the three popular areas, such as classification, clustering, associate and trend discovery. Readers who are interested in the background of metaheuristics, bio-inspired optimization or swarm intelligence are referred to some surveys (Cantú-Paz& Kamath, 2001). Cantú-Paz and Kamath illustrated diverse possibilities in which the power of metaheuristics in the form of evolutionary algorithm scan be used to improve the data analytics especially for massive data sets. Some technical difficulties encountered in applying metaheuristics are discussed. Binitha and Sathya (2012) surveyed over a collection of bio-inspired optimization algorithms, taxonomy on their behaviors. A comparison of the algorithms in terms of application areas and control parameters is provided.

2.1 Classification

One of the most detailed thesis by Raffaele (2006) is devoted to verify that nature-inspired optimization algorithms, especially GA and Ant Colony Optimization (ACO) indeed help solve the problem of combinational search space. In particular, the thesis demonstrated that GA and ACO can be used as metaheuristics temples in implementing Classification and Regression Trees (CART) classifier. A prototype classifier is coded in Java software by using a very fast procedure; it was anticipated that the work will provide a flexible framework to support future development of other nature-inspired algorithms to be coded as CART. A Forward Search-based methodology was proposed in the thesis for improving the stability of the decision trees.

Bursa lately (2013) applied a similar ACO decision tree algorithm, for analyzing 32 different biomedical datasets. It was shown that integrating decision tree despite other classifiers yield a best result; the decision tree induced by ACO method is better than other state-of-the-art classifier implementations. The advantage of the proposed method is achieved by the robustness from mimicking the self-organization behaviour of ants which was incorporated into the logics of decision tree induction mechanisms. Using the concept of elitism and diverse population approach, good solutions refines in iterations. In the thesis an error-based pruning and an adaptive measure for the control of pheromone values in the reference matrix was proposed.

Parpinelli et al (2002) has implemented a software program called Ant-Miner for finding the best predicate rules for classification. Without inducing a decision tree or similar classifier model, Ant-Miner extracts classification rules heuristically from data. The optimization principles are the same as those in (Bursa, 2013) (Raffaele, 2006) in terms of finding the best decision rules or branches of decision trees from pheromone matrix, except without an induced model. The authors compared the performance of Ant-Miner with a classification rule discovery algorithm called CN2. They noticed that Ant-Miner provides a higher accuracy and the generated rules are simpler in length than those discovered by CN2.

The basic logic of Ant-Miner and many of its similar variants is outlined as follows. In the classification task the objective is to classify each instance of a dataset to one of several predefined classes. The class assignment is done based on the values of the predictor attributes associated with the dataset. In the rule discovery process the resultant rules are expressed in the format of IF-THEN rules, whose consequent part specifies the class predicted for cases. The values of the predictor attributes in the antecedent part of the rules are then sought from a huge combinatorial search space heuristically by the search algorithm, while disqualified rules that lead to false prediction or poor accuracy would be discarded and good ones retained. In the context of rule discovery, ACO finds a good combination of logical conditions for each possible rule, from many different combinations of values of the predictor attributes mapping the predefined classes. Some irrelevant rules are pruned to avoid overfitting and to improve the simplicity of the rule.

Gorea (2009) extended the concept of Ant-Miner by integrating ACO and classification by clustering algorithm. The authors aimed at using the proposed classification method for solving problems in the application area of semantic Web mining. Based on their metadata Web resources are clustered. Subsequently automatic classification of Web pages is made available by judging the similarities of the testing pages and the clustered groups.

Instead of ACO, Sousa et al (2004) attempted implementing Particle Swarm Optimization (PSO) and J48 which is one of the most popular decision tree based on CART for rule discovery. PSO is inherently derived from the schooling behavior and interactions between many simple autonomous agents called particles. The authors improved the PSO as a variant regarding the support of attribute type and temporal complexity. The new algorithms are put under tests with some commonly used data sources which considered as a de facto standard for testing the reliability and ranking of rule discovery algorithms. The results demonstrated that PSO Data Mining Algorithms are competitive with other evolutionary techniques, and they are flexible enough to be applied in different application domains.

In addition to cooperative ants and swarming particles, the bio-inspired foraging behavior of honey bees is looked into by Shukran et al (2011) as clues for building classifiers. The authors proposed a new tool in 2011 called Artificial Bee Colony[1] (ABC) algorithm in solving combinatorial problems in classification tasks. ABC is similar to PSO except that it has simpler control parameter; actually there is only one – the number of bees in the colony. As a metaheuristics, ABC has ability in performing local search similar to Differential Evolution algorithm as well as global optimal searching faculties by the onlookers and scout bees. Therefore it provides a good balance between intensification and diversification when it comes to searching for the best solution in the search space. In general the ABC version of classification algorithm consists of the following major steps: 1. Constructing the rules by selecting predictor attributes and target classes; 2.Evaluating the fitness function whose fitness is quantified as the amount of nectar; 3.Exchanging local search strategy between teams of employed bees and onlookers via dances; 4. Rule discovery; 5.Rule pruning; and 6.Prediction strategy. Experiments were done to compare ABC algorithm and found that it is competitive over some popular and standard classification algorithms.

There are several variants based on Bee algorithms; one of them is called Honey Bee Mating Optimization (HBMO) algorithm. HBMO is exploited by Marinaki et al (2010) in implementing a Nearest Neighbour based classifier for performing feature selection for financial classification. HBMO is inspired by the mating behavior of honey bees, where the algorithm starts from a single queen bee without any family and evolves to the growth of a colony with family having more reproductive queens. In the work of Marinaki et al (2010), the performance of the HBMO method in task of financial classification with the objective function of credit risk assessment was tested. The results are compared with those of PSO, ACO, GA and Tabu search algorithm. The HBMO and ABC algorithms utilize typical random explorative search to locate promising locations in an evolutionary manner. At the same time, the meta-procedure uses the exploitative search on the remote locations to explore for the global optimum. In principle, the Bee type of metaheuristics is an improved version of GA. The unique characteristic of Bee algorithms is to improve local search while maintaining the global search ability of random mutation of GA.

Oliveira et al surveyed several bio-inspired metaheuristics in (Oliveira et al., 2007). Three computational tools that implemented bio-inspired metaheuristics for data mining tasks are analyzed comparatively. The first tool developed the Ant Colony metaphor called Ant-miner; the second tool uses the Artificial Immune System which is a relatively new biologically-inspired paradigm, called IFRAIS. The third one equips with a fuzzy GA method, namely FGS. The comparative survey of metaheuristics that are used in extracting rules from databases confirms the importance of discovering knowledge to be done accurately using metaheuristics. The comparison results showed that in terms of classification accuracy Ant-miner and offered superior performances over C4.5 and CN2. But still they are under rated by FGS. It is validated that the power of fuzzy logic that has an edge in dealing linguistic terms in text mining and for discovering fuzzy knowledge rules, which in turn help enhance the performance FGS and IFRAIS which are fuzzy in nature. Meanwhile, Ant-Miner beats IFRAIS and FGS by execution time. It is fast without the burden of fuzzy logic module. Overall Ant-Miner and IFRAIS are far better than C4.5 in performance. Between Ant-Miner and IFRAIS, the number of prediction rules generated by the IFRAIS is always fewer than the amount of rules extracted by Ant-Miner. Moreover, Ant-Miner appears to be very competitive in extracting the rules with most number of linguistic terms. This advantage is attributed by the pruning mechanism in Ant-Miner that helps further simplify the amount of rules, making them concise. The comparative results and analysis reveal that potentially there are plenty of rooms in future extension over these algorithms by upgrading the effectiveness of the metaheuristics.

Soliman et al in (Soliman, 2012) innovatively designed an associative classifier which is also known as classification by associative rules (CAR), by using a bio-inspired algorithm called Quantum-Inspired Artificial Immune system (QAIS). The authors represented each CAR as an immune cell, collectively after each generation, a pool of immune cells is obtained which represent a set of class association rules. There are implicitly two parts in the rule selection process: rule discovery by generating immune cells and rule evaluation via selecting only the fit ones. Starting from an initial random population, new rules are generated and discovered from the testing dataset. The population of immune cells increases through iterative generations and inputs of testing data. The fittest rules which have the maximum confidence values and highest confidence measure as the affinity in immune system are selected. They also would have to satisfy the conditional constraints if any, in each round. The process terminates when generation count exceeds the given maximum number of generations. Then the classification initialized after the CARs from memory pool are obtained. The concept of QAIS is founded on the quantum theory and clonal selection theory. The proposed system is demonstrated to be able to produce association rules efficiently in a very large search space for classification. By using a Q-gate mutation operator the diversity of immune cells can be kept in check in the search space, leading the direction of the search. Therefore the system is able and suitable for working with highly complex search space of association rules. By evaluating and comparing with benchmark datasets, QAIS performed well with superb accuracy and good affinity values. Each discovered rule is checked at the end of each generation, disqualified rules are eliminated from the immune cell pool.

2.2 Clustering and Others

Clustering is one of the popular data mining methods aiming at representing a large dataset by a concise collection of clusters. It helps a user to obtain abstract views of data that are segmented in groups. Also clustering plays a central role in knowledge discovery and the amount of dataset we collect becomes increasingly larger than ever, cluster partitioning of huge datasets must be fast and accurate. Therefore severe computational requirements are imposed on the traditional clustering techniques. Recently a family of metaheuristics emerged with the aim of meeting the performance requirements for empowering clustering algorithms by partitioning the dataset into an optimal number of groups with optimized group memberships for the data points.

Some of the pioneer research teams, led by Handl and Meyer (2002) and Ramos et al (2002) in the early millennium worked on modifying the original K-means algorithm in order to improve the cluster convergence and to obtain an optimal number of clusters. In 1999, Monmarche et al (1999) integrated the ACO algorithm into K-means algorithm. Their hybrid was then compared to traditional K-means under the test of different datasets with classification error deemed as performance criterion. However this criterion is not suitable for ordinary clustering. In 2003, Kanade and Hall (2003) extended the previous work by hybridizing ACO with fuzzy clustering method, called Fuzzy Ant algorithm. At the start, the ant based clustering forms raw clusters. Then fuzzy clustering algorithms are used to rearrange these clusters. The ants that represent the centroids pull the data points to form heaps. The centroids of the heaps reform and reshape along the process of optimization to form new heaps until they stabilized and final clusters emerged.

In addition to ACO, PSO was also used to form new hybrids such as PSO-based clustering algorithm that was proposed by Omran et al. (2002) in 2002. Their results showed that PSO based method outperformed K-means, fuzzy clustering some other modern clustering algorithms. A quantization error was used as a fitness measure in the PSO-based clustering for judging the goodness of a clustering algorithm. Subsequently there exist several other variants too, such as hybridizing PSO with the Self Organizing Maps (SOM)(Xiao, 2003);and that was used for clustering gene expression data. Promising results were also shown by applying the hybrid PSO-SOM over the gene expression data of Yeast and Rat Hepatocytes too. In the latter years, other hybrids like GA and K-means, PSO and Differential Evolution for better partitioned clustering than the original K-means have been seen as well.

When it comes to applications, Tang et al (2012a) attempted clustering Web data by using hybrids of several metaheuristics and K-means in the Web environment. The data to be clustered are so called Web Intelligence data which are dynamic in terms of updates, loosely structured and composed of complex attributes and multimedia elements. The authors evolved K-means by adding optimization ability through a collection of bio-inspired optimization methods. They are PSO Clustering (C-PSO) and Clustering with Ant Colony Optimization (C-ACO) and Clustering Fireflies (C-FF), Cuckoos (C-Cuckoo), Bats (C-Bat) and Wolves (C-WSA). These hybrid clustering algorithms are stress-tested over a collection of Web Intelligence data retrieved from different data sources. It was found that some contemporary hybrids outperformed their precedent C-PSO. The improvement mainly comes from the ability that metaheuristics can avoid the formation of clusters falling into local optima and get trapped there. The other implicit factors are due to the measures of the distance between any pair of data points. Jafar and

Sivakumar(2013) hence tested C-PSO by trying different distance measures including Euclidean, Manhattan and Chebyshevover some popular medical benchmark as well as artificially generated data set. It was shown from their experiment that C-PSO coupled with Chebyshev distance measure achieves better fitness values than the rest of the distance measures. Chebyshev distance measure is well known for its ability in measuring very high-dimensional data in a huge hyperspace. That offers the search agents of metaheuristics to explore far and wide for finding the best configuration of clusters.

An interesting alternative to bio-inspired optimization algorithms as fore-mentioned, is Black Hole algorithm which is rather nature-inspired, inspired by the black hole phenomenon. Hatamlou (2013) proposed a new Black Hole algorithm integrated with K-means. He mentioned that nature has always been a source of inspiration. The black hole algorithm (BH) which is similar to other population-based metaheuristics begins with an initial randomly population of candidate solutions, and it has a user-defined optimization objective function. Assume that soon after big-bang the universe is scattered with black holes. Each iteration represents some trillions of years of time. At each iteration cycle the universe evolves and the creator somehow picks the best candidate selected to be the black hole. According to the BH algorithm, the selected candidates then start pulling other candidates around it, they are called stars. If a star gets too close to the black hole, it will be consumed by the black hole and is extinct forever. By this way, a new star as a new candidate solution is randomly formed (by the star dust in the void), the new star is then born to be placed in the search space and a new search repeats. To validate the performance of the BH algorithm, the author applied it to solve the NP-hard clustering problem. The experimental results show that the BH algorithm performs better than other metaheuristics for a number of benchmark datasets.

Besides association and clustering which dominate two of the major data mining families of techniques, there are other data mining tasks to be empowered by metaheuristics. Zarnaniet al. (2006) attempted to discover spatial trend from GIS spatial data using ACO. It is know that very large repositories of spatial data are uncommon nowadays that are drawn from various applications of GIS, environmental studies, banking, sensor-network etc. The increasing demand for knowledge residing inside these spatial data has given rise to the importance of the field of Spatial Data Mining. Since the repository volume is so huge spatial knowledge discovery algorithms face technical challenges. In (Zarnani et al., 2006), two novel nature-inspired algorithms for efficient discovery of spatial trends are proposed. The algorithms are developed by incorporating ACO and Evolutionary Search (ES) in trend discovery. Empirically the task of trend discovery is tested and compared in terms of efficiency from the two algorithms given a real-life banking spatial database. The results yielded from experiments clearly reveal the improvement in effectiveness and performance as observed from the trend discovery process, when they were compared to the previously proposed metaheuristics methods.

Jaiswal and Dubey (2013) modified association rule mining by adding in the optimization function of GA. GA is shown to be able to generate good quality association rules. The quality is defined by the authors in four aspects: accuracy, completeness, comprehensibility and interestingness. GA algorithms are powerful and they are well known for their widely applicable stochastic search and optimization power as inspired by the life science concepts of natural selection. The advantage of applying GA is to discover high level prediction rules come from the process of global search. GA can cope better with attribute interaction iteration by iteration, than the traditional greedy rule induction algorithm which is often used generalizing some data mining model. The objective of this paper is to locate all the qualified frequent itemsets from a given transaction dataset using GA. As an experiment a large dataset was tested and the results confirm the effectiveness of applying GA for association rule mining.

2.3 Challenges and Prospective

Metaheuristics have been proven successfully in many cases in enhancing the performance of data mining tasks. Some selected examples are shortlisted in the previous section. In general they help increase the prediction or classification accuracy, effectiveness or completeness by avoiding local optima. However, the benefits do not come without a price. Though the optimization methods are geared to opt for the best, they have certain drawbacks – a major one of them is time consumption due to high computational demand.

As early as1996, Poli (1996) who applied GA for image processing, has noticed and commented that a tremendous demand in computational resources for the fitness evaluations. This high demand hinders researchers from conducting extensive study of these systems, especially in complex image processing applications as concurred by Ebner and Zell (1999). Time-consuming is a well-known sentiment among similar researchers as it typically takes several days to a week to complete the optimization over image processing tasks. This essentially prevents the availability of real-time machine vision system to be used in an adaptive or changing environmental condition.

To address the time-consuming issue, researchers in the subsequent years recommended using sampling methods. Instead of processing all pixels from a given image for evaluating the fitness of the current candidate solution, a small sample set taken from the pixels should be used. Other researchers suggested that the performance would be on par to the original heuristics methods, if only a recorded set of globally fit states would be used to seed the randomization of the GA for each image. This way would minimize a lot of repetitions on random trails throughout the optimization process. Computation time therefore would be reduced. Some proposed applying edge detection filters to shrink the amount of pixels from the full image; and some looked into the prospects of exploiting the inherent modular execution properties of GA for enabling parallelism in computation.

It was concluded that from the algorithm perspective, the repetitive evaluation of the classification step, so called fitness function lead to the long time consumption. A common solution without modifying the metaheuristics algorithm or compromising the full scale of optimization is the use of parallel or distributed processing. Between algorithmic changes such as sampling and custom operators redesign, and parallel/distributed processing, some debate was going on. In one way or another, it is certain that they can aid in simplifying the heavy computation in classification and clustering tasks when performed in metaheuristics style, making the optimization more scalable for large datasets.

An alternative method without the need of hacking into the metaheuristics or expensive parallel computing is to reduce the original feature set by removing the irrelevant ones, as pointed out in (Cantú-Paz & Kamath, 2001). It was mentioned that the complexity required for learning a concept in the metaheuristics optimization is proportional to the dimension of the feature space. This increase may even be exponential for high-dimensional classification problems. Features or attributes may well associate with the costs and sensitivity of the data mining model. Therefore it makes sense to perform feature subset selection which identifies and chooses only that useful subset of features to be used in the classification. The training dataset would be reduced in sizes when the redundant attributes are removed. The easiest and most intuitive approach is to get rid of irrelevant features by referring to domain knowledge. For instance of text mining documents, be it classification or clustering, obviously some stop-words like "a, an, the, of, that" etc should be taken away. However, in many other application domains the users or scientists which as bioinformatics would have little clues about which words or features belong to the irrelevant attributes. Worse still, some features may appear to be irrelevant when they are viewed individually, but they may have dependency or non-linear relationship when it comes to inducing a complex prediction model.

Fong et al (2013) attempted a wrapper approach for selecting optimal features by combining different metaheuristics search methods with different types of classifiers. The advantage of this approach include flexibility where different metaheuristics and classification algorithms can inter-change (plug and play, so-called), and simplicity without modification of the metaheuristics functions. By this wrapped approach, the fitness value evaluated from each candidate of feature subset during the stochastic optimization process improves as it iterates progressively. However it may be still computationally intensive in its execution which depends on the choices of metaheuristics algorithm and the classification algorithm, it can preserve the inductive and representational classification mappings of the learning algorithm. Some pioneers researchers in the 90's Brill et al (1990) and Brotherton and Simpson (1995) have tried it on K-nearest neighbor classification algorithm, neural networks and GA by encoding the features as simple binary representations in the GA chromosomes. Vafaie and DeJong (1998) exploited similar concept by using decision tree for feature selection for classification. Recently in (Fong et al., 2013), a collection of metaheuristics such as BAT, PSO and WSA, and classifiers like Decision Tree, Naiive Bayes and Neural Networks have been formulated as a unified algorithm for finding an optimal feature subset with satisfactory accuracies and within reasonable time. Two case studies using such methods are narrated in the following sections on examples of classifying online social comments and clustering for image segmentation respectively, using metaheuristics in a wrapper approach.

3. CASE STUDY – METAHEURISTICS FOR CLASSIFICATION

In classification, feature selection (FS) is a computational process that picks from the original feature set the most influential features in order to enhance classification performance. The selection is considered as optimization process that scouts for an ideal subset of features so the representative power is sustained for modeling the classification mapping between the feature values and the target classes. It is generally agreed that there is no universal FS approach that will always work the best at different situations for all types of data. One of the approaches for working with different choices of classifiers as wide as possible, is to equip classification with a metaheuristic stype of FS. So that different types of metaheuristics optimizers can work with various classifiers, yet the following limitations which are generally found by other methods could be solved: 1), the length of the resultant feature subset is assumed fixed. Users would have to explicitly set an upper limit for the subset dimension. The drawback is that the search is restricted to only the combinations of features within that given dimensions. 2), the feature shrinks into minimum size. There is no standard that controls how many features should be eliminated removed. Users would have to set a threshold value himself, to which the selected feature subset will reduce minimum to. 3), many FS are custom made for one or few types of classifiers and metaheuristics by embedding the logics into one another. It is not of a generic design.

Therefore the authors opted to design a flexible metaheuristics for finding an optimal feature subset, called Swarm Search (Fong et al., 2013) for classification tasks. In this case study the performances of the Swarm Search FS would be put under test for text mining classification task. The classifiers that are empowered by Swarm Search FS (FS-SS) would have to classify over a social network dataset that comes with an extremely large amount of features. The raw testing dataset is downloaded from Online Social Networks Research at The Max Plank Institute for Software Systems (http://socialnetworks.

mpi-sws.org/data-imc2007.html). This original data was crawled from YouTube (www.youtube.com) is a popular video-sharing site that includes a social network. The data was obtained on January 15th, 2007. After being anonymized with information that can potentially identifies a user was removed, it has 1,157,827 users indexed with numeric user identifiers, 4,945,382 friend links, 4.29 average number of friends per user, 79.1% fraction of links symmetric, 30,087 number of user groups and 0.25 average number of groups memberships per user. The original dataset is a sequential list of all of the user-to-user links. Each instance contains a pair of two user identifiers separated by a tab, indicating a link exists in a forward direction from one user to the other.

The classification objective is to distinguish the group membership of a user that belongs to by examining the user's relationships to the other users that s/he connects to. The list of linked pairs is transposed into a 1,157,827 × 1,157,827 huge sparse matrix, with a '1' signifying a connection between a user from the row and a user from the column, '0' otherwise. As such the sparse matrix is indeed very sparse having a 98.5657% of empty entries. Taking randomly 3,000 users who have non-empty relations as testing samples, the rest of them are used for training a classification model.

3.1 FS-SS Model Design

The design of an improved feature selection using metaheuristics is presented, which is flexible in adapting different classifiers and optimizer together; the optimal feature subset would be sought on the fly without setting a subset length. The framework is based on a wrapper-based design which is comprised of two cooperative modules: Classifier for classification algorithms and Optimizer for metaheuristics, which is shown in Fig.1. The Feature Selector module extracts a part of the full dataset as instructed by the Optimizer module. The Feature Selector then supplies the required data in partitions of training data and testing data to the Classifier. The Classifier induces a model, tests it and evaluates the accuracy by the fitness function; then it will decide whether the current fitness should either replace the recorded fitness or to stop running should the termination criteria are met.

The classification process is inherently embedded into the metaheuristic that searches heuristically for the suitable candidate of feature subset from the full dataset. The execution of FS-SS has dual phases. Firstly, a new candidate of feature subset is explored and evaluated by the Optimizer Module according to the mechanism of the metaheuristic algorithm. At the initial run, a candidate subset is picked at random. Secondly, the Classifier Module, a classifier model does the learning and testing, and records the performance usually in terms of accuracy or error rate which is the ratio of correctly (or incorrectly) classified instances over the total amount of instances. The two phases alternate and run continually until the stopping criterion is satisfied.

Without the need of trying out every possible feature subset which will be too many in number, FS-SS would be able to find the feature subset that is most currently optimum at any time. The current candidate of feature subset may be the best as far as the search has advanced in the search space. The absolute best candidate that is also the global best will remain unknown unless every state in the search space has been tried. Assume the original feature set of size K, $F=\{f_1, f_2, \ldots f_k\}$, FS-SS attempts to construct a classification model in each iteration which has an accuracy rate a by using an optimal feature subset $G \in F$ such that $a(F) \geq a(G)$, where G is one of all the possible subsets that exist in the hyperspace of H. Three metaheuristic algorithms are applied in this experiment, namely Bat Algorithm (BAT), Particle Swarm Optimization (PSO) and Wolf Search Algorithm (WSA).

Figure 1. Process model of the proposed Swarm Search

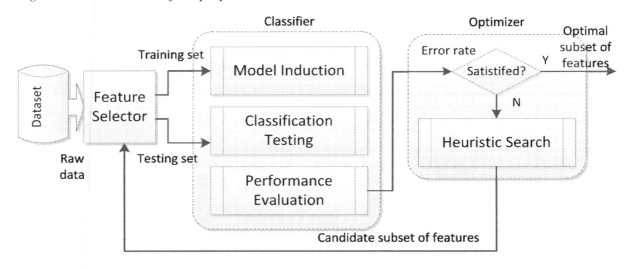

BAT is a relatively modern metaheuristic, invented by Yang (2010). The searching behavior of BAT was inspired by the echolocation ability of micro-bats. Some sonar technique is used by micro-bats, called, echolocation, to scout their environment for hunting prey and avoiding obstacles in the dark. During echolocation, a very loud sound pulse in high frequency is emitted; the echoes that bounce back from the surrounding objects are listened. The echo pulses vary in tunes and they correspond to their hunting strategies, depending on the on the sizes of the species. Most bats use short, frequency-modulated signals to sweep through about an octave, while others more often use constant-frequency signals for echolocation. Their signal bandwidth variation depends on the species, and often increased by using more harmonics. Three generalized rules control the operation of the bat algorithm:

1. All bats use echolocation to sense distance, and they also know the difference between food/prey and background barriers by instinct.
2. Bats fly randomly with velocity v_i at position x_i with a fixed frequency f_{min}, varying wavelength λ and loudness A_0 to search for prey. They can automatically adjust the wavelength of their emitted pulses, and adjust the rate of pulse emission $r \in [0,1]$, depending on the proximity of their target;

Although the loudness can vary in many ways, we assume that the loudness varies from a large and positive A_0 to a minimum constant value A_{min}. The new solution x_i^t and velocities v_i^t at time step t are given by

$$f_i = f_{min} + (f_{max} - f_{min})\beta \tag{1}$$

$$v_i^t = v_i^{t-1} + (x_i^t - x_*)f_i \tag{2}$$

$$x_i^t = x_i^{t-1} + v_i^t \tag{3}$$

where $\beta \in [0,1]$ is a random vector having a uniform distribution. Here x_* is the current global best location which is located after comparing all the solutions among n bats. As the product λf_i is the velocity increases, either f_i or λ_i is used to adjust the velocity change while fixing the other factor constant. Initially each bat is randomly assigned a frequency which is drawn uniformly from $[f_{min}, f_{max}]$. For local search, once a solution is selected among the current best solutions, a new solution for each bat is generated locally using random walk.

$$X_{new} = x_{old} + \in A^t \tag{4}$$

where $\varepsilon \in [-1,1]$ is a random number, while $A^t = <A_i^t>$ is the average loudness of all the bats at this time step. The update of the velocities and positions of bats have some similarity to PSO as f_i essentially controls the pace and range of the movement of the swarming particles. The loudness and rate of pulse emission have to be updated accordingly as the iterations progress. As the loudness decreases once a bat has found its prey, the rate of pulse emission increases

$$A_i^{t+1} = \alpha A_i^t, \quad r_i^{t+1} = r_i^0 \left[1 - exp\left(-\gamma t\right)\right] \tag{5}$$

$$A_i^t \to 0, r_i^t \to r_i^0, ast \to \infty \tag{6}$$

PSO is inspired by the swarm behavior such as fish, birds and bees schooling in nature. The term called Swarm Intelligence was coined since PSO became popular. The dual movement of a swarming particle is defined by its social cognition and that of its own. Each particle is attracted towards the position of the currently global best g^* and its own locally best position l_i^* in history. While at the same time with the effect of the attraction, it has a tendency of moving randomly. Let l_i and v_i be the location vector and velocity for particle i, respectively. The new velocity and location and location updating formulas are determined by

$$v_i^{t+1} = v_i^t + \alpha \varepsilon_1 \left[g^* - l_i^t\right] + \beta \epsilon_2 \left[l_i^* - l_i^t\right] \tag{7}$$

$$l_i^{t+1} = l_i^t + v_i^{t+1} \tag{8}$$

where ε_1 and ε_2 are two random vectors, and each entry taking the values between 0 and 1. The parameters α and β are the learning parameters or acceleration constants, typically $\alpha \approx \beta \approx 2$.

WSA (Tang et al., 2012a) is one of the latest metaheuristic algorithms by the authors. The search design as the name suggested is based on wolves' hunting behavior. Three simplified rules that govern the logics of WSA are presented as follow.

1. Each wolf has a fixed visual area with a radius defined by v for X as a set of continuous possible solutions. In 2D, the coverage would simply be the area of a circle by the radius v. In hyper-plane, where multiple attributes dominate, the distance would be estimated by Minkowski distance, such that

$$v \leq d\left(x_i, x_c\right) = \left(\sum_{k=1}^{n}\left|x_{i,k} - x_{c,k}\right|^{\lambda}\right)^{1/\lambda}, \; x_c \in X \tag{9}$$

where x_i is the current position; x_c are all the potential neighboring positions near x_i and the absolute distance between the two positions must be equal to or less than v; and λ is the order of the hyper space. For discrete solutions, an enumerated list of the neighboring positions would be approximated. Each wolf can only sense companions who appear within its visual circle and the step distance by which the wolf moves at a time is usually smaller than its visual distance.

2. The result or the fitness of the objective function represents the quality of the wolf's current position. The wolf always tries to move to better terrain but rather than choose the best terrain it opts to move to better terrain that already houses a companion. If there is more than one better position occupied by its peers, the wolf will chose the best terrain inhabited by another wolf from the given options. Otherwise, the wolf will continue to move randomly in Brownian motion.

    The distance between the current wolf's location and its companion's location is considered. The greater this distance, the less attractive the new location becomes, despite the fact that it might be better. This decrease in the wolf's willingness to move obeys the inverse square law. Therefore, we get a basic formula of betterment.

$$(r) = \frac{I_o}{r^2}, \tag{10}$$

where I_o is the origin of food (the ultimate incentive) and r is the distance between the food or the new terrain and the wolf. It is added with the absorption coefficient, such that using the Gaussian equation; the incentive formula is

$$\beta\left(r\right) = \beta_o e^{-r^2} \tag{11}$$

where β_o equals to I_o.

3. At some point, it is possible that the wolf will sense an enemy. The wolf will then escape to a random position far from the threat and beyond its visual range. The movement is implemented using the following formula

$$x(i) = x(i) + \beta_o e^{-r^2}\left(x(j) - x(i)\right) + escape() \tag{12}$$

where *escape*() is a function that calculates a random position to jump to with a constraint of minimum length; v, x is the wolf, which represents a candidate solution; and $x(j)$ is the peer with a better position as represented by the value of the fitness function. The second term of the above equation represents the change in value or gain achieved by progressing to the new position. r is the distance between the wolf and its peer with the better location. Step size must be less than the visual distance.

A candidate solution vector is encoded in each representative search agent in the metaheuristic (BAT/PSO/WSA). The format is a subset of feature indices, the length of a solution vector is variable and it is also the length of the feature subset. At initialization, the vector size is arbitrarily selected in random for each search agent. So they have different subset lengths to start with, in a way similar to placing the search agents in random dimensions of the search space. Each search agent has a variable k, which is the current length of feature subset it represents, where $1 \leq k \leq K$. K is a constant that is maximum cardinality of the search space that is also the maximum number of the original features. When FS-SS runs, the search agent moves in steps in the same dimension in each local step movement. The agent explores feature subsets in the same dimension. It changes its dimension occasionally. The occasional events are similar in context to the escape function in WSA, mutation in GA, or sudden direction change in other swarm-type of algorithms where a search agent deviates by large degree from its proximity which is the current dimension or subset length in this case. The occurrence of this sudden change is programmed with a pre-defined probability. When it occurs, k is assigned with other random value than its current one. In this way, the search agent is able to "hop" far out of its local proximity to a new dimension which it may not have visited before.

FS-SS works by following the steps below:

Step 1. Initialize all variables. Randomly assign a different values and length for the feature subset to the search agents.

Step 2. Compute the fitness of each search agent by the objective function. Rank the search agents in order by their fitness. Nominate the search agent which has the highest score in fitness as the most promising solution.

Step 3. Do local search to find a current best solution. The mechanism of the local search varies depending on the metaheuristic algorithms used. Generally the local search tries to update the currently most promising solution, and it keeps doing so until some terminal condition is reached. Velocities are updated in the swarming particles for PSO. For BAT, the currently best position and the corresponding velocities are ranked according to the loudness and the pulse rate. Each WSA agent is updated through these three iterative procedures – firstly move to a random walk position; secondly, check whether the agents should swarm and merge with other peers; thirdly check if an escape should occur by a random function.

Step 4. Change the positions of the search agents in the same dimension by random walk.

Step 5. Check if the optimization should exit the loop; Go back to Step 2.

Step 6. Stop and display the results.

3.2 FS-SS Experiment

In order to validate the efficacy of FS-SS especially for datasets that have very huge dimensionality, a combination of popular classification algorithms and metaheuristics have been for experimentation. A list of feature such wrapper-based feature selection methods that are used in experiments are shown in Figure 2.

BAT and PSO possess certain swarming behavior in their search movements which are governed by the velocities of the whole group as well as that of individual agents or particles. A single leader is always found in the swarm that steers the major direction of every remaining peer. At the same time the agents roam locally but they somehow still flock towards the leader's global direction.

In the experiment, the main performance indicator is the mean error rate ranging from 0 to 1, the same error is also used as a stopping criterion. The optimization program is set to explore and seek the solution repeatedly until the difference in the improvement of the average error rate for a new iteration drops below 1.0×10^{-6}. The other stopping control is the upper limit of iteration that is fixed at 100,000,000 cycles. The limit is for preventing the search to take exceedingly long. The YouTube dataset under test, with 1,157,827 dimensions, sum up to $2^{1,157,827}$ combinatorial feature subsets in the search space. This astronomically huge number apparently prevents most computers from doing an exhaustive search. FS-SS however will still require some length of run time for a stochastically optimal result, which may be better than no results at all by deterministic approach (see figure 3).

Figure 2. Different FS-SS models by combining various metaheuristics and classification algorithms.

Method abbreviation	Classifier	Metaheuristic	Approach
FS-PSO-PN	Pattern Network	Particle swarm optimization	Swarm
FS-PSO-DT	Decision Tree	Particle swarm optimization	Swarm
FS-PSO-NB	Naive Bayes	Particle swarm optimization	Swarm
FS-BAT-PN	Pattern Network	Bat algorithm	Swarm
FS-BAT-DT	Decision Tree	Bat algorithm	Swarm
FS-BAT-NB	Naive Bayes	Bat algorithm	Swarm
FS-WSA-PN	Pattern Network	Wolf search algorithm	Semiswarm
FS-WSA-DT	Decision Tree	Wolf search algorithm	Semiswarm
FS-WSA-NB	Naive Bayes	Wolf search algorithm	Semiswarm

Figure 3. Different FS-SS models by combining various metaheuristics and classification

FS using PSO		FS using BAT		FS using WSA	
Parameter	value	Parameter	value	Parameter	value
Populations	5	A (loudness)	0.5	Visual distance	1
c_1	1.5	R (pulse rate)	0.5	Escape distance	5
c_2	1.5	Populations	5	Escape probability	0.25
		Q_{min}	0	Population	5
		Q_{max}	0.2		

For a fair comparison, five search agents are used and the other parameters are carefully chosen for each metaheuristic, as the parameters are quite sensitive to influencing the final performance. They have been pre-tuned by sampling a small dataset for the best results. The parameters do vary for different metaheuristic methods. For instance, in BAT algorithm, the search agent's position is affected by the bat's echo pulse rate and echo loudness. Tuning the loudness and emitted pulse to the best effectiveness is needed for different proximity of their target. 0.5 are set for both of them which should yield a balance between intensification and exploration. Two learning parameters are associated with PSO, c_1, c_2. Typically they should be set equal $c_1=c_2$ with value lower than 2, that has been adopted widely in the literature. In our experiment, we choose 1.5that is moderately lower than 2. Each search agent in WSA has a visual radius and an escape parameter that decides how often a wolf dashes far away from the current position. The jump distance should be much longer than the visual radius. Here we set the escape distance 5 which is five times longer than the range of the wolf's eye sight. The programs are coded in Matlab R2010b. The computing environment is a Dell Precision T3610 Workstation with an Intel Xeon Processor E5-1650v2 (6 Core 3.5GHz, 12M, Turbo+) and with 32GB, DDR3 RDIMM Memory.

Three types of performance indicators on which the experiment is centered for FS-SS: average error rate, time consumption in seconds and the proportion of features finally sought in the feature subset. By these three performance indicators, Table 1 tabulates the experiment results. For visual comparison, the time consumption and dimension reduction relative to the original feature length normalized to a range of [0,1]. Hence the results of the three performance indicators can be charted and visually compared together as shown in Figure 4.

With respect to the classification error, we can observe that in Table 1 NB is the worst and the Decision Tree is best whose accuracies of each SS-FS reached almost 100%. These two classification algorithms performed quite extremely when it comes to sparse matrix. Decision tree can growth a large number of decision rules being able to cater for even the very non-linear mapping relations between the feature values and the classes. NB on the other hand assumes each attribute is independent of each other, and it relies on rigid priori probabilities which do not cater well for contradictory cases. Although the error rate of PN is not the lowest, its credibility is the highest. Comparing over the three FS-SS methods using PN classifier, the BAT's error rate is the lowest. Naive Bayes that integrated with each SS method does not only have a high error rate but also it costs a lot of time. In the radar chart in Figure 4 we can see

Table 1. Experiment results of FS-SS in different combinations of classifiers and metaheuristics

Algorithms	Error rate	Time (s)	%Time	Selected features	%Dimension
FS-PSO-PN	0.011236	3106.28	0.315557151	2250	0.75
FS-PSO-DT	0	2122.71	0.215639492	2865	0.955
FS-PSO-NB	1	9399.74	0.9548898	1971	0.657
FS-BAT-PN	0.005618	4297.76	0.43659631	1479	0.493
FS-BAT-DT	0	2929.8	0.297628952	2394	0.798
FS-BAT-NB	1	8540.29	0.867581108	1284	0.428
FS-WSA-PN	0.2808989	4104.64	0.416977196	1758	0.586
FS-WSA-DT	0	4276.03	0.43438872	2433	0.811
FS-WSA-NB	1	9843.79	1	1320	0.44

Figure 4. Radar chart of FS-SS performance by different combinations of classifiers and metaheuristics

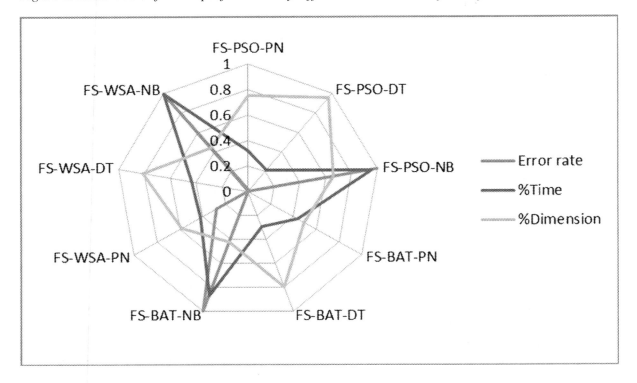

that in Decision tree classifier regardless of which metaheuristics that it works with selected the most amounts of features in the process. This is due to its tree branch growing nature, by that it can create as many rules as required by the data.

Lastly, from Table 2 and Figure 5, we can see the aggregated results by only the metaheuristics methods while the results for the classifiers are averaged. We are more concerned for the metaheuristics because that is what the search is about when it comes into such extreme case of very large sparse matrix. Although the degree of sparseness high, in this experiment we dealt with the words' low frequency area. It is observed that from the aggregated results WSA metaheuristic did not achieve a good performance as one would expect; it even has the worst in accuracy/time, that WSA took the longest time though the error rate is the lowest. This could be explained by WSA's semi-swarm nature. The wolf agents operated independently and sometimes they merge when the peer agents are met within visual range. In spare matrix, the useful information may be concentrated particular in some patches of areas. Most of the five wolves may be waste their efforts searching in the waste fields of the matrix, and only few may be able to hit the useful area by random escape. Even though, only the exception wolves are doing meaningful search in the useful area, the rest of the wolf agents are hardly attracted to come. The long running time implies that once the wolves are separated in their searches, they would hardly meet and hence converge together to a final optimum. In contrast, PSO and BAT have agents that flock together; so once any of these agents gets on to a good terrain, its fitness increases thereby becoming a leader that pulls the rest of the agents to swarm along. The same idea applies when one of the swarming agents finds a very good optimum; the rest would easily converge because they move near of each other as a whole school. From

Table 2. Averaged results of FS-SS by metaheuristics methods

Algorithms	Error rate	%Time	%Dimension
FS-PSO	0.3370787	0.49536	0.79
FS-BAT	0.335206	0.53394	0.57
FS-WSA	0.4269663	0.61712	0.61

Figure 5. Radar chart of averaged FS-SS performance by metaheuristics methods

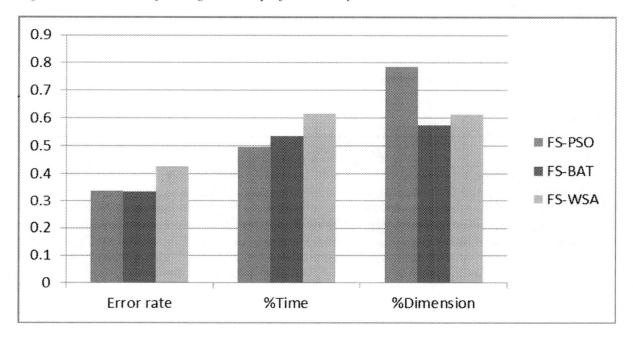

the results of Table 2 and Figure 3, the PSO's performance is stable and great, followed by the BAT metaheuristic which achieved satisfactory performance results too.

Thus, in this experiment it is shown that WSA may no longer be a fit candidate to deal with sparse matrix in some extremely large social network data especially when the distribution of feasible areas in the very huge search space is uneven. Much of the time WSA would have its search agents busy searching in the voids. PSO and BAT on the other hand demonstrated some stability in performance in this case.

4. CASE STUDY – METAHEURISTICS FOR CLUSTERING

Traditional K-means clustering algorithm assigns membership to data points by estimating the hyper-distance between each pair of data point and centroid, using an iterative partitioning strategy. Through iterations, the membership designation gets refined progressively until certain stopping criteria are met. The stopping condition usually is when the sum of intra-distances of the data points within a cluster are reduced and the inter-distances are extended to the most. However, given the many data points and almost infinite possibilities in arranging the clusters among them, the final quality of the clustering results often may not reach the very best. The quality actually depends on how the values of the initial centroids got started in the design of K-means.It is well-known that these initial centroid positions are randomly initiated, and the random start can differ in each run. Over such random chance, it is likely that K-means at the end get stuck into local optima thinking falsely that the best has already been obtained. But it may be far from the global best of the ground truth.

As a matter of ground truth, the final centroids should be scattered tactfully in a manner that the clusters formed around them exhibit the greatest quality; this is the situation so-called global optimum. It happens when the data points in all the formed clusters possess maximum intra-similarities and minimum inter-similarities. However, K-means does not guarantee a global optimal clustering result and it is infamous for having resultant clusters stuck at local optima, it lacks of an efficient mechanism to further explore for the best results. Just like the previous case study present, finding the global optimum for K-means is NP-hard, implying infeasibility in computation if it were to be done by brute-force in trying all the different random initiations of centroid values. In (Tang et al., 2012b), the universal integration of any metaheuristics optimization algorithm into K-means was first proposed by the authors. A step further into exploiting its application in image segmentation is attempted here. To begin with the integration, some assumption is made. The formation of centroids which to be calculated stochastically from beginning to convergence, would be managed by the search agents of the metaheuristic algorithms. The evolution of the optimization works by following the principle that the centroids which are to be repositioned in each generation must enable forming the new clusters with better results. Naturally it makes sense to attain the optimal configuration of centroids by formulating the quality of the final clusters as an objective or fitness function. Let cen_{jv} be the centroid or the center point of the jth cluster in the hyper-dimensional search space characterized by v^{th} attribute. $W_{i,j}$ is the membership of data point x_i that indicate whether it exists in cluster j. The centroid location can be computed by Equation (14) for a set of attributes v for each particular cluster j. The fitness function for the clustering task is then specified as equation (15)

$$w_{i,j} = \begin{cases} 1, & x_i \in cluster_j \\ 0, & x_i \notin cluster_j \end{cases} \tag{13}$$

$$cen_{j,v} = \frac{\sum_{i=1}^{S} w_{i,j} x_{i,v}}{\sum_{i=1}^{S} w_{i,j}}, j = 1..K, v = 1..K * D \tag{14}$$

where S is the number of search agents in the metaheuristic population, K is the total number of clusters and j is the active cluster now being processed. The maximum dimension of attributes is D for the data-set, a centroid is therefore located by a tuple of size D. In the design of our mathematical model cen is a 2D matrix of size $K \times D$ holding all the values of the centroids (the cluster centers) indicated by $cen_{j,v}$.

$$F(cen) = \sum_{j=1}^{K} \sum_{i=1}^{S} w_{i,j} \sum_{v=1}^{K*D} \left(x_{i,v} - cen_{j,v} \right)^2 \tag{15}$$

The computation process seeks through the cen matrix up to $K \times D$ times to check the attribute values of the data point x for measuring the similarity distance between each pair of x and $cen_{j,v}$. This program iterates for each cluster v and proceeds in time. In the optimization process, a particular combination of centroids of all the clusters is represented as a centroids vector by each search agent in the $K{\times}D$ dimensional search space. The best search agent being found in each generation is supposed to produce the best clustering result given its representative centroid positions. The metaheuristic clustering is therefore evaluated by a minimization function which aims at minimizing the distances among the data points in a cluster. So the smaller the value it is, the better the fitness an agent represents.

$$clmat_{i,j} = \min_{k \in K} \left\{ \| x_i - cen_k \| \right\} \tag{16}$$

The scopes of the variables are as follow $i=1..N$, $j=1..S$, and $k=1..K$. The double lines notation in Equation (16) indicates that is a Euclidean distance function. Depending on the metaheuristic algorithm being used, the optimization will guide the search agents to find the fittest best centroids. In this case study, we used four hybrids, which are resulted from combining four metaheuristic optimization algorithms into K-means. The capital letter C denotes 'clustering', the four hybrid algorithms are called C-Wolf, C-Firefly, C-Bat and C-PSO respectively. The mathematical formulation of the four clustering models as well as their design blueprint (Tang et al., 2012b) based on which researcher can mix and match with other metaheuristics at well, is given in (Fong et al., 2014). Thus the details are not repeated here, readers are referred to the previous publication (Fong et al., 2014) for in-depth information.

In this case study experiment, the four hybrid clustering algorithms against the original K-means are put under test of an image segmentation task. The core of image analysis is image segmentation by pixel colors. It has a wide range of application areas like robotics, computer vision, GIS remote sensing, medical microscopy, multi-media retrieval and recognition, etc., just to name a few. Acting as a core technology for computer vision, the quality of image segmentation results actually rely mostly on the underlying clustering algorithm being used. K-means is such a common choice, yet metaheuristics serve as an optimizer to further enhance its performance. In color image segmentation the regions of the image depending on the color features are grouped into a certain set of clusters by gauging the intra-cluster distance and inter-cluster distance between each image pixel and the centroid within the cluster.

In the experiment, a color image by an 8MB high-resolution photo is made up of 5184×3456 pixels. The spatial information in terms of x- and y-axis coordinate of the pixel position in the image, and together with the color information RGB for each pixel that make up five attributes, describe each pixel. The RGB information, ranges from 0 in complete darkness to 255 in full intensity. We know that a pixel of an image is comprised of 256 independent intensity levels of red light, green light and blue light. Each data point of the 5184×3456=17,915,904 pixels is constructed as a five-dimensional matrix that represent the pixel position information relative to the picture, and its RGB information, such as [x, y, R, G, B]. The ranges of the variables are $0{\leq}x{\leq}5184$, $0{\leq}y{\leq}3456$, $0{\leq}R{\leq}255$, $0{\leq}G{\leq}255$ and $0{\leq}B{\leq}255$. The relevant image data are technically harvested by using a built-in function *imread(image-name)* in Matlab that first constructs a three-dimensional matrix, and applying *impixel()* returns the RGB values of each pixel. The final five-dimensional matrix is computed by using a custom-written software program that computes the x-y locations of the pixels and tallies them with the corresponding RGB information for each pixel.

The experiment is run over a testing image whose pixels are to be clustered using $k=2$. The image is a street scene of the city Antwerp, with Altocumulus cloud formation. Altocumulus refers to heaped clouds which is a good testing benchmark for visually determining the visual clarity of image segmentation. The compositions of the heaped clouds are nevertheless similar, making it challenging for a binary clustering to attempt separating the white clouds from the background of blue sky. The street scenes has houses of similar shapes and shades, again making it challenging, subtly, for testing the efficacy of the K-mean clustering algorithm empowered by different metaheuristics.

The performance is again measured by inter-similarity and intra-similarity across and within the same cluster, as well as time consumption for the optimizer to run in seconds in forming the best clusters by their search agents. The parameters settings are same as those listed in Figure 3 and in (Fong et al., 2014). The performance results are tabulated in Tables 2. The winning performance result by one of the four hybrid clustering algorithms or K-means is marked with a red asterisk as distinction. The comparison results with regards of inter-cluster distance, intra-cluster distance and CPU time consumption are charted in Figures 6, 7 and 8 respectively. The original images under test and the segmented images by the various clustering algorithms are shown in Figures 9a, 9b, 9c, 9d, 9e and 9f respectively.

As it can be seen obviously in Table 3, PSO performed the best in terms of achieving in average of all clusters the longest inter-similarity, the shortest inter-similarity and it took up reasonable convergence time. The poorest metaheuristic perhaps again is WSA that has relatively short inter-similarity and long intra-similarity, followed by Bat algorithm. These two algorithms have in common of semi-swarm nature, where each search agent operates independently and less likely they would swarm in their search like how their counterpart PSO would do. Firefly on the other hand performed very badly for inter-similarity too, implying that again this semi-swarm type of metaheuristic failed to outreach to places where the centroids are placed far apart in the search space. This could allegedly be due to being stuck in some local optima too. For CPU time consumption, K-means is the fastest to complete the execution because

Figure 6. Results in inter-distance for different metaheuristic clustering methods, in bar chart

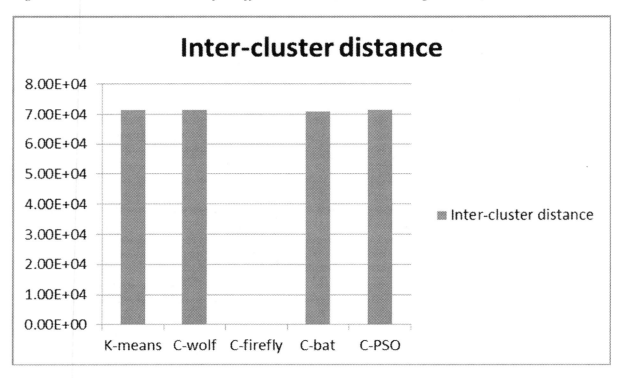

Figure 7. Results in intra-distance for different metaheuristic clustering methods, in bar chart

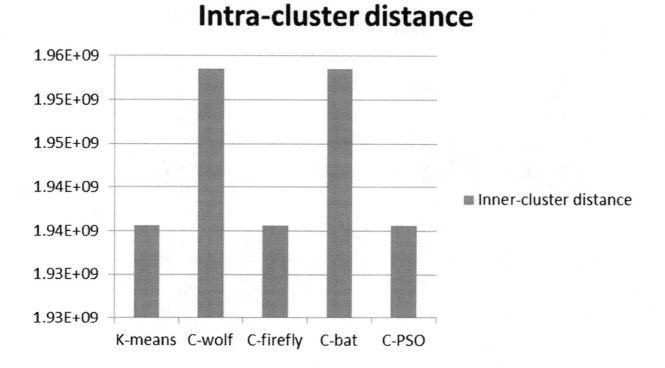

Figure 8. Results in CPU time consumption for different metaheuristic clustering methods, in bar chart

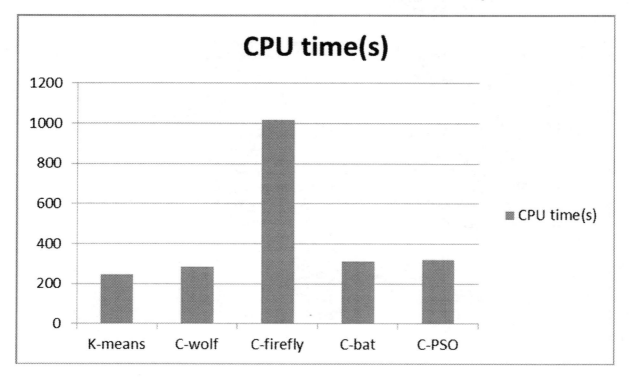

Figure 9. a-9f. Original image and segmented image by different metaheuristic clustering methods

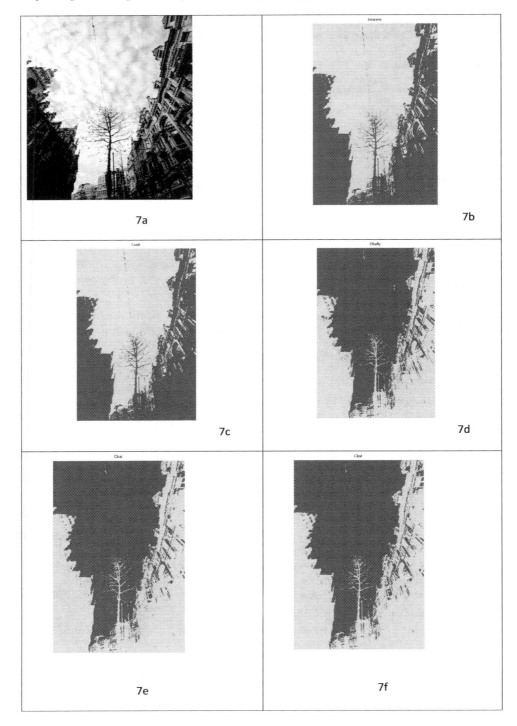

Table 3. Comparison of performance results for different metaheuristic clustering methods

Performance Comparison			
Algorithms	Inter-cluster distance	Inner-cluster distance	CPU time(s)
K-means	1.8142e+5	2.5541e+8	160.2645*
C-Wolf	1.7534e+5	2.5273e+8	223.5515
C-Bat	1.8125e+5	2.5793e+8	250.0147
C-PSO	2.0102e+5*	2.4998e+8*	250.7541
C-Firefly	0.4564	2.5273e+8	941.8844

it was done without any optimization on the centroid positions. Nevertheless the metaheuristic methods did not increase too much in multitudes. C-Firefly however took an exceptionally long time to converge, probably due to the problem of local optima where the search agents got stuck in and struggling to come out. The experiment results reveal an interesting phenomenon which is in agreement with the other case study done earlier – semi-swarm metaheuristic methods like WSA runs short of achieving the best global optimum especially in very large search space where the meaningful data points are not well distributed. In the case of image segmentation, the heaped clouds are concentrated in the center of the photo interlaced to a great extent with the blue hues from the sky background. Similar drawbacks are observed from other semi-swarm metaheuristic methods like Bat and Firefly too. PSO which swarm as a united flock of search agents manage to achieve good global optimum in sparse matrix and unevenly distributed color hues (cloud and sky) like the image used in this case study. This is double confirmed by the bar charts as depicted in Figures 6, 7 and 8.

In Figure 9, where the visual outputs of the image segments by different metaheuristic methods are show, one can see that Firefly reproduce certain noise as two stains on the backdrop of the sky, in sub Figure 9d. WSA in sub Figure 9c suffers from losing some structural distortion on the outlines of the houses.

5. CONCLUSION

In this book chapter, we have reviewed, discussed and shown by experiments that metaheuristic algorithms can complement data mining algorithms. Hybrids of both families of methods are possibly built, and they help select optimal features subsets, offer accurate classification, and produce quality clustering results with high integrity. The choice of metaheuristics and choice of data mining algorithms are diverse and they should not be limited to only those shown in this article. Metaheuristics are especially useful when the data mining tasks require further optimization whose fitness can be quantified by a properly defined fitness function. While metaheuristic methods do indeed offer an edge in performance by finding a best sometimes globally best solution, they do come at a price, namely the demand for extra computation resources in performing stochastic searches. Nevertheless, as computer technology advances by leaps nowadays, processors are becoming faster and cheaper in mass production. Integrating metaheuristic algorithms into data mining still would have certain prospect despite the extra computation cost.

Two case studies in particular are demonstrated in this article with the aim of proving the viability of integrating metaheuristics into data mining process. In the first case, we showed that feature selection, classification and swarm search by metaheuristics can be possibly integrated into one software program, called FS-SS. It can efficiently find an optimal subgroup of features from a very huge search space. Also there is no need for the user to fix the feature subset size as FS-SS would take care of automatically finding the optimal length of the feature subset. The mechanism of FS-SS is meant to be flexible such that different optimizers and classifiers can just be interchangeably integrated. As a comparative study, several popular classification algorithms coupled with several various contemporary metaheuristic methods are integrated as one in the experimentation. We tested FS-SS in a case of social network analysis where the relations of users forming an extremely huge affinity matrix over which FS-SS finds the relevant features and does classify testing users into their belonging groups. From the experiment results however, it is observed that semi-swarm type of method like Wolf Search Algorithm is being compromised by its autonomous searching characteristics, leading to poor final fitness. It is speculated that the search agents stuck at local optima in regions of search space which contain meaningless relations.

The second case study looks at improving the clustering integrity for traditional K-means clustering algorithm. Metaheuristic methods are called to help avoid choosing the centroids of the clusters which may be stuck at local optima for K-means depend solely on the random values of initial centroids. Metaheuristics have advantages in guiding iterative computation to search for global optima while avoiding local optima. The algorithms however take extra time in the search process. An experiment on image segmentation is carried out, we show the results of the evaluation over the quality of the final clusters. The same phenomenon is observed that PSO being a pure swarming metaheuristic did the best in finding the best quality clusters for image segments, and semi-swarm types like Wolf, Bat and Firefly are being rated down relatively. Further studies and investigations are planned to solve this phenomenon as future work.

REFERENCES

Barricelli, N. A. (1954). Esempinumerici di processi di evoluzione. *Methodos*, 45–68

Binitha, S., & Sathya, S. (2012) A Survey of Bio-inspired Optimization Algorithms, *International Journal of Soft Computing and Engineering (IJSCE)*, 2(2), 137-151

Brill, F. Z., Brown, D. E., & Martin, W. N. (1990). *Genetic algorithms for feature selection for counter propagation networks*. Technical Report. No.IPC-TR-90-004. Charlottesville, VA: University of Virginia, Institute of Parallel Computation

Brotherton, T. W., & Simpson, P. K. (1995). Dynamic feature set training of neural nets for classification. In McDonnell, J.R., Reynolds, R.G., & Fogel, D.B. (Eds.), Evolutionary Programming IV. 83-94. Cambridge, MA: MIT Press

Bursa, M. (2013). *Ant-inspired Metaheuristics for Biomedical Data Mining* [PhD thesis]. Czech Technical University in Prague.

Cantú-Paz, E., & Kamath, C. (2001). On the Use of Evolutionary Algorithms in Data Mining. In H. A. Abbass, R. A. Sarker, & C. S. Newton (Eds.), Data Mining: A Heuristic Approach. Hershey: Idea Group Publishing.

Ebner, M., & Zell, A. (1999). Evolving a task specific image operator. In R. Poli et al. (Ed.), *Evolutionary Image Analysis, Signal Processing and Telecommunications* (pp. 74-89). Berlin: Springer-Verlag.

Fayyad, U., Piatetsky-Shapiro, G., Smyth, P., & Uthurusamy, R. (1996). *Advances in knowledge discovery and data mining.* Menlo Park, CA: AAAI Press/The MIT Press.

Fong, S., Deb, S., Yang, X-S, & Zhuang, Yan. (2014, June). Towards Enhancement of Performance of K-means Clustering Using Nature-Inspired Optimization Algorithms, *The Scientific World Journal*, Article no. 564829.

Fong, S., Zhuang, Y., Tang, R., Yang, X.-S., & Deb, S. (2013). Selecting Optimal Feature Set in High-Dimensional Data by Swarm Search. *Journal of Applied Mathematics, 590614*, 18. doi:10.1155/2013/590614

Gorea, D. A. (2009, January). *Interoperability and Integration of Processes of Knowledge Discovery in Databases* [PhD thesis]. University Alexandru Ioan Cuza Iasi.

Handl, J., & Meyer, B. (2002). Improved ant-based clustering and sorting in a document retrieval interface. *Proceedings of the Seventh International Conference on Parallel Problem Solving from Nature (PPSN VII)*, (pp. 913-923). Springer-Verlag, Berlin, Germany. doi:10.1007/3-540-45712-7_88

Hatamlou, A. (2013, February). Black hole: A new heuristic optimization approach for data clustering. *Information Sciences, 222*(10), 175–184. doi:10.1016/j.ins.2012.08.023

Jafar, O. A. M., & Sivakumar, R. (2013, March). A Study of Bio-inspired Algorithm to Data Clustering using Different Distance Measures, *International Journal of Computer Applications, 66*(12), 33-44.

Jaiswal, A., & Dubey, G. (2013, May). Identifying Best Association Rules and Their Optimization Using Genetic Algorithm, *International Journal of Emerging Science and Engineering (IJESE), 1*(7), 91-96.

Kanade, P. M., & Hall, L. O. (2003), Fuzzy Ants as a Clustering Concept, In *Proceedings of the 22nd International Conference of the North American Fuzzy Information Processing Society* (NAFIPS03), 227-232.

Marinaki, M., Marinakis, Y., & Zopounidis, C. (2010). Honey Bees Mating Optimization algorithm for financial classification problems. *Applied Soft Computing, 10*(3), 806–812. doi:10.1016/j.asoc.2009.09.010

Monmarche, N., Slimane, M., & Venturini, G. (1999). *Ant Class: discovery of clusters in numeric data by a hybridization of an ant colony with the k means algorithm* [Report No. 213]. Laboratoired Informatique, Universite de Tours.

Oliveira, R. L., Lima, B. S. L. P., & Ebecken, N. F. F. (2007). A comparison of bio-inspired metaheuristic approaches in classification tasks. *WIT Transactions on Information and Communication Technologies, 38*, 25–32.

Omran, M., Salman, A., & Engelbrecht, A. P. (2002). Image Classification using Particle Swarm Optimization, In *Proceedings of Conference on Simulated Evolution and Learning*, 1, 370-374.

Parpinelli, R. S., Lopes, H. S., & Freits, A. A. (2002, August). Data Mining with an Ant Colony Optimization Algorithm. *IEEE Transactions on Evolutionary Computation, 6*(4), 321–332. doi:10.1109/TEVC.2002.802452

Poli, R. (1996). Genetic programming for feature detection and image segmentation. In T. Fogarty (Ed.), Evolutionary Computing, in Lecture Notes in Computer Science, 1143, 110-125. Springer-Verlag. doi:10.1007/BFb0032777

Raffaele, M. (2006) Nature inspired Optimization Algorithms for Classification and Regression Trees [PhD thesis]. Università degli Studi di Napoli Federico II.

Ramos, V., Muge, F., & Pina, P. (2002). Self-Organized Data and Image Retrieval as a Consequence of Inter-Dynamic Synergistic Relationships in Artificial Ant Colonies. *Soft Computing Systems: Design, Management and Applications*, 87, 500–509.

Shukran, M. A. M., Chung, Y. Y., & Yeh, W. C. (2011, August). Artificial Bee Colony based Data Mining Algorithms for Classification Tasks, *Modern Applied Science. Canadian Center of Science and Education*, 5(4), 217–231.

Soliman, O. S., Bahgat, R., & Adly, A. (2012). Associative Classification using a Bio-Inspired Algorithm, In *Proceedings of the Tenth Australasian Data Mining Conference (AusDM 2012)*, Sydney, Australia, 119-125.

Sousa, T., Silva, A., & Neves, A. (2004, May). Particle swarm based Data Mining Algorithms for classification tasks. Journal of Parallel Computing, 30(5-6), 767-783.

Tang, R., Fong, S., Yang, X.-S., & Deb, S. (2012, December). Nature-Inspired Clustering Algorithms for Web Intelligence Data. *Proceedings of IEEE/WIC/ACM International Conferences on Web Intelligence and Intelligent Agent Technology (WI-IAT)* (pp. 147-153).

Tang, R., Fong, S., Yang, X.-S., & Deb, S. (2012a, August 22-24). Wolf search algorithm with ephemeral memory. *Proceedings of IEEE Seventh International Conference on Digital Information Management (ICDIM 2012)* 165-172. Macau. doi:10.1109/ICDIM.2012.6360147

Tang, R., Fong, S., Yang, X.-S., & Deb, S. (2012b, August 22-24). Integrating Nature-inspired Optimization Algorithms to K-means Clustering. Proceedings of *IEEE Seventh International Conference on Digital Information Management (ICDIM 2012)* (pp. 116-123). Macau.

Vafaie, H., & DeJong, K. (1998). Feature space transformation using genetic algorithms. *IEEE Intelligent Systems & their Applications*, 13(2), 57–65. doi:10.1109/5254.671093

Xiao, X., Dow, E. R., Eberhart, R. C., Miled, Z. B., & Oppelt, R. J. (2003). Gene Clustering Using Self-Organizing Maps and Particle Swarm Optimization. *Proceedings of the 17th International Symposium on Parallel and Distributed Processing (PDPS '03)*. Washington DC. doi:10.1109/IPDPS.2003.1213290

Yang, X.-S. (2010). A New Metaheuristic Bat-Inspired Algorithm. In J. R. Gonzalez, et al (Eds.), Nature Inspired Cooperative Strategies for Optimization, 65-74. doi:10.1007/978-3-642-12538-6_6

Zarnani, A., Rahgozar, M., & Lucas, C. (2006). Nature-Inspired Approaches to Mining Trend Patterns in Spatial Databases, *Intelligent Data Engineering and Automated Learning – IDEAL 2006. Lecture Notes in Computer Science*, 4224, 1407–1414. doi:10.1007/11875581_167

KEY TERMS AND DEFINITIONS

Bat Algorithm: It is a metaheuristic based on the echolocation behaviour of microbats with varying pulse rates of emission and loudness.

Clustering: It is the task of grouping a set of objects in such a way that objects in the same group are more similar to each other than to those in other groups by some unsupervised learning algorithms.

Feature Selection: It reduces the dimensionality of data by selecting only a subset of features (predictor variables) to create a model with accuracy on par or better than that of a model induced by the full set of features.

Metaheuristic: In computer science and mathematical optimization, a metaheuristic is a higher-level procedure or heuristic designed to find, generate, or select a heuristic (partial search algorithm) that may provide a sufficiently good solution to an optimization problem.

Nature-Inspired Optimization Algorithms: It is in general a modern field of research that embraces computational techniques inspired by nature and natural systems. The algorithms enable development of new computational tools for solving complex, usually conventionally-hard problems. This often leads to the synthesis of natural patterns, behaviors and organisms, and may result in the design of novel computing systems that use natural media with which to compute.

Swarm Intelligence: It is the collective behavior of decentralized, self-organized systems, natural or artificial.

Wolf Search Algorithm: It is a metaheuristic that imitates the way wolves search for food and survive by avoiding their enemies.

ENDNOTES

[1]   http://mf.erciyes.edu.tr/abc/

Chapter 6
Artificial Immune Optimization Algorithm

Waseem Ahmad
International College of Auckland, New Zealand

ABSTRACT

Artificial immune system (AIS) is a paradigm inspired by processes and metaphors of natural immune system (NIS). There is a rapidly growing interest in AIS approaches to machine learning and especially in the domain of optimization. Of particular interest is the way human body responds to diseases and pathogens as well as adapts to remain immune for long periods after a disease has been combated. In this chapter, we are presenting a novel multilayered natural immune system (NIS) inspired algorithms in the domain of optimization. The proposed algorithm uses natural immune system components such as B-cells, Memory cells and Antibodies; and processes such as negative clonal selection and affinity maturation to find multiple local optimum points. Another benefit this algorithm presents is the presence of immunological memory that is in the form of specific memory cells which keep track of previously explored solutions. The algorithm is evaluated on two well-known numeric functions to demonstrate the applicability.

INTRODUCTION

Nature, through millions of years of learning has found efficient, robust and innovative methods for dealing daily challenges. The primary mechanism for these methods is 'neo-Darwinism', which is evolution by natural selection underpinned by modern genetics. This has led to the emergence of a relatively recent area of computing called 'evolutionary computing', which refers to a collection of nature-inspired techniques for solving hard problems in computer science. The computing algorithms inspired by such natural process are genetic algorithms (Goldberg, 1989; Jones, Willett, & Glen, 1995), simulated annealing (Goodsell & Olson, 1990; Kirkpatrick, Gelatt, & Jr., 1983), particle swarm optimization (PSO) (Kennedy & Eberhart, 1995) and ant colony optimization (ACO) (Shelokar, Jayaraman, & Kulkarni, 2004; Zhang, Yen, & Zhongshi, 2014). The contribution of these algorithms their contributions in various subfields of machine learning is well established and recognized in the literature. All of these algorithms

DOI: 10.4018/978-1-4666-8513-0.ch006

take their inspirations at the level of an individual organism or in populations of organisms. In recent few decades, our understanding of genetics has increased significantly. However, there is relatively less focus by computational researchers to develop novel computing algorithms inspired by genetic mechanisms. Natural immune system is an example of area that is less explored by computational researchers. In this chapter, our primary focus is to look into various processes and functions of natural immune system and propose a novel optimization algorithm.

In 1782 Jenner discovered that a smallpox viral attack can be prevented if people are injected with a small amount of the cowpox virus – a weaker form of the smallpox virus found in cattle. This is a form of vaccination, where a weaker form of pathogen is introduced in living organisms to immunize the body from stronger pathogens of the same kind. This finding formulate the basis for a new field of science called natural immune system. Natural Immune System (NIS) are known to possess learning and adaptive capabilities for dealing with pathogens not previously encountered and for finding preventative solutions for disinfection once infection is identified. Moreover, such disinfection can take place in a timely manner so that, in some cases, the organism does not even notice that it has been infected. Since there appears to be no supervision of the NIS (i.e. there appears to be no equivalent to a central executive in the organism for dealing with NIS), an AIS approach will need to be adaptive and cooperative. Also, once a pathogen is dealt with, the NIS has a 'memory' of that pathogen should it be encountered again. Because of these adaptive and learning aspects, previous AIS research has been located in the machine learning literature. However, our knowledge of the molecular biology underlying NIS is growing constantly and new discoveries being made that indicate that the NIS for multi-cellular organisms are much more complex than originally thought.

The early researchers of AIS considered that an immune system-inspired algorithm can only work in the pattern recognition domain due to its alignment with the human immune system and its pathogen recognition and elimination capabilities. The researchers have been using AIS algorithms on a number of different application domains such as computer security (Harmer, Williams, Gunsch, & Lamont, 2002; Kim, Greensmith, Twycross, & Aickelin, 2005), clustering/classification (Ayara, Timmis, Lemos, & Forrest, 2005; L. N. d. Castro & Timmis, 2002c; L. N. d. Castro & J. Zuben, 2000; Timmis, Neal, & Hunt, 2000; Watkins, Timmis, & Boggess, 2004), optimization (L. N. d. Castro & J. Zuben, 2000; Khaled, Abdul-Kader, & Ismail, 2010) and robotics (Lau, Bate, & Timmis, 2009; Whitbrook, Aickelin, & Garibaldi, 2007, 2008, 2009). Hart and Timmis (Hart & Timmis, 2008) presented a general review of application areas where AIS has been applied. The authors, based on a natural grouping of published work, classified AIS application areas into 12 distinct groups (Table 1) (Hart & Timmis, 2008). A reflection of these groupings can also be found in (L. N. d. Castro & F. J. V. Zuben, 2000).

These 12 groups can be re-classified into three more generalized and distinct groups; Anomaly Detection, Optimization and Learning (Hart & Timmis, 2008). It can be seen from Table 1 that groups such as anomaly detection, virus detection and computer security can be classified as Anomaly Detection. Numeric function optimization and combinatorial optimization can be considered as 'Optimization' group. Learning group can be formed to contain image processing, web mining, clustering/classification and bio-informatics.

AISs are local search algorithms where hypermutation is used to explore neighboring search space. The random population of solutions are inserted during the course of the algorithm to encourage global search. One of the drawbacks of introducing a randomly generated population of B-cells is that the algorithm can tend to repeat local searches due to the presence of a basis of attraction. Basis of attraction can be defined as follows: *'Given any local optima, consider the set of all points in the search space*

Table 1. Main application areas of AIS

Major	Minor
Clustering/Classification	Bio-informatics
Anomaly Detection	Image Processing
Computer Security	Control
Numeric Function Optimization	Robotics
Combinatorial Optimization	Virus Detection
Learning	Web Mining

that have the property that starting local search from there, finishes at that local optima.' Most of the approaches in the literature do not address this problem, with the exception of 'tabu search' (Chelouah & Siarry, 2000). Tabu search does this by keeping a memory (the tabu list) of recent moves, which are disallowed for a certain period.

The generation and presence of memory cells is a salient feature of an NIS. In the context of AIS approaches, memory cells are points in a search space that have been visited in the past and there is no need to revisit them. Existing AIS optimization approaches do not utilize this feature. The salient feature of our proposed HAIS-optimization in comparison with existing AIS optimization algorithms is its more effective and novel role of memory cells. The algorithm proposed in this chapter uses concepts of natural immune systems and principles of tabu search to find better solutions by not considering paths that are already explored.

NATURAL IMMUNE SYSTEM – AN INTRODUCTION

Innate and adaptive/acquired immune systems are two main parts of our natural immune system. Innate immune system does not adapt or changes throughout our life spam. It consists of specific cells that helps eradicate different types of micro-organisms and harmful cells. The main component of innate immune system is leucocytes or white blood cells and they do not divide or reproduce to mount an immune response. Typical leucocytes are natural killer cells and phagocytes (macrophages, neutrophils and dendritic cells). Out of these all, dendritic cells are most important. One reason is their location that is in contact with the external environment, such as the skin and mucus. Second, and more important is their functionality, since they link the innate and adaptive immune systems through antigen presentation. Antigens are any particle (coats, capsules, cell walls, toxins) of bacteria, viruses and other micro-organisms. If the innate immune system cannot deal with a pathogen, the adaptive/acquired system is triggered.

The main component of the adaptive immune system is white blood cells, called lymphocytes. Lymphocytes are normally in a passive state until they encounter specific molecules called antigens (either 'self' or 'non-self' antigens). Lymphocytes are normally of two types, class-T and class-B lymphocytes. B-lymphocytes secrete proteins that bind to the antigens, whereas T-lymphocytes perform a variety of functions, including recognizing and killing the cells which are bearing non-self antigens on their surfaces. They can also kill cancerous cells. Each lymphocyte can recognize only one type of antigen by having a single type of antigen receptor with unique specificity. Each antigen leaves a genetic blueprint on class-B and class-T lymphocytes, resulting in a quick and effective response to a repeat attack by

Figure 1. A snapshot of humoral-mediated response

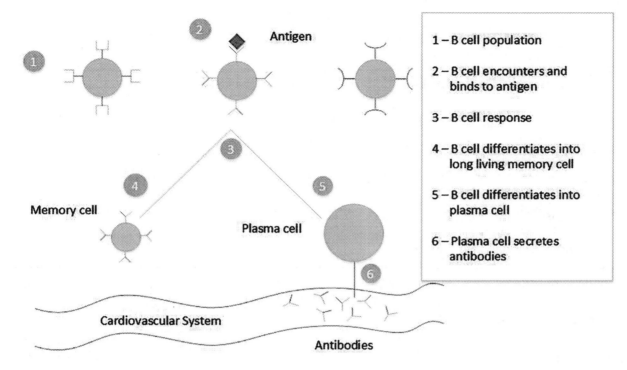

similar antigens. This phenomenon is referred to as immunology memory. If the immunity is mediated by T lymphocytes, it is called cell mediated immunity and on the other hand if it is mediated by antibody secretion produced by B cells it is called humoral immunity (a snapshot is presented in Figure 1). In this chapter, our focus is on humoral mediated aspects of adaptive immune systems.

B cells produced in the bone marrow remain there until maturation, and when they are released they have a unique receptor on their membrane called the Ig receptor, due to their link to a specific immuno-globulin (Ig) super-family. When a B cell encounters an antigen, it is stimulated by receptor occupation and reacts in two ways: first it produces a B-memory cell and secondly it produces an effector-B cell. The memory B cell too has an Ig receptor on its membrane that keeps looking for similar antigens. When plasma or effector-B cells lose their Ig receptor they grow larger in size and start producing antibodies which are released into the free circulation to combat the antigens. These antibodies are the hyper-mutated copies of stimulated B cells. The new B cells which have not encountered any antigens are called naïve cells. Such cells have a life span of about a week unless they interact with antigens. The life span of memory cells is much longer than regular B cells and they can survive for many years. This is one way that immunological memory keeps track of the diseases or viruses that have been encountered in the past.

The immune system works through a process called negative clonal selection. This is one method of differentiating between self and non-self. The immune system destroys all the antibodies which are similar to self to avoid a self-destructive immune response. This record of non-self keeps updating as new antigens or viruses are encountered. This negative selection process takes place in the thymus. Only those antibodies that interact with antigens are selected for proliferation and differentiation and all others are placed in an inactive or passive state. The main feature of clonal selection theory is that proliferated cells will have receptors of the same specificity as the original B cell with hyper-mutation rates for altering the specificity of antibodies that are dependent on the affinity measure (similarity measure) between antigens and antibodies.

BASIC CONCEPTS OF AN ARTIFICIAL IMMUNE SYSTEM (AIS)

We have explained main processes involved in NISs. In order to map processes and information available in an NIS to an AIS, a few considerations are necessary, regardless of the area of application:

- How to represent antigens, antibodies and B-cells?
- What are memory cells in computational AISs?
- How to calculate affinity between antigen and antibody receptors?
- How to perform clonal selection?
- What does hypermutation mean?

Here, we answer these questions in the context of AISs in a machine learning paradigm. All the unseen data instances are usually considered as antigens. In the example of a cancer dataset, the task is to classify all data instances/records into either a normal group or cancer group, with or without seeing an original class label. Regardless of biological differences, there is little to distinguish in the use between antibodies and B-cells in the literature. Antibodies are data items which we have already seen and classified, whereas B-cells can be regarded as data clusters. Memory cells are also data items which we have already seen. The main difference between antibodies and memory cells is that the former are generalized forms of already seen data and the latter are specializations of seen data instances. The antigens and antibodies must be represented in the same way, e.g. as a number of continuous or discrete variables or features.

The affinity or similarity measure is one of the most important factors in designing an AIS and it depends on the representation scheme of antigens and antibodies. For example, consider an antigen = [1 1 0 0 1] and an antibody = [0 1 0 1 1]. There is a similarity score of 3 as there are three matching indices. If the representations of data items are real variables, various other distance measures can also be applied such as Euclidean distance, Manhattan distance, Mahalanobis distance and Hamming distance. Essentially, these measures return a magnitude of similarity or dissimilarity, which can be considered as the affinity between an antigen and an antibody.

Mutation in AIS is the same as that performed in genetic algorithms. For example, for binary string, one or more bits are randomly flipped, and in real-value string, one or more values are changed to other values. There are different ways that mutation can be implemented in an AIS. For example, the mutation rate can be higher or lower depending on the affinity between antigen and antibodies. When a new data instance is introduced into an AIS, it is compared against all existing antibodies, and those antibodies with a threshold higher than some specified level (affinity) get stimulated and activated. Once an antibody is activated it undergoes clonal selection. Clonal selection is the process of generating more antibodies by activated antibodies to achieve a higher affinity level between antigen (new data instance) and antibodies. In AIS, clonal selection is responsible for exploring local search space to find better solutions. The process of fine-tuning antibodies receptors (moving of antibodies towards new data instance) towards an antigen is called affinity maturation.

De Castro and Timmis (L. N. d. Castro & Timmis, 2002c) proposed a framework for AIS. In the case of other nature-inspired computational techniques (e.g. neural networks and genetic algorithms) frameworks already exist which can help considerably in the development of AIS systems. For instance, one framework for designing an artificial neural network (Liao & Wen, 2007; Ripley, 1996) consists of artificial neurons, interconnecting weights on neurons, and a learning algorithm (L. N. d. Castro & Timmis, 2002c; Ripley, 1996). An artificial neural network can be designed by arranging together artificial neurons in various layers (input layer, hidden layer and output layer). During the training or learning process, the artificial neurons undergo an adaptive process by which weights associated with those artificial neurons are adjusted and quantified and finally knowledge is acquired from the system. In the case of genetic/evolutionary algorithms, an initial population of chromosomes is generated, which during the learning process undergoes reproduction, genetic variations and selection. As a result of this learning process a population of evolved chromosomes (individuals) arises. In summary, the framework for designing an evolutionary algorithm is the generation of an initial population of chromosomes, and the procedures for reproduction, genetic variations and selection. The authors (L. N. d. Castro & Timmis, 2002c) derived some simple rules for designing any nature-inspired algorithm. It must have:

- "A representation of the components of the system
- A set of mechanisms to evaluate the interaction of individuals with the environment and each other. The environment is usually simulated by a set of input stimuli, one or more fitness function(s), or other mean(s) and
- Procedures of adaptation that govern the dynamics of the system, i.e. how its behavior varies over time" (L. N. d. Castro & Timmis, 2002c).

The framework for designing AIS algorithms is represented as a layered approach in Figure 2. The AIS system consists of three components: representation, affinity measure, and immune algorithms (L. N. d. Castro & Timmis, 2002c). To build an AIS, the first step is to know the application domain. The application knowledge will help the representation of the AIS system. The affinity measure also depends on the representation of AIS system. One or a combination of distance measures can be used for the affinity measure. Each of these distance measures have their own biases (Freitas, 2002; Jain, 2010) and an affinity measure must therefore be selected with great care as it can affect the final solution obtained by the system. Finally, the final layer is the selection of appropriate immune system-based algorithms. Some of the proposed AIS algorithms are negative selection, positive selection, clonal selection, and the immune network algorithm (Hart & Timmis, 2008). The details regarding these algorithms are presented the next section.

LITERATURE REVIEW

The NIS, by its very nature, does not perform optimization. The goal of any computational optimization is to find an optimal solution. On the other hand, the objective of an NIS is to evolve to find the best possible response (solution) under existing conditions (Hart & Timmis, 2008), and sometimes it has to work under contradicting conditions. This does not stop AIS researchers using AIS in an optimization domain, however. AIS has produced a number of optimization algorithms on the clonal selection principles such

Figure 2. AIS layered framework (Hart & Timmis, 2008)

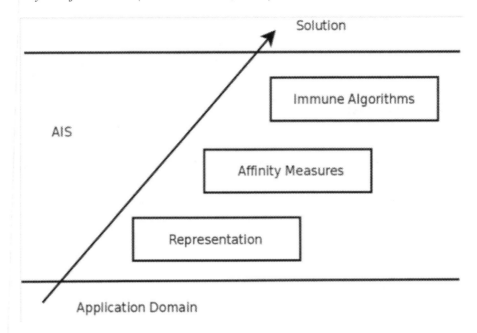

as CLONALG (L. N. d. Castro & J. Zuben, 2000), opt-aiNet (L. N. d. Castro & Timmis, 2002a), B-cell algorithm (BCA) (Kelsey & Timmis, 2003), and opt-IA (Cutello, Nicosia, & Pavone, 2004).

CLONALG (de Castro and von Zuben, 2000) is a clonal selection algorithm originally specified for binary character recognition and engineering optimization but can be adapted for clustering. CLONALG can be described as follows, where antibodies are regarded as cells (Brownlee, 2005):

- **Initialise:** Prepare an initial random antibody pool.
- **Loop:** Present the antigens to the antibodies and calculate affinity values for each antibody depending on the similarity between the antibody and the antigens.
- **Select:** A set of antibodies are selected from the entire antibody pool that have the highest affinity with the antigen.
- **Clone:** This set of selected antibodies is cloned in proportion to their affinity (the higher the affinity, the more an antibody is cloned).
- **Mutate (Affinity Maturation:** Mutate the clones in direct inverse proportion to their affinity (the lower the fitness, the more a cloned antibody is mutated).
- **Measure clonal affinity:** Calculate affinity values for each cloned antibody depending on the similarity between the cloned antibody and the antigens.
- **Select candidates:** The antibodies (original and cloned) with the highest affinity are selected for survival in the next generation.
- **Diversify:** Add a number of newly generated random antibodies.
- **Return:** to Loop until some termination condition is satisfied.

This generic algorithm can be fine-tuned depending on the problem being dealt with. For instance, if binary classification is required, the class of antigen can be used in the affinity measure to produce just two antibodies that are highly tuned to their respective antigens. The algorithm reflects several immune system principles, including the match between antigens and antibodies and the somatic hypermutation and clonal selection of those antibodies that match antigens.

Al-Sheshtawi (Al-Sheshtawi, Abdul-Kadir, & Ismail, 2010) used CLONALG, opt-IA and BCA on numerical optimization problems and found that the results obtained were comparable with other state-of-the-art optimization techniques. All these approaches use cloning, mutation and selection to build a population of solutions. The authors of aiNet (L. N. d. Castro & Zuben, 2002) stated some of the benefits AIS can provide while doing optimization: it (a) performs exploration and exploitation of search space through memory cells and antibodies, (b) finds multiple local optimal solutions, (c) maintains many local optimal solutions and (d) has a predefined stopping criteria. An advanced version of opt-aiNet was proposed by Xuhua and called mopt-aiNet, which uses several novel operators such as multi-population, a dynamic hypermutation operator and dynamic memory cell formation (Xuhua & Feng, 2009). An AIS model for numerical constraint optimization problems based on CLONALG was proposed by Aragon *et al.* (Aragon, Esquivel, & Coello, 2007). A new mutation operator was introduced that used two different methods for mutation (low and high mutation rates) based on feasibility or non-feasibility of the clones produced. The low mutation of feasible clones helps in exploitation, whereas the high mutation of infeasible clones is useful in exploration of the search space. In recent work, Wang (Wang & Xu, 2010) adopted a cluster mechanism to divide a single population into sub-populations for hypermutation and selection. The author also uses a hybrid mutation operator consisting of Gaussian mutation and Cauchy mutation to obtain diversity in antibodies and affinity maturation. This was done to achieve better fitness on the population of antibodies as well as to obtain a global optimal solution. El-Wahed (El-Wahed, Zaki, & El-Refaey, 2010) proposed an AIS and neural network hybrid optimization algorithm for finding better solutions near the pareto-optimal frontier. Woldemariam (Woldemariam & Yen, 2010) introduces the notion of vaccination in AIS algorithm to solve function optimization problems. Vaccine is extracted by dividing the search space into equal subspaces. These vaccines are then introduces into the algorithm to enhance exploration of global and local solutions. Castro and Zuben introduced a Bayesian artificial immune system optimization algorithm (P. A. D. Castro & Zuben, 2009) and later upgraded it to multi-objective optimization (MOBAIS) (P. A. D. Castro & Zuben, 2008). The authors replaced traditional cloning and mutation operators with a Bayesian network representing a joint distribution of promising solutions. Another advantage of MOBAIS is its ability to automatically control the population size. The algorithm showed comparative results with other benchmarked multi-objective optimization approaches. Yap *et al.* (Yap, Koh, & Tiong, 2011) presented an improved version of clonal selection algorithm. The empirical results are compared against Genetic Algorithms (GAs) and Particle Swarm Optimization (PSO) in terms of accuracy and stability for single and multi-objective function optimization. Author concluded that PSO is fast in obtaining optimal values, however, it suffers from premature convergence and hence struck in local optimal solutions. Gas converge slowly and able to find better optimal solutions. A variant of AIS has been able to find consistently much better results than other approaches.

Zhang et al. (Zhang et al., 2014) presented an AIS algorithm inspired by B-cells for constraint optimization. The concepts of activated B-cells and inactivated B-cells are mapped to feasible region and infeasible region of the search space. Activated B-cells are responsible for exploration in feasible regions through clonal selection, recombination and hypermutation operators. Whereas, the positioning of inactivated B-cells are updated along the feasibility boundary and then inactivated B-cells exploit the region close to the boundaries of feasibility region. There is a knowledge sharing between activated and inactivated B-cells. A multi-objective optimization based on the concepts of immune network theory is presented by (Tsang & Lau, 2013), where empirical results are compared against other state of the art approaches.

An AIS algorithm inspired by the functionality of T-cells was proposed by Aragon *et al.* (Aragon, Esquivel, & Coello, 2010) for solving optimization problems. This algorithm consists of four components, namely virgin cells (VC), effector cells (CD4 and CD8), and memory cells (MC). The main objective of this algorithm was to explore possible solution space using local and global search operators. An extensive and global search is performed using CD4 and CD8, whereas fine-tuning of candidate memory cells is performed by exploring neighborhood operators (with low mutation rate). An extension of this work for dynamic optimization problems is presented in (Aragon, Esquivel, & Coello, 2011) and called the Dynamic T-cell (DTC) algorithm.

HAIS-OPTIMIZATION ALGORITHM

The proposed HAIS-Optimization algorithm is a variant of already published work humoral- mediated clustering algorithm by (Ahmad & Narayanan, 2010). HAIS algorithm was originally proposed for unsupervised learning. In this section, an overview of HAIS is presented followed by description of HAIS-Optimization algorithm.

The main components of HAIS algorithms are B-cells, Antibodies and Memory cells. The algorithm start with pre-defined B-cells (clusters). Antigens are considered to be unseen or un-clustered data. The algorithm mainly works on three layers, as shown in Figure 3. First layer consists of Memory cells. Second layer consists of antibodies generated by existing B-cells and finally third layer is responsible for creating new B-cell. The similarity between antigen and antibodies/memory cells is calculated by pairwise square normalized Euclidean distance. Antigens are randomly selected from the pool of antigens, one at a time and presented to first layer. If first layer cannot capture antigen (based on some threshold value), antigen is presented to second layer. However, if captured at first layer or second layer, certain actions are performed. If first two layers cannot capture antigen; it is presented to layer three, where new B-cell is created with same receptor values as antigen. This is an iterative process; at the end of each iteration all B-cells are evaluated and less stimulated B-cells (small clusters) are removed. Remaining B-cells update their centroids according to captured antigens. This whole process is repeat until some pre-defined criteria is met.

After a brief description of HAIS clustering algorithm, now we will describe HAIS-Optimization algorithm. The following are the parameters used (Table 2) in the proposed algorithm

The algorithm starts by generating a random number of B-cells ('N'). These B-cells are also placed into the pool of memory cells (M-cells). Each of the B-cells in the system generates 'n' number of antibodies using a pre-defined mutation rate. Now, all antibodies with affinity (fitness) greater than the parent B-cell are selected. The antibody with highest affinity is kept separated and called b-Ab. At this step (Step h), if the antibody pool is not empty, we perform a negative selection. A negative selection is first performed between newly generated antibodies and subsequently between antibodies and existing M-cells. After performing a negative selection, if the antibody pool is not empty then we perform three tasks: (a) evolve the parent B-cell receptor towards the b-Ab; (b) generate new B-cells for each of the antibodies left in the pool; and (c) assign all these newly generated B-cells to M-cells. However, if the antibody pool is empty and the fitness of the b-Ab is higher than that of the parent B-cell, the B-cell and

Figure 3. A snapshot of the HAIS Algorithm

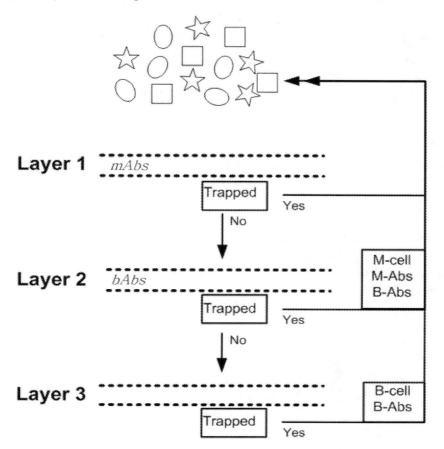

Table 2. Parameters used in the proposed algorithm

Parameter	Description
Gen	Number of generation the algorithm is run
N	Minimum size of B-cell Population
g	Number of antibodies selected based on the criteria of affinity
n	Number of antibodies generated from each stimulated B-cell
Mut	Mutation rate – fixed
NegT	Negative clonal selection threshold
Peaks	Number of best final M-cells selected

M-cell receptors are evolved towards the b-Ab. Otherwise the parent B-cell is removed from the population of B-cells. At the end of each generation, the size of the population of B-cells is calculated and if it is below 'N', new B-cells are generated. However, before introducing new B-cells into the population of existing B-cells, a negative selection (against existing M-cells) is performed.

The outcome of this algorithm is in the form of a set of evolved M-cells. These M-cells are points explored in a search space and subsequently a set of best memory cells can be selected from them.

a)

b)   Randomly select **'N'** number of B-cells

c)   Generate Memory cells pool, and M cells:= B-cells

d)   **Repeat:**

e)   **For each B-cell**

f)   Generate **'n'** antibodies based on **'Mut'** mutation rate

g)   Select antibodies with higher fitness than parent B-cell

h)   Select antibody with highest affinity **(b-Ab)**

i)   **If** not empty (antibodies)

    i)   Perform negative selection between antibodies

    ii)   Perform negative selection between M-cells and selected antibodies

    iii)   Select maximum of **'g'** antibodies

    iv)   **If** not empty (antibodies)

        (a)   Evolve parent B-cells towards **b-Ab**

        (b)   Generate new B-cells for each of the antibody

        (c)   M cells = M cells + new B-cells

    v)   Else

        (a)   **If** fitness of **b-Ab** is better than B-cell

            1.   Evolve parent B-cell towards **b-Ab**

            2.   Evolve related M cell receptors towards **b-Ab**

        (b)   Else

            1.   Remove B-cell

j)   Else

    i)   Remove B-cell

k)   **End For loop**

l)   **If** size of B-cell population is less than **'N'**

    (a)   Generate new B-cells (Add them into the B-cell population after performing negative selection with M cells)

m)   **Until termination condition**

EXPERIMENTAL RESULTS

Following are the two functions used to evaluate the performance of our proposed HAIS-optimization algorithm. The parameters used for these experiments are in Table 3.

$$f = 10.2 + (x^2 - 10\cos(2\pi x)) + (y^2 - 10\cos(2\pi y)) \; [-2,2] \tag{1}$$

Table 3. Parameter values used for experiments

Parameters	Values
Gen	25
N	20
g	10
n	100
Mut	12
NegT	0.15
Peaks	16

$$f = \sin(x + y^2) \ [-2,2] \tag{2}$$

In Figure 4, the black round marks are the M-cells obtained during the process of HAIS and red-round marks near the peaks are final number of M-cells selected from the pool of all obtained memory cells. From the Figure it can clearly be seen that 16 best memory cells are selected (Red marks). The memory cells (black marks) are regarded as memory of the proposed optimization system and it help to stop ex-

Figure 4. M-cells obtained using the HAIS algorithm on Equation 1

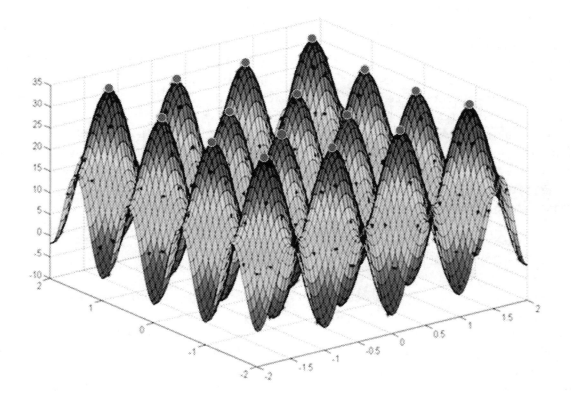

ploring the path that has already been explored in the past. This process saves us a lot of computational time and effectively helps to find local optimum solutions.

We can see from the Figure 5 (top) that the algorithm started with 22 B-cells and by the end of second generation there were 26 B-cells present in the system. Generation 3 has maximum number of B-cells and from generation 4 onwards, we have maintained 20 B-cells that is minimum requirement that we have to maintain. The algorithm is totally run for 25 generations. Figure 5 (middle) represents average fitness value of B-cells at the end of each generation. This graph is fluctuating because of the introduction of random population of B-cells at the end of each generation. Figure 5 (bottom) is showing a very nice converging trend. The graph represents average fitness value of best memory cells at the end of each iteration. The average fitness was very low in the beginning however, only after 5 generation, the algorithm started to converge to its local optimum points. The original 16 points, as well as the corresponding fitness values obtained by the algorithm are shown in Table 4. The x and y values are shown in first 2 columns and function values obtained is shown in last column (maximum and minimum values between 34.3145 and 30.6281).

In Figure 6, the black round marks are the M-cells obtained during the process of HAIS and red-round marks near the peaks are final number of M-cells selected from the pool of all obtained memory cells. From the Figure it can clearly be seen that 16 best memory cells are selected. The memory cells (Red marks) are regarded as memory of the proposed optimization system and it help to stop exploring the path that has already been explored in the past. This process saves us a lot of computational time and effectively helps to find local optimum solutions.

We can see from the Figure 7 (top) that the algorithm stated with 22 B-cells and by the end of second generation there were 26 B-cells present in the system. Generation 3 has maximum number of B-cells and from generation 4 onwards, we have maintained 20 B-cells that is minimum requirement that we have to maintain. The algorithm is totally run for 25 generations. Figure 7 (bottom) is showing a very nice converging trend. The graph represents average fitness value of best memory cells at the end of each iteration. The average fitness was very low in the beginning however, only after 5 generation, the algorithm started to converge to its local optimum points. . The original 16 points, as well as the corresponding fitness values obtained by the algorithm are shown in Table 5. The x and y values are shown in first 2 columns and function values obtained is shown in last column.

Here, we have demonstrated with simple two numeric function that the HAIS algorithm can also be fine-tuned to solve optimization problems. In the HAIS-optimization algorithm, the population of B-cells is evolved towards local optimum solutions and randomly generated B-cells are introduced into the existing population of B-cells when the total size of the population decreases to a pre-defined threshold. This random generation of B-cells is helpful in finding global search space.

CONCLUSION

In this chapter we have described a novel humoral-inspired optimization algorithm inspired by memory cells, plasma cells, immunoglobulin receptors and antibody concepts. The experimental results indicate that dynamic growth and reduction of the number of B-cells (potential optimal solutions), together with population of memory cells, achieve effective optimization. Results on numerical functions demonstrate the feasibility of the approach when numbers of local peaks are known to exist in the search space. In future work the focus will be to extend this algorithm further to deal with multi-objective optimization

Figure 5. Size of B-cell population, average fitness and best fitness of M-cells obtained at the end of each generation

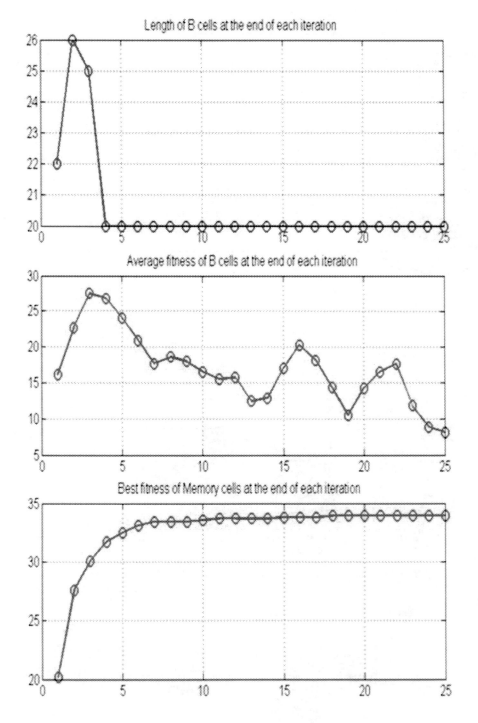

Table 4. List of obtained best M-cells

x	y	f
1.5041	-1.5022	34.7145
1.5012	1.5054	34.7138
-1.5195	-1.5054	34.6942
-1.4863	1.5575	34.1533
1.5068	0.501	32.7121
-1.5078	0.4999	32.7114
0.5008	-1.5025	32.7069
0.5041	1.5139	32.7047
1.5084	-0.496	32.7042
-1.5064	-0.4944	32.6993
-0.5103	1.5125	32.6961
-0.5184	-1.5048	32.6617
0.4969	0.5007	30.6956
-0.5028	-0.5129	30.6813
-0.5023	0.4908	30.6752
0.4888	-0.4887	30.6281

Figure 6. M-cells obtained using the HAIS algorithm on Equation 2

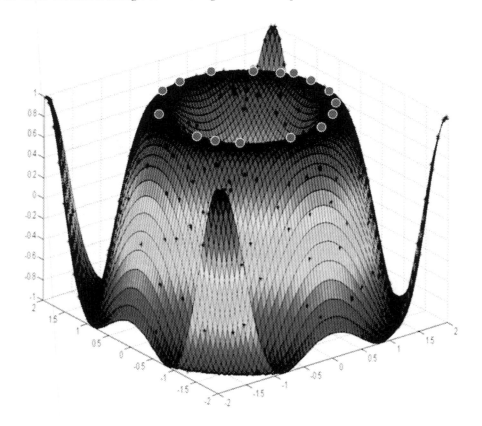

Figure 7. Size of B-cell population, average fitness and best fitness of M-cells obtained at the end of each generation

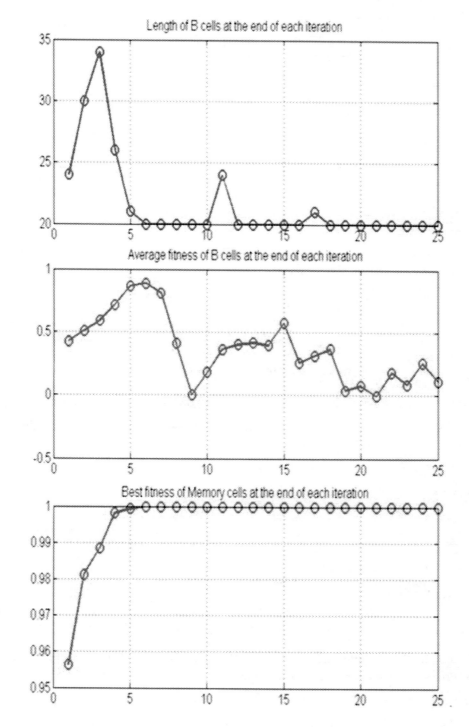

Table 5. List of obtained best M-cells

x	y	f
-1.1845	-0.4096	1
1.0449	-0.6921	1
0.8333	0.9362	1
-1.0623	-0.6651	1
-0.2284	1.2324	1
1.1659	0.4594	1
0.7325	-1.0167	1
-0.8247	-0.9434	1
1.2178	-0.2949	1
-1.1534	0.4913	1
-0.6507	1.0706	1
1.2435	0.1602	1
-0.1789	-1.2399	1
0.3037	1.2152	1
0.3849	-1.1938	1
1.0775	0.6379	1

that is more challenging task. Also, future emphasis will be on constructing a better dynamic framework for reinforced directed mutation and self-evolving memory cell affinity criteria where different memory cells can merge to formulate super-memory cells. It will be interesting to compare this algorithm in terms of accuracy and convergence speed with other state of the art algorithms to really find the placement of this work in the existing literature.

REFERENCES

Ahmad, W., & Narayanan, A. (2010). Humoral-mediated Clustering. Proceedings of the IEEE 5th International Conference on Bio-Inspired Computing: Theories and Applications (BIC-TA 2010) (pp. 1471-1481). doi:10.1109/BICTA.2010.5645279

Al-Sheshtawi, K. A., Abdul-Kadir, H. M., & Ismail, A. A. (2010). Artificial Immune Clonal Selection Algorithms: A Comparative Study of CLONALG, opt-IA and BCA with Numerical Optimization Problems. *International Journal of Computer Science and Network Security, 10*(4), 24–30.

Aragon, V. S., Esquivel, S. C., & Coello, C. A. C. (2010). Artificial Immune System for Solving Global Optimization Problems. *Inteligencia Artificial, 46*, 3–16. doi:10.4114/ia.v14i46.1500

Aragon, V. S., Esquivel, S. C., & Coello, C. A. C. (2011). A T-cell Algorithm for Solving Dynamic Optimization Problems. *Information Sciences, 181*(17), 3614–3637. doi:10.1016/j.ins.2011.04.028

Aragon, V. S., Esquivel, S. C., & Coello, E. S. (2007). Artificial Immune System for Solving Constrained Optimization Problems. *Intelligencia Artificial, 11*(35), 55–66.

Ayara, M., Timmis, J., de Lemos, R., & Forrest, S. (2005). Immunising Automated Teller Machines. In C. Jacob, M. Pilat, P. J. Bentley, & J. I. Timmis (Eds.), Artificial Immune Systems (pp. 404-417). doi:10.1007/11536444_31

Castro, L. N. d., & Timmis, J. (2002a). An Artificial Immune Network for Multimodal Function Optimisation. *Proceedings of IEEE World Congress on Evolutionary Computation*, 669-674.

Castro, L. N. d., & Timmis, J. (2002c). Artificial immune system: a new computational intelligence approach, 380. London: Springer-Verlag.

Castro, L. N. d., & Zuben, F. J. V. (2000). Artificial Immune Systems: Part II - A Survey of Applications [Technical Report - RT DCA 02/00]. Retrieved from ftp://ftp.dca.fee.unicamp.br/pub/docs/vonzuben/lnunes/rtdca0200.pdf

Castro, L. N. d., & Zuben, F. J. V. (2002). aiNet: An Artificial Immune Network for Data Analysis. In H. Abbass, R. Sarker, & C. Newton (Eds.), Data Mining: A Heuristic Approach, Idea Group Publishing. doi:, 231-260. doi:10.4018/978-1-930708-25-9.ch012

Castro, L. N. d., & Zuben, J. (2000). The Clonal Selection Algorithm with Engineering Applications. *Workshop Proceedings of GECCO, Workshop on Artificial Immune Systems and Their Applications,* 36-37. Las Vegas.

Castro, P. A. D., & Zuben, F. J. V. (2008). MOBAIS: A Bayesian Artificial Immune System for Multi-Objective Optimization. *Proceedings of the 7th International Conference*, 48-59.

Castro, P. A. D., & Zuben, F. J. V. (2009). BAIS: A Bayesian Artificial Immune System for the Effective Handling of Building Blocks. *Information Sciences, 179*(10), 1426–1440. doi:10.1016/j.ins.2008.11.040

Chelouah, R., & Siarry, P. (2000). Tabu Search applied to global optimization. *European Journal of Operational Research, 123*(2), 256–270. doi:10.1016/S0377-2217(99)00255-6

Cutello, V., Nicosia, G., & Pavone, M. (2004). Exploring the capability of immune algorithms: A characterization of hypermutation operators. *Proceedings of the Third International Conference on Artificial Immune System (ICARIS'04)*, 263-276. doi:10.1007/978-3-540-30220-9_22

El-Wahed, W. F., Zaki, E. M., & El-Refaey, A. M. (2010). Reference Point Based Multi-Objective Optimization Using Hybrid Artificial Immune System. *Universal Journal of Computer Science and Engineering Technology, 1*, 24–30.

Freitas, A. A. (2002). *Data mining and knowledge discovery with evolutionary algorithms*. New York: Springer-Vlag Berlin Heidelberg. doi:10.1007/978-3-662-04923-5

Goldberg, D. E. (1989). *Genetic Algorithms in Search Opimization and Machine Learning*. Reading, MA: Addison-Wesley.

Goodsell, D. S., & Olson, A. J. (1990). Automated Docking of Substrates to Proteins by Simulated Annealing. Proteins. *Structure, Function, and Bioinformatics, 8*(3), 195–202. doi:10.1002/prot.340080302 PMID:2281083

Harmer, P. K., Williams, P. D., Gunsch, G. H., & Lamont, G. B. (2002). An artificial immune system architecture for computer security applications. *IEEE Transactions on Evolutionary Computation, 6*(3), 252–280. doi:10.1109/TEVC.2002.1011540

Hart, E., & Timmis, J. (2008). Application area of AIS: The Past, The Present and the Future. Applied Soft Computing, 8(1).

Jain, A. K. (2010). Data Clustering: 50 Years Beyond K-means. *Pattern Recognition Letters, 31*(8), 651–666. doi:10.1016/j.patrec.2009.09.011

Jones, G., Willett, P., & Glen, R. C. (1995). Molecular Recognition of Receptor Sites using a Genetic algorithm with a Description of Desolvation. *Journal of Molecular Biology, 245*(1), 43–53. doi:10.1016/S0022-2836(95)80037-9 PMID:7823319

Kelsey, J., & Timmis, J. (2003). Immune inspired somatic contiguous hypermutation for function optimisation. *Proceedings of Genetic and Evolutionary Computation Conference - GECCO* (pp. 207–218).

Kennedy, J., & Eberhart, R. C. (1995). Particle swarm optimization. *Proc. IEEE Int'l. Conf. on Neural Networks, IV*, (pp. 1942-1948). doi:10.1109/ICNN.1995.488968

Khaled, A., Abdul-Kader, H. M., & Ismail, N. A. (2010). Artificial Immune Clonal Selection Algorithm: A Comparative Study of CLONALG, opt-IA and BCA with Numerical Optimization Problems. *International Journal of Computer Science and Network Security, 10*(4), 24–30.

Kim, J., Greensmith, J., Twycross, J., & Aickelin, U. (2005). Malicious Code Execution Detection and Response Immune System inspired by the Danger Theory. *Proceedings of Adaptive and Resilient Computing Security Workshop (ARCS-05)*.

Kirkpatrick, S., Gelatt, C. D., & Jr, M. P. V. (1983). Optimization by Simulated Annealing. *Science, 220*(4598), 671–680. doi:10.1126/science.220.4598.671 PMID:17813860

Lau, H., Bate, I., & Timmis, J. (2009). An Immuno-engineering Approach for Anomaly Detection in Swarm Robotics. *Proceedings of 8th International Conference* (pp. 136–150).

Liao, S. H., & Wen, C. H. (2007). Artificial neural networks classification and clustering of methodologies and applications – literature analysis from 1995 to 2005. *Expert Systems with Applications, 32*(1), 1–11. doi:10.1016/j.eswa.2005.11.014

Ripley, B. D. (1996). *Pattern Recognition and Neural Networks*. Cambridge, UK: Cambridge University Press. doi:10.1017/CBO9780511812651

Shelokar, P. S., Jayaraman, V. K., & Kulkarni, B. D. (2004). An ant colony approach for clustering. *Analytica Chimica Acta, 509*(2), 187–195. doi:10.1016/j.aca.2003.12.032

Timmis, J., Neal, M., & Hunt, J. (2000). An artificial immune system for data analysis. *Bio Systems, 55*(1-3), 143–150. doi:10.1016/S0303-2647(99)00092-1 PMID:10745118

Tsang, W. W., & Lau, H. Y. (2013). An Artificial Immune System-based Many-Objective Optimization Algorithm with Network Activation Scheme. *Advances in Artificial Life, ECAL, 12*, 872–873.

Wang, S., & Xu, X. (2010). A novel immune clonal selection optimization algorithm. *Proceedings of International Conference on Computer Application and System Modeling* (ICCASM'10), 391-395.

Watkins, A., Timmis, J., & Boggess, L. (2004). Artificial Immune Recognition System (AIRS): An Immune-Inspired Supervised Learning Algorithm. *Genetic Programming and Evolvable Machines, 5*(3), 291–317. doi:10.1023/B:GENP.0000030197.83685.94

Whitbrook, A. M., Aickelin, U., & Garibaldi, J. M. (2007). Idiotypic Immune Networks in Mobile Robot Control. *IEEE Transactions on Systems, Man, and Cybernetics. Part B, Cybernetics, 37*(6), 1581–1598. doi:10.1109/TSMCB.2007.907334 PMID:18179075

Whitbrook, A. M., Aickelin, U., & Garibaldi, J. M. (2008). An Idiotypic Immune Network as a Short-Term Learning Architecture for Mobile Robots. *Proceedings of 7th International Conference* (pp. 266–278).

Whitbrook, A. M., Aickelin, U., & Garibaldi, J. M. (2009). The Transfer of Evolved Artificial Immune System Behaviours Between Small and Large Scale Robotic Platforms. *Proceedings of the 9th international conference on artificial evolution (EA'09)*.

Woldemariam, K. M., & Yen, G. G. (2010). Vaccine-Enhanced Artificial Immune System for Multi-modal Function Optimization. *IEEE Transactions on Systems, Man, and Cybernetics, 40*(1), 218–228. doi:10.1109/TSMCB.2009.2025504 PMID:19635706

Xuhua, S., & Feng, Q. (2009). An optimization Algorithm Based on Multi-population Artificial Immune Network. *Proceedings of Fifth International Conference on Natural Computation*, 379-383. doi:10.1109/ICNC.2009.574

Yap, F. W., Koh, S. P., & Tiong, S. K. (2011). Mathematical Function Optimization using AIS Antibody Remainder method. *International Journal of Machine Learning and Computing*, 1(1), 13-19.

Zhang, W., Yen, G. G., & Zhongshi, H. (2014). Constrained Optimization Via Artificial Immune System. *IEEE Transactions on Cybernetics, 44*(2), 185–198. doi:10.1109/TCYB.2013.2250956 PMID:23757542

KEY TERMS AND DEFINITIONS

Antibodies: Proteins in the human immune system to identify and neutralize pathogens.

Antigen: Any substance that causes immune system to stimulate or react to produce antibodies.

B Cells: A type of white bold cells that produces antibodies. These are also known as B lymphocytes.

Humoral: Relating to the antibodies secreted by the B cells that circulate in bodily fluids.

Memory Cells: Are B-cells subtype that are formed following primary infection. In the case of reinfection, these cells can trigger faster immune response.

Optimization: Is the problem of finding single or a set of solution from all feasible solutions.

Pathogen: Microorganisms capable of causing disease.

Chapter 7

The Role of Hypermutation and Affinity Maturation in AIS Approaches to Clustering

Waseem Ahmad
International College of Auckland, New Zealand

Ajit Narayanan
Auckland University of Technology (AUT), New Zealand

ABSTRACT

In recent years, several artificial immune system (AIS) approaches have been proposed for unsupervised learning. Generally, in these approaches antibodies (or B-cells) are considered as clusters and antigens are data samples or instances. Moreover, antigens are trapped through free-floating antibodies or immunoglobulins. In all these approaches, hypermutation plays an important role. Hypermutation is responsible for producing mutated copies of stimulated antibodies/B-cells to capture similar antigens with higher affinity (similarity) measure and responsible to create diverse pool of solutions. Humoral-Mediated Artificial Immune System (HAIS) is an example of such algorithms. However, there is currently little understanding about the effectiveness of hypermutation operator in AIS approaches. In this chapter, we investigate the role of the hypermutation operator as well as affinity threshold (AT) parameters in order to achieve efficient clustering solutions. We propose a three-step methodology to examine the importance of hypermutation and the AT parameters in AIS approaches to clustering using basic concepts of HAIS algorithm. Here, the role of hypermutation in under-fitting and over-fitting the data will be discussed in the context of measure of entropy.

INTRODUCTION

Clustering is one of the most intensively researched areas in the unsupervised learning and data mining disciplines. Clustering seeks to group similar data into clusters (groups) so that data instances within a group have maximum similarity while instances across different clusters have a high degree of dissimilarity. Clustering also depends on the nature of the data and the desired results or intuition (Tan,

DOI: 10.4018/978-1-4666-8513-0.ch007

Steinbach, & Kumar, 2006). Therefore many clustering algorithms exist which use different induction principles. Recently, researchers have turned to natural phenomena for inspiration to develop new clustering algorithms. Underpinning this interest is an inclination with the nature and the emergence of complex learning behaviors and intelligence out of unstructured, unsupervised and decentralized processes, such as those in natural immune systems (NISs).

There is a rapidly growing interest in immune system inspired approaches to machine learning. Of particular interest is the way the human body responds to diseases and new pathogens as well as adapting to remain immune for long periods after a disease has been combated. Immune system processes consist of two phases: recognition of invaders, and response. It has been established that the NIS can adequately distinguish between threat and non-threat at a basic level. Also of interest is the way that the NIS can identify a self-cell (which is not to be reacted to) but which has been subsequently damaged in some way and might present a threat to the body (and which must be reacted to). In other words, the NIS is dynamic in that it can re-structure (re-classify or re-cluster) in the light of new information so that it provides protection against not only outside invaders but also inside dangers. All these NIS concepts, if carefully and systematically used, could confer great benefit in the area of machine learning. Apart from above mentioned characteristics, NISs also demonstrate the following capabilities:

- **Learning:** An NIS continuously learns and adapts from the pathogens to trigger an appropriate immune response.
- **Diversity:** An NIS consists of various cells and organs, which help to mount an immune response when seen or unseen pathogens are encountered.
- **Specialization/Generalization:** An NIS has capabilities of specialization and generalization through the presence of memory cells and generation of antibodies, respectively.
- **Memory:** Memory of previously encountered viruses and pathogens is kept in the form of memory cells, so that if the same pathogen attacks the immune system in the future, it can trigger a fast and more effective response.
- **Multi-layered:** An NIS has various layers. The first layer of defense is human skin and various body secretions. Apart from that innate and adaptive immune systems are the two main layers in an NIS to provide protection against various pathogens.
- **Decentralized process:** An NIS is decentralized in nature, meaning it does not have any central control.
- **Noise tolerance:** An NIS is tolerant to noise, and a perfect match between pathogen and immune cell receptors is not required to trigger an immune response.
- **Dynamic system:** An NIS is constantly under attack by new pathogens and therefore it is constantly changing and adapting to new pathogens. As pathogens and viruses are evolving all the time, an NIS has to be dynamic to trigger an appropriate immune response.

One of the key components of AIS clustering algorithms is hypermutation, which is the process of generating cloned but mutated copies of antibodies (Abs) so that antigens (Ags) can be captured and dealt with more effectively by the immune system. This process maximizes the chances of producing an Ab that is even closer in approximation to the Ag, resulting in: (1) a more efficient handling of the current Ag; and (2) better capturing capabilities for future Ags that could be variants of currently captured one. The biological mechanism underlying this process is referred to as 'affinity maturation'. Most of the AIS clustering algorithms assume that mutation (hypermutation) plays an important role in deciding class memberships of data instances and hence finding better clustering solutions. One such example is the HAIS algorithm (Ahmad & Narayanan, 2010a). HAIS is inspired by the role of immunoglobulins (Igs) and Abs in the humoral-mediated response triggered in NISs. However, despite the importance of hypermutation in AIS approaches to clustering, there is relatively little understanding of its effects on clustering algorithms. Apart from hypermutation; Antigen (Ag) or data instances presentation order and initial clustering centroids play an important role in finding better clustering solutions. In this chapter, the initial clustering (centroids) starting points and Ag presentation order are kept fixed to evaluate the effects of different mutation rates on the algorithm and therefore shed some light on how hypermutation can affect clustering solutions. Here, we propose a three-step methodology to evaluate the effectiveness of hypermutation in the HAIS clustering algorithm. In Step 1, a hierarchical clustering method is used to get initial data partitioning. The centroids of each cluster are then used as a starting point for the HAIS algorithm. Step 2 evaluates different Ag presentation orders based on the initial starting point (obtained in Step 1). Different affinity threshold (AT) parameters produce different Ag presentation orders. The Ag presentation order that gives the best clustering is selected and used in the third step. Finally, in Step 3, the initial starting point and Ag presentation order selected in the previous steps are respectively used to observe the effects of different mutation rates. Different mutation rates are used to demonstrate the effectiveness of the mutation operator. Consequent over-fitting and under-fitting by the mutation operator will also be discussed in this chapter in the context of the HAIS clustering approach.

AIS CLUSTERING: AN OVERVIEW

Many nature-inspired clustering algorithms (metaheuristic and stochastic) have been developed over the years. The contributions of simulated annealing, genetic algorithms, ant colony optimization, particle swarm and self-organizing maps to clustering are well recognized. A survey of some of these algorithms can be found in (Jain, Murty, & Flynn, September 1999; Rokach & Maimon, 2005).

As noted in the Introduction, AIS (and immunoinformatics) refers to computational paradigms inspired by natural immune systems (Castro, 2003; Dasgupta & Gonzalez, 2003; Forrest & Hofmeyer, 2000; Forrest, Perelson, Allen, & Cherukuri, 1994; Hunt & Cook, 1996; Timmis & Knight, 2001; Timmis, Neal, & Hunt, 2000). In artificial immune system (AIS) approaches to clustering, the fundamental principle is to represent cluster centroids as B cells or antibodies, and data samples as antigens, so that the antigens are attracted to antibodies/ B cells, given some similarity measure. Matching of antibodies and antigens is done by pair-wise comparison, typically using squared Euclidean distance or some other similarity measure. Antibodies/B-cells are cloned and hyper-mutated to generate a more diverse set of samples to trap more similar antigens (data samples) in future.

The main work done in the AIS supervised learning is the Artificial Immune Recognition System (AIRS) by Watkins et al (Watkins, Timmis, & Boggess, 2004). One of the main AIS algorithms for unsupervised clustering was proposed by De Castro et al (Castro & Zuben, 2002), Artificial Immune network (aiNet). It utilizes the concepts of memory cells, clonal selection and hyper mutation. This is a two stage clustering algorithm. In the first step, a number of memory cells are generated from the original data and then in stage 2 a minimum spanning tree (MST) is used to obtained the number of clusters in the data. Qing (Qing, Liang, Bie, & Gao, 2010) incorporated aiNet algorithm with the k-means clustering algorithm, where the AIS algorithm is employed first to train the network and then the k-means clustering algorithm is used on the final set of antibodies generated by aiNet to find clustering solutions.

Another AIS clustering algorithm is clonal selection algorithm called CLONALG (Brownlee, 2005). This algorithm was originally designed for binary character recognition and engineering optimization, however, it can be adapted for unsupervised learning. This algorithm is inspired by the B-cell activation process, which results in the generation of plasma cells and antibodies that are subsequently released into the bloodstream to capture similar antigens. The main components of this algorithm are antibodies, cloning and hypermutation, and affinity measure and selection.

An AIS clustering algorithm is proposed by Younsi et al (Younsi & Wang, 2004) which is also similar to CLONALG. The immune system inspired clonal selection process is replaced with a random generation of new B-cells (clusters). It is a two phase algorithm. Recognition of antigens is performed in the first phase, and then memory cells produced by the first phase are used to find clusters in the data by building an inter-connected network of memory cells. Recently another AIS clustering algorithm has been proposed inspired by the humoral mediated response triggered by adaptive immune system (Ahmad & Narayanan, 2010a). It is an iterative process where antigens are presented to the algorithm randomly and then compared against existing memory cells and/or antibodies before being presented to B-cells bearing Igs on their surface. A clear distinction is made in this algorithm between Igs, antibodies and B-cells. That is, this system uses B-cells whose surface consists of Ig receptors in the initial phase to capture antigens. Once, a B-cell is activated by its Igs, only antibodies matter for the purpose of capturing antigens. For the purpose of this chapter, however, Igs are no longer separated from antibodies.

HUMORAL-MEDIATED CLUSTERING ALGORITHM (HAIS)

The inspiration of HAIS algorithm (Ahmad & Narayanan, 2010a) is based on the humoral immune repose triggered in natural immune systems. B-cells and their Igs, antigens, memory cells, antibodies and affinity threshold are the main components of this algorithm. The algorithm starts with 10% of data instances and considers each instance as an individual B-cell. The main idea here is that B-cells are considered as clusters and these B-cells generate memory cells as well as antibodies. New samples (pathogens) are trapped through antibodies. Two types of antibodies are produced: one is generated by B-cells (b-Abs) while the others are generated by memory cells (m-Abs). The similarity between an Ag and antibodies is calculated by the pair-wise square normalized Euclidean distance.

HAIS algorithm works mainly in three layers. At the first layer, m-Abs' try to trap Ags. If the entrapment is successful, then the stimulated m-Ab brings the Ag to its respective B-cell. If not, then the Ag goes to the second layer, where it is compared against existing b-Abs. If an Ag is captured, then the stimulated b-Ab will bring the Ag to its respective B-cell, which holds on to it till the end of the cycle. Moreover, after entrapment the B-cell produces a memory cell which further generates m-Ab, which is an exact copy of the captured Ag. B-cell also produces b-Abs', which are mutated copies of the captured Ag. If this layer fails to capture the Ag, then a new B-cell is generated which will hold onto this Ag and also generate b-Abs. At the end of each successful entrapment of Ags, similarities among B-cells are calculated and, if similarity between two B-cells is greater than the network measure threshold (NT), both B-cells form an inter-connected cluster (cluster mergence).

This is an iterative algorithm: at the end of each iteration, B-cells are evaluated and less stimulated B-cells (small clusters) are removed through natural killer cells. Surviving B-cells update their centroids according to the samples captured. All the antibodies generated by B-cells or memory cells are also removed, whereas some M percent of memory cells near to the centroid of B-cells are carried to the next cycle. All the parameters (AT, NT and DT) are updated before the start of the next cycle. This whole process is repeated until there is no change in the number of surviving B-cells for two consecutive cycles.

Two important parameters used in this HAIS algorithm are affinity measure threshold (AT) and network measure threshold (NT). The AT parameter is used to trap similar antigens whereas NT is used to merge similar B-cells. The algorithm starts with the same value for AT and NT. The parameter NT decreases whereas AT increases with iterations. At the end of each cycle parameter AT and NT are updated. The AT parameter is updated based on the values of α, β and γ. More details about these parameters can found in (Ahmad & Narayanan, 2010a, 2010e).

PROPOSED THREE-STEP METHODOLOGY

For AIS, the similarity measure based on the affinity between Ag features and Ab feature receptors is calculated using the following normalized Euclidean expression:

$$D = \frac{1}{f} \sum_{i=1}^{f} | A_i - B_i |$$

(1)

where f is a number of features in the data and A_i and B_i are the absolute values of the Ag and Ab features respectively.

The methodology is divided into three steps. In Step 1, initial clustering is obtained using hierarchical clustering. Step 2 is performed to select an Ag presentation order, ideally giving the lowest clustering error without using any mutation. Finally, Step 3 is used to perform mutation at different rates to achieve a better clustering solution on the Ag presentation order obtained in Step 2.

Step 1: Initial Clustering

In generative clustering approaches, a good starting point plays a very important role in finding good groupings in the data. The model-based Gaussian hierarchical clustering algorithms approach (Fraley, 1999), which is a well-established hierarchical model-based method, is used for the initial partitioning. In this method, at each step in the algorithm pairs of clusters are merged so as to maximize the likelihood function f_k ($X_i \backslash u_k$,cov_k) (Fraley & Raftery, 1998; Martinez & Martinez, 2005):

$$f_k\left(X_i|\mu_k,cov_k\right) = \frac{\exp\left[-\frac{1}{2}\left(X_i - \mu_k\right)^T cov_k \left(X_i - \mu_k\right)\right]}{\left(2\pi\right)^{d/2}\left|cov_k\right|^{1/2}}$$

(2)

where X represent the data, μ_k and cov_k denote the mean and covariance respectively of the kth cluster.

Three different clustering algorithms, namely hierarchical Euclidean distance, K-means clustering, and hierarchical model-based clustering algorithms were tested for the initial partition of the data, from which the hierarchical model-based approach was chosen on account of its superior performance.

Figure 1. Overview of the two-layered algorithm

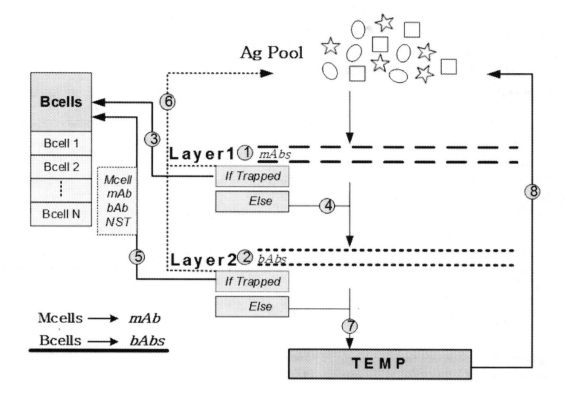

Step 2: Finding Antigen Presentation Order

A variant of the HAIS was used to demonstrate the effectiveness of the algorithm using datasets where numbers of clusters and class membership of instances are already known. HAIS is a stochastic algorithm, so that different runs can produce different outcomes. The motivation for Step 2 is to get an established Ag presentation order that gives better clustering outcomes based on minimum error against true class labels. Furthermore, in this step no mutation is used, which means that Abs are true data instances without any variation. This step is helpful in investigating the effects of different AT parameters in the HAIS algorithm.

With the number of clusters and initial starting points now being obtained from hierarchical clustering, the third layer of the original HAIS algorithm that deals with generations of new clusters was removed and replaced with a temporary storage unit (TEMP) which is shown in Figure 1. TEMP only stores Ags that cannot be trapped at an existing affinity value (AT). These Ags are subsequently put back into the Ag Pool for re-selection after updating the AT parameter.

Step 2 of the algorithm operates on two layers (see Figure 1). At the first layer (Layer 1) any memory cell Abs (m-Abs) that already exist trap Ags that are similar as they are released from the Ag Pool and present them to their respective B-cells (Step 3 in Figure 1). The second layer (Layer 2) gets activated if the first layer fails to trap the Ag. At this second layer, the stimulated B-cell Abs (b-Abs) bring the captured Ag to its respective B-cell and also perform certain actions (Step 5 in Figure 1), such as generating a memory cell which results in the generation of further m-Abs, generating *k* numbers of b-Abs and also performing a negative clonal selection on the newly generated b-Abs. The stimulation level of Ag to m-Ab is set 10 times higher than that of b-Abs to Ag. If the second layer fails to capture the Ag, it is stored at TEMP (Step 7 in Figure 1), which later dumps all Ags back to the Ag Pool (Step 8 in Figure 1). After each successful capture, the algorithm goes back and randomly selects another Ag from the Ag Pool (Step 6 in Figure 1). If there is no selection of an Ag for one complete cycle, the AT parameter is increased appropriately (discussed in next section). This whole process is repeated until all Ags are captured by B-cells.

The above algorithm is highly dependent on the AT parameter, which controls the convergence of the algorithm. The algorithm starts with a small value of AT and, as the immune system matures, the value of AT is increased by some pre-defined quantity to attract and capture Ags with relatively less similarity. This parameter will be discussed in depth in the next section.

In Step 2, no mutation (0% mutation) is used, which means that m-Abs and b-Abs are exact copies of captured Ags. This stage is used to select the Ag presentation order that gives the best clustering results without the influence of a mutation operator. This AT increment continues until all Ags are allocated to their respective B-cells (clusters). The importance of this step is to obtain the best Ag presentation order. Then, in Step 3, the same Ag presentation order is used to allocate Ags to respective B-cells using different mutation rates.

Affinity Threshold (AT) Parameter

In clustering, data instances that are situated closer to the centroids of the clusters should be assigned first and the data instances further away can be left until the size of the cluster gradually increases and those instances come within range of the cluster. Each cluster can acquire only the data instances that are in its calculated neighborhood radius. Once there are no more data instances within that radius, the radius is increased by some pre-defined quantity to capture the data instances which were out of reach earlier. The same idea is used here in this algorithm, which initially subjects Abs to a very high AT value to get stimulated in order to capture Ags that are highly similar to the Abs. As the clustering process progresses, the affinity threshold is reduced to capture Ags with less, but still enough, similarity to warrant inclusion in the cluster.

Consider the data instances/points in Figure 2. In the case of the cluster containing rectangular-shaped data, Cluster 1 should commit to Ags A and C first. The same principle applies to Cluster 2, which should first acquire Ags D and B rather than committing to Ag E, which is located quite far from both clusters and at this point can belong to either. The initial value of the AT is defined by the expression:

$$AT = \left(\frac{1}{N} \sum_{i=1}^{f} s\left(X_i \right) \right) * \alpha \qquad (3)$$

where s is the standard deviation and X_i is the ith data feature, f is the number of features, and N is the total number of instances in the data.

Standard deviation is the square root of variance and is a widely used measure of dispersion and variability. Sums of standard deviation calculated across all the features represent the total variation or dispersion in a dataset, which when divided by the total number of instances gives the average dispersion of an instance and generates a small starting value of AT. This AT does not stay the same but it changes

Figure 2. Importance of distance measure in cluster analysis

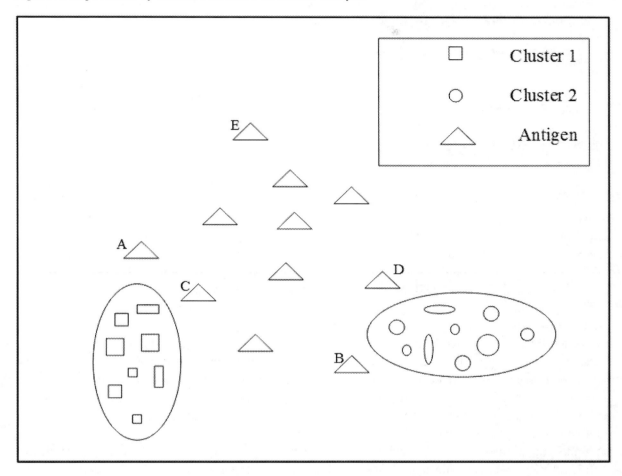

(increases) as the algorithm proceeds. AT increases when no data instances are captured by Abs in one complete cycle and there are still Ags left to be captured.

The updating of AT can be done in many ways. The simplest is to increase the AT_{inc} by a fixed amount each time when necessary. That technique is not very effective on sparse data, where the algorithm will be forced to perform many redundant cycles. Another approach is to increase it dynamically, and this is the approach adopted here. The AT is incremented by:

$$A T_{inc} = \min \left(affinity \right) + \left[\frac{1}{N} \sum_{i=1}^{f} s\left(X_i \right) \right] * \beta \tag{4}$$

where *affinity* is the distance measured between b-Abs and Ags and β is another user-defined parameter.

AT_{inc} has two parts: the first finds the next closest distance from Abs to Ags and the second is the initial *AT* (Equation 3) value with different increasing factor (β), which is to ensure that more than one instance gets selected in the next cycle. The parameters α and β control the rate of convergence. If the values of α and β are set too high then the algorithm converges too quickly. Similarly, if the value is set too low, the algorithm may not converge quickly enough.

Step 3: Effect of Different Mutation Rates

The initial cluster centroids (starting points) were obtained from Step 1, and Step 2 provided a fixed Ag presentation order. Now, in Step 3, a one-shot approach is used to allocate all Ags to B-cells, in the same order as that obtained in Step 2. Many runs can now be performed using variable mutation rates, with a fixed Ag presentation order and fixed initial clustering. Finally, different mutation rates were used to find and evaluate different clustering solutions.

The only difference at this stage from Step 2 is that there are only two layers are activated and any selected Ag must be assigned to one of these two layers, and no TEMP is used (Figure 3). At this level b-Abs are generated with different mutation rates to evaluate the effects of different mutations while generating Abs to capture Ags. Fifty runs (cycles) were performed for each mutation rate. The mutation rates used varied from 5% to 50%. We allowed each feature to mutate within a given specified upper and lower limit. Mutation was designed in such a way that each selected feature could mutate both ways (positively and negatively) at random, rather than just in one direction.

In Step 3, the algorithm starts by generating a number of B-cells. The number of B-cells is equal to the known number of clusters in the data. Those B-cells are placed at the centroids of the clusters obtained by Step 1. The B-cells then capture g of the nearest neighbor Ags (data instances). The value of the g parameter depends on the number of clusters and total number of instances in the data. Now, these B-cells generate k numbers of cloned and mutated copies of captured b-Abs to capture similar Ags in the future. The k Abs produced are dependent on two main factors. Firstly, the number of features in the data: the higher the number of features, the higher the number of Abs generated should be to find good enough samples to attract similar Ags. Secondly, the mutation rate: the higher the mutation rate, the higher the number of Abs should be to ensure sufficient diversity in the system. This k parameter directly influences the time the algorithm takes to run. The Ag captured by each B-cell is considered the memory cell, and this stimulated memory cell will generate respective m-Abs with a very small mutation rate to capture similar Ags. For the experiments done in this chapter, the m-Abs are exact copies of captured Ags.

EXPERIMENTAL RESULTS AND DISCUSSION

Four well-known datasets, namely Iris, Wine, Thyroid and Breast Cancer Wisconsin (see appendix A) were used to show the effectiveness of the proposed methodology. Each of the datasets selected shows different degrees of data complexity, which demonstrates the feasibility of the methodology. The hierarchical clustering was performed on normalized data whereas Steps 2 and 3 were performed on raw data except for the Wine data, where normalized data was used in all three steps.

When the hierarchical model-based clustering algorithm was used on the Iris data, it produced 15 clustering errors. The cluster membership is map against the true class membership of iris data to obtain clustering errors. There are number of external and internal criteria present in the literature to evaluate the quality of clustering results obtained by algorithms (Rokach & Maimon, 2005). In this chapter, an above mentioned external cluster evaluation method will be used with an objective to minimize the

Figure 3. A one-shot modified HAIS algorithm using fixed B-cell centroids and fixed Ag presentation order.

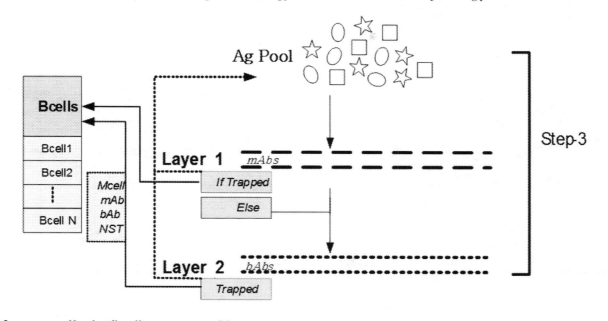

Memory cells Antibodies ⟶ *mAb*

B cell Antibodies ⟶ *bAbs*

clustering errors. The lower clustering error represents higher quality cluster formation and vice versa. The confusion matrix obtained can be seen below:

	Group1	Group2	Group3
Cluster 1	50	0	0
Cluster 2	0	49	1
Cluster 3	0	14	36

In Step 2 (with variable Ag presentation orders), the algorithm was run for 50 times, each time with different α and β parameters. The results obtained using different α and β parameters can be seen in the Figure 4 (without mutation). The lower values of α and β mean fewer ways to present Ags or less randomness in the Ag presentation order. On the other hand, the higher values of α and β mean more ways to present Ags to the algorithm.

In the legend of Figure 4, AB21 denotes α and β values of 1 and 2 respectively. It can be observed from Figure 4 that with AB21 the number of clustering errors oscillates between 4 and 6. The second-best set of parameter values was obtained by using AB22, which gave a minimum of 6 clustering errors. Out of the α and β parameters listed in Figure 4, it can be seen that AB21 consistently gave better clustering results (meaning fewer clustering errors) without using any mutation rate. Figure 4 also shows the importance of different data presentation orders for clustering solutions given AT parameter. Figure 4 demonstrates that a lower AT parameter produces less fluctuation in terms of variations obtained in clustering results, whereas a higher AT parameter produces higher fluctuation is clustering results.

Figure 4. Iris data clustering errors using various α and β values with 0% mutation (Step 2), with the x-axis representing the number of runs and the y-axis the number of clustering errors obtained.

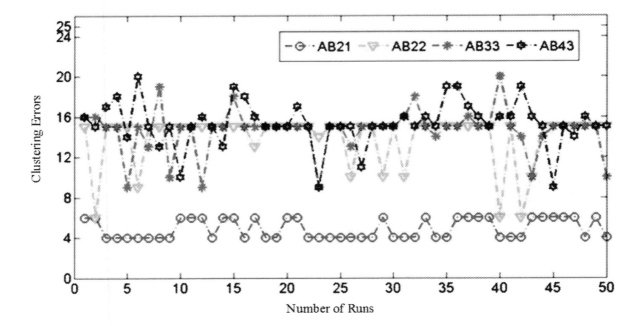

A summary of the experimental results given in Figure 4 in terms of minimum, maximum and average clustering errors found using different α and β parameters is given in Table 1. In Table 1, errors mean clustering error obtained by the proposed methodology. These results suggest that AB21 has the least errors and that its error average is also the lowest. The worst average of clustering errors of 15.288 was obtained from AB43. The experiments were also performed using other values of α and β, but only four are shown here. The purpose of conducting these experiments is to show that even without using mutation, α and β influence the final clustering solution and that the AT parameter plays an important role in AIS clustering algorithms. Another aspect of these results is that running the algorithm for 50 times with the same AB21 and the same initial clustering mean produces different clustering outcomes. This underlines the importance of the way Ags are presented to the system for selection (Ag presentation order). The purpose of this three-step methodology is to fix the cluster starting point as well as the order of presentation in order to observe the effects of different mutation rates on the clustering outcome.

Table 1. Summary of Figure 4

	Min. Errors	Max. Errors	Avg. Errors
AB21	4	6	4.8846
AB22	6	15	13.75
AB33	9	20	14.577
AB43	9	20	15.288

To explain the behavior of mutation rates, the Ag presentation order showing 15 clustering errors was selected (Step 2). Here, a fixed Ag presentation order was used that has been obtained by using AB22 parameter values (see Figure 4). The mutation rates of 5%, 10%, 15%, 20%, 30% and 40% were used and each was run 50 times, as shown in Figure 5. Different colors and shapes represent different mutation rates, defined in the legend of Figure 5. A summary of Figure 5, in terms of minimum, maximum and average clustering errors, can be seen in the Table 2. When the mutation rate was 5%, the oscillation was minimal but as the mutation rate increased the oscillation in the clustering solutions increased also. The clustering error without mutation was 15, therefore 15 can be considered as the mean point or point of reference for this experiment. It can be seen that for mutation rates of 5%, 10%, 15% and 20%, the oscillation is around the mean point, whereas in the case of mutation rates of 30% and 40% the clustering errors are much higher and away from the mean point. More specifically, with a mutation rate of 5% the error curve is not too far from 15 (the average is 15.67 in Table 2).

The best and worst clustering solutions were 14 and 18 errors, respectively, for the 5% mutation rate. However, with a 10% mutation rate the oscillation becomes higher and it had best and worst clustering solutions of 5 and 19 errors respectively. The lowest clustering error of 4 was found with a mutation rate of 15%. The clustering results gradually degrade from this point onwards for all the remaining mutation rates. This experiment suggests that mutation plays an important role in finding better clustering solutions. When the mutation rate is kept too low, it cannot generate a diverse enough population of Abs to match the Ags as they are introduced to the system; as a consequence the results are not much different from 0% or no mutation. On the other hand, in the case of too high a mutation rate the Abs cover too much feature space, which results in bad clustering solutions. Abs not only represent already seen

Figure 5. Various mutation rates M5 to M40 (5% to 40%) are applied to an Ag presentation order with 15 clustering errors

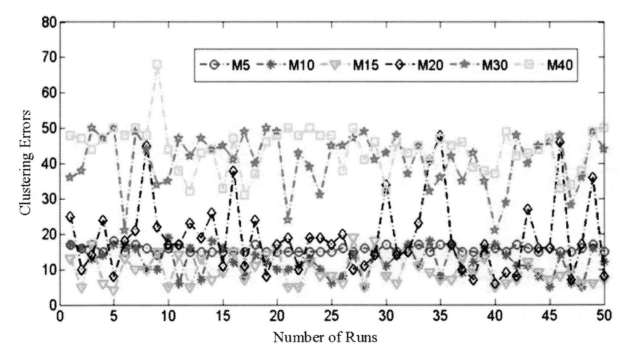

Table 2. Summary of Figure 5

Mutation	Min. Errors	Max. Errors	Avg. Errors
M5	14	18	15.67308
M10	5	19	12.23077
M15	4	19	9.596154
M20	6	48	19.48077
M30	21	50	40.82692
M40	31	68	44.21154

samples but also 'predict' future samples that should belong to the same cluster. Hence, low mutation rates suffer from under-fitting when predicting future samples based on existing samples, whereas too high a mutation rate cause over-fitting.

Using α and β values of 2 and 1 respectively returned the minimum number of clustering errors (4) in the previously explained experiment. The same Ag presentation order can be used to investigate the effects of mutation rates on clustering error. In particular, it will be possible to determine whether different mutation rates using the Ag presentation order show the same behavior as in Figure 5 (using an Ag presentation order with 15 clustering errors). The results obtained using mutation rates of 5%, 10%, 15%, 20% and 30% can be seen in Figure 6. The same trend can be seen as for the previous experiment (with 15 clustering errors). The role of mutation can now be clearly seen in Table 3, which is a summary of Figure 6. A minimum clustering error of 2 was found when a mutation rate of 15% was used as

Figure 6. Various Mutation rates M5 to M30 (5% to 30%) are applied to an Ag presentation order with 4 clustering errors

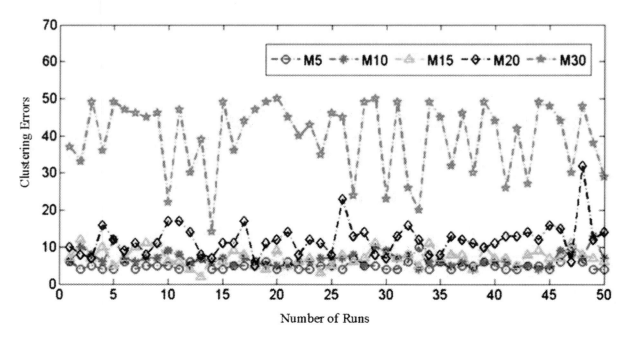

Table 3. Summary of Figure 6

Mutation	Min. Errors	Max. Errors	Avg. Errors
M5	4	10	5.173077
M10	4	13	6.788462
M15	2	12	7.230769
M20	5	32	12.26923
M30	14	50	39.42308

Table 4. Datasets information (three-step methodology)

Datasets	α	β	Mutation	Min. Errors	Max. Errors	Avg. Errors
Iris Data	2	1	15%	2	12	7.23
Thyroids Data	15	5	40%	11	44	22.19
Wisconsin Data	15	7	50%	17	29	23.09
Wine Data	3	2	15%	6	22	13.26

compared with 4 clustering errors without mutation. This experiment suggests that including mutation rate in the HAIS clustering algorithm does provide extra benefit in terms of reducing clustering error, if it is tuned correctly.

The best results found using the proposed methodology on all datasets can be seen in Table 4. The α and β parameters were obtained manually, by trying various combinations, while 50 runs were performed against each mutation rate to get the best results.

The comparison of clustering errors found at the end of each step is shown in Table 5, which suggests improved results at Step 3 from both the previous steps. Note that in the results obtained at the end of Step 3 (after applying sub-optimal AT and mutation rates) for all four real-world datasets, the final clustering results are superior only when applying the hierarchical clustering algorithm (Step 1). These results were obtained using only 50 runs in Step 3; much better results can be obtained if Step 3 is repeated for more iterations (explained below). One of the reasons for the observed oscillations at Step 3 is the use of intra-cluster B-cell negative selection (negative selection of Abs for each cluster or B-cell separately) and allowing Abs to enforce natural selection pressure across all clusters. This approach was applied under the assumption that clusters can overlap in Euclidean space, which forms the basis of using intra-cluster (and not inter-cluster) B-cell negative selection. All these fluctuations (in clustering results) at the level of AT and hypermutation in Figures 4, 5 and 6 can also be explained using the norm of entropy.

The various mutation rates can also be explained in terms of the entropy of a system. Entropy is defined as a number of ways the constituents of a system can be re-arranged, in such a way that a change would not be noticed (Carroll, 2010). Different systems can vary from a low entropy state to a high entropy state. Low entropy means there are fewer possible arrangements exist (the system is more organized), whereas in a high entropy state many possible arrangements exist (less organized system). Entropy can be explained using the simple example shown in Figure 7, where (a) shows some randomly located gas molecules in a box. The system is considered to be a closed system and gas molecules move

Table 5. Step-wise clustering errors information

Datasets	Step-1	Step-2	Step-3
Iris Data	15	4	2
Thyroids Data	23	20	11
Wisconsin Data	23	29	17
Wine Data	7	9	6

around in the box. There are many ways the system in (a) can re-arrange itself so that no difference is noticeable. Therefore, it can be said that the system in (a) is in a high entropy state. On the contrary, the system in (b) is said to be in a low entropy state as there are fewer arrangements existing. According to Sean Carroll (Carroll, 2010), a low entropy state can be achieved from a high entropy state, but it takes a much longer time. Therefore, if the system in high entropy (a) is left for a long time, due to the random motion of gas molecules all the configurations attainable will be attained and it is possible that the molecules with re-arrange themselves into the configuration shown in (b), which is a low entropy state. Entropy is defined as:

$$E = k.\log(N) \tag{5}$$

where N = number of states and k is the Boltzmann's constant.

Now the question requiring an answer is: How can clustering be related to entropy? Clustering algorithms can mainly be classified into deterministic and stochastic algorithms. In deterministic algorithms, different runs of the same algorithm using the same data produce the same clustering results. One example of such algorithms is hierarchical clustering algorithms (Step 1). On the other hand, stochastic algorithms produce variable clustering results across different runs. Therefore, in the light of the entropy definition explained earlier, deterministic algorithms can be categorized into systems (algorithms) having a low or zero entropy state and stochastic algorithms, which oscillate between different clustering solutions, can be regarded as systems having a high entropy state. The HAIS algorithm is a stochastic algorithm, meaning it can produce different clustering outcomes on various runs, which suggests it has high entropy. The important question here is to consider what are the most important factors or parameters in the HAIS that make it such a stochastic algorithm.

Figure 7. Fluctuations in a closed system (gas molecules) occasionally lead from a high entropy state (a) to a low entropy state (b)

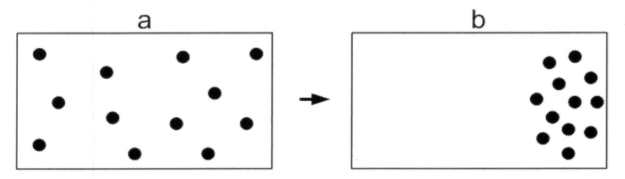

In this chapter, the two most important features of the HAIS are investigated, namely the AT parameter and hypermutation. The results shown in Figure 4 indicate that a low AT is equivalent to a low entropy state and a high AT equivalent to a high entropy state. A low AT parameter such as that of AB21 has only two possible arrangements (4 and 6 clustering errors), but as the AT parameter value is increased, the system showed many more possible arrangements (more fluctuations in clustering results). The minimum errors obtained on the Iris data at AB21 and AB43 were 4 and 7 respectively when only 50 runs are used. Now, an interesting experiment would be to see whether a system with higher AT (e.g. AB43) that is left for a longer time (more runs) randomly fluctuates to a low entropy state that corresponds to a low clustering error configuration. The experiment was run using AB43 for 1000 iterations. The results can be seen in Figure 8 below and suggest a higher level of fluctuations (meaning high entropy) in the clustering results. The four clustering errors earlier obtained using AB21 were obtained many times in the 1000 iterations using AB43, which proves that a low entropy state can be obtained from higher entropy state but, due to the random fluctuations, it can take a longer time. Another important feature of this experiment was that it achieved a minimum of 3 clustering errors, which also demonstrates the HAIS's capacity to find better clustering solutions while exploring wider search space by increasing the AT parameter. This experiment also showed that there is a trade-off between local search and global search for finding optimal clustering solutions. AB21 was consistently able to find 4 and 6 clustering errors, but even though AB43 on average found fewer efficient clustering solutions, it did find a clustering solution with 3 errors, i.e. better than those of AB21. Therefore, we can characterize algorithms

Figure 8. Iris data clustering errors using AB43 (Step 2). The x-axis represents the number of runs and the y-axis the number of clustering errors obtained.

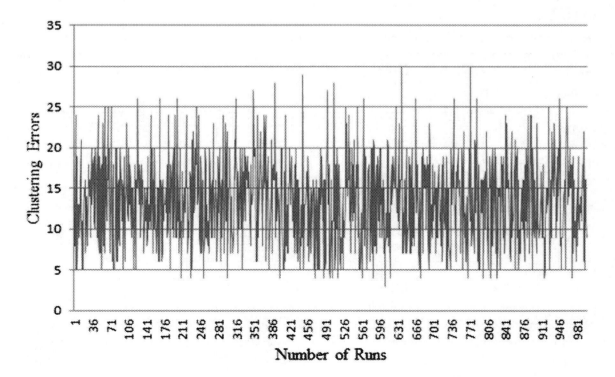

Figure 9. Various mutation rates (5% to 30%) with 4 clustering errors at Step 2. The x-axis represents the number of runs whereas y-axis the number of clustering errors obtained.

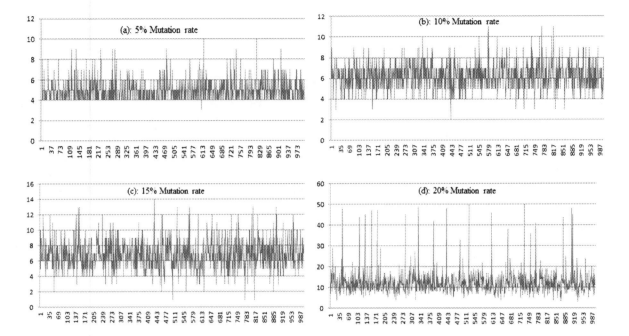

(or algorithmic settings) that produce more fluctuations as systems with high entropy, and vice versa. The same behavior can be observed in hypermutation. As the rate of mutation is increased, the system is transformed from a low entropy state to a high entropy state (see Figure 9). An Ag presentation order of 4 clustering errors was used to demonstrate this idea. The same setting was run for 1000 iterations using 5% to 30% mutation rates. A 15% mutation rate has found the lowest number of clustering errors (clustering error of 1).

Here we are interpolating the idea of the number of possible states N (which is proportional to the entropy value E) to the range of clustering solutions (fluctuation in clustering errors) obtained. In these experiments, N is equivalent to AT as well as N is equivalent to mutation rate. From the experiments conducted here, it can be concluded that a low AT or low mutation rate describes a low entropy state and a high AT or high mutation rate characterizes a high entropy state.

PROPOSED ENHANCEMENTS

Experiments performed above clearly indicate that mutation plays an important role in finding better clustering solutions. However, there is too much variation in the clustering results. This variation comes from the introduction of random mutation. Due to this random mutation, antibodies spread out in all directions equally, that introduces the noise in the system. This factor can be controlled by adding directed mutation. One way of achieving directed mutation is generating antibodies based on the covariance of each of the B-cell (cluster). Another possibility of random noise is the fact that only once antibody is needed to capture antigen. In other words, only one antibody decides the membership of any antigen. A better approach will be to increase this stimulation threshold from one to n (n can be any reasonable odd number). Once this threshold is achieved (n antibodies are stick to antigen), the cluster membership of antigen will be decided based on the majority vote. This process will introduce more stability into the existing algorithm. Therefore, at this stage, two enhancements to the existing algorithm are proposed.

Mutation = RandomMutation + DirectedMutation

ActivationThreshold = n

Random Mutation is the process of generating antibodies based on the localized knowledge, whereas, Direct Mutation is the process of generating antibodies based on the provisional global knowledge.

To investigate the effectiveness of our revised algorithm, Ag presentation order (iris dataset) with 15 clustering error is selected. The role of new mutation parameter and activation threshold can be seen in Figure 10, where much improved and stable clustering results are achieved in comparison to only using random mutation and single activation threshold. In these experiments activation threshold of 15 was used to decide the membership of any antigen. Average of 6.28 clustering errors was obtained over 50 iterations with minimum and maximum clustering error of 2 and 12, respectively. This experiment suggests that the directed mutation as well as high activation threshold is important to get better clustering solutions. In the future, more rigorous experimentations are required to completely validate this claim.

Figure 10. Clustering results obtained by using directed mutation and activation threshold of 15.

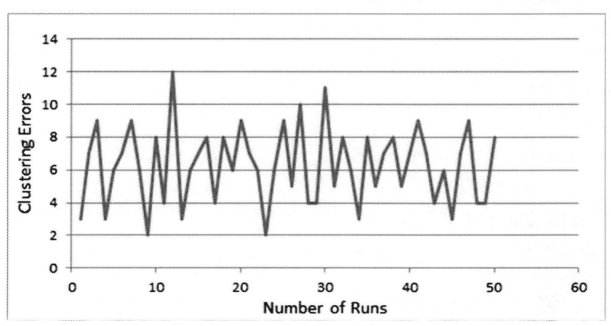

Final Pool of Antibodies

Final pool of antibodies is obtained by aggregating antibodies from local knowledge (random mutation) and global knowledge (directed mutation).

mvnrnd is a function that takes in mean and covariance of data and returns a matrix of random numbers chosen from normal distribution

normrnd is a function that given a mean of data and degree of variation; returns a matrix of random numbers chosen from normal distribution

CONCLUSION

Both affinity measure (AT) and hypermutation play critical parts in any AIS algorithm. The aim of this chapter was to determine the effects of both parameters on unsupervised clustering while using the HAIS algorithm. AT is a similarity criterion that is very important in defining the boundaries of Ab receptors (in terms of shape space) and the vicinity they interact in (put another way, AT helps to distinguish self, known and seen search space from unknown, non-self and unseen search space). Hypermutation is another critical component of the AIS and getting the mutation rate right is important for effective Ag-Ab match and capture.

There are three main parameters that can influence the clustering outcomes in the HAIS algorithm: (1) initial B-cell placement; (2) similarity measure (AT); and (3) mutation rate. The main focus of this chapter was to investigate the effects of different affinity measures and mutation rates on the HAIS algorithm. We have demonstrated with experimental results on real-world datasets that both AT and mutation play an important role in finding better clustering solutions. The experimental results indicate that mutation, along with the AT parameter and the initial B-cell starting point, helps the HAIS algorithm produce better clustering results. The implications are not clear for other AIS approaches to clustering given that they have other parameters. Nevertheless, the role of mutation can be expected to play a key part in other AIS approaches to clustering. For example, the aiNet and CLONALG algorithms use similarity thresholds to select strong affinity Abs. These similarity thresholds act in a similar manner to our mutation rate. We have also tried to map the behavior of two core parameters of the HAIS algorithm, namely AT and mutation, onto entropy. In this chapter we have argued that a low AT or mutation rate can be linked to a low entropy state and a high AT or mutation rate to a high entropy state.

REFERENCES

Ahmad, W., & Narayanan, A. (2010a). Humoral-mediated Clustering. *Proceedings of the IEEE 5th International Conference on Bio-Inspired Computing: Theories and Applications* (pp. 1471-1481). doi:10.1109/BICTA.2010.5645279

Ahmad, W., & Narayanan, A. (2010e). Outlier Detection using Humoral-mediated Clustering. *Proceedings of IEEE World Congress on Nature and Biologically Inspired Computing* (pp. 45-52).

Brownlee, J. (2005). Clonal Selection Theory and CLONALG: The Clonal Selection Classification Algorithm (CSCA). Technical Report 2-02, CISCP, Swinburne University of Technology.

Carroll, S. (2010). *From Eternity to Here: The Quest for the Ultimate Theory of Time*. USA: Dutton.

Castro, L. N. d. (2003). Artificial immune systems as a novel soft computing paradigm. *Soft Computing*, 7(8), 526-544.

Castro, L. N. d., & Zuben, F. J. V. (2002). aiNet: An Artificial Immune Network for Data Analysis. In H. Abbass, R. Sarker, & C. Newton (Eds.) Data Mining: A Heuristic Approach (pp. 231-260). Hershey: Idea Group Publishing. doi:. doi:10.4018/978-1-930708-25-9.ch012

Dasgupta, D., & Gonzalez, F. (2003). Artificial immune system (AIS) research in the last five years. *Proceedings of the Congress on Evolutionary Computation* (pp. 123–130). doi:10.1109/CEC.2003.1299565

Forrest, S., & Hofmeyer, S. (2000). Immunology as information processing. In L. Segel & I. Cohen (Eds.), *Design Principles for Immune System and Other Distributed Autonomous Systems. Oxford University Press, 361.*

Forrest, S., Perelson, A., Allen, L., & Cherukuri, R. (1994). Self-nonself discrimination in a computer. *Proceedings of IEEE Computer Society Symposium on Research in Security and Privacy* (pp. 202-212). doi:10.1109/RISP.1994.296580

Fraley, C. (1999). Algorithms for model-based Gaussian hierarchical clustering. *SIAM Journal on Scientific Computing, 20*(1), 270–281. doi:10.1137/S1064827596311451

Fraley, C., & Raftery, A. (1998). How Many Clusters? Which Clustering Method? Answers Via Model-Based Cluster Analysis. *The Computer Journal, 41*(8), 578–588. doi:10.1093/comjnl/41.8.578

Hunt, J. E., & Cook, D. E. (1996). Learning using an artificial immune system. *Journal of Network and Computer Applications, 19*(2), 189–212. doi:10.1006/jnca.1996.0014

Jain, A. K., Murty, M. N., & Flynn, P. J. (1999, September). Data Clustering: A Review. *ACM Computing Surveys, 31*(3), 265–323. doi:10.1145/331499.331504

Martinez, W. L., & Martinez, A. (2005). Model-based Clustering Toolbox for MATLAB. *Naval Surface Warfare Center.*

Qing, J., Liang, X., Bie, R., & Gao, X. (2010). A New Clustering Algorithm Based on Artificial Immune Network and K-means Method. *Proceedings of Sixth International Conference on Natural Computation* (pp. 2826-2830). doi:10.1109/ICNC.2010.5583507

Rokach, L., & Maimon, O. (2005). *Clustering Methods. Data Mining and Knowledge Discovery Handbook* (pp. 321-352).

Tan, P. N., Steinbach, M., & Kumar, V. (2006). Cluster analysis: basic concepts and algorithms. Introduction to Data Mining (pp. 487-568). Addison-Wesley.

Timmis, J., & Knight, T. (2001). AINE: An Immmunological Approach to Data Mining. *Proceedings of 2013 IEEE 13th International Conference on Data Mining* (pp. 297-304).

Timmis, J., Neal, M., & Hunt, J. (2000). An artificial immune system for data analysis. *Bio Systems, 55*(1-3), 143–150. doi:10.1016/S0303-2647(99)00092-1 PMID:10745118

Watkins, A., Timmis, J., & Boggess, L. (2004). Artificial Immune Recognition System (AIRS): An Immune-Inspired Supervised Learning Algorithm. *Genetic Programming and Evolvable Machines, 5*(3), 291–317. doi:10.1023/B:GENP.0000030197.83685.94

Younsi, R., & Wang, W. (2004). A New Artificial Immune System Algorithm for Clustering. *Lecture Notes in Computer Science, 3177*, 58–64. doi:10.1007/978-3-540-28651-6_9

KEY TERMS AND DEFINITIONS

Affinity Maturation: During repeating exposure to same antigens, B cell produced antibodies with increased affinity for antigen.

B Cells: A type of white blood cell that produces antibodies. These are also known as B lymphocytes.

Clustering: Grouping together data instances in such a way that data instances within each group has maximum similarity and maximum dissimilarity against other groups.

Entropy: Is a measure of the number of ways the constitutes of a system can be arranged.

Hypermutation: A mechanism by which activated B cells generate enormous diversity against foreign pathogen.

Immunity: The condition of being able to resist a particular disease.

Memory Cells: It is immune system's way to keeping track of past pathogenic attacks. These are B cells formed following primary infection. In the case of reinfection, these cells can trigger faster immune response.

Chapter 8
Cancer Pathway Network Analysis Using Cellular Automata

Kalyan Mahata
Government College of Engineering and Leather Technology, India

Anasua Sarkar
Government College of Engineering and Leather Technology, India

ABSTRACT

Identification of cancer pathways is the central goal in the cancer gene expression data analysis. Data mining refers to the process analyzing huge data in order to find useful pattern. Data classification is the process of identifying common properties among a set of objects and grouping them into different classes. A cellular automaton is a discrete, dynamical system with simple uniformly interconnected cells. Cellular automata are used in data mining for reasons such as all decisions are made locally depend on the state of the cell and the states of neighboring cells. A high-speed, low-cost pattern-classifier, built around a sparse network referred to as cellular automata (ca) is implemented. Lif-stimulated gene regulatory network involved in breast cancer has been simulated using cellular automata to obtain biomarker genes. Our model outputs the desired genes among inputs with highest priority, which are analysed for their functional involvement in relevant oncological functional enrichment analysis. This approach is a novel one to discover cancer biomarkers in cellular spaces.

INTRODUCTION

For a given type of cancer, there are often stimulating factors that produces different patterns of gene expression in patient data. Analyzing them, it reveals the discovery of gene networks and regulatory pathways involved in those tumor formations (Sarkar, 2013). In this respect, the gene expression profiles in breast cancer has been analysed extensively recently. This reveals the identification of breast cancer molecular subtypes and the development of prognostic and predictive gene signatures, resulting in an

DOI: 10.4018/978-1-4666-8513-0.ch008

improved knowledge on the heterogeneity of breast cancer and its biomarkers (Perou et al., 2000; Sorlie et al., 2001; Sorlie, 2003; Sotiriou, 2009).

In pioneering work, (Perou et al., 2000) classified the expression of approximately 8,000 genes in samples from 42 breast cancer patients into specific 'intrinsic subtypes' of primary breast carcinomas. Later, Sorlie et al. (Sorlie et al., 2001) experiments for correlations between gene expression patterns and clinically relevant parameters to detect the breast cancer subtypes. They reveal the prognostic markers with respect to overall and relapse-free survival among a subset of patients who had received uniform therapy (Sorlie et al., 2001; Sorlie, 2003).

Sotiriou and Pusztai (Sotiriou, 2009) define that there are three approaches for analyzing the global gene expression profiling to obtain genomic signatures. In 'top-down' approach, tumor or cell line gene expressions are correlated with the clinical outcome of patients to identify prognostic gene signatures. In 'bottom-up' approach, a gene expression signature is defined to be a prognostic predictor which is related to a particular biological pathway or process. Third, among the list of candidate genes, some biomarkers are prospectively selected based on previous biological knowledge like recurrence score signature (Sotiriou, 2009).

In complex disease states such as breast cancer, genes may overlap in their involvement of relevant pathways and networks and may influence the disease significantly. Therefore, the shared neighbourhood in gene expression networks exhibits the significance of one gene in the network. In a rank-based network analysis (Corban et al., 2010), they construct the networks of similarity among gene expression profiles based on shared neighborhood. The hierarchical agglomerative clustering is used to group nodes in clusters by computing a rank on the log odds ratio based on Poisson parameter over shared neighbors. The nodes with highest ranking on degrees and neighbourhoods with cross-connectivity, which belong to some dense bipartite networks, are selected (Corban et al., 2010). Implicit notion of applying such analysis to biologically important tumor gene expression profiles, is to rank genes according to their correlated expression patterns in gene expression networks of cancer cell line.

We present an integrated approach to detect cancer biomarkers using cellular automata, which we experiment over the gene expression profiles in a data set (Icardi et al., 2012) of 6 samples of leukemia inhibitory factor effect on breast cancer cell line. We analyse the LIF-responsive genes in MCF7 cells. We develop the correlation expression network over these genes using the shared neighborhood ranking score method (Corban et al., 2010). Therefore, we choose significant genes based on their ranking values to simulate the cellular automata approach over their ranking score matrices in both control and LIF-stimulated expression stages. The 2-dimensional analysis in cellular automata over these two stages, chooses finally the most significant 4 biomarkers based on our newly developed algorithm to traverse gene networks in cellular space. We further analyse the extended biological KEGG pathways associated with those selected biomarkers using DAVID (http://david.abcc.ncifcrf.gov/) (Huang, 2009). The detailed analysis of the GO annotations of those identified biomarkers also exhibits how the priority in shared neighbourhood is reflected in the priority in biological functions to detect biomarker oncogenes.

LITERATURE REVIEW

Cellular Automata is a powerful tool to model the complex dynamic system. To bridge between bioinformatics with artificial intelligence, CA is played a vital role.

Protein synthesis is done by CA nowadays which shows extraordinary results. Previously, cellular automata has been applied to predict protein attributes using pseudo amino acid composition (Xiao et al., 2011).To implement it, the pseudo amino acid composition (PseAAC) was developed and stimulated in a series of modes of PseAAC to deal with proteins or proteins-related systems. They defined the space-time evolvement rules of cellular automata, which can represent a protein sequence by a unique image, called cellular automata (CA) image (CAI). They showed that many important features of long and complicated amino acid sequences can be clearly revealed through their CAIs (Xiao et al., 2011).

Hodgeweg (Hodgeweg, 2010) described Multilevel Cellular Automata. He defined the microscopic entities (states) and their transition rules themselves as adjusted by the mesoscale patterns which are generated from themselves. Recently, Pokkuluri (Pokkulri, 2014) proposed clonal-based cellular automata approaches to address different problems in bioinformatics. Chakrabarti et al. (Chakrabarti et al., 2013) proposed a pattern classifier based on the sparse network of cellular automata.

Xuan Xiao (Xiao et al., 2011) described the technique to use CA in protein synthesis. (Ghosh et al., 2012) defined a Restricted Five Neighborhood Cellular Automata (R5NCA) can be used for protein structure prediction. However, till no work has been done on cancer pathway network analysis using cellular automata.

MATERIALS AND METHODS

Data Source and Preprocessing

The expression profile of GSE35696 (Icardi et al., 2012) was downloaded from Gene Expression Omnibus-GEO database (http://www.ncbi.nlm.nih.gov/geo/) of NCBI (National Center of Biotechnology Information) based on GPL570 [HG-U133_Plus_2] Affymetrix Human Genome U133 Plus 2.0 Array. The GDS4388 data set (Icardi et al., 2012) shows the leukemia inhibitory factor (LIF) effect on MCF7 breast cancer cell line, has been used for our experiments here. The flowchart of our approach has been shown in Figure 1. The gene expression profiles are on MCF7 cells stimulated with LIF cytokine to activate signal transducer and activator of transcription 3 (STAT3). STAT3 transcription factor is a potent oncogene. The analysis over this dataset provides insight into the role of LIF cytokine to stimulate STAT3 activity. The clusterMaker2 (ClusterMaker) plugin in Cytoscape has been used to normalize the dataset with log2 scaling and unit variance and replacing missing value with row means.

Microarray-Based Gene Expression Profiling

The differentially coexpressed gene analysis reveals the groups of coexpressed genes under different conditions (Sotiriou et al., 2003) to conclude many biological hypotheses. 3182 genes in the chosen dataset have been selected for our experiment based on their higher expression value (>10.0) in the first stage of the experiment. In this study, among all selected genes, a correlation network based on Pearson correlation distance metric for any pair of genes is being computed (ClusterMaker2).

Figure 1. Flowchart of our hybrid ranking based Cellular Automata model for data mining of cancer gene expression networks

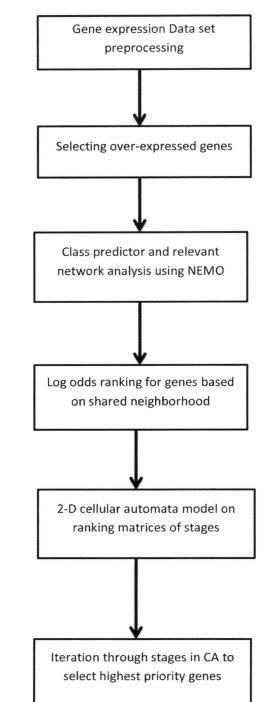

Class Predictor and Relevant Network Analysis using NEMO

In the chosen dataset GDS4388 (Icardi et al., 2012), we have selected 6 samples, namely - GSM873554 (RL_siRNA_LIF1h_rep1), GSM873557 (RL_siRNA_LIF1h_rep2), GSM873561 (RL_siRNA_LIF1h_rep3), GSM873553 (RL_siRNA_NS_rep1), GSM873556 (RL_siRNA_NS_rep2) and GSM873560 (RL_siRNA_NS_rep3). We have chosen the expressions of 3182 gene in these LIF stimulated and non-stimulated siRNA stages for our experiments. In the correlation network developed over this data, we compute a ranking based on shared neighborhood and their priority in clusters (Corban et al., 2010).

The NEMO algorithm was originally developed for identifying densely connected and bipartite network modules in networks (Corban et al., 2010). We for the first time, apply the NEMO algorithm on the biological network to obtain the stage-specific priority rankings based on log odds score for shared neighbours of the selected 3182 genes in both stages separately. These ranking matrices are selected for further analysis.

The community finding algorithm NEMO (Corban et al., 2010), based on a log odds score of shared neighbors has been used to find ranking of genes in both stages. This method combines a uniquely computed neighbour-sharing score with hierarchical agglomerative clustering to identify diverse network communities. NeMo has no adjustable parameters. No a-priori number of network modules needs tobe defined. (Corban et al., 2010) established that NeMo with complete-linkage can identify more networks with 100% reconstruction fidelity. NeMo can uniquely identify both dense network and dense bipartite structures in a single approach.

This method uses hierarchical agglomerative clustering as part of its procedure to compute ranking. The log odds score rxy has been defined (Corban et al., 2010), for observing sxy number of shared neighbors between nodes x and y. A shared neighbor is a node z that satisfies x~z and y~z, where ~ represents adjacency in the graph representing either directed or undirected network. The null hypothesis in the methods states that s_{xy} number of shared neighbors between x and y is from a random network model. Apparently, s_{xy} ~$Poisson(\lambda)$. The parameter λ is defined as the Poisson parameter for s_{xy} under the null hypothesis. (Corban et al., 2010) defined the score r_{xy} approximately as equals to the log odds ratio between the probability of s_{xy} under the alternative and null hypotheses.

$$r_{xy} \approx s_{xy} \ln\left[\frac{s_{xy}}{\lambda}\right] - \left|s_{xy} - \lambda\right| \qquad (1)$$

The score r_{xy} is computed for all node pairs x and y. The hierarchical agglomerative clustering using complete-linkage clustering is further performed on the data. All the nodes are sorted in descending order based on the ranking score r_{xy}.

Cellular Automata Method

Cellular Automata (CA) are defined to be the discrete spatially-extended dynamical systems to study models of physical systems (Smith, 1971). It evolves the computational devices in discrete space and time. A CA, which is seeded with any state from the set of states with all 0 and single 1 at different position, generates a fixed number of unique patterns. Cellular automata method is different form k-NN classifier, as it considers the states in discrete time domain. The k-NN classifier considers only the k

Table 1. Look-up table for Rule 30

Present State	111	110	101	100	011	010	001	000
Rule	(7)	(6)	(5)	(4)	(3)	(2)	(1)	(0)
Next State	0	0	0	1	1	1	1	0

nearest points in a specific class are chosen based on the distance and assigning the class of the majority to the current point. In cellular automata, every new generation in the grid is created based on the output of the rules using the states of neighborhood cells in present time.

Stephen Wolfram (Wolfram, 1986) proposes its simplest CA in a form of a spatial lattice of cells. Each cell stores a discrete variable at time t that refers to the present state of the cell. The next state of the cell at $(t+1)$ is affected by its state and the states of its neighbors at time t. In the earlier works, researchers consider 3-neighborhood (self, left and right neighbors) CA, where a CA cell is having two states, either 0 or 1. The next state of each cell of such a CA is

$$S_i^{t+1} = f(S_{i-1}^t, S_i^t, S_{i+1}^t) \qquad (2)$$

where f is the next state function. S_{i-1}^t, S_i^t and S_{i+1}^t are the present states of the left neighbor, self and right neighbor of the i th CA cell at a time t. The f can be expressed as a look-up table as shown in Table 1. The decimal equivalent of the 8 outputs in table 1, is called 'Rule' R_i (Wolfram, 1983). In a two-state 3-neighborhood CA, there can be a total of 2^8 (256) rules.

One such rule is 30 in Table 1. Rule 30 CA can generate a sequence of random patterns. Scientists observed in their experiments that an n-cell rule 30 CA, seeded with a state all 0 and single 1, generates a state with fair distribution of 0 and 1 after n iterations. However, it is not guaranteed that after n iterations no all 0 pattern will come. It can be proved that for every, $n > 1$, an n-cell Rule 30 CA seeded with any state with all 0 and single 1 at different positions, generates a non-zero states after $n/2$ iterations.

Using Wolfram's classification scheme, Rule 30 is a class III rule (Wolfram, 1986), displaying aperiodic, chaotic behavior. Rule 30 of the elementary cellular automata (CA) was among the first rules, in which Stephen Wolfram noticed the appearance of intrinsic randomness in a deterministic system. When initialized with a single black pixel there is a pattern behavior down both sides of the unfolding CA which gives way to the randomly patterned center, as shown in Figure 2. This rule is of particular interest because it produces complex, seemingly-random patterns from simple, well-defined rules. In fact, Mathematica uses the center column of pixel values as one of its random number generator.

If the leftmost and right most cells are neighbors of each other, the CA is defined to be with periodic boundary; otherwise it is a null boundary CA. Cellular automata can further be divided as deterministic and probabilistic (or, stochastic). Elementary CA as stated above is deterministic in nature. On the other hand, in case of probabilistic CA, the next state of each cell is updated based on not only the present states of its neighbors but also on a predetermined probability.

However, in our present work, we have not used 3-neighborhood or Rule 30 for our experiments. Our neighborhood grid definition of 2-dimensional CA model has been described below. In our proposed model, we adopt the 2-dimensional CA with null boundary condition. We have used deterministic CA for our experiments.

Figure 2. Example of Wolfram Rule 30

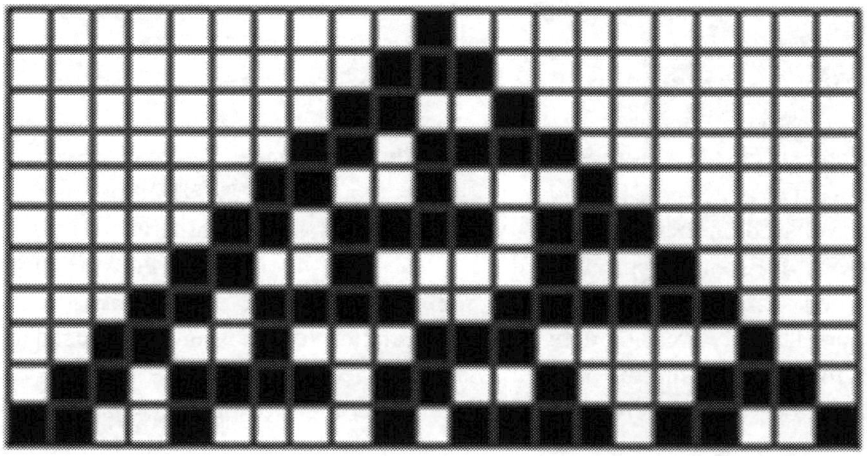

In our 2-dimensional CA models for both stages, we have considered the states of the cells in each CA according to the ranking priority of the genes in sorted order in that stage. The cells in CA (genes) with highest ranking value is considered as in state *0*, while the states of other cells increase with the decrease in order of ranking values in that stage. Our 2-dimensional CA model has been depicted in the flowchart in Figure 1.

The first stage CA is developed based on the ranking matrix of non-stimulated gene clusters in correlation network on chosen dataset. Now if among 4 neighbors (left, right, top, bottom), at least two neighbors show lower ranking values (higher states), the priority of current cell increases to be an important regulatory gene. Therefore, in this case, the present state of current cell decreases by 1 towards *0* state. Similarly, if more than *2* neighbors have higher ranking values (lower states) than current cell, the next state of current cell increases by *1*, to make it less significant to be potential biomarker gene.

We iterate through the CA matrices of both non-stimulated and LIF-stimulated stages for genes, until final *10* genes are being selected as in state *0* in both stages. We then compare highest priority *10* genes from both stages and consider the common genes among them. These common *4* genes for these cells of CAs from two stages, are the most significant nodes in the correlation networks to be effective in LIF stimulation on breast cancer cell line.

Gene Ontology and Canonical Pathway Analysis

We used DAVID (Huang, 2009) to perform GO annotation and KEGG pathway enriching analysis for the top 4 genes selected in our correlation networks using cellular automata based priority flow approach between stages.

RESULTS

In this section, we have explained the results obtained by our novel 2-dimensional cellular automata approach over the chosen gene correlation network model of breast cancer based on log-odds ranking score. We further chose 4 highest priority nodes from our CA model and further analyze their significance to be the genomic signature based on their GO annotations and KEGG pathway analysis results.

Class Predictor Analysis Identifies Genomic Signatures of Breast Cancer

From the perspective of systems biology, the functionally related genes are frequently coexpressed across a set of samples (Hu et al., 2005 ; Pujana et. al, 2007; Zhang et al., 2009). In our approach, we cluster coexpressed genes based on their expression values in the dataset and generate the correlation network over them. The NEMO scores (Corban et al., 2010) over all nodes in the coexpression network have also been computed. These show the significance of each node with respect to its shared neighborhood in the Pearson correlation expression network. These ranking matrices have been used as inputs to each stage in our CA model for further priority enhancing between stages.

The constructed correlation network with clusters is comprised of more than 10,000 nodes. Overexpressed 3182 genes in both stages have been selected for further experiment. Finally our CA model

Figure 3. Correlation network of top 4 nodes with their first neighbors. White nodes represent highest priority nodes, gray nodes represent their first neighbor nodes, and lines represent the regulation relationships between them.

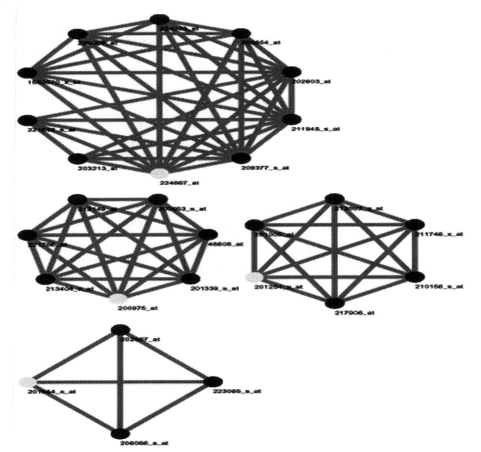

chose 4 nodes to be with highest priority ranking. The first neighbor network for these 4 highest priority nodes are visualized using Cytoscape software in Figure 3.

Gene Ontology Analysis

We use GATHER (Chang & Nevins, 2006) to perform GO annotation and the relevant GO terms for each gene are shown in Table 2. Table 2 shows the GO terms, the number of genes with the annotation and P-value (<0.01). From the gene ontology terms, it is clear that all proteins are mostly in protein/macromolecule metabolism and cellular/macromolecule biosynthesis.

Relevant research in cancer biology states that many of the genes, that can initiate tumorigenesis and progress cancer, are intricately linked to metabolic regulation. Therefore, all GOs for selected genes are related to cancer metabolism or synthesis. If macromolecule biosynthesis increases extremely in one cell, it leads to cancer. The GO macromolecule biosynthetic process defines a biological process, which shows the chemical reactions and pathways resulting in the formation of a macromolecule, any molecule of high relative molecular mass. The structure of macromolecules essentially comprises the multiple repetition of units derived, actually or conceptually, from molecules of low relative molecular mass. Therefore, potential cancer biomarkers may be those who increase macromolecule synthesis/metabolism extensively in one cell to produce cancer growth. This GO annotation (macromolecule synthesis/metabolism) includes 3 of our selected markers (GYG, PPT1, RPS6).

Enrichment of KEGG Pathway

In order to obtain the functional annotation and pathway analysis of genes in our result, we input all the Probe IDs into DAVID (The Database for Annotation, Visualization and Integrated Discovery) for KEGG (Kyoto Encyclopedia of Genes and Genomes) term enrichment analysis (Huang, 2009). The DAVID identifies canonical pathways associated with a given list of genes by calculating the hyper geometric test p-value for probability that association between this set of genes and a canonical pathway (Huang, 2009). We chose p-value <0.05 as the cut-off criterion.

Four gene names are selected for the selected 4 Probe IDS. These genes are GYG1, C1ORF151, PPT1 and RPS6. The relevant gene names and Entrez gene IDs as obtained from DAVID (Huang, 2009) for

Table 2. The enriched GO terms of selected 4 markers with P-value less than 0.01

Gene Ontology	Number of Input Genes with the Annotation	P-Value
GO:0044267~cellular protein metabolism	2	0.006
GO:0019538~protein metabolism	2	0.006
GO:0009059~macromolecule biosynthesis	2	0.0008
GO:0044260~cellular macromolecule metabolism	3	0.002
GO:0043170~macromolecule metabolism	3	0.002
GO:0044249~cellular biosynthesis	2	0.002
GO:0009058~biosynthesis	2	0.002

Table 3. KEGG pathway analysis and cancer subtype with Pubmed IDs

Probe ID	Entrez Gene ID	Gene Name	KEGG Pathway		Cancer Subtype	PubMed ID
			ID	Description		
224867_at	440574	C1ORF151	UN-ANNOTATED GENE		Breast cancer	17932254, 22495314
201554_x_at	2992	GYG1	hsa2992	glycogenin 1	Breast cancer	16959974
201254_x_at	6194	RPS6	hsa04150	mTOR signaling pathway	Breast cancer	16959974
			hsa03010	Ribosome		
			hsa04910	Insulin signaling pathway		
200975_at	5538	PPT1	hsa00062	Lysosome	Breast cancer	16959974, 22608084
			hsa04142	Fatty acid elongation in mitochondria		

relevant Affymetrix Probe IDs, have been shown in respective rows in Table 3. As shown in Table 3, the selected 3 genes (GYG1, PPT1 and RPS6) are mainly enriched in some important pathways, such as Ribosome, Calcium signaling pathway, Lysome, Fatty acid elongation in mitochondria etc. The other gene C1ORF151 is an un-annotated genes in KEGG pathway. Specific cancer subtypes for each gene, as we have found in Catalogue of Somatic Mutations In Cancer (COSMIC) (Forbes et al., 2010), are also included in each row. Relevant PubMed IDs for verification of cancer subtypes are also shown in last column.

Sjöblom T et al (Sjoblom et al., 2010) experiment with several consensus coding sequences, which are relevant to breast and colorectal cancers. Most of our selected genes belong to the results of their experiments, namely – GYG1, PPT1 and RPS6. Two Breast cancer studies in UK have also included our genes in their list namely, COSU385 and COSU414. Breast Invasive Carcinoma (TCGA, US) imports from ICGC (COSU414) study includes GYG1, PPT1 and RPS6 genes. Moreover, Breast Cancer – UK study (COSU385) includes GYG1, C1ORF151 and PPT1 genes. Therefore, these surveys exhibit the importance of the significance of the selected genes in breast cancer study.

CONCLUSION

Cellular automata is a well-known method in data mining to generates classifications in different dynamic models. We utilize it on a dynamic biological system to generate classes of highest ranking genes with a priority upgradation between stages. We experiment CA to detect potential cancer biomarkers from their correlation networks. The detection is helpful in diagnosis and measuring the prediction accuracy for clinical treatment. Microarrays are used several times for detecting biomarkers (Bredel et al., 2005; Zhang et al., 2010), as they can analyze thousands of gene expressions in human genome simultaneously (Sarkar, 2009; Maulik, 2009; 2010). In this work, we analyze MCF7 breast cancer cell line expression in non-stimulated and LIF-stimulated stages in our integrated 2-dimensional CA approach. We utilize the computational ranking methods with CA to uncover biomarkers that are potentially overexpressed in networks and therefore significant in breast cancer. We identify total 4 genes to have the highest priority based on our hybrid implementation of cellular automata over rank-based correlation network over the chosen dataset. The log-odds ratios of ranking among shared neighbors in the correlation networks over the dataset, have been computed and utilized as the ranking score in our approach. We compute ranking of significant genes in the correlation networks in both stages and then perform cellular automata based iterative selection of higher priority genes in both stages. We then consider only the common 4 highest priority genes in both stages, for further functional enrichment analysis. After correlation network formation and cellular automata analysis, we find that the mRNAs 224867_at, 201554_x_at, 201254_x_at and 200975_at may play important roles in breast cancer and are significant for LIF cytokine stimulation. On account of further functional enrichment analysis, three among them, except 224867_at (un-annotated gene) are considered as potential breast-cancer-related factors from this computational approach. They may be used as biomarkers for breast cancer, however more laboratory-based pathological works are needed to validate our result. In our further extended research works in this field, we shall further analyze the graphical maps obtained by our CA model over some simulated and real life biological data sets.

REFERENCES

Perou, C., Sørlie, T., Eisen, M. B., van de Rijn, M., Jeffrey, S. S., & Rees, C. A. et al. (2000). Molecular portraits of human breast tumours. *Nature, 406*(6797), 747–752. doi:10.1038/35021093 PMID:10963602

Sørlie, T., Perou, C.M., Tibshirani, R., Aas, T., Geisler, S., Johnsen, H., … Børresen-Dale, A.L. (2001). Gene expression patterns of breast carcinomas distinguish tumor subclasses with clinical implications. *Proc Natl Acad Sci U S A., 98(19),* 10869–74.

Sorlie, T., Tibshirani, R., Parker, J., Hastie, T., Marron, J. S., & Nobel, A. et al. (2003). Repeated observation of breast tumor subtypes in independent gene expression data sets. *Proceedings of the National Academy of Sciences of the United States of America, 100*(14), 8418–8423. PMID:12829800

Sotiriou, C., & Pusztai, L. (2009). Gene-expression signatures in breast cancer. *The New England Journal of Medicine, 360*(8), 790–800. doi:10.1056/NEJMra0801289 PMID:19228622

Sarkar, A., & Maulik, U. (2013). Cancer Gene Expression Data Analysis Using Rough Based Symmetrical Clustering, Handbook of Research on Computational Intelligence for Engineering, Science, and Business (pp. 699-715) USA: IGI Global.

Sarkar, A., & Maulik, U. (2009). Parallel Point symmetry Based Clustering for Gene Microarray Data. *Proceedings of Seventh International Conference on Advances in Pattern Recognition-2009 (ICAPR)* (pp. 351-354). Kolkata. IEEE Computer Society, Conference Publishing Services (CPS).

Maulik, U., & Sarkar, A. (2010). Gene Microarray Data Analysis Using Parallel Point Symmetry-Based Clustering. In U. Maulik, S. Bandyopadhyay, & J. T. L. Wang (Eds.), *Computational Intelligence and Pattern Analysis in Biological Informatics.* Hoboken, NJ, USA: John Wiley & Sons, Inc. doi:10.1002/9780470872352.ch13

Maulik, U. & Sarkar, A., (20013), Searching remote homology with spectral clustering with symmetry in neighborhood cluster kernels, *PLoS ONE, 8(2), e46468.*

Corban, G. R., Rachit, V., & Bader, J. S. (2010). NeMo: Network Module identification in Cytoscape. *BMC Bioinformatics, 11*(Suppl 1), S61. doi:10.1186/1471-2105-11-S1-S61 PMID:20122237

Laura, I., Moria, R., Gesellchen, V., Eyckerman, S., & Cauwer, L. D. (2012). The Sin3a repressor complex is a master regulator of STAT transcriptional activity. *Proceedings of the National Academy of Sciences of the United States of America*, *109*(30), 12058–12063. doi:10.1073/pnas.1206458109 PMID:22783022

Huang, D. W., Sherman, B. T., & Lempicki, R. A. (2009). Systematic and integrative analysis of large gene lists using DAVID Bioinformatics Resources. *Nature Protocols*, *4*(1), 44–57. doi:10.1038/nprot.2008.211 PMID:19131956

Huang, D. W., Sherman, B. T., & Lempicki, R. A. (2009). Bioinformatics enrichment tools: Paths toward the comprehensive functional analysis of large gene lists. *Nucleic Acids Research*, *37*(1), 1–13. doi:10.1093/nar/gkn923 PMID:19033363

ClusterMaker. (n. d.). Retrieved from http://www.cgl.ucsf.edu/cytoscape/cluster/clusterMaker.html

Sotiriou, C., Neo, S.-Y., McShane, L. M., Korn, E. L., Long, P. M., & Jazaeri, A., ... Liu, E. T. (2003). Breast cancer classification and prognosis based on gene expression profiles from a population-based study. *Proceedings of the National Academy of Sciences of the United States of America*, 100(18), 10393–10398. doi:10.1073/pnas.1732912100

Smith, A. R. III. (1971). Two-dimensional Formal Languages and Pattern Recognition by Cellular Automata. *Proceedings of IEEE Conference Record of 12th Annual Symposium on Switchinh and Automata Theory*. doi:10.1109/SWAT.1971.29

Wolfram, S. (1986). Cryptography with cellular automata. *Lecture Notes in Computer Science*, *218*, 429–432. doi:10.1007/3-540-39799-X_32

Wolfram, S. (1983). Statistical mechanics of cellular automata. *Reviews of Modern Physics*, *55*(3), 601–644. doi:10.1103/RevModPhys.55.601

Zhang, J., Xiang, Y., Jin, R., & Huang, K. (2009) Using Frequent Co-expression Network to Identify Gene Clusters for Breast Cancer Prognosis. *International Joint Conference on Bioinformatics, Systems Biology and Intelligent Computing (IJCBS). Shanghai: IEEE Computer Society*. doi:10.1109/IJCBS.2009.29

Hu, H., Yan, X., Huang, Y., Han, J., & Zhou, X. J. (2005). Mining coherent dense subgraphs across massive biological networks for functional discovery. *Bioinformatics (Oxford, England)*, *21*(Suppl 1), i213–i221. doi:10.1093/bioinformatics/bti1049 PMID:15961460

Pujana, M. A., Han, J. D., Starita, L. M., Stevens, K. N., Tewari, M., & Ahn, J. S. et al. (2007). Network modeling links breast cancer susceptibility and centrosome dysfunction. *Nature Genetics*, *39*(11), 1338–1349. doi:10.1038/ng.2007.2 PMID:17922014

Forbes, S. A., Tang, G., Bindal, N., Bamford, S., Dawson, E., & Cole, C. et al. (2010). COSMIC (the Catalogue of Somatic Mutations in Cancer): A resource to investigate acquired mutations in human cancer. *Nucleic Acids Research*, *38*(Database issue), D652–D657. PMID:19906727

Sjöblom, T., Jones, S., Wood, L. D., Parsons, D. W., Lin, J., & Barber, T. D. et al. (2006). The consensus coding sequences of human breast and colorectal cancers. *Science*, *314*(5797), 268–274. doi:10.1126/science.1133427 PMID:16959974

Zhang, J., Xiang, Y., Ding, L., Keen-Circle, K., Borlawsky, T. B., & Ozer, H. G. et al. (2010). Using gene co-expression network analysis to predict biomarkers for chronic lymphocytic leukemia. *BMC Bioinformatics*, *11*(Suppl 9), S5. doi:10.1186/1471-2105-11-S9-S5 PMID:21044363

Bredel, M., Bredel, C., Juric, D., Harsh, G. R., Vogel, H., & Recht, L. D. et al. (2005). Functional Network Analysis Reveals Extended Gliomagenesis Pathway Maps and Three Novel MYC-Interacting Genes in Human Gliomas. *Cancer Research*, *65*(19), 8679–8689. doi:10.1158/0008-5472.CAN-05-1204 PMID:16204036

Chang, J. T., & Nevins, J. R. (2006). GATHER: A Systems Approach to Interpreting Genomic Signatures. *Bioinformatics (Oxford, England)*, *22*(23), 2926–2933. doi:10.1093/bioinformatics/btl483 PMID:17000751

Xiao, X., & Chou, K.-C. (2011). Using Pseudo Amino Acid Composition to Predict Protein Attributes Via Cellular Automata and Other Approaches. *Current Bioinformatics*, *6*(2), 251–260. doi:10.2174/1574893611106020251

Paulien Hogeweg. (2010) Multilevel Cellular Automata as a Tool for Studying Bioinformatic Processes. Simulating Complex Systems by Cellular Automata Understanding Complex Systems, 19-28. Springer.

Pokkuluri, K. S., & Babu, I. R. (2014). Clonal-Based Cellular Automata in Bioinformatics. *Journal of Advance Research in Applied Artificial Intelligence & Neural Network*, *1*(1), 1.

Chakrabarti, T., Saha, S., & Sinha, D. (2013). A Cellular Automata Based DNA Pattern Classifier. *Biometrics and Bioinformatics*, *5*(9), 1.

Ghosh, S., Maiti, N. S. & Chaudhuri, P. P. (2012) *Theory and Application of Restricted Five Neighborhood Cellular Automata (R5NCA) for Protein Structure Prediction.*

ADDITIONAL READING

Sharan, R., Maron-Katz, A., & Shamir, R. (2003). CLICK and EXPANDER: A system for clustering and visualizing gene expression data. *Bioinformatics (Oxford, England)*, *19*(14), 1787–1799. doi:10.1093/bioinformatics/btg232 PMID:14512350

DeRisi, J., Iyer, V., & Brown, P. (1997). Exploring the metabolic and genetic control of gene expression on a genome scale. *Science*, *282*, 257–264. PMID:9381177

Chu, S. (1998). The transcriptional program of sporulation in budding yeast. *Science*, *202*(5389), 699–705. doi:10.1126/science.282.5389.699 PMID:9784122

Cho, R. J., Campbell, M. J., Winzeler, E. A., Steinmetz, L., Conway, A., & Wodicka, L. et al. (1998). A genome-wide transcriptional analysis of the mitotic cell cycle. *Molecular Cell*, *2*(1), 65–73. doi:10.1016/S1097-2765(00)80114-8 PMID:9702192

Dhilon, I., Marcotte, E., & Roshan, U. (2003). Diametrical clustering for identifying anticorrelated gene clusters. *Bioinformatics (Oxford, England)*, *19*(13), 1612–1619. doi:10.1093/bioinformatics/btg209 PMID:12967956

Horn, D., & Axel, L. (2003). Novel clustering algorithm for microarray expression data in a truncated svd space. *Bioinformatics (Oxford, England)*, *19*(9), 1110–1115. doi:10.1093/bioinformatics/btg053 PMID:12801871

Bandyopadhyay, S., Mukhopadhyay, A., & Maulik, U. (2007). An improved algorithm for clustering gene expression data. *Bioionformatics.*, *23*(21), 2859–2865. doi:10.1093/bioinformatics/btm418 PMID:17720981

Tou, J. T., & Gonzalez, R. C. (1974). *Pattern recognition principles*. Reading, MA: Addison-Wesley.

Chen, Y. L., & Hu, H. L. (2006). An overlapping cluster algorithm to provide non-exhaustive clustering. *European Journal of Operational Research*, *173*(3), 762–780. doi:10.1016/j.ejor.2005.06.056

Bandyopadhyay, S., & Saha, S. (2007). GAPS: A clustering method using a new point symmetry-based distance measure. *Pattern Recognition*, *10*(12), 3430–3451. doi:10.1016/j.patcog.2007.03.026

Bandyopadhyay, S., & Saha, S. (2008). A point symmetry based clustering technique for automatic evolution of clusters. *IEEE Transactions on Knowledge and Data Engineering*, *20*(11), 1–17. doi:10.1109/TKDE.2008.79

Kim, S. Y. (2001). Effect of data normalization on fuzzy clustering of DNA microarray data. *BMC Bioinformatics*, *17*, 309–318. PMID:16533412

Hvidsten, T. R., Laegreid, A., & Komorowski, J. (2003). Learning rule-based models of biological process from gene expression time profiles using gene ontology. *Bioinformatics (Oxford, England)*, *19*(9), 1116–1123. doi:10.1093/bioinformatics/btg047 PMID:12801872

Kanungo, T., Mount, D., Netanyahu, N., Piatko, C., Silverman, R., & Wu, A. (2002). An efficient k-means clustering algorithm: Analysis and implementation. *IEEE Transactions on Pattern Analysis and Machine Intelligence*, *24*(7), 881–892. doi:10.1109/TPAMI.2002.1017616

Kalyanaraman, A., Aluru, S., Brendel, V., & Kothari, S. (2003). Space and time efficient parallel algorithms and software for EST clustering. *IEEE Transactions on Parallel and Distributed Systems*, *14*(12), 1209–1221. doi:10.1109/TPDS.2003.1255634

Rajko, S., & Aluru, S. (2004). Space and time optimal parallel sequence alignments. *IEEE Transactions on Parallel and Distributed Systems*, *15*(12), 1070–1081. doi:10.1109/TPDS.2004.86

Jiang, K., Thorsen, O., Peters, A. E., Smith, B. E., & Sosa, C. P. (2008). An efficient parallel implementation of the hidden markov methods for genomic sequence-search on a massively parallel system. *IEEE Transactions on Parallel and Distributed Systems*, *19*(1), 15–23. doi:10.1109/TPDS.2007.70712

Liu, W., & Schmidt, B. (2006). Parallel pattern-based systems for computational biology: A case study. *IEEE Transactions on Parallel and Distributed Systems*, *17*(8), 750–763. doi:10.1109/TPDS.2006.109

Rajasekaran, S. (2005). Efficient parallel hierarchical clustering algorithms. *IEEE Transactions on Parallel and Distributed Systems*, *16*(6), 497–502. doi:10.1109/TPDS.2005.72

Chen, L., Pan, Y., & Xu, X. (2004). Scalable and efficient parallel algorithms for Euclidean distance transform on the LARPBS model. *IEEE Transactions on Parallel and Distributed Systems*, *15*(11), 975–982. doi:10.1109/TPDS.2004.71

Hollander, M., & Wolfe, D. (1999). Nonparametric statistical methods (2nd ed.). USA: Wiely.

Wen, X. (1998). Large-scale temporal gene expression mapping of central nervous system development. *Proceedings of the National Academy of Sciences of the United States of America*, *95*, 334–339.

Iyer, V. R. (1999). The transcriptional program in the response of human fibroblasts serum. *Science*, *283*(5398), 83–87. doi:10.1126/science.283.5398.83 PMID:9872747

Ashburner, M., Ball, C. A., Blake, J. A., Botstein, D., Butler, H., & Cherry, J. M. et al.The Gene Ontology Consortium. (2000). Gene ontology: Tool for the unification biology. *Nature Genetics*, *25*(1), 25–29. doi:10.1038/75556 PMID:10802651

Shahrour, F. A. (2004). FatiGO: A web tool for finding significant associations to gene ontology terms with groups of genes. *Bioinformatics*, *20*(4), 578–580. doi:10.1093/bioinformatics/btg455 PMID:14990455

KEY TERMS AND DEFINITIONS

Cellular Automata: A cellular automata is a discrete, dynamical system composed of very simple, uniformly interconnected cells.

Correlation Network: Weighted correlation network analysis, also known as weighted gene co-expression network analysis, is one very popular data mining method for studying biological networks based on pairwise correlations between expression variables.

Ranking: The gene ranking method is based on the comparison of network trees, which are extracted from the correlation network obtained for each shared neighborhood in our method.

Section 3

Chapter 9
Knowledge Extraction from Information System Using Rough Computing

D. P. Acharjya
VIT University, India

ABSTRACT

The amount of data collected across various sources in real life situations is never in its complete form. That is, it is never precise or it never gives definite knowledge. It always contains uncertainty and vagueness. Therefore, most of our traditional tools for formal modelling, reasoning and computing can not handle efficiently. Therefore, it is very challenging to organize this data in formal system which provides information in more relevant, useful, and structured manner. There are many techniques available for knowledge extraction form this high dimensional data. This chapter discusses various rough computing based knowledge extraction techniques to obtain meaningful knowledge from large amount of data. A real life example is provided to show the viability of the proposed research.

INTRODUCTION

At the present age of Internet, a huge repository of data is available across various domains. It is due to the wide spread of distributed computing which involves dispersion of data geographically. In addition, these data are neither crisp nor deterministic due to presence of uncertainty and vagueness. Analyzing these data for obtaining meaningful information is a great challenge for human being. Therefore, it is very difficult to extract expert knowledge from the universal dataset. Also, there is much information hidden in the accumulated voluminous data. It is observed that, most of our traditional tools for knowledge extraction are crisp, deterministic and precise in character. So, it is essential for a new generation of computational theories and tools to assist human in extracting knowledge from the rapidly growing voluminous digital data. Knowledge discovery in databases (KDD) is the field that has evolved into an important and active area of research because of theoretical challenges associated with the problem of discovering intelligent solutions for huge data. Knowledge discovery and data mining is the rapidly

DOI: 10.4018/978-1-4666-8513-0.ch009

growing interdisciplinary field which merges database management, statistics, computational intelligence and related areas. The basic aim of all these is knowledge extraction from voluminous data.

The processes of knowledge discovery in databases and information retrieval appear deceptively simple when viewed from the perspective of terminological definition (Fayaad, 1996). The nontrivial process of identifying valid, novel, potentially useful, and ultimately understandable patterns in data is known as knowledge discovery in databases. It consists of several stages such as data selection, cleaning of data, enrichment of data, coding, data mining and reporting. The different stages are shown in the following figure 1. In addition, closely related process of information retrieval is defined by Rocha (2001) as "the methods and processes for searching relevant information out of information systems that contain extremely large numbers of documents". However in execution, these processes are not simple at all, especially when executed to satisfy specific personal or organizational knowledge management requirements. It is also observed that, usefulness of an individual data element or pattern of data elements change dramatically from individual to individual, organization to organization, or task to task. It is because of the acquisition of knowledge and reasoning that involve in vagueness and incompleteness. In addition, knowledge extraction or description of data patterns generally understandable is also highly problematic. Therefore, there is much need for dealing with the incomplete and vague information in classification, concept formulation, and data analysis.

Figure 1. The KDD process

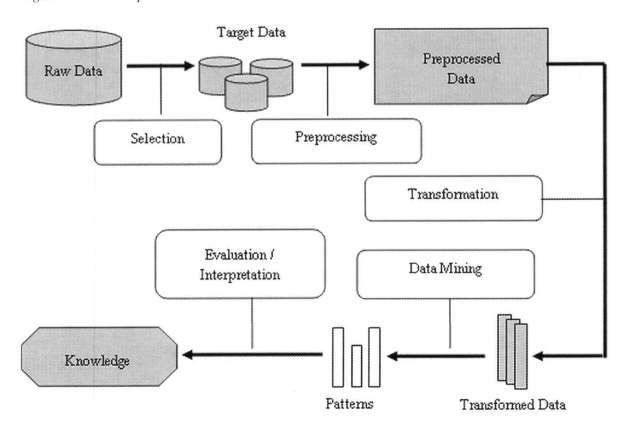

The problem of uncertainties and vagueness has been tackled for a long time by logicians, mathematicians and computer scientists, particularly in the area of knowledge extraction and artificial intelligence. There are various approaches to solve such problems. The earliest and most successful one is being the notion of fuzzy sets by L. A. Zadeh (1965) that captures impreciseness in information. On the other hand rough set of Z. Pawlak (1982) is another attempt that captures indiscernibility among objects to model imperfect knowledge (Pawlak & Skowron, (2007a, 2007b, 2007c)). In addition, many other advanced methods such as rough set with similarity (Slowinski & Vanderpooten, 2000), rough fuzzy sets and fuzzy rough set (Dubois & Prade, 1990), rough set on fuzzy approximation spaces (Acharjya & Tripathy, 2008), rough set on intuitionistic fuzzy approximation spaces (Acharjya & Tripathy, 2009), dynamic rough set (Li & Hu, 2007), covering based rough set (Zhu & Wang, 2007) were discussed by different authors to extract knowledge from the huge amount of data. Universe can be considered as a large collection of objects and each object is associated with some information with it. In order to obtain some knowledge about the universe, we need to extract some information about these objects. However, uniquely identification is not possible in case of all objects due to lack of sufficient amount of information. Hence, it is essential to classify these objects into similarity classes to characterize and to obtain knowledge about the universe. In recent years, rough computing is an approach which is widely used to extract knowledge from the universe.

This chapter discusses various rough computing techniques that are used in extracting knowledge from the universe. The chapter is organized as follows: It starts with an introduction followed by information system. Information system is followed by foundations of rough set. This is further followed by indiscernibility and almost indiscernibility relation. Extension of rough set such as rough set on fuzzy approximation space and rough set on intuitionistic fuzzy approximation spaces is presented next. Further order information system is presented. A real life application is further presented followed by a conclusion. Finally, a complete reference is provided at the end of the chapter.

INFORMATION SYSTEM

The fundamental objective of inductive learning and data mining is to learn the knowledge for classification. But, we may not face with a simply classification while dealing real world problems. Ordering of objects is one such problem. Before we discuss knowledge extraction techniques using rough computing, one must know about an information system. An information system contains a finite set of objects typically represented by their values on a finite set of attributes. Such information system may be conveniently described in a tabular form in which each row represents an object whereas each column represents an attribute. Each cell of the information system contains an attribute value. Now, we define formally an information system as below.

An information system is a table that provides a convenient way to describe a finite set of objects called the universe by a finite set of attributes thereby representing all available information and knowledge. The attribute sets along with the objects in an information system consists of the set of condition attributes and decision attributes. Therefore it is also named as decision table (Pawlak, 1981). Let us denote the information system as $I = (U, A, V, f)$, where U is a finite non-empty set of objects called the universe and A is a non-empty finite set of attributes. For every $a \in A$, V_a is the set of values that attribute a may take. Also $V = \bigcup_{a \in A} V_a$. In addition, for every $a \in A$, $f_a: U \rightarrow V_a$ is the information function (Tripathy, Acharjya & Cynthya, 2011).

For example, a sample information system is presented in Table 1 in which $U = \{x_1, x_2, x_3, x_4, x_5, x_6, x_7\}$ represents a nonempty finite set of objects; and $A = \{$Humidity, Windy, Temperature$\}$ be a finite set of attributes. In particular, object x_1 is characterized in the table by the attribute value set (humidity, high), (windy, yes), and (temperature, hot) which form the information about the object. The information system presented in Table 1 is a qualitative system, where all the attribute values are discrete and categorical (qualitative).

In the information system shown in Table 2, $U = \{x_1, x_2, x_3, x_4, x_5\}$ represents a set of patients and A = {Temperature, Blood Pressure, Cholesterol} represents a finite set of attributes. In particular, object x_1 is characterized in the table by the attribute value set (temperature, 98.7), (blood pressure, 112), and (cholesterol, 180) which form the information about the object. This information system is a quantitative system, since all the attribute values are non categorical (Acharjya & Geetha, 2014).

ROUGH SET IN KNOWLEDGE EXTRACTION

In real world, invent of computers, communication technologies, and database systems have created a new space for knowledge extraction. Therefore, data handling and data processing is of prime importance in recent years. In the hierarchy of data processing, data is the root which transforms into information and further refined to avail it in the form of knowledge. It is well established fact that right decision at right time provides an advantage to any organization. Knowledge extraction specifies the collection of the right information at the right level and utilize for the suitable purposes. The real challenge arises when larger volume of inconsistent data is presented for extraction of knowledge and decision making. The

Table 1. Qualitative information system

Objects	Humidity	Windy	Temperature
x_1	High	Yes	Hot
x_2	Low	No	Cool
x_3	Normal	No	Mild
x_4	Low	Yes	Cool
x_5	High	No	Hot
x_6	High	Yes	Hot
x_7	Normal	No	Mild

Table 2. Quantitative information system

Object	Temperature (F)	Blood Pressure	Cholesterol
x_1	98.7	112	180
x_2	102.3	143	184
x_3	99	125	197
x_4	98.9	106	193
x_5	100.3	134	205

major issue lies in converting large volume of data into knowledge and to use that knowledge to make a proper decision. Though present technologies help in creating large databases, but most of the information may not be relevant. Therefore, attribute reduction becomes an important aspect for handling such voluminous database by eliminating superfluous data. Rough set theory developed by Z. Pawlak (1982, 1991) used to process uncertain and incomplete information is a tool to the above mentioned problem. In addition, it has many applications in all the fields of science and engineering. One of its strength is the attribute dependencies, their significance among inconsistent data. At the same time, it does not need any preliminary or additional information about the data. Therefore, it classifies imprecise, uncertain or incomplete information expressed in terms of data.

ROUGH SET

The rough set philosophy was developed based on the assumption that with every object of the universe of discourse, we associate some information (data, knowledge). Objects characterized by same information are indiscernible (similar) in view of the available information about them. The indiscernibility relation obtained in this way is the mathematical foundation of rough set theory. In this section we give some definitions and notations as developed by Z. Pawlak (1982), which shall be referred in the rest of the paper.

Let U be a finite nonempty set called the universe. Suppose $R \subseteq U \times U$ is an equivalence relation on U. The equivalence relation R partitions the set U into disjoint subsets. Elements of same equivalence class are said to be indistinguishable. Equivalence classes induced by R are called elementary concepts. Every union of elementary concepts is called a definable set. The empty set is considered to be a definable set, thus all the definable sets form a Boolean algebra and (U, R) is called an approximation space. Given a target set X, we can characterize X by a pair of lower and upper approximations. We associate two subsets $\underline{R}X$ and $\overline{R}X$ called the R–lower and R–upper approximations of X respectively and are given by

$$\underline{R}X = \bigcup\{Y \in U \,/\, R : Y \subseteq X\} \tag{1}$$

and

$$\overline{R}X = \bigcup\{Y \in U \,/\, R : Y \cap X \neq \phi\} \tag{2}$$

The R–boundary of X, $BN_R(X)$ is given by $BN_R(X) = \overline{R}X - \underline{R}X$. We say X is rough with respect to R if and only if $\overline{R}X \neq \underline{R}X$, equivalently $BN_R(X) \neq \phi$. X is said to be R–definable if and only if $\overline{R}X = \underline{R}X$ or $BN_R(X) = \phi$. So, a set is rough with respect to R if and only if it is not R–definable.

INDISCERNIBILITY RELATION

Universe can be considered as a large collection of objects. Each object is associated with some information (data, knowledge) within it. In order to find knowledge about the universe we need to process these attribute values. Therefore, we require sufficient amount of information to uniquely identify, classify these objects into similar classes and to extract knowledge about the universe. The classification of the objects of the universe is done based on indiscernibility relation among these objects. It indicates that objects of a class cannot discern from one another based on available set of attributes of the objects (Pawlak, 1982; Tripathy & Acharjya, 2011). The indiscernibility relation generated in this way is the mathematical basis of rough set theory. Any set of all indiscernible objects is called an elementary concept, and form a basic granule (atom) of knowledge about the universe. Any union of the elementary sets is referred to be either crisp (precise) set or rough (imprecise) set. Let $P \subseteq A$ and $x_i, x_j \in U$. Then we say x_i and x_j are indiscernible by the set of attributes P in A if and only if the following (3) holds.

$$f(x_i, a) = f(x_j, a), \forall\, a \in P \tag{3}$$

For example, given the attributes humidity, windy, and temperature $\{x_1, x_6\}$ are indiscernible. Similarly, the other indiscernible classes obtained are $\{x_2\}$, $\{x_3, x_7\}$, $\{x_4\}$ and $\{x_5\}$. In general each object x_i, $i = 1, 2, ..., 7$ is compared with each other cell wise to find the indiscernibility in the attribute value. From the data set Table-1, on considering the attributes $A = \{$humidity, windy, temperature$\}$, we get the family of equivalence classes of A, i.e., the partition determined by set of attributes A, denoted by U/A or $I(A)$. Therefore,

$$U/A = \{\{x_1, x_6\}, \{x_2\}, \{x_3, x_7\}, \{x_4\}, \{x_5\}\}$$

On considering the target set $X = \{x_1, x_2, x_6, x_7\}$; objects x_3 and x_7 are the boundary-line objects, where

$$\underline{A}X = \bigcup\{Y \in U/A : Y \subseteq X\} = \{x_1, x_2, x_6\} \quad \text{and}$$
$$\overline{A}X = \bigcup\{Y \in U/A : Y \cap X \neq \phi\} = \{x_1, x_2, x_3, x_6, x_7\}$$

Furthermore, considering the attributes $P \subseteq A$, we can associate an index (i.e. $\alpha_A(X)$) called the accuracy of approximation for any set $X \subseteq U$ as follows:

$$\alpha_A(X) = \frac{\text{cardinality of } \underline{A}X}{\text{cardinality of } \overline{A}X} = \frac{|\underline{A}X|}{|\overline{A}X|}$$

For example, $\alpha_A(X) = \frac{3}{5}$, where $X = \{x_1, x_2, x_6, x_7\}$; and $A = \{$humidity, windy, temperature$\}$. From the information system given in Table 1, it is clear that object x_2 has no windy, whereas object x_4 is windy and they are indiscernible with respect to the attributes humidity, and temperature. Hence, windy cannot be characterized in terms of attributes and attribute-value pair (humidity, low) and (temperature, cool).

ALMOST INDISCERNIBILITY RELATION

Universe can be considered as large collection of objects. Every object has certain attributes and the attribute values portray some information about that particular object. Objects that belong to same category of information are indiscernible (Pawlak (1981, 1991)). This is known as indiscernibility and it is the basis of Pawlak's Rough set theory. Indiscernibility relation is an equivalence relation where all identical objects of set are considered as elementary. But in many real life applications the data collected from various sources, it has been observed that two different objects x_i and x_j may have attribute values that are not exactly identical but are almost identical. For example in Table 2 the temperature of objects x_1, x_3 and x_4 are almost identical rather exactly identical. Keeping in view this context Acharjya and Tripathy (2008, 2010) generalized Pawlak's approach of indiscernibility to almost indiscernibility relation with the introduction of fuzzy proximity relation. This has further generalized to with the help of intuitionistic fuzzy proximity relation (Acharjya & Tripathy, 2009).

Any set of all almost indiscernible objects is called an elementary concept, and forms a granule (atom) of knowledge about the universe. To decide amount of identity between two attribute values, we use intuitionistic fuzzy proximity relation on each domain of attributes. This domain of attributes helps the universal set to create an intuitionistic fuzzy approximation space on the universe.

The motivation behind this chapter is that the notion of almost indiscernibility relation is a generalization of indiscernibility relation with the use of intuitionistic fuzzy proximity relation and is mainly applicable on information systems where the attribute values are not subjective having vague or imprecise meaning rather than quantitative. Also, the notion of intuitionistic fuzzy approximation space defined with the help of intuitionistic fuzzy proximity relation is a generalization of Pawlak's (1982) approximation space. Therefore, the rough set on intuitionistic fuzzy approximation space (Acharjya & Tripathy, 2009) generalizes the Pawlak's rough set and provides better result in real life situations under study. Now, in the succeeding sections we provide the basic foundations of rough set on fuzzy approximation space and rough set on intuitionistic fuzzy approximation space.

ROUGH SET ON FUZZY APPROXIMATION SPACES

The basic idea of rough sets, introduced by Pawlak depends upon the notion of equivalence relations defined over a universe. However, equivalence relations in real life situations are relatively rare in practice. Therefore, efforts have been made to make the relations less significant by removing one or more of the three requirements of an equivalence relation. A fuzzy relation is an extension of the concept of a relation on any set U. Fuzzy proximity relations on U are much more general and abundant than equivalence relations. The concept of fuzzy approximation space which depends upon a fuzzy proximity relation defined on a set U is a generalization of the concept of knowledge base. So, rough sets defined on fuzzy approximation spaces extend the concept of rough sets on knowledge bases as discussed by Acharjya and Tripathy (2008). We unfold the background of this article in this section, by presenting the fundamental concepts, notations and results on rough sets on fuzzy approximation spaces, and these are all bases our discussion starts from.

Let U be a universe. We define a fuzzy relation on U as a fuzzy subset of $(U \times U)$. A fuzzy relation R on U is a fuzzy proximity relation if $\mu_R(x,x)=1$ for all $x \in U$ and $\mu_R(x,y) = \mu_R(y,x)$ for $x,y \in U$. Let R be a fuzzy proximity relation on U. Then for a given $\alpha \in [0,1]$, we say that two elements x and y are α similar with respect to R if $\mu_R(x,y) \geq \alpha$ and we write $xR_\alpha y$ or $(x,y) \in R_\alpha$. Two elements x and y in U are said to be α identical denoted by $xR(\alpha)y$ if either x is α similar to y or x is transitively α similar to y, that is, there exists a sequence $u_1, u_2, u_3, \ldots, u_n$ in U such that $xR_\alpha u_1, u_1 R_\alpha u_2, u_2 R_\alpha u_3, \ldots, u_n R_\alpha y$.

If x and y are α identical with respect to fuzzy proximity relation R, then we write $xR(\alpha)y$, where the relation $R(\alpha)$ for each fixed $\alpha \in [0,1]$ is an equivalence relation on U. The pair (U,R) is called a fuzzy approximation space. The rough set of X, in the generated approximation space $(U,R(\alpha))$ is denoted by $(\underline{X}_\alpha, \overline{X}_\alpha)$ and is defined with respect to R_α^*, the family of equivalence classes of $R(\alpha)$. The α lower approximation of X, $\underline{X}_\alpha$ and α upper approximation of X, $\overline{X}_\alpha$ are defined as follows:

$$\underline{X}_\alpha = \cup \{Y : Y \in R_\alpha^* \text{ and } Y \subseteq X\} \tag{4}$$

$$\overline{X}_\alpha = \cup \{Y : Y \in R_\alpha^* \text{ and } Y \cap X \neq \phi\} \tag{5}$$

The target set X is said to be α discernible if and only if $\underline{X}_\alpha = \overline{X}_\alpha$ and X is said to be α rough if $\underline{X}_\alpha \neq \overline{X}_\alpha$. It is also noticed that $R(\alpha)$ is not exact indiscernibility relation defined by Pawlak, rather it can be considered as an almost indiscernibility relation on U. The almost indiscernibility relation $R(\alpha)$ reduces to Pawlak's exact indiscernibility relation when $\alpha = 1$ and thus it generalizes Pawlak's indiscernibility relation. The family of all equivalence classes of $R(\alpha)$ i.e. the partition generated for $\alpha \in [0,1]$ is denoted by $U/R(\alpha)$. If $(x,y) \in R(\alpha)$, then we say that x and y are α indiscernible. These are the basic building blocks of rough set on fuzzy approximation space.

ROUGH SET ON INTUITIONISTIC FUZZY APPROXIMATION SPACES

In real life situations, we accumulate lot of information which may be insufficient and not necessarily important to us. Processing such vague and insufficient information, Zadeh (1965) introduced the concept of fuzzy set. Though it has wide acceptability today, but it has certain limitations in choosing membership functions. To this end, many researchers proposed many methods such as "twofold fuzzy sets" by Dubosis and Prade (1987); "L-fuzzy set" by Gougen (1967); "Toll sets" by Dubosis and Prade (1980) and "Intuitionistic fuzzy sets" by Atanasov (1986). However, intuitionistic fuzzy set theory introduced by Atanasov is quite useful and applicable in many real life problems. It is because, till this date there is no unique method which can determine the membership values of an element in a fuzzy set. These problems are situation dependent. In addition, the membership value for an object cannot be determined for a particular situation due to less significant information about the object. Similar kind of problem arises when non membership values are getting determined. This estimation can be stated as in-deterministic. In fuzzy set theory we do not consider this in-deterministic part and we already assumed that membership values of all objects exists. But, it is not true in many real life problems. In fuzzy set theory, if μ be the degree of membership of an element x, then the degree of non membership of x is calculated using mathematical formula with the assumption that full part of the degree of membership is determinism and in-deterministic part is zero. At the same time, intuitionistic fuzzy set theory reduces to fuzzy set theory if in-deterministic part is zero. Therefore, intuitionistic fuzzy set model is a generalized and better model over fuzzy set model. Thus, rough sets on intuitionistic fuzzy approximation spaces is a generalized and better model then rough set on fuzzy approximation space (Acharjya, 2009). The different properties of rough sets on intuitionistic fuzzy approximation space are studied by Tripathy (2006).

For completeness of the chapter, the definitions, notations and results on rough sets on IF-approximation space as studied by Acharjya and Tripathy (2009) is presented. The basic concepts of rough sets on intuitionistic fuzzy approximation space use the standard notation μ for membership and v for non-membership.

Definition 1 An intuitionistic fuzzy relation R on a universal set U is an intuitionistic fuzzy set defined on $U \times U$.

Definition 2 An intuitionistic fuzzy relation R on U is said to be an intuitionistic fuzzy proximity relation if the following properties hold.

$$\mu_R(x,x)=1 \text{ and } v_R(x,x)=0 \ \forall x \in U$$

$$\mu_R(x,y) = \mu_R(y,x), \ v_R(x,y) = v_R(y,x) \ \forall x,y \in U$$

Definition 3 Let R be an intuitionistic fuzzy (IF) proximity relation on U. Then for any $(\alpha,\beta) \in J$, where $J = \{(\alpha, \beta) \mid \alpha, \beta \in [0,1] \text{ and } 0 \leq \alpha+\beta \leq 1\}$, the (α,β) -cut '$R_{\alpha,\beta}$' of R is given by

$$R_{\alpha,\beta} = \{(x,y) \mid \mu_R(x,y) \geq \alpha \text{ and } v_R(x,y) \leq \beta\}$$

Definition 4 Let R be a IF-proximity relation on U. We say that two elements x and y are (α,β)-similar with respect to R if $(x,y) \in R_{\alpha,\beta}$ and we write $xR_{\alpha,\beta}y$.

Definition 5 Let R is an IF-proximity relation on U. We say that two elements x and y are (α,β)-identical with respect to R for $(\alpha,\beta) \in J$, written as $xR(\alpha,\beta)y$ if and only if $xR_{\alpha,\beta}y$ or there exists a sequence of elements $u_1, u_2, u_3, \ldots, u_n$ in U such that $xR_{\alpha,\beta}u_1, u_1R_{\alpha,\beta}u_2, u_2R_{\alpha,\beta}u_3, \ldots, u_nR_{\alpha,\beta}y$. In the last case, we say that x is transitively (α,β)-similar to y with respect to R.

It is also easy to see that for any $(\alpha,\beta) \in J$, $R(\alpha,\beta)$ is an equivalence relation on U. We denote $R^*_{\alpha,\beta}$ the set of equivalence classes generated by the equivalence relation $R(\alpha,\beta)$ for each fixed $(\alpha,\beta) \in J$.

Definition 6 Let U be a universal set and R be an intuitionistic fuzzy proximity relation on U. The pair (U,R) is an intuitionistic fuzzy approximation space (IF-approximation space). An IF-approximation space (U,R) generates usual approximation space $(U,R(\alpha,\beta))$ of Pawlak for every $(\alpha,\beta) \in J$.

Definition 7 The rough set on X in the generalized approximation space $(U,R(\alpha,\beta))$ is denoted by $(\underline{X}_{\alpha,\beta}, \overline{X}_{\alpha,\beta})$, where

$$\underline{X}_{\alpha,\beta} = \bigcup\{Y \mid Y \in R^*_{\alpha,\beta} \text{ and } Y \subseteq X\} \tag{6}$$

and

$$\overline{X}_{\alpha,\beta} = \bigcup\{Y \mid Y \in R^*_{\alpha,\beta} \text{ and } Y \cap X \neq \phi\} \tag{7}$$

Definition 8 Let X be a rough set in the generalized approximation space $(U,R(\alpha,\beta))$. Then the (α,β)-boundary of X with respect to R denoted by $BNR_{\alpha,\beta}(X)$ as $BNR_{\alpha,\beta}(X) = \overline{X}_{\alpha,\beta} - \underline{X}_{\alpha,\beta}$.

Definition 9 Let X be a rough set in the generalized approximation space $(U, R(\alpha, \beta))$. Then X is (α, β)-discernible with respect to R if and only if $\overline{X}_{\alpha,\beta} = \underline{X}_{\alpha,\beta}$ and X is (α, β)-rough with respect to R if and only if $\overline{X}_{\alpha,\beta} \neq \underline{X}_{\alpha,\beta}$.

PROPERTIES OF ROUGH SET ON IF APPROXIMATION SPACES

This section states the properties of (α, β)-lower and (α, β)-upper approximations as established by Tripathy (2006). The relations (10), (11), (14) and (15) can be extended to any finite number of rough sets on intuitionistic fuzzy approximation spaces. The inclusions (14) and (15) imply that knowledge contained in a distributed knowledge base defined over intuitionistic fuzzy approximation space is less than the integrated one. Let X and Y be rough sets in the generalized approximation space $(U, R(\alpha, \beta))$; $(\alpha, \beta) \in J$. Then the following properties hold.

$$\underline{X}_{\alpha,\beta} \subseteq X \subseteq \overline{X}_{\alpha,\beta} \tag{8}$$

$$\underline{\phi}_{\alpha,\beta} = \phi = \overline{\phi}_{\alpha,\beta}, \quad \underline{U}_{\alpha,\beta} = U = \overline{U}_{\alpha,\beta} \tag{9}$$

$$\overline{(X \cup Y)}_{\alpha,\beta} = \overline{X}_{\alpha,\beta} \cup \overline{Y}_{\alpha,\beta} \tag{10}$$

$$\underline{(X \cap Y)}_{\alpha,\beta} = \underline{X}_{\alpha,\beta} \cap \underline{Y}_{\alpha,\beta} \tag{11}$$

$$X \subseteq Y \Rightarrow \underline{X}_{\alpha,\beta} \subseteq \underline{Y}_{\alpha,\beta} \tag{12}$$

$$X \subseteq Y \Rightarrow \overline{X}_{\alpha,\beta} \subseteq \overline{Y}_{\alpha,\beta} \tag{13}$$

$$\underline{(X \cup Y)}_{\alpha,\beta} \supseteq \underline{X}_{\alpha,\beta} \cup \underline{Y}_{\alpha,\beta} \tag{14}$$

$$\overline{(X \cap Y)}_{\alpha,\beta} \subseteq \overline{X}_{\alpha,\beta} \cap \overline{Y}_{\alpha,\beta} \tag{15}$$

APPLICATION TO DEPENDENCY OF KNOWLEDGE

After introducing the concept of rough set on intuitionistic fuzzy approximation space, Tripathy (2006) generalized the concepts of dependency of knowledge. If $x \in A$, then the equivalence class is given by $X(\alpha, \beta)$ for all $(\alpha, \beta) \in J$. If $P \subseteq A$, then we define,

$$P(\alpha, \beta) = \bigcap_{X(\alpha,\beta) \in P(\alpha,\beta)} X(\alpha, \beta).$$

Let $I=(U,A)$ be an information system and let $P, Q \subseteq A$. Then for $(\alpha, \beta) \in J$, the set of attributes Q, (α, β)-depends on the set of attributes P in I denoted by   if $POS_{P(\alpha,\beta)}(Q(\alpha,\beta))=U$, where

$$(\alpha, \beta) - POS_P(Q) = \bigcup_{X \in Q(\alpha,\beta)} \underline{PX}_{\alpha,\beta}.$$

Sets of attributes $P, Q \subseteq A$ are (α, β)-equivalent denoted by $P \overset{(\alpha,\beta)}{=} Q$ if $P \overset{(\alpha,\beta)}{\to} Q$ and $Q \overset{(\alpha,\beta)}{\to} P$. Similarly, Sets of attributes $P, Q \subseteq A$ are (α, β)-independent, denoted by $P \overset{(\alpha,\beta)}{\neq} Q$ if neither $P \overset{(\alpha,\beta)}{\to} Q$ nor $Q \overset{(\alpha,\beta)}{\to} P$. Clearly for $(\alpha, \beta) \in J$, $(\alpha, \beta) - POS_P(Q)=U$ if and only if $P(\alpha,\beta) \subseteq Q(\alpha,\beta)$. The set of attributes Q may or may not (α, β)-depend on the set of attributes P. But there may exist, some amount of rough (α, β)-dependency. Attributes $Q(\alpha,\beta)$ -depends by a degree $k(\alpha,\beta)$; $0 \leq k(\alpha,\beta) \leq 1$ on the set of attributes P (in I), symbolically $P \overset{k(\alpha,\beta)}{\underset{(\alpha,\beta)}{\to}} Q$, where

$$k(\alpha, \beta) = \frac{Card\ [POS_{P(\alpha,\beta)}(Q(\alpha,\beta))]}{Card\ (U)}$$

and

$$(\alpha, \beta) - POS_P(Q) = \bigcup_{X \in Q(\alpha,\beta)} \underline{PX}_{\alpha,\beta}.$$

(i)   If $k(\alpha,\beta)=1$, then $Q(\alpha,\beta)$-depends totally on P.
(ii)   If $0<k(\alpha,\beta)<1$, then $Q(\alpha,\beta)$-depends roughly on P and if $k(\alpha,\beta)=0$, we say that Q and P are (α,β)-independent.

TOPOLOGICAL CHARACTERIZATION OF ROUGH SET ON IF APPROXIMATION SPACE

Similar to the types of usual rough sets and rough sets on fuzzy approximation spaces, four types of rough sets over intuitionistic fuzzy approximation space are defined. The physical interpretations of these kinds of rough sets and set theoretic operations such as union and intersection are discussed by Acharjya & Tripathy (2009).

Type 1: If $\underline{X}_{\alpha,\beta} \neq \varphi$ and $\overline{X}_{\alpha,\beta} \neq U$, then the set X is roughly $R_{\alpha,\beta}$ - definable.

Type 2: If $\underline{X}_{\alpha,\beta} = \varphi$ and $\overline{X}_{\alpha,\beta} \neq U$, then the set X is internally $R_{\alpha,\beta}$ - undefinable.

Type 3: If $\underline{X}_{\alpha,\beta} \neq \varphi$ and $\overline{X}_{\alpha,\beta} = U$, then the set X is externally $R_{\alpha,\beta}$ - undefinable.

Type 4: If $\underline{X}_{\alpha,\beta} = \varphi$ and $\overline{X}_{\alpha,\beta} = U$, then the set X is totally $R_{\alpha,\beta}$ - undefinable.

ORDERED INFORMATION SYSTEM

An information system represents all available information and knowledge about the objects under consideration. Objects are only measured by using a finite number of properties without considering any semantic relationships between the attribute values of a particular attribute (Yao, 2000). Different values of the same attribute are considered as distinct symbols without any connections, and therefore horizontal analyses to a large extent are considered on simple pattern matching. Hence, in general one uses the trivial equality relation on values of an attribute as discussed in standard rough set theory (Pawlak, 1982). However, it is observed in many real life applications that the attribute values are not exactly identical rather almost identical. It is because objects characterized by the almost same information are almost indiscernible in the view of available information as discussed in table 2. Generalized information system may be viewed as information system with added semantics. For the problem of knowledge extraction, order relations on attribute values are introduced (Yao & Ying, 2001). However, it is not appropriate in case of attribute values that are almost indiscernible.

An ordered information system (OIS) is defined as   where, I is a standard information system and $\prec_a$ is an order relation on attribute a. An ordering of values of a particular attribute a naturally induces an ordering of objects:

$$x \prec_{\{a\}} y \Leftrightarrow f_a(x) \prec_a f_a(y)$$

where, $\prec_{\{a\}}$ denotes an order relation on U induced by the attribute a. An object x is ranked ahead of object y if and only if the value of x on the attribute a is ranked ahead of the value of y on the attribute a. For example, the information system presented in Table 1 becomes an ordered information system on introducing the following ordering relations.

$\prec_{\text{Humidity}}:$ High $\prec$ Normal $\prec$ Low

$\prec_{\text{Windy}}:$ Yes $\prec$ No

$\prec_{\text{Temperature}}:$ Hot $\prec$ Mild $\prec$ Cool

For a subset of attributes $P \subseteq A$, we define:

$$x \prec_P y \Leftrightarrow f_a(x) \prec_a f_a(y) \quad \forall\, a \in P$$

$$\Leftrightarrow \bigwedge_{a \in P} f_a(x) \prec_a f_a(y)$$

$$\Leftrightarrow \bigcap_{a \in P} \prec_{\{a\}}$$

Therefore, an object *x* is ranked ahead of *y* if and only if *x* is ranked ahead of *y* according to all attributes in *P*. It is a straightforward generalization of the standard definition of equivalence relations in rough set theory (Pawlak, (1982, 1991), where the equality relation is used. Knowledge extraction based on order relations is a concrete example of applications on generalized rough set model with almost indiscernibility relations. This is because exactly ordering is not possible when the attribute values are almost identical. For $\alpha=1$, and $\beta=0$ the almost indiscernibility relation, reduces to the indiscernibility relation and thus it generalizes the Pawlak's indiscernibility relation.

AN EXAMPLE OF KNOWLEDGE EXTRACTION

For demonstration of above concepts, an information system of a group of institutions of India is taken into consideration. The basic objective of this case study is to rank the institutions based on their attribute values. Table 3 below specifies the attribute descriptions that influence the ranking of the institutions. The institutes can be judged by the outputs, which are produced. The quality of the output can be judged by the placement performance of the institute and is given highest weight with a score 385 which comes to around 24% of total weight. To produce the quality output the input should be of high quality. The major inputs for an institute are in general intellectual capital and infrastructure facilities. Accordingly the scores for intellectual capital and an infrastructure facility are fixed as 250 and 200 respectively that weight 15% and 12% of total weight. The student placed in the company shall serve the company up to their expectation and it leads to recruiter's satisfaction and is given with a score of 200 which comes around 12%. At the same time student's satisfaction and extra curricular activities plays a vital role for prospective students is given with a score 60 and 80 respectively of weight 4% and 6% of the total weight. Many other factors that do not have impact on ranking the institutions have not considered. It is obvious that, institution that excel in all attributes being an ideal case for securing highest rank. But such type of cases is rare in practice.

The intuitionistic fuzzy proximity relation $R(x_i,x_j)$ which identifies the almost indiscernibility among the institutions x_i and x_j is defined as below:

$$\mu_R(x_i,x_j) = 1 - \frac{|V_{x_i} - V_{x_j}|}{\text{Max range}}$$

and

$$\nu_R(x_i, x_j) = \frac{|V_{x_i} - V_{x_j}|}{2(V_{x_i} + V_{x_j})}$$

The membership and non-membership relations have been adjusted such that the sum of their values should lie in [0, 1] and also must be symmetric. The first requirement necessitates a major of 2 in the denominators of the non-membership relations.

The institute with more intellectual capital, having high infrastructure, better placement opportunities for students in high profile organizations and higher student satisfaction measure is an ideal case

Table 3. Attribute descriptions table

Attribute	Notation	Possible Range	Attribute	Notation	Possible Range
Intellectual capital (IC)	a_1	[1 – 250]	Recruiters satisfaction score (RS)	a_4	[1 – 200]
Infrastructure facility (IF)	a_2	[1 – 200]	Students satisfaction score (SS)	a_5	[1 – 60]
Placement performance (PP)	a_3	[1 – 385]	Extra curricular activities (EC)	a_6	[1 – 80]

for highest rank. But it may not be possible for an institute to excel in all the above fields. However, some of the parameters considered above may have higher influence on the rank than other parameters. The importance of parameters depends upon the control parameters and so varies along with the values of these parameters. In fact, it has been observed that if we increase the values of α and decrease the value of β more and more parameters become indispensable. In view of the length of the paper and to make our analysis simple, a small universe of 10 institutions and the information pertaining to them are presented in the Table 4. The identities of the institutions are kept confidential as they do not affect our analysis. The data collected is considered to be the representative figure and tabulated below in Table 4. Intuitionistic fuzzy proximity relations R_i; $i=1, 2, 3,\ldots,6$ corresponding to attributes IC, IF, PP, RS, SS and EC are given in Table 5, Table 6, Table 7, Table 8, Table 9 and Table 10 respectively.

On considering the degree of dependency values $\alpha \geq 0.92$, $\beta < 0.08$ for membership and non-membership values respectively, it is observed from Table 5 that $\mu_{R_1}(x_1, x_1) = 1$, $\nu_{R_1}(x_1, x_1) = 0$;

$$\mu_{R_1}(x_1, x_2) = 0.992, \nu_{R_1}(x_1, x_2) = 0.002$$

and

$$\mu_{R_1}(x_1, x_3) = 0.989, \nu_{R_1}(x_1, x_3) = 0.003 .$$

Table 4. Small universe of information system

Institutions	IC	IF	PP	RS	SS	ECA
x_1	229	151	304	169	56	49
x_2	227	143	298	169	53	79
x_3	226	145	266	167	54	63
x_4	191	110	316	163	41	64
x_5	179	117	247	160	53	53
x_6	148	102	180	147	43	27
x_7	131	78	138	145	46	25
x_8	124	61	130	142	38	9
x_9	88	58	121	143	40	34
x_{10}	92	48	100	137	32	2

Table 5. Intuitionistic fuzzy proximity relation for attribute IC

R_1	x_1	x_2	x_3	x_4	x_5	x_6	x_7	x_8	x_9	x_{10}
x_1	1, 0	0.992, 0.002	0.989, 0.003	0.848, 0.045	0.802, 0.061	0.676, 0.108	0.61, 0.135	0.581, 0.149	0.437, 0.222	0.451, 0.214
x_2	0.992, 0.002	1, 0	0.997, 0.001	0.856, 0.043	0.81, 0.058	0.684, 0.106	0.618, 0.133	0.589, 0.147	0.445, 0.22	0.46, 0.212
x_3	0.989, 0.003	0.997, 0.001	1, 0	0.859, 0.042	0.813, 0.058	0.686, 0.105	0.621, 0.132	0.591, 0.146	0.448, 0.219	0.462, 0.211
x_4	0.848, 0.045	0.856, 0.043	0.859, 0.042	1, 0	0.954, 0.016	0.827, 0.064	0.762, 0.092	0.732, 0.106	0.589, 0.184	0.603, 0.175
x_5	0.802, 0.061	0.81, 0.058	0.813, 0.058	0.954, 0.016	1, 0	0.873, 0.048	0.808, 0.077	0.778, 0.091	0.635, 0.17	0.649, 0.162
x_6	0.676, 0.108	0.684, 0.106	0.686, 0.105	0.827, 0.064	0.873, 0.048	1, 0	0.935, 0.029	0.905, 0.044	0.762, 0.126	0.776, 0.117
x_7	0.61, 0.135	0.618, 0.133	0.621, 0.132	0.762, 0.092	0.808, 0.077	0.935, 0.029	1, 0	0.97, 0.014	0.827, 0.098	0.841, 0.089
x_8	0.581, 0.149	0.589, 0.147	0.591, 0.146	0.732, 0.106	0.778, 0.091	0.905, 0.044	0.97, 0.014	1, 0	0.857, 0.084	0.871, 0.075
x_9	0.437, 0.222	0.445, 0.22	0.448, 0.219	0.589, 0.184	0.635, 0.17	0.762, 0.126	0.827, 0.098	0.857, 0.084	1, 0	0.986, 0.01
x_{10}	0.451, 0.214	0.46, 0.212	0.462, 0.211	0.603, 0.175	0.649, 0.162	0.776, 0.117	0.841, 0.089	0.871, 0.075	0.986, 0.01	1, 0

Table 6. Intuitionistic fuzzy proximity relation for attribute IF

R_2	x_1	x_2	x_3	x_4	x_5	x_6	x_7	x_8	x_9	x_{10}
x_1	1, 0	0.956, 0.015	0.966, 0.011	0.792, 0.08	0.827, 0.065	0.751, 0.098	0.632, 0.161	0.549, 0.212	0.532, 0.224	0.485, 0.258
x_2	0.956, 0.015	1, 0	0.99, 0.004	0.836, 0.065	0.871, 0.05	0.795, 0.084	0.676, 0.147	0.593, 0.2	0.576, 0.212	0.529, 0.246
x_3	0.966, 0.011	0.99, 0.004	1, 0	0.825, 0.069	0.86, 0.054	0.785, 0.087	0.666, 0.15	0.583, 0.203	0.565, 0.215	0.519, 0.249
x_4	0.792, 0.08	0.836, 0.065	0.825, 0.069	1, 0	0.965, 0.015	0.96, 0.019	0.84, 0.085	0.757, 0.142	0.74, 0.155	0.693, 0.194
x_5	0.827, 0.065	0.871, 0.05	0.86, 0.054	0.965, 0.015	1, 0	0.925, 0.034	0.806, 0.1	0.723, 0.156	0.705, 0.169	0.659, 0.207
x_6	0.751, 0.098	0.795, 0.084	0.785, 0.087	0.96, 0.019	0.925, 0.034	1, 0	0.881, 0.066	0.798, 0.124	0.78, 0.138	0.734, 0.177
x_7	0.632, 0.161	0.676, 0.147	0.666, 0.15	0.84, 0.085	0.806, 0.1	0.881, 0.066	1, 0	0.917, 0.06	0.9, 0.074	0.853, 0.116
x_8	0.549, 0.212	0.593, 0.2	0.583, 0.203	0.757, 0.142	0.723, 0.156	0.798, 0.124	0.917, 0.06	1, 0	0.983, 0.015	0.936, 0.058
x_9	0.532, 0.224	0.576, 0.212	0.565, 0.215	0.74, 0.155	0.705, 0.169	0.78, 0.138	0.9, 0.074	0.983, 0.015	1, 0	0.954, 0.044
x_{10}	0.485, 0.258	0.529, 0.246	0.519, 0.249	0.693, 0.194	0.659, 0.207	0.734, 0.177	0.853, 0.116	0.936, 0.058	0.954, 0.044	1, 0

Table 7. Intuitionistic fuzzy proximity relation for attribute PP

R_3	x_1	x_2	x_3	x_4	x_5	x_6	x_7	x_8	x_9	x_{10}
x_1	1, 0	0.987, 0.004	0.904, 0.033	0.967, 0.01	0.853, 0.052	0.678, 0.128	0.57, 0.187	0.55, 0.2	0.525, 0.215	0.472, 0.252
x_2	0.987, 0.004	1, 0	0.917, 0.028	0.954, 0.015	0.866, 0.047	0.691, 0.124	0.583, 0.184	0.563, 0.196	0.539, 0.212	0.485, 0.249
x_3	0.904, 0.033	0.917, 0.028	1, 0	0.87, 0.043	0.949, 0.019	0.774, 0.097	0.666, 0.159	0.646, 0.172	0.622, 0.188	0.568, 0.227
x_4	0.967, 0.01	0.954, 0.015	0.87, 0.043	1, 0	0.819, 0.062	0.645, 0.138	0.537, 0.196	0.517, 0.208	0.492, 0.224	0.439, 0.259
x_5	0.853, 0.052	0.866, 0.047	0.949, 0.019	0.819, 0.062	1, 0	0.825, 0.079	0.717, 0.141	0.697, 0.154	0.673, 0.171	0.619, 0.211
x_6	0.678, 0.128	0.691, 0.124	0.774, 0.097	0.645, 0.138	0.825, 0.079	1, 0	0.892, 0.065	0.872, 0.079	0.847, 0.098	0.794, 0.142
x_7	0.57, 0.187	0.583, 0.184	0.666, 0.159	0.537, 0.196	0.717, 0.141	0.892, 0.065	1, 0	0.98, 0.014	0.955, 0.033	0.902, 0.79
x_8	0.55, 0.2	0.563, 0.196	0.646, 0.172	0.517, 0.208	0.697, 0.154	0.872, 0.079	0.98, 0.014	1, 0	0.975, 0.019	0.922, 0.065
x_9	0.525, 0.215	0.539, 0.212	0.622, 0.188	0.492, 0.224	0.673, 0.171	0.847, 0.098	0.955, 0.033	0.975, 0.019	1, 0	0.947, 0.046
x_{10}	0.472, 0.252	0.485, 0.249	0.568, 0.227	0.439, 0.259	0.619, 0.211	0.794, 0.142	0.902, 0.79	0.922, 0.065	0.947, 0.046	1, 0

Table 8. Intuitionistic fuzzy proximity relation for attribute RS

R_4	x_1	x_2	x_3	x_4	x_5	x_6	x_7	x_8	x_9	x_{10}
x_1	1, 0	1, 0	0.99, 0.003	0.97, 0.009	0.955, 0.14	0.89, 0.035	0.88, 0.038	0.865, 0.043	0.87, 0.042	0.84, 0.52
x_2	1, 0	1, 0	0.99, 0.003	0.97, 0.009	0.955, 0.14	0.89, 0.035	0.88, 0.038	0.865, 0.043	0.87, 0.042	0.84, 0.52
x_3	0.99, 0.003	0.99, 0.003	1, 0	0.98, 0.006	0.965, 0.11	0.9, 0.032	0.89, 0.035	0.875, 0.04	0.88, 0.039	0.85, 0.049
x_4	0.97, 0.009	0.97, 0.009	0.98, 0.006	1, 0	0.985, 0.005	0.92, 0.026	0.91, 0.029	0.895, 0.034	0.9, 0.033	0.87, 0.043
x_5	0.955, 0.14	0.955, 0.14	0.965, 0.11	0.985, 0.005	1, 0	0.935, 0.021	0.925, 0.025	0.91, 0.03	0.915, 0.028	0.885, 0.039
x_6	0.89, 0.035	0.89, 0.035	0.9, 0.032	0.92, 0.026	0.935, 0.021	1, 0	0.99, 0.003	0.975, 0.009	0.98, 0.007	0.95, 0.018
x_7	0.88, 0.038	0.88, 0.038	0.89, 0.035	0.91, 0.029	0.925, 0.025	0.99, 0.003	1, 0	0.985, 0.005	0.99, 0.003	0.96, 0.014
x_8	0.88, 0.038	0.865, 0.043	0.875, 0.04	0.895, 0.034	0.91, 0.03	0.975, 0.009	0.985, 0.005	1, 0	0.995, 0.002	0.975, 0.009
x_9	0.87, 0.042	0.87, 0.042	0.88, 0.039	0.9, 0.033	0.915, 0.028	0.99, 0.003	0.99, 0.003	0.995, 0.002	1, 0	0.97, 0.011
x_{10}	0.84, 0.52	0.84, 0.52	0.85, 0.049	0.87, 0.043	0.885, 0.039	0.96, 0.014	0.96, 0.014	0.975, 0.009	0.97, 0.011	1, 0

Table 9. Intuitionistic fuzzy proximity relation for attribute SS

R_5	x_1	x_2	x_3	x_4	x_5	x_6	x_7	x_8	x_9	x_{10}
x_1	1, 0	0.95, 0.014	0.967, 0.009	0.75, 0.077	0.95, 0.014	0.783, 0.066	0.833, 0.049	0.7, 0.096	0.733, 0.083	0.6, 0.136
x_2	0.95, 0.014	1, 0	0.983, 0.005	0.8, 0.064	1, 0	0.833, 0.52	0.883, 0.035	0.75, 0.082	0.783, 0.07	0.65, 0.124
x_3	0.967, 0.009	0.983, 0.005	1, 0	0.783, 0.068	0.983, 0.005	0.817, 0.057	0.867, 0.04	0.733, 0.087	0.767, 0.074	0.633, 0.128
x_4	0.75, 0.077	0.8, 0.064	0.783, 0.068	1, 0	0.8, 0.064	0.967, 0.012	0.917, 0.029	0.95, 0.019	0.983, 0.006	0.85, 0.062
x_5	0.95, 0.014	1, 0	0.983, 0.005	0.8, 0.064	1, 0	0.833, 0.052	0.883, 0.035	0.75, 0.082	0.783, 0.07	0.65, 0.124
x_6	0.783, 0.066	0.833, 0.52	0.817, 0.057	0.967, 0.012	0.833, 0.052	1, 0	0.95, 0.017	0.917, 0.031	0.95, 0.18	0.817, 0.073
x_7	0.833, 0.049	0.883, 0.035	0.867, 0.04	0.917, 0.029	0.883, 0.035	0.95, 0.017	1, 0	0.867, 0.048	0.9, 0.035	0.767, 0.09
x_8	0.7, 0.096	0.75, 0.082	0.733, 0.087	0.95, 0.019	0.75, 0.082	0.917, 0.031	0.867, 0.048	1, 0	0.967, 0.013	0.9, 0.043
x_9	0.733, 0.083	0.783, 0.07	0.767, 0.074	0.983, 0.006	0.783, 0.07	0.95, 0.18	0.9, 0.035	0.967, 0.013	1, 0	0.867, 0.056
x_{10}	0.6, 0.136	0.65, 0.124	0.633, 0.128	0.85, 0.062	0.65, 0.124	0.817, 0.073	0.767, 0.09	0.9, 0.043	0.867, 0.056	1, 0

Table 10. Intuitionistic fuzzy proximity relation for attribute EC

R_6	x_1	x_2	x_3	x_4	x_5	x_6	x_7	x_8	x_9	x_{10}
x_1	1, 0	0.631, 0.115	0.831, 0.06	0.821, 0.063	0.953, 0.018	0.726, 0.143	0.692, 0.167	0.499, 0.342	0.812, 0.09	0.407, 0.462
x_2	0.631, 0.115	1, 0	0.8, 0.056	0.81, 0.053	0.679, 0.097	0.357, 0.242	0.323, 0.262	0.13, 0.395	0.443, 0.197	0.039, 0.476
x_3	0.831, 0.06	0.8, 0.056	1, 0	0.99, 0.003	0.879, 0.042	0.557, 0.196	0.523, 0.218	0.33, 0.372	0.643, 0.147	0.239, 0.47
x_4	0.821, 0.063	0.81, 0.053	0.99, 0.003	1, 0	0.869, 0.045	0.547, 0.199	0.513, 0.221	0.32, 0.373	0.633, 0.15	0.229, 0.47
x_5	0.953, 0.018	0.679, 0.097	0.879, 0.042	0.869, 0.045	1, 0	0.679, 0.16	0.644, 0.183	0.452, 0.352	0.764, 0.108	0.36, 0.465
x_6	0.726, 0.143	0.357, 0.242	0.557, 0.196	0.547, 0.199	0.679, 0.16	1, 0	0.966, 0.026	0.773, 0.248	0.914, 0.056	0.681, 0.434
x_7	0.692, 0.167	0.323, 0.262	0.523, 0.218	0.513, 0.221	0.644, 0.183	0.966, 0.026	1, 0	0.807, 0.227	0.88, 0.081	0.716, 0.427
x_8	0.499, 0.342	0.13, 0.395	0.33, 0.372	0.32, 0.373	0.452, 0.352	0.773, 0.248	0.807, 0.227	1, 0	0.687, 0.287	0.909, 0.327
x_9	0.812, 0.09	0.443, 0.197	0.643, 0.147	0.633, 0.15	0.764, 0.108	0.914, 0.056	0.88, 0.081	0.687, 0.287	1, 0	0.596, 0.446
x_{10}	0.407, 0.462	0.039, 0.476	0.239, 0.47	0.229, 0.47	0.36, 0.465	0.681, 0.434	0.716, 0.427	0.909, 0.327	0.596, 0.446	1, 0

Thus, the institutions x_1, x_2, x_3 are (α,β)-identical. Similarly, x_4, x_5 are (α,β)-identical; x_6, x_7, x_8 are (α,β)-identical and x_9, x_{10} is (α,β)-identical. Therefore, we get

$$U \, / \, R_1^{\alpha,\beta} = \{\{x_1,x_2,x_3\},\{x_4,x_5\},\{x_6,x_7,x_8\},\{x_9,x_{10}\}\}$$

It indicates that, the values of the attribute intellectual capital (IC) are classified into four categories namely very high, high, moderate, low and hence can be ordered. Similarly, the different equivalence classes obtained from Table 6, 7, 8, 9 and 10 corresponding to the attributes IF, PP, RS, SS, and EC are given below.

$$U \, / \, R_2^{\alpha,\beta} = \{\{x_1,x_2,x_3\},\{x_4,x_5,x_6\},\{x_7\},\{x_8,x_9,x_{10}\}\}$$

$$U \, / \, R_3^{\alpha,\beta} = \{\{x_1,x_2,x_4\},\{x_3,x_5\},\{x_6\},\{x_7,x_8,x_9,x_{10}\}\}$$

$$U \, / \, R_4^{\alpha,\beta} = \{\{x_1,x_2,x_3,x_4,x_5,x_6,x_7,x_8,x_9,x_{10}\}\}$$

$$U \, / \, R_5^{\alpha,\beta} = \{\{x_1,x_2,x_3,x_5\},\{x_4,x_6,x_7,x_8,x_9\},\{x_{10}\}\}$$

$$U \, / \, R_6^{\alpha,\beta} = \{\{x_1,x_5\},\{x_2\},\{x_3,x_4\},\{x_6,x_7\},\{x_8\},\{x_9\},\{x_{10}\}\}$$

From the above analysis, it is clear that the attribute EC classify the universe into seven categories. Let it be poor, low, average, good, very good, excellent, and outstanding and hence can be ordered. Similarly, the attributes IF, and PP classify the universe into four categories. Let it be low, moderate, high and very high and hence can be ordered. The attribute SS classify the universe into three categories namely good, very good, and excellent. Since the equivalence class $U \, / \, R_4^{\alpha,\beta}$ contains only one category, the universe is (α,β) -indiscernible according to the attribute RS and hence do not require any ordering while extracting knowledge from the information system. Therefore, the ordered information system of the small universe Table 4 is given in Table 11.

$\prec_{\text{IC}}$: Very high $\prec$ High $\prec$ Moderate $\prec$ Low

$\prec_{\text{IF}}$: Very high $\prec$ High $\prec$ Moderate $\prec$ Low

$\prec_{\text{PP}}$: Very high $\prec$ High $\prec$ Moderate $\prec$ Low

$\prec_{\text{SS}}$: Excellent $\prec$ Very good $\prec$ Good

$\prec_{\text{EC}}$: Outstanding $\prec$ Excellent $\prec$ Very good $\prec$ Good $\prec$ Average $\prec$ Low $\prec$ Poor

Table 11. Ordered information table of the small universe

Institutions	IC	IF	PP	SS	EC
x_1	Very high	Very high	Very high	Excellent	Very good
x_2	Very high	Very high	Very high	Excellent	Outstanding.
x_3	Very high	Very high	High	Excellent	Excellent
x_4	High	High	Very high	Very good	Excellent
x_5	High	High	High	Excellent	Very good
x_6	Moderate	High	Moderate	Very good	Average
x_7	Moderate	Moderate	Low	Very good	Average
x_8	Moderate	Low	Low	Very good	Low
x_9	Low	Low	Low	Very good	Good
x_{10}	Low	Low	Low	Good	Poor

Now, in order to rank the institutions we assign weights to the attribute values. In order to compute the rank of the institutions x_k; $k = 1, 2, \ldots, 10$ we add the weights of the attribute values and rank them according to the total sum obtained from highest to lowest. However, it is identified that in some cases the total sum remains same for certain institutions. It indicates that these institutions cannot be distinguished from one another according to the available attributes and attribute values. In such cases, using further analysis techniques actual ranking of the institutes can also be found out. On considering the weights of outstanding, excellent, (very high, very good), (high, good), (moderate, average), low and poor as 7, 6, 5, 4, 3, 2 and 1 respectively the ordered information system for ranking the institutions is given in Table 12. From the computation given in Table 12 shows that the institution x_2 belongs to the first rank whereas x_1 and x_3 belongs to third rank. Similarly, the ranks of the other institutions can also be obtained from the Table 12.

Table 12. Ranking of institutions

Institutions	IC	IF	PP	SS	EC	Total Sum	Rank
x_1	Very high (5)	Very high (5)	Very high (5)	Excellent (6)	Very good (5)	26	2
x_2	Very high (5)	Very high (5)	Very high (5)	Excellent (6)	Outstanding (7)	28	1
x_3	Very high (5)	Very high (5)	High (4)	Excellent (6)	Excellent (6)	26	2
x_4	High (4)	High (4)	Very high (5)	Very good (5)	Excellent (6)	24	3
x_5	High (4)	High (4)	High (4)	Excellent (6)	Very good (5)	23	4
x_6	Moderate (3)	High (4)	Moderate (3)	Very good (5)	Average (3)	18	5
x_7	Moderate (3)	Moderate (3)	Low (2)	Very good (5)	Average (3)	16	6
x_8	Moderate (3)	Low (2)	Low (2)	Very good (5)	Low (2)	14	8
x_9	Low (2)	Low (2)	Low (2)	Very good (5)	Good (4)	15	7
x_{10}	Low (2)	Low (2)	Low (2)	Good (4)	Poor (1)	11	9

FUTURE RESEARCH DIRECTIONS

This chapter extends the concept of rough set to rough set on fuzzy approximation spaces and rough set on intuitionistic fuzzy approximation spaces. A real life application is presented to show the viability of the extended concept. Future work will be carried out in the direction of multigranulation and its applications. The study of topological properties, approximation of classification, rough equality and its applications is a major concern. These results and applications are to be addressed and studied.

CONCLUSION

This Chapter extends the concepts of rough set to rough set on fuzzy approximation spaces. Further rough set on fuzzy approximation space is extended to rough set on intuitionistic fuzzy approximation space. Ordering of objects is a fundamental issue in decision making and plays a vital role in the design of intelligent information systems. Here, we have integrated ordering rules and rough set on intuitionistic fuzzy approximation spaces. The main objective of integration is to expand the domain of application of rough set on intuitionistic fuzzy approximation space. We have taken a real life example of ranking 10 institutions according to different attributes. We have shown how analysis can be performed by taking rough set on intuitionistic fuzzy approximation space and ordering of objects as a model for extraction of knowledge from information system. The concepts developed are very much useful for their application in knowledge extraction and design of knowledge bases.

REFERENCES

Acharjya, D. P. (2009). Comparative study of rough sets on fuzzy approximation spaces and intuitionistic fuzzy approximation spaces. *International Journal of Computational and Applied Mathematics*, *4*(2), 95–106.

Acharjya, D. P., & Mary, A. G. (2014). Privacy Preservation in Information System. In B. Tripathy & D. Acharjya (Eds.), *Advances in Secure Computing, Internet Services, and Applications* (pp. 49–72). Hershey, PA: IGI Global; doi:10.4018/978-1-4666-4940-8.ch003

Acharjya, D. P., & Tripathy, B. K. (2008). Rough sets on fuzzy approximation spaces and applications to distributed knowledge systems. *International Journal of Artificial Intelligence and Soft Computing*, *1*(1), 1–14. doi:10.1504/IJAISC.2008.021260

Acharjya, D. P., & Tripathy, B. K. (2009). Rough sets on intuitionistic fuzzy approximation spaces and knowledge representation. *International Journal of Artificial Intelligence and Computational Research*, *1*(1), 29–36.

Atanasov, K. T. (1986). Intuitionistic Fuzzy Sets. *Fuzzy Sets and Systems*, *20*(1), 87–96. doi:10.1016/S0165-0114(86)80034-3

Dubosis, D., & Prade, H. (1980). *Fuzzy sets and systems: Theory and applications*. New York: Academic Press.

Dubosis, D., & Prade, H. (1987). Twofold fuzzy sets and rough sets-some issues in knowledge representation. *Fuzzy Sets and Systems*, *23*(1), 3–18. doi:10.1016/0165-0114(87)90096-0

Fayaad, U. M. (1996). Advances in knowledge discovery and data mining. In U. M. Fayaad, G. Piatetsky-Shapiro, P. Smyth, & R. Uthurusamy (Eds.), *American Association for Artificial Intelligence* (pp. 1–57). California: *(AAAI) press.*

Goguen, J. A. (1967). L–fuzzy sets. *Journal of Mathematical Analysis and Applications*, *18*(1), 145–174. doi:10.1016/0022-247X(67)90189-8

Li, D. Y., & Hu, Bao Qing (2007). A kind of dynamic rough sets. *Proceedings of the Fourth International Conference on Fuzzy Systems and Knowledge Discovery (FSKD)* (pp. 79-85). doi:10.1109/FSKD.2007.51

Pawlak, Z. (1981). Information systems: Theoretical foundations. *Information Systems*, *6*(3), 205–218. doi:10.1016/0306-4379(81)90023-5

Pawlak, Z. (1982). Rough sets. *International Journal of Computer Information Science*, *11*(5), 341–356. doi:10.1007/BF01001956

Pawlak, Z. (1991). *Rough sets: Theoretical Aspects of Reasoning about Data*. The Netherlands: Kluwer Academic Publishers. doi:10.1007/978-94-011-3534-4

Pawlak, Z., & Skowron, A. (2007a). Rudiments of rough sets. *Information Sciences*, *177*(1), 3–27. doi:10.1016/j.ins.2006.06.003

Pawlak, Z., & Skowron, A. (2007b). Rough sets: Some extensions. *Information Sciences*, *177*(1), 28–40. doi:10.1016/j.ins.2006.06.006

Pawlak, Z., & Skowron, A. (2007c). Rough sets and Boolean reasoning. *Information Sciences*, *177*(1), 41–73. doi:10.1016/j.ins.2006.06.007

Rocha, L. M. (2001). TalkMine: A soft computing approach to adaptive knowledge recommendation. In Loia, V. and Sessa, S. (Eds.), Soft Computing Agents: New Trends for Designing Autonomous Systems, Series on Studies in Fuzziness and Soft Computing (pp. 89-116). New York: Springer. doi:10.1007/978-3-7908-1815-4_4

Slowinski, R., & Vanderpooten, D. (2000). A generalized definition of rough approximations based on similarity. *IEEE Transactions on Knowledge and Data Engineering*, *12*(2), 331–336. doi:10.1109/69.842271

Tripathy, B. K. (2006). Rough sets on intuitionistic fuzzy approximation spaces. *Proceedings of the 3rd International IEEE Conference on Intelligent Systems (IS06)* (pp.776-779). London: IEEE Xplore. doi:10.1109/IS.2006.348519

Tripathy, B. K., & Acharjya, D. P. (2010). Knowledge mining using ordering rules and rough sets on fuzzy approximation spaces. *International Journal of Advances in Science and Technology*, *1*(3), 41–50.

Tripathy, B. K., & Acharjya, D. P. (2011). Association rule granulation using rough sets on intuitionistic fuzzy approximation spaces and granular computing. *Annals Computer Science Series*, *9*(1), 125–144.

Tripathy, B. K., Acharjya, D. P., & Cynthya, V. (2011). A framework for intelligent medical diagnosis using rough set with formal concept analysis. *International Journal of Artificial Intelligence & Applications*, 2(2), 45–66. doi:10.5121/ijaia.2011.2204

Yao, Y. Y. (2000). Information tables with neighborhood semantics. In B. V. Dasarathy (Ed.), Data Mining and Knowledge Discovery: Theory, Tools, and Technology (Vol. 2, pp. 108-116). Bellingham, Washington: Society for Optical Engineering.

Yao, Y. Y., & Sai, Ying. (2001). Mining ordering rules using rough set theory. *Bulletin of International Rough Set Society*, 5, 99–106.

Zadeh, L. A. (1965). Fuzzy sets. *Information and Control*, 8(3), 338–353. doi:10.1016/S0019-9958(65)90241-X

Zhu, W., & Wang, F. Y. (2007). On three types of covering rough sets. *IEEE Transactions on Knowledge and Data Engineering*, 19(8), 1131–1144. doi:10.1109/TKDE.2007.1044

KEY TERMS AND DEFINITIONS

Almost Indiscernibility: Attribute values that are not exactly identical but almost identical are termed as almost indiscernible.

Data Reduction: Therefore, attribute reduction becomes an important aspect for handling such voluminous database by eliminating superfluous data.

Fuzzy Proximity Relation: A fuzzy relation which is fuzzy reflexive and fuzzy symmetric is termed as fuzzy proximity relation.

Information System: An information system contains a finite set of objects typically represented by their values on a finite set of attributes.

Intuitionistic Fuzzy Proximity Relation: An intuitionistic fuzzy relation which is intuitionistic fuzzy reflexive and intuitionistic fuzzy symmetric is termed as fuzzy proximity relation.

Knowledge: Any set of all indiscernible objects is called an elementary concept, and form a basic granule (atom) of knowledge about the universe.

Knowledge Discovery in Databases: The nontrivial process of identifying valid, novel, potentially useful, and ultimately understandable patterns in data is known as knowledge discovery in databases.

Knowledge Extraction: Knowledge extraction specifies the collection of the right information at the right level and utilize for the suitable purposes.

Order Information System: An order information system is an information system in which all attribute values are ordered with some order relation.

Rough Set: A model, proposed by Pawlak to capture imprecision in data through boundary approach.

Rough Set on Fuzzy Approximation Space: A model that capture almost indiscernibility in data using fuzzy proximity relation through boundary approach.

Rough Set on Intuitionistic Fuzzy Approximation Space: A model that capture almost indiscernibility in data using intuitionistic fuzzy proximity relation through boundary approach.

Topological Characterization: The properties of sets taken as a whole without considering the properties of individual objects.

Chapter 10
Data Mining Techniques on Earthquake Data:
Recent Data Mining Approaches

Negar Sadat Soleimani Zakeri
University of Tabriz, Iran

Saeid Pashazadeh
University of Tabriz, Iran

ABSTRACT

Active faults are sources of earthquakes and one of them is north fault of Tabriz in the northwest of Iran. The activation of faults can harm humans' life and constructions. The analysis of the seismic data in active regions can be helpful in dealing with earthquake hazards and devising prevention strategies. In this chapter, structure of earthquake events along with application of various intelligent data mining algorithms for earthquake prediction are studied. Main focus is on categorizing the seismic data of local regions according to the events' location using clustering algorithms for classification and then using intelligent artificial neural network for cluster prediction. As a result, the target data were clustered to six groups and proposed model with 10 fold cross validation yielded accuracy of 98.3%. Also, as a case study, the tectonic stress on concentration zones of Tabriz fault has been identified and five features of the events were used. Finally, the most important points have been proposed for evaluation of the nonlinear model predictions as future directions.

INTRODUCTION

Active faults are counted as seismological active regions. Many researchers are interested to study these faults and destructive historical earthquakes (Zhang, Zhang, Yang, & Su, 2014). Occurrence of earthquakes on one hand and daily development of urban regions and critical facilities in seismic zones on the other hand, are sufficient factors for showing importance of reviewing seismo-tectonic analysis methods for predicting earthquake magnitude and its future occurrence time (Ennis, 2010), (Elmi, Ganjpour Sales, Tabrizi, Soleimanpour, & Mohseni, 2013). Earthquake is sudden motion of the ground caused by re-

DOI: 10.4018/978-1-4666-8513-0.ch010

leasing energy of stored stress in the fault (Peng, Yang, Zheng, Xu, & Jiang, 2014). After stop of fault's motion, its waves continue to move along the ground. Many important and populous cities are placed in active faults' zones. Significant earthquakes have been reported in the recent centuries, while geodesy studies show a significant amount of deformation on both slip sides of fault that emphasize risks of new activities of fault (Orihara, Kamogawa, & Nagao, 2014). Therefore, the analysis of earthquake data is so important (Peng et al., 2014). The kinesiology of the earthquake and its computer modeling is one of the most challenging issues in modern geophysics (Ruiz et al., 2014). After large earthquakes, seismologists are able to express many phenomena associated with earthquake. They will be able to provide successful predictions using information of events and their occurrence order, but it is still difficult to predict earthquakes because of its high complex structure (Dologlou, 2008). Seismic data mining by computer modeling, computer simulation and artificial intelligence techniques can be used to study this phenomenon. Automatic learning techniques can be used to extract relationships between different phenomena and earthquakes (Uyeda, 2013). They can be used to obtain more accurate forecasting based on automated reasoning algorithms (Peng et al., 2014). Different countries like China and Japan which are located in earthquake-prone regions of the world have paid much attention to earthquake predicting sites for dealing with earthquake disasters (Kako, Arbon, & Mitani, 2014; Y. Wang, Li, Chen, & Zou, 2014).

In following part of this chapter basic and well known analyzing methods of seismic data are introduced. In related works, brief review classification and different methods that are used for analysis of the earthquake data are investigated. Then proposed method is presented. A short history behind the earthquakes, the types of data which are used for processing the occurrence of earthquake, databases of a case study that the valid seismic data can be taken from is presented. Also, preprocessing techniques such as normalization the data, data mining methods such as k-means clustering algorithm as a preprocessing step for categorizing the data that can be used for modeling the earthquake function based on related parameters and features to predict the magnitude of earthquake in terms of time and location by ANNs are discussed in section of proposed approach. In section results and discussion section, results of study is presented and discussed. In future research direction section some notes those are important and critical and must be considered in study of seismic data is discussed and finally conclusion is presented.

PRELIMINARY CONCEPTS AND BASIC METHODS

According to literature investigation, learning algorithms or data mining methods and in some cases combinations of these two methods are used as high-level classification methods in studies of earthquake data in the seismic regions. Each method has its own subdivisions. The learning algorithms are also known as machine learning algorithms in computer science. Most common methods that are used for this issue are ANNs, fuzzy systems and SVMs. Different types of neural networks have been used in different literature. Recurrent neural networks, PNNs, feed forward neural networks, SVMs and fuzzy based algorithms were used for predicting time and location of earthquakes. Collected data from various parts of the world and different extracted features such as sequence number, occurrence time are used by these methods while existing noises were removed along the preprocessing steps.

Clustering is the most important category of methods with different types of algorithms for clustering time series which have sequential nature or by using agglomerative hierarchical clustering algorithm to extract a temporal pattern for predicting an event. Most of the methods took the advantage of two universal laws including the Gutenberg-Richter (G-R) and the Omori to demonstrate the increasing effect of each earthquake on the future earthquakes (Console, Murru, & Catalli, 2006). Different unsupervised clustering algorithms exists which are employed to perform a visual data mining. Another automatic classification method of the seismic phenomenon is self-organized feature map (SOM) (Roy, Matos, & Marfurt, 2010).

Non-linear and multi-dimensional scaling and analysis of the earthquake clustering is another combinational model that introduced in 2003 and 2005 (Dzwinel et al., 2003, 2005). In this study, the results of both data space and feature space clustering were used to make a decision about fault analysis response. Combination of data mining and fuzzy logics (Preethi & Santhi, 2011), the combination of k-means and Gaussian mixture as a pattern recognition method (Kuyuk, Yildirim, Dogan, & G. Horasan, 2012), multivariate analysis (Dzwinel, Kaneko, Boryczko, & Ben-Zion, 2003), extracting association patterns in multi-sequence earthquake data (Miura & Okada, 2012), designing a decision support system (Somodevilla et al., 2012), the K-nearest neighbor graph (KNN) method (Leon & Atanasiu, 2006) are some other studies that carried out in this era. It shows an active trend for the earthquake predictions in terms of magnitude value and time of occurrence.

There are different factors that cause occurrence of the earthquake. In the normal case, the crustal plates of the earth move alongside each other in different directions. During this movement some crust plates may lock together and energy accumulates over time. After specific threshold this energy is released and makes earthquakes (Adeli & Panakkat, 2008). The other influencing factors are temperature of the earth, temperature of the water, Radon gas concentration in oil and etc. (Niksarlioglu & Kulahci, 2013). The Gutenberg-Richter (G-R) law is one of the important universal relations that was applied almost in all the researchers in this field and shows the magnitude distribution (Console, Murru, &Catalli, 2006). This relation is also called inverse power law and represents the relation between the magnitude and frequency of earthquake. This law is defined by equation $\log_{10}^{N} = a - bM$; where a and b are the seismicity constants and N is the number of the earthquakes with magnitude equal or greater than M (Panakkat & Adeli, 2007).

RELATED WORKS

Northwest of Iran, as a part of Alp-Himalia ring with the development of complex tectonic history, active faults, and destructive historical earthquakes, is one of the seismically active regions of the Iranian Plateau (Ardalan, Hajiuni, & Zare, 2013). In the Northwest of Iran, the shear motions which led to the creation of strike-slip faults make the Tabriz fault one of the most important region of interest. Beyond this, Tabriz is one of the most important and populous cities of Iran and about 1.6 million people are living in this active strike area. This city was destroyed by earthquake several times over the past histories. The last destructive earthquake is told to be traced back to more than 200 years ago (Djamour, Vernant, Nankali, & Tavakoli, 2011; Karimzadeha et al., 2013). In the recent centuries, a significant earthquake has not been reported for this city while geodesy studies show a significant amount of deformation on both slip sides of Tabriz fault that emphasize the risks of new activities of fault (Gheitanchi, Mirzaei, & Bayramnejad, 2004; Hessami et al., 2003).

In 2009, Panakkat and Adeli used a recurrent neural network to predict the time and location of the earthquakes (Panakkat & Adeli, 2009). They used the related data of Southern California and the San Francisco Bay regions to evaluate their proposed method. The input of the network was an eight dimensional vector which was calculated in their previous paper published in 2007 (Panakkat & Adeli, 2007). Their proposed ANN was a two-hidden layer network with ten nodes that was the best structure. As a result, the authors concluded that the recurrent neural network was suitable for the large earthquakes rather than small or moderate ones.

Also, they presented a PNN and used the same indicators as inputs of their proposed network. The advantage of PNN was its high speed, because unlike other neural networks, PNN didn't calculate any learning rules, as it escaped complex calculations of learning steps. The results showed that this network unlike the previously introduced neural network can present a good prediction performance for the moderate magnitude earthquakes (Adeli & Panakkat, 2009; Panakkat & Adeli, 2007, 2009).

Another prediction method used a feed forward neural network based on the Northern Red Sea area datasets (Alarifi, Alarifi, & Al-Humidan, 2012). Its particular specification was the use of sequence number instead of the time of occurrence. They stated that it was easy for neural network to learn target sequence.

As another application of the neural networks, in 2000 Wang et al. introduced a network for mid-term predictions using the seismic catalog of china (W. Wang, WU, & Song, 2000). After the pre-processing stage which tried to omit influence of the aftershocks, effective parameters in midterm prediction was introduced and then the prior interval and the current interval were used as inputs of their ANN design. The seismic alert system is an example of learning method's application that utilizes the back propagation ANN combined with genetic algorithms and proposed in 2012 (Robles G. & Hernandez-Becerril, 2012). The aim of this system was to find relations between desired region and seismic regions. Designed system can recognize pattern of the desired region using mentioned methods.

In 2006, the research conducted by Wei et al. reported an example for application of SVM applied for seismic predictions of future strong earthquakes in Chinese mainland (Wei et al., 2006). As a comparison, a back propagation ANN was also designed and the results showed that the success rate of SVM method was 6% better than ANN and this result is related to higher generalization capability of SVM (Wei et al., 2006).

A fuzzy based system study was developed on earthquake data around Zagros range as another application of the learning algorithms (Andalib, Zare, & Atry, 2009). In order to construct the system, an expert's knowledge was used to form fuzzy rules. The extracted rules were sent to the fuzzy inference system (FIS) and when the FIS was ready to infer, the crisp variables were converted to fuzzy variables. Then, the fuzzy variables were given to FIS as input and related output was derived. According to the authors' opinion, most error free parameters provided by the expert may lead to act as a high performance system.

Data mining as second major category of method for analyzing earthquake data has a lot of subgroups. But, in here the important ones that are used in the literature will be introduced. Clustering is one of the most important methods of data mining has different types. The researches in this field are presented as follows. One of the researches in this field is clustering time series that was presented by Liao in 2005 (Liao, 2005). As, the earthquake data can be considered as a sample of time series with a sequential nature, it can be used to apply time series clustering on the earthquake dataset. This method is a multivariate method that uses agglomerative hierarchical clustering algorithm. In 2009, Aydin et al also used time series to extract a temporal pattern for predicting an event (Aydin, Karakose, & Akin, 2009).Another paper for earthquake clustering was presented based on the physical and stochastic models(Console et al., 2006). In this paper, the authors used two universal laws including the G-R and the Omori. This method was based on the theory that each earthquake had an increasing effect on the future earthquakes.

The Japanese seismicity was studied by this model and could be described by observations with a high likelihood (Console et al., 2006).

On the other hand, another literature study tried to compare different unsupervised clustering algorithms and evaluated them by a visual data mining methodology (Marroquín, Brault, & Hart, 2009). In order to compare different algorithms, it utilized three types of data sets. The clusters in these data sets were well-separated, intermediate-separated, and overlapped. The algorithms were examined and compared with partition model, expectation maximization (EM) strategy, agglomerative method, divisive method, neural gas algorithm and SOM algorithm. Finally, according to the results, the authors concluded that SOM algorithm was the best among others (Marroquín et al., 2009).

In 2005, a web client-server system named WEB-IS was proposed by constructing an interactive system for data mining, analyzing and visualizing the seismic data all over the world (Yuen et al., 2005). Fast access to earthquake data anywhere in the world is one of the important issues in this research. So to facilitate analysis and the visualization, the data sources were located in a grid framework. The java message passing system was used to communicate between clients consisting of both users and resources. The authors believed that the proposed system would help to improve communication between data sources and the researches in this field. Therefore, it led to further success in the earthquake prediction realm (Yuen et al., 2005).

PROPOSED APPROACH AND RECOMMENDATIONS FOR CASE STUDY (NORTHWEST OF IRAN)

Strike-slip and right-lateral fault in Tabriz accompanied by the Northwest-Southeast flow is known as a major and effective fault in the Azerbaijan area. Its mechanism is strike-slip with the dip-slip reverse component and the fault plate is almost vertical (Dzwinel et al., 2003). This fault, with a length of around 600 km in the Northwest of Iran starts from Zanjan and passes through North of Tabriz toward West. It passes through Morrow and Mishow mountains and Khoy and Maku cities and reaches to Ararat mountain in Turkey that located in Northwest of Azerbaijan Caucasus (Dzwinel et al., 2005). The movements and displacements in this fault have contributed to creation of Sahand volcano. Also, springs along the fault and the seismic activity show that this fault is an active fault. However, in the North of Tabriz airport, Miocene rocks have been thrust over the Quaternary alluvial deposits, but the review of historical earthquakes of past 100 years in Tabriz has no evidence of fault activity. It is worth mentioning that it is being told that renewed movements of the fault with devastating earthquakes are likely to happen.

Tele-seismic data related to different decades of twentieth century have many errors in epicenter and focal depth of earthquakes. With completion of the seismic recording system and increasing the number of seismic stations, this error has also been reduced. So far, the entire catalog of twentieth century earthquakes of Iran is unpublished and currently first decade's data of this century is not available. Based on qualitative and quantitative improvements in global seismology devices, instrumental earthquake data are divided into two major earthquakes, 1) prime instrumental earthquake data (1900-1963) and 2) new instrumental earthquake data (1964 until now). In this research, to collect instrumental earthquakes catalogs, data from different references have been collected and used (Alarifi et al., 2012; Aydin et al., 2009; Leon & Atanasiu, 2006; Liao, 2005; Miura & Okada, 2012; Robles G. & Hernandez-Becerril, 2012; Somodevilla et al., 2012; Wei et al., 2006). Each event in this research is represented by a tuples with five fields (features) like (*i.e.*, $P_i = (T_i, X_i, Y_i, M_i, D_i)$) where T_i is the occurrence time of the event i.

Table 1. The ranges of values for each features of dataset

	Min	**Max**
T_i (Time of Occurrence)	1965	2012
X_i (Longitude of the Event)	45.8530	47.2800
Y_i (Latitude of the Event)	37.6090	38.4000
M_i (Magnitude of the Event)	1	5.1000
D_i (Depth of the Event)	0.1000	65

X_i and Y_i represents longitude and latitude of event i, M_i is the magnitude and D_i is the depth of it. Ranges of values for each feature are demonstrated in Table 1. The dataset have been normalized to be prepared for the next step (i.e., k-means clustering). Two databases were used. The first database includes 759 records of the Tabriz zone with radius of 100 Km and the second database includes 1239 data of this zone with the radius of 20 Km.

Clustering is one of basic methods of data mining which is the process of dividing large amount of data into smaller and meaningful groups such that members of each group have more similarity with each other. K-means as a clustering method, calculates the distances between data points to extract the clusters in different iterations. Although, k-means is known as a simple method but it is used as a basic method for most of various clustering algorithms. This method has an iterative structure and each iteration are accomplished in two steps, first step is obtaining the cluster centers by calculating the mean value of the samples in each cluster and second step is assigning each sample to nearest cluster by calculating its distance from the cluster center. At beginning that there is no clusters, k points are selected randomly known as cluster centers. This process is done iteratively until the clusters are not changed or the convergence condition is satisfied (Chamundeswari, Pardasaradhi Varma, & Satyanarayana, 2012). Ultimate goal of this algorithm is to obtain the clusters that data in each cluster are more similar to each other and the data in different clusters are less similar to each other. The main problem in using the clustering techniques is determining the suitable algorithm, best criterions for stopping clustering's iterations and appropriate number of clusters. Determining the number of clusters depends solely on the researchers' experience and the experimental evidences obtained from the geological analysis.

The normalized dataset is given to k-means clustering algorithm to make clusters according to geographical location of events. As mentioned before, selecting the number of the clusters is based on the experience and in this research according to the geological studies about Tabriz fault, 6 clusters have been chosen for clustering the data set which is very close to what the geologists have obtained experimentally.

ANN is one the branches of the artificial intelligence that is based on learning algorithms. Data set is divided into two groups, the training dataset and the testing dataset. The network can be trained by different training algorithms. The algorithm used in this research is the Levenberg-Marquardt (LM) backpropagation algorithm that is used to train network which is known as fastest method in multilayer networks (Pradeep, Srinivasu, Avadhani, & Murthy, 2011). This algorithm updates the weight and the bias values according to Levenberg-Marquardt optimization method. The disadvantage appointed to this algorithm is its high memory usage.

Our goal is to extract meaningful clusters from the seismic data of Tabriz fault by utilizing the artificial intelligence methods. For this purpose, data mining methods and clustering algorithms are used to determine the seismic zones in the Tabriz fault zone. Aim of clustering is classifying event patterns based on the special and common features and identifying groups those are near to each other. According to the most of the mentioned related works, using artificial neural network is suggested to predict magnitude and time of the future earthquakes. But in this study the ANN is used for another purpose and application named as clustering. This study is consisting of two stages. First, applying the k-means algorithm to cluster the dataset based on the location parameters. The statistical results of clusters stage will be derived. Second, the results are used to train proposed ANN and predict the cluster type as an output. Data for analysis is not enough therefore k-means clustering method can be used to obtain clustering groups as an output. But, when number of data is big especially on the huge earthquake dataset, the k-means method will be applied for its statistical nature for decreasing the extensive computing and increasing the speed of the algorithm. So, the ANN designed in this study can calculate and construct the clusters faster than before by the help of k-means clustering as a preprocessing step. In fact, this research trains the results of the k-means clustering values by the neural network. The algorithm used to train this neural network is Levenberg-Marquardt (LM) back propagation algorithm that is the best one for multilayer networks. When there is just one hidden layer, it is easy to find the optimum solution but when there is more than one hidden layer, the amount of computation will be increased and it becomes hard to find the solution. In such cases, the Levenberg-Marquardt algorithm is the fastest way to reach the optimal solution as it doesn't calculate the Hessian matrix and makes use of approximation of this matrix (Fu, Li, Fairbank, Wunsch, & Alonso, 2014; Nguyen, Nguyen, Ling, & Nguyen, 2013; Pradeep et al., 2011; Zhu & Zhang, 2013).

As is shown in Figure 1, proposed network has four layers consisting of input layer, output layer and two hidden layers. The details regarding the number of the neurons and the transfer functions related to each layer are shown in Table 2 which shows the best performance. ANN receives a 5 dimensional vector as specified in Table 1 at five input neurons. Given the number of the segments and the clusters, its output is a 6 dimensional binary vector based on the one out of k encoding scheme that just one of the outputs can be 1 to represents cluster number (*i.e.,* *(1,0,0,0,0,0)*, *(0,1,0,0,0,0)*,*(0,0,1,0,0,0)*,*(0,0,0,1,0,0)*, *(0,0,0,0,1,0)* and *(0,0,0,0,0,1)*).

RESULTS AND DISCUSSIONS

The harmful nature of earthquakes shows importance of studying about Tabriz fault. The ANN as an intelligent system is a useful tool for learning non-linear events to make predictions. Proposed ANN was for predicting the cluster of each event. To reach this goal, current study consists of two stages. At first step, a statistical data mining algorithm is used for making multiple clusters (i.e., k-means clustering) from provided dataset. This algorithm makes six clusters of the occurred events on Tabriz fault dataset over time including the longitude and the latitude parameters. Results of clustering are used for training the ANN. Computed clusters coincide with clusters obtained by geological studies. After conducting different experiments, Levenberg-Marquent algorithm is resulted as best training algorithm for these datasets. This algorithm was used to train the network and two hidden layer was determined to obtain optimal results in this network.

There were two main goals to perform this study. The first one is related to the huge number of the earthquake events and using the ANN which tries to make cluster prediction faster while the data set becomes larger. As k-means algorithm will be slow on large number of data. The second one is to participate all of the parameters in the ANN prediction that was hard to do by k-means clustering algorithm.

Figure 1. Architecture of proposed artificial neural network.

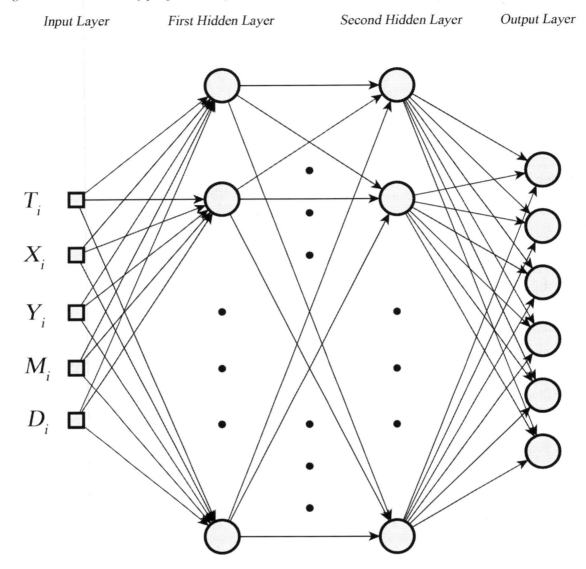

Table 2. Specifications of layers in proposed artificial neural network

	Number of Neurons	Activation Function of Layer
Layer1(Input Layer)	5	Tangent sigmoid
Layer2(Hidden Layer1)	10	Tangent sigmoid
Layer3(Hidden Layer2)	8	Tangent sigmoid
Layer4(Output Layer)	6	Purelin (Linear Transfer)

Parameters are time, longitude, latitude, depth and magnitude of the events and all of them were used for training the ANN. So, result of prediction depends on all of these five parameters. The network was also examined by two different data sets related to this fault and in both cases; the correct prediction rate was about 98%. By obtaining an optimistic result, proposed network which achieved a high accuracy can be used on other data setsor the updated data set of this fault.

After applying pre-processing stage to collected data of Tabriz fault, normalizing the dataset was accomplished. In order to acquire the segments of this fault, the k-means algorithm was applied over the normalized data set. The result of this clustering is shown at Figure 2. As Figure 2 shows, six segments of the Tabriz fault is determined that coincide by the segments that was obtained by the geological studies. At the next step, results of clustering were trained by proposed ANN described before. First, the data set was divided into 10 parts. 10 experiments were done by this network and in each experiment 9 parts were used to train the network and remained one part was used to test the network. To prevent the overtraining of ANN a 10 fold cross validation was used. Thus, each category was appeared once in the test set in each experiment. The final average of the prediction rate for the proposed network is 97.42%. The prediction rate for each category in each experiment in the best case, worst case and the average case is specified in Table 3.

Figure 2. Clusters of earthquake data related to Tabriz fault by K-means clustering algorithm in terms of longitude and latitude of events

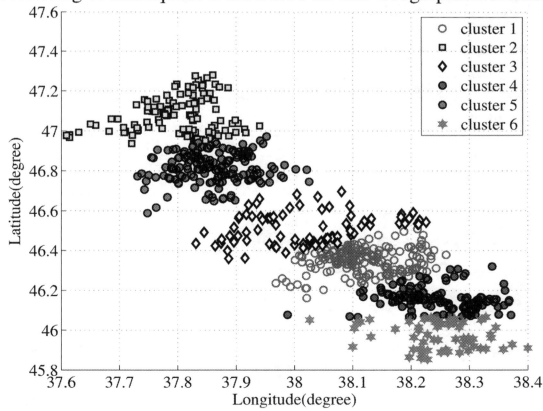

Table 3. Prediction accuracy of the proposed artificial neural network using first dataset

Categories	Worst Case	Average Case	Best Case
1	90.78%	94.46%	98.68%
2	90.78%	92.75%	94.73%
3	97.36%	99.20%	100%
4	96.05%	97.18%	98.68%
5	98.68%	99.20%	100%
6	96.05%	98.02%	98.68%
7	97.36%	98.94%	100%
8	96.05%	98.55%	100%
9	94.73%	96.31%	98.68%
10	97.33%	99.59%	100%
Mean of All	95.52%	97.42%	98.95

The best case occurred when weights of the ANN model are set randomly that gives best result, the worst case occurred when the ANN model's weights and biases are randomly set and not a good performance has been achieved. In other words, for each testing group multiple runs have been conducted to demonstrate the performance of proposed ANN model while considering the random selection of weights and biases. However, the results in Table 4 which are obtained from the second dataset (with more data) show no outstanding differences in comparison with the results in Table 3 which belongs to the first dataset (with less data). However, it shows that when a large database is used, the ANN will be trained and performs better than when it was trained on smaller database.

Table 4. Prediction accuracy of the proposed artificial neural network using second dataset

The Categories	The Correct Prediction Rate
1	97.58%
2	99.19%
3	97.58%
4	100%
5	98.38%
6	98.38%
7	96.77%
8	97.58%
9	99.19%
10	98.38%
Mean of all	**98.30%**

FUTURE RESEARCH DIRECTIONS

There are four important issues which should be considered when proposing a nonlinear model for data mining. These are including 1) the type and the selected time periods of data, 2) the preprocessing techniques such as principle component analysis complying with the minimum requirements, 3) k-fold cross validation to avoid extra biases, and 4) using an adequate measurement tool such as AIC, BIC, or AICc in situations where R-squared or adjusted R-squared are not performing well for assessing the performance of the nonlinear models.

For an example, we have carefully studied the recently published interesting article by Zamani et al in the journal of Earth Science Informatics entitled "Application of neural network and ANFIS model for earthquake occurrence in Iran" who proposed applications of RBF and ANFIS model by using spatial and temporal features of a region of interest mentioned as Qeshm, Iran (Zamani, Sorbi, & Safavi, 2013). However, there are some issues that should be considered when proposing nonlinear models for predicting activity values ranging from the first stage (i.e., gathering the required data) to the last stage (i.e., the validation and generalization of the model). In this article, the authors have gathered the spatial data from two datasets (i.e., catalogues of the U.S geological survey (USGS) and international institute of earthquake engineering and seismicity (IIEES)) and no catalogues have been mentioned for temporal dataset. However, the time periods for the registered events in IIEES is starting from 2006. There is no reason for selecting different periods of times while considering the spatial and temporal dataset. The way of merging data of multiple sources is important especially when they may have overlapped time intervals. Some preprocessing techniques are required for data preparation. These preprocessing must be selected accurately because they make big influences on the results of study. It should be taken a good consideration while using principal component analysis (PCA) on low dimension dataset (i.e., 5 features for spatial and 3 features for temporal properties) which may leads to lose the important seismic data (Astel, Astel, & Biziuk, 2008; Chakrabarti, Kumar, Singh, & Dimitrova, 2012; Xu & Brereton, 2005). Generally, PCA is effectively used as a tool to reduce the dimensionality of the huge data and existing noise to cover most of the characteristics of the data which results in uncorrelated and orthogonal components (Bai et al., 2013; Yao, Coquery, & Le Cao, 2012). PCA assumes that input data follows the multivariate normal distribution and is not useful on the other types of distribution such as super-Gaussian (Yao et al., 2012). If a research a method is used that is appropriate for data with Poisson or Gaussian distribution, then it must be proved that data set have appropriate distribution. From nonlinear structure of the seismic data results that it cannot follow the normal distribution. However, PCA decides based on the highest variance achieved by components which is more likely than 80-90%, hence, the second highest variance in selecting the first component for temporal data covers less than 80% and the resulted R-squared is shown as promising which is not fair. Regarding the evaluation section of the RBF and ANFIS models, the some authors have assessed their proposed nonlinear models based on only R-squared, however, in 2010, Spiess and Neumeyer have shown that R-squared is an inadequate measurement tool for nonlinear models by using a Monte Carlo approach applied to nine various nonlinear models ranging from three to five parameters (Spiess & Neumeyer, 2010). Spiess and Neumeyer have emphasized that these kinds of misunderstandings are mostly related to differences among the mathematical background of statisticians and other researchers without considering the initial requirements of a tool (Spiess & Neumeyer, 2010). R-squared and its other variations are frequently used for fitting nonlinear models; however they are designed to fit linear data models (Miaou, Lu, & Lum, 1996; Nagelkerderde, 1991). In conclusion, the world researchers and reviewers of well-known journals are encouraged to consider that R-squared is not an appropriate tool for validating the performance of a nonlinear model, in turn, based on the important evaluation results achieved by Spiess and Neumeyer on nine models and ten measurements of goodness of fit, they should use other methods such as Akaike information criterion (AIC) (Akaike, 1973, 1974, 1978), Bayesian information criterion (BIC) (Schwarz, 1978) or the bias-corrected AIC (AICc) (Spiess & Neumeyer, 2010) for this purpose which have showed significant performance in comparison to simple R-Squared or adjusted R-Squared. Moreover, the authors have emphasized that they have not done a cross-validation on their spatial data model, however, cross validation is part of validating a model and omitting this part will result in extra biases in improving the performances of the RBF and ANFIS models.

CONCLUSION

Is this case study, after reviewing the most recent studies on data mining techniques related to earthquake data, the earthquake data of Tabriz fault was studied using k-means algorithm and a 4 layered ANN trained by the Levenberg-Marquardt backpropagation algorithm. The dataset consists of the earthquake data of Tabriz fault. Each event in this dataset has five features, two of them are related to geographical location of the event and the three remaining ones are related to time, magnitude, and depth of each event respectively. After normalizing the data set that is collected from different references, a statistical clustering scheme was extracted by using k-means clustering algorithm that divides the fault dataset into six segments according to their location parameters. When number of the events increases, this approach needs much time to reach the result. Due to high speed of ANN, the results of the first part were used to train and test proposed ANN. After accomplishing the experiments over the dataset, the network operated well and accuracy of event clustering at it's the best average is 97.42%. Therefore, the proposed ANN can be used to make a meaningful clustering of Tabriz fault while facing huge amount of data. As a future work, this method can be used by other features of the events to find out if they have a successful result or not. For the future trends of researches on earthquakes, few points of clarifications on the workflow of validating nonlinear predictive models on a sample study has been demonstrated.

REFERENCES

Adeli, H., & Panakkat, A. (2009). A probabilistic neural network for earthquake magnitude prediction. *Neural Networks*, 22(7), 1018–1024. doi:10.1016/j.neunet.2009.05.003 PMID:19502005

Akaike, H. (1973). Information theory and an extension of the maximum likelihood principle. *Proc 2nd Inter Symposium of Information Theory* (pp. 267-281).

Akaike, H. (1974). A new look at the statistical model identification. *IEEE Transactions on Automatic Control*, 19(6), 716–723. doi:10.1109/TAC.1974.1100705

Akaike, H. (1978). On the likelihood of time series model. *The Statistician*, 27(3/4), 217–235. doi:10.2307/2988185

Alarifi, A. S. N., Alarifi, N. S. N., & Al-Humidan, S. (2012). Earthquakes magnitude predication using artificial neural network in northern Red Sea area. *Journal of King Saud University – Science*, 24, 301–313.

Andalib, A., Zare, M., & Atry, F. (2009). A fuzzy expert system for earthquake prediction, case study: the Zagros range. *Proceedings of the Third International Conference on Modeling, Simulation and Applied Optimization*. Sharjah, U.A.E.

Ardalan, A., Hajiuni, A., & Zare, M. (2013). Aftershocks following the 9 April 2013 Bushehr earthquake, Iran. *PLoS Currents*, *5*. doi: doi:10.1371/currents.dis.76750ede500e61b81d7f2ba9edfb2373 PMID:24042232

Astel, A., Astel, K., & Biziuk, M. (2008). PCA and multidimensional visualization techniques united to aid in the bioindication of elements from transplanted Sphagnum palustre moss exposed in the Gdansk City area. *Environmental Science and Pollution Research International*, *15*(1), 41–50. doi:10.1065/espr2007.05.422 PMID:18306887

Aydin, I., Karakose, M., & Akin, E. (2009). The prediction algorithm based on fuzzy logic using time series data mining method. *Proceedings of World Academy of Science: Engineering & Technology*.

Bai, L., Gao, B., Tian, S., Cheng, Y., Chen, Y., Tian, G. Y., & Woo, W. L. (2013). A comparative study of principal component analysis and independent component analysis in eddy current pulsed thermography data processing. *The Review of Scientific Instruments*, *84*(10), 104901. doi:10.1063/1.4823521 PMID:24182145

Chakrabarti, B., Kumar, S., Singh, R., & Dimitrova, N. (2012). Genetic diversity and admixture patterns in Indian populations. *Gene*, *508*(2), 250–255. doi:10.1016/j.gene.2012.07.047 PMID:22892377

Chamundeswari, G., Pardasaradhi Varma, G., & Satyanarayana, C. (2012). An experimental analysis of k-means using Matlab. *International Journal of Engineering Research & Technology*, *1*(5), 1–5.

Console, R., Murru, M., & Catalli, F. (2006). Physical and stochastic models of earthquake clustering. *Tectonophysics*, *417*(1-2), 141–153. doi:10.1016/j.tecto.2005.05.052

Djamour, Y., Vernant, P., Nankali, H. R., & Tavakoli, F. (2011). NW Iran-eastern Turkey present-day kinematics: Results from the Iranian permanent GPS network. *Earth and Planetary Science Letters*, *307*(1-2), 27–34. doi:10.1016/j.epsl.2011.04.029

Dologlou, E. (2008). Possible relationship between seismic electric signals (SES) lead time and earthquake stress drop. *Proceedings of the Japan Academy. Series B, Physical and Biological Sciences*, *84*(4), 117–122. doi:10.2183/pjab.84.117 PMID:18941291

Dzwinel, W., Yuen, D. A., Boryczko, K., Ben-Zion, Y., Yoshioka, S., & Ito, T. (2003). Cluster analysis, data-mining, multi-dimensional visualization of earthquakes over space, time and feature space. *Earth and Planetary Science Letters*, 1–11.

Dzwinel, W., Yuen, D. A., Boryczko, K., Ben-Zion, Y., Yoshioka, S., & Ito, T. (2005). Nonlinear multidimensional scaling and visualization of earthquake clusters over space, time and feature space. *Nonlinear Processes in Geophysics*, *12*(1), 117–128. doi:10.5194/npg-12-117-2005

Elmi, A., Ganjpour Sales, J., Tabrizi, A., Soleimanpour, J., & Mohseni, M. A. (2013). Orthopedic injuries following the East Azerbaijan earthquake. *Trauma Mon*, *18*(1), 3–7. doi:10.5812/traumamon.8322 PMID:24350141

Ennis, W. J. (2010). Disaster management, triage-based wound care, and patient safety: Reflections on practice following an earthquake. *Ostomy/Wound Management, 56*(11), 61–69. PMID:21131698

Fu, X., Li, S., Fairbank, M., Wunsch, D. C., & Alonso, E. (2014). Training recurrent neural networks with the levenberg-marquardt algorithm for optimal control of a grid-connected converter. *IEEE Trans Neural Netw Learn Syst.* doi: 10.1109/TNNLS.2014.2361267

Gheitanchi, M. R., Mirzaei, N., & Bayramnejad, E. (2004). Pattern of seismicity in Northwest Iran, revealed from local seismic network. *Geoscience, 11*, 104–111.

Hessami, K., Pantosti, D., Tabassi, H., Shabanian, E., Abbassi, M. R., Feghhi, K., & Solaymani, S. (2003). Paleoearthquakes and slip rates of the North Tabriz fault, NW Iran: Preliminary results. *Annals of Geophysics, 46*(5), 903–915.

Kako, M., Arbon, P., & Mitani, S. (2014). Disaster health after the 2011 great East Japan earthquake. *Prehospital and Disaster Medicine, 29*(1), 54–59. doi:10.1017/S1049023X14000028 PMID:24451332

Karimzadeha, S., Cakirb, Z., Osmano˘gluc, B., Schmalzled, G., Miyajimaa, M., Amiraslanzadeha, R., & Djamoure, Y. (2013). Interseismic strain accumulation across the North Tabriz fault (NW Iran) deduced from InSAR time series. *Journal of Geodynamics, 66*, 53–58. doi:10.1016/j.jog.2013.02.003

Leon, F., & Atanasiu, G. M. (2006). *Data mining methods for GIS analysis of seismic vulnerability. Proceedings of the First International Conference on Software and Data Technologies.*

Liao, T. W. (2005). Clustering of time series data—a survey. *Pattern Recognition, 38*(11), 1857–1874. doi:10.1016/j.patcog.2005.01.025

Marroquín, I. D., Brault, J.-J., & Hart, B. S. (2009). A visual data-mining methodology for seismic facies analysis: Part 1-Testing and comparison with other unsupervised clustering methods. *Geophysic, 74*(1), 1–11. doi:10.1190/1.3046455

Miaou, S. P., Lu, A., & Lum, H. S. (1996). Pitfalls of using r-squared to evaluate goodness of fit of accident prediction models. *Transportation Research Record, 1542*, 6–13. doi:10.3141/1542-02

Miura, T., & Okada, Y. (2012). *Extraction of frequent association patterns co-occurring across multisequence data. Proceedings of the International Multi Conference of Engineers.*

Nagelkerderde, N. J. D. (1991). A note on a general definition of the coefficient of determination. *Biometrika, 78*(3), 691–692. doi:10.1093/biomet/78.3.691

Nguyen, L. B., Nguyen, A. V., Ling, S. H., & Nguyen, H. T. (2013). Combining genetic algorithm and Levenberg-Marquardt algorithm in training neural network for hypoglycemia detection using EEG signals. *Conference Proceedings; ... Annual International Conference of the IEEE Engineering in Medicine and Biology Society. IEEE Engineering in Medicine and Biology Society. Conference, 5386-5389.* doi: doi:10.1109/EMBC.2013.6610766 PMID:24110953

Orihara, Y., Kamogawa, M., & Nagao, T. (2014). Pre-seismic changes of the level and temperature of confined groundwater related to the 2011 Tohoku Earthquake. *Scientific Reports, 4*, 6907. doi:10.1038/srep06907 PMID:25366123

Panakkat, A., & Adeli, H. (2007). Neural Network Models for Earthquake Magnitude Prediction Using Multiple Seismicity Indicators. *International Journal of Neural Systems*, *17*(1), 13–33. doi:10.1142/S0129065707000890 PMID:17393560

Panakkat, A., & Adeli, H. (2009). Recurrent neural network for approximate earthquake time and location prediction using multiple seismicity indicators. *Computer-Aided Civil and Infrastructure Engineering*, *24*(4), 280–292. doi:10.1111/j.1467-8667.2009.00595.x

Peng, C., Yang, J., Zheng, Y., Xu, Z., & Jiang, X. (2014). Early magnitude estimation for the MW 7.9 Wenchuan earthquake using progressively expanded P-wave time window. *Scientific Reports*, *4*, 6770. doi:10.1038/srep06770 PMID:25346344

Pradeep, T., Srinivasu, P., Avadhani, P. S., & Murthy, Y. V. S. (2011). Comparison of variable learning rate and Levenberg-Marquardt back-propagation training algorithms for detecting attacks in Intrusion Detection Systems. *International Journal on Computer Science and Engineering*, *3*(11), 3572–3581.

Preethi, G., & Santhi, B. (2011). Study on techniques of earthquake prediction. *International Journal of Computers and Applications*, *29*(4), 55–58. doi:10.5120/3549-4867

Robles, G. C. M. A., & Hernandez-Becerril, R. A. (2012). Seismic alert system based on artificial neural networks. World Academy of Science, Engineering & Technology(66), 813-818.

Roy, A., Matos, M., & Marfurt, K. J. (2010). Automatic seismic facies classification with kohonen self organizing maps – a tutorial. *Geohorizons Journal of Society of Petroleum Geophysicists*, 6-14.

Ruiz, S., Metois, M., Fuenzalida, A., Ruiz, J., Leyton, F., & Grandin, R. et al. (2014). Intense foreshocks and a slow slip event preceded the 2014 Iquique Mw 8.1 earthquake. *Science*, *345*(6201), 1165–1169. doi:10.1126/science.1256074 PMID:25061132

ADDITIONAL READING

Schwarz, G. (1978). Estimating the dimension of a model. *Annals of Statistics*, *6*(2), 461–464. doi:10.1214/aos/1176344136

Somodevilla, M. J., Priego, A. B., Castillo, E., Pineda, I. H., Vilariño, D., & Nava, A. (2012). Decision support system for seismic risks. *Journal of Computer Science and Technology*, *12*(2), 71.

Spiess, A. N., & Neumeyer, N. (2010). An evaluation of R2 as an inadequate measure for nonlinear models in pharmacological and biochemical research: A Monte Carlo approach. *BMC Pharmacology*, *10*(1), 6. doi:10.1186/1471-2210-10-6 PMID:20529254

Uyeda, S. (2013). On earthquake prediction in Japan. *Proceedings of the Japan Academy. Series B, Physical and Biological Sciences*, *89*(9), 391–400. doi:10.2183/pjab.89.391 PMID:24213204

Wang, W., Wu, G.-F., & Song, X.-Y. (2000). The application of neural network to comprehensive prediction by seismology prediction method. *Acta Seismologica Sinica*, *13*(2), 210–215. doi:10.1007/s11589-000-0012-0

Wang, Y., Li, J., Chen, H., & Zou, Z. (2014). The time process of post-earthquake recovery: The Yao'an earthquake in China. *Disasters*, *38*(4), 774–789. doi:10.1111/disa.12083 PMID:25196336

Wei, W., Yue, L., Guo-zheng, L., Geng-feng, W., Qin-zhong, M., Li-fei, Z., & Ming-zhou, L. (2006). Support vector machine method for forecasting future strong earthquakes in Chinese mainland. *Acta Seismologica Sinica*, *19*(1), 30–38. doi:10.1007/s11589-001-0030-6

Xu, Y., & Brereton, R. G. (2005). Diagnostic pattern recognition on gene-expression profile data by using one-class classification. *Journal of Chemical Information and Modeling*, *45*(5), 1392–1401. doi:10.1021/ci049726v PMID:16180916

Yao, F., Coquery, J., & Le Cao, K. A. (2012). Independent principal component analysis for biologically meaningful dimension reduction of large biological data sets. *BMC Bioinformatics*, *13*(1), 24. doi:10.1186/1471-2105-13-24 PMID:22305354

Yuen, D. A., Kadlec, B. J., Bollig, E. F., Dzwinel, W., Garbow, Z. A., & da Silva, C. R. S. (2005). Clustering and visualization of earthquake data in a grid environment. *Visual Geosciences*, *10*(1), 1–12. doi:10.1007/s10069-005-0023-z

Zamani, A., Sorbi, M. R., & Safavi, A. A. (2013). Application of neural network and ANFIS model for earthquake occurrence in Iran. *Earth Science Informatics*, *6*(2), 71–85. doi:10.1007/s12145-013-0112-8

Zhang, Q., Zhang, Y., Yang, X., & Su, B. (2014). Automatic recognition of seismic intensity based on RS and GIS: A case study in Wenchuan Ms8.0 earthquake of China. *The Scientific World Journal*, *878149*. doi: doi:10.1155/2014/878149 PMID:24688445

Zhu, X., & Zhang, D. (2013). Efficient parallel Levenberg-Marquardt model fitting towards real-time automated parametric imaging microscopy. *PLoS ONE*, *8*(10), e76665. doi:10.1371/journal.pone.0076665 PMID:24130785

KEY TERMS AND DEFINITIONS

Artificial Neural Networks: ANNs are computational models inspired by an animal's central nervous system which is capable of machine learning as well as pattern recognition.

Clustering Algorithms: They are described as the task of grouping a set of objects in such a way that objects in the same group are more similar to each other than to those in other groups. k-means and fuzzy c-means are examples.

Data Mining: They are some kinds of techniques that include the computational process of discovering patterns in large data sets involving methods at the intersection of artificial intelligence, machine learning, statistics, and database systems.

Earthquake: An earthquake is caused as a result of a sudden release of energy in the Earth's crust that creates seismic waves.

Evolutionary Algorithms: These are known as a subset of evolutionary computation, or a generic population-based metaheuristic optimization algorithm.

Fuzzy Systems: Fuzzy system is an alternative to traditional notions of set membership and logic that has its origins in ancient Greek philosophy, and applications at the leading edge of Artificial Intelligence.

North Tabriz Fault: The North Tabriz Fault is a major seismogenic fault in Northwest of Iran. The last damaging earthquakes on this fault occurred in 1721.

Self-Organizing Map (SOM) or Self-Organizing Feature Map (SOFM): SOM is used to map the input data to a small dimension of space and is trained like an artificial neural network in an unsupervised manner.

Support Vector Machines: SVMs are supervised learning models with associated learning algorithms that analyze data and recognize patterns, used for classification and regression analysis.

Chapter 11
An Evaluation of C4.5 and Fuzzy C4.5 with Effect of Pruning Methods

Tayyeba Naseer
PMAS Arid Agriculture University, Pakistan

Sohail Asghar
COMSATs Institute of Information Technology, Pakistan

ABSTRACT

Classification is a supervised learning technique in data mining classify historical data. The decision tree is easy method for inductive inference. The decision tree induction process has three major steps – first complete decision tree is constructed to classify all examples in the training data, the second is pruning this tree to decrease misclassification rate and the third is processing the pruned tree to improve the classification. In this chapter, the empirical comparison of pruning the tree created by C4.5 and the fuzzy C4.5 algorithm. C4.5 and Fuzzy C4.5 decision tree algorithms are implemented using the JAVA language in Eclipse tool. In this chapter, first decision tree is built using C4.5 and Fuzzy C4.5 and five famous pruning techniques is used to evaluate trees and the comparison is achieved between pruning methods for refining the size and accuracy of a decision tree. Cost-complexity pruning produce the smaller tree with minimum increase in error for C4.5 and Fuzzy C4.5 decision trees.

INTRODUCTION

"Data mining is refers to as mining or extracting knowledge from huge data set", according to (Jiawei et *al.,* 2006). Data mining is the solicitation of explicit algorithms for mining patterns from data. The term data mining has habitually been used by statisticians, data analysts and the management information systems (MIS) communitie. Data mining can carry out in numerous terms or to some level diverse meaning from data mining such as data dredging, knowledge mining from data, pattern analysis, data archaeology and knowledge extraction. Machine learning is part of data mining. It rose over the late 1980s had made excessiveprogresses all through the 1990s and is expected to endure in the 21st century

DOI: 10.4018/978-1-4666-8513-0.ch011

(John 1989). Clustering, data reduction, prediction, classification, association, or data transformation etc. Are several areas of data mining used to solve diverse types of problems. The development of effectual and dynamic data mining algorithms to process data; and the decreasing cost of computational impact, enabling the use of computationally tough methods for data exploration. Data mining is categorized in two types (Guoxiu 2005).

1.   Supervised Learning
2.   Unsupervised learning

Supervised learning is the task of machine learning of persuading a function of categorized data. The data used for inferring learning is called training data, it contains set of training examples. However, in supervised learning, examples are the pairsentailing of an input item and aessentialefficiency value which is also known as a managerial indication (Nitesh 2003). A supervised learning algorithm inspects the training data and produces a reliant function, which can be designed for recording inventive examples. Finest situation will allow the algorithm to fittingly fix the class labels for unseen examples. Classification is one of the instances of supervised learning techniques (Guoxiu 2005).

In unsupervised learning, all the observations are estimated to be elicited by hidden variables, that is, the clarifications are hypothesized to be at the end of the fundamental series, (Guoxiu 2005). In unsupervised learning, examples entail of input items only, they do not pair with output values. Clustering is an eminent example of unsupervised learning.

In our daily life and in the working environment we often solve numerous decisions – making problems. Conferring to the real-world, we make a decision based on our past experiences (Semra & Ersoy 2010). Machine learning field frequently lets computers implement or come up with new ideas for the precise result; various decision making methods exist, such as Decision Trees, Bayesian learning and Artificial Neural Networks. The decision tree methods are the emphasis of this investigation. Respectively each technique has its own advantages and drawbacks. The decision tree is one of the foremost use machines learning method for making decisions in pattern recognition (Guoxiu 2005).

The decision tree is a figurativemethodology used in numerous regions because of its benefits, more precise, effective, influential and easy for data preparation and also easy to understand for non – practical peoples (Quinlan 1986), (Wang, Yeung & Tsang 2001) and (Semra & Ersoy 2010). The supplementary benefit is that it can categorize numerical and categorical both types of data.

The first symbolic inductive learning algorithm was CLS [2], it is the prototype of decision tree, and then various additional decision tree algorithms, e.g. ID3, CART, C4.5, SPRINT, SLIQ and BOAT were proposed. C4.5 and CART (a beneficiary of ID3) is the two renowned and extensively used algorithms. CART was developed by Statisticians, while C4.5 (Quinlan 1986) was developed by a computer scientist in the field of machine learning. Decision-tree inductions comprises of three main phases:

Phase 1. Creating the complete decision tree to classify all the training data instances
Phase 2. Pruning the decision tree to show statistical constancy
Phase 3. And tendering out the pruned tree to raise understandability.

Decision Tree is also known as a nested hierarchy of branches like tree because it has different levels for indicating the information, and each branch, division demonstrates the features of the dataset using symbols called nodes. Each node can be divided into binary or multi – way split, this riven is based on attributes value is called branches, each branch represents the value of that attribute or feature (Sison & Chong 1994). Each node stipulates the test for attribute of the instance and each descendent branch resembles to one of the possible values of the attributes (Nitesh 2003). If that test is true, then it goes to the next node or if the test is false then it will check the other branches of the test. Classification start from topmost node is called the root node. Nodes with class value and have no downward node is called terminal nodes or leaf node (Pal 2001), all the records of the branch have an alike class label is not separated more, and the leaf resultant to it is categorized with the class (Guoxiu 2005). Nodes between the root node and leaf nodes are called internal nodes or sub – nodes.

The decision tree is known as a massively apprehensive classifier with respect to negligible perturbations in example training data. If changes are made in the data set, then the decision tree structure is completely different. Some intellectuals have recommended Fuzzy Decision Tree (e.g. Fuzzy C4.5) to overwhelmed this problem by employing the fuzzy set theory to define the associated degree of attribute values, the admiration of subordinate relations among every attribute values and different examples.

Fuzzy set theory is applied on C4.5 to attain Fuzzy C4.5 and it is an extension of the C4.5 algorithm. The fuzzy decision tree is generated by using indefinite sets defined by a user for all features and develops nominal fuzzy entropy to select long attributes (Wang, Yeung & Tsang 2001). However, the effect of this Fuzzy ID3 is deprived in knowledge accuracy.

To overcome the problem, knowledge precision two critical constraints, leaf decision threshold and fuzziness control parameter have been used. Furthermore the lowest fuzzy entropy, numerous criteria has been predictable to select protracted attributes, such as the point of the reputation of attribute effect to the classification and least classification vagueness, etc.

The procedure of cutting off non – predictive parts of a tree or least reliable sub-tree is called "pruning." (Eibe 2000), by eliminating redundant structure, pruning recovers the accuracy of the tree and also licensed size. They form a vital component of real learning algorithms since many datasets of real – world are noisy, they contain an amount of ambiguity that is either effects of the method in which the data is composed or inherent in the area, or together.

The pruning machine's productivity, manages the size and accuracy of the resulting tree (Eibe 2000). Rather, pruning should not ever eradicate any structure that is correctly predicted, it only evacuates those parts of a tree that are indeterminate due to noise, this decision constructed on the data. Consequently pruning method requires a delicate mechanism that practices the given observations to detect whether there is a unassertive relationship between the mechanisms of a model and the domain. There are two root pruning methods:

1. Pre – pruning
2. Post – pruning

Pre – pruning is pragmatic to the tree throughout building of the tree, stops development of the tree using certain mathematical calculation. Post – pruning is applied after the construction of the complete tree. There are frequent post pruning techniques originate in literature proposed by researchers, (Eibe 2000).

In this chapter, we describe the C4.5 and Fuzzy C4.5 algorithms for construction of the decision tree. And five renowned pruning algorithms like Cost, Complexity Pruning, Pessimistic Error Pruning, Minimum Error Pruning, Reduced Error Pruning and Critical Value Pruning algorithms are describing. Comparison of C4.5 and Fuzzy C4.5 is described and discussed by showing experimental results. Effects of pruning methods are measure using two parameters, i.e. size and accuracy of the decision tree. Different pruning methods have different effects for different datasets. This analysis shows that the Fuzzy C4.5 is succeed to generate more accurate tree as compare to the performance of C4.5 algorithms. When pruning techniques are applied of these decision trees, some pruning algorithms leave the tree un-prunes, and some methods reduce the size of the tree and increace accuracy. Cost- complexity pruning generate smaller and moe accurate tree for C4.5 decision tree algorithm and Pessimistic error pruning, show better results for different domain datasets by generating smaller and more accurate tree for fuzzy C4.5 decision tree algorithm. Minimum error puning failed to produce the smaaler tree, and mostly leave the tree un prune. For this analysis, Chi-Square test is applied to decision tree for both C4.5 and fuzzy C4.5, also for the result of pruning methods to check the accuracy of the tree.

MATERIAL AND METHODS

Decision Tree

Many methods of decision analysis exist; one of the standard techniques used for classification is the decision tree. It is a figurative structure of node branches and leaves (John 1989). The decision tree has been efficaciously applied to many areas such as Finance, Banking and Insurance, Business management, Medical decision making for analysis and selection of a suitable treatment and more (Guoxiu 2005) and (Semra & Ersoy 2010). Many eminent algorithms of decision tree are found in literature, C4.5 and fuzzy C4.5 are both renowned algorithms use for construction of the tree.

The example decision tree is given (Guoxiu 2005) is given for public transport dataset the resulting tree shows that if *Traffic Jam* is *long* and *wind* is *strong*, then people will choose to take the public transportation or if the *wind* is *weak*, then people will not take the public transportation.

CRITERIA FOR COMPARISON

For comparing the decision tree built using C4.5 and Fuzzy C4.5 many parameters are use the main two criteria's are the size and classification error or accuracy of the tree. In this research, these two parameters are used for performing the assessment of the decision tree algorithm and pruning possessions on decision tree.

Size

Measure selected for the comparison is the size of the tree; here the question arises that why the size of the tree? The answer is, small model is better than larger ones by (Eibe 2000). The intricacy of statistical model is inferior for prediction of assessment data but it will recover and better for training data. In this experimental study, we measure the size of the tree by, total number of nodes, including the root node, internal nodes and leave nodes have been selected as a measure of the size of the decision tree. Number of leaves fluctuates for binary and multi-valued attributes both, for binary distribution attributes, the number of leave nodes will be one additional than entire number of internal nodes by Minger (1989). For multi-valued qualities number of nodes will be grander. In this experiment total number of nodes including root node, internal nodes and leave nodes have been selected as a measure of size of decision tree. This measure is used in both comparisons, i.e. effect of C4.5 and Fuzzy C4.5 for five fuzzy multivariate datasets of different domains and also evaluate the effects of pruning on decision trees.

Accuracy

Here accuracy is measured by the classification error. This refers to the diagnostic ability of the decision tree to classify the data set used for training the model and for testing the model Minger (1989). It does not reflect the predictions for different classes accessible within the dataset that's why it is also analyses as a basic measure for measuring the performance of the decision tree. Here the accuracy is measured by total number of classification error in complete tree and Chi-Square X^2 test is applied for measuring the accuracy of the tree.

DECISION TREE

The symbolic structure of nodes, leave and branch tree is a decision tree (John 1989). Many algorithms of decision tree exist in the literature like CART, ID3, C4.5, SPRINT and Fuzzy C4.5 etc. It is one of the standard classification learning techniques of data mining used for making predictions based on past experience. It has been magnificently applied to many fields such as Banking, Insurance, Finance, Business management and Medical diagnosis (Guoxiu 2005) and (Semra and E. ÖZ. 2010). Many eminent algorithms of decision tree are found in literature, C4.5 and fuzzy C4.5 are both eminent algorithms use for construction of the tree.

C4.5 Algorithm

C4.5 algorithm is an extended form of Interactive Dichotomizer 3 (ID3) algorithm developed by Quinlan created on the Concept Learning System (CLS) algorithm (Earl et *al.* 1966). It is most often used decision tree algorithm in data mining field for the prediction of future using historical data; it is famous because of effectiveness and easiness to use.

   This approach uses historical data with diverse features. Different types of data are available like categorical and real data or continuous data. Every feature in the dataset is known as attributes. The dataset is divided into two parts, i.e. Training data and test data. The data used to build the decision tree is called training data, after the construction of the decision tree test data is applied to decision tree to check the accuracy of the tree. For an attribute selection this algorithm uses statistical measures based on probability, i.e. Entropy (E) and Information Gain (IG).

   An Entropy is described that how descriptive a definite input attribute is about the class attribute for subset of training data. The Entropy is defined as follows by (Semra and Ersoy. 2005)

$$E\left(S\right) = \sum_{i}^{N} - P_i * Log_2 P_i$$

where P_i is the quantity of the class C_i in the samples *set* $S = \{x_1, x_2, ..., x_k\}$.

$$P_i = \frac{\sum x_k \in C_i}{S}$$

The information gain (IG) of an attribute *At* of the sample dataset is described as follows by (Semra and Ersoy. 2005)

$$IG(S, At) = E(S) - \sum_{i \in Val(A)} \frac{|S_i|}{|S|} E(S_i)$$

It is a greedy approach because it selects the attribute with highest information gain for split; highest information gain means how well the attribute discriminates between the class values (Guoxiu. 2005). It is recursive algorithm, that selected the attribute for the split and the dataset is partitioned into subsets until all data instances are correctly classified to the respective class value. The resulting tree consists of nodes and branches each node represents the attributes and each branch of the tree. The decision tree is recognized as best tree with least classification errors and small in size. The basic purpose of this method is to generate the series of rules that help in future decisions for better results the basic concept of the decision tree algorithm are described below

1. All nodes other than leaf nodes represent input attribute and ach branch of that attribute represents the feasible test value of that attribute.
2. Leaf nodes represent the class value that is expected to be predicted.
3. The informative attributes will be selected for the non-leaf node as input attributes.

Complete procedure of constructing a decision tree is described.

Step 1: Calculate the class entropy by using the formula E (S)

Figure 1. C4.5 Algorithm

In pseudo code, the general *C4.5* algorithm for building decision trees is

1. Check for base cases
2. for each attibute *S*
   - Find the normalized information gain from splitting on all *S*
3. Let *Si_best* be the attributes with the highest normalized information gain
4. Create a decision *node* that splits *Si_best*
5. Recurse on the sublists obtained by splitting on *Si_ best*, and add those nodes as children of the *node*

Figure 2 explains that how to calculate the info about class, attribute by specifying again, both *yes* and *no* class values. Now separate partial tree for all the attributes will be constructed and entropy and information gain will be calculated against each class value.

$$E\left(Play\right) = -Play_{yes} \log_2 Play_{yes} - Play_{No} \log_2 Play_{No}$$
$$= -\frac{9}{14}\log_2\frac{9}{14} - \frac{5}{14}\log_2\frac{5}{14} = -\frac{9}{14}\log_2\frac{9}{14} - \frac{5}{14}\log_2\frac{5}{14}$$
$$= 0.94\,bits$$

Step 2: Construct the partial decision tree and then compute the information gain of each attribute. For this data set of Golf is used to construct the decision tree. It has two values of the class attribute *"Play", Yes and no.* The data set contains four categorical attributes, partial tree of all the attibutes are created against the class value yes or no. Entropy and information gain is calculated for all the attributes.

Figure 3 shows the partial tree with calculation of entropy and information gain against each value of the attribute for the following attributes (a) *Outlook*, (b) *Temperature*, (c) *Humidity* and (d) *Windy*.

Step 3: Attribute with the highest information gain will be selected and shown from figure 3 the gain of *Outlook* is highest and it will be selected as root node. The *outlook* is selected to split as root node, it is categorical attribute so this attribute is split against its all three values *'Sunny'*, *'Overcast'* and *'Rainy'* and partitions are shown in figure 3.

Figure 2. Class attribute "play"

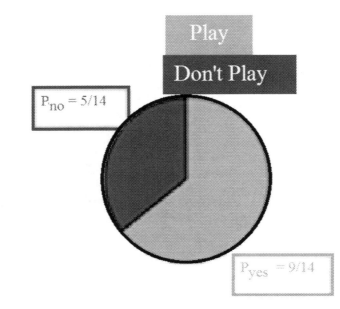

Figure 3. Partial trees for all the attributes (a) Outlook, (b) Humidity, (c) temperature and (d) Windy

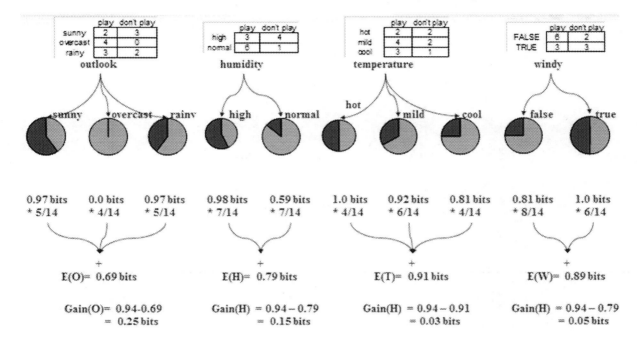

If the value of any attribute belongs to any one class, then this value will be assigned a class value and become leaf node. As shown in figure 5. *Overcast* show that it belongs to the class value *Yes*, so it will assign a class value and selected as leaf nodes. The rest of the two values sunny and rainy show misclassifications.

Step 4: First we will check the rest of the attributes with *Sunny* and *Rainy* value of *Outlook* attribute. Regenerate the data set from table 1 against the *Outlook* attribute value Sunny and Rainy shown in table 2 and 3. Generate the partial tree against *Sunny* and *Rainy* value of the *Outlook* attribute.

Figure 5 shows the partial tree from Table 2 against *Outlook* is *Sunny*. Highest information gain attribute is selected, from Figure 5 *Humidity* is selected for further split against *Oultook* is *Sunny*.

Figure 5 shows the partial tree from table 3 against *Outlook* is *Rainy*. Highest information gain attribute is selected from, Figure 5 *Windy* is selected for further split against *Oultook* is *Rainy*.

The complete decision tree is constructed by further splitting the attributes *Humidity* against *Outlook* is *Sunny* and *Windy* against *Outlook* is *Rainy*. Figure 7 shows the complete decision tree constructed by using Table 1.

Fuzzy C4.5

The fuzzy decision tree is an dynamic method to extract information on ambiguous classification problems. The fuzzy decision tree is an extended form of the typical decision tree. Fuzzy set theory is applied to define the data set and tree developing and pruning are combined to accomplish the tree structure. Using

Figure 5. Sub tree Information gain calculation against outlook is sunny

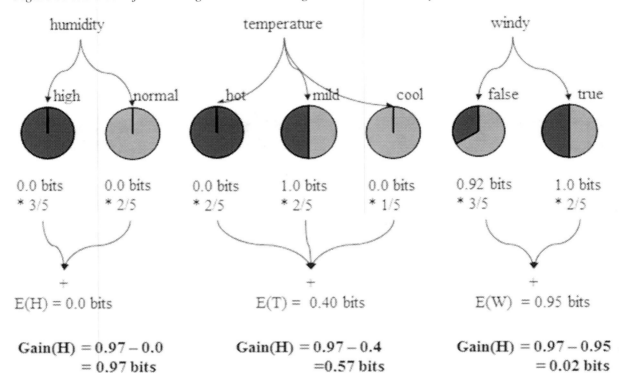

$$E(H) = 0.0 \text{ bits} \qquad E(T) = 0.40 \text{ bits} \qquad E(W) = 0.95 \text{ bits}$$

$$\textbf{Gain(H)} = 0.97 - 0.0 \qquad \textbf{Gain(H)} = 0.97 - 0.4 \qquad \textbf{Gain(H)} = 0.97 - 0.95$$
$$= 0.97 \textbf{ bits} \qquad\qquad = 0.57 \textbf{ bits} \qquad\qquad = 0.02 \textbf{ bits}$$

Table 1. Sample dataset

Outlook	Temp	Humidity	Windy	Play
Sunny	Hot	High	False	No
Sunny	Hot	High	True	No
Overcast	Hot	High	False	Yes
Rainy	Mild	High	False	Yes
Rainy	Cool	Normal	False	Yes
Rainy	Cool	Normal	True	No
Overcast	Cool	Normal	True	Yes
Suny	Mild	High	False	No
Suny	Cool	Normal	False	Yes
Rainy	Mild	Normal	False	Yes
Suny	Mild	Normal	True	Yes
Overcast	Mild	High	True	Yes
Overcast	Hot	Normal	False	Yes
Rainy	Mild	High	True	No

Table 2. Outlook is sunny

Outlook	Temp	Humidity	Windy	Play
Sunny	Hot	High	False	No
Sunny	Hot	High	True	No
Suny	Mild	High	False	No
Suny	Cool	Normal	False	Yes
Suny	Mild	Normal	True	Yes

Table 3. Outlook is rainy

Outlook	Temp	Humidity	Windy	Play
Rainy	mild	High	False	Yes
Rainy	Cool	Normal	False	Yes
Rainy	Cool	Normal	True	No
Rainy	Mild	Normal	False	Yes
Rainy	Mild	High	True	No

Figure 4. Root node tree

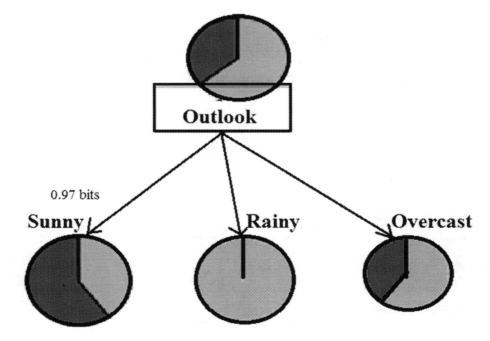

Figure 6. Sub tree information gain calculation against outlook is rainy

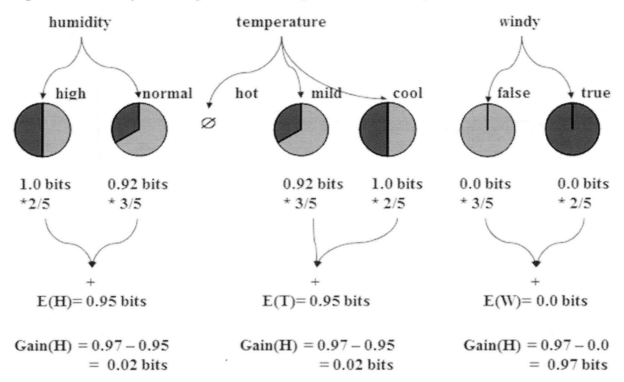

Figure 7. Complete decision tree for the golf dataset

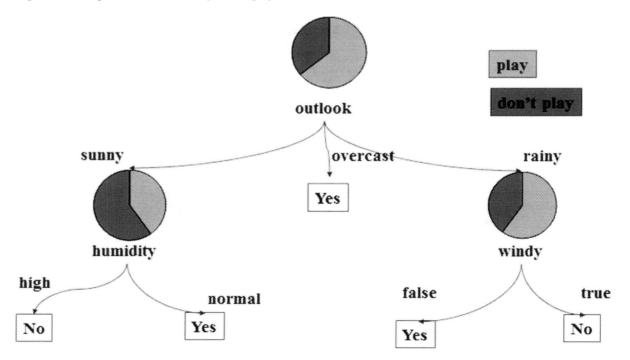

these processes, fuzzy sets are define for continuous attributes and tree is carried using discrete features only. Central steps of the fuzzy tree training process were presented by (Marcos et *al.*, 2010) as follow:

1. Fuzzy database defined;
2. Fuzzify the training set using fuzzy database;
3. Compute entropy and information gain for all attributes to split the training samples and grow a tree till all examples are classified or all attributes are used;

Fuzzy set theory is applied to the training data before tree induction. Then the measure of traditional decision tree classification is applied to the fuzzy dataset for tree induction.

Fuzzy Representation of Sample Data Set

Data can be of various types, but generally two different types of data are found, i.e. continuous and categorical. It is easy to handle categorical data in data analysis. In the decision tree most of the algorithm requires categorical data since it is easy to split an attribute designated as highest gain. In categorical data all potential values are used in each branch of the tree as a branch test for splitting the tree. Categorical data can be binary form, i.e. True/false or Yes/No and can also have multiple categories, i.e. low, medium and high or below-average, average and generous.

But handling with real data or translating real data into a categorical form is not an easy, tt required clustering or partition. For this divider, boundaries of real attributes are defined which is not so easy task, number of boundaries differs for different attribute because it have great effect on the results (Guoxiu. 2005). Here datasets are clustered into parts (Low and High) and then the boundaries are defined using the following steps.

After calculating the cluster center membership functions are defined using the low and high cluster center value. Membership function helps to convert the continuous value into a categorical form, each attribute has its own membership function and membership value is calculated according to the function that we define. Following are the membership functions for low and high by (Guoxiu. 2005) and (Semra and Ersoy. 2005).

Figure 8. Cluster defining algorithm

1. Attributes are sorted in ascending order.
2. Now attributes are partially into *2* equal parts.
3. For *lower* boundary calculates the average of last *15%* data instances of *Part 1*.
4. For *higher* boundary calculates the average of first *15%* data instances of *Part 2*.
5. Use this *lower* and *higher* value as cluster center.

$0 \; x \leq 1$

$$\mu_{high} = \frac{x-h}{h-l} \; l < x < h$$

$1 \; x \geq h$

$0 \; x \geq h$

$$\mu_{low} = 1 - \frac{x-h}{h-l} \; l < x < h$$

$1 \; x \leq 1$

- l denotes the lower cluster center and
- h denotes the higher cluster center.

Use membership functions to replace the data set with fuzzy expression and merged it with C4.5 algorithm to form Fuzzy C4.5. *Labor Relation Datasets* used to as an example. Boundaries are defined according to the obligations of the dataset. The dataset has total 16 features in which eight continuous attributes and eight categorical attributes and fuzzy representation is applied to all eight continuous attributes. Membership functions are erected as *Low* and *High*.

Then define the membership functions for fuzzy set x *(Low and High)* μ_x are defined distinctly using the method as described above and boundaries are intended using that boundary, membership function is calculated using equation μ_{low} and μ_{high} of all attributes. These membership functions are applied to the sample data set for the fuzzy depiction of the dataset. The sum of the membership values essential be equal to one so fuzzy values are computed for *Labor Relation* dataset using the following membership functions for fuzzy continuous attributes. Figure 6represents the graphical view membership function of two continuous attributes of labor relation datasets constructed using the cluster center point.

Attribute Wages Increase First Year (WIFY)

$0 \; x \leq 3.5$

$\mu_{high} = 1.09x - 4.847 \; 3.5 < x < 4.41$

$1 \; x \geq 4.41$

$0 \; x \geq 4.41$

$\mu_{low} = 5.84 - 1.09x \; 3.5 < x < 4.41$

$1 \; x \leq 3.5$

Figure 9. Membership function of an attribute WIFY

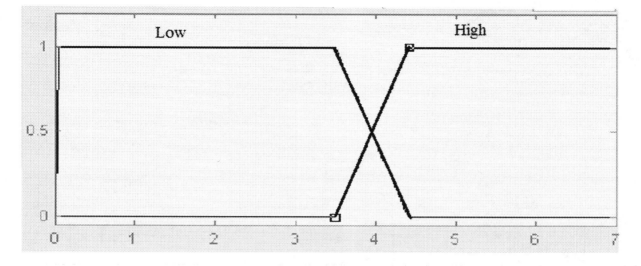

Fuzzy Information Gain and Entropy

Here the class entropy formula in fuzzy remains same as C4.5 decision tree algorithm using probability, thus its mean entropy of *the Labor Relation dataset* of the class attribute using the formula is

$$E\left(S\right) = \sum_{i}^{N} - P_i * Log_2 P_i$$

$E(S) = E(42 \text{ Bad and } 71 \text{ Good}) = 0.952$

Due to fuzzy expression, fuzzy entropy and fuzzy information gain will be used and the formula of fuzzy entropy and information gain are a slightly different. It use membership function value instead of probability. Membership function value is applied to all fuzzy or continuous attributes.

The fuzzy entropy (E_f) of attributes At for sample set $S = \{x_1, x_2, x_{3v}, \ldots, x_j\}$ using μ_{ij} the membership value of the jth pattern and i^{th} class value will be

$$E_f\left(S, A\right) = -\sum_{j=1}^{c} \frac{\sum_{j}^{N} \mu_{ij}}{S} \log_2 \frac{\sum_{j}^{N} \mu_{ij}}{S}$$

And information gained (IG_f) will calculate using the following formula by computing the difference of information contents of the class attribute and entropy of the attribute

$$IG_f\left(S, A\right) = E_f\left(S\right) - \sum_{c \subseteq A}^{N} \frac{\left|S_c\right|}{\left|S\right|} * E_{fS}\left(S_c, A\right)$$

Figure 10. Root node tree with highest information gain

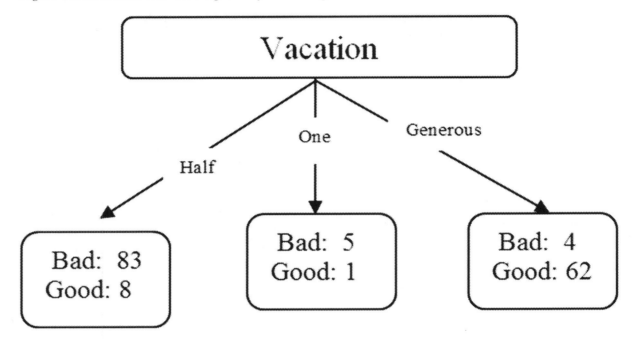

Therefore

- $E_f(S)$, the entropy of the set S of sample training examples in the node.
- $|S|$ is the proportions of the subset $S_c \subseteq S_f$ of training samples x_j with c attributes.
- The *Size* of the sample set is presented by set $|S|$.

Example Calculations of fuzzy attribute *Wages Increased First Year (WIFY)*

$$H_f\left(WIFY, low\right) = -\frac{30.0}{47.6}\log_2\frac{30.0}{47.6} - \frac{17.6}{47.6}\log_2\frac{17.6}{47.6} = 0.950$$

$$G_f\left(S, Duration\right) = 0.952 - \frac{47.6}{113}H_f\left(WIFY, low\right) - \frac{65.4}{113}H_f\left(WIFY, High\right) = 0.154$$

Attribute with highest information gain is selected and here *Vacation* attribute is selected as the root node and is used to split as shown in Figure 10.

Thresholds

The learning of fuzzy decision tree stops till all the instances of the sample data at each leaf node belong to one class value. If tree growth will not stop, then it resultant tree will have poorer accuracy. Two thresholds are used for defining the stopping criteria for improving the accuracy of tree (Umano et *al.* 1994).

Fuzzy Control Threshold θ_r

For stopping the growth of the tree, calculate the proportion of the sample set for class C_k, and define the threshold. If the value of the proportion is equal to or greater than the threshold θ_r then stop tree expansion process. Level of threshold is defined wisely because the threshold has an excessive impact on the result.

For example, the ratio of subset dataset for class *bad* and class *Good* is calculated from figure 10. If the coherent branch *one* is calculated for class *good* is 16.7% and *bad* is 83.3%, threshold θ_r is 80% than stop expanding the tree but if threshold θ_r is 85% then expand the node.

Leaf Node Decision Threshold θ_n

This threshold is used for defining any node as leaf nodes. If the number of instances of node is more than the threshold than expand tree for that node otherwise stop expanding the tree. If we increase the threshold than it shows the great effect on the accuracy of the tree.

For example *Labor relation* dataset contains 113 data instances and where θ_n is 5% than 5% of 113 is 4, so if a node has less than 4 instances than stop expanding the tree.

Recursively apply this process for expanding the tree till all instances will be classified correctly. Figure 11 shows the entire fuzzy decision tree of Labor relation dataset.

Figure 11. Fuzzy decision tree for labor relation dataset

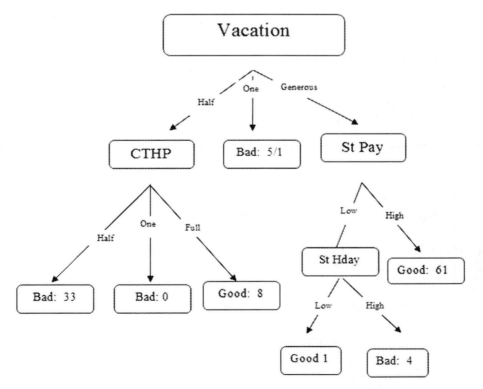

Figure 12. Fuzzy C4.5 algorithm

1   Create a *Root* node that has a set of fuzzy data with membership value 1

1   Create a *Root* node that has a set of fuzzy data with membership value 1

2   If a node t with a fuzzy set of data D satisfies the following conditions, then it is a leaf node and assigned by the class name

- The proportion of a class C_k is greater than or equal to θ_r,

$$\frac{|D^\alpha|}{|D|} \geq \theta_r$$

- the number of a data set is less than θ_n

- there are no attributes for more classifications

3 If a node D does no satisfy the above conditions, then it is not a leaf-node. And an new sub-node is generated as follow:

- For A_i's ($i=1,...,L$) calculate the information gain G(2.8), and select the test attribute A_{max} that maximizes them.

- Divide D into fuzzy subset $D_1, ..., D_m$ according to A_{max}, where the membership value of the data in D_j is the product of the membership value in D and the value of $F_{max,j}$ of the value of A_{max} in D.

- Generate new nodes $t_1, ..., t_m$ for fuzzy subsets $D_1, ..., D_m$ and label the fuzzy sets $F_{max,j}$ to edges that connect between the nodes t_j and t

- Replace D by D_j ($j=1, 2, ..., m$) and repeat from 2 recursively.

(Janikow 1998) presented the amendment of representative decision tree with fuzzy illustration to achieve the advantages of together decision tree and fuzziness. They explore the capabilities of both frameworks to get complete accuracy and in result they express that it is suitable work for stationary problems with both continuous and categorical datasets. It allows for processing unpredictable, noisy and imperfect data with real values. (Chaing and Jane 2002) have presented and compare the performance of fuzzy classification tree and C4.5 of uncertainties in a biochemical laboratory diagnose dataset. The accuracy rate of Fuzzy tree is better than the C4.5. C4.5 does not focus upon the distribution of data which cause improper classification (Chaing and Jane 2002). Fuzzy tree allows multiple prediction associated with degree of pruning and focuses on the data distribution. The fuzzy classification tree is very useful for large amount of data with uncertainty.

(Guoxiu 2005) and (Semra & Ersoy 2010) Presents the comparative study of Interactive Dichotomizer 3 (ID3), Fuzzy ID3 (FID3) and Probabilistic Fuzzy ID3 algorithm (PFID3). Two third dataset is used for training they used 9 pairs of threshold to experimentation. Leaf decision threshold is very important because as threshold increase performance also increase (Guoxiu 2005). They have compared the average performance of ID3, fuzzy ID 3 and probabilistic fuzzy ID3 and the results shows that the performance of FID3 and PFID3 is better than ID3. The foremost alteration is because of well define sample space (Guoxiu 2005).The best quality results of all three method are shown and according to the results the best gain is achieved by PFID3 and then FID3 is in second position and IF3 remain at last with 0.557 gain respectively. The fuzziness control threshold is very significant (Semra & Ersoy 2010).

(John 1989). perform an empirical comparison of pruning methods for ID3 algorithm and concludes that, PEP is fastest, simple method and also the showed tremendous result of some datasets, MEP is the least accurate method. Virtuous results are attained by Error – complexity pruning, CVP and REP by producing less error rate. (Mehta M. *et al.* 1995) presented a novel pruning algorithm that automatically attained the main goal pruning by reducing the misclassification rate. Minimum Description Length pruning produces a small tree with less error rates, more accurate and fast result when compared with other pruning techniques. (Esposito *et al.* 1997) perform the comparison for investigating six pruning methods, to understand the theoretical substance, strengths, weaknesses and computational complexity of their formulation. (Esposito *et at.* 1997) *a*lso discuss the characteristics of pruning methods. REP find the smallest tree with a low error rate belong to separate pruning sets. The experiment shows that the REP method achieves an unbiased evaluation of the learning to under-prune / over-prune observed in each method.

(Bradford and Clayton. 1998). Describe the experimental study of various pruning algorithms for decision tree. Empirical comparison was implemented with respect to mean square error, log loss and loss. How pruning suffers bias and variance is also presented. (Bradford and Clayton. 1998). Results show that not any one pruning algorithm captured best performance over all datasets in term of loss, log loss and MSE. Very less difference is between MSE and loss and also for the method which did not use loss matrices. Various features of Pruning methods are discussed by (Dipiti, et *al.* 2010). A new MLPC algorithm that combines pruning and building the tree is proposed. For the evaluation *Credit Card Database* is used with and without pruning. It reduces the complexity of creating the decision tree when fewer nodes are extended during the tree construction phase.

COMPARISON C4.5 AND FUZZY C4.5

Modification of general decision tree algorithm with fuzzy representation is presented by (Janikow 1998) to achieve the benefits of both fuzziness and decision tree. The complete tree building process is explained and it is recommended that the fuzzy decision tree framework is appropriate for stationary problems with both categorical and continuous data sets. (Chaing and Jane 2002) compare the performance of C4.5 and fuzzy classification tree for biochemical laboratory diagnose dataset to avoid the uncertainty problem. Partition boundaries for continuous attribute complicate the decision from C4.5 but the accuracy rate of Fuzzy tree is better than the C4.5, because Fuzzy tree focuses on the data distribution, it allows numerous predictions related to the degree of pruning. Comparative study of Interactive Dichotomizer 3 (ID3), Fuzzy ID3 (FID3) and Probabilistic Fuzzy ID3 algorithm (PFID3) was presented by (Guoxiu 2005) for Iris data set. They use two third dataset for training and 9 pair of thresholds is used to experiment. (Semra & Ersoy 2010) also presented the comparative study for the evaluation of the learning achievements of student datasets. The result shows that FID3 and PFID3 work better than ID3.

Table 4. Dataset detail

S. No	Dataset	Features			Number of Instance			Number of Class Values	Missing Value
		Total	Categorical	Real	Total	Training 80%	Test 20%		
1.	Labor Relation	17	8	9	No	113	25	No	2
2.	Glass Identification	11	1	10	No	171	43	No	6
3.	Statlog (Heart)	14	9	5	No	216	54	No	2

C4.5 and fuzzy C4.5 is compared using two main measures size and accuracy of the tree. The first parameter *Size* of the tree is important smaller tree is better than larger one by (Eibe 2000), here size is measured by total number of nodes in the tree including the root node, internal nodes and leaf nodes. The second parameter *Accuracy* of the tree is measured by the classification error. Number of instances incorrectly classified describes the accuracy of the tree. Chi square test is used to check the accuracy of the tree for errors.

Dataset Detail

In this enquiry three datasets from UCI Machine Learning Repository area used. UCI Machine Learning Repository is collection of databases used in experiential data analysis of machine learning algorithms. The library was formed by David Aha and companions at UC Irvine in 1987. This website has been broadly used as a prime source of machine learning datasets by students, researchers and educators. Following three datasets are used from UCI Machine Learning Repository. Characteristics of the datasets and training and test set distribution are described in the table 4.

Glass Identification Data Set

This dataset was created by *B. German* and was donated by *VinaSpiehler* Ph.D. DABFT Diagnostic Products Corporation. A comparison test was conducted by Vina of her rule-based system. In determining the type of the glass was float or not. This is multivariate dataset used for classification problems, this dataset have 214 number of instances of ten continuous attributes and last attribute is class type and glass are classified into seven classes and only six class labels are available in this dataset.

Labor Relations

This data was not created by individual; it is result of collective effort of monthly publications, labors, industrial relations information service Canada. And this is donated by Stan Matwin, Computer Science Dept. University of Ottawa. This dataset also includes all collective agreements in personal service sector, business in Canada in 87. According to the requirement of my work preprocessing is performed in this dataset. Originally this dataset consist of 57 data instances and having missing values. To avoid the missing values pre-processing is applied using WEKA tool. Data instances are increased to 148. This dataset shows the behavior of labors in two class values *Good or Bad*. Data set contain different continuous and categorical attributes.

Statlog (Heart) Data Set

This dataset use various attribute to show the absences and presence of heart disease. It is a multivariate database consists of 13 continuous and categorical attributes, 270 data instances and 2 class labels. This dataset have no missing values.

Table 4 shows describe the general characteristics of dataset and division of dataset. Features of datasets are Total (T), Real (R) and Categorical (C), instances and missing values. It also shows the distribution of data instances in test and training data. 80% of total data is used to train the model. And 20% data is used to test the classical learning.

The performance of the decision tree is measured by the size of the tree, classification error and Chi-Square Test X^2 is applied to check the accuracy of the tree because fewer the errors more accurate the model will be. Here are the some recommendations from the results that we receive.

Table 5 shows the results of C4.5 and fuzzy C4.5 for different domains of data and graphical representation of the table 5 is shown in figure 13 (a) tree size, (b) classification error and (c) Chi-Square test.

According to the Size of the Tree

Following are the results of comparison of C4.5 and Fuzzy C4.5 according to size of the tree from table 5 and as shown from figure 13 (a)

1. C4.5 is succeed to generate the smaller for the following two data sets
    a. Glass Identification and
    b. Statlog Heart dataset
2. From *Labor Relation* dataset smaller tree is constructed by Fuzzy C4.5

According to the Number of Classification Error

Following are the results of comparison of C4.5 and Fuzzy C4.5 according to number of misclassification errors of the tree from table 5 and as shown from figure 13 (b)

1. C4.5 generate the smaller error for the following two data sets
    a. Glass Identification and
    b. Statlog Heart dataset

Table 5. Comparison of C4.5 and Fuzzy C4.5

S. No	Dataset	Tree Size		Classification Errors		Chi-Square X^2	
		C4.5	Fuzzy C4.5	C4.5	Fuzzy C4.5	C4.5	Fuzzy C4.5
1.	Labor Relation	13	11	1	1	1.678	1.678
2.	Glass Identification	37	119	16	55	45.3	38.2
3.	Statlog (Heart)	76	96	12	13	127.1	126.5

Figure 13. Comparison of C4.5 And Fuzzy C4.5 without pruning

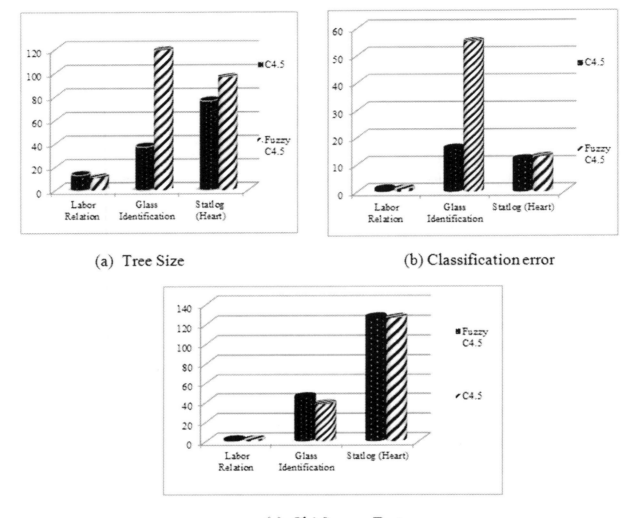

(a) Tree Size

(b) Classification error

(c) Chi Square Test

2.   For *Labor Relation* dataset the performance of C4.5 and Fuzzy C4.5 is equal, so they generate the same number of errors.

According to the Chi-Square Test X^2

Following are the results of comparison of C4.5 and Fuzzy C4.5 according to errors using chi-square error of the tree from table 5 and as shown from figure 13 (c)

1.   C4.5 generate the smaller error when the test is applied for the only datasets
    a.   Labor Relation Dataset

2.   For *Labor Relation* dataset the performance of C4.5 and Fuzzy C4.5 is equal, so they generate the same errors when the test is applied.
3.   Fuzzy C4.5 succeed to generate the smaller error for all the three datasets
     a.   Glass Identification and
     b.   Labor Relation Dataset
     c.   Statlog Heart dataset
4.   Performance of Fuzzy C4.5 is better than C4.5 because it succeeds to generate the more accurate tree with minimum error.

Pruning Methods

Classifier performance can be improved by eliminating error–prone modules. It also rushes supplementary inquiry of the patterns for the purpose of information attainment. Apparently, it will not eliminate analytical parts of the tree. Accordingly, the pruning technique imposes a measure for deciding a set of splits is predictive or not, or it would be joined into only higher disjoint.

Classifying the data using C4.5 and fuzzy C4.5 will outcome the large dimension tree, statistical tests of pruning area applied to diminish the size of the tree till implication level (Minger 1989). The data consists of vagueness in many real time problems; there are two unlike causes of uncertainty (Minger 1989)

1. Miss-Measurement Values of attributes are erroneously measure or missing, due to incorrect recording, transcription, measurement, or perception.
2. Occurrence of inappropriate factors Recording of inappropriate features affects the result, so it will not be recorded. It has more implication than real-world problem nails.

In pruning the less reliable branches of the tree which have high uncertainty are abolished or replace by the leaf node. Classification error rate will be decreased on separate test data and increase error rate on the training data (Minger 1989). The decision tree pruning is detected as sound diligence after tree creation has two central reasons

1.   Decrease decision tree size
2.   Increase the decision tree accuracy.

Different results are achieved by applying altered pruning techniques on decision tree. Some methods gave the smaller tree as a result and increase the accuracy of the tree. Pruning the decision tree up to 25% will increase the accuracy (Marcos et *al.*, 2010)

Cost–Complexity Pruning (CCP)

Cost-complexity pruning was proposed in 1984 by Breiman *et al.*, also known as error – complexity pruning. This method checks for the size of the tree and errors. It has two steps (Wang *et al.* 2001),

1.   The first step is to construct a sequence of trees T_0, DT_1,…,DT_r,and where the original un-prunes tree is denoted by DT_0 and root tree is DT_r.

2. In the second step, select one tree from a sequence of pruned trees as the final tree, based on its general error estimate. It will select the sub–trees to prune which will result less increase in degree of error per pruned leaf node by using the following measure $a = \dfrac{\varepsilon\left(Prune\left(DT, dt\right), S\right) - \varepsilon\left(DT, S\right)}{\left|Leaf\left(DT\right)\right| - 1}$

    ○ ■ Where Error cost of node t if the selected sub tree T_t is prune, can be measured as

$\varepsilon(Prune(DT, dt), S) = r(t_i) \times p(t_i)$

    ○ $\varepsilon(DT; S)$ indicate the degree of errors for the sample set S in the subtree DT
    ○ Prune(DT, dt) indicates the prune tree achieved by swapping the sub tree 10.4018/978-1-4666-4940-8.ch003in DT with an appropriate leaf node value.
    ○ |Leaf(DT)| indicates the total number of leaf nodes in sub-tree DT.
    ○ Change in error is a measure of quantity α defined to be increased error of every leaf of the sub-tree.
    ○ I – Sub tree leaves
    ○ $\left|N_{T_t}\right|$ – Quantity of leaf nodes in sub tree T_t
    ○ ■ $\varepsilon(DT, S)$– The error rate of node t

$\varepsilon\left(DT, S\right) = \dfrac{Number\ of\ error\ on\ node\ t}{Number\ of\ training\ examples}$

    ○ ■ $p(t_i)$– The amount of data on total training dataset

$p\left(t_i\right) = \dfrac{Number\ of\ training\ example\ in\ sub\ tree}{Total\ number\ of\ training\ examples}$

    ○ ■ $R\left(T_{t_i}\right)$ - The error cost if the sub tree T is not pruned.

$R\left(T_{t_i}\right) = \sum R\left(i\right)$

This algorithm will compute α for all sub trees and then prune all those sub trees which illustrate the smallest value. The CART algorithm practices this algorithm to generate gradually smaller pruned tree. This method takes explanation of both the size of the tree and number of errors of the tree (Minger. 1998). The best pruned tree is then selected (Earl et al.1966).

Reduced Error Pruning (REP)

A new pruning method based on a separate pruning set proposed by Quinlan in 1987. This method is simple and easy to understand for the pruning decision tree. A series of pruned trees are produced by this method by applying test data on the complete tree directly (Minger 1989). This is a bottom-up traversal approach and produce a smaller version of the pruned tree based on pruning settings (Esposito et *al*. 1997). The main advantage of this method is that it only visits each node only once for pruning evaluation that's why it has linear computational complexity.

Start with a complete decision tree and run a separate test set on it and write the errors on each non leaf node of the tree and count the number of errors occurs at each leaf node. Compute the number of errors if sub tree is kept or if it is pruned. Select the node to prune with maximum difference, this process will be continued until more pruning will result an increase in misclassification rate. This method will produce the smallest tree with respect to pruning set. If the pruning set is small then it will produce a smaller tree than the original tree.

The working of this method is as follows: it starts with the complete tree T and run test data through it. It will total the classification errors at the correspondingly inner nodes of the tree that made on the sample test data if the node is pruned and convert a leaf node. Pruned node will have less misclassification on test data, if we replace the sub tree t by the mainstream of its class value of the leaf then the misclassification will occur (Dipiti et al. 2010). If the error rate of pruned tree is smaller or equal to the original tree T than replace the sub tree by leaf node otherwise, stop pruning tree process. The restriction of this method is that no sub tree t comprises the sub tree with the same possessions.

The tree will lead to over prune if test sample is much smaller than the training data. This technique will yield the smallest tree with respect to pruning set. Number of sub trees will be there with same difference, but it is not specified by Quanlin (1987) which tree will be preferred for such situation e.g. smallest or largest sub tree.

Pessimistic Error Pruning (PEP)

Quinlan in 1993 advised a method which uses pessimistic statistical correlation test for the binomial distributions; no separate test data are required in this method for pruning method. An error estimate is calculated from training data, hence the separate pruning set is not required (Eibe. 2000). Moreover in pessimistic pruning algorithm a constant is added to the training error of a sub tree by condescendingly that each leaf usually classifies a definite segment of an example imperfectly. ½ divided by the quantity of instances covered by the leaf is taken as a fraction. It is used to make the typical distribution more appraised to the binomial distribution if the sample space is small. In pruning process, this modification is used the adjusted error estimation for the leaf is lesser or equal to the attuned error of the tree plus one standard error of the ultimate estimation. Following measures are used for the calculation

The estimate for the misclassification rate for a node is calculated as follows:

$$r\left(t\right) = \frac{e\left(t\right)}{N\left(t\right)}$$

T – Represents the node
$e(t)$ – number or misclassified example
$N(t)$ – number of training example set

The estimate for the misclassification rate for sub tree *it* is calculated as follow:

$$r\left(t\right) = \frac{\sum e(i)}{\sum N(i)}$$

$\sum e(i)$– *Represent the sum of errors on leaf nodes*
i– it will cover all leaves of the sub tree *t*

The rate with the continuity correction for a node is calculated as follows:

$$r^*(T_t) = \frac{e(t) + \dfrac{1}{2}}{N(t)}$$

The rate with the continuity correction for sub tree *t* is calculated as follows:

$$r'\left(T_t\right) = \frac{\sum\left(e\left(i\right) + \dfrac{1}{2}\right)}{\sum N\left(i\right)} = \frac{\sum e\left(i\right) + \dfrac{N_{Tt}}{2}}{\sum N\left(i\right)}$$

N_T – number or leave nodes

According to the equation 2.7 and 2.8 N(i) and $\sum N(i)$ Refer to the same training examples so the equations for the node is simplified as

$$n'\left(t\right) = e\left(t\right) + \frac{1}{2}$$

Equation for sub tree *t* as follow

$$n'\left(T_t\right) = \sum e\left(i\right) + \frac{N_T}{2}$$

The decision tree will make fewer error than the consistent node with the training data, this will not happen if a corrected figure is used, because it just not depend upon number of error it also depend upon number of leaves (Minger 1989). Standard Error (SE) for the number of misclassification is defined for the rate of misclassification that given earlier.

$$SE\left(n'\left(T_t\right)\right) = \sqrt{\frac{n'\left(T_t\right) \times \left(N\left(t\right) - n'\left(T_t\right)\right)}{N\left(t\right)}}$$

If the value of $n'\left(t\right)$ is less than $n'\left(T_t\right) + SE\left(n'\left(T_t\right)\right)$ Then the sub-tree will be changed by the leaf node having the leading class label. The sub tree will not be pruned and keep by the algorithm if $n'\left(t\right)$ is greater than $n'\left(T_t\right) + SE\left(n'\left(T_t\right)\right)$.

The condition is based on the statistical confidence-interval for spaces. Any node no matters leave or internal node will be selected to prune. When any leaf nodes of the sub tree are selected to be prone than convert the selected sub tree into leaf node with prominent class value, or selected node is an internal node than all successors trees will be eliminated and that convert the internal sub tree into leaf node, resulting in a relatively fast pruning (Bradford and Clayton 1998).

Critical Value Pruning (CVP)

(John 1989) suggested post-pruning technique (Umano *et al.* 1994) based on the measure used for tree building and check the value for certain threshold value. it is a bottom-up approach comparable to reduced-error pruning. This pruning method calculates the strength and importance of the node using the calculation done at the time of tree construction. The goodness or gain is used to select the best split attribute on the node (Minger 1989), this value of goodness reflects that how the attribute is selected for the split at the node. This measure will maximize the value of splitting measure. Absolutely, a threshold is designated as critical value to select a node for pruning. Then, a sub tree is eliminated and converted to leaf node if the value of the measure will be smaller than the critical value, or if the value is greater than the threshold then the classifier will keep the sub tree. The pruning, rate has obviously altered with the increase or decrease in critical value greater the critical value results smaller tree. This method consists of two major steps (Umano *et al.* 1994)

1. Sequence of the tree will be pruned with growing critical values.
2. Measure the implication of the pruned tree entirely and best tree will be selected from a sequence of pruned trees.

The larger the value of the threshold is nominated than the degree of pruning is large and the size of the pruned tree is smaller the pruned tree. A series of pruned trees will be generated using different critical values and then the best tree will be selected with least increase in error. On the other hand, one more additional limitation is forced:

- If the sub tree even contains one node whose goodness value is greater than the threshold, then that node will not pruned. Only those sub trees are selected to prune if all its leading nodes are leaf nodes (Eibe 2000).

Overall, a value of the threshold is in the range 0.9500 - 0.9995 (95% - 99.95%) is suitable to produce a set of pruned trees (Minger 1989). This method selects the low analytical accuracy sub trees reasonably and has a strong leaning towards under prune is the main is advantages of this pruning algorithm (Dipiti et al. 2010).

Minimum Error Pruning (MEP)

Niblett and Bratko (1987) proposed a technique pursuing for a single tree that minimize the expected errors. called minimum error pruning. Error rate estimated of all nodes with and without pruning is compared with this method (Wang *et al.* 2001). The expected error rate of leaf is calculated using following measure (Esposito et al. 1997). It is identical to pessimistic error pruning method. Drived the class count from the training data is also used by this method. It differs from the pessimistic error pruning method in a way like the count is attuned in order to reflect the performance of the leaf simplification more thoroughly. This method is developed to find the single tree of minimum error rate in classifying separate dataset (Minger 1989). This does not mean that it will use separate test data for pruning, simply the error is estimated for unseen cases (Esposito et al. 1997).

Calculate the predictable error rate E_k of each inner node if the sub-tree is pruned is also called stated error. And also calculate the expected error rate E_k of same node of each branch if the sub tree is not pruned by combining the probability of observation along each branch is called dynamic error (Esposito et al. 1997). Expected error be contingent upon the number of classes k it affects the grade of pruning. If the expected error rate of pruning the node is larger than the expected error rate of not pruning than keep the sub tree, otherwise replace the sub tree with the leaf node.

$$E_k = \frac{n_t - n_c\left(t\right) + k - 1}{n_t + k}$$

- E_k– represents expected error rate that is, the proportion of wrong classification
- n_t – Number of training examples observed on sub tree t
- $n_c(t)$ – Number of observations belongs to the leading class at node t
- k – Number of classes

If pruning the sub node does not increase the error, then pruning that node is accepted.

This is a recursive procedure, mean while the error rate of all branches is calculated until you cannot know that the branch itself to be pruned or not.

COMPARISON OF PRUNING METHODS

Effects of pruning are measured for the decision tree constructed C4.5 and Fuzzy C4.5. Different pruning methods show different results, some of them remain the tree un-prunes and some prune the tree slightly, we have tested the impact for the following datasets of UCI repository for the two major parameters of decision tree analysis, i.e. size and accuracy of the tree.

Table 6. Pruning effects on C4.5 and Fuzzy C4.5 for tree size

S. No	Dataset	Tree Size									
		C4.5					Fuzzy C4.5				
		CCP	CVP	MEP	PEP	REP	CCP	CVP	MEP	PEP	REP
1.	Labor Relation	**8**	13	13	13	13	**8**	10	10	**8**	20
2.	Glass Identification	**19**	25	37	27	33	69	89	**63**	**63**	105
3.	Statlog (Heart)	37	49	44	**22**	49	48	70	58	**17**	84

Figure 14. Effects of pruning on (a) C4.5 And (b) Fuzzy C4.5

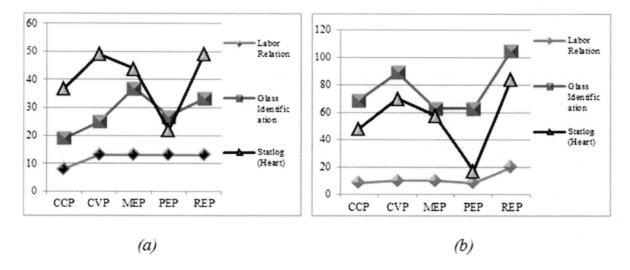

(a)   *(b)*

Table 6 shows the results of pruning with respect to the size of the tree for C4.5 and fuzzy C4.5. Graphical representation of the tree size is shown in figure 14 shows the impacts of pruning for (a) C4.5 and (b) Fuzzy C4.5.

Impact of Pruning When Applied to C4.5

Following are the recommendations when five pruning methods are applied on C4.5 from table 6 and as shown from figure 14 (a)

1. CCP succeeds to generate the smaller tree for the following two data sets
   a. Glass Identification and
   b. Labor Relation dataset
2. PEP also shows the best results, but it generates the smallest tree for only one dataset.
   a. Statlog (Heart) dataset
3. PEP also prunes the Glass Identification dataset, but didn't succeed to generate the smallest tree.
4. MEP leave the tree un-prune for two datasets

    a.   Glass Identification and

    b.   Labor Relation dataset

5.   CVP and REP also try to reduce the size if the tree but failed to produce the smallest tree.

Impact of Pruning When Applied to Fuzzy C4.5

Following are the recommendations when five pruning methods are applied on Fuzzy C4.5 from table 6 and as shown from figure 14 (b)

1.   CCP succeeds to generate the smaller tree for the only one dataset

    a.   Labor Relation dataset

2.   PEP also shows the consistent results by generating the smallest tree for all three datasets.

    a.   Glass Identification and

    b.   Labor Relation dataset

    c.   Statlog (Heart) dataset

3.   In *Labor Relation* dataset results or CCP and PEP shows the same results by generating the smaller tree.

4.   In Glass Identification dataset results or PEP and MEP shows the same results by generating the smaller tree.

5.   CVP and REP also try to reduce the size if the tree but failed to produce the smallest tree from any of the datasets.

        To evaluate the accuracy of the tree *Chi-Square Test X^2* is used which is used to measure the error, here it is applied to the results of the tree after pruning to show the effects with respect to the error, lesser the error more will be the accuracy.

        Table 7 shows the results of pruning with respect to the *Chi-Square Test X^2* for error to C4.5 and fuzzy C4.5. Graphical representation of the *Chi-Square Test X^2* is showed in figure 15 shows the impacts of pruning for (a) C4.5 and (b) Fuzzy C4.5.

Impact of Pruning When Applied to C4.5

Following are the recommendations when five pruning methods are applied on C4.5 from Table 7 and as shown from Figure 15 (a)

1.   CCP succeeds to generate the smaller tree with little increase in error for the following two data sets

    a.   Glass Identification and

    b.   Labor Relation dataset

2.   PEP succeeds to generate the smaller tree with less increase in error for only one dataset.

    a.   Statlog (Heart) dataset

3.   For *Labor Relation* dataset only CCP reduced the size of the tree which cause change in error of the tree rest of all pruning methods leaves it un-prune.

Table 7. Pruning effects on C4.5 and Fuzzy C4.5 with Chi-Square Test X^2

S. No	Dataset	Classification Error									
		C4.5					Fuzzy C4.5				
		CCP	CVP	MEP	PEP	REP	CCP	CVP	MEP	PEP	REP
1.	Labor Relation	**1.60**	1.67	1.67	0	1.67	**1.678**	1.679	1.679	**1.678**	1.679
2.	Glass Identification	**42.2**	44.3	45.6	43.6	44.7	37.2	**34.9**	36.5	37.4	37.5
3.	Statlog (Heart)	124.8	126.5	125.9	**119.1**	126.5	121.8	125.2	124.0	**116.2**	127.1

Figure 15. Effect of pruning on (a) C4.5 and (b) Fuzzy C4.5

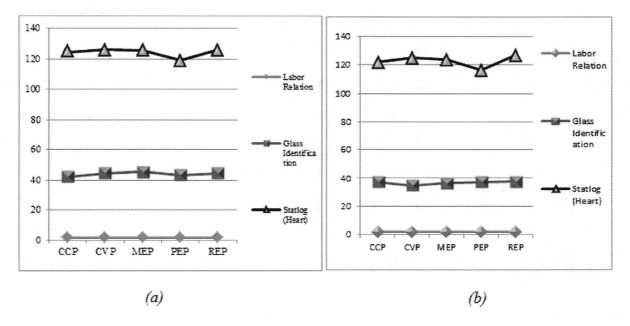

(a)   (b)

Impact of Pruning When Applied to Fuzzy C4.5

Following are the recommendations when five pruning methods are applied on Fuzzy C4.5 from Table 7 and as shown from Figure 15 (b).

1. PEP generates more accurate, smallest tree by showing less errors for following two datasets.
   a. Labor Relation dataset
   b. Statlog (Heart) dataset
2. For *Labor Relation* dataset results or CCP and PEPshows the same results by generating the smaller tree with minimum error
3. CVP succeeds to generate more accurate tree but failed to produce the smaller tree by showing less errors for following dataset.
   a. Glass Identification

CONCLUSION

Comparison of C4.5 and Fuzzy C4.5 is performed using three data sets from UCI repository is performed and the results show that the performance of Fuzzy C4.5 is better than the C4.5 in term of accuracy rate. Fuzzy C4.5 generated the more accurate tree for all three dataset. For *Labor Relation* dataset the performance of both C4. 5 and fuzzy C4.5 is equal in term of accuracy, but fuzzy C4.5 generate smaller tree as compare to C4.5. The effect of Pruning is also evaluated for both C4.5 and Fuzzy C4.5, the results implies

- When pruning is applied on C4.5,
  - CCP generates the smaller tree with minimum increase in error for
- *Glass Identification*
- Labor *Relation dataset,*
  - PEP also shows the best results by generating the smaller tree for *Statlog (Heart)* dataset.
- Most of the pruning methods leave tree un-prunes.
- When pruning is applied on Fuzzy C4.5
  - CCP also succeeds to generate the smaller tree for *Labor Relation* dataset
  - PEP also shows the consistent results by generating the smallest tree for all three datasets.
  - MEP also generates the smaller tree after pruning for *Glass Identification*dataset.
- When Chi-Square test is applied to check the accuracy of the tree
  - CCP, PEP shows good results by producing a minimum error for C4.5 and Fuzzy C4.5 both.
  - CVP also shows minimum error for *Glass Identification*dataset when applied on Fuzzy C4.5.
- CCP and PEP work best for both continuous and categorical data for generating small size and more accurate tree when applied on C4.5 and Fuzzy C4.5.

REFERENCES

Bradford, J. P., Clayton, K., Ron, K., Cliff, B., & Carla, E. B. (1998). Pruning Decision Trees with Misclassification Costs. Machine Learning ECML-98. *Lecture Notes in Computer Science, 1398*, 131–136. doi:10.1007/BFb0026682

Dipiti, D. P., V. M. Wadhai, & J. A. Gokhale. (2010). Evaluation of Decision Tree Pruning Algorithms for Complexity and Classification Accuracy. International Journal of Computer Applications (0975 – 8887), 11(2), 23- 29.

Earl, B. H., Janet, M., & Philip, J. S. (1966). *Experiments in Induction.* New York: Academic Press.

Eibe, F. (2000). *Pruning Decision Trees and Lists* [Thesis].

Esposito, F., Maerba, D., Semeraro, G., & Kay, J. (1997). A Comparative Analysis of Methods for Pruning Decision Trees. *IEEE Transactions on Pattern Analysis and Machine Intelligence, 19*(5), 476–491.

Glass Identification Dataset. Retrieved from http//archive.ics.uci.edu/ml/datasets/Glass+Identification

Janikow, C. Z. (1998). Fuzzy Decision Trees Issues and Methods, IEEE Transaction on Systems. *Man and Cybernetics – Part B Cybernetics, 28*(1), 5–12.

Jen, C., & Jane, Y. H. (2002). Fuzzy Classification Trees for Data analysis. *Fuzzy Sets and Systems, 130*(1), 87–99. doi:10.1016/S0165-0114(01)00212-3

Jiawei, H., Micheline, K., & Jian, P. (2006). Data Mining, Southeast Asia Edition Concepts and Techniques Book. Guoxiu, L. (2005). A comparative study of three Decision Tree algorithms ID3, Fuzzy ID3 and Probabilistic Fuzzy ID3 [Thesis].

John, M. (1989). An Empirical Comparison of Pruning Methods for Decision Tree Induction. Kluwer Academic Publishers, Boston. Manufactured in The Netherlands. *Machine Learning, 4*(2), 227–243. doi:10.1023/A:1022604100933

Labor Relation Dataset. Retrieved from http//archive.ics.uci.edu/ml/datasets/Labor+Relations

Marcos, E. C., Maria, C. M., & Helosia, A. C. (2010). Evaluation of the pruning impact on Fuzzy C4.5. *Congresso Brasileiro de Sistemas Fuzzy., 1*(1), 257–264.

Marcos, E. C., Maria, C. M., & Helosia, A. C. (2012). *Fuzzy DT - A Fuzzy Decision Tree Algorithm Based on C4.5.*

Nitesh, V. C. (2003). C4.5 and Imbalanced Datasets Investigating the effect of sampling method, probabilistic estimate, and decision tree structure. Workshop on Learning from Imbalanced Datasets II, ICML, Washington DC.

Pal, R. N., & Chakraborty, S. (2001). Fuzzy Rule Extraction from ID3-Type Decision Trees for Real Data. *IEEE Transactions on Systems, Man, and Cybernetics. Part B, Cybernetics, 31*(5), 745–753. doi:10.1109/3477.956036 PMID:18244839

Quinlan, J. R. (1986). Induction of Decision Trees. *Machine Learning, 1*(1), 81–106. doi:10.1007/BF00116251

Quinlan, J. R. (1990). Decision Trees and Decision-Making, IEEE Transaction on Systems. *Man and Cybernetics, 20*(2), 339–336. doi:10.1109/21.52545

Semra, E., & Ersoy, Ö. Z. (2010). Comparison of Id3, Fuzzy Id3 and Probabilistic Id3 Algorithms in the Evaluation of Learning Achievements. *Journal of Computing*, (12), 20-25.

Sison, L. G., & Chong, E. K. P. (1994). Fuzzy Modeling by Induction and Pruning of Decision Trees. *Proceedings of IEEE symposium on intelligent control* (pp. 166-171).

Statlog Heart Dataset. Retrieved from http//archive.ics.uci.edu/ml/machine-learning-databases/statlog/heart/

Umano, M., Okamoto, H., Hatono, I., Tamura, H., Kawachi, F., Umedzu, S., & Kinoshita, J. (1994). Fuzzy Decision Trees by Fuzzy ID3 Algorithm and Its Application to Diagnosis Systems. In *Proceedings of the third IEEE Conference on Fuzzy Systems* (Vol. 3, pp. 2113-2118). Orlando.

Wang, X. Z., Yeung, D. S., & Tsang, E. C. C. (2001). A Comparative Study on Heuristic Algorithms for Generating Fuzzy Decision Trees. *IEEE Transactions on Systems, Man, and Cybernetics. Part B, Cybernetics, 31*(2), 215–226. doi:10.1109/3477.915344 PMID:18244783

KEY TERMS AND DEFINITIONS

Accuracy: The degree to which the result of a measurement, calculation, or specification conforms to the standard or a correct value.

Analysis: Analysis of data is a process of cleaning, inspecting, modeling and transforming data with the goal of discovering useful information, suggesting conclusions, and supporting decision-making.

Chi-Square: It is a statistical method assessing the goodness of fit between a set of observed values and those expected theoretically.

Data Mining: Data mining is refers to as mining or extracting knowledge from huge data set.

Decision Tree: The symbolic structure of nodes, leave and branch tree is a decision tree.

Misclassification: The values which are classify incorrectly; assign to the wrong category.

Pattern: A regular and comprehensive form or sequence apparently in the way in which something happens or is done.

Pruning: Pruning is a technique in machine learning that reduces the size of decision trees by removing sections of the tree that provide little power to classify instances. Pruning reduces the complexity of the final classifier, and hence improves predictive accuracy by the reduction of overfitting.

Uncertainty: The estimated amount or percentage by which an estimated or calculated value may differ from the true value.

Chapter 12
An Empirical Evaluation of Feature Selection Methods

Mohsin Iqbal
University Institute of Information Technology, Pakistan

Saif Ur Rehman
University Institute of Information Technology, Pakistan

Saira Gillani
Corvinus University of Budapest, Hungary

Sohail Asghar
COMSATS Institute of Information Technology, Pakistan

ABSTRACT

The key objective of the chapter would be to study the classification accuracy, using feature selection with machine learning algorithms. The dimensionality of the data is reduced by implementing Feature selection and accuracy of the learning algorithm improved. We test how an integrated feature selection could affect the accuracy of three classifiers by performing feature selection methods. The filter effects show that Information Gain (IG), Gain Ratio (GR) and Relief-f, and wrapper effect show that Bagging and Naive Bayes (NB), enabled the classifiers to give the highest escalation in classification accuracy about the average while reducing the volume of unnecessary attributes. The achieved conclusions can advise the machine learning users, which classifier and feature selection methods to use to optimize the classification accuracy, and this can be important, especially at risk-sensitive applying Machine Learning whereas in the one of the aim to reduce costs of collecting, processing and storage of unnecessary data.

1. INTRODUCTION

Considering feature selection extensively in the field of theory, such as machine learning and data mining for wide applications in gene expression microarray analysis, image analysis and word processing. Feature Selection of crucial importance in these areas, because it helps to improve the performance of the device to predict learning models by eliminating variables redundant, irrelevant and noisy, and provide

DOI: 10.4018/978-1-4666-8513-0.ch012

simpler models that facilitate the best explanation for a complex process of random, and provide cost a large amount of experimental measurements in practice, revealing subset of variables that can be studied closely to causal inference. Selection of feature (also known as variable selection, Subspace selection, or dimensional reduction) is Procedure to select a subset of the original feature set by eliminating redundant and less informative sub features so that it contains only the best Features discriminatory (Morita et al.; 2003). Feature selection works as (i) improve the prediction performance of the predictor, (ii) Helps more cost effective predictor and predictor do faster, and (iii) Provides a better understanding of the fundamental process that generates data (Guyon & Elisseeff. 2003).

The feature is irrelevant or noisy does not provide any valuable information to predict the concept of a goal and redundant feature does not add any additional information that may be useful for predicting the concept of goal (Dash & Liu, 1997). Feature subset selection helps in a number of ways, such as it reduces ineffective features to save time, computing and data storage, Features associated with enhanced performance and predictive prevents excessive manner, and provides a description of more than one occasion Target concept. Feature selection is a combinatorial optimization problem as it includes a feature set N Features can be very large, exclusive research. There are two types of feature selection method, i.e. filter method and wrapper method (Guyon & Elisseeff, 2003; Dash & Liu, 1997; Isabelle, 2003).

Filter based methods evaluate each feature independent through some classifiers e.g. statistical measure. As compared to other methods filter based method are light weighted, very efficient and fast to compute. Shed by hand wrapper based method assess the quality of a set of feature using a specific learning algorithm by internal cross-validation to evaluate the usefulness of a selected feature subset along with some search method (Heuristic search). Wrapper method is very slow, more expensive as compared to filter method, but wrapper method is best in terms of predictive accuracy (Yu & Huan, 2003).

Feature selection is furthermore useful within the data analysis process, as shows which features are for prediction, a lot more these features are related. Irrelevant features, using redundant features, severely affect the accuracy of this learning machine. Thus, feature subset selection is able to identify and remove because the irrelevant and redundant information as they possibly can. Many feature subset selection methods have been completely proposed and studied for machine learning applications. An existing feature selection approaches generally owned by these two categories: wrapper and filter. Wrappers include the target classifier as a part of their performance evaluation, while filters employ evaluation functions independent from the target classifier. Since wrappers train a classifier to evaluate each feature subset, they're just a whole lot more computationally intensive than filters. Hence, filters become more practical than wrappers in high-dimensional include spaces. Their computational complexity is low, nonetheless accuracy of this learning algorithm will be guaranteed.

From this chapter, we experiment with an alternative approach, which iteratively removes one after the other feature of this worst estimated quality. In each iteration it utilizes an important classifier model, which subsequently plays a great role with the procedure, to compute its accuracy. After performing all iterations, we buy a feature set, which enables the classifier to create its maximum classification accuracy of the guidance data. In this particular evaluation, we commence with discovering which feature selection method just about the most successful, i-e. Can enable the classifier to create its highest accuracy by removing a very high selection of unimportant features.

In the literature, there are many studies of feature selection methods; including on why prefer filter to wrapper method (Doraisami & Golzari, 2008), and for classification (Dash & Liu, 1997; Brank, 2002). In our study, for comparison, we used 10 datasets for feature selection methods and classification algorithms with respect to their influence.

In this particular experiment part, we present an empirical evaluation of five different filter methods to the include selection: *Information Gain (IG), Gain Ratio (GR), One-R, Symmetrical Uncertainty (SU)* and *Relief-f*, and three different wrapper methods to the include selection: *Bagging, Naïve Bayes* and *Random Forest*. Among these feature selection methods, comparison of filter and wrapper methods to other approaches presents a novelty, since practically no such empirical comparisons have been performed in the related work yet. The aim is to reduce the features and the ability to classify quickly and accurately.

The rest of this chapter is formed as follows. Section 2 provides a detailed review of similar publication and the related work. Section 3 provides a brief review of feature selection methods that describe a feature subset selection technique and classification algorithms. In section 4 illustrates the dataset. Section 5 report experimental and discussion of the results obtained. The conclusion is given in the last section.

2. BACKGROUND AND RELATED WORK

As the world grows in complexity, overwhelming us when using the data it generates, data mining becomes a common a solution to elucidating the patterns that underlie it (Witten et al, 2011). The manual steps involved in data analysis become tedious as scale data grows and also lots of dimensions increases, so the process of data analysis requires to be computerized. While in the presence of hundreds of features, the researchers observe that extremely common that a large number of features are usually not informed because they are either irrelevant or redundant with respect to the class concept. In various words, learning can be carried out more efficiently and effectively with just relevant and non-redundant features. Nonetheless, the number of possible feature subsets grows exponentially when using the increase of dimensionality. Findings any optimal subset will likely be intractable as well as some problems relating to feature selection have been completely proven NP-hard (Qiang et al, 2012).Suppose we are going to give the typical problem in which we wish optimizing a performance from a particular classifier by removing many different features in which presence hinders the classification accuracy. A typical solution to this is often by computing weights in the available features and choose only especially those with weight above an actual threshold. Nonetheless, really procedure would require the data which values work to use when the thresholds to prevent yourself from either disregarding unnecessary relevant features or considering unnecessary irrelevant ones. Additionally, the optimality to a chosen feature subset may well be a valid classification algorithm and necessarily in the other, that mean the perfect threshold can vary greatly within the classifier to classifier.

While in the broader context, feature selection, plus feature transformation, is certainly a dimensionality reduction approach. Methods of feature selection are usually categorized into two classes. The main group features methods which return superior estimate from each feature and also second class features methods that aim at selecting a subset of good quality features. Even though the previous can wind up being transformed to latter by selecting for only features above pre-defined threshold value, then adjust while in the other direction just always possible.

The feature selection methods are generally also divided to filter, wrapper and embedded methods (Blum & Langley.1997; Guyon & Elisseeff. 2003). The most important are defined as the estimating functions and used to provide a preprocessing step to estimate the quality in given features. The wrapper methods explore feature quality by moving via the feature subset space and additionally observing the impact of selected feature fixed at an important classification method which therefore acts as a black box. The third group, the embedded methods, is an integral area of particular learning algorithm (e. g.

Boosting, random forests) as they are resulting the properties within the underlying learning algorithm. With the related work, many categorizations and comparisons of this feature selection methods contain previously been performed. Published research from this field focuses mostly on the progress new feature selection methods, theoretical and empirical comparisons of feature selection approaches and helpful applications of such methods. From this section we present this related work, categorized in keeping with their personal main contributions. With the following Section 3, we briefly describe the feature selection approaches, relating to which we focus from this chapter.

Much of research publications in this region focus mostly over the wrapper methods. Ferri et al. (Ferri et al, 1994) compare wrapper methods, sequential forward selection (SFS), sequential floating in advance selection (SFFS) and genetic algorithms (GA) for high dimensional feature selection. Their goal was basically to check that the properties within the evaluated methods change when offered a problems about various difficulty magnitudes. Consistent with their research, the SFFS method gives achievement even meant for high dimensional problems. GA approach performs better you might find, but due to its stochastic nature the issues may well be you might find worse. This motivated the authors to produce a composite feature selection method, which combines one of the best parts of both methods. Similarly, Hall and Holmes (Hall & Holmes, 2003) compared the information gain, ReliefF, PCA, correlation-based feature selection, consistency-based feature evaluation in addition to a modified SFS algorithm, when in combination with C4. 5 and Naive Bayes classifiers. Authors get a general conclusion the fact that the feature selection is normally necessary for boosting the performance within the learning algorithms. They even observe that there isn't a single algorithm which could perform more optimally regardless of the situation. Similar findings are presented by Kudo and Sklansky (Kudo & Sklansky, 1997) who compare a wide range feature selection methods among which we find SFS, SFFS, sequential backward selection (SBS) and GA while using the commence with the medium and huge in scale problems. They conclude that many methods has its advantages/problems and propose a unified style of comparing an assortment of feature selection methods. The same authors (Kudo & Sklansky, 1998) later also compared two types of classifier-independent feature selection methods and proposed a two-stage feature selection. The recent comes with the advantage of experiencing the performance boost owing to more difficult feature evaluations which is used in the actual stage. Blum and Langley (Blum & Langley.1997) reviewed the feature selection algorithms, Working on each of the key issues: the drawback of important feature selection and also problem of important examples selection. Kohavi and John focuses mostly over the wrapper methods, similarly visited the relation between optimal feature subset selection and also the relevance of individual features. They phase out two problems present when using the wrapper methods: overheating and high computational overhead (Kohavi & John, 1997). Besides performing an all-inclusive post on the feature selection method, Dash and Liu also systematically described the steps to performing the feature selection (subset generation, subset evaluation, stopping criterion, valida-tion), categorized and theoretically evaluated advantages and disadvantages of specific methods (Dash & Liu, 1997). There are few works that compare examples of the classification algorithms. Panda et al. Compared the performance of NB, Id3 and J48 algorithms for network intrusion detection. Using the authors NB performs more advanced than Id3 and J48 for overall classification accuracy. Nonetheless, inexperienced authors include that DTs (Id3 and J48) are robust in detecting unique intrusion/attacks, stunning NB (Panda & Patra, 2008). The authors compared the ranking performance of NB classifier with DT (C4.4) classifier (Zhang & Su, 2004). The experiments conducted by using 15 datasets from the UCI data repository Asuncion & Newman, 2007). According to the experimental results NB algorithm outperforms the C4.4 (Provost & Domingos, 2002). [11] algorithm in 8 datasets, ties in 3 datasets and loses in 4 dataset. The average AUC of NB is 90. 36%, which is substantially higher than the average 85. 25% of C4. 4. Considering these results, the authors argue that NB performs well in ranking, just as it does in classification.

3. FEATURE SELECTION METHODS

Most of the feature selection methods and algorithms since the 1970. It illustrates the common steps and processes of all the selection tasks and also demonstrated the key concepts of the algorithms. Feature selection methods are also used in other field of research like pattern recognition, text classification, statistics and machine learning. We can't use the full set of feature because it is too expensive and may be some of the features not relevant to the classification task and the other may be redundant. Feature selection is the process to generate candidate feature subset from the original set of feature, and try to find the best one among the candidate subset according to some evaluation function. It may be too expensive because this procedure is exhaustive. The other methods are random or heuristic where certain guideline is used for the selection; these methods reduce the computational complexity by compromising performance. Four basic steps in feature selection methods are shown in Figure 1 (Dash & Liu, 1997).

1. Generation = generates candidate feature subset.
2. Evaluation = evaluates the generated candidate feature subset and output a relevancy value.
3. Stopping criterion = determines whether a subset is relevant or irrelevant.
4. Validation = verifies subset validity.

There exist five different evaluation methods. Some literature categories the first four as a filter approach and the final one as a wrapper approach (See Table 1).

Figure 1. Feature selection process (Dash & Liu, 1997)

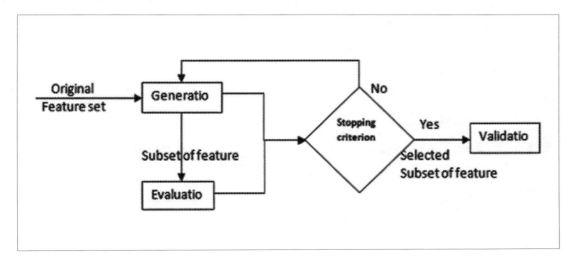

Table 1. Comparison among the various evaluation methods

Method	Generality	Time	Accuracy
Distance	Yes	Low	-
Information	Yes	Low	-
Dependency	Yes	Low	-
Consistency	Yes	Moderate	-
Classifier error rate	No	High	Very high

- Generality = how the method is general towards difference classifier?
- Time = in terms of time their complexity?
- Accuracy = Accuracy of resulting classification task?

Feature selection is the process of removing the feature among the entire feature set because some of the features are relevant, redundant and noisy thus not contributing to the learning process. So it reduces the dimension of a feature space, increase algorithm speed because the irrelevant feature can include noisy data affecting the accuracy of the resulting model (Doraisami & Golzari,2008).Using feature selection methods, costs of data handling become smaller and understands ability can be improved (Arauzo-Azofra et al,2011).

Generally, feature selection methods are divided into three categories, filters, wrappers and embedded methods. Feature selection methods are differing in three ways (Guyon & Elisseeff. 2003). (i) Searching techniques (ii) evaluation (prediction of the classifier) (iii) estimation (cross-validation or statistical test).

3.1 Filter Method

Filter method evaluates each feature to measure how relevant a feature is to the target. Then filter method rank the feature by their relevance indices and take the superior ones (see Figure 2).

Figure 2. Evaluation of feature using filter method (Guyon & Elisseeff, 2003)

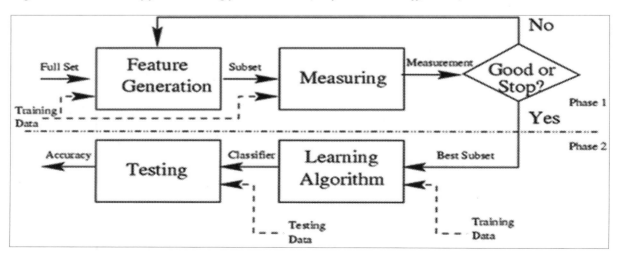

Filter method filters out redundant or irrelevant attributes before machine learning occurs, that search is done independently of the machine learning algorithms. Filter methods are relatively robust against over-fitting and may fail to select the useful feature. These methods are very efficient and fast to compute. The main disadvantage of filter methods is a feature is not useful by itself can be very useful when combined with others. Filter method can miss it (Guyon & Elisseeff. 2003; Dash & Liu, 1997).

In filter methods, there are two different processes, first selection of best subset feature and then induction. Search the best subset and ranked according to the relevance to the class label, and finally the subsets of features are selected according to a threshold value (Witten & Hall, 2011). For each subset of features the feature selection algorithms have an evaluation value, if the evaluation value is greater than the threshold, the feature are selected. In this chapter threshold is defined as 0.1 (Predefined by user). In this study, five filter algorithms used for the feature selection;

Relief-F (Kira & Rendell, 1992), One-R (Holte, 1993), Gain Ratio (Mitchell, 1997), Information Gain (Cover & Thomas, 2006) and Symmetrical Uncertainty (Press, 1988), following is a detailed explanation of the algorithms mentioned;

3.1.1 Relief-f

The *Relief-f* algorithm is generic, successful attribute estimator. They can detect condition dependencies between attribute and provide a unified view on the attribute estimation in classification and regression. In addition, the quality estimates have a natural explanation. And they are often seen as a model before learning the step likable feature subset selection method applied, they actually have been used successfully in a variety of settings, for example, to select the partition or boot building constructive induced phase decision or regression tree learning method as an attribute weights and inductive logic programming. The Relief-f algorithm has regularly been seen as a feature subset select methods.

While Relief algorithms have ordinarily been viewed as feature subset selection strategies that square measure applied in a very attractive step before the model is learned (Kira and Rendell, 1992), Dietterich says Relief-f is one of the most successful pre-processing algorithms to date (Dietterich, 1997).

Algorithm Relief-F
Input: for each training instance a vector of attribute values and the class value
Output: The vector W of estimation of the qualities of attribute

1.   set all weights W[A]:=0.0;
2.   **for** i:= 1 **to** *m* **do begin**
3.   randomly select an instance R_i ;
4.   find K nearest hits H_j;
5.   **for** each class $C \neq class$ (R_i) **do**
6.   from class C find K nearest misses M_j (C)

for A:= 1 **to** a **do**

$$W\left[A\right] := W\left[A\right] - \sum_{j=1}^{k} diff\left(A, R_i, H_j\right) / \left(m.k\right) +$$

$$\sum_{C \neq class(R_i)} \left| \frac{P(C)}{1 - p(class(R_I))} \right| \sum_{j=1}^{K} diff\left(A, R_i, H_j\right) / (m.k);$$

8. **end;**

Kira and Rendell give a key idea for relief-f algorithm in figure 1,the Relief-f algorithm estimate the standard of attributes in line with however well their values distinguish between instances that square measure close to one another. For that purpose, given a randomly chosen instance *Ri*(line 3), Relief searches for its two nearest neighbours: one from same category, referred to as nearest hit H, and the other from the different category, referred to as nearest miss M (line 4).Line 5 & 6 updates the quality estimation W[A] for all attributes A depending on their values .If Ri and H have different values of the attribute A then the attribute A separates two instances with same category which isn't fascinating thus we have a tendency to decrease the quality estimation W [A]. On the other hand, if instances RI and M have totally different values of the attribute A then the attribute A separate 2 instances with totally different category values that has desirable thus we had a tendency to increase the standard estimation W [A]. The whole process is repeated for M times, wherever m could be a user-defined parameter.

3.1.2 One-R

One-R, short for "One Rule", may be a simple, yet accurate, the classification algorithmic program that generates one rule for every predictor within the information, then selects the rule with the tiniest total error as its "one rule". To make a rule for a predictor, we have a tendency to construct a frequency table for every predictor against the target. It's been shown that One-R produces rules solely slightly less correct than progressive classification algorithms whereas manufacturing rules that area unit simple for humans to interpret.

Listing 1. Algorithm One-R

```
For each predictor,
      For each value of that predictor, make a rule as follows;
            Count how often each value of the target (class) appears
            Find the most frequent class
            Make the rule assign that class to this value of the predictor
      Calculate the total error of the rules of each predictor
Choose the predictor with the smallest total error.
if outlook = sunny    then play = yes        ... makes 2 errors in 4 records
if outlook = overcast then play = yes        ... makes 0 errors in 5 records
if outlook = rainy    then play = no          ... makes 2 errors in 5
records
total of 4 errors in 14 cases. Likewise,
if humidity = high then play = yes        ... makes 3 errors in 7 records
if humidity = normal then play = no        ... makes 1 error  in 7 records
```

It seems that very easy association rules, involving only one attribute within the condition part, typically work revoltingly well in applying with real-world information. Suppose within the weather information, you would like to be able to predict the value of play. The idea of the *One-R* (one-attribute-rule) algorithm (shown in Listing 1) is to seek out the one attribute to use that produces fewest prediction errors.

Also for a total of 4 errors in 14 cases. The other two attributes, each produces 5 errors at best, so the One-R algorithm chooses at random between singing outlook and humidity as the one decisive attribute.

3.1.3 Information Gain

Given entropy (*E*) as a measure of the contamination in a collection of items it is to conceivable evaluate the adequacy of a feature in classifying the training data (Mitchell, 1997 and Quinlan, 1992).

$$IG(S, A) = E(S) - \sum_{V(A)} \frac{|S_v|}{|S|} . E(S_v) \dots\dots\dots\dots \tag{1}$$

$$E(S) = \sum_{C} -\frac{|S_c|}{S} . \log_2 \frac{|S_c|}{|S|} \dots\dots\dots\dots \tag{2}$$

Information Gain (IG) measures the normal reduction of entropy created by partitioning the illustrations as indicated by attribute A. In the equation 1& 2:

I.   *S* is the item collection,
II. |S| its cardinality;
III.   *V (A)* is the set of all possible values for attribute *A*;
IV.   *Sv* is the subset of *S* for which *A* has value *v*;
V.   *C* is the class collection *Sc* is the subset of *S* containing items belonging to class *c*.

3.1.4 Gain Ratio

The *Information gain* (IG) measure feature attributes with numerous values over those with few values ((Mitchell, 1997). *Gain Ratio* (GR) overcomes this issue by presenting an additional term taking into record how the feature splits the data.

$$GR(S, A) = \frac{IG(S, A)}{SI(S, A)} \dots\dots\dots\dots \tag{3}$$

$$SI(S, A) = -\sum_{i=1}^{d} \frac{|S_i|}{|S|} . \log_2 \frac{|S_i|}{|S|} \dots\dots\dots\dots \tag{4}$$

Si is *d* subsets of examples resulting for partitioning *S* by the *d* valued feature *A*. In some special cases *Si* can be zero, if *Si (S,A) = 0* for feature *A*. Then define

GR(S,A) = IG(S,A) .

3.1.5 Symmetrical Uncertainty

The *Symmetrical Uncertainty* (SU) model adjusts for the inherent bias of IG by isolating it by the total of the entropies of *X* and *Y*(Hall and Smith, 1998).

$$SU = 2\frac{IG}{H\left(Y\right) + H\left(X\right)} \ldots\ldots\ldots\ldots \tag{5}$$

Because of the correction factor 2, SU takes values which are normalized to the range [0,1]. The knowledge of one feature completely predicts when a value of SU = 1 and if SU = 0 then *X* and *Y* are uncorreleted . The SU is biased towards features with fewer values, similar to Gain-Ratio (GR).

3.2 Wrapper Method

In wrapper method (John et al, 1994), Wrapper ranks the feature subset by the prediction performance of a classifier on a given feature subset, wrapper takes a subset of the feature set, evaluates the classifier performance on this feature subset and then another subset is evaluated on this classifier. The subsets that have maximum performance on this classifier are selected (Dash & Liu, 1997; John & Kohavi,1997). The main idea behind this approach is shown in figure 3, the learning algorithm is considered as a black box. The classification result of wrapper method is compared to the correct label with the data in the evaluation stage. Based on the prediction error, we will decide how to search next or stop search. Searching combinatorial subset is NP-hard and prone to over-fitting (Novakovic, 2010).

Figure 3. Evaluation of features using wrapper method (John et al, 1994)

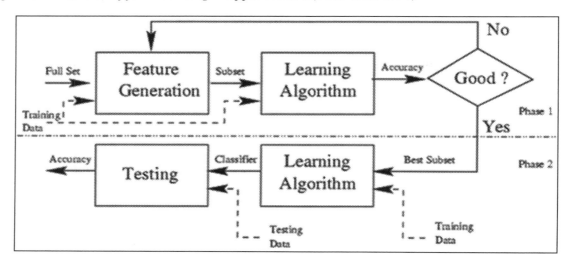

The main disadvantages of wrapper method are, it is very slow, higher computational cost and danger for over fitting.

The wrapper methods search the best subset of feature by starting with an empty set of selected features (John & R. Kohavi, 1997). According to the performance of classifier wrapper methods evaluate the subset. In wrapper methods, learning algorithm usually use error rate or accuracy as an evaluation criterion (Yudong & Lenan, 2011;Marinakis & Marinaki, 2008) . The learning algorithms act as a black box (see Figure 3). In this chapter, we use three learning algorithms for feature subset selection the algorithms are: Bagging, Naive Bayes and Random Forest. These algorithms are run on a different feature subset, the subset that has highest evaluation are selected. Wrapper methods have a strong forecasting capability while filter methods have a high computational efficiency.

Many classification algorithms were used to solve the problem of feature selection. In this study, we used three classification algorithms; Naive Bayes (John & Langley, 1995), J48 (Decision Tree) (Quinlan, 1992) and Multilayer Perceptron (MLP) as an Artificial Neural Network (Rosenblatt, 1962).

3.2.1 Bagging

Bagging may be a methodology for improving the results of machine learning classification algorithms. This technique was developed by Leo Breiman and its name was deduced from the phrase "bootstrap aggregating"(Breiman, 1994). In case of classification into 2 attainable classes,a classification algorithm creates a classifier $H:D \rightarrow \{-1,1\}$ on the bottom of a training set of example description D. The bagging methodology creates a sequence of classifiers Hm, $m=1,..., M$ in reference to modifications of the training set. We have a tendency to experimented with the subsequent textile algorithmic program (Breiman, 1994).

Algorithm Bagging

1. Initialization of the training set D
2. for m = 1, ..., M
   2.1 Creation of a new set D_m of the same size D by random selection of training examples from the set D (some of the examples can be selected repeatedly and some may not be selected at all).
   2.2 Learning of a particular classifier $Hm: Dm \rightarrow R$ by a given machine learning algorithm based on the actual training set Dm.
3. Compound classifier H is created as the aggregation of particular classifiers

Hm: m = 1 ..., M and an example di is classified to the class C_j in accordance with the number of votes obtained from particular classifiers H_m

$$H\left(d_i, c_j\right) = SIGN\left(\sum_m^M \alpha_m H_m\left(d_i, c_j\right)\right)$$

If it's potential to influence the learning procedure performed by the classifier H_m directly, classification error are often decreased conjointly by H_m whereas keeping parameters *am* constant.

3.2.2 Naive Bayes

A Bayes classifier could be a straightforward probabilistic classifier supported applying Bayes' theorem (from Bayesian statistics) with sturdy (naive) independence assumptions. A lot of descriptive term for the underlying probability model would be "independent feature model".

According to Baye's rule

$$P\left(\frac{A}{B}\right) = \frac{P\left(B/A\right)P\left(A\right)}{P\left(B\right)} \ldots\ldots\ldots\ldots \tag{6}$$

I. $P\ (A|B)$ is defined as the probability of observing A given that B occurs.
II. $P\ (A|B)$ is called posterior probability.
III. $P\ (B|A),\ P\ (A)$ and $P\ (B)$ are called prior probabilities.

Bayes' theorem provides a relationship between the posterior probability and therefore the prior probability. It permits one to discover the probability of observing A given B when the individual probabilities of A and B are known, and the probability of observing B given A is additionally known.

Naive Bayes (Langley et al., 1992) is a simple probabilistic classifier. Bayes' hypothesis gives an approach to ascertain the probability of a hypothesis focused around its prior probability. It utilizes all attributes and permits them to settle on commitments to the decision as though they were all just as important and independent of each other. Given a set of attributes as input, it predicts the output value, which is one of the target attributes.

Naïve_Bayes_Learn (Example)

For each target value V_j

$$\hat{P}\left(V_j\right) \leftarrow estimatep\left(V_j\right)$$

For each attribute value a_i of each attribute a

$$\hat{P}\left(a_i / | v_j\right) \leftarrow estimateP(a_i \mid v_j)$$

Classify_New_Instances (x)

$$V_{NB} = arg_{v_j \in V}\hat{P}\left(V_j\right)\prod_{a_i \in x}\hat{P}(a_i \mid v_j)$$

3.2.3 Random Forest

We expect that the user thinks about the development of single classification trees. Random Forests become numerous classification trees. To order another item from an input vector, put the input vector down each of the trees in the forest. Each one tree gives an order, and we say the tree "votes" for that class. The forest picks the classification having the most votes (over all the trees in the forest).

Each one tree is grown as follows:

1. In the event that the number of cases in the training set is N, sample N cases at random, however with substitution, from the first information. This sample will be the training set for developing the tree.
2. if there are M data variables, a number m<<M is defined such that at every node, m variables are chosen at random out of the M and the best split on these m is utilized to split the node. The estimation of m is held consistent amid the forest growing.
3. Each one tree has developed to the biggest degree conceivable. There is no pruning.

(Breiman, 2001) random forest was demonstrated that the forest error rate relies on upon two things:

*   The relationship between any two trees in the forest. Increasing the connection increases the forest error rate .

Listing 2. Random Forest Algorithm

```
To generate c classifiers:
for i = 1 to c do
Randomly sample the training data D with replacement to produce D_i
Create a root node, N_i containing D_i
Call Build Tree (N_i)
end for
Build Tree (N):
If N contains instances of only one class then
return
else
Randomly select x% of the possible splitting features in N
Select the feature F with the highest information gain to split on
Create f child nodes of N, N_1, ..., N_f, where F has f possible values (F_1, ...,
F_f)
    For i = 1 to f do
    Set the contents of N_i to D_i, where D_i is all instances in N that match
    F_i
    Call Build Tree (N_i)
    end for
end if
```

The quality of every individual tree in the forest. A tree with a low error rate is a strong classifier. Increasing the quality of the individual trees decreases the forest error rate.

3.2.4 Decision Tree (J48)

A decision tree is a prediction machine-learning model that chooses the target value (dependent variable) of a new sample based on various attribute values of the variable data. The internal nodes of a decision tree signify the different attributes, the extensions between the nodes let us know the conceivable values that these characteristics can have in the observed sample, while the terminal nodes let us know the final value (classification) of the dependent variable.

J48 classifier is known as simple C4.5 decision tree for classification.J48 creates a binary tree. C4.5 decision tree is mostly used in classification problem. Using C4.5 algorithm, a tree is constructed to model the classification process. When a tree is built on training data, it is applied to each tuple in the database and result in classification for the tuple (Margaret et al. 2006).

Algorithm J48

INPUT:D //Training data
OUTPUT: T //Decision tree
DTBUILD (*D)
{$T=\varphi$;
$T=$ Create root node and label with splitting attribute;
$T=$ Add arc to root node for each split predicate and label;
for each arc **do**
$D=$ Database created by applying splitting predicate to D;
If stopping point reached for this path, **then**
$T'=$ create leaf node and label with the appropriate class;
Else
$T'=$ DTBUILD(D);
$T=$ add T' to arc;}

While assembling a tree, J48 disregards the missing values, i.e. the quality of that item can be anticipated focused around what is thought about the attribute values for alternate records. The fundamental thought is to divide the data into range based on the attribute values for that item that are found in the training sample. J48 allows classification via either decision trees or rules generated from them (William, 1999).

3.2.5 Multilayer Perceptron (MLP)

Multi-Layer Perceptrons (MLPs) constitute an essential class of feed-forward Artificial Neural Networks (ANNs), created to replicate learning and speculation abilities of people with an attempt to model the functions of biological neural networks. They have numerous potential applications in the regions of Artificial Intelligence (AI) and Pattern Recognition (PR). Handwritten numeral recognition is a benchmark issue of PR. It has a clearly characterized business essentials and a level of trouble that makes it testing, yet it is not all that substantial as to be completely intractable. The MLP algorithm works like this:

Algorithm Multilayer Perceptron

1. First apply the inputs to the network and work out the output – remember this initial output could be anything, as the initial weights were random numbers.
2. Next work out the error of neuron B. The error is What you want – What you actually get, in other words:

$$Error_B = Output_B \ (1\text{-}Output_B) \ (Target_B - Output_B)$$

The *"Output (1-Output)"* term is necessary in the equation because of the Sigmoid
Function – if we were only using a threshold neuron it would just be
(Target – Output).

3. Change the weight. Let W^+_{AB} be the new (trained) weight and W_{AB} be the initial weight.

$$W^+_{AB} = W_{AB} + (Error_B \ x \ Output_A)$$

Notice that it is the output of the connecting neuron (neuron A) we use (not B). We update all the weights in the output layer in this way.

4. Calculate the Errors for the hidden layer neurons. Unlike the output layer we can't calculate these directly (because we don't have a Target), so we Back Propagate them from the output layer (hence the name of the algorithm). This is done by taking the Errors from the output neurons and running them back through the weights to get the hidden layer errors. For example, if neuron A is connected as shown in B and C then we take the errors from B and C to generate an error for A.

$$Error_A = Output_A \ (1 - Output_A) \ (Error_B \ W_{AB} + Error_C \ W_{AC})$$

Again, the factor *"Output (1 - Output)"* is present because of the sigmoid squashing function.

5. Having obtained the Error for the hidden layer neurons now proceed as in stage 3 to change the hidden layer weights. By repeating, this method we can train a network of any number of layers.

Optical Character Recognition (OCR) of handwritten numerals is integral to numerous business applications related to perusing sums from bank checks, separating numeric information from filled in structures, translating written by hand pin codes from mail pieces etc. The work introduced here basically goes for making the convenience of the MLP as an example classifier contrasted with the Nearest Neighbor (NN) classifier utilized as a suboptimal traditional classifier. MLPs are fit for going past the restricted set of straightly divisible issues and tackling subjectively unpredictable issues (accepting that the computational resources are unbounded),an incredible arrangement of exertion has been given to the advancement of MLP training algorithms.

3.3 Embedded Methods

Embedded methods are similar to wrappers, search for the best subset. These methods have selected the features based on some criterion that are generated by the learning process, search the best subset by adding or removing a feature from the generated feature set, so the prediction errors are lower for new features. Embedded methods are like a model building, e.g. decision tree or artificial neural network (Guyon & Elisseeff, 2003; Ladha & Deepa, 2011). Very important when we have a large number of features but small sample size. Automatically shut down unnecessary features. Embedded methods are less computationally expensive and less prone to over-fitting.

4. DATASET

In this study, for experiments ten data sets are taken from the Data Mining Repository of University of California, Irvine (UCI) (Newman et al, 1998). Description of these datasets is shown Table 2.

5. RESULTS AND DISCUSSION

In this chapter, Weka 3.7.8 Data Mining tool was used to compare the performance of classification algorithms, for classification the default parameter were used (Hall et al,2009). For all experiments we used 10-fold cross validation with default parameters.

The goal of our experimental evaluation would rank the feature selection methods by their effectiveness, which we measure by how the removal of weak features influences the performance of numerous

Table 2. Description of the datasets

Data Set	Example	Feature	Classes
Anneal	898	39	5
Audiology	226	69	24
Breast-Cancer	286	9	2
Diabetes	768	8	2
Hepatitis	155	19	2
Lumphography	148	18	4
Page-Blocks	5473	10	5
Segment	2310	19	7
Vowel	990	13	11
Zoo	101	16	7

Table 3. Classification accuracy rate of NB algorithm using filter method

Dataset	NB	Naïve Bayes Using Filter Methods				
		IG	GR	RF	One-R	SU
Anneal	75.83	75.5	**79.84**	**90.42**	75.83	75.5
Audiology	73.45	**75.66**	73.00	68.14	73.45	67.7
Breast-Cancer	71.68	70.28	70.28	66.78	71.68	71.68
Diabetes	76.30	75	-	-	76.3	75
Hepatitis	84.51	83.87	83.23	83.87	84.51	83.22
Lumphography	83.11	80.4	77.7	77.02	83.11	77.7
Page-Blocks	90.85	**92.62**	**94.60**	-	90.85	**93.90**
Segment	80.22	79.87	79.31	**87.06**	80.22	79.00
Vowel	63.74	**67.88**	**67.68**	56.06	**63.94**	63.73
Zoo	95.05	95.05	95.05	**96.04**	95.05	**96.04**

classifiers. The testing was performed iteratively by estimating top-quality the features, at each step, removing the feature of this worst estimated quality, and re-computing the classifier performance of the reduced data set with *10-fold cross validation*. Each experiment, we recorded a very high classification accuracy of this include removal sequence with all the accompanying selection of features.

In Table-4, Multilayer Perceptron (MLP) is not affected by filter selection methods as much as Naive Bayes and J48. Only three data sets have been affected. Information Gain, Gain Ratio and Symmetrical Uncertainty have a positive effect. No increase in accuracy has been observed in other Filter Selection Methods. Figure 4 shows the comparison of accuracy using MLP.

To have biasness of this testing, we classified 20% of randomly selected examples belonging to the original data set for the final testing examples, well before performing, here's a great looking do a search for the right performing range features at the remaining 80% of this instance. These independent examples where would always appraise the performance of this classifier of the reduced feature set, that's

Figure 4. Accuracy of MLP classifier using the wrapper method

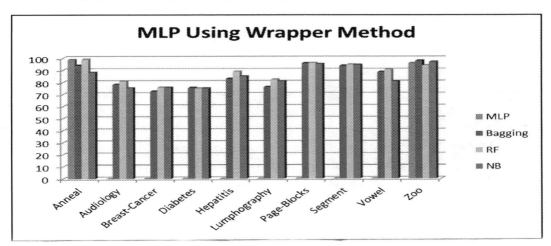

Table 4. Classification accuracy rate of J48 algorithm using filter method

Dataset	J48	J48 Using Filter Methods				
		IG	GR	RF	One-R	SU
Anneal	90.98	**91.53**	**91.75**	82.07	90.98	**91.53**
Audiology	77.88	**78.31**	**82.74**	74.34	**78.32**	72.12
Breast-Cancer	75.52	70.28	70.28	66.78	75.52	70.28
Diabetes	73.82	73.04	-	-	73.82	73.04
Hepatitis	83.87	81.29	81.94	82.58	83.87	83.87
Lumphography	78.38	75.00	77.03	75	78.13	78.13
Page-Blocks	96.88	**96.99**	97.11	-	96.88	97.10
Segment	96.93	**96.97**	96.40	96.70	96.93	96.50
Vowel	81.52	**82.02**	81.41	70.51	81.21	78.28
Zoo	92.08	91.09	90.01	**93.07**	90.1	**94.06**

Figure 5. Accuracy of J48 classifier using the filter method

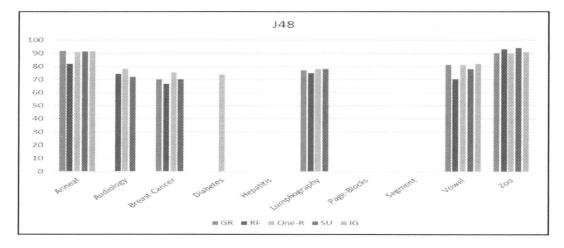

also the best result of your evaluated classifier/feature selector/domain combination. Inside a, the testing data were separated belonging to the feature set selection algorithm, which makes the result less biased good chosen classifier algorithms. See that received been not feasible to gauge the past classification accuracy with cross-validation approach, considering that best performing range feature in each training fold may just be different.

In filter algorithms, five feature selection methods are used to select the subset of feature before passing the best subset to the learning algorithm. To choose the best subset 0.1 threshold value is chosen. Accuracies (in %) of classification algorithms are expressed in Table II, Table III and Table IV. The column named full present the accuracy value before the feature selection methods using all features. As compared to the entire value of the data goes down the highlighted cell indicates the increase in accuracy.

On same datasets, we implement the wrapper methods; select the best feature subset using wrapper subset evaluators. In wrapper subset evaluator, use three classifiers for best subset, the classifier is Naive Bayes, Random Forest and Bagging. The classification results from wrapper methods are compared with the correct label with the data in the evaluation phase. Accuracies of classification algorithms are shown in Table 5, Table 6 and Table 7.

These feature selection methods are evaluated through a well-known classifier, Naive Bayes in Table-2. The highlighted cells represent the highest classification value for that particular data set. Naive Bayes classifier achieved improved or comparable. We have applied the Naïve Bayes classifier with five filter methods on ten data sets. Information Gain, Gain ratio and Relief-F is mostly affected by increase in accuracy. Especially for Anneal dataset using Relief-F method accuracy has increased 14.59% that is the largest among all. For audiology dataset Information Gain performs better. With Breast-Cancer, Diabetes, Hepatitis and Lumphography using the filter method no effect has been observed. With Page-Blocks, Segment, Vowel and Zoo datasets, we have observed an increase in accuracy using filter method. Figure-5 shows the comparison of accuracy using Naïve Bayes.

Table 5. Classification accuracy rate of MLP algorithms using feature selection

Dataset	MLP	MLP Using Filter Methods				
		IG	GR	RF	One-R	SU
Anneal	98.77	86.97	92.2	96.21	98.77	86.97
Audiology	83.18	82.74	82.74	72.57	83.63	72.12
Breast-Cancer	64.68	**70.28**	**70.28**	**66.78**	65.38	**70.28**
Diabetes	75.39	74.08	-	-	75.39	74.08
Hepatitis	80	**84.51**	**83.23**	78.06	80	**85.16**
Lumphography	84.46	79.73	80.41	79.73	83.11	81.08
Page-Blocks	96.22	**96.31**	96.02	-	96.22	**96.42**
Segment	96.06	96.02	95.80	95.76	96.06	96.06
Vowel	92.73	79.39	79.29	64.43	92.02	67.78
Zoo	96.04	96.04	96.04	96.04	96.04	96.04

Table 6. Classification accuracy rate of MLP algorithms using feature selection

Dataset	MLP	MLP Using Wrapper Method		
		Bagging	RF	NB
Anneal	98.77	94.21	**99.11**	88.31
Audiology	83.18	78.32	80.97	75.42
Breast-Cancer	64.68	**72.73**	**75.87**	**75.87**
Diabetes	75.39	**75.65**	75.13	75.26
Hepatitis	80	**83.23**	**89.03**	**85.16**
Page-Blocks	96.22	95.91	96.13	95.18
Segment	96.06	93.9	94.94	94.59
Vowel	92.73	88.69	90.81	80.81
Zoo	96.04	**98.02**	94.05	**97.03**

Table 7. Classification accuracy rate of MLP algorithms using feature selection

Dataset	J48	J48 Using Wrapper Method		
		Bagging	RF	NB
Anneal	90.98	92.43	90.98	79.96
Audiology	77.88	**80.1**	77.88	76.55
Breast-Cancer	75.52	**75.87**	75.17	75.17
Diabetes	73.82	**75.91**	**75.26**	**74.74**
Hepatitis	83.87	**84.51**	81.94	**85.16**
Lumphography	78.38	**79.73**	**82.43**	**79.05**
Page-Blocks	96.88	**97.26**	**96.93**	**96.91**
Segment	96.93	96.93	96.88	96.49
Vowel	81.52	**82.32**	81.31	**81.82**
Zoo	92.08	**98.02**	97.03	**95.05**

Figure 6. Accuracy of MLP classifier using filter method

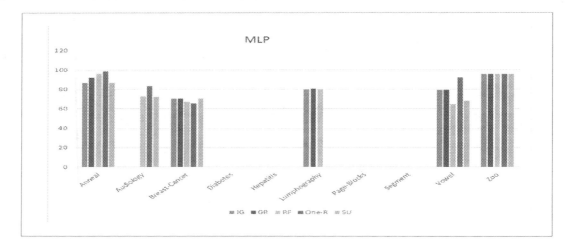

In Table 3, Accuracy using J48 classifier is given. Information Gain, Gain ratio and Symmetric Uncertainty showed an increase in accuracy. Information gain has performed better using J48 classifier while with Relief-F and One-R we have found less change in accuracy. Figure-6 shows the comparison of accuracy using J48.

On the same datasets, we have applied the Wrapper Methods. In this method we select the attribute as wrapper subset evaluator and classify the best subsets with three techniques Bagging, Random Forest and Naive Bayes. When the best subset is selected, then these subsets pass through the classifiers that are Naïve Bayes, J48 and MLP.

Table 5 indicates that the MLP is not affected by the wrapper subset evaluator as much as J48 and Naive Bayes. Five of the datasets have an increase in accuracy; four data sets are affected. Breast cancer is the maximum increase in accuracy is 11.92%. Figure-8 shows the comparison of accuracy using MLP.

Figure 7. Accuracy of J48 classifier using the wrapper method

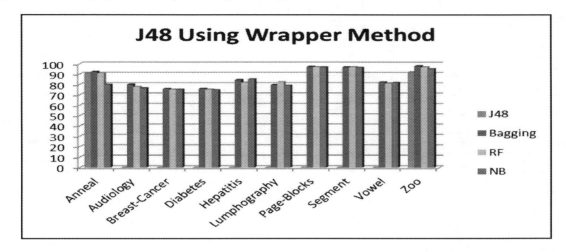

Figure 8. Accuracy of NB classifier using the wrapper method

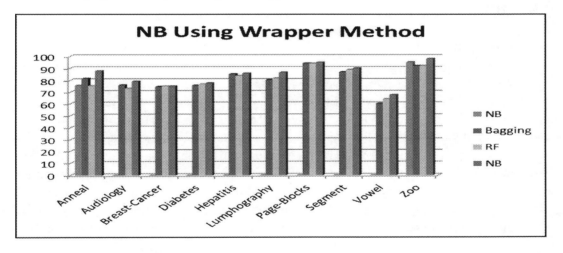

Table 6 indicates that J48 (Decision Tree) datasets are less affected as compared to Naive Bayes. Wrapper subset selection methods positively affected eight of the data sets. The zoo data set is most affected; increase in accuracy is 5.94%. Figure 7 shows the comparison of accuracy using J48.

According to Naive Bayes classifier, shown in Table-7, all the datasets have been affected using wrapper subset evaluation that is accuracy is increased. The anneal data set is most affected as the largest difference; the increase in accuracy is *11.92%*. Figure 8 shows the comparison of accuracy using NB.

As compared to filter method the wrapper method is confirmed as the best option when it can be applied. In this chapter, a wrapper methods produces the best results as compared to filter methods. Both Filter and Wrapper Methods reduced the number of features and the increased classification accuracy, while some state-of-the-art methods yields poor results, either in number of features reduced, classification accuracy, or both. These results are produced by using commonly used feature selection methods.

Table 8. Classification accuracy rate of MLP algorithms using feature selection

Dataset	NB	NB Using Wrapper Method		
		Bagging	RF	NB
Anneal	75.83	**81.51**	75.5	**87.75**
Audiology	73.45	**76.1**	73.45	**79.2**
Breast-Cancer	71.68	**74.82**	**75.17**	**75.17**
Diabetes	76.30	75.91	**76.82**	**77.73**
Hepatitis	84.51	**85.16**	83.87	**85.81**
Lumphography	83.11	80.41	81.76	**86.49**
Page-Blocks	90.85	**94.19**	**94.01**	**94.94**
Segment	80.22	**86.84**	**88.83**	**90.04**
Vowel	63.74	60.3	**64.04**	**67.68**
Zoo	95.05	92.08	92.08	**98.02**

6. CONCLUSION AND FUTURE WORK

Mine meaningful pattern from the huge amount of data, it becomes a difficult task. Feature selection methods reduce the number of dimensions of the dataset, so the data become easy to understand and more comprehensible. In this chapter, we have reviewed various feature selection methods and explained the basic concepts of filter and wrapper methods. We have reviewed five filters based feature selection techniques and three wrapper based feature selection techniques. For filter methods we have used Information Gain, Gain Ratio, One-R, Relief-f and Symmetrical Uncertainty. Four wrapper methods we have used Bagging, Random Forest and Naïve Bayes. We have also used Naïve Bayes, J48 and MLP classifiers for a classification model. In this Empirical Evaluation, we have checked the feature selection methods on three classifiers J48, Naive Bayes and MLP uses ten datasets. As compared to filter methods, the wrapper methods returned better results. The wrapper methods produced better accuracy rate. Experiments regarding the feature selection methods yielded very encouraging results. Ease of application and the simplicity along with greater predictive accuracy are strong motivations for the proposed method.

The results have shown that Wrapper methods, Bagging and Naïve Bayes, performed better in terms of the highest percentage of testing domains with significant increase of classification accuracy. Among the classifier, J48 and MLP has also shown to perform better in our evaluation procedure by achieving the most frequent significant improvement in the classification accuracy on the testing domains. The above feature selection methods and the classifiers mostly achieve their highest accuracies in the iteration in which the lowest number of features remained in the domain as compared to other feature selection methods and classifiers. This empirical evaluation speaks in favor, especially of the bagging and Naïve Bayes performance, using which we successfully manage to remove more features of the worse quality and therewith improve the accuracy of the classifier. The combination of Bagging and Naïve Bayes wrapper feature selector and J48 and Naïve Bayes classifier achieved the highest score, appearing to be the most suitable choice for the usage in an environment where similar feature selection procedures have been performed. To conclude our empirical evaluation has provided the indication about the appropriateness of the tested feature selection methods for optimization of the classifiers accuracies.

When faced with such a task with real world applications, the achieved results may ease the decision which features selection method and classifier to use to implement the prediction tasks. In the form of future work you can easily search the performance within the information theoretic feature selection algorithms for other high dimensional datasets when i decided i wanted to find which method achieves record significantly greater results. Furthermore you can easily search that the performance changes while we are by using different discretization methods, as an illustration that the performance changes as soon as use varied lots of boxes while in the equal width approach or what is going on while we are with all the equal frequencies approach.

REFERENCES

Anderson, G. (2009). Random Relational Rules [PhD thesis].

Arauzo-Azofra, A., Aznarte, J. L., & Benítez, J. M. (2011). Empirical study of feature selection methods based on individual feature evaluation for classification problems. *Expert Systems with Applications*, *38*(7), 8170–8177. doi:10.1016/j.eswa.2010.12.160

Asuncion, A., & Newman, D. J. (2007). UCI Machine Learning Repository Irvine, CA: University of California, School of Information and Computer Science Blum, A. L., & Langley, P. (1997). Selection of relevant features and examples in machine learning. *Artificial Intelligence*, *97*(1–2), 245–271.

Brank, J., Grobelnik, M., Milic-Frayling, N., & Mladenic, D. (2002). Interaction of Feature selection Methods and Linear Classification Models. *Proceedings of the ICML-02 Workshop on Text Learning*.

Breiman, L. (1994). Bagging predictors [Technical Report 421]. *University of California at Berkeley*.

Breiman, L. (2001). Random forests. *Machine Learning*, *45*(1), 5–32. doi:10.1023/A:1010933404324

Buddhinath, G. & Derry, D. (n. d.). A Simple Enhancement to One Rule Classification. *Department of Computer Science & Software Engineering University of Melbourne*.

Cover, T. M., & Thomas, J. A. (2006). *Elements of information theory* (2nd ed.). Hoboken, N.J.: Wiley-Interscience.

Dash, M., & Liu, H. (1997). Feature selection for classification. *Intelligent Data Analysis*, *1*(1-4), 131–156. doi:10.1016/S1088-467X(97)00008-5

Dash, M., & Liu, H. (1997). Feature Selection for Classification. *Intelligent Data Analysis*, *1*(3), 131–156. doi:10.1016/S1088-467X(97)00008-5

Dietterich, T. G. (1997). Machine Learning Research: *Four Current Directions. AI Magazine*, *18*(4), 97–136.

Doraisami, S., & Golzari, S. (2008). *A Study on Feature Selection and Classification Techniques for Automatic Genre Classification of Traditional Malay Music*. Content-Based Retrieval, Categorization and Similarity.

Ferri, F., Pudil, P., Hatef, M., & Kittler, J. (1994). Comparative Study of Techniques for Large-Scale Feature Selection. In E.S. Gelsema, & L.N. Kanal (Eds.), Pattern Recognition in Practice IV, Multiple Paradigms, Comparative Studies and Hybrid Systems (pp. 403–413).

Guyon, I. (2003). An introduction to variable and feature selection. *Journal of Machine Learning Research*, *3*, 1157–1182.

Guyon, I., & Elisseeff, A. (2003, March). An Introduction to Variable and Feature Selection JMLR Special Issue on Variable and Feature Selection. Kernel Machines Section, 1157-1182.

Hall, M., Frank, E., Holmes, G., Pfahringer, B., Reutemann, P., & Witten, I. H. (1997). The WEKA data mining software: an update. In SIGKDD Explorer Newsletter (2009), 10-18.

Hall, M. A., & Holmes, G. (2003). Benchmarking attribute selection techniques for discrete class data mining. *IEEE Transactions on Knowledge and Data Engineering*, *15*(6), 1437–1447. doi:10.1109/TKDE.2003.1245283

Hall, M. A., & Smith, L. A. (1998). Practical feature subset selection for machine learning. *Proceedings of the 21st Australian Computer Science Conference (pp. 181–191)*.

Holte, R. (1993). Very Simple Classification Rules Perform Well on Most Commonly Used Datasets. *Machine Learning*, *11*(1), 63–90. doi:10.1023/A:1022631118932

John, G., & Kohavi, R. (1997). Wrapper for feature subset selection. In *Artificial intelligence* (pp. 273–324). Elsevier Science.

John, G., Kohavi, R., & Pfleger, K. (1994). Irrelevant features and the subset selection problem. *Proceedings of Fifth International Conference on Machine Learning (pp.* 121-129). doi:10.1016/B978-1-55860-335-6.50023-4

John, G., & Langley, P. (1995). Estimating Continuous Distributions in Bayesian Classifiers. *Proceedings of Eleventh Conference on Uncertainty in Artificial Intelligence (pp- 338-345)*.

Kira, K., & Rendell, L. A. (1992). A practical approach to feature selection. *Proceedings of the ninth international workshop on Machine learning*. Aberdeen, Scotland, United Kingdom.

Kira, K., & Rendell, L. A. (1992). A practical approach to feature selection. In D. Sleeman and P. Edwards (Eds.), *Machine Learning: Proceedings of International Conference (ICML'92)* (pp. 249–256). Morgan Kaufmann.

Kohavi, R., & John, G. H. (1997). Wrappers for feature subset selection. *Artificial Intelligence*, *97*(1–2), 273–324. doi:10.1016/S0004-3702(97)00043-X

Kudo, M. & Sklansky, J. (1997). A Comparative Evaluation of Medium- and Large-Scale Feature Selectors for Pattern Classifiers. *Proceedings of the First International Workshop on Statistical Techniques in Pattern Recognition (pp.91–96)*. Prague, Czech Republic.

Kudo, M., & Sklansky, J. (1998). Classifier-independent feature selection for two-stage feature selection, Syntactical and Structural Pattern Recognition/Statistical. *Pattern Recognition*, 548–554.

Ladha, L., & Deepa, T. (2011). Feature Selection Methods and Algorithms. *International Journal on Computer Science and Engineering, 3*(5), 1787-1797.

Langley, P. L., Wayne, I., & Thompson, K. (1992). An Analysis of Bayesian Classifiers. *Proceedings of the Tenth Conference on Artificial Intelligence (pp. 233-228). San Jose, California, USA.*

Lei, Y., & Huan, L., (2003). Feature Selection for High-Dimensional Data: A Fast Correlation-Based Filter Solution. *Proceedings of the Twentieth International Conference on Machine Leaning (pp.* 856-863).

Margaret, D. H. (2006). *Data mining, introductory and Advanced Topics.* Pearson Education.

Marinakis, Y., Marinaki, M., & Dounias, G. (2008). Particle swarm optimization for pap-smear diagnosis. *Expert Systems with Applications, 35*(4), 1645–1656. doi:10.1016/j.eswa.2007.08.089

Mitchell, T. M. (1997). *Machine learning.* Boston: WCB/McGraw-Hill.

Morita, M. E., Sabourin, R., Bortolozzi, F., & Suen, C. Y. (2003). Unsupervised Feature Selection Using Multi-Objective Genetic Algorithm for Handwritten Word Recognition. *Proceedings of the 7th International Conference on Document Analysis and Recognition* (pp.666-670). Edinburgh, Scotland. doi:10.1109/ICDAR.2003.1227746

Newman, D. J., Hettich, S. C., Blake, L., & Merz, C. J. (1998). *UCI Repository of machine learning databases, University California Irvine.* Department of Information and Computer Science.

Novakovic, J. (2010). The Impact of Feature Selection on the Accuracy of Naive Bayes Classifier. Proceedings of *18th Telecommunications forum TELFOR.*

Panda, M., & Patra, R. M. (2008). A comparative study of data mining algorithms for network intrusion detection. *Proceedings of 1st International Conference on Emerging Trends in Engineering and Technology.* doi:10.1109/ICETET.2008.80

Press, W. H. (1988). Numerical recipes in C: the art of scientific computing, (2nd Ed). New York.

Provost, F., & Domingos, P. (2002). Tree induction for probability based ranking. In Machine Learning (Vol 52, No 3). (2003). Netherland: Kluwer Academic Publisher.

Qiang, S., Ren, D., & Pan, S., (2012). Feature Selection Ensemble. *Turing-100, 10, 289–306.*

Quinlan, R. (1992). *C4.5: Programs for Machine Learning.* San Mateo: Morgan Kaufmann.

Rosenblatt, F. (1962). *Principles of Neurodynamics: Perceptrons and the Theory of Brain Mechanisms.* Spartan.

William, E. S., Jerrold, H. M., & Luis, G. V. (1999). Choosing Data-Mining Methods for Multiple Classification: Representational and Performance Measurement Implications for Decision Support. *Journal of Management Information Systems, 16*(I), 3.

Witten, I. H., Frank, E., & Hall, M. A. (2011). *Data mining practical machine learning tools and techniques.* Burlington: Morgan Kaufmann publisher.

Witten, I. H., & Hall, M. A. (2011). *Data mining: practical machine learning tools and techniques.* Amsterdam, Boston: Morgan Kaufmann.

Yudong, Z., & Lenan, W. (2011). *Bankruptcy Prediction by Genetic Ant Colony Algorithm* (pp. 459–463). Advanced Materials Research.

Zhang, H., & Su, J. (2004). Naive Bayesian classifiers for ranking. *Proceedings of ECML2004 15th European Conference on Machine Learning*. Pisa, Italy. doi:10.1007/978-3-540-30115-8_46

KEY TERMS AND DEFINITIONS

Classification: Classification is a technique used for discovering classes of unknown data.

Data Mining: Data mining is a form of knowledge discovery essential for solving problems in a specific domain.

Feature Selection: Feature selection is a process that chooses a subset of features from the original features so that the feature space is optimally reduced according to a certain criterion.

Filter Method: the attribute selection method is independent of the data mining algorithm to be applied to the selected attributes and assess the relevance of features by looking only at the intrinsic properties of the data. In most cases a feature relevance score is calculated, and low scoring features are removed. The subset of features left after feature removal is presented as input to the classification algorithm.

Wrapper Method: In the wrapper approach the attribute selection method uses the result of the data mining algorithm to determine how good a given attribute subset is. In this setup, a search procedure in the space of possible feature subsets is defined, and various subsets of features are generated and evaluated. The major characteristic of the wrapper approach is that the quality of an attribute subset is directly measured by the performance of the data mining algorithm applied to that attribute subset.

Section 4

Chapter 13
Data Mining Driven Rule Based Expert System for Medical Billing Compliance:
A Case Study

Umair Abdullah
Foundation University, Pakistan

Aftab Ahmed
Foundation University, Pakistan

Sohail Asghar
Comsats Institute of Information Technology, Pakistan

Kashif Zafar
National University of Computer and Emerging Sciences, Pakistan

ABSTRACT

Most of the data mining projects generate information (summarized in the form of graphs and charts) for business executives and decision makers; however it leaves to the choice of decision makers either to use it or disregard it. The manual use of the extracted knowledge limits the effectiveness of data mining technology considerably. This chapter proposes an architecture, in which data mining module is utilized to provide continuous supply of knowledge to a rule based expert system. Proposed approach solves the knowledge acquisition problem of rule based systems and also enhances effective utilization of data mining techniques (i.e. by supplying extracted knowledge to rule based system for automated use). The chapter describes the details of a data mining driven rule based expert system applied in medical billing domain. Main modules of the system along with the final analysis of performance of the system have also been presented.

DOI: 10.4018/978-1-4666-8513-0.ch013

INTRODUCTION

It was in early 2009, manager of a medical billing company was concerned about the implementation of special instructions given by medical providers (clients of the company) regarding their medical bills. There were approximately 500 special instructions in the form of conditions and associated actions (e.g. apply modifier 76 in a medical bill if diagnosis code 708.47 is used in it). Fact that billing codes and rules are quarterly updated made the problem worse. It was not possible for the team working on billing software – which was a desktop application – to encode those conditions and actions in the billing software. So the task was assigned to two different teams (each with two members) in parallel. One team used conventional programming technique and developed a 'Claim Scrubber'. The Scrubber had initially 250 special instructions implemented as part of code. The Scrubber with 250 checks was quickly moved to production by integrating it with Electronic Medical Record (EMR) – prime software - of the company. The second team was a bit slow, only developed an inference engine of a Rule Based System (RBS) using structured query language (U. Abdullah, Sawar, & Ahmed, 2009). So, the RBS with just 50 special instructions (implemented in the form of production rules) was integrated with billing software which was being used by data entry operators of the company.

In 2009, both software, were operational in their specific places (i.e. Scrubber in EMR and RBS in billing software). RBS team gradually added more rules to its system, while Scrubber team was finding it difficult to maintain existing ones. After six month, (i.e. around Aug 2009), the Claim Scrubber has 30 new checks added to it (total 280), while RBS has 145 new rules (total 195) (Umair Abdullah, Jamil Sawar, & Ahmed, 2009). Moreover, RBS was found to be more flexible, dynamic and logically powerful as compared to the Scrubber (Umair Abdullah et al., 2009). Therefore, by the end of year 2009, the Scrubber was abandoned – replaced by RBS. As of today – after five years – RBS has approximately 2500 productions rules with two teams working on it; one team of programmers for maintaining/extending the code of RBS and the second team is of domain experts, responsible for maintaining the knowledge base of the RBS. Now, in the medical billing company no medical claim is submitted to insurance without sign-off from the RBS. User interface of the RBS has been enhanced by provision of a Knowledge Editor (Umair Abdullah, Ahmed, & Sawar, 2012), which allows the domain experts to edit, update, and manage production rules by themselves. Knowledge acquisition process (i.e. adding new rules) has been speed-up by the implementation of a data mining module (Umair Abdullah, Ahmed, Asghar, & Zafar, 2014).

Success of RBS has not been a simple straight forward process. Various issues came along, and were resolved by RBS team to make the system successful. These issues have been presented in generalized form, along with the proposed solution in the next section.

PROBLEM STATEMENT

Raw data – of any application domain – coming from multiple heterogeneous sources need to be processed for the implementation of business rules according to the business need/logic. Implementing business logic with the help of conventional programming techniques is not feasible. Proposed solution for the implementation of business logic is in the form of a Rule Based System (RBS) module integrated with main data processing software.

Domain experts having knowledge of business rules coordinate with RBS developers for the editing, debugging, updating and management of rules. This coordination requirement leads to the problem of inefficiency in operational process. Knowledge editor – a Graphical User Interface (GUI) based front end – is the proposed solution for the problem of developing, editing, debugging, updating and managing the production rules of RBS. Domain experts with the help of easy to use knowledge editor may do all the rule related tasks by themselves. However, knowledge engineers (i.e. domain experts) using knowledge editor for management of rules can only develop those rules for which they have knowledge.

It is a tedious task to identify new rules from data. The slow manual knowledge acquisition process may result in failure of the whole system. For knowledge acquisition data mining techniques can play vital role. A production rule mining module can ensure continuous, authentic (i.e. on the basis of evidence from data) and fast supply of knowledge to the rule based system. Knowledge engineers may just need to validate the extracted rules (with the help of knowledge editor) before moving them to operation. The final result is an efficient, dynamic, flexible and powerful system for implementation of business logic.

Above problem statement and proposed solution are generic. Customization will be required when working in any specific application domain. Section 3 presents a generalized architecture, which is customized for medical billing domain in section 4. Before going to the conclusion in section 5, section 4 presents technical details of the internal components the RBS.

PROPOSED ARCHITECTURE OF DATA MINING DRIVEN RULE BASED EXPERT SYSTEM

This section describes a generalized architecture of data mining driven rule based expert system. As shown in Figure 1, data from multiple sources comes to the main database, where it is 'scrubbed' by the RBS before sending it to data sinks, where it has to be processed. The term 'scrubbing' refers to performing small legitimate changes for cleansing of data (Umair Abdullah et al., 2009).

Without RBS, data sinks will receive un-cleaned, dirty data with many errors, inconsistencies and omissions. As a result corrected information will be required for processing at data sinks, which in turn will request it from data sources. This whole process will cause delay in data acceptance at data sinks. To solve this inefficiency RBS is introduced to operate on central data repository to identify missing or inconsistent data and request it from data source layer prior to sending the data to sinks. Cleansing of data at central data base improves the efficiency of the system.

RBS comprises of four components; an inference engine, a knowledge base, a knowledge editor, and a rule mining module. Knowledge editor is preferably web based so that many domain experts (acting as knowledge sources) may connect to the system and update the knowledge base. Remaining chapter describes the transformation of the generalized architecture (stated above) to the specific domain of medical billing.

IMPLEMENTATION OF DATA MINING DRIVEN RULE BASED SYSTEM FOR MEDICAL BILLING

This section describes the specialized implementation of the generalized architecture (presented in previous section) as a data mining driven rule based system developed in medical billing domain for cleansing/scrubbing of medical data.

Figure 1. A generic architecture of data mining driven rule based expert system

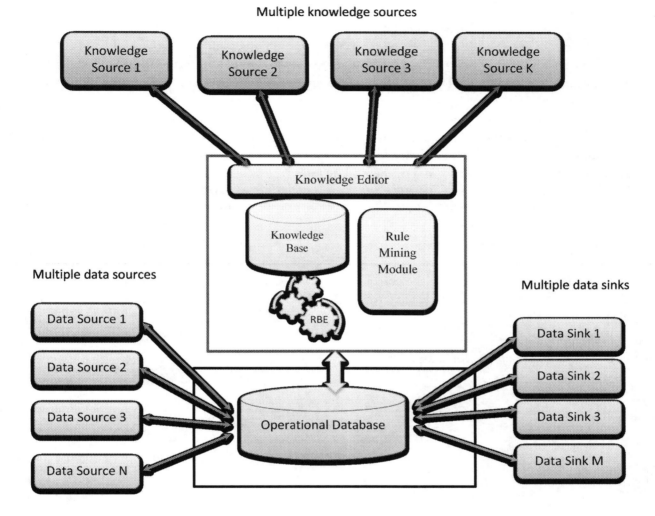

This practical work has been carried out at a medical billing company situated in a custom built software technology park. Data from hundreds of medical practices which includes hundred thousands of patients and millions of medical claims, stored in the main operational database of the company, has been used for demonstrating the proposed solution. Production rule mining has been used as learning methodology which involves extraction of production rules in the form of SQL queries. Extracted rules are supplied to the rule based system that is also developed in SQL language. Graphical User Interface (GUI) based knowledge editor is provided to the knowledge engineers for validation of extracted knowledge, manual knowledge editing and knowledge management. Before going to the details of RBS, next subsection introduce the target application domain i.e. medical billing.

Medical Billing Process

Medical billing is the process of submitting medical claims to insurances and following up on the submitted claims in order to receive payment for services rendered by a healthcare provider. It is an interaction between a healthcare provider and the insurance company (payer). The entirety of this interaction is known as the billing cycle. This process can take several days to several months for completion and requires several interactions before a resolution is reached.

A typical medical billing process cycle is shown in Figure 2. The interaction begins with the office visit of a patient on a preset appointment time. Patients make appointments before visiting the doctors (also known as providers). In this chapter, terms 'provider' and 'doctor' have been used interchangeably. Appointments' details are also saved to support the billing process. Appointment detail includes date and time, visit reason of the patient, patient name and number etc. It also includes eligibility information of the patient which can be checked from insurance servers at real time. Thus doctors may know the current status of patient insurance, even before the patient's visit. A doctor or staff typically creates or updates the patient's medical record. The record contains information of treatments and demographic information including patient's name, social security number, home telephone number, office telephone number and address, his/her insurance policy identity number. If the patient is a dependent, then guarantor information is included in patient's record. On first visit, providers usually assign one or more diagnoses to the patient.

Figure 2. Typical medical billing cycle

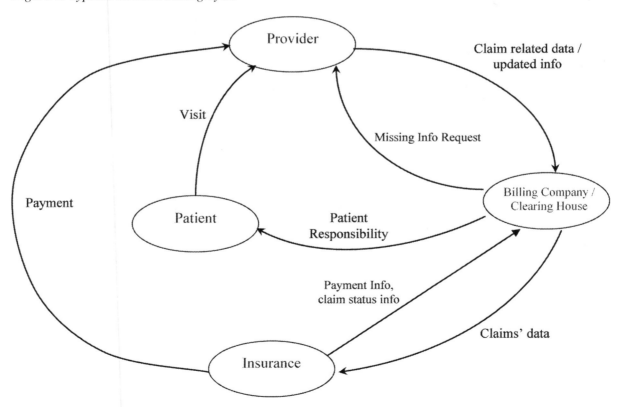

The correct level of service is determined by evaluating background information (history) obtained from the patient, the complexity of the medical decision making, and the extent of physical examination. Current Procedural Terminology (CPT) database is used to translate level of service into a five digit procedure code. Standardized ICD-10 database is used to translate verbal diagnosis into a numerical code. These two types of codes, CPTs and ICDs, along with patient information are sent to billing company or a clearing house which in turn sends the data to medical insurances. The insurance company (i.e. payer), processes the claims to assess the payment level. Three factors: patient eligibility, provider credentials, and medical necessity, are used to determine payments. Payment rates are already agreed upon by the provider and the insurance company. Provider is notified in the form of Explanation of Benefits (EOB) or Remittance Advice for the paid or rejected claims. Until a claim is fully paid or the provider accepts an incomplete reimbursement, exchange of claims and rejections continues several times.

In medical billing domain, due to similarities in diagnoses codes and high complexity of claims and/ or errors the frequency of rejections and over payments is high (often reaching 50%) (Wicklund, 2008). Insurance companies also deny certain services that are beyond their scope. Certain portion of billed amount, approved by the insurance yet not paid, is identified as patient's responsibility. It is sent to the patient for reimbursement (Carl_Mays_II, 2008).

A practice that has interactions with the patient must now - under Health Insurance Portability Accountability Act (HIPAA) of 1996 - send most billing claims for services via electronic means. Prior to actually performing service and billing a patient, the care provider may use software to check the eligibility of the patient for the intended services with the patient's insurance company. This process uses the same standards and technologies as an electronic claims transmission with small changes in the transmission format. Therefore, most providers use medical billing service from some company to electronically communicate with insurances. Many practice management software automate this communication process hiding the technical details from the user.

Simplified view of Medical billing process is shown in Figure 3. It resembles our generic architecture shown in Figure 1, except that RBS is missing. Multiple providers work as data sources, generate patients and claims data.

Figure 3. Simplified medical billing cycle

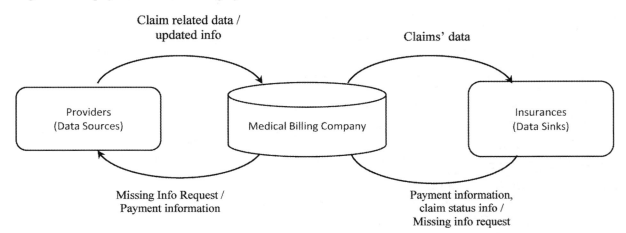

A medical billing company serves as intermediate data repository and submits the claims' data (on behalf of providers) to multiple insurances. Insurances resemble data sinks and do processing of medical claims.

As described in previous section RBS can be introduced at the middle layer for cleansing of medical claims so that faulty claims may not travel to data sinks and get rejected. RBS can identify and send the faulty claims back to providers for correction and updating of missing/incorrect information. Architecture of such a system is described in the next section along with the details of its internal components.

Architecture of Data Mining Driven Rule Based System

Published in (Ahmed, Abdullah, & Sawar, 2010) architecture of a data mining driven rule based system specific for medical billing compliance is shown in Figure 4. Billing software is the main component with

Figure 4. Proposed architecture of data mining driven rule based system

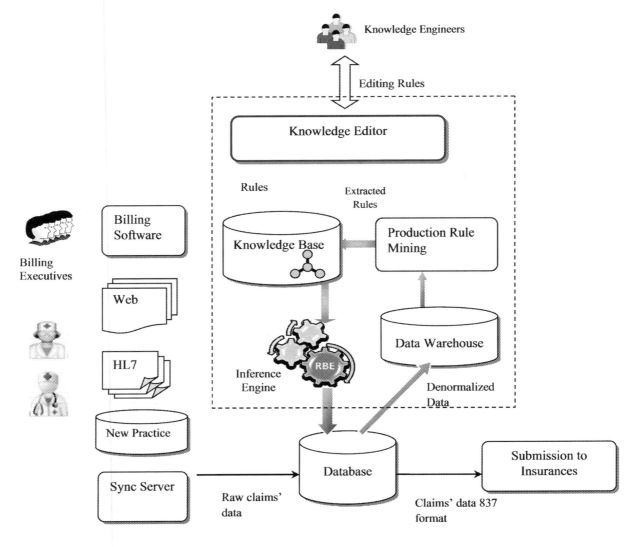

which most of the users interact. Billing executives use it for inserting, updating, and modifying claims' data. Domain experts use it for pulling various types of reports, importing data and following up claims.

Billing software triggers Rule Based Engine (RBE) to perform billing compliance related checks on a claim being saved. RBE applies production rules on the claim (which is being saved at a particular moment) and informs the user about faults found in the claim being submitted. RBE also performs scrubbing activity, defined as 'then-part' of the production rules. Main database contains claim related data, input from billing software, Web sites, Health Level 7 (HL7) files, data imported from database of new practices and data sent by sync server (synchronization server). Electronic Data Interchange (EDI) module gets data from the database and converts it into text files in specific format (like 837 format) which is acceptable for the insurances. Submission module sends these files to the insurances via Internet.

Data mining driven rule based expert system is represented by the dotted box in Figure 4. It has four major components (enclosed in dotted box). Knowledge Editor (KE) is shown on top left corner of dotted box which consists of a form based graphical user interface. Knowledge is in the form of production rules stored in knowledge base, shown at top right corner of the system.

RBE is depicted in the form of gear at bottom left area of dotted box. Rule engine has been developed in Structured Query Language (SQL) in the form of stored procedures (U. Abdullah et al., 2009). Remaining blocks in RBS belongs to data mining module. These include 'data warehouse', and production rule mining module. Domain experts use knowledge editor to add new knowledge to the knowledge base (in the form of production rule) or verify any new rules found by production rule mining module. Brief descriptions of each component of the system's architecture are given in the following sub-sections.

External Components

Proposed system is represented by dotted box in Figure 4. Many modules interacting with it from outside can be termed as external components. Descriptions of these external modules are given below:

Medical Billing Software

Daily three shifts (8 hours each) of billing executives use medical billing software to insert medical claims' data into the main operational database of the company. Medical billing software is custom built software designed and developed for healthcare data entry.

Company's Website

Medical providers use company's Website to view status of their medical bills. They can use Website for adding new patients, appointments and other related information which is directly stored in main database of the company.

EMR and Synchronization Server

Many doctors use EMR of the company, especially after the health reform done by the US government, which requires medical practitioners to use EMRs in order to get incentives and avoid penalties (Ishtiaq & Ali, 2010). EMR developed by the company is certified for 'meaningful use' which means its users can get incentive amounts and avoid penalties. EMR of the company is a desktop application which stores data in Microsoft SQL Server at the backend installed at doctor's office. Medical claims' data is copied from practice (doctor's) office to the main database server of the company over the Internet by custom built data synchronization software (shown as 'sync server' at bottom left of Figure 4).

Import Files (HL7, Amazing Charts)

Many clients of the company use EMRs of other companies like MediSoft (Medisoft, 2009), and Amazing Charts etc. These EMRs export data in the form of text files in Health Level 7 (HL7) format. HL7 is standard format for transferring medical data between different locations. A module in medical billing software, imports these HL7 files containing medical billing data to the main operational database of the company.

Servers of New Practices

Complete patients' data of new practices which joins the company is imported directly into the main database of the company with the help of SQL scripts manually developed by IT department. Data of new practices has a lot of information missing in it. Insurances are mapped with those already coded in the company's database. Similarly, a lot of transformation is required for new practice's data. Due to the required transformations and data changes, many inconsistencies creep into new practice's data. To find those inconsistencies, RBS processes all the claims imported into the main database before submitting to insurances.

Domain Users

There are different types of users, who use RBS and medical billing related software. Different types of users have different qualifications, experiences, and qualities.

Medical Providers

Term 'medical provider' is used for doctors, physicians, surgeons, skilled nurses, and any person who can claim for reimbursement of healthcare services provided to patients. Few years back providers were mainly concerned with patient checkup and treatment, they rarely used any software or Website. Most of the providers were doing paper work for their duties. In recent years, many providers have started using EMR, Websites, and other healthcare related software.

Practices' Office Staff

Even if providers fully use EMR, staff at provider's office also needs to use desktop or Web-based EMR to enter information of patients. When a patient comes to visit a provider, office staff of provider inserts basic data of the patient like demographics, vital signs, and past medical history etc. into the electronic database prior to check up from provider. In this way much time of the provider is saved. Some providers have their staff for billing related activities i.e. submitting claims to insurances and doing follow up till payments are received. This is termed as 'in-house billing'.

Billing Executives

Medical paper bills in the form of scanned images are received by the medical billing company where billing executives insert medical data into the main operational database of the company by reading data from the scanned images and using billing software of the company. Billing executives are simple graduates with a little background in computer science. At initial level, they just enter data. After some years of experience they start claims' follow up by communicating with insurances. In Figure 4, billing executives are shown on left side near the 'Billing Software'.

Domain Experts

Persons with comprehensive knowledge of medical billing can be termed as domain experts. Normally, billing executives having medical billing experience of more than three years can be termed as domain experts. Users with this much experience, are normally working as Team leads and Managers in operation department. They supervise the billing activities done by billing executives.

Knowledge Engineers

A selected group of domain experts works as knowledge engineers. They use knowledge editor to edit rules and manage knowledge base of the system. They do analysis related to rules category, severity and priority. They coordinate with domain users to improve the knowledge base and justify the challenged rules. They also coordinate with team of developers, who develop and maintain the RBS for improving the knowledge base and knowledge editor of the data mining driven rule based system.

Knowledge Engineers monitor the performance of individual rules, enable, disable, and modify them on the basis of their analysis and feedback from operations. Knowledge engineers are shown at upper side of Figure 4. They use Knowledge editor and medical billing software and also use emails for communicating and coordinating with other teams.

RBS Developers

A group of programmers who work on development and maintenance of RBS is known as RBS development team. They have qualification related to computer science and/or software engineering, and have knowledge of computer programming languages. They use knowledge editor and Microsoft SQL Server Management Studio for editing of knowledge base.

Main modules of the system are 'rule based engine' and 'knowledge editor'. Initially rules were developed by RBS programmers directly in SQL environment. Later knowledge editor was built by RBS development team so that knowledge engineer could build rules by themselves.

Internal Components of the System

Modules inside the Rule Based System (RBS) are termed as internal components. In Figure 4, main box with dotted lines represents the RBS. It has four main components; 'knowledge base', 'knowledge editor', 'rule based engine', and 'data mining based learning module'.

Rule Engine

The Rule Based Engine (RBE) has been implemented using structured query language (U. Abdullah et al., 2009). Rule engine applies all the rules on a given claim and finds out errors/ faults. Each rule is equivalent to a check with some actions associated with it. Each rule has been implemented as 'where' clause of a SQL query. 'Select' portion of the rule query is attached by the rule engine at runtime.

The logical flow of rule engine is very simple i.e. take one claim at a time, keeping in view the rule priority and meta-rules, apply all rules on it one by one, and execute 'then-part' of those rules for which rule conditions are true. The above simple logic has been explained as logical design of the rule based engine shown in Figure 5.

In first phase, for a given claim all the meta-rules are executed one by one. When a meta-rule returns true then its related rules are selected. At the end of this phase all applicable rules are separated from non-applicable rules of the claim.

In the second phase, rule engine applies all these selected rules individually on the given claim and identifies the inconsistencies and errors. Each rule is like a condition with some action part associated to it and implemented as a "where" clause of a SQL query. For example the check of "missing date of birth" will be implemented as "*select @rowcnt = count(*) where '<DOB>' = ''*". The token <DOB> is a logical variable and will be replaced by its value. RBE will get its value from the claim at runtime. For example, if <DOB> is blank then rule query after replacing the value of logical variable will become:

select @rowcnt = count(*) where '' = ''

In above rule query, 'where' clause is true so @rowcnt SQL variable will get value 1 indicating the error of "patient date of birth missing". Suppose date of birth of the patient is not missing i.e. it is "08/20/2009", then rule query after replacing value of logical variable <DOB> will become:

select @rowcnt = count(*) where '08/20/2009' = ''

In this case @rowcnt SQL variable will get 0 value (as condition is false in 'where' clause), thus indicating that error of "patient date of birth missing" has not occurred.

To understand the working of rule engine let us discuss another data inconsistency example; according to medical billing knowledge the date of service of a patient cannot be earlier than his/her date of birth (i.e. a patient cannot be treated before his/her birth). It could only happen due to manual data entry mistake. So the check of 'date of birth follows date of service' is implemented as '*select @rowcnt = count(*) where '<DOB>' > '<DOS>'* '. where <DOB> (i.e. date of birth of the patient) and <DOS> (i.e. date of service of the patient's claim) are logical variables and will be replaced by their respective values from the claim (being processed at) at runtime. Suppose, the date of birth of the patient is '25/01/10' and date of service (mistakenly entered) is '20/01/10'. The rule query after replacing the values of logical variables will become:

select @rowcnt=count(*) where '25/01/10' > '20/01/10'

Figure 5. Rule engine design (logical)

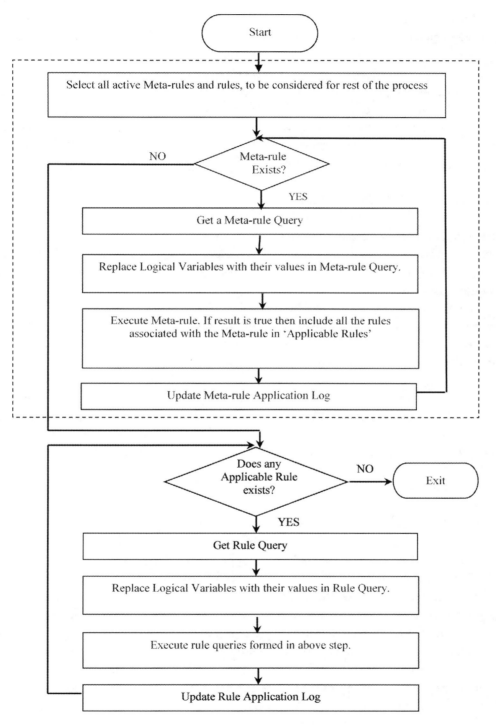

Now 'where' clause is true so @rowcnt (a SQL variable) will get value 1, indicating the error of 'patient date of birth follows date of service'. So, the claim having these values of date of service and date of birth will be identified by RBS as faulty claim and hence will be blocked from submission to insurance.

Rule engine described above is only effective when sufficient amount of billing knowledge is provided to it in the form of production rules. Manual entry of production rules with the knowledge editor is not efficient way of supplying a continuous supply of rules to the system. Therefore, a production rule mining module has been developed to extract rules from rejected claims. Production rule mining algorithm – described in coming sections – works on rejected and corrected versions of medical claims present in a data warehouse. Next subsection describes the design of the Datawarehouse followed by the section explaining rule mining module itself.

Data Warehouse of the System

As construction and maintenance of data warehouse requires a lot of resources (such as time, money, human resource etc.), therefore, it was important to decide whether to construct a data warehouse or to utilize a regularly backed up copy of operational database, for applying data mining algorithms to extract new production rules from data.

Main reason for developing a data warehouse is that, when a claim is rejected by insurance, record of the claim is modified in operational database to remove the rejection reason. After modification, corrected claim is resubmitted to the insurance. In this way, the data with which claim was rejected is modified in operational database. However that data is important for the production rule mining module, to learn new production rules and to avoid future rejections. Operational database contains either information of unpaid claims (not yet corrected), or paid claims (with correct, clean data) accepted by the insurances, while the data warehouse contains all the historic records of claims i.e. faulty data rejected from insurances and final clean data for which claims were accepted and paid by the insurances.

Published in (Ahmed, Zafar, Siddiqui, & Abdullah, 2013), design of the data warehouse based on medical billing data is shown in Figure 6. Data warehouse has been designed to extract production rules on the basis of those rejected claims which get paid after manual correction. Operational data of the organization may not be used for this purpose as rejected versions of claims are corrected and sent back to insurance for reimbursement. Operationally it is not suitable to keep all modified versions of a claim in an operational database; therefore, only final corrected (and paid) version of a claim is kept in operational database. Data is in normalized form in operational database and it is required to be in denormalized form in data warehouse, for efficiency purpose and for easy selection.

Another major difference between operational database and data warehouse is the use of primary keys. In operational database, primary keys are logical i.e. IDs are generated with some logic (e.g. 'Practice code' appended with 'serial number' to form a patient ID); while in data warehouse, primary key is physical i.e. an auto generated serial number which increments when new record (or even an existing record) is inserted. Physical primary key is used in all dimension tables and fact tables of the data warehouse.

In all companies and organizations which are related to medical billing or medical claim processing, entities of medical billing process are almost same e.g. patient, provider, and payer etc. Therefore data warehouse design presented here, after making required changes, can be utilized in any application related to medical claim processing.

Data warehouse derived from the operational database - shown in Figure 6 - is approximate star schema with 16 dimension tables and 3 fact tables.

Figure 6. Proposed data warehouse design (approximate star schema)

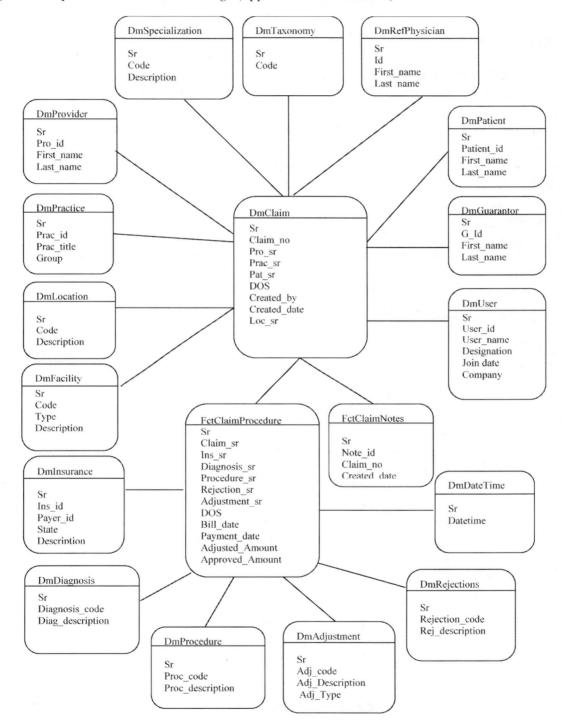

Data Mining Based Learning Module

Data mining based learning module is based on the production rule mining algorithm (Umair Abdullah et al., 2014) outlined in Figure 7. It has four major steps; at step one it produces a 'What-Table' (i.e. what has been done by the users to corrected the rejected versions of claims) with the help of 'R-Table' i.e. table containing only rejected versions of claims, and a 'C-Table' i.e. table containing corrected versions of those claims. At second step 'when-table' is produced (i.e. count the occurrences of specific values in specific columns when the claims were rejected due to a specific reason). At third step both 'what-table' and 'when-table' are merged in order to show count of when what action was performed by the users in order to correct the claims. And finally at the fourth step production rules are generated with the help of user action rule action mapping table.

Proposed algorithm is for application domains in which same object has accepted state, which was previously in rejected state. Such as, a student passing a previously failed course, a medical claim accepted by insurance which got rejected initially due to some missing information. Algorithm tries to find difference between accepted and rejected states of same object, and check all other objects of same rejection type.

Proposed algorithm try to find what corrective action is done by the user on a rejected record so that it got corrected on the basis of counts.

Figure 7. Outline of production rule mining algorithm

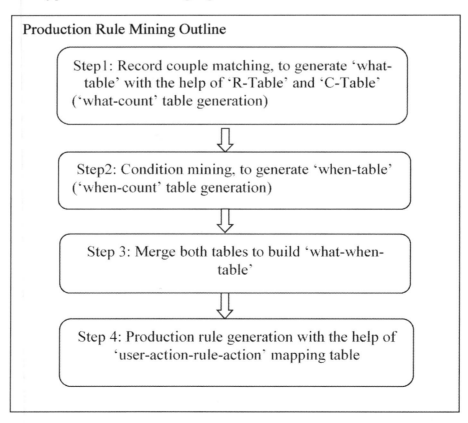

Definition: A 'record-couple' (RC) is collection of two states of an object i.e. current accepted one and previous rejected one stored in the dataset in the form of two tuples/records of a Table

```
Record Couple = Ĉ = {R, C}
R = <V_eid, R_1, R_2, R_3, ....., R_m>
C = <V_eid, C_1, C_2, C_3, ....., C_m>
V_eid = V_eid            and ∃ i: R_i ≠ C_i
```

Where 'R' is represents rejected record, and 'C' is the corrected record. 'R_i' is value of ith attribute in rejected record and 'C_i' is value of ith attribute in accepted record. 'V_{eid}' is value of primary key, having same value (i.e. 'V_{eid}') in 'R' and 'C' implies that both records belong to the same object.

Difference between corrected and rejected/faulty versions of records (within a record-couple) is actually action done by the user (in order to remove the fault). 100% confidence for an action means same action is performed in all record- couples (for same error). Similar attribute values in all records of a dataset helps to determine 'when' that action should be performed (which constitutes condition part of the production rule).

Input a data set 'D' of n record-couples (each record-couple has a rejected and a corrected record), along with a threshold confidence ĉ, algorithm produces list L of production rules.

$$D = \{ \hat{C}_1, \hat{C}_2, \hat{C}_3, ..., \hat{C}n \}$$

Algorithm Steps:

1. From all record-couples of the dataset D to identify 'focused-attributes' (i.e. columns which has different values in rejected tuple and in corrected tuples).
2. Generate 'R-Table' and 'C-Table' from dataset D containing only rejected-values and accepted values respectively.
3. From 'R-Table' and 'C-Table' obtain additional information about 'Focused Attributes' like their minimum and maximum lengths, list of wrong values (from R-table) and list of correct values (from C-Table), any fixed symbols compulsory (present in all correct values) etc.
4. For i = 1 to n, (where $\hat{C}_i$ is i^{th} record-couple of dataset D).

Match all attributes of R (rejected tuple of $\hat{C}_i$) and C (corrected tuple of $\hat{C}_i$) to update 'What-count' table with what has been done within a record couple (i.e. which column inserted/update/deleted).

5. From all records of dataset D (including rejected and corrected versions) identifies which columns have same values and prepare a 'when-count' table.
6. Create a merged 'What-When-count' table by combining 'what-count' and 'when-count' tables on the basis of primary key attributes.
7. Apply following sub algorithm to generate rule list L.
   Rule List: L = { }
   Action: nil
   Condition: nil
   Rule: nil

1. For each ith row of 'what-when-table' do;
1.1 Suppose WWij is count value of ith row (what$_i$) and jth column (When$_j$)
1.2 ∀ WWij > $\hat{c}$: Condition = When$_j$ ^ Condition
1.3 Action = *action* (What$_i$)
1.4 Rule = Condition ➔ Action
1.5 L = Rule U L
2. Return rule list L

'Action (What$_i$)' returns call of the function action which is stored as rule-action in 'user-action rule-action mapping' table. Confidence of a production rule can be calculated by equation (1) as follow;

$$Confidence \ (\text{Rule}) = \frac{B}{|D|} \ \text{--------} \tag{1}$$

where 'B' is count of records in which both 'What' (Action) and 'When' (condition) exist, and |D| represents total number of records in a dataset. Threshold confidence is the minimum confidence value of a rule which allows generation of the rule. Its value is adjusted by the user at runtime.

Proposed algorithm is tested on a medical claim dataset. Table 1 – to be used by the Algorithm – given below, shows mapping of rule-action and user-action in medical billing domain.

Test Dataset: A test data of 500 record-couples associated with rejection *"Subscriber primary identifier invalid for payer, it must be 8 to 14 alpha-numeric characters"* was used for testing the algorithm.

Table 2, shows a sample of 5 record-couples related to this rejection. Gray records (with SR 1, 3, 5, 7, 9) are rejected ones while others (with SR 2, 4, 6, 8) are corrected records of corresponding claims.

User added preceding 0 to make the length of the policy number '04513678' valid for the payer (valid length is 8 to 14 alphanumeric characters).

A table containing only corrected tuples extracted from all record couples of a rejection is termed as 'C-Table'. Similarly table containing all rejected tuples extracted from all record couples of a rejection, is termed as 'R-Table'. R-Table of test dataset is shown as Table 3.

Table 1. Sample 9 records of 'User-Action-Rule-Action' mapping table

SR	Reason/ What	Action of production rule
1	Datetime is less than other datetime column	Store second column value as datetime of the first column
2	Datetime is greater than other datetime column	Store second column value as datetime of the first column
3	Predefined suffix missing	Append the suffix
4	Predefined prefix missing	Attach the prefix
5	Required character missing inside string value	Insert the required character at specified position
6	Negative value stored while positive value required	Change the sign to + ive
7	Value from invalid list inserted	Block the claim
8	Value not from predefine list of values	Block the claim
9	*Default action*	Block the claim

Table 2. A portion of test dataset showing record couples of the rejection

SR	Claim No	Payer Code	Patient Account	Policy No	....
1	10023	500114	203	4513678	....
2	10023	500114	203	04513678	....
3	10045	500114	506		....
4	10045	500114	506	100000035185	....
5	10060	500114	423		....
6	10060	500114	423	100000122291	....
7	10045	500114	506		....
8	10045	500114	506	100321112WA	....
9	10060	500114	423		....
10	10060	500114	423	102220778WA	....

Table 3. A portion of R-Table of rejection dataset

SR	Claim No	Policy Number	Payer Code
1	10023	4513678	500114
3	10045		500114
5	10060		500114
7	10045		500114
9	10060		500114

Table 4. A sample portion of C-Table of rejection dataset

SR	Claim No	Policy Number	Payer Code
2	10023	04513678	500114
4	10045	100000035185	500114
6	10060	100000122291	500114
8	10045	100321112WA	500114
10	10060	102220778WA	500114

Table 5. A portion of what-table containing count of user actions

SR	Action	Couple Count
1	Policy number inserted	250
2	Policy number modified (due to invalid length)	173

C-Table generated from 'C' (i.e. corrected) tuples of all record-couples of the rejection dataset, is shown as Table 4 as follow;

From C-Table (Table 4) given above format returned by string generalization function is: '\N\N\N\N\N\N\N\N\N\N\n\n\x\x'.

Table 5 is the 'what-table' generated at step 1, containing count of actions identified by matching rejected and corrected records within all record couples of a rejection. A portion of 'When-Table' (step 2 of algorithm outline) is shown in Table 6 given below.

Table 7 , is 'what-when table' generated at third step of production rule mining algorithm, by merging 'what-table' and 'when-table' tables.

Encircled values are above threshold (i.e. 50 in this case) set by the user. Condition and action of encircled values are used by rule generation algorithm (A4) to generate production rules in the form;

'When' (Condition) => 'What' (Action)

In this case condition 1 is that 'for payer 500114, patient's policy number is blank', condition 2 is 'for payer 500114, length of policy number is less than 8' and condition 3 is 'for payer 500114, length of policy number is greater than 14'. Note that these length limits are identified by string matching algorithm while forming template pattern. Following rules have been extracted by the production rule mining algorithm.

<payer id> = 500114 AND <policy_number> = '' ➔ block the claim

<payer id> = 500114 AND Length (<policy_number>) < 8 ➔ block the claim

<payer id> = 500114 AND Length (<policy_number>) > 14 ➔ block the claim

Table 6. A portion of when-table containing claim count for each attribute value of focused columns

SR	Column	Value	Couple Count
1	Policy number		250
2	Policy number length less than	8	107
3	Policy number length greater than	14	66
4	Payer code	500114	500

Table 7. A portion of what-when (action–condition) count table

SR	What\When	Condition 1	Condition 2	Condition 3
1	Policy number inserted	250	0	0
2	Policy number modified	0	107	66

Note that the last rule generation step has taken action part of above rules from 'user action-rule action' mapping table.

With the help of production rule mining module, knowledge engineers have been able to insert more and accurate knowledge thus increasing the effectiveness of the RBS deployed for scrubbing medical claims. Extracted rules are in the form of SQL queries directly usable by rule based engine. The production rule mining module works at the background, on a data warehouse. Therefore it does not have any direct influence on the performance of operational database. Advantage of data mining module is that it provides drill down information as an evidence for the piece of knowledge extracted from data warehouse. On the basis of data evidence, domain expert simply needs to accept or reject the rule. A knowledge editor has been provided to domain experts to do validate the extracted rules (Umair Abdullah et al., 2012).

Knowledge Editor

A graphical user interface based knowledge editor has been developed to allow knowledge engineers to add, update, delete, and manage rules, meta-rules, and logical variables. Domain experts can use it to verify mined rules, test and debug all rules. In classical rule based system, logical variables get their values by matching with the working memory elements (Hayes-roth, 1985). In this system whole database serves the purpose of working memory and logical variables get their value(s) by executing a SQL query associated with each of them.

Advantage of the knowledge editor can be visualized in rule development process before and after the implementation of the knowledge editor, as shown in Figure 8 and Figure 9 respectively.

Flow of rule development process prior to knowledge editor is shown in Figure 8. Domain user initiates a rule by sending a piece of knowledge to rule development group (comprising of knowledge engineers). It is a group of domain experts with normally more than five years of experience and in-depth knowledge of medical billing. The group of knowledge engineers then analyzes of information received,

Figure 8. Rule development process before knowledge editor

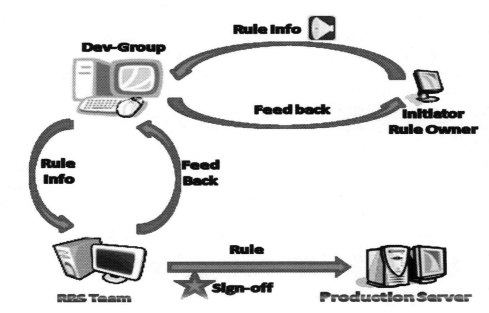

Figure 9. Rule development process after knowledge editor

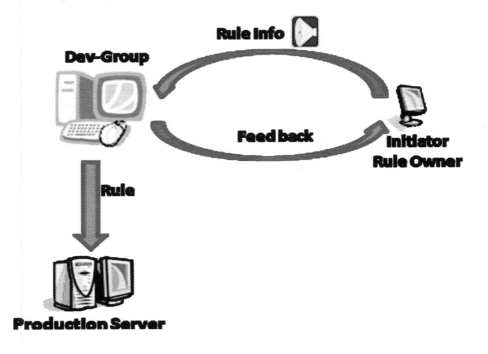

confirms its validity, and sends the refined information to RBS team for development of the rule. Since there was no user interface available for knowledge engineers, so they were dependent on RBS team for development of production rules. RBS team was using Microsoft SQL Server Management Studio to write production rules in the form of SQL queries. The process was time consuming and involves chances of error, miscommunications and false assumptions.

The flow of rule development process after the implementation of knowledge editor is shown in Figure 9. Now it is more simplified, efficient, and less error prone.

Rule initiator sends the piece of knowledge to the domain experts. Domain experts (knowledge engineers) of rule development group can develop rules with the help of graphical user interface of knowledge editor software which is developed and maintained by RBS team. Rule creation process has been speed up due to the knowledge editor. It provides graphical interface to knowledge engineers for developing rules, meta-rules, and logical variables. Production rule editor opens in main window, which is shown in Figure 10. Knowledge editor generates SQL queries of rules, meta-rules and logical variables by itself, while the user has to interact with the graphical user interface only.

A list of rules is appearing on the left side of the editor window shown in Figure 10. User can switch to meta-rules and logical variables by clicking their respective radio buttons present above the rule list. User can search and select any rule from the list in order to edit it. Data of the selected rule appears on the main area of the window. SQL query of the rule, generated by the rule editor, is shown in 'Rule SQL Query' section of knowledge editor window. Upper half of the Form shows attributes related to the rule, which includes rule name, description, status, meta-rule, rule owner, reference etc. Every rule name should be unique i.e. no two rules in the knowledge base are allowed to have the same name. Rule description is a piece of information in English describing the rule.

Figure 10. Knowledge (rule) editor main window

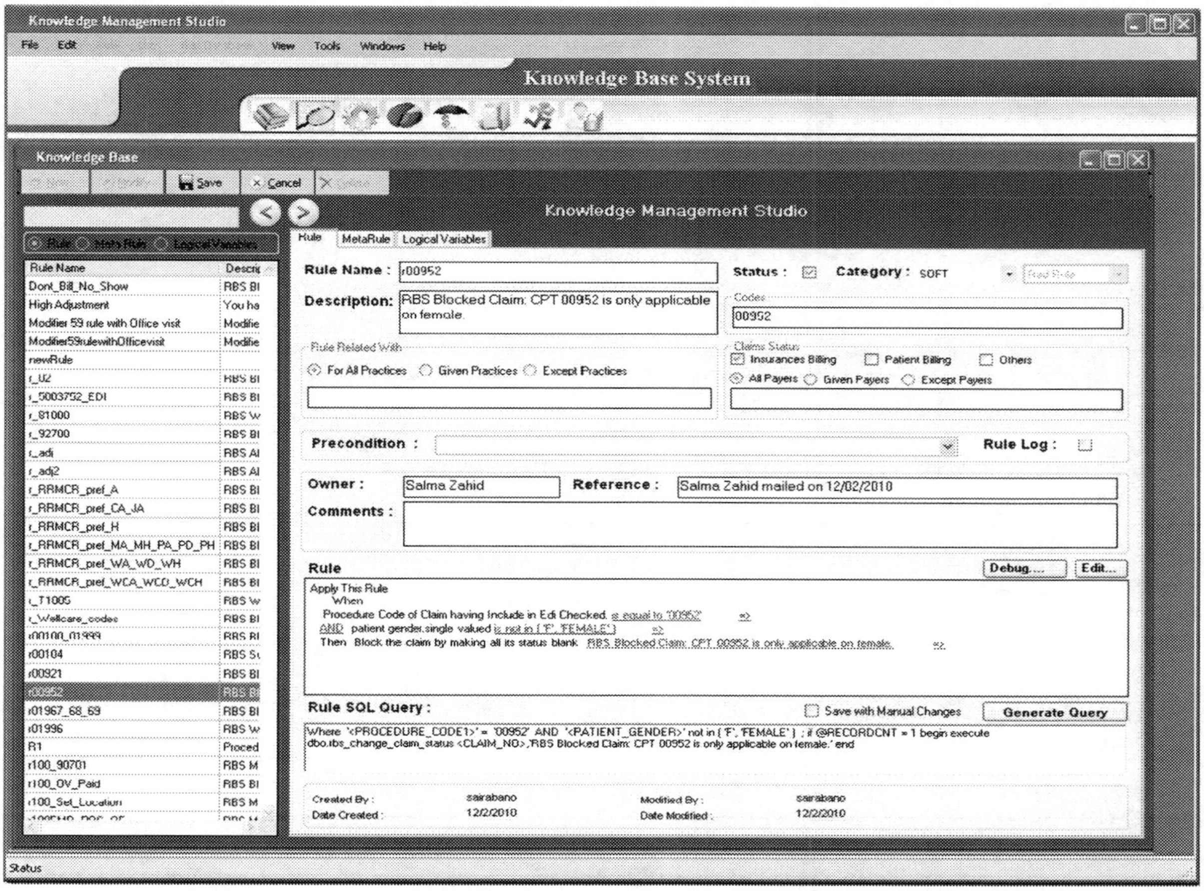

Other two important attributes are 'reference' and 'rule owner'. Often it happens that when a rule is moved to operation, it is challenged by some domain users. Reference attributes help knowledge engineering team to keep track of knowledge source of the rule, and 'rule owner' defends the rule and convinces domain users about the authenticity and validity of the rule. In some cases, a rule needs to be modified or even fully rolled back from the operation.

On main production rule editor window, the middle portion (labeled as 'Rule') is the main rule developing area. It is the working area of the user (i.e. knowledge engineer) where he/she can define rule conditions and action. If user wants to add more conditions, he/she can click 'Edit' button to open an information segment window shown in Figure 11. User can click a hyperlink to open rule condition window shown in Figure 12 and build a rule condition. The last hyperlink, after 'then' is action part of the rule. It opens rule action window where user can select some predefined actions and input rule message.

Information segment window has two parts. Upper panel is the list of data attributes/columns related to claim, patient, insurance, practice, and provider etc. Required information segment is included in a rule to define a rule condition. Popup menus (shown in Figure 11) have been provided to join multiple conditions with the help of logical operators i.e. 'and', 'or', 'not'. From popup menu user can insert

Figure 11. Information segment window

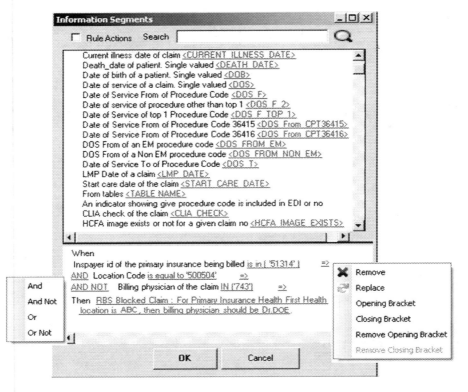

Figure 12. Rule condition window

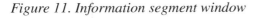

opening and closing parenthesis to make rule condition more logical. User can build conditions on main rule developing area of either main window or information segment window.

In rule developing area values are in the form of hyperlinks. When a user clicks the hyperlink, a rule condition window opens up (shown in Figure 12). A condition is basically a collection of conditional operator in the middle, left operand and right operand on left and right side respectively. Rule condition window allows the user to build a condition. Left operand is normally a logical variable associated with information segment which was added in the rule on information segment window.

Right operand can be another logical variable or a single specific value; like, in example rule of previous section, insurance code of Health First i.e. 515314 (a specific value) used as right operand in one of the rule conditions. Right operand can be a list of more than one values when user selects 'in' or 'not in' as conditional operator. Right operand can be two values when user chooses 'between' operator.

Domain expert with the help of knowledge management window – shown in Figure 13 - can check, uncheck, and unmark the check box for any rule of any server to move, delete, or disable the particular rule on particular server. All actions selected by the user on rules' grid are then listed in 'Actions list' shown on right hand side of Figure 13. Knowledge manager can finally review the actions and if satisfied, he/she can click 'Apply' button to perform all the actions mentioned in actions list. User can exclude any specific action by double clicking it or cancel all actions by pressing 'Clear All' button.

Figure 13. Rule management window

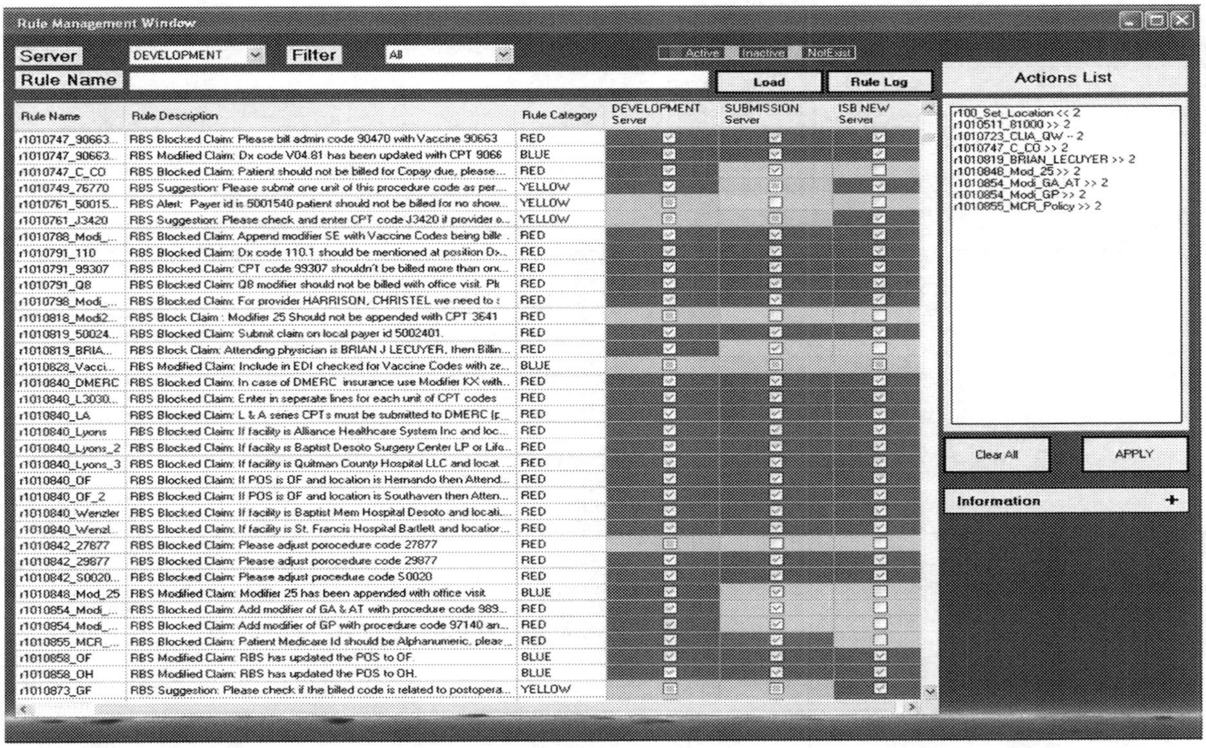

Table 8. A sample of 20 rules from the knowledge base of the system

SR	Rule_Name	Description	Condition
1	r_02	RBS Blocked Claim: Vaccine is not payable by Medicaid in practice state	Where '<PRAC_STATE>' in ('CO', 'IA', 'ID', 'IN', 'KS', 'ME', 'NE', 'VT', 'NH', 'NM', 'SD', 'OR') AND '<PROCEDURE_CODE>' in ('90632', '90659', '90707', '90716', '90718', '90733', '90746', '90732') AND '<PRO_REJ_TYPE>' = '02' AND '<PRI_STATUS>' = 'R' AND '<N_INSPAYER_ID>' in ('5002448', '5004916', '5004171', '5002453', '5004164', '5002459', '5002460', '5003427', '5004170', '5003736') AND '<PRACTICE_CODE>' not in ('238') ; if @RECORDCNT = 1 begin execute dbo.rbs_change_claim_status <CLAIM_NO>' end
2	r_92700	RBS Modified Claim: Procedure code 92700 used with 92612	Where '<PROCEDURE_CODE1>' = '92612' AND charindex('92700','<PROC_ALL>') = '0' AND '<PRACTICE_CODE>' not in ('238') ; if @RECORDCNT = 1 begin execute dbo.rbs_apply_Procedure_code <CLAIM_NO>,'92700' end
3	r00952	RBS Blocked Claim: CPT 00952 is only applicable on female.	Where '<PROCEDURE_CODE1>' = '00952' AND '<PATIENT_GENDER>' not in ('F', 'FEMALE') ; if @RECORDCNT = 1 begin execute dbo.rbs_change_claim_status <CLAIM_NO> end
4	r1010520_ECHOCode	SIR: RBS Blocked Claim: According to Special Instructions, Replace ECHO code with 93306	Where '<N_P_INSPAYER_ID>' = '5002492' and '<PROCEDURE_CODE1>' in ('93307','93325','93320'); if @RECORDCNT = 1 begin execute dbo.rbs_change_claim_status <CLAIM_NO> end
5	r1010520_Modi_LC_LD_RC	SIR: RBS Blocked Claim: According to Special Instructions, if CPT code is in range 92980-92982, restrict user to add modifier LC, LD OR RC	Where '<PROC_LC_LD_RC>' in ('92980','92981','92982'); if @RECORDCNT = 1 begin execute dbo.rbs_change_claim_status <CLAIM_NO> end
6	r1010539_Modi_QW	RBS Modified Claim: Entered QW modifier With CPT 81003 and 82570 as per provider special instructions	Where '<N_INSPAYER_ID>' = '5002495' AND '<PROC_QW>' in ('81003', '82570') ; if @RECORDCNT = 1 begin execute dbo.rbs_apply_modifier <CLAIM_NO>, 'QW' end
7	r1010652_L3020_Units	RBS Blocked Claim: Enter separate lines for each unit of CPT L3020	where '<PROC_UNITS>' = 'L3020' ; if @RECORDCNT = 1 begin execute dbo.rbs_change_claim_status <CLAIM_NO> end
8	r1010681_MCD	RBS Blocked Claim: Medicaid patients cannot be billed, so adjust the due amount or bill to Medicaid.	Where '<CLAIM_PAYER_ID>' = '5002447' AND '<PATIENT_STATUS>' in ('N', 'R') ; if @RECORDCNT = 1 begin execute dbo.rbs_change_claim_status <CLAIM_NO>end
9	r1010712_81002	RBS Blocked Claim: Please append modifier QW with CPT code 81002.	Where '<PROC_QW>' = '81002' ; if @RECORDCNT = 1 begin execute dbo.rbs_apply_modifier <CLAIM_NO>,'QW' end
10	r1010720_OV	RBS Modified Claim: Office and well care code used in the claim, appended modifier 25 with office visit code.	Where '<PROCEDURE_CODE1>' between '99381' and '99397' AND '<PROC_25>' between '99201' and '99215' ; if @RECORDCNT = 1 begin execute dbo.rbs_apply_modifier <CLAIM_NO>,'25' end
11	r1010723_CLIA_QW	RBS Modified Claim: Added modifier QW with CLIA waived test	Where '<PROC_QW>' in ('80047', '80048', '80051', '80053', '80061', '80069', '80101', '80178', '81002', '81003', '81007', '81025', '82010', '82040', '82044', '82055', '82120', '82150', '82247', '87807', '87808', '87880', '87899', '87999', '89300', '89321', 'G0328', 'G0430', 'G0431') ; if @RECORDCNT = 1 begin execute dbo.rbs_apply_modifier <CLAIM_NO>,'QW' end
12	sir255_5002492_728	SIR: RBS Modified Claim: For primary payer MEDICARE(payer id 5002492), If CPT code is 20550, 20552, 20553 used, then change ICD 721.3 or 721.0 with 728.85	Where '<N_P_INSPAYER_ID>' = '5002492' and '<PROCEDURE_CODE>' IN ('20550', '20552','20553') and ('<CDX_CODE>' in ('721.0','721.3')); If @RECORDCNT = 1 begin execute dbo.rbs_Replace_ICD <claim_no>,'728.85' end

Continued on following page

Table 8. Continued

SR	Rule_Name	Description	Condition
13	sir339_5002450	SIR: RBS Modified Claim: if payer is Medicaid FL (5002450) then referring physician must have Medicaid PIN updated or PA number must exist	Where '<N_P_INSPAYER_ID>' = '5002450' and ('<REFERRING_PHY_PIN>'='' And '<PA_NUMBER>' = '') ; if @RECORDCNT = 1 begin execute dbo.rbs_update_pa_number <CLAIM_NO>,'5002450' end
14	sir339_5002481_QW	SIR: RBS Modified Claim: Add modifier QW with CPT codes 87880 or 86318.	Where '<N_P_INSPAYER_ID>' = '5002481' and '<PROC_QW>' in ('87880','86318') ; If @RECORDCNT = 1 begin execute dbo.rbs_apply_modifier <CLAIM_NO>,'QW' end
15	sir360_Bill_Hanna	SIR: RBS Modified Claim: If primary payer id is 5002437,5002438,5002439, then billing physician should be HANNA, DINA	Where '<N_P_INSPAYER_ID>' in ('5002437','5002438','5002439') and '<BILLING_PHYSICIAN_A>' != '564' ; IF @RECORDCNT = 1 begin execute dbo.rbs_set_billing_phy <CLAIM_NO>,'564' end
16	sir371_DXV04	SIR: RBS Modified Claim: For CPTs 90658 DX code must be V04.81	Where '<PROCEDURE_CODE1>' = '90658' AND (NOT(charindex('V04.81','<DX_ALL>')>0)); IF @RECORDCNT = 1 begin execute dbo.rbs_apply_dx_code <CLAIM_NO>,'V048.1' end
17	sir400_Modi_GP	SIR: RBS Modified Claim: Add modifier GP with CPT code 97032.	Where '<PROC_GP>' = '97032' ; IF @RECORDCNT = 1 begin execute dbo.rbs_apply_modifier <CLAIM_NO>,'GP' end
18	sir419_Pt_Billing	RBS Modified Claim: Adjust the patient due amount as according to special instructions, billing team will not bill patient for the balance under $1.	Where convert(float,'<AMT_DUE>') < convert(float,'1') AND '<PATIENT_STATUS>' in ('N', 'R') ; if @RECORDCNT = 1 begin execute dbo.rbs_change_claim_status <CLAIM_NO> end
19	sir424_Modi_25	SIR: RBS Modified Claim: Add modifier 25 with office visit when used with CPT code 69210.	Where '<PROC_25>' in ('99201','99202','99203','99204','99205','99211','99212','99213','99214','99215') And Charindex('69210','<PROC_ALL_IN>')>0 ; IF @RECORDCNT = 1 begin execute dbo.rbs_apply_modifier <CLAIM_NO>,'25' end
20	sir426_AA	SIR: RBS Modified Claim: According to Special instructions, if secondary payer status is New or Rebill, then uncheck AA box	Where '<AA>' = '1' and '<SEC_STATUS>' in ('N','R') ; if @RECORDCNT = 1 begin execute dbo.rbs_un_check_AA_box <CLAIM_NO> end

Knowledge Base

Success of the system primarily depends upon quality and quantity of knowledge present in the knowledge base of the system. Knowledge base of the RBS is collection of production rules, implemented in the form of SQL statements. These rules are applied by inference engine of the RBS. If 'condition-part' is true, then 'action-part' is executed which performs updates in medical billing database. Meta-rules and logical variables are also part of the knowledge base. Meta-rules act as preconditions of rules. One meta-rule, when found true, triggers a group of rules associated with it. Logical variables are symbols to access attribute values for specific claims. Logical variables are used in rules and meta-rules. Logical variables are replaced with claim specific values when a rule or meta-rule is tried by rule based engine.

Table 8 given below shows a sample of 20 business rules – out of 2500 currently in operation - implemented in the form of productions rules with the help of 'where' clause of SQL queries. The prefix 'SIR' in rule name and description stands for 'Special Instruction Rule' i.e. rule developed against special instruction of any specific provider.

RBS has the 'scrubbing' ability i.e. it can tweak the claim for obvious, valid, and legitimate change. Rules with 'RBS Modified Claim' in descriptions show scrubbing ability of the system.

Key point of the system described in this chapter is that it merges data mining (production rule mining), and rule based expert systems technology - with implementation in relational database environment. Utilization of the extracted and learned knowledge is an important issue. Extracted knowledge can be best utilized if fed to an expert system. Further, this process of fetching and utilization of knowledge is improved as both (learning module and the expert system) are implemented in relational database environment. Rule engine has been successfully developed and deployed in the form of SQL stored procedures. Knowledge editor, data warehouse and production rule mining modules have also been developed in relational database environment.

Due to RBS, claim rejection rate has been reduced. Prior to the implementation of RBS, daily average rejection rate was 4.98% i.e. out of 100 claims approximately 5 claims got rejected. After the implementation of RBS, daily rejection rate has reduced to 2.70%. Rejections have been reduced by 54%. With the help of RBS, the company has been able to automate special instructions of providers and apply knowledge oriented checks and corrective actions on medical claims. Process remained dependent on developers and SQL programmers till the development of knowledge editor. Domain experts having no knowledge of SQL queries can develop rules easily. While underlying SQL queries are generated by the knowledge editor. However, even after the provision of knowledge editor, rule development process remained slow till the inclusion of data mining module. Data mining module boosted the speed of knowledge acquisition.

System is successfully running in the medical billing company. No claim is submitted to insurances without sign-off from RBS. What can be the crucial point for the success of the system? Various factors have contributed to the success of the system. Selecting SQL as implementation environment of RBS made the data availability and processing easy. Knowledge Editor provided GUI to domain experts for easy management of knowledge. Besides all these points RBS was stuck with knowledge acquisition bottle neck, which was resolved by the data mining module. In our view the data mining module has played a vital role for the success of the rule based expert system.

The generalized architecture proposed in this chapter can be specialized for any real life application domain which requires large number of knowledge oriented data consistency requirements.

CONCLUSION

Business logic can be best implemented with RBS technology. Four components; 'inference engine', 'knowledge base', 'knowledge editor' and 'production rule mining module' have been proposed as essential components of an RBS. This chapter presented a generalized architecture of such a data mining driven rule based system which is then specialized for medical billing domain. In the knowledge base, rules are represented as SQL queries with associated attributes. Rule engine has been developed using SQL in the form of stored procedures. Knowledge editor provides an interface to domain experts to manually edit the knowledge base. To speed up the knowledge acquisition process and to find the useful hidden information, a production rule mining module has been implemented. Billing executives use medical billing software to feed data into the database. Domain experts perform analysis of the data and do knowledge engineering tasks like editing rules, validating rules, and following up the claims blocked by the system due to medical billing errors. The RBS has been successful and is operational in the company since 2010. No claim is submitted to insurance companies without sign-off from RBS. Generalized architecture presented in this chapter can be mapped to other knowledge rich domain by incorporating knowledge of the domain to the knowledge base of the system in the form of production rules.

ACKNOWLEDGMENT

Thanks to the healthcare IT Company, MaxRemindHealth (www.mremind.com) for providing excellent research environment.

REFERENCES

Abdullah, U., Ahmed, A., Asghar, S., & Zafar, K. (2014). Record-Couple Based Production Rule Mining Algorithm : Tested in Medical Billing Domain. *Journal of Applied Environmental and Biological Sciences, 4*(8S), 275–280.

Abdullah, U., Ahmed, A., & Sawar, M. J. (2012). Knowledge Representation and Knowledge Editor of a Medical Claim. *Journal of Basic and Applied Scientific Research, 2*(2), 1373–1384.

Abdullah, U., Jamil Sawar, M., & Ahmed, A. (2009). Comparative Study of Medical Claim Scrubber and a Rule Based System. Proceedings *2009 International Conference on Information Engineering and Computer Science* (pp. 1–4). Wuhan, China. doi:10.1109/ICIECS.2009.5363668

Abdullah, U., Sawar, M. J., & Ahmed, A. (2009). Design of a Rule Based System Using Structured Query Language. Proceedings of *2009 Eighth IEEE International Conference on Dependable, Autonomic and Secure Computing* (pp. 223–228). doi:10.1109/DASC.2009.78

Ahmed, A., Abdullah, U., & Sawar, M. J. (2010). Software Architecture of a Learning Apprentice System in Medical Billing. *Proceedings of the World Congress on Engineering 2010* (Vol. I, pp. 52–56). London, UK.

Ahmed, A., Zafar, K., Siddiqui, A. B., & Abdullah, U. (2013). Data warehouse design for knowledge discovery from healthcare data. *Proceedings of the World Congress on Engineering* (Vol. III, pp. 1589–1594). London, UK.

Carl_Mays_II. (2008). *Don't Leave Money on the Table - Use a Claim Scrubber*. Retrieved from http://EzineArticles.com/?expert=Carl_Mays_II

Hayes-Roth, F. (1985). Rule-based systems. *Communications of the ACM, 28*(9), 921–932. doi:10.1145/4284.4286

Ishtiaq, M., & Ali, K. (2010). *Meaningful Use of EHR, the HITECH Act*. EHR Incentives & the Final Rule.

The Total Revenue Cycle Solution for Physicians. (2009). *Medisoft*. Retrieved from www.slcsoftware.com

Wicklund, E. (2008). Alpha II brings "claims scrubbing" to the medical billing market Healthcare IT News.

KEY TERMS AND DEFINITIONS

Claim Scrubber: A software which performs minor, legitimate changes to the data of a medical bill before its submission to insurances.

Data Mining: A body of knowledge (within computer science domain) concerned with extraction of knowledge from huge volumes of data.

Domain Expert: A person with expert level knowledge of any specific application domain (e.g. in this book chapter 'Medical Billing' is application domain).

Knowledge Editor: A graphical user interface based software which helps knowledge engineers in editing and managing of knowledge of the rule based system.

Knowledge Engineer: A domain expert which add, edit, and manage knowledge of a rule based expert system.

Medical Billing: An iterative process of submitting medical claims to insurances for reimbursement of services rendered by a healthcare professional to a patient.

Medical Claim: The term interchangeably used with 'Medical Bill' refers to the details of a patient visit (i.e. checkup and treatment) to a healthcare professional. It includes patient demographic data, his/her insurance information, diagnosis, and treatment codes along with charged amount.

Production Rule Mining: Process of extracting production rules from volumes of data, where production rule is an implication of the form $X \rightarrow Y$ where X is collection of conditions and Y is some action which should be performed when X conditions are true.

Rule Based Expert System: The term interchangeably used with 'Rule Based System (RBS)' represents a software having expert level knowledge – in the form of production rules – about any specific application domain.

Chapter 14
A Web Backtracking Technique for Fraud Detection in Financial Applications

Tasawar Hussain
Mohammad Ali Jinnah University, Pakistan

Sohail Asghar
COMSATS Institute of Information Technology, Pakistan

ABSTRACT

The web based applications are maturing and gaining the confidence of their users gradually, however, www still lacks the mechanism to stop the hackers. The implementing the adhesive security measures such as intrusion deduction systems and firewalls, are no more useful breaker for online frauds. The Web Backtracking Technique (WBT) is proposed for fraud detection in online financial applications by applying the hierarchical sessionization technique on the web log file. The web log Hierarchical Sessionization enhances the focused groups of users from web log and paves the path for in-depth visualization for knowledge discovery. User clicks are compared with user profiles for change in previous user click records. Those transactions which do not conform to business rules are stopped from business activities. The WBT analyzes suspicious behavior and will produce reports for security and risk mitigation purposes Furthermore, suspicious transactions are mined for the up-gradation of business rules from hierarchical sessionization. The proposed WBT is validated against the university web log data.

INTRODUCTION

In 1990, internet was made available to public. Since then it has revolutionized the world and made it a global village. In the last two decades, the numbers of websites have grown from few hundreds to 650 million websites and thousands of new web pages are being added to this mega stream per day. Moreover, today we have more than 3 billion active users of the internet. This exponential growth of World Wide Web (www) has become the single largest knowledge repository with the world. Thousands of transactions are being carried out on the daily basis to execute the various web based businesses.

DOI: 10.4018/978-1-4666-8513-0.ch014

From sea to space, the web is working as a knowledge backbone to provide the basic level information to advance research. The web is the most powerful and cost effective media to deliver services to its users. Consequently, business community prefers internet for their services and users feel free to avail the web services (Mohammad Pourzarandi & Tamimi, 2013). The web is providing its services in all most every walk and department of life irrespective of geographical boundaries (Hussain & Asghar, 2013). The internet is simple in nature to deliver the services and motivated the organizations (Hawwash & Nasraoui, 2010) for online e-business for more competitive environment and challenges.

As the websites and users are growing day by day, millions of user clicks are being recorded per second. The websites lack the user feedback mechanisms (Hussain & Asghar, 2013) to improve the websites and provide to the point web knowledge to its users. The web mining tools are effectively supporting the web to study and analyze the websites. The web mining is the application of data mining techniques (Bari & Chawan, 2013) and web mining itself is divided into three broad categories, namely *web structure mining (wsm)*; *web content mining(scm)*; and *web usage mining(wum)*.

The website consists of web pages in a tree structure and are linked with each other via hyperlink. Each web page consists of web objects that is the core of the knowledge for web users. Website, web pages and web objects provide the website structure. The application of data mining techniques on web structure is commonly known as web structure mining. The information retrieval is a one of the major challenge of the World Wide Web and wsm is playing a pivotal role to provide the structural knowledge about the web pages for linked analysis.

Web contents are very important and play the key role to deliver the web services to the end users. Through wcm, we mine the web page contents for knowledge and information retrieval and extract the useful patterns. The internet is like an ocean of knowledge and to the point knowledge retrieval is a difficult task. By applying the data mining techniques we can mine the web contents for efficient search query results (Chaniara and Sherasiya, 2014). For structural knowledge about the web contents, the hybrid web techniques based on wsm and wcm are applied.

In web usage mining, data mining techniques are applied on the users' data available in the form of web log files (Sharma, 2013). These log files are maintained on the web server (the server hosting the banks' website). When client interact with the website to avail the desired service, log file captures the users' surfing on a website and each activity of the user is recorded. These log files contain the hidden knowledge about the users' traversal during the surfing. The primary objective of web log files is for the maintenance of the server not for the data mining. To extract the hidden knowledge from the log file is complex data mining exercise. Without deploying the proper data mining system, the accurate and precise hidden knowledge can't be mined. The analysis of web log file is providing various benefits to the website owner and website developers such as performance of web server; smartness of website; user click stream history; user profiles; user sessions; predictions; and fraud detections.

The unrestrained growth of the internet has not only opened the new competitive markets for business, however, has also given free hand to hackers to play fraudulent activities. The web-based applications are the most vulnerable to security threats and attacks (Garg & Singh, 2013; S.Mirdula & D.Manivannan, 2013). The hackers are not only devastating the confidence of clients, however, are posing serious threats to online business (Meyer, 2008). According to National Fraud Authority UK, in 2012, cyber attackers are plundering money around £1.1 billion per annum (Harrison, 2012) and the ratio of online fraud losses in the USA is in million dollars annually, while in India the losses are around 22.90 billion rupees (Jassal & Sehgal, 2013). The online fraud data is not available in Pakistan and other developing countries as these countries have no online fraud monitoring and gauging systems.

Figure 1. Detection of Web attack (Meyer, 2008)

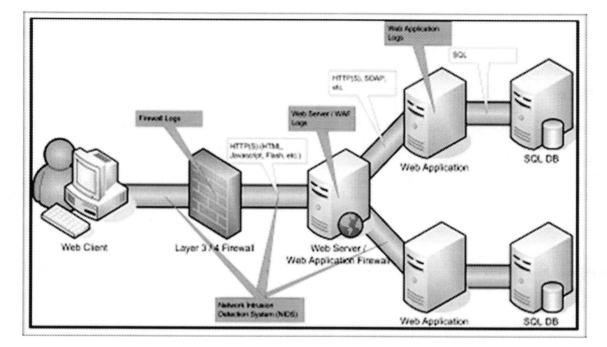

Websites consist of web pages which are designed and developed by using various tools and scripting languages such as PHP, Python, ASP, JSP, Perl, VB and Java scripts (Khochare, Chalurkar, & B.B.Meshram, 2013). Web application works as an intermediary between users and web server databases. Consequently, web applications are more vulnerable to security attacks such as SQL Injection; Cross Site Scripting (XSS); Cross-site Request Forgery (CSRF); Broken Authentication and Session Management; Security Misconfiguration; and Sensitive Data Exposure etc.

Web sites are prone and are always vulnerable to security attacks (Garg & Singh, 2013) due to their structures and hackers attack these vulnerabilities for their own goals (Mohammadpourzarandi & Tamimi, 2013). Web applications follow the seven-layered OSI model for the normal business procedures. Each layer is dedicated for specific job to communication.

Detection of web attack is a challenging job (Hallgren, Mauritzson, & Sabelfeld, 2013) as web application and web database server both are exposed to end users. Similarly, there are a number of tools available to hacker for spoofing and sniffing web applications. Different measures are being applied to detect the web attacks and to minimize the web vulnerabilities at different layers of the OSI model (Figure 1.)

In our proposed research, web log file is used as the primary source to detect the frauds in web applications by applying the various data mining techniques. Proper and enhanced analysis of the log file can reveal many interesting aspects about users and websites. Correspondingly, a Fraud Detection System can also be developed by applying Data Mining techniques on this web log file. Fraud Detection System will analyze suspicious behavior and will produce reports for security and risk mitigation purposes.

Motivation

In this chapter, we are interested in to design and develop a data mining framework to implement the data mining techniques to model the real world problem as an online fraud detection system. The proposed framework will be implemented in banking industry of Pakistan by applying web mining techniques. Web log file is the primary raw source for knowledge discovery. At the preprocessing level of web log file, hierarchical clustering classifier will be proposed and categorical similarity measure will also be proposed for clustering. Similarly, at pattern discovery level, the introduction of the constraint template library will be a new research direction and theory to model the problem in multi-way in accordance with pre-defined objectives of web mining such as fraud detection and risk management. To achieve the mining objectives, a generic hierarchical algorithm will be proposed. In the last phase, pattern analysis will be performed to extract the business rules to govern the web application without disturbing the normal web application business.

BACKGROUND

Hyper Text Transfer Protocol (HTTP) and Hyper Text Transfer Protocol Secure (HTTPS) are the standard protocol to monitor and govern the internet traffic. According to Meyer (2008) HTTP is request and response mechanism between user web browser and web server. User requests for specific services over internet in proper format and web server responds accordingly. The user request is in the form:

http://en.wikipedia.org/wiki/#q=query

where http: is protocol; //en.wikipedia.org is host; the wiki is resource location; and #q=query is user query request.

The user request is composed of header (user request) and request message body (Gupta, Saikia, & Sanghi, 2007). Subsequently web server parses the user request and responds to user accordingly with proper status successful or page not found etc.

The HTTP response can be captured by hackers by requesting the web server along with legitimate user.

HTTPS is a certificate based authentication (CA) protocol, which provides secure communication channel between web user; a user's browser; and web server over the socket secure layer (SSL). Asghari, Eeten, Arnbak, & Eijk, (2012) conceptualize the security vulnerabilities of HTTPS. HTTPS can facilitate illegitimate user. Correspondingly, CA requires the proper updates of patches and in the same way any segment of poor coding can be bypassed by SSL.

Both the protocols are still vulnerable and provide no such mechanism for end users and web operators for the safety of their communication. The user traversals and clicks can be seized by hackers for any misuse to distort the trust of end users.

According to Khandelwal, Shah, Bhavsar, & Gandhi, (2013) firewall are used in web applications for secure transactions by end users with application. It acts as intermediary between web users (Internet) and web servers. Firewall mechanism is to protect the unauthorized access to the web resources. The firewall provides hardware and software solution to protect the system from unauthorized access. Firewall operates on port 80 while it restricts all the other ports.

The authors also discussed the various firewall techniques such as packet-filtering; application-gateway; circuit-level gateway; and proxy server. The firewall works on the network layer of the OSI model and hackers can exploit the other OSI model layer such as session; presentation; and application layer. Similarly firewall operates on port 80 which can be manipulated by hackers by using attacks like SQL injections, cross scripting and Trojan horse etc. Firewall is also a costly solution for web applications and yet no foolproof secure firewall is available.

Garg & Singh (2013) have discussed the role of SQL injection in web application attack. It is the most common weapon of hackers to exploit the code anomalies by issuing a series of SQL queries to bypass the normal security measures of web application. The sample code for SQL injection can be:

```php
<?php
<form action="sql.php" method= "POST" />
<p>Name: <input type= "text" name= "name" />
<br /> <input type= "submit" value= "Add Comment" /></p> </form>
 $query = "SELECT * FROM users WHERE username = '{$_POST['username']}";
 $result = mysql_query($query);
function save_email ($user, $message)
{ $sql= "insert into message (user, message)values ('$user', '$message')";
 return mysql_query($sql);}
?>
```

Hackers sometime modify the original user query to get the basic information of genuine user by applying inner and outer joins along with OR and AND operators in where clause. The authors have also discussed the various preventive measures such as use of latest and upgraded software releases. Similarly, login to a database as a super user is also discouraged.

(Jovanovic, Kruegel, & Kirda, (2013)) and Garg & Singh, (2013)) have discussed the cross-site scripting vulnerability of dynamic web applications. The hackers inject the malicious code through different scripting languages such as java, vb etc in user browser. When the user executes the malicious (crafted) code, the hacker can steal the precious information about the user. The sample XSS code is, such as:

```php
<form action="search.php" method=  "GET" />
 <p>Please enter your name: <input type= "text" name= "user_name" />
<br /> <input type= "submit" value= "Go" /></p><br> </form>
 <?php echo "<p>Welcome   <br />"; echo ($_GET[user_name]); ?>
```

This code can be exploited by the hacker to get the information about the user and the database.

```
http://www.website_url/clean.php?user_name=
<script>alert(Warning! Unauthorized Access);</script>
```

The user profile can be hacked by hacker by launching XSS email scripting attack. A fake email is sent to the user and when user clicks on url, the user profile can also be transmitted through a web server. Through cross-site attack, user cookies; blogs; and comment area can be exploited by hacker for information.

Most of the prevention techniques modify the user's browser to limit the cross-site scripting, however, change in browser can ignite the vulnerability.

According to (Jovanovic, Kirda, & Kruegel, 2006) CSRF exploits the user active session. When a user establishes session with trusted website and parallel uses the hacker's web site. Hacker snatches the cache of the user's browser and send HTTP requests through user. In this way a hacker manipulates the website integrity. The authenticated user login to the online banking system to transfer the money to another account. The user request form for money transfer will be of the form;

```
<form action= "transfer.php" method= "get">
To:<input type= "text", name="to"/>
Amount:<input type="text" name="amount"/>
<input type="submit" value="submit"/>
</form>
```

The hacker injects the false script and sends it to the web server via the user's browser. The snap shot of hackers' script is as under:

```
<form action= "https://www.onlinebank.com/transfer.php" method= "post">
<input type= "text", name= "to" value= "1111-11"/>
<input type=  "text" name= "amount" value= "55555.55"/>
<input type=  "submit"/>
</form>
<script type= "text/javascript">
document.forms[0].submit();
<script/>
```

In this way, a hacker may get the amount be transferred to his/her account or hacker may be able to get the information about the legitimate user and about his bank account.

As we have studied the various techniques which hacker apply to snatch the precious user information and play the fraudulent activities to shake the user interest and confidence in online web business. There are so many other techniques are available in the literature which shows that the growing trend in hacking and it is non-stop. As the web is getting to be more and more intelligent to safe the vital interests, similarly hackers are using the same information technology tools for more efficiently.

We have concluded that web hacking is an endless path. When we are an internet user, we are at a risk of to be hacked. The best remedy to mitigate the hacking risk is how secure, we can move to the net. We cannot limit the hackers; however, we can adopt the measures to reduce the hacking risk. The self-protection is first and last lesson to reduce the hacking and make our web application more secure.

Financial Fraud Scenario

As we have discussed in the chapter 1 & 2, websites are open to everybody and internet is a safe haven for the hackers. There are number of hacking tools are available to exploit the users and websites. Nowadays, hacking has become an active job cum hobby throughout the world. Financial websites are more targeted to steal the precious user and owner information as well as money laundering.

Figure 2. Session hacking scenario

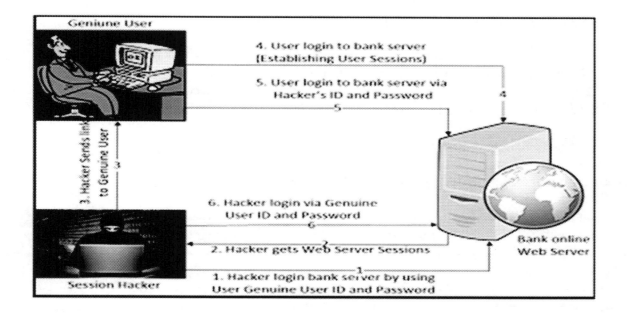

The hackers apply a number of techniques to hack the credentials of genuine users as we have discussed in the literature review chapter. Sometimes they apply composite techniques for hacking.

In this financial fraud scenario, the hacker is applying a session hacking technique to establish a session with an online banking web server through stealing the genuine user session (Figure 2.). The hacker sends the online banking link to user to establish the session with a bank. The genuine user following the url link establishes links to the online banking web server. The hackers captures the genuine user credentials.

Problem Statement

Let $L=\{(T,A) \mid T_a$ be the user transactions & A set be the web log attributes $\}$ be a web log file and let B be the set of business logic rules for a specific website. Let $T`: L \to T_a \mid T` \in L \wedge T` \subseteq T_a$ where $T`$ be those transactions whose T_a does not conform to B.

Objectives and Goals of Proposed Research

The extraction of useful knowledge from web log file is a challenging and complex job as because log files are to help administrator to monitor the error occurrence not for mining purpose. Consequently, we required state of the art data mining techniques to extract useful knowledge from log files. This proposed system will contribute in research by proposing new research techniques. A web log is the major data source for this proposed research that lists actions that have occurred. With enhanced web log file analysis, the proposed system will be applied in the banking sector for fraud detection. The proposed System is a Web-based security solution that will signal the threat of fraud before customers fall prey to the perpetrators. Fraud Detection System analyzes suspicious behavior and produces reports for security and risk mitigation purposes. Unlike network security solutions, Fraud Detection System reports suspicious activity before it escalates into fraud, identity theft or other crimes.

1. The proposed system will provide a real-time protection by transparently monitoring user behavior to identify anomalies, then calculating the risk associated with a particular transaction. If a risk is identified, step-up authentication can be automatically invoked— to complete the transaction.
2. Define and Development of Risk Management Policy
3. Automate the conceptual framework for online fraud detection based on risk policy.
4. Send email/SMS to customers and management.

The Proposed Conceptual Framework (WBT)

To gauge the user transactions as legitimate or illegitimate is a challenging research problem. The proposed framework will be completed in different phases and the brief description of the proposed framework along with different phases and implementation plan as under:

Web applications are placed on any web server for public access and users throughout the world can access these applications. For financial institutions, only specific users are allowed to access the services of web application. Users are provided the login ID and password for the access, but IP, location, browsers and OS cannot be restricted. The Firewall is helpful in many ways to control the unauthorized access, nonetheless when users are wearing he legitimate veils, it is almost impossible to stop that user and it is behind the scope of the firewall. The proposed framework WBT (Figure 3) works parallel with the firewall and web server without affecting the normal transactions of users. The main objective of proposed WBT is to expose the unauthorized users; stop them from being committing fraudulent activities; and help the website owners and administrators to prepare the risk management policies to update the business rules for future use. The Figure 2 describes the high level conceptual framework for fraud detection and risk management. The different steps of WBT are being described in following paragraphs.

The internet connects millions of people and delivers services to its users. When a user access the specific website, the user credentials are verified and validated as per prescribed business rules of the website.

The users can be legitimate and illegitimate (hackers), the user transaction passes through the firewall and send to the authentication server via business rules. If the user is verified by the server and then the user is allowed to surf the website. In parallel, user's transactions are stored in transaction server in the form of web log files. The log files are further investigated for any discrepancy in transactions. If the user transactions do not conform to the business logic of the website, the user transactions are stooped and no business can be done with the web application. Business logic is the core and crux of this research. The business logic has business rules from website organizers and from user's transaction analysis (Log files). Acknowledgement server plays a cruiser role to send acknowledgment via SMS (Short Messaging Service) by using telephone service providers or it acts as an email server. It can send emails to the user for further verification of account and transaction validation. Similarly, it sends emails to website organizers about the odd behavior of user along with details of transaction stoppage. In the next section, we will discuss *Business Logic* in details, that will further elaborate the proposed research.

Figure 3. Proposed conceptual framework for Web backtracking technique

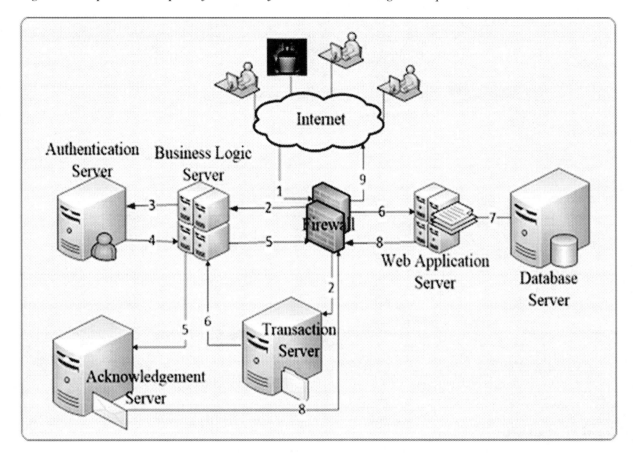

Proposed Business Logic Flow Model

The business logic works on the basis of web log file (user transactions) and output is business rules; transaction stoppage etc. (Figure 4).

Web Usage Data and Preprocessing

In this phase, we will take a web log file as a primary data source. As log file contains the all click data of users. The snapshot of the log file is given in Figure 5. The log file contains the number of raw entries such as images; audio; video; and crawler entries due to the design nature of the website. The entries are irrelevant for the mining purpose and has to be eliminated before applying the data mining techniques.

For our experimental results, we took the log file of a website of 4574 KB with 20408 log entries. After applying preprocessing techniques for web log cleansing such as data cleaning; data filtering; and data integration, the actual and useful record size is reduced to 6038. These records are helpful for further processing and identifying the useful patterns from web log to further investigate the user behavior and trends.

Figure 4. Proposed business logic flow model

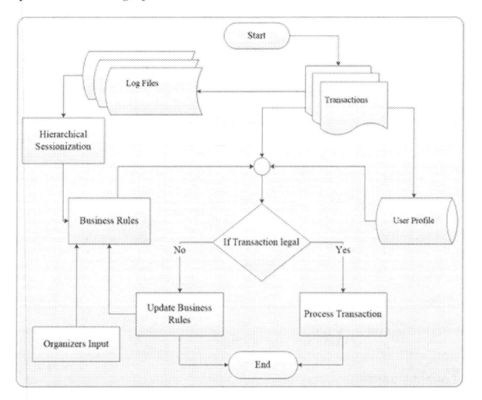

WebLog Sessionizations

The user session is a time span between login and logout of a website by a user. During the session, user traverse the different web pages of website and spend different time to different pages as per his/ her interest. The user clicks are recorded in the web log on the basis of the IP address and user sessions are also identified on the basis of IP Addresses. These sessions are helpful to personalize the data and hierarchical clustering is performed based on these sessions. As users are traversing the same website with different objectives. They are visiting the same pages and spending different time on these pages. During the sessionizations process, we also calculated the number of pages visited by different users and time spent by each user to visit these pages in a session. As users have many things in common, such as a website; pages; and time spent, accordingly, there is a strong correlation between the users. Consequently, hierarchical clustering is the ultimate choice for the more enhanced visualization of web log.

Web Personalization and Hierarchical Clustering

Log sessionization is performed on the basis of IP Address, however, users have option to user different browsers, different OS and different version of HTTP. Even users have an option to use website from different geographical locations. These minor changes can be treated as risk mitigation for the user analysis and studying the user trends. In this proposed research, we personalize the user's traverses which are

Figure 5. Log file snapshot

```
111.68.99.242 - - [20/Mar/2013:00:47:42 -0700] "GET /uims/index.php?dept_id=32 HTTP/1.1" 200 33952 "http://www.uaar.edu.pk/cms-
home.php" "Mozilla/4.0 (compatible; MSIE 8.0; Windows NT 6.1; Trident/4.0; SLCC2; .NET CLR 2.0.50727; .NET CLR 3.5.30729; .NET CLR
3.0.30729; Media Center PC 6.0; InfoPath.3; .NET4.0C)"111.68.99.242 - - [20/Mar/2013:00:47:43 -0700] "GET /css/stylesheet.css
HTTP/1.1" 304 - "http://www.uaar.edu.pk/uims/index.php?dept_id=32" "Mozilla/4.0 (compatible; MSIE 8.0; Windows NT 6.1; Trident/4.0;
SLCC2; .NET CLR 2.0.50727; .NET CLR 3.5.30729; .NET CLR 3.0.30729; Media Center PC 6.0; InfoPath.3; .NET4.0C)"111.68.99.242 - -
[20/Mar/2013:00:47:43 -0700] "GET /css/style.css HTTP/1.1" 304 - "http://www.uaar.edu.pk/uims/index.php?dept_id=32" "Mozilla/4.0
(compatible; MSIE 8.0; Windows NT 6.1; Trident/4.0; SLCC2; .NET CLR 2.0.50727; .NET CLR 3.5.30729; .NET CLR 3.0.30729; Media Center
PC 6.0; InfoPath.3; .NET4.0C)"111.68.99.242 - - [20/Mar/2013:00:47:44 -0700] "GET /js/jquery-1.3.1.min.js HTTP/1.1" 304 -
"http://www.uaar.edu.pk/uims/index.php?dept_id=32" "Mozilla/4.0 (compatible; MSIE 8.0; Windows NT 6.1; Trident/4.0; SLCC2; .NET CLR
2.0.50727; .NET CLR 3.5.30729; .NET CLR 3.0.30729; Media Center PC 6.0; InfoPath.3; .NET4.0C)"111.68.99.242 - -
[20/Mar/2013:00:47:44 -0700] "GET /js/jquery.dropdown.js HTTP/1.1" 304 - "http://www.uaar.edu.pk/uims/index.php?dept_id=32"
"Mozilla/4.0 (compatible; MSIE 8.0; Windows NT 6.1; Trident/4.0; SLCC2; .NET CLR 2.0.50727; .NET CLR 3.5.30729; .NET CLR 3.0.30729;
Media Center PC 6.0; InfoPath.3; .NET4.0C)"111.68.99.242 - - [20/Mar/2013:00:47:44 -0700] "GET /js/hoverIntent.js HTTP/1.1" 304 -
"http://www.uaar.edu.pk/uims/index.php?dept_id=32" "Mozilla/4.0 (compatible; MSIE 8.0; Windows NT 6.1; Trident/4.0; SLCC2; .NET CLR
2.0.50727; .NET CLR 3.5.30729; .NET CLR 3.0.30729; Media Center PC 6.0; InfoPath.3; .NET4.0C)"203.128.31.123 - -
[20/Mar/2013:00:47:43 -0700] "GET /albums/STIeOAgAxDHHFCx8.jpg HTTP/1.1" 200 110657
"http://www.uaar.edu.pk/photogallery/newgallery.php" "Mozilla/5.0 (Windows NT 6.1) AppleWebKit/537.22 (KHTML, like Gecko)
Chrome/25.0.1364.172 Safari/537.22"111.68.99.242 - - [20/Mar/2013:00:47:45 -0700] "GET /images/logo.png HTTP/1.1" 304 -
"http://www.uaar.edu.pk/uims/index.php?dept_id=32" "Mozilla/4.0 (compatible; MSIE 8.0; Windows NT 6.1; Trident/4.0; SLCC2; .NET CLR
2.0.50727; .NET CLR 3.5.30729; .NET CLR 3.0.30729; Media Center PC 6.0; InfoPath.3; .NET4.0C)"111.68.99.242 - -
[20/Mar/2013:00:47:45 -0700] "GET /images/logo-text.png HTTP/1.1" 304 - "http://www.uaar.edu.pk/uims/index.php?dept_id=32"
"Mozilla/4.0 (compatible; MSIE 8.0; Windows NT 6.1; Trident/4.0; SLCC2; .NET CLR 2.0.50727; .NET CLR 3.5.30729; .NET CLR 3.0.30729;
```

unique and different from the previous click history. This personalization helps to identify the business rules for a specific website.

For hierarchical clustering of web log, we opted the research work of (Hussain & Asghar, 2013). We calculated the number of web pages visited by the user in a session. After performing preprocessing, we obtained the 1609 sessions. Moreover, we calculated the chi square values based on the parameters of a number of web pages and a session time in each session. The chi square value of each session is computed with every other session and the highest chi square value shows the strong correlation between these two sessions. If more than one sessions have the same higher value, than first occurrence is considered a more appropriate pair of related sessions. This is the first level hierarchy. We also computed the average of the most related pairs, for the calculation of next hierarchy level and for the height of related session in dendogram.

Results Evaluation

On the basis of the proposed algorithm (Figure 6), we got the 11 levels of hierarchical clusters of web log. Figure 3.2 is an illustration of chi square based sessionization of web log. Each image of Figure3.2 represents the hierarchical clustering combination of session at each level.

For the analysis of our proposed hierarchical clustering classifier, we used the precision and recall measures to evaluate the clustering results. We computed the True Positive (TN), True Negative (TN), False Positive (FP) and False Negative (FN) in each hierarchy level for the analysis of placements of clusters in that particular level. The results The precision and recall are also shown by the Figures 7 and 8 respectively.

Figure 6. Hierarchy levels of Web log sessionization (Hussain & Asghar 2014)

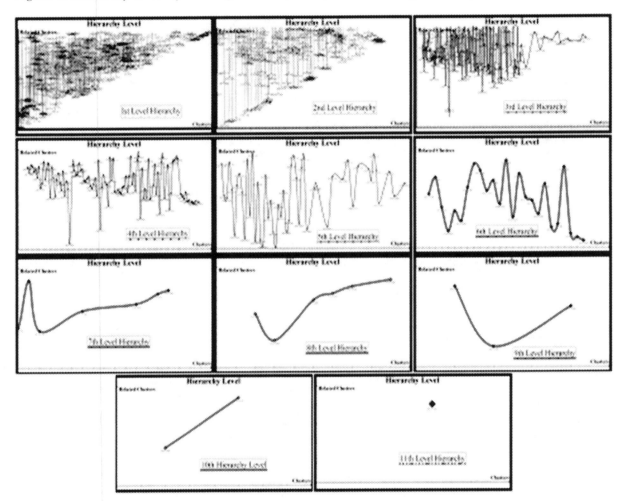

We also compare the proposed Chi-HAC with the research work of Murray, Lin, & Chowdhury (2006) and Hussain & Asghar (2010). We implemented the classifier of Murray, Lin, & Chowdhury (2006) with a few minor changes without affecting the original essence of the classifier. The data set used for the experiment was web log file of the university web site. We compare the three classifiers on the basis of precision and recall measure to find out the goodness of classifiers Figure 7. & 8. The graphs indicate the better results of proposed Chi-HAC over the both published work.

CONCLUSION

The focus of this research and study is the introduction of the importance of web log mining for the in-depth analysis of users' behavior and provide the strong backtrack mechanism to identify the fraud risk without affecting the normal business of web applications. We reviewed the different techniques to overcome the catastrophe of being hacked for fraudulent activities. The report is useless until we endorse

Figure 7. Comparison of classifers at each hierarchy level (Precision) (Hussain & Asghar 2014)

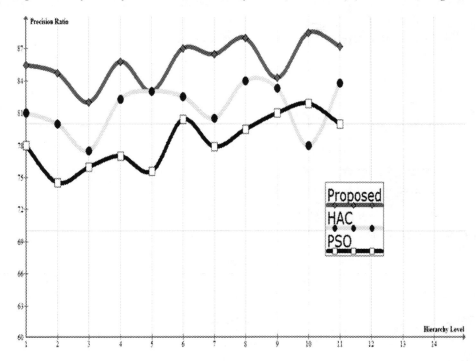

Figure 8. Comparison of classifers at each hierarchy level (Recall) (Hussain & Asghar 2014)

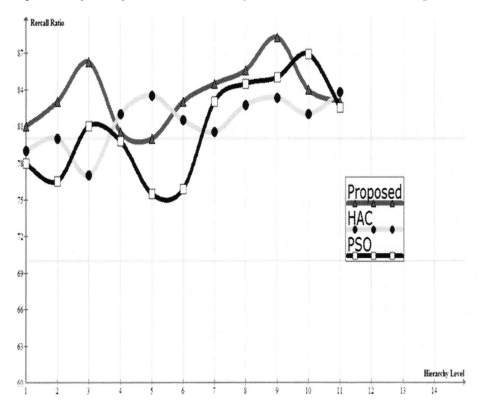

the conclusion with some recommendation with vivid research direction. Keeping in view clear research dimension, it is useful if we split this section into problem statement and research objective so that we can make a clear distinction between the issue and its possible solution as an outcome of this research.

REFERENCES

Abro, Q. M. M., Bhutto, A. & Memon, N. A. (2011). Customer's perceptions on e-banking: a case study of HBL Jamshoro. *Mehran university research journal of engineering & technology*, 30(4), 681-688.

Ahmad, S. (2013). Web Mining Pedagogy: The Theoretical Support. *International Journal of Computing. Intelligent and Communication Technologies*, 2, 17–22.

Akhtar, M. H. (2002). X-efficiency Analysis of Commercial Banks in Pakistan: A Preliminary Investigation. *Pakistan Development Review*, 567–580.

Aladwani, A. M. (2001). Online banking: A field study of drivers, development challenges, and expectations. *International Journal of Information Management*, 21(3), 213–225. doi:10.1016/S0268-4012(01)00011-1

Asghari, H., Eeten, M. J. G. V., Arnbak, A. M., & Eijk, N. A. N. M. V. (2012). Security Economics in the HTTPS Value Chain. *Proceedings of TPRC 2012: The research conference on communication, information and internet policy.*

Atkins, B., & Huang, W. (n. d.). A study of social Engineering in Online Frauds. *Open Journal of Social Sciences*, 1, 23–32.

Baloach, Q. B., Khan, M. I., & Alam, A. (2008). Online Banking Services: A Comparative Study of Islamic and Conventional Banks of Pakistan. *Journal of Managerial Sciences*, IV, 67–95.

Banstola, A. (2007). Prospects and Challenges of E-banking in Nepal. *The Journal of Nepalese Business Studies*, IV, 96–104.

Bargh, J. A. & Mckenna, K. Y. A. (2004). *The internet and social life.*

Bari, P. & Chawan, P. M. (2013). Web Usage Mining. *Journal of Engineering, Computers & Applied Sciences (JEC&AS)*, 2.

Barth, A., Jackson, C., & Mitchell, J. C. (2008). Robust defenses for cross-site request forgery. Proceedings of the 15th ACM conference on Computer and communications security (pp. 75-88). New York.

Berendt, B., Mobasher, B. & Spiliopoulou, M. (2002). Web Usage Mining for E-Business Application. *ECML/PKDD-2002 Tutorial.*

Bhasin, D. M. L. 2006. Data Mining: A Competitive Tool in the Banking and Retail Industries. *Banking and Finance*, 7.

Brunswick, S. (2009). eCommerce fraud – time to act? *Card Technology Today*, 21(1), 12–13. doi:10.1016/S0965-2590(09)70019-2

Chaniara, J. M., & Sherasiya, F. (2014). Survey on ameliorate data extraction in web mining by clustering the web log data. *Development*, *1*(12).

Dashore, P., & Jain, S. K. (2009). Fuzzy Rule Based System and Metagraph for Risk Management in Electronic Banking Activities. *IACSIT International Journal of Engineering and Technology*, *1*(1), 5. doi:10.7763/IJET.2009.V1.18

Desai, A. B., & Deshmukh, D. R. (2013). Data mining techniques for Fraud Detection. *International Journal of Computer Science and Information Technologies*, *3*, 1–4.

Esakkiraj, S., & Chidambaram, S. (2013). A Predictive Approach for Fraud Detection Using Hidden Markov Model. [IJERT]. *International Journal of Engineering Research & Technology*, *2*, 1–7.

Garg, A., & Singh, S. (2013). A Review on Web Application Security Vulnerabilities. *International Journal of Advanced Research in Computer Science and Software Engineering*, *3*, 222–226.

Grossmann, W., Hudec, M., & Kurzawa, R. (2004). Web usage mining in e-commerce. *International Journal of Electronic Business*, *2*(5), 480–493. doi:10.1504/IJEB.2004.005881

Gupta, N., Saikia, A., & Sanghi, D. D. (2007). *WEB APPLICATION FIREWALL*. Kanpur: Indian Instituite of Technology.

Hallgren, P. A., Mauritzson, D. T., & Sabelfeld, A. (2013). A Lightweight Approach to Web Application Integrity. Proceedings of ACM PLAS'13. Seattle, WA, USA: ACM.

Harrison, S. (2012). *Annual Fraud Indicator*. National Fraud Authority.

Hawwash, B. & Nasraoui, O. (2010). Mining and tracking evolving web user trends from large web server logs.

Hinde, S. (2005). Identity theft & fraud. *Computer theft & fraud*.

Hoehle, H., Scornavacca, E., & Huff, S. (2012). Three Decades of Research on Consumer Adoption and Utilization of Electronic Banking Channels: A Literature Analysis. *Decision Support Systems*, *54*(1), 122–132. doi:10.1016/j.dss.2012.04.010

Huang, Y.-W., Huang, S.-K., Lin, T.-P., & Tsai, C.-H. (2003). Proceedings of Web Application Security Assessment by Fault Injection and Behavior Monitoring. WWW 2003. Budapest, Hungary: ACM.

Hussain, T., Asghar, D. S., & Fong, S. (2010a). A Hierarchical Cluster Based Preprocessing Methodology for Web Usage Mining. Proceedings of *6th International Conference on Advanced Information Management and Service (IMS)*. Seoul, South Korea.

Hussain, T., Asghar, D. S., & Masood, D. N. (2010b). Hierarchical Sessionization at Preprocessing Level of WUM Based on Swarm Intelligence. *Proceedings of 2010 6th International Conference on Emerging Technologies (ICET)*. Islamabad.

Hussain, T., Asghar, D. S., & Masood, D. N. (2010c). *Web Usage Mining: A Survey on Preprocessing of Web Log File. Information and Emerging Technologies (ICIET), 2010*. Karachi, Pakistan: IEEE.

Hussain, T., & Asghar, S. (2013). Evaluation of similarity measures for categorical data. *The Nucleus: The Scientific Journal of Pakistan Atomic Energy* Commission, *50*, 387–394.

Hussain, T., & Asghar, S. (2013). Web mining: Approaches, applications and business intelligence. *International Journal of Academic Research Part A*, *5*(2), 211–217. doi:10.7813/2075-4124.2013/5-2/A.32

Jassal, R. K., & Sehgal, R. K. (2013). Online Banking Security Flaws: A Study. *International Journal of Advanced Research in Computer Science and Software Engineering*, *3*, 1016–1021.

Jianxi. Zhang, Zhao, P., Shang, L. & Wang, L. (2009). Web usage mining based on fuzzy clustering in identifying target group. *Proceedings of ISECS International Colloquium on Computing, Communication, Control, and Management* (pp. 209-212). IEEE.

Jones, S., & Gupta, O. K. (2006). Web Data Mining: A Case Study. *Communications of the IIMA*, *6*, 6.

Jovanovic, N., Kirda, E., & Kruegel, C. (2006, August 28-September 1). Preventing Cross Site Request Forgery Attacks. *Securecomm and Workshops*. Baltimore, MD.

Jovanovic, N., Kruegel, C. & Kirda, E. (2013). Pixy: A Static Analysis Tool for Detecting Web Application Vulnerabilities.

Julisch, K. (2010). *Risk-Based Payment Fraud Detection*. Zurich.

Kaleem, A., & Ahmad, S. (2008). Bankers' Perceptions of Electronic Banking in Pakistan. *Journal of Internet Banking and Commerce*, *13*, 1–16.

Kaleem, A., & Ahmad, S. (2009). Determinants of SMEs' perceptions of electronic banking in Pakistan. *International Journal of Electronic Finance*, *3*(2), 133–148. doi:10.1504/IJEF.2009.026356

Kaur, M. & Anupnandy (n. d.). Web Logs Conversion to Improve the Analysis of Web Usage Data for Web Usage mining in E-Learning. *International Journal of Computer Science and its Applications*, 6.

Khandelwal, S., Shah, P., Bhavsar, K. & Gandhi, D. S. (2013). Frontline Techniques to Prevent Web Application Vulnerability. *International Journal of Advanced Research in Computer Science and Electronics Engineering*, 2.

Khiyal, M. S. H., Khan, A., Bashir, S., Khan, F. H., & Aman, S. (2011). Dynamic Blind Group Digital Signature Scheme in E-Banking. *International Journal of Computer and Electrical Engineering*, *3*, 514–519. doi:10.7763/IJCEE.2011.V3.371

Khochare, N., Chalurkar, S., & Meshram, B.B. (2013). Web Application Vulnerabilities Detection Techniques Survey. *International Journal of Computer Science and Network Security,* 13.

Lee, K.-W., Tsai, M.-T., & Lanting, M. C. L. (2011). From marketplace to marketspace: Investigating the consumer switch to online banking. *Electronic Commerce Research and Applications*, *10*(1), 115–125. doi:10.1016/j.elerap.2010.08.005

Li, S., Shah, S. A. H., Khan, M. A. U., Khayam, S. A., Sadeghi, A.-R., & Schmitz, R. (2010). Breaking e-Banking CAPTCHAs. *Proceedings of the 26th Annual computer Security Application Conference*. Austin, Texas. New York: ACM.

Li, X., & Zhang, S. (2010). Application of Web Usage Mining in e-learning Platform. Proceedings of *International conference on E-Business and E-Government.* doi:10.1109/ICEE.2010.353

Meyer, R. (2008). *Detecting Attacks on Web Applications from Log Files. SANS Institute 2008. Mobarek.* D. A. E-banking practices and customer satisfaction- a case study in Botswana.

Mirdula, S., & Manivannan, D. (2013). Security Vulnerabilities in Web Application- An Attack Perspective. *International Journal of Engineering and Technology,* 5.

Mohammadpourzarandi, P. D. M. E. & Tamimi, R. (2013). The Application of Web Usage Mining In E-commerce Security. *International Journal of Information Science and Management.*

Moore, T., Clayton, R., & Anderson, R. (2009). The Economics of Online Crime. *The Journal of Economic Perspectives, 23*(3), 3–20. doi:10.1257/jep.23.3.3

Murray, G. C., Lin, J., & Chowdhury, A. (2006, November 3-9). Identification of User Sessions with Hierarchical Agglomerative Clustering. *Proceedings of ASIS&T annual meeting.* Austin, Texas, USA.

Nawrocki, M. (2013). A Survey on Web Usage Mining, Applications and Tools. *American Journal of Computing and Computation,* 3.

Nitsure, R. R. (2003). E-banking: Challenges and Opportunities. *JSTOR, Economic and Political Weekly,* 38(51/52), 5377-5381.

OWASP. (2013). *The Ten Most Critical web Application security Risks. The Open Web Application Security Project.* OWASP.

Paget, F. (2009). Financial Fraud and Internet Banking: Threats and Countermeasures [Report]. McAffee Avert Labs.

Pahl, C. (2003). Data mining for the analysis of content interaction in web-based learning and training systems.

Phua, C., Lee, V., Smith, K. & Gayler, R. (2005). A Comprehensive Survey of Data Mining-based Fraud Detection Research. *Artificial Intelligence Review,* 14.

Raymond, D. & Conti, G. (2013). A Control Measure Framework to Limit Collateral Damage and Propagation of Cyber Weapons.

Reavley, N. (2005). Securing online banking. *Card Technology Today, 17*(10), 12–13. doi:10.1016/S0965-2590(05)70389-3

Report, S. (2012). *Payment Systems Review.* Islamabad.

RSA Online Fraud Report. ([REMOVED HYPERLINK FIELD]2012). Available: http://www.emc.com/domains/rsa/index.htm

Rusch, J. J. (2003). *Computer and Internet Fraud: A Risk Identification Overview.* Computer Fraud & Security.

Sarma, G. & Singh, P. K. (2010). Internet Banking: Risk Analysis and Applicability of Biometric Technology for Authentication. *International Journal of Pure and Applied Sciences and Technology,* 1, 14.

Shah, M., & Clarke, S. (2009). *E-Banking Management: Issues, Solutions, and Strategies*. Hershey, New York: Information Science Reference. doi:10.4018/978-1-60566-252-7

Shariq, S. (2006). *Internet Banking in Pakistan* [Master Thesis]. Lulea University of Technology.

Sharma, R. (2013). A Framework to Compare Web Mining Types. *International Journal of Advanced Research in Computer Science and Software Engineering, 3*, 144–148.

Siddiqui, M. H., Ali, S. I., Zaman, S., Javed, M. A., Raheja, R., Shafiq, U. & Masood, R. (2011). Branchless Banking Regulations. State Bank of Pakistan.

van Meer, G.J.L., & van Raaij, F. (2003). A suitable research methodology for analyzing online banking behaviour. *Journal of Internet banking and commerce, 32*.

Vogt, P., Nentwich, F., Jovanovic, N., Kirda, E., Kruege, C. & Vigna, G. (2013). Cross-Site Scripting Prevention with Dynamic Data Tainting and Static Analysis.

Yousafzai, S. Y., Pallister, J. G., & Foxall, G. R. (2005). Strategies for Building and Communicating Trust in Electronic Banking: A Field Experiment. *Psychology and Marketing, 22*(2), 181–201. doi:10.1002/mar.20054

Zhang, Q. (2009). Study on Fraud Risk Prevention of Online Banks. *Proceedings of International Conference on Networks security, Wireless Communications and Trusted Computing*. doi:10.1109/NSWCTC.2009.312

KEY TERMS AND DEFINITIONS

Backtracking: Is a general algorithm for finding all (or some) solutions to some computational problems, notably constraint satisfaction problems, which incrementally builds candidates to the solutions, and abandons each partial candidate c ("backtracks") as soon as it determines that c cannot possibly be completed to a valid solution.

Data Mining: Is an analytic process designed to explore data (usually large amounts of data - typically business or market related - also known as "big data") in search of consistent patterns and/or systematic relationships between variables, and then to validate the findings by applying the detected patterns.

Hierarchical Sessionization: Is a systematic approach to build the hierarchy of sessions based on given criteria (similarity measure) and web log attributes. These sessions can further be used for discovery enhanced visualization of web log.

Knowledge Visualization: Is the process of analyzing patterns for knowledge extraction for the in-depth study of the whole data mining process and objectives.

Online Frauds: The use of Internet services or software with Internet access to defraud victims or to otherwise take advantage of them; for example, by stealing personal information, which can even lead to identity theft. A very common form of Internet fraud is the distribution of rogue security software. Internet services can be used to present fraudulent solicitations to prospective victims, to conduct fraudulent transactions, or to transmit the proceeds of fraud to financial institutions or to others connected with the scheme.

Pattern Discovery: By applying the data mining techniques on the web log data, patterns are identified which exhibit the similar behavior and the most frequent sub set of data items that indicate the specific interest.

Web Usage Mining: Is the application of data mining techniques to discover patterns from the web or Web usage mining is the process of extracting useful information from server logs. Web usage mining is a key source to study the user traversing behavior on a particular website.

Chapter 15
Segmentation of Crops and Weeds Using Supervised Learning Technique

Noureen Zafar
University Institute of Information Technology, Pakistan

Saif Ur Rehma
University Institute of Information Technology, Pakistan

Saira Gillani
Corvinus University of Budapest, Hungary

Sohail Asghar
COMSATS Institute of Information Technology, Pakistan

ABSTRACT

In this article, segmentation of weeds and crops has been investigated by using supervised learning based on feed forward neural network. The images have been taken from the satellite imaginary for a specified region on the geographical space in Pakistan and perform edge detection by classical image processing scheme. The obtained samples are classified by data mining, based on artificial neural network model based on linear activation function at the input and output layer while threshold ramp function at hidden layer. A scenario based results are obtained at a huge samples of the weeds of the corn field and crop in the form of the mean square error based fitness evaluation function. The given scheme has the perks on the existed schemes as applicability of the designed framework, ease in implementation and less hardware needed for implementation.

1. INTRODUCTION

In Pakistan, agriculture is fundamental to economic augmentation and improvement. It comprises 21.4 percent of total GDP, provides employment to 45 percent of the labor force of the country and plays important role in development of important sectors of the economy of Pakistan. Weeds are dangerous

DOI: 10.4018/978-1-4666-8513-0.ch015

for crops because they reduce the quantities of herbicides applied to fields. Its control is one of the areas which demands automation. Weeds provide damaging consequences like negative impacts on plants, soil and underground aquifers and also reduction in crop yield. It increases the cost of cultivation, reduces the quality of the field and is also harmful to human beings and animals. Weed control thresholds have been used to reduce the cost and avoid unacceptable yield loss.

Many researchers have done work in agriculture; Kianiet et al. (2010) worked on crops and weeds using Wavelet transformation and artificial neural network (ANN). He detected weeds present in the inter-row and those that lie inside the two crops. He contains small number of images and does not involve work on mixed weeds. (Kianiet *et al.*, 2010). Kargar B et al. (2013) classified weed and crop using Wavelet transformation. He sprayed the specific weed plant not the whole crop. His work includes the small amount of dataset. Moreover, Light conditions also affected the performance of detection of weed and crop. (Kargar B *et al.*, 2013).

Jeonet et al. (2011) described the recognition of weed and crop. He used different techniques like statistical threshold value estimation method, normalized excessive green conversion and median filter, adaptive image segmentation, artificial intelligence and morphological feature calculation. The demerit of his work lied in the fact that it could not recognize the two occluded plants as two separate entities. Piron et al.,[6] worked to detect the weeds found in carrots. He merged the multispectral and stereoscopic data. Hecomputerized the different parameter values regarding altitude support weed detection. Multispectral and stereoscopic acquisition methods were used for improving in-row weed detection. His mechanical technique was victorious for premature stages but not for afterwards expansion stages. The planned method was foundation on the creation of the probability density function of plant altitude from stereoscopic multispectral images restricted to the sown group. (Jeon *et al.*, 2011).

Burgos et al. (2011) worked on computer vision system that successfully distinguished between weed territory and yield rows under unrestrained illumination in real-time.The system depended on two parts, FIP and RCRD. The difficulty was that FIP was incapable to execute a correct difference under all conditions. The blend of FIP and RCRD was time-consuming.The trouble had an insignificant solution, due to fluctuation conditions of lighting, moisture, vegetation development, different weed variety, and due to the resemblances existing. (Burgos et al., 2011). Dionisio Andújaret al. (2013) proposed the LiDAR (Light Detection and Ranging) a remote-sensing technique for the measurement of the distance between the sensor and a target. This procedure was based on the hypothesis that weed species with different heights could be precisely detected and discriminated using non-contact ranging sensors such as LiDAR. He used LiDAR sampling system method.The CDA showed the capabilities and limitations of the system. When performing a four group (i.e., four weed species) discriminated analysis, canonical functions could not discriminate correctly among groups. However, when CDA analysis was performed using two groups, one for S. halfpence and one for the other weed species, 77.7 percent of the unique cluster belongings were correctly classified for S, although sensor readings did not allow discriminating the two dicotyledonous species. (Dionisio Andújar *et al.,* 2013).

Montalvo et al. (2012) proposed a new method, for crop row detection in corn ground with lofty weed strain. The computer vision system is built to be mounted onboard a portable agricultural vehicle. The images are detained under image perception, being exaggerated. He applies different image processing techniques like image segmentation, double thresholding, and crop row detection. Image segmentation is dependent on the function of a plants directory, the double thresholding attained the division between weeds and crops and the crop row detection. (Montalvo *et al.*, 2012). Montalvo et al. (2013) worked tocorrectly identify all plants without any difficulty of greenness loss. His proposed a mechanical expert system that deals with image segmentation methods. He used SVM, AES, DEM and Otsu's methods for detection of weeds. In this paper results are not too good. (Montalvo *et al.*, 2013).

Jiang et al. (2010) aimed to be mounting a new method which can detect crop strips to lead agricultural machines to work in actual time even all external causes occurred.Image division method and Hough transform methods were used in this research. The main defect in his research was that agriculture robots were unable to find the satisfactory result and also failed in centerlines of the row when inter-row spaces were too thin. (Jiang *et al.*, 2010). Peng (2010) described a healthy weed identification method. He worked on the small value color weed images with the aforementioned image distort. The anticipated design based on three parts. Image matte was utilized to fragment the mud and the plant. He proposed a generative learning technique in order to deal with distort images. In the end, weed identification was achieved through the unclear colour knowledge base on the subspace technique. Time factor was main drawback in his work. (Peng ., 2010). Dejan et al. (2010) proposed the method of automatic weed detection and treatment in grasslands.The main intention of his work was the use of the third dimension that was altitude knowledge. He used edge detection, analysis of the boundary with help of the elliptic Fourier descriptors and support vector machine methods.This technique needed more computation. Under more complicate conditions (dock between clover or other broad leafed plants) the recognition rate was improved but still it was not satisfactory. (Dejan *et al.*, 2010).

Cordill et al. (2011) dealt the problem of accomplishment of mechanical adjacent row weed control in corn field. The purpose was to eliminate adjacent weeds found in corn field. He used stalk sensing, a control algorithm and mechanical weeding mechanism methods.Performance was not good in damaged plants. More effort was essential to recognize the grounds of misapprehend the positions of the corn plants. (Cordill *et al.*, 2011).Midtiby (2011) anticipatedthe system that made a distinction between weed and maize plants. He used an herbicide for the detection of weeds. He also used velocity estimator, plant recognizer, and nearest neighbor methods.The scheme was not capable to successfully manage weeds less than 11 mm X 11 mm. Inconvenience was also linked in dropping adequate herbicide on the tiny vegetation or a mixture of both. (Midtiby., 2011).Tewariet et al.(2014) presented the growth of a microcontroller based technology for site precise herbicide application with automatic weed detection technique. He used machine vision and image processing techniques or specific amount of herbicide application. In this technique the wastage of herbicide was also avoided. (Tewari *et al.*, 2014). Asif et al. (2013) aimed to improve the evaluation of the weed invasion through modifications and review of literature in yield loss prediction models. (Asif *et al.*, 2013).

Komi *et al.*(2007) worked with detection of weeds and their categorization. Inexpensive RGB colours and spectral (400 to 1000 nm) were used for this purpose. Weed identification was based on non-overlapping of full leaves. They used the technique of linear discriminant analysis and median filter. This paper did not give correct result or output in case of overlapping leaves. Moreover, the non-overlapping leaves consumed more time and in this way performance was ineffective. (Komi *et al.*, 2007).

Tellaeche*et al.*(2007) proposed the method of detection of weeds using Bayes and Support vector machine. This paper not only detected weed but also involved spray where weed appeared. It failed the robustness of the proposed solution against Illumination variability. (Tellaeche *et al.*, 2007).

Ishak et al.(2007) identified weeds based on broad and narrow leaves. This paper is using AI popular technique, ANN and image processing technique, edge detection, curve detection and ROI. It is perfect for detection of broad weed type but not efficient for detection of narrow weed type. (Ishak *et al.*, 2007).

Siddiqi *et al.*(2009) work on weeds recognizes on the basis of whether it is narrow or broad and investigates the presence and absence of weeds. They used the Erosion and Dilation segmentation algorithm for detection of weeds. This paper provides the efficient results for one type of weed detection but fail to detect other types of weeds. Their worked not provide the adoptive weed recognition and classification method. (Siddiqi *et al.,* 2009).

Siddiqi *et al.*(2009) differentiated between crop and inter-row weeds using Edge Link Detector. This paper work is efficient for detection of one type of weed class known as broad and narrow leaves weeds but give incorrect results in other classes of weeds. They also failed in classifying mixed weeds.

The reminder of this paper is as follows; the artificial neural network modeling along with the edge detection using fuzzy logic is narrated in section 2 and section 3, respectively. In section 4 the proposed methodology has been revealed. The simulation and discussion on the results has been presented in section 5 while last section concludes the findings of this article along with some directions for the future research. (Siddiqi *et al.,* 2009).

2. ARTIFICIAL NEURAL NETWORK

ANN is a system which processes information that has certain common performance characteristics with biological neural system. Neuron is simple elements where information processing take place. Between neuron signals are passed over connection links .A weight is associated to each connection link that is usually multiplied with the transmitted signal.

ANN has universal capabilities for approximation and contains some features and attributes that are similar with human nervous system. It contains some suppositions such as neurons are used to handle information processing. Secondly information or waves are traveled between cells over connection links and weight is contained by each link. Each neuron applies a threshold function (it should be differentiable, continuous and monotonically non-decreasing) to its net input to determine its output signal. The basic biological neuron system is given in Figure 1.

Figure 1. Basic biological neuron

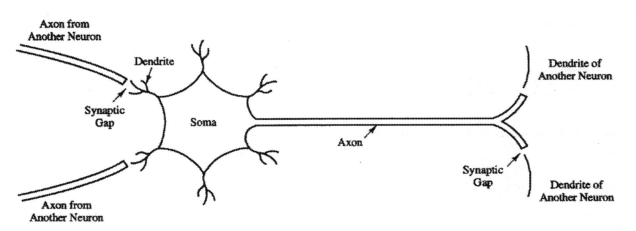

Figure 2. A very simple neural network based on input, output and a hidden layer

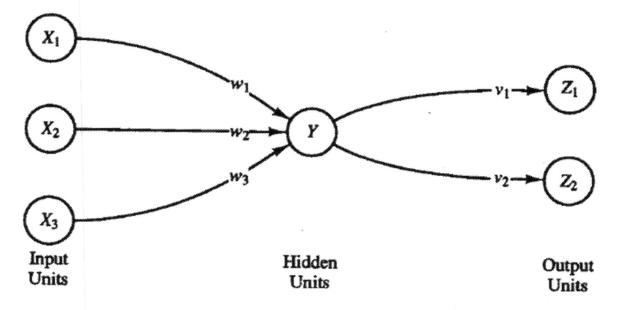

Neural network model is duplicate of human nervous system. Human brain contained billions of cells called neurons. Electromechanical signals are used for make association between neurons. The source of the signals is synapses. The location of synapses is terminal of neurons. Neural network, contained many units and cells similar to human nervous system. Limit of neurons are depended on the scenario of the specified problem in hand. As shown in Figure 2 each neuron has its own weights as shown in w1, w2 and w3.The weights are either positive or negative. There are many ways to organize neurons, one way of doing this is feed forward neural network. As shown in Figure 2 is feed forward neural network.

There is no restriction of levels in Ann. In feed forward neural network every level passed information to immediate next level until information is reached by the last or final level. Neural network creates connection between neurons .As shown in Figure 3 neural network contained three layers .Layer first is known as input layer that is from X_1 to X_N. Second layer is known as hidden layer that is from Z_1 toZ_p. Third layer is the final layer or output layer. Composite network contains many layers.

Neural network function $f(x)$ in mathematics is defined as the composition of other functions $g_i(x)$, which is further well-defined as the conformation of other function.

A widely used sum of weights is defined as,$f(x) = K(\sum_i w_i g_i(x))$.

3. EDGE DETECTION USING FUZZY LOGIC

In edge detection technique, we take the image in jpg format and then convert image from RGB to gray-scale and then apply edge detection. Edge detection eliminated all the background and highlight the original image. In edge detection technique, we first subtract the background from the image and then a graph appeared that showed different colors of an image. The transformation is applied for the targeted image; this will provide the gray-scale image. Then we applied fuzzy logic on it. In fuzzy logic we applied

Figure 3. Feed forward neural network model

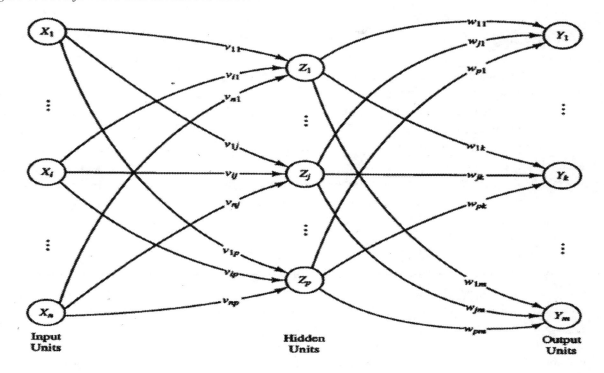

Gaussian membership function on it. We also changed the values of weights and bias. We have taken three values of biases and three values of weights. Now we compare the image with reference to x-axis and y-axis. Finally we have received a graph that identified the graph on change the value of x-axis and change the value of y-axis. We have received the original gray-scale image. Now this gray-scale image converted to sharp edge image.

Conventional logic includes the generalization of Fuzzy logic, in which there is a even alteration from right to wrong. It provides the understandable presentation of data. It deals with rules. The purpose of fuzzy logic is to tackle overlapping values. The fundamentals of fuzzy logic are resulting from the premises. A fuzzy set B in Y is characterized by a association function (MF) $\mu_B(Y)$, It contains the interval between 0 to 1. (y in B is dependent on $\mu_B(Y)$ for the purpose of value of membership). That is, the fuzzy set B on a universe of discourse Y is defined as:

$$B = \{(y, \mu_B(Y)) \mid y \in Y\}.$$

The MF is characterized by subjective measures and not probability functions. MF's have multiple types such astrapezoidal, Generalized bell, the Sigmoidal functions, Gaussian, Z-shaped, triangular and S-shaped.

4. PROPOSED METHODOLOGY

In constructing intelligent systems fuzzy logic and neural networks are corresponding tools. Neural networks are computational structures that are low in level, but with raw data it performs well. Fuzzy logic uses linguistic information obtained from domain experts. However fuzzy systems are unable to modify themselves to a new environment. While on the other side neural networks can learn but are incomprehensible to the user. The learning and computational abilities of neural networks and explanation and humanly knowledge representation abilities of fuzzy systems get combine together in integrated neuro-fuzzy systems. Due to this composition fuzzy system become proficient of learning, while neural network become more evident. Expert knowledge can be incorporated into the structure of the neuro-fuzzy system. At the same time, the connectionist structure avoids fuzzy inference, which entails a substantial computational burden. A neural network which is in function a like to a fuzzy inference model. It can be skilled to develop IF-THEN fuzzy rules and determine membership functions for input and output variables of the system.

In the given proposed method of crop and weed detection using supervised learning techniques; we exploited Neuro-Fuzzy technique for detection of weeds found in corn field. We first of all take the satellite images of weeds and then with the help of edge detection technique convert the RGB image into Gray-Scale. And then different images are converted to 560 x 420 dimensions.387 images of nine species of weeds has been taken for applying the given scheme. Then we apply edge detection on it. Edge detection using fuzzy logic highlighted the weed and dims all the expressions. Now we applied different membership function like Gaussian membership function and trim membership function etc. Gaussian membership function has given best results. So we also adjusted the weights and bias.

Now we picked edge detected image and apply classification method that is ANN. It has given hundredpercent accuracy for detection of achyranthusaspera, convolvulusarvensis, carthamusoxycantha, cynodon dactylon, atura alba, euphorbia helioscopia, silybummarianum, sorghum halepense and amaranthushybridus.

Table 1. Proposed algorithm

Algorithm Weed Identification
Input: Images set
Output: Weed detection at flower stage
Step#1 Pre-processing
e. Read the images one by one
f. Back ground subtraction
g. Convert image in gray scale
h. Resizing the images
Step#2 Edge detection using fuzzy logic
g. Compute the magnitude of gradient
h. Fuzzy inference system
i. Add variable function
j. Add membership function
k. Parse rules function
l. Defuzzification
Step#3 Apply artificial neural network

In this research, we proposed the method of crop and weed detection using supervised learning techniques. So we used Neuro-Fuzzy technique for detection of weeds found in corn field. We first of all took the images of weeds at flower stage and then with the help of edge detection technique converted the RGB image into Gray-Scale. We took 386 images of nine species of weeds and resized those images. Then we applied edge detection using fuzzy logic to highlight the weeds and to dim all the expressions. Now we applied Gaussian membership function and trim membership function. Gaussian membership function has given the best results. So we also adjusted the weights and bias. Finally, we picked edge detected images and applied classification method that was ANN. It has given 100 percent accuracy for detection of nine weed species (see Table 1).

4.1 Read the Images in JPG Format

We read our images in jpg format. In this way we get the numeric values of an image as shown in figure 3.

4.2 Surf of Each Image

From the *I* components in matrix I, and using x=1:8: end and y=1:8: end, where [0 255] = size (I) a shaded surface in three-dimensions is created by Surf (I). 'I' is a single-valued function representing height which is defined over a grid which is geometrically rectangular. I specify the color data and surface height such that color and surface height are proportional to each other.

4.3 Edge Detection Using Fuzzy Logic

Edges of an image are considered a type of crucial information that can be extracted by applying detectors with different methodology. Edge detection is a type of image segmentation techniques which determines the presence of an edge or line in an image and outlines them in an appropriate way. The main purpose of edge detection is to simplify the image data in order to minimize the amount of data to be processed. Generally, an edge is defined as the boundary pixels that connect two separate regions with changing image amplitude attributes such as different constant luminance and tristimulus values in an image. The detection operation begins with the examination of the local discontinuity at each pixel element in an image. Amplitude, orientation, and location of a particular sub area in the image are essentially important characteristics of possible edges. Based on these characteristics, the detector has to decide whether each of the examined pixels is an edge or not.

4.4 Background Subtraction

In background subtraction, first of all we used the morphological function. In which we create the disk shaped structuring element with a radius of 15 pixels as shown in figure 4 and 5, 6 and 7 respectively. In this way background is subtracted from the image. The morphological opening was used to take out minute objects from an image while preserving original size and shape of larger objects in subject images. Morphology is a vast set of image processing operations that can process images on the basis of their shapes. In morphological operations a structuring element is applied to a specific input image to generate an output image of exactly same size. In a morphological operation, the value of every pixel of the output image depends on evaluation of the parallel pixel in the given input image with its neighbors.

Figure 4. Image value of species 1

```
93   74   61   68   91   78   88   89   86   79   96   86   56   30   32   94   92   91   73   83   36
101  99   73   57   81   92   91   91   92   86   89   79   39   26   39   40  130   81   87   88   83
19  101  102   63   57   81   84   88   95   96   96   79   26   28   29   52  109  108   92   85   94
 4   37   93   59   55   89   90   88   91  101   99   35   25   49   48   52   91  118   94  101   98
21    0   51   95   79   79   92   95   99  113   83   36   20   37   59   46   39  126  103   99   99
23   19    2   71  101   75   86   99  111  120   69    7   24   37   63   18    0  104  107   99  103
19   34   14   17   89   90   86   97  126  119   50   12   30   35   22   10   15   53  134  104  103
24   30   27   24   35   95   97   96  119   84   28   47   74   45   28   68   54   20  139   98  111
30   38   34   36   21   71  103   87  117   71   16   70   87   65   61   55   41   10  106  103  127
24   34   33   27   34   12   85  102   96   65   49   79   67   72   78   50   52   23   64  120  126
28   29   28   30   24    7   53  103  100   68   58   67   65   80   81   61   51   47   18  144  115
36   19   42   45   38   43   47   83   84   64   59   62   75   78   71   78   67   41   25  113  110
28   23   46   37   36   47   52   54   66   65   70   72   77   76   73   76   74   59   24   34  106
36   31   37   40   39   38   41   53   59   65   66   70   77   78   76   74   65   85   55   26   39
28   36   36   36   38   47   45   40   48   58   58   63   75   76   73   81   78   75  105    0  172
38   34   10   58   45   47   54   64   69   67   62   64   73   78   72   78   79   82   79  102  226
23   31   27   39   57   55   55   57   64   70   72   71   71   74   70   78   90   90   20  223  218
14   37   25   35   53   63   67   69   73   77   68   62   73   73   76   72   84   31  241  245  205
14   25   33   18   36   61   69   69   76   63   67   73   78   88   69   82   46  244  240  237  242
23   32   25   32    8   61   66   68   67   68   66   69   74   80   69   68  242  244  226  228  247
32   33   27   29   25   24   76   75   69   69   76   78   63   79   81  219  242  225  228  232  221
30   30   24   27   30   10   53   81   76   71   72   88   74   76  192  241  218  226  225  231  225
28   29   27   30   25   23   22   67   87   76   73   73   73  133  234  211  225  230  219  224  229
25   27   28   29   24   30   14   37   75   84   71   68   87  182  229  220  222  222  228  230  222
26   30   32   28   32   26   36   15   52   82   73   70   88  196  236  218  218  219  223  221  222
```

Figure 5. Surf of species 1

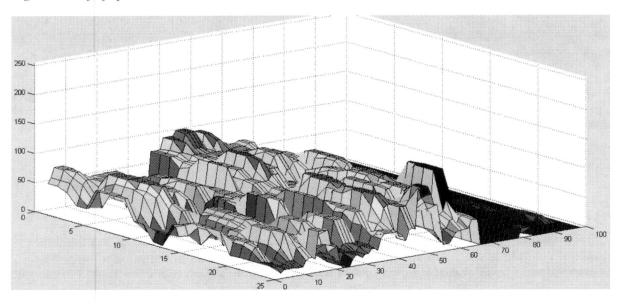

Figure 6. Back Propagation Neural Network

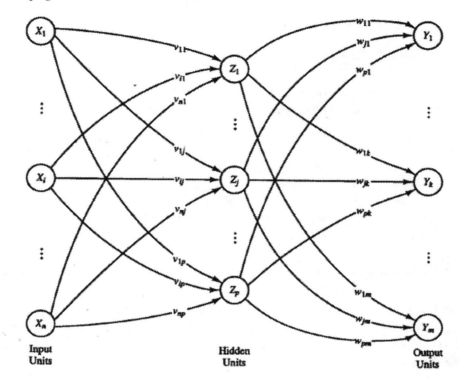

Figure 7. Vector diagram of neural network

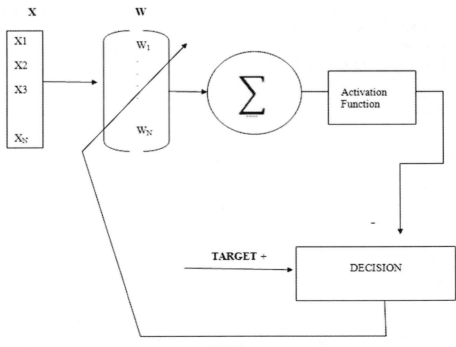

A person can build a morphological operation by selecting the shape and size of the neighborhood that is actually sensitive to specific feature and shape in the input image.

4.5 Convert RGB to Gray Scale Image

Although the preservance of the quality of image is an important issue, but we are adjusting the parametric values to get a raw data in the form of binary values rather than real as in true colored image. We are preferring grayscale on RGB because it eliminates the saturation information and hue while retaining the luminance. We tried to produce perceptually plausible grayscale results and retain the information about the original colour image as much as possible. We convert our image in gray scale image by using colormap function. A colormap is an m-by-3 matrix of real numbers between 0.0 and 1.0. Each colour is defined by a unique row, that is, each row is an RGB vector. So the kth colour is defined by the kth row of the matrix representing the colormap, where map (k,:) = [r(k) g(k) b(k)]) specifies the intensity of red, green, and blue. Colormap (map) sets the colour to the matrix map.

4.6 Resize Each Image

Matrix computation should be made symmetric as per the programming rules. So, the images have been taken in png format that will provide a consistent size. This function is used to subsample and filter the digital data. Optimization of the filter is used to compare the resolution to a particular target being displayed. Moreover, the high resolution pixel data also remains accessible for future application and storage.

4.7 Compute the Magnitude of Gradient

Convolution of two *functions* IX and IY produces a third function which is a modified version of one of the original functions, Convolution give the overlapped area between the two functions, which is given as a function of the amount that one of the original functions is *translated*. C = conv2(E, F) computes the two-dimensional convolution of matrices E and F (shown in Listing 1).

Listing 1.

```
If
E= matrix describing two-dimensional finite impulse response (FIR) filter
    F=matrix filtered in two-dimensions
    size(E) =[me, ne], size(F)= [mf, nf], size(C)= [mc, nc]
then
    mc = max([me+mf-1,me,mf]) and n= max([ne+nf-1,ne,nf]).
    C = conv2(h1, h2, E) first convolves E with the vector h1 along the rows
and then with the vector   h2 along the columns
         The size of C is given by:
         If n1 = length(h1), n2 = length(h2),  then mc = max([me, n1,
me+n1-1]) and
    nc = max([ne+n2-1, ne, n2]). A subsection of the two-dimensional convo-
lution is proceeded by C =  conv2(..., shape), as specified by the shape pa-
rameter.
```

4.8 Fuzzy Inference System

This function creates new FIS structures. newfis has up to seven input arguments, and the output argument is a FIS structure. FIS contains seven arguments such as fis name, fis type, method and range. In FIS structure we contained edgefis as fis name, input as fistype, IX as method and range is between 1 to -1.

4.9 Add Variable to Fuzzy Inference System

In fuzzy inference system we contained the function add variable. In this add variable function we contained four arguments and the arguments are FIS name, input, IX or IY and range between -1 to 1.

4.10 Add Membership Function

The graphical demonstration of scale participation of every input is known as membership function. It assigns a weighting to each of the inputs being processed, elaborates functional overlap between various inputs, and finally signifies an output response. In our research we used Gaussian and trim membership function. In our research we used add membership function and the arguments of add membership function contained FIS name, input type of variable, 1 as a index of the variable, Gaussian and trim membership functions, [sx, [0 0 0 0]] and [sy, [0 0 0 0]] as vector of parameters.

4.11 Parse Rules

Parse rule is the function that is used in FIS structure. There are three formats of rules (symbolic, verbose and indexed).We use verbose format in our research that is in English language. Parse rule function contained 2 arguments. In our research the first argument is edgefis as FIS structure and rules as a second argument.

4.12 Pre allocate the Output Matrix/Defuzzification of Data

In Matlab, arrays are dynamic in size. We used zeros function that resized our images array. In this way we received the edge detected image. That is smoother and noise free edge detected image using fuzzy logic.

4.13 Back Propagation Neural Network

Neural network model is duplicate of human nervous system. Human brain contained billions of cells called neurons. Electromechanical signals are used for making association between neurons. The source of the signals is synapses. The location of synapses is terminal of neurons. Neurons constantly obtained waves.

Axon produced the output. Neural network, contained many units and cells similar to human nervous system. Limit of Neurons are depended on the scenario. As shown in figure 6 each neuron has its own weights as shown in w1, w2 and w3. The weights are either positive or negative. There are many ways to organize neurons; one way of doing this is back propagation neural network. As shown in figure 6 is feed forward neural network. There is no restriction of levels in Ann. In back propagation neural networks every level passes information to immediate next level until information is reached by the last or final level. Neural network creates connection between neurons. As shown in figure 4 neural network contained three layers .Layer first is known as input layer that is from X_1 to X_N. Second layer is known as hidden layer that is from Z_1 to Z_p. Third layer is the final layer or output layer. Composite network contains many layers. Neural netw ork function f(x) in mathematics is defined as the composition of other functions $g_i(x)$, which is further well-defined as the conformation of other function.

A widely used sum of weights is defined as, $f(x) = K (\sum_i w_i g_i(x))$

In our research we have used the used back propagation $\in$ neural network with one layer. The mathematical description of our proposed ann solution is as follow

$$NeuralNetworkapprox(Y_{approx}) = f\sum_{i=1}^{N}(x_i w_i)\,\forall w_i \in R$$

$$F(X) = \begin{cases} 0 & if\ Y_{approx} \leq 0 \\ Y_{approx} & if\ 0 < Y_{approx} < 1/2 \\ 1 & if\ Y_{approx} \geq 1/2 \end{cases}$$

Error = D(n)- neural network approx

Figure 8. Proposed Method

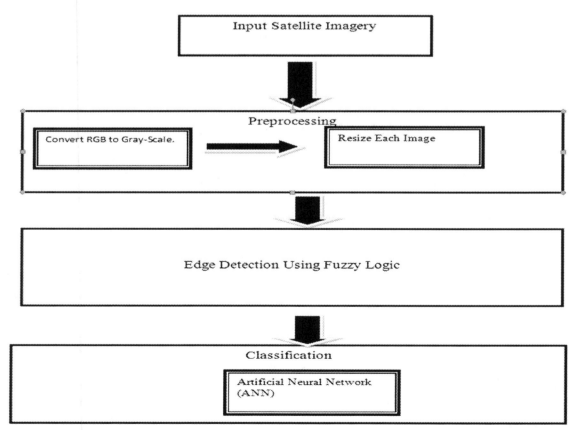

Table 3. Image reading and timing profiles

Function Name	Calls	Total Time	Self Time
P	1	14.418s	11.513s
Imread	386	2.901s	0.150s
Imagesci/ private/ readpng	386	2.476s	0.637s
Imagesci/ private/ pngreadc(MEX-file)	386	1.663s	1.663s
Images/ private/ imftype	386	0.255s	0.012s
Imagesci/ private/ ispng	386	0.166s	0.166s
ismember	386	0.156s	0.062s
Ismember > ismemberR2012a	386	0.094s	0.094s
imformats	386	0.077s	0.024s
Imformats > find_in_registry	386	0.053s	0.053s
Imread > parse_inputs	386	0.020s	0.020s
Imagesci/ private/ readpng > parse_args	386	0.020s	0.020s
std	9	0.004s	0.000s
var	9	0.004s	0.004s

Table 2. Parameter setting/values using Fuzzy logic and ANN

Parameters	Values/Setting
Image Type	Png
Dimensions	560X420
Width	560pixels
Height	420pixels
Bit Depth	32

Table 4. Statistical analysis for different species

System specifications	IV. Processor: Intel(R) Pentium(R) CPU B950@ 2.10GHz V. RAM: 2.00 GB VI. Windows edition:window7 enterprise			
Specie No	**Mean**	**Min**	**Max**	**STD**
Species1	1.7149e+08	165944727	174648401	1.897607599363925e+06
Species2	1.6403e+08	152831487	172187476	5.321317663300054e+06
Species3	1.7129e+08	162422859	175728517	2.413328586197289e+06
Species4	1.6772e+08	152036821	174220855	4.935322775798350e+06
Species5	1.7236e+08	166664565	175324365	2.031588545658133e+06
Species6	1.7245e+08	163637148	175896684	2.818956730813235e+06
Species7	1.7475e+08	172242288	176244333	1.044093984411532e+06
Species8	1.7431e+08	169252767	176176002	2.037776452696190e+06
Species9	1.7211e+08	158150100	176713068	4.080540886773737e+06

Figure 9. RGB to Gray Scale conversion

SPECIES	ORIGINAL IMAGE	GRAY-SCALE IMAGE
SPECIES 1		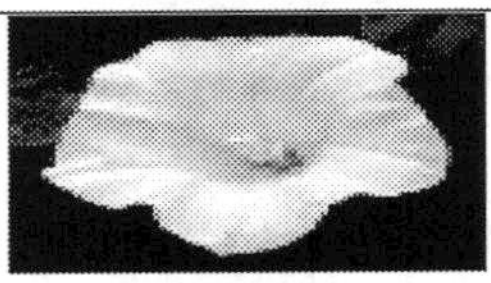
SPECIES 2		

Figure 10. Edge detection in species 1

Original Image	Graph Show Different Colours Of Image
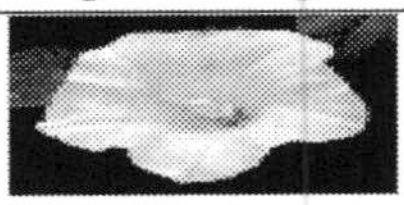	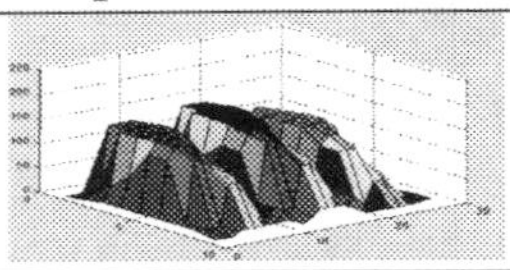
Transformation	Input Gray-Scale Image
	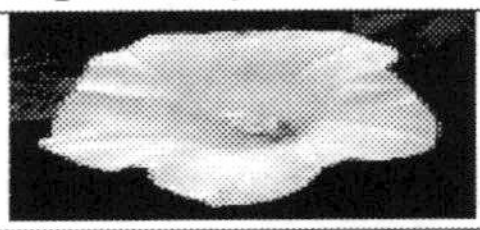
Gray-Scale With Reference To X-Axis	Gray-Scale With Reference To Y-Axis
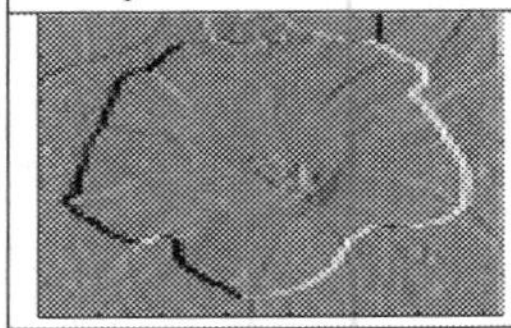	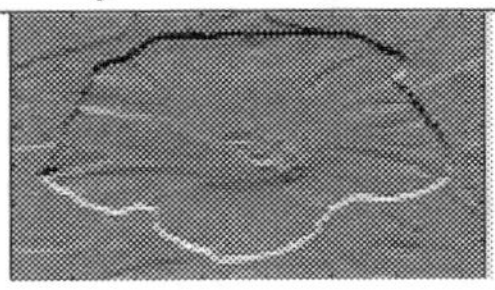
Fuzzy Logic Graph	Original Gray-Scale Image
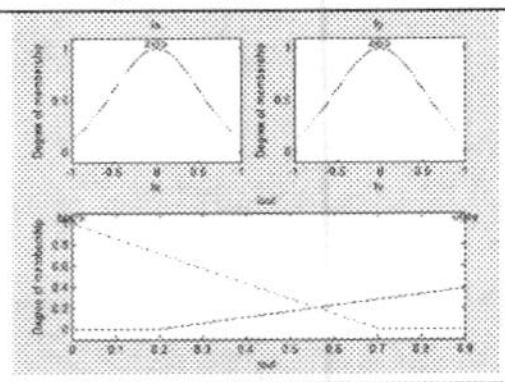	
Edge Detected Image	
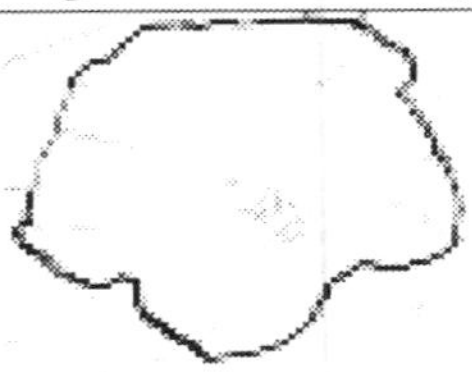	

Figure 11. Edge detection in species 2

Original Image	Graph Show Different Colours Of Image
	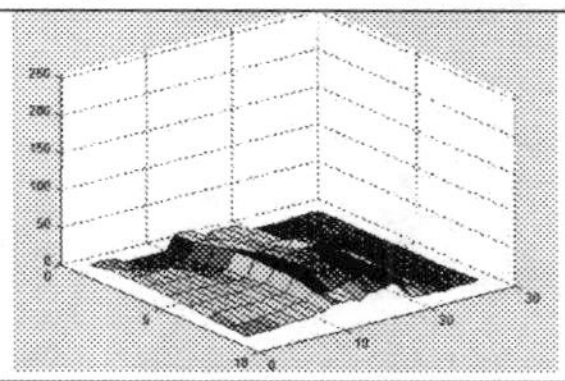
Transformation	Input Gray-Scale Image
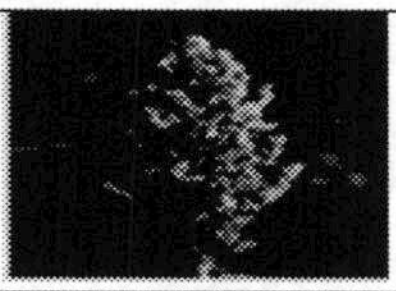	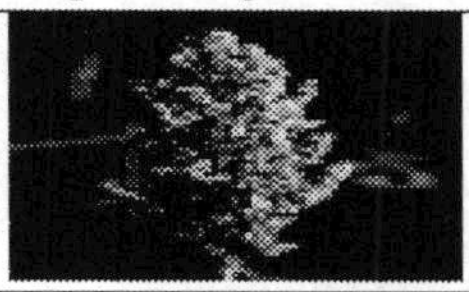
Gray-Scale With Reference To X-Axis	Gray-Scale With Reference To Y-Axis
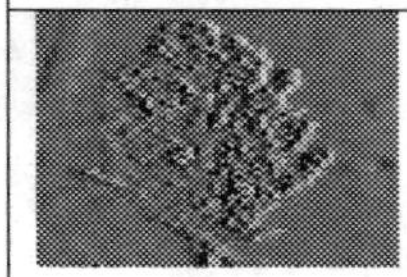	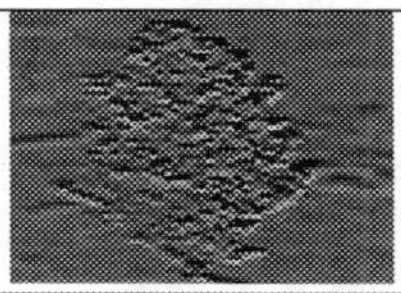
Fuzzy Logic Graph	Original Gray-Scale Image
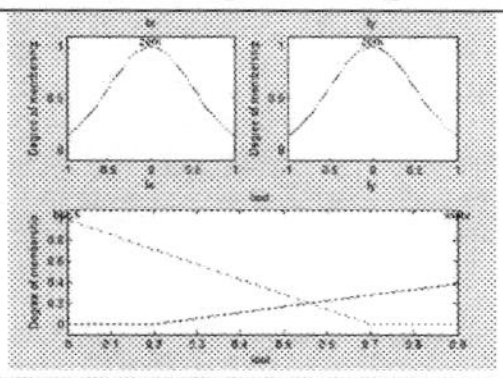	
Edge Detected Image	
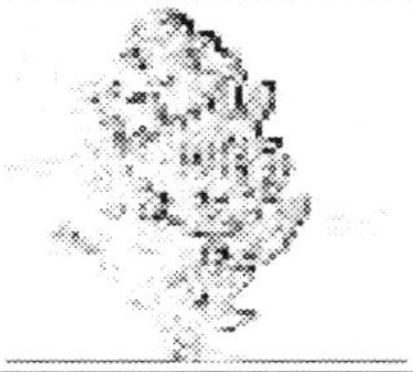	

D(n) = Mean(Sum(imread,2))

Y_{approx} = Neural network approximated solution

F(X) = Activation function

D(n) = Desired target

In D(n) we calculated the centroid of each image. Imread function is used to read each image in png format and 2 is used to calculate the sum of row and then find the average. In this way we calculate the centroid of each image. D(n) is minus from the value that is calculated through neural network (Y_{approx}). Then the difference is error. So adjust the weights in order to minimize the error rate.

Figure 12. Edge detection in specie 3

Original Image	Graph Show Different Colours Of Image
	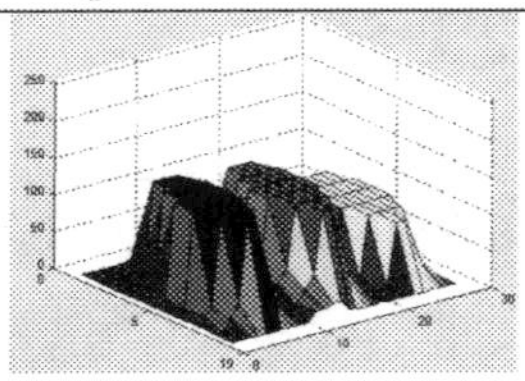
Transformation	Input Gray-Scale Image
	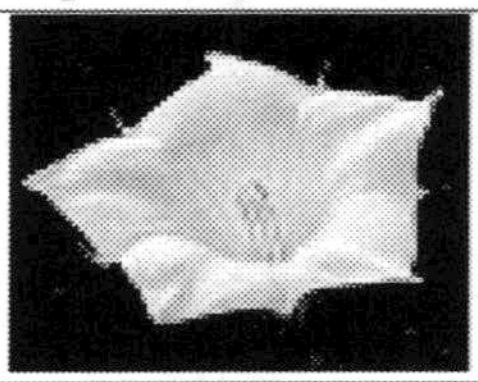
Gray-Scale With Reference To X-Axis	Gray-Scale With Reference To Y-Axis
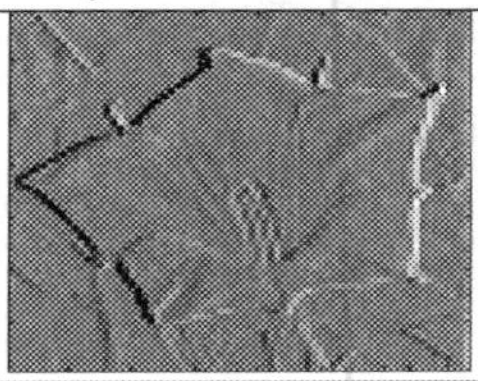	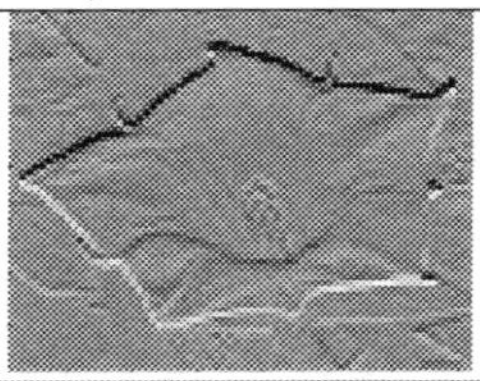
Fuzzy Logic Graph	Original Gray-Scale Image
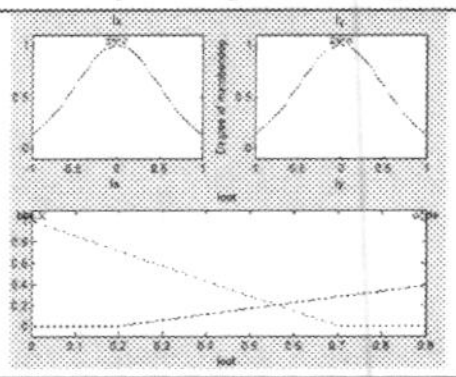	
Edge Detected Image	
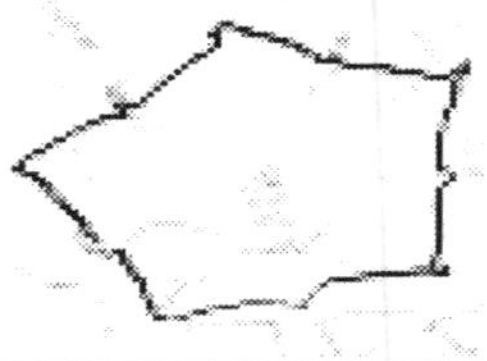	

5. SIMULATION AND RESULTS

For experimentation we have used Matlab R2013a (8.1.0.604) with windows 7 enterprise 32 bit operating system installed on Processor: DELL Inspiron Intel Pentium inside with 2GB memory. We have used edge detection using fuzzy logic and then applied artificial neural network as a classifier. This table defined the overall time for execution of artificial neural network. In this table file p.m takes 11.513 seconds and imread instruction has taken 2.901 seconds, standard deviation 0.004 seconds and variance 0.004 seconds (see figure 8).

Figure 13. Edge detection in specie 4

Original Image	Graph Show Different Colours Of Image

Transformation	Input Gray-Scale Image

Gray-Scale With Reference To X-Axis	Gray-Scale With Reference To Y-Axis
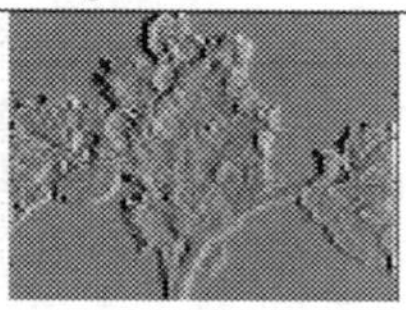	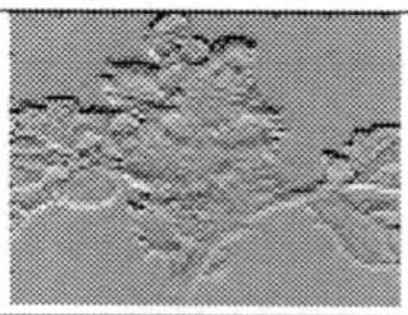
Fuzzy Logic Graph	Original Gray-Scale Image
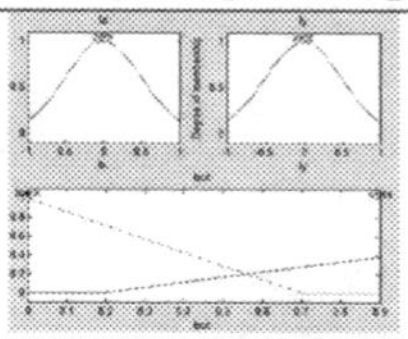	
Edge Detected Image	
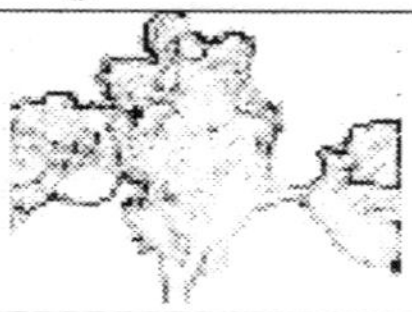	

In our research work, we have worked in satellite imagery. We worked on two types of weeds of corn field. Each image type is png format and dimension is 560X420 pixels. The height is 420 pixels and width is 560 pixels. Each image has bit depth 32. The basic parameters setting or values taken for the simulation is provided in Table 2 while different functions used for reading the images along with their timing profile is provided in Table 3.

Table 4 defines the system specification on which the simulations have been performed. As the fuzzy methods are stochastic in nature so one good result cannot validate the applicability of the proposed scheme so statistical analysis has been taken based on the statistical modes mean that define the average value, Min, the minimum range obtained for the specie, Max defines the highest value for that specie and STD provides the standard deviation in the in the results from the mean value.

Figure 14. Edge detection in specie 5

Original Image	Graph Show Different Colours Of Image

Transformation	Input Gray-Scale Image

Gray-Scale With Reference To X-Axis	Gray-Scale With Reference To Y-Axis
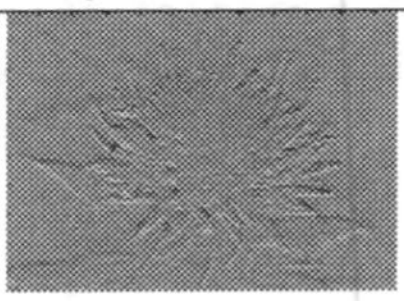	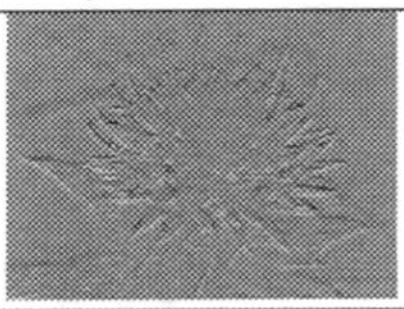
Fuzzy Logic Graph	Original Gray-Scale Image
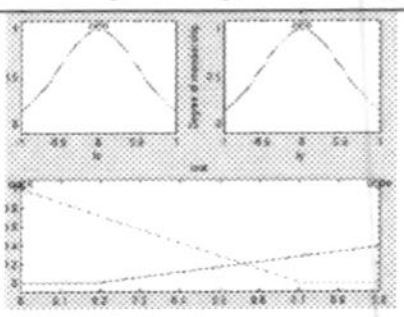	
Edge Detected Image	

First of all, we performed preprocessing of each image because image size of all the images must be same, otherwise it will create an error in Matlab. In first step, we switch all images from RGB to gray-scale. Original images are in .jpg format and dimension is 73X69 and when we convert the image from RGB to Gray scale then the image dimension was 560X420 (see figure 9).

In edge detection technique, we take the image in jpg format and then convert image from RGB to gray-scale .Then apply edge detection. Edge detection eliminated all the background and highlight the original image. In edge detection technique we first subtract the background from the image, a graph appeared that showed different colors of an image we then applied transformation on it which basically targeted the image. Now we get the gray-scale image. Then we applied fuzzy logic on it. In fuzzy logic we applied Gaussian membership function on it.

We also changed the values of weights and bias. We have taken three values of biases and three values of weights. Now we compare the image with reference to x-axis and y-axis. Finally we have received a graph that identified the graph on change the value of x-axis and change the value of y-axis. We have

Figure 15. Edge detection in specie 6

Original Image	Graph Show Different Colours Of Image
	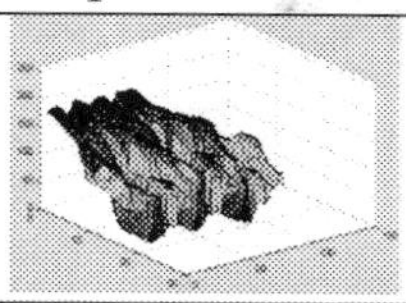
Transformation	Input Gray-Scale Image

Gray-Scale With Reference To X-Axis	Gray-Scale With Reference To Y-Axis
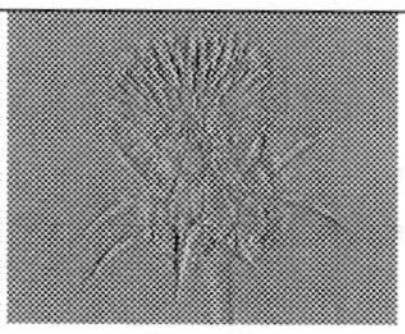	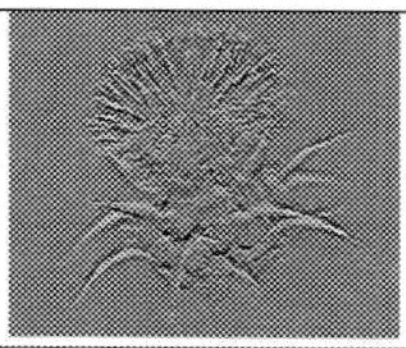
Fuzzy Logic Graph	Original Gray-Scale Image
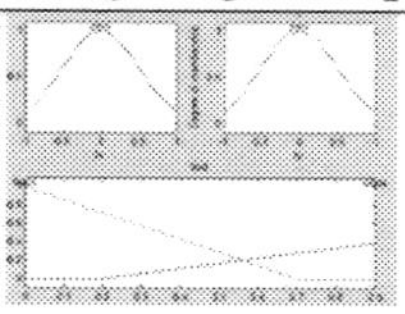	
Edge Detected Image	

received the original gray-scale image. Now this gray-scale image converted to sharp edge image. Conventional logic includes the generalization of Fuzzy logic, in which there is an even alteration from right to wrong. It provides the understandable presentation of data and deals with rules. The purpose of fuzzy logic is to tackle overlapping values. The fundamentals of fuzzy logic are resulting from the premises. A fuzzy set B in Y is characterized by an association function (MF) $\mu_B(Y)$, It contains the interval between 0 to 1. (y in B is dependent on $\mu_B(Y)$ for the purpose of value of membership). That is, the fuzzy set B on a universe of discourse Y is defined as

$$B = \{(y, \mu_B(Y)) \mid y \in Y\}.$$

The MF is characterized by subjective measures and not probability functions. MF's have multiple types such as trapezoidal, Generalized bell, the Sigmoidal functions, Gaussian, Z-shaped, triangular and S-shaped (see figure 10).

Figure 16. Edge detection in specie 7

Original Image	Graph Show Different Colours Of Image
	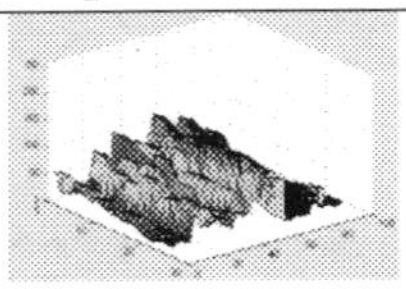
Transformation	Input Gray-Scale Image
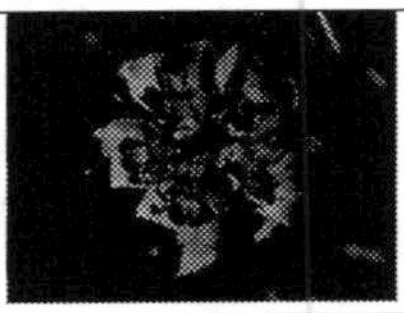	
Gray-Scale With Reference To X-Axis	Gray-Scale With Reference To Y-Axis
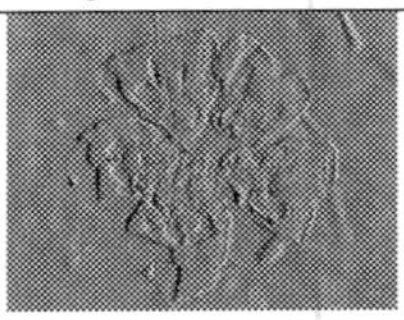	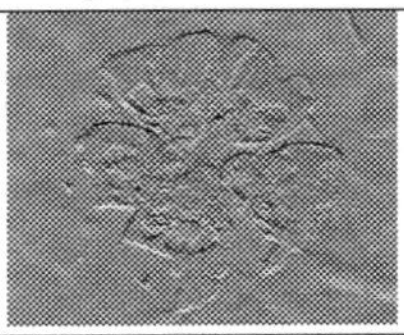
Fuzzy Logic Graph	Original Gray-Scale Image
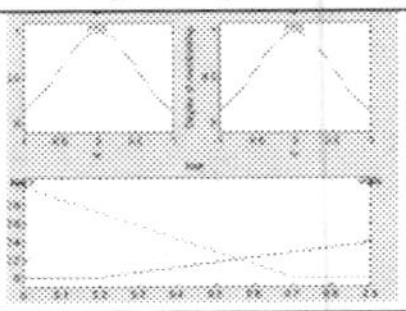	
Edge Detected Image	

Figures 11 to 18 are the examples of nine species. The whole images described the conversion of simple image into sharp image. Now in this way our image is noise free. It improved our results. It is the weed commonly found in maize field. We took 387 images of weeds.

The percentage of accuracy for the test data is presented in Table 5.

6. CONCLUSION AND FUTURE WORK

In this research study, based on the results and discussion following conclusions have been obtained:

The given frame work is validated with the extensive simulation and the results has been obtained in good agreement with the actual detection of the weeds.

The scheme is successfully applied for accuracy weeds under consideration as achyranthusaspera, convolvulusarvensis, carthamusoxycantha, cynodondactylon, aturaalba, euphorbia helioscopia, silybummarianum, sorghum halepense and amaranthushybridus.

Figure 17. Edge detection in specie 8

Original Image	Graph Show Different Colours Of Image
	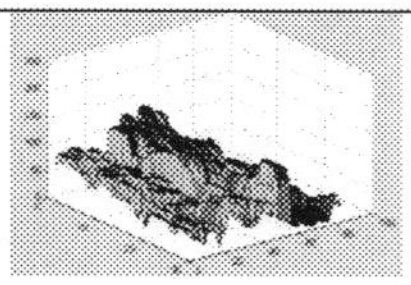
Transformation	Input Gray-Scale Image
	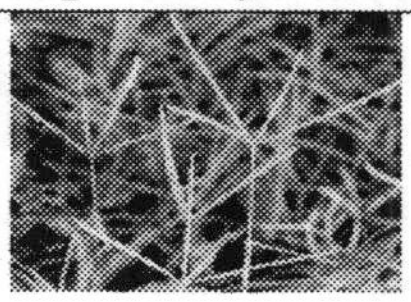
Gray-Scale With Reference To X-Axis	Gray-Scale With Reference To Y-Axis
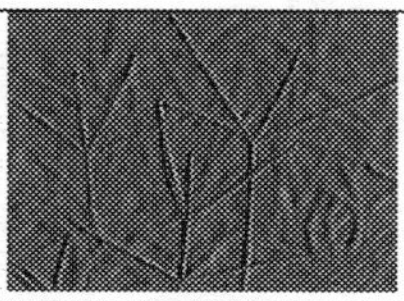	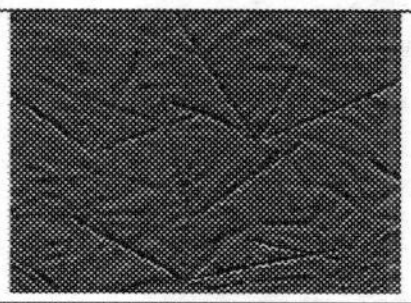
Fuzzy Logic Graph	Original Gray-Scale Image
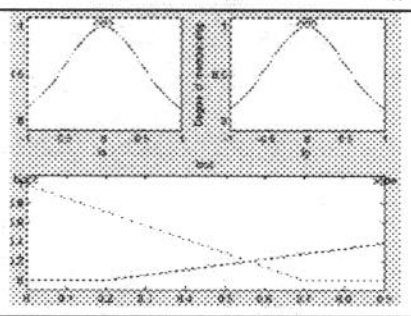	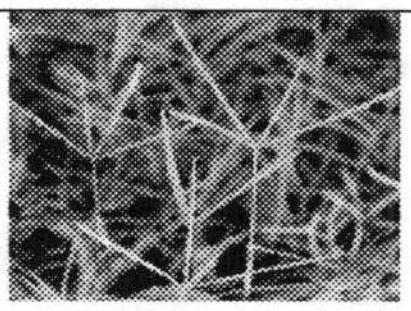
Edge Detected Image	

The statistical analysis provides the robustness in the scheme by Monti Carlo simulations performed for a data set of 386 images. This work is helpful in the classification of mixed weeds. The proposed scheme is applicable for weed classification. It is a narrow spectrum application. This scheme provides the economical solution for farmers which increases the crop yield and reduces the detrimental effects of spray on crops.

In future, one can exploit different neural network models hybrid with soft computing techniques. Our future goal is to extend this work to the leaves as well as on seed stage.

The level of accuracy for the matching for the true classification is found to be 100 percent for neuro-fuzzy algorithm.

The one of the hidden advantages are applicability of the designed framework, ease in implementation and less hardware needed for implementation.

Figure 18. Edge detection in specie 9

Original Image	Graph Show Different Colours Of Image
	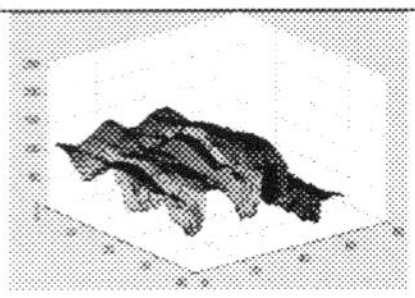
Transformation	Input Gray-Scale Image

Gray-Scale With Reference To X-Axis	Gray-Scale With Reference To Y-Axis

Fuzzy Logic Graph	Original Gray-Scale Image
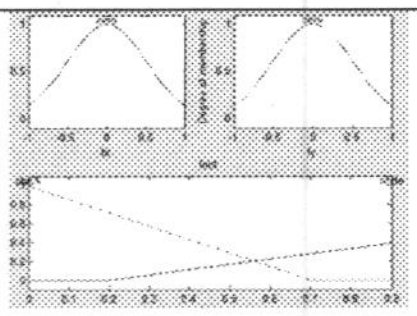	
Edge Detected Image	

Table 5. Percentage of accuracy for the test data

SPECIES TYPES	SPECIES1	SPECIES2	SPECIES3	SPECIES4	SPECIES5	SPECIES6	SPECIES7	SPECIES8	SPECIES9
CORRECTLY CLASSIFIED%	100%	100%	100%	100%	100%	100%	100%	100%	100%
MIS-CLASSIFIED%	0%	0%	0%	0%	0%	0%	0%	0%	0%

REFERENCES

Ali, A., Streibig, J. C., & Andreasen, C. (2013). Yield loss prediction models based on early estimation of weed pressure. *Crop Protection (Guildford, Surrey)*, *53*, 125–131. doi:10.1016/j.cropro.2013.06.010

Andújar, D., Escolà, A., Rosell-Polo, J. R., Fernández-Quintanilla, C., & Dorado, J. (2013). Potential of a terrestrial LiDAR-based system to characterise weed vegetation in maize crops. *Computers and Electronics in Agriculture*, *92*, 11–15. doi:10.1016/j.compag.2012.12.012

Burgos-Artizzu, X. P., Ribeiro, A., Guijarro, M., & Pajares, G. (2011). Real-time image processing for crop/weed discrimination in maize fields. *Computers and Electronics in Agriculture*, *75*(2), 337–346. doi:10.1016/j.compag.2010.12.011

Cordill, C., & Grift, T. E. (2011). Design and testing of an intra-row mechanical weeding machine for corn. *Biosystems Engineering*, *110*(3), 247–252. doi:10.1016/j.biosystemseng.2011.07.007

Ishak, A. J., Mokri, S. S., Mustafa, M. M., & Hussain, A. (2007, December). Weed Detection utilizing Quadratic Polynomial and ROI Techniques.

Ishak, A. J., Mustafa, M. M., Tahir, N. M., & Hussain, A. (2008). Weed Detection System using Support Vector Machine.

Jiang, G. Q., Zhao, C. J., & Si, Y. S. (2010, July). A machine vision based crop rows detection for agricultural robots. In *Wavelet Analysis and Pattern Recognition (ICWAPR), 2010 International Conference on* (pp. 114-118). IEEE. doi:10.1109/ICWAPR.2010.5576422

Kiani, S., Azimifar, Z., & Kamgar, S. (2010, May). Wavelet-based crop detection and classification. In *Electrical Engineering (ICEE), 2010 18th Iranian Conference on* (pp. 587-591). IEEE. doi:10.1109/IRANIANCEE.2010.5507003

Komi, P. J., Jackson, M. R., & Parkin, R. M. (2007). Plant Classification Combining Colour and Spectral Cameras for Weed Control Purposes. *2007 IEEE International Symposium on Industrial Electronics*, 2039–2042. doi:10.1109/ISIE.2007.4374921

Midtiby, H. S., Mathiassen, S. K., Andersson, K. J., & Jørgensen, R. N. (2011). Performance evaluation of a crop/weed discriminating microsprayer. *Computers and Electronics in Agriculture*, *77*(1), 35–40. doi:10.1016/j.compag.2011.03.006

Montalvo, M., Guerrero, J. M., Romeo, J., Emmi, L., Guijarro, M., & Pajares, G. (2013). Expert Systems with Applications Automatic expert system for weeds / crops identification in images from maize fields. *Expert Systems with Applications*, *40*(1), 75–82. doi:10.1016/j.eswa.2012.07.034

Montalvo, M., Pajares, G., Guerrero, J. M., Romeo, J., Guijarro, M., & Ribeiro, A. et al. (2012). Automatic detection of crop rows in maize fields with high weeds pressure. *Expert Systems with Applications*, *39*(15), 11889–11897. doi:10.1016/j.eswa.2012.02.117

Montalvo, M., Pajares, G., Guerrero, J. M., Romeo, J., Guijarro, M., Ribeiro, A., & Cruz, J. M. (2012). Expert Systems with Applications Automatic detection of crop rows in maize fields with high weeds pressure. *Expert Systems with Applications*, *39*(15), 11889–11897. doi:10.1016/j.eswa.2012.02.117

Nejati, H., Azimifar, Z., & Zamani, M. (2008). Using Fast Fourier Transform for Weed Detection in corn fields.

Peng, Z. (2010). Image-blur-based Robust Weed Recognition. *Tc, 10*, 8.

Piron, A., Leemans, V., Lebeau, F., & Destain, M. (2009). Improving in-row weed detection in multispectral stereoscopic images. Computers and Electronics in Agriculture, 69(1), 73–79.

Šeatović, D., Kutterer, H., & Anken, T. (2010, September). Automatic weed detection and treatment in grasslands. Proceedings of ELMAR, 2010 PROCEEDINGS (pp. 65-68). IEEE.

Shirzadifar, A. M. (2013). Automatic Weed Detection System and Smart Herbicide Sprayer Robot for com fields, 468–473.

Siddiqi, M. H., Ahmad, I., & Sulaiman, S. B. (2009, March). Edge link detector based weed classifier. Proceedings of *Digital Image Processing, 2009 International Conference on* (pp. 255-259). IEEE. doi:10.1109/ICDIP.2009.64

Siddiqi, M. H., Ahmad, I., & Sulaiman, S. B. (2009b). Weed Recognition Based on Erosion and Dilation Segmentation Algorithm. Proceedings of *2009 International Conference on Education Technology and Computer* (pp. 224–228). doi:10.1109/ICETC.2009.62

Tellaeche, A., BurgosArtizzu, X. P., Pajares, G., & Ribeiro, A. (2007). A Vision-based Classifier in Precision Agriculture Combining Bayes and Support Vector Machines. Proceedings of *2007 IEEE International Symposium on Intelligent Signal Processing*, 1–6. doi:10.1109/WISP.2007.4447561

Tewari, V. K., Kumar, A. A., Nare, B., Prakash, S., & Tyagi, A. (2014a). Microcontroller based roller contact type herbicide applicator for weed control under row crops. *Computers and Electronics in Agriculture, 104*, 40–45. doi:10.1016/j.compag.2014.03.005

Tewari, V. K., Kumar, A. A., Nare, B., Prakash, S., & Tyagi, A. (2014b). Microcontroller based roller contact type herbicide applicator for weed control under row crops. *Computers and Electronics in Agriculture, 104*, 40–45. doi:10.1016/j.compag.2014.03.005

Weed Science Society of Pakistan. (n. d.). Retrieved from http://en.wikipedia.org/wiki/file:Pakistan_agriculture.png

Weiss, U., Biber, P., Laible, S., Bohlmann, K., & Zell, A. (2010, December). Plant species classification using a 3d lidar sensor and machine learning. Proceedings of *Machine Learning and Applications (ICMLA), 2010 Ninth International Conference on* (pp. 339-345). IEEE.

Xanthium strumarium, (1998), (1996), 6–38.

KEY TERMS AND DEFINITIONS

Artificial Neural Network: ANN is a system which processes information that has certain common performance characteristics with biological neural system.

Edge Detection: It is a type of image segmentation techniques which determines the presence of an edge or line in an image and outlines them in an appropriate way .The main purpose of edge detection is to simplify the image data in order to minimize the amount of data to be processed.

Fuzzy Inference System: This function creates new FIS structures. newfis has up to seven input arguments, and the output argument is a FIS structure. FIS contains seven arguments such as fis name, fis type, method and range.

Fuzzy Logic: Fuzzy logic uses linguistic information obtained from domain experts. It deals with overlapping values.

Membership Function: The graphical demonstration of scale participation of every input is known as membership function. It assigns a weighting to each of the inputs being processed, elaborates functional overlap between various inputs, and finally signifies an output response.

Parse Rules: Parse rule is the function that is used in FIS structure. There are three formats of rules (symbolic, verbose and indexed).

Weed Detection: Identification of weeds (unwanted plants).

Chapter 16
A Supervised Learning Model for AGV Perception in Unstructured Environment

Rizwan Aqeel
University Institute of Information Technology, Pakistan

Saif Ur Rehman
University Institute of Information Technology, Pakistan

Saira Gillani
Corvinus University of Budapest, Hungary

Sohail Asghar
COMSATS Institute of Information Technology, Pakistan

ABSTRACT

This chapter focuses on an Autonomous Ground Vehicle (AGV), also known as intelligent vehicle, which is a vehicle that can navigate without human supervision. AGV navigation over an unstructured road is a challenging task and is known research problem. This chapter is to detect road area from an unstructured environment by applying a proposed classification model. The Proposed model is sub divided into three stages: (1) - preprocessing has been performed in the initial stage; (2) - road area clustering has been done in the second stage; (3) - Finally, road pixel classification has been achieved. Furthermore, combination of classification as well as clustering is used in achieving our goals. K-means clustering algorithm is used to discover biggest cluster from road scene, second big cluster area has been classified as road or non road by using the well-known technique support vector machine. The Proposed approach is validated from extensive experiments carried out on RGB dataset, which shows that the successful detection of road area and is robust against diverse road conditions such as unstructured nature, different weather and lightening variations.

DOI: 10.4018/978-1-4666-8513-0.ch016

INTRODUCTION

An AGV is a kind of vehicle having ability to navigate autonomously (Wit et al., 2004). An AGV comprises of four major interrelated components (Crane et al., 2007), (a) - Perception; (b) - Planning; (c) -Control; (d) - Intelligence. Of all the four components, perception is the most vital component as it detects, classify, track and predict the future position of different objects of environment such as road, obstacle, pedestrian, etc. (Ilas, 2013). As it can be seen from **Figure 1.**

Accurate detection, classification, tracking and prediction guarantee safe navigation of an AGV from the source towards the destination and can be helpful in avoidance of accidents and collisions of an AGV. The Road is an important object of the environment where AGV navigates to reach its destination. Road detection has gained researcher's attention in recent years as an important research problem because of complex environmental conditions like cloudy or rainy weather, muddy roads, shadows, unstructured road and night time driving etc.

Research contributions have productively achieved for road detection based on data mining techniques in recent decades. During the road detection, pattern identification and classification is needed and according to (Laskshmi and Raghunandhan., 2011) data mining is the process of discovering patterns. In (Maurya et al., 2011), (Song and Civco., 2004), (Qin et al., 2013), (Wen Hung., 2013), different data mining techniques such as support vector machine, Bayesian, k-means clustering and artificial neural network has been used for solving road detection problem. Some research works (Vitor et al., 2013), (Shang et al., 2013) even examines this problem under diverse conditions like rainy, sunny or cloudy weather. Existing approaches are based on features, activity and model for the road detection, which are successful under given and specific road conditions, however, these algorithms likely to perform poorly as the road condition changes.

Figure 1. Perception phase of AGV

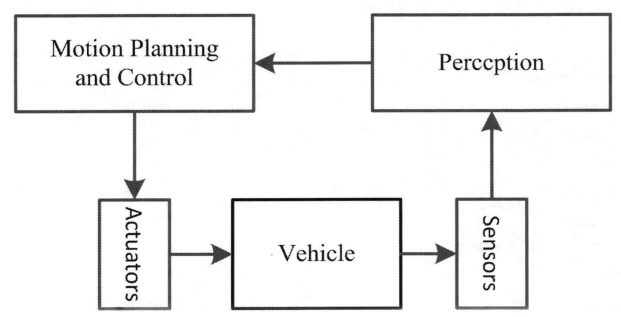

Numerous rural roads do not have sharp, smoothly curving edges and a uniform surface appearance which affects the performance and accuracy issues in traditional vision-based road-following methods. Different rural region's roads do not have sharp, smoothly curving edges and a consistent surface emergence which prevents the accomplishment of traditional vision-based road-following methods. Also, thorough lighting fluctuations and weather conditions make the problem more complex. Among common algorithms, features are the most important factors to distinguish the road surface from the background. But in actual unstructured environments, especially when affected by varying weather and lighting conditions, road surfaces are variable and existing algorithms have poor results. There are some problems in unstructured road detection: (i) Features in the same scene appear different under different weather conditions and variable lighting conditions, and they cannot be matched accurately. (ii) The same attribute of a feature seem appear in both the road surface and background. As shown in Figures 2 and 3.

Given a set of sensing devices, i.e. LADAR, IRs, RGB Camera mounted over AGV with their captured data, it is required to detect unstructured road area, generate a classified output (road/non road).

The purpose of this chapter is to provide a classification model for unmarked roads, marking lane segments with lanes based on the road size information and once we have correct lane segments of unmarked roads.

Figure 2. Structured road

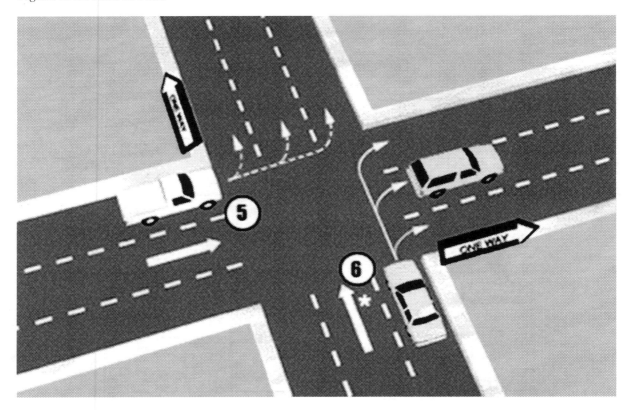

Figure 3. Unstructured road

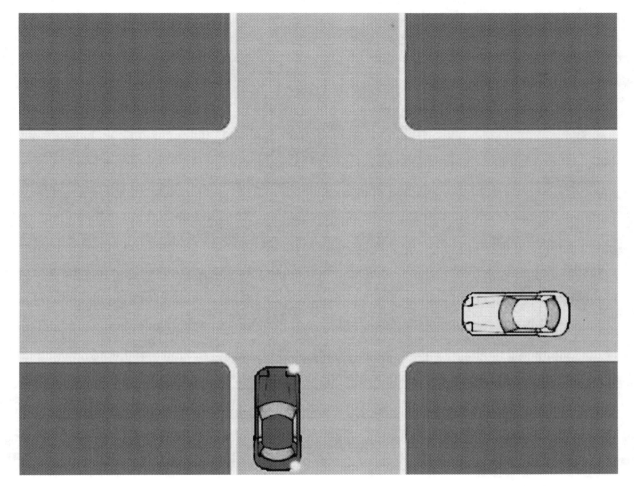

Literature Review of Existing Methodologies

The primary objective of this section is to review the literature on existing techniques and methodologies for data classification using supervised learning generally during the perception phase of autonomous system's working.

There is a significant contribution of Data mining in the field of an Autonomous Ground Vehicle (AGV) which is one of the progressing fields today. Before discussing certain domain (AGV) problems it is necessary to briefly describe AGV, its common components and their interaction to carry out its sensing and navigating tasks.

An AGV is capable of intelligently navigating through various terrains under dynamic physical conditions and environments. For this purpose the vehicle uses different types of sensors, that is, LADAR (Laser Detection and Ranging), IR (Infrared) and (RGB) camera. The LADAR uses optical sensing technology, which detects the presence of environmental objects such as cars, obstacles, pedestrian and cyclists from the vehicle. The (RGB) camera is used for electronic motion video/picture acquisition to collect real world data and make high level decisions on the basis of that data, for example, to detect road area for safe navigation of AGV from source to destination. In detail after getting the data from multiple sensors the AGV makes use of the classification technique/method on the image/signal to detect the presence of road area. Based on the road detection result (s), the AGV may decide to move in the same direction, maintaining the same speed or it may change any or both of these or may even stop. Here some research contributions are discussed that laid the ground for general AGV architecture.

An AGV is normally of a particular size and it is possible for it to detect navigational area ahead of it. The unstructured environment makes road detection a challenging research problem because in the real world we may encounter cases like broken, muddy, snowy and flooded roads, roads with some smooth and some rough surface, urban roads with some muddy portion, or urban with some rural portion. This real scenario can affect identification of road.

Initially we discuss the important research contributions in order to resolve certain issues regarding unstructured road detection. The justification of discussing these techniques is because of their prime importance.

In an effort to resolve the problem of road detection while traveling in unstructured environments and having no prior knowledge of the appearance of the ground or location, Maurya et al. (2011) proposed an independent technique based on K Mean clustering, which filters the area having the same road features.

Naturally terrains exist with distinct ground and atmospheric conditions that need to be identified and classified while an AGV is navigating through them. Features such as AVG of RGV values, histogram of RGB values, histogram of difference of RGB values, advanced RGB value and advance RGB values are used extensively by different research authors in order to find unstructured road area but few of research authors has explained the reason to choose such features. Shang et al. (2012) devised a way to decide which features are more important, so the author has used Support vector machine to analyze the importance of each feature during the process of road detection. Afterwards a novel algorithm has been proposed based on hybrid features which are important for road detection. Similarly, many other contributions such as Zhou et al. (2007) consider the problem of road detection under rapidly changing environment. A self learning, adapting and classification based algorithm has been provided. Their approach is capable of automatically updating its training data based on the road environment condition that makes the algorithm dynamic under diverse road condition. However, the updating of training data for every road condition has a dramatic effect on the performance of the proposed approach.

Some kind of natural processes raises different environmental changes. These changes may alter road detection and classification approach because road type and its conditions have also been changed. Liu et al., (2014) has been achieved under unfavorable road conditions such as fuzzy edges, change in ambient light and shadows road side. FCM (Fuzzy Clustering Means) Algorithm has been used for road detection as the author considers road detection as a pixel clustering problem. FCM has been applied under four different road conditions. Results show that FCM is more robust for road detection when the road is distributed by shadow and lights. Color information is taken as a classification feature which makes it difficult to discriminate the shadows on the road from the road side objects. It does not deal with different light situations and also pay huge computation cost in shape of adaptive learning.

Above literature focuses to increase the road detection ability of AGV but different performance overheads are identified in the critical review. Different contributions focus either on AGV performance or its accuracy. There is always a tradeoff between these two objectives. We need an adjustable model in which based on our needs, we could increase performance while not compromising on accuracy or vice versa. By adding more sensors we could definitely increase accuracy and may probably be compromising on performance and vice versa could be achieved by having less number of sensors.

In (Gao, Song, & Yang, 2012) authors have presented a novel method for detecting drivable area on unstructured urban roads based on region growing using seed points. Experimental results shown by the author suggest that the proposed algorithm is effective under complex traffics scenes and stable for real time drivable road detection.

In (Kong, Audibert, & Ponce, 2010) authors have worked on the road parameter by identifying a road segment from one single image. The approach is based on road vanishing point estimation using a novel scheme called locally adaptive Soft Voting (LASV) algorithm.

Road detection based on color vision system has been proposed by Jill and Charles (Crisman & Thorpe, 1991) for unstructured roads. The authors have built a system named USCARF which uses pixel based clustering with similar colors and locations for road detection.

Alvarez et al., (Álvarez, López, Gevers, & Lumbreras, 2014), have considered high level cues such as color, vanishing points, Lane markings and road shapes for detection road. Propose method extracts information on the image and pixel level to obtain a diversified ensemble of cues which is used as input of probabilistic framework. The Author has acquired data set consisting of acquiring Geo referenced images using on board camera and a GPS antenna. A confidence map for road detection is presented (B. Wang, Frémont, & Rodríguez, 2014) that is based on likelihood theory that performs better on non flat road surface and over-saturation images.

A novel road detection approach based on super pixels and anisotropic heat diffusion has been proposed in (Xiao & Hu, 2014). Experimental results have shown that proposed algorithm is strong and robust for various kinds of road scenes like highway and urban.

An algorithm for estimating the road ahead of a host vehicle based on the measurements from several onboard sensors: such as a camera, a radar, wheel speed sensors, and an inertial measurement unit has been proposed by Garcia (Crane et al., 2007). The author has proposed a novel rat model that is more able to describe the road ahead with higher accuracy than the usual polynomial model.

A new road area detection method has proposed (Bui & Hieu, 2013) that is based on texture orientation estimation and vanishing point detection. This method first estimates a vanishing point using a texture-based soft voting algorithm proposed in our recent study. After that, texture orientations and color information are combined in order to generate a histogram for estimating two most dominant road borders. The area of road is defined as a region between the two detected road borders and below the estimated vanishing point. Their proposed method has been implemented and tested in 1000 road images which contain large variations in color, texture, lighting conditions and the surrounding environment.

Existing research approaches, considers structured environment for AGV navigation, but less consideration has been given to unstructured environment. If we consider road analysis, for instance, we can see that road with proper lanes has been considered for road detection, but in our case we are using unstructured road environment for road detection. As we can see from the classification model that it achieves unstructured road detection using clustering and classification. The presented classification model considers unstructured road detection which makes it novel from different earlier research approaches.

EXPERIMENTATIONS AND RECOMMENDATIONS

To resolve the issue of road detection under diverse conditions, we proposed a model named "Classification Model for Perception in AGV's (CMPA)" which is effective under rapidly changing road conditions. Rather than considering traditional approaches, our proposed model achieves road detection by

Figure 4. Supervised learning model for AGV perception

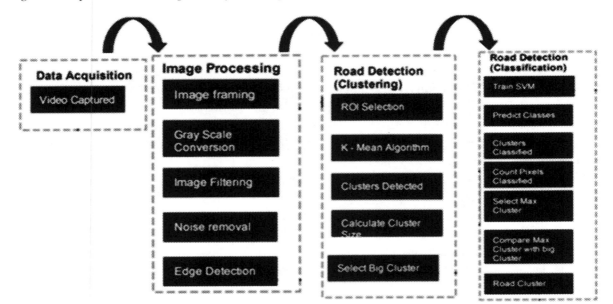

combining classification and clustering techniques, i.e. support vector machine (SVM) and K-Means Clustering Algorithm respectively. The Proposed model is mainly based on two steps, it first finds the big cluster among all the detected clusters ahead of the vehicle using K-Mean Clustering algorithm, secondly detected clusters are then passed to a trained classifier i.e Support vector Machines for road/ non road classification. As shown in **Figure 4.**

DATA ACQUISITION

For the first step real RGB dataset (recorded video) is given as input of diverse unstructured environments and selected random samples of images for applying our proposed algorithm in **Figure 5.**

IMAGE PROCESSING

After acquisition of real time data set of different unstructured environments, we did some basic image processing which is known as preprocessing (see **Figure 6.**) Preprocessing step includes noise removal from images, histogram equalization of gray scale values, applying filters. As shown in figure 6.

ROAD EXTRACTION

After preprocessing step, road extraction has been performed using the cluster based approach. Our road extraction approach is based upon two steps, by first selecting the biggest clusters from sample image and

Figure 5. Data acquisition

Figure 6. Image processing

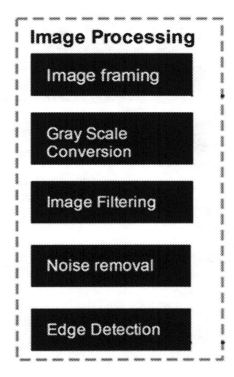

then classifying the pixels of the big cluster as road or non road pixels. As we know that during driving a car or any vehicle, there is 80% of the time, the road is in front of the vehicle horizontally and 20% of the times we can say we have something else then the road, so we need to detect the biggest cluster in front of the vehicle horizontally. To achieve this, we created a rectangular window horizontally and using image coordinates, we have extracted road area, i.e. the region of interest, from this eliminate another scene parameters such as sky, trees, etc. The selected region is known as Region of Interest i.e. ROI.As shown in **Figure 7.**

Furthermore, we have applied to an efficient clustering algorithm on our ROI for detecting of clusters of pixels. K-Mean clustering algorithm has been selected for finding different clusters from our region of interest. The k-means algorithm is applied to the dataset, returning k cluster centers. As shown in **Figure 8.**

Figure 7. Road detection clustering

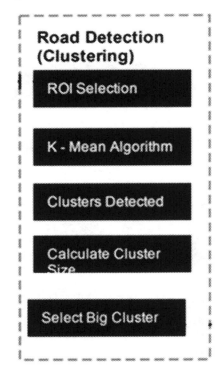

Figure 8. Road detection classification

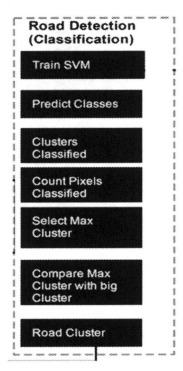

Once we have pixel clusters available, we need to estimate the size of every cluster by counting the number of pixels for each cluster, we selected the biggest cluster inside the pixel window.

In the final step of our model, we used the pixels of big clusters for classification as road or non road pixels. Support vector machines have been developed in the years 90 by the team of Vladimir Vapnik. They have been developed initially for the supervised classification, example of perception to linearly separate positive examples from the negative ones in different examples submitted to the analysis. Every example, must be represented by a vector of dimension n. The method searches the hyper plane that separates the two classes of examples. It guarantees that the margin between the nearest of positives and negatives is maximal. The interest of this approach is the selection of the Support Vectors that represents discriminative vectors with which are determined the hyper plan. The Examples used for research of the hyper plan are then useless and only these support vectors are used to analyze a new case. The trained classifier i.e. support vector machine is then applied to all pixels of clusters and turn the big cluster into classified cluster.

EXPERIMENTS, RESULTS, AND DISCUSSIONS

Experiments were performed on different selected images. The selected images were taken and basic image processing techniques have been applied to remove noise and enhance image quality. Later, the images were converted into grayscale images.

DATA ACQUISITION

Real time data has been acquired by mounting an RGB camera over a car on an unstructured highway road. As it can be seen from **Figure 9** that there are different environment objects exist, such as we have sign board in from of us, different cars are moving around in the environment, road pavements, road intersections, trees with having variable height and width. From all these existing road objects, we have to filter road area.

PREPROCESSING

Next, experiments were performed over the extracted frame, it is necessary to perform some image processing techniques over extracted frames in order to improve image quality. For improving the quality of the image for further analysis, different images in **Figure 10, Figure 11, and Figure 12** shown below display the enhancement techniques such as histogram equalization for enhancement of contrast, applying different filters for modifying or enhancing image features.

ROAD EXTRACTION (K-MEAN CLUSTERING)

Furthermore, we have applied K-Means clustering for finding different clusters. K-Mean is partitioning method of clustering, which partitions data into mutually exclusive clusters and returns the index of

Figure 9. Real time dataset

Figure 10. Video framing

the cluster to which it has assigned each observation. As shown in the **Figure 13.** After that, we have calculated the size of each cluster by counting the pixels of each cluster. As it can be seen from the below table, i.e.(**Table 1 Cluster and Sizes**) we have 3 clusters identified from our region of interest and

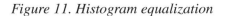

Figure 11. Histogram equalization

Figure 12. Image filtering

ROAD EXTRACTION (SUPPORT VECTOR MACHINE CLASSIFICATION)

Finally, we have applied support vector machine for classification of big cluster pixels. We have used binary svm classifier as our data set has only two classes' i.e. road or non road pixels. Following figure shows the results of our binary classifier.As shown in **Figure 14.**

Figure 13. Clusters Using K – Mean

Table 1. Clusters and sizes

Cluster No	Cluster Size
1	6979
2	20596
3	2875
Big Cluster	2nd
Total Number of Pixels	30750

Figure 14. SVM classification results

RESULTS FOR DIFFERENT DATA SET

Results shown on different data sets in below figures, i.e. shown in Figures 15 through 22.

CONCLUSION AND FUTURE WORK

In this chapter, a new classification model for improving perception phase of AGV has been proposed. Our classification model first processes the images by applying basic image processing techniques.

Figure 15. Results on snowy conditions

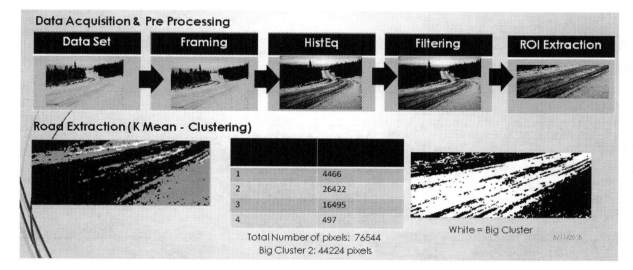

Figure 16. Results on muddy conditions

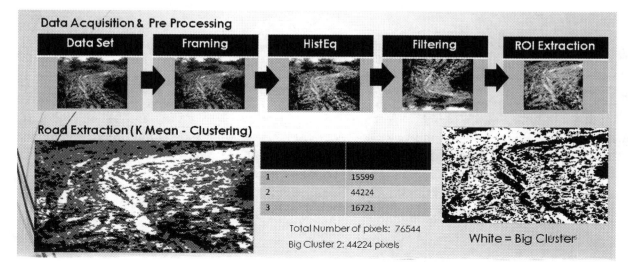

Figure 17. Results on poor lighting conditions

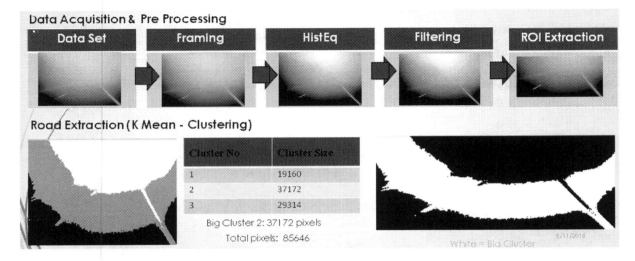

Figure 18. Results on bumpy, water, muddy conditions

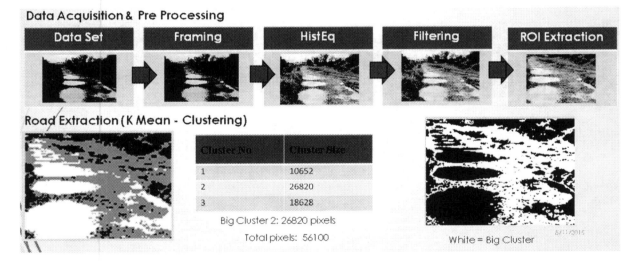

After that, achieves road extraction from images by applying first pixel clustering and then using a classifier to detect road pixels. In order to estimate the road size and segmenting the road, we applied pixel count and by setting the threshold value. After that we marked the road with proper road lane markings. The experimental results show that our model achieves the best results of road markings. Future work includes detection of obstacles for these segments and detection the vehicle segment and then guiding the vehicle to change his lane segment if it is in the obstacle segment.

Figure 19. Classification results

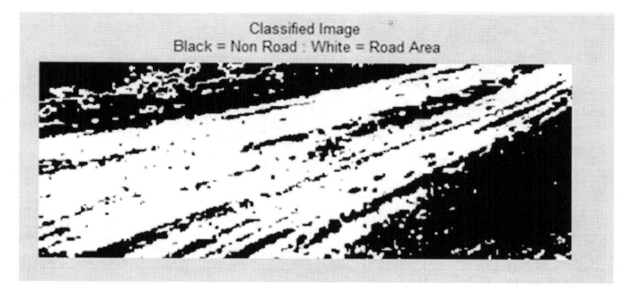

Figure 20. Classification results

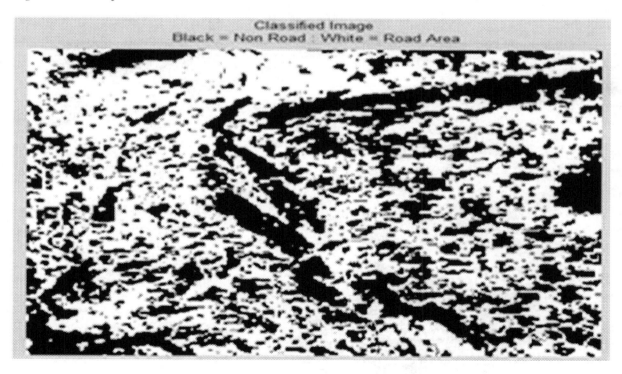

Figure 21. Classification results

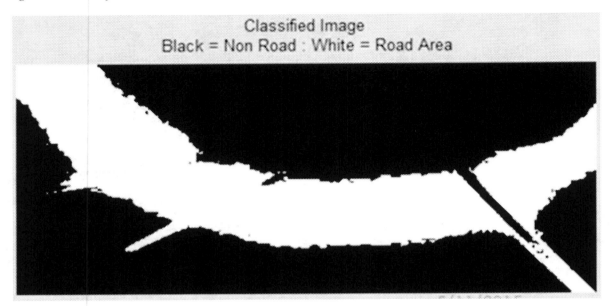

Figure 22. Classification results

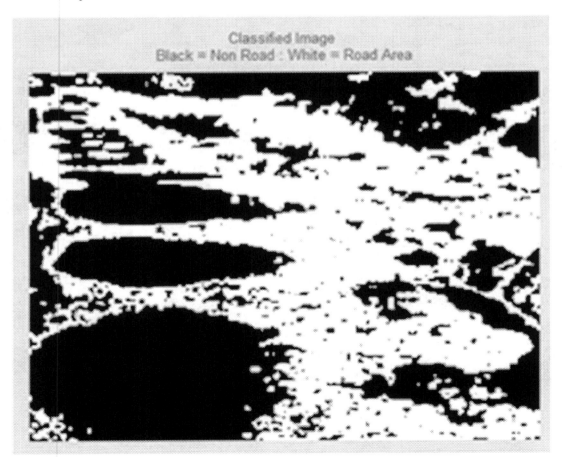

REFERENCES

Aizawa, T., Tanaka, A., Higashikage, H., Asokawa, Y., Kimachi, M., & Ogata, S. (2002). *Road surface estimation robust against vehicles' existence for stereo-based vehicle detection.* Paper presented at the Proceedings of the Intelligent Transportation Systems, 2002. doi:10.1109/ITSC.2002.1041186

Álvarez, J. M., López, A. M., Gevers, T., & Lumbreras, F. (2014). Combining priors, appearance, and context for road detection. *IEEE Transactions on Intelligent Transportation Systems, 15*(3), 1168–1178. doi:10.1109/TITS.2013.2295427

Benenson, R., Petti, S., Fraichard, T., & Parent, M. (2006). *Integrating perception and planning for autonomous navigation of urban vehicles.* Paper presented at the Intelligent Robots and Systems, 2006 IEEE/RSJ International Conference. doi:10.1109/IROS.2006.281806

Bui, & Hieu, T. (2013). *Road area detection based on texture orientations estimation and vanishing point detection.* Paper presented at the SICE Annual Conference. Nagoya, Japan.

Chen, H., Yin, L., & Ma, L. (2014). *Research on road information extraction from high resolution imagery based on global precedence.* Paper presented at the Earth Observation and Remote Sensing Applications (EORSA), 3rd International Workshop. doi:10.1109/EORSA.2014.6927868

Chiku, T., & Miura, J. (2012). *On-line road boundary estimation by switching multiple road models using visual features from a stereo camera.* Paper presented at the Intelligent Robots and Systems (IROS), IEEE/RSJ International Conference. doi:10.1109/IROS.2012.6385746

Coombs, D., Murphy, K., Lacaze, A., & Legowik, S. (2002, August 6). Driving Autonomously Off-road up to 35 km/h. Proceedings of the IEEE Intelligent Vehicles Symposium 2000, pp. (186–191). Dearborn, MI, USA.

Crane, C., Armstrong, D., Arroyo, A., Baker, A., Dankel, D., & Garcia, G. et al. (2007). Team gator nation's autonomous vehicle development for the 2007 DARPA Urban challenge. *Journal of Aerospace Computing, Information, and Communication, 4*(12), 1059–1085. doi:10.2514/1.33342

Crisman, J. D., & Thorpe, C. E. (1991). *Unscarf-a color vision system for the detection of unstructured roads.* Paper presented at the Robotics and Automation, 1991 IEEE International Conference. doi:10.1109/ROBOT.1991.132000

Gao, Y., Song, Y., & Yang, Z. (2012). *A real-time drivable road detection algorithm in urban traffic environment Computer Vision and Graphics* (pp. 387–396). Springer.

Ilas, C. (2013). *Perception in autonomous ground vehicles.* Paper presented at the Electronics, Computers and Artificial Intelligence (ECAI), 2013 International Conference

Kong, H., Audibert, J.-Y., & Ponce, J. (2010). General road detection from a single image. *Image Processing. IEEE Transactions on, 19*(8), 2211–2220.

Lalonde, J.-F., Vandapel, N., Huber, D. F., & Hebert, M. (2006). Natural terrain classification using three-dimensional ladar data for ground robot mobility. *Journal of Field Robotics, 23*(10), 839–861. doi:10.1002/rob.20134

Lorigo, L. M., Brooks, R. A. & Grimson, W. E. L. 1997. Visually-guided obstacle avoidance in unstructured environments Proceedings of the *IEEE Conference on Intelligent Robots and Systems.*

Moghadam, P., & Dong, J. F. (2012). *Road direction detection based on vanishing-point tracking.* Paper presented at the Intelligent Robots and Systems (IROS) 2012 IEEE/RSJ International Conference. doi:10.1109/IROS.2012.6386089

Naeem, M., Asghar, S., Irfan, S. R., & Fong, S. (2010). *Multilevel classification scheme for AGV perception.* Paper presented at the Advanced Information Management and Service (IMS) 2010 6th International Conference on.

Rahman, A., Verma, B., & Stockwell, D. (2012). *An hierarchical approach towards road image segmentation.* Paper presented at the Neural Networks (IJCNN) The 2012 International Joint Conference on. doi:10.1109/IJCNN.2012.6252403

Serfling, M., Schweiger, R., & Ritter, W. (2008). *Road course estimation in a night vision application using a digital map, a camera sensor and a prototypical imaging radar system.* Paper presented at the 2008 Intelligent Vehicles Symposium. doi:10.1109/IVS.2008.4621312

Shashidhara, H., & Aswath, A. (2014). *A Novel Approach to Circular Edge Detection for Iris Image Segmentation.* Paper presented at the 2014 Fifth International Conference. doi:10.1109/ICSIP.2014.56

Tanzmeister, G., Friedl, M., Lawitzky, A., Wollherr, D., & Buss, M. (2013). *Road course estimation in unknown, structured environments.* Paper presented at the Intelligent Vehicles Symposium (IV). doi:10.1109/IVS.2013.6629537

Velat, S. J., Lee, J., Johnson, N., & Crane III, C.D. (2007). Vision Based Vehicle Localization for Autonomous Navigation. *Computational Intelligence in Robotics and Automation.* Jacksonville, FI

Waghule, D. R., & Ochawar, R. S. (2014). *Overview on Edge Detection Methods.* Paper presented at the Electronic Systems, Signal Processing and Computing Technologies (ICESC), 2014 International Conference. doi:10.1109/ICESC.2014.31

Wan, Y., Jia, S., & Wang, D. (2013). *Edge Detection Algorithm Based on Grey System Theory Combined with Directed Graph.* Paper presented at the Image and Graphics (ICIG), 2013 Seventh International Conference. doi:10.1109/ICIG.2013.42

Wang, B., Frémont, V., & Rodríguez, S. A. (2014). *Color-based road detection and its evaluation on the KITTI road benchmark.* Paper presented at the Intelligent Vehicles Symposium Proceedings, 2014 IEEE. doi:10.1109/IVS.2014.6856619

Wang, Y., Ewert, D., Schilberg, D., & Jeschke, S. (2013). *Edge extraction by merging 3D point cloud and 2D image data.* Paper presented at the Emerging Technologies for a Smarter World (CEWIT), 2013 10th International Conference and Expo. doi:10.1007/978-3-319-08816-7_61

Xiao, D., & Hu, X. (2014). *Road detection based on superpixels and anisotropic heat diffusion.* Paper presented at the Digital Information and Communication Technology and it's Applications (DICTAP), 2014 Fourth International Conference. doi:10.1109/DICTAP.2014.6821724

Zhang, L., Zhou, W.-H., & Liu, J.-L. (2007). *A robust road segmentation method.* Paper presented at the Wavelet Analysis and Pattern Recognition, 2007. ICWAPR'07. International Conference. doi:10.1109/ICWAPR.2007.4420799

KEY TERMS AND DEFINITIONS

Autonomous Ground Vehicle: It is an unmanned ground vehicle, having driven capabilities, but physically no driver exists. It navigates from source to destination using planning, control, perception and intelligence elements.

Image Filtering: Image filtering is a technique used to enhance the image quality. Generally image filtering is performed to emphasize certain features of the image.

K Mean Clustering: Clustering is an unsupervised learning technique in which instances have no class labels prior. Clustering algorithm generally learns and builds model by itself and provide class labels to newly instances.

Pixels: Smallest image element from image is formed. A pixel can be located by its address based on screen coordinates.

Support Vector Machines: Classification technique used to find class of a provided instance. Generally, support vectors build a hype plane having a maximum width which is actually the max distance between the two classes of data.

Unstructured Environment: A kind of environment having no proper parameters for driving such as cracks, poor light, rain, no proper lanes and road edges etc.

354

Compilation of References

Abdullah, U., Ahmed, A., & Sawar, M. J. (2012). Knowledge Representation and Knowledge Editor of a Medical Claim. *Journal of Basic and Applied Scientific Research, 2*(2), 1373–1384.

Abdullah, U., Ahmed, A., Asghar, S., & Zafar, K. (2014). Record-Couple Based Production Rule Mining Algorithm : Tested in Medical Billing Domain. *Journal of Applied Environmental and Biological Sciences, 4*(8S), 275–280.

Abdullah, U., Jamil Sawar, M., & Ahmed, A. (2009). Comparative Study of Medical Claim Scrubber and a Rule Based System. Proceedings *2009 International Conference on Information Engineering and Computer Science* (pp. 1–4). Wuhan, China. doi: doi:10.1109/ICIECS.2009.5363668

Abdullah, U., Sawar, M. J., & Ahmed, A. (2009). Design of a Rule Based System Using Structured Query Language. Proceedings of *2009 Eighth IEEE International Conference on Dependable, Autonomic and Secure Computing* (pp. 223–228). doi:10.1109/DASC.2009.78

Abro, Q. M. M., Bhutto, A. & Memon, N. A. (2011). Customer's perceptions on e-banking: a case study of HBL Jamshoro. *Mehran university research journal of engineering & technology*, 30(4), 681-688.

Acharjya, D. P. (2009). Comparative study of rough sets on fuzzy approximation spaces and intuitionistic fuzzy approximation spaces. *International Journal of Computational and Applied Mathematics, 4*(2), 95–106.

Acharjya, D. P., & Mary, A. G. (2014). Privacy Preservation in Information System. In B. Tripathy & D. Acharjya (Eds.), *Advances in Secure Computing, Internet Services, and Applications* (pp. 49–72). Hershey, PA: IGI Global; doi:10.4018/978-1-4666-4940-8.ch003

Acharjya, D. P., & Tripathy, B. K. (2008). Rough sets on fuzzy approximation spaces and applications to distributed knowledge systems. *International Journal of Artificial Intelligence and Soft Computing, 1*(1), 1–14. doi:10.1504/IJAISC.2008.021260

Acharjya, D. P., & Tripathy, B. K. (2009). Rough sets on intuitionistic fuzzy approximation spaces and knowledge representation. *International Journal of Artificial Intelligence and Computational Research, 1*(1), 29–36.

Adeli, H., & Panakkat, A. (2009). A probabilistic neural network for earthquake magnitude prediction. *Neural Networks, 22*(7), 1018–1024. doi:10.1016/j.neunet.2009.05.003 PMID:19502005

Aggarwal, C., & Yu, P. (2001). Outlier Detection for High Dimensional Data.*Proc. of the ACM SIGMOD International Conference on Management of Data.*

Agrawal, R. M., Heikki; Srikant, Ramakrishnan; Toivonen, Hannu; Verkamo, A. Inkeri. (1997). Fast Discovery of Association Rules. *Artificial Intelligence.*

Ahmad, W., & Narayanan, A. (2010). Humoral-mediated Clustering. Proceedings of the IEEE 5th International Conference on Bio-Inspired Computing: Theories and Applications (BIC-TA 2010) (pp. 1471-1481). doi:10.1109/BICTA.2010.5645279

Ahmad, W., & Narayanan, A. (2010e). Outlier Detection using Humoral-mediated Clustering. *Proceedings of IEEE World Congress on Nature and Biologically Inspired Computing* (pp. 45-52).

Ahmad, S. (2013). Web Mining Pedagogy: The Theoretical Support. *International Journal of Computing. Intelligent and Communication Technologies, 2*, 17–22.

Ahmed, A., Zafar, K., Siddiqui, A. B., & Abdullah, U. (2013). Data warehouse design for knowledge discovery from healthcare data. *Proceedings of the World Congress on Engineering* (Vol. III, pp. 1589–1594). London, UK.

Ahmed, A., Abdullah, U., & Sawar, M. J. (2010). Software Architecture of a Learning Apprentice System in Medical Billing.*Proceedings of the World Congress on Engineering 2010* (Vol. I, pp. 52–56). London, UK.

Aizawa, T., Tanaka, A., Higashikage, H., Asokawa, Y., Kimachi, M., & Ogata, S. (2002). *Road surface estimation robust against vehicles' existence for stereo-based vehicle detection.* Paper presented at the Proceedings of the Intelligent Transportation Systems, 2002. doi:10.1109/ITSC.2002.1041186

Akaike, H. (1973). Information theory and an extension of the maximum likelihood principle.*Proc 2nd Inter Symposium of Information Theory* (pp. 267-281).

Akaike, H. (1974). A new look at the statistical model identification. *IEEE Transactions on Automatic Control, 19*(6), 716–723. doi:10.1109/TAC.1974.1100705

Akaike, H. (1978). On the likelihood of time series model. *The Statistician, 27*(3/4), 217–235. doi:10.2307/2988185

Akhtar, M. H. (2002). X-efficiency Analysis of Commercial Banks in Pakistan: A Preliminary Investigation. *Pakistan Development Review*, 567–580.

Aladwani, A. M. (2001). Online banking: A field study of drivers, development challenges, and expectations. *International Journal of Information Management, 21*(3), 213–225. doi:10.1016/S0268-4012(01)00011-1

Alarifi, A. S. N., Alarifi, N. S. N., & Al-Humidan, S. (2012). Earthquakes magnitude predication using artificial neural network in northern Red Sea area. *Journal of King Saud University – Science, 24*, 301–313.

Ali, A., Streibig, J. C., & Andreasen, C. (2013). Yield loss prediction models based on early estimation of weed pressure. *Crop Protection (Guildford, Surrey), 53*, 125–131. doi:10.1016/j.cropro.2013.06.010

Al-Sheshtawi, K. A., Abdul-Kadir, H. M., & Ismail, A. A. (2010). Artificial Immune Clonal Selection Algorithms: A Comparative Study of CLONALG, opt-IA and BCA with Numerical Optimization Problems. *International Journal of Computer Science and Network Security, 10*(4), 24–30.

Álvarez, J. M., López, A. M., Gevers, T., & Lumbreras, F. (2014). Combining priors, appearance, and context for road detection. *IEEE Transactions on Intelligent Transportation Systems, 15*(3), 1168–1178. doi:10.1109/TITS.2013.2295427

Andalib, A., Zare, M., & Atry, F. (2009). A fuzzy expert system for earthquake prediction, case study: the Zagros range. *Proceedings of the Third International Conference on Modeling, Simulation and Applied Optimization.* Sharjah, U.A.E.

Anderson, G. (2009). Random Relational Rules [PhD thesis].

Anderson, C. (2006). *The Long Tail: Why the Future of Business Is Selling Less of More.* Hyperion.

Andújar, D., Escolà, A., Rosell-Polo, J. R., Fernández-Quintanilla, C., & Dorado, J. (2013). Potential of a terrestrial LiDAR-based system to characterise weed vegetation in maize crops. *Computers and Electronics in Agriculture, 92*, 11–15. doi:10.1016/j.compag.2012.12.012

Antunes, C. M., & Oliveira, A. L. (2001). Temporal data mining: Proceedings of the KDD Workshop on Temporal Data Mining

Appice, A., Ceci, M., & Malerba, D. (2003). MR-SMOTI: A Data Mining System for Regression Tasks Tightly-Coupled with a Relational Database. *Proceedings of KDID-2003*.

Aragon, V. S., Esquivel, S. C., & Coello, C. A. C. (2010). Artificial Immune System for Solving Global Optimization Problems. *Inteligencia Artificial, 46*, 3–16. doi: doi:10.4114/ia.v14i46.1500

Aragon, V. S., Esquivel, S. C., & Coello, C. A. C. (2011). A T-cell Algorithm for Solving Dynamic Optimization Problems. *Information Sciences, 181*(17), 3614–3637. doi:10.1016/j.ins.2011.04.028

Aragon, V. S., Esquivel, S. C., & Coello, E. S. (2007). Artificial Immune System for Solving Constrained Optimization Problems. *Intelligencia Artificial, 11*(35), 55–66.

Arasu, A., Babu, S., & Widom, J. (2002). *An Abstract Semantics and Concrete Language for Continuous Queries over Streams and Relations*. Stanford. Retrieved from http://ilpubs.stanford.edu:8090/563/

Arauzo-Azofra, A., Aznarte, J. L., & Benítez, J. M. (2011). Empirical study of feature selection methods based on individual feature evaluation for classification problems. *Expert Systems with Applications, 38*(7), 8170–8177. doi:10.1016/j.eswa.2010.12.160

Ardalan, A., Hajiuni, A., & Zare, M. (2013). Aftershocks following the 9 April 2013 Bushehr earthquake, Iran. *PLoS Currents, 5*. doi: doi:10.1371/currents.dis.76750ede500e61b81d7f2ba9edfb2373 PMID:24042232

Arning, A., Agrawal, R., & Raghavan, P. (1996). A Linear Method for Deviation Detection in Large Databases. *Proc. of 1996 Int. Conf. Data Mining and Knowledge Discovery (KDD'96)* (pp. 164–169). Portland, OR.

Asghari, H., Eeten, M. J. G. V., Arnbak, A. M., & Eijk, N. A. N. M. V. (2012). Security Economics in the HTTPS Value Chain. *Proceedings of TPRC 2012: The research conference on communication, information and internet policy*.

Asghar, S., Alahakoon, D., & Hsu, A. (2004). Enhancing OLAP functionality using self-organizing neural networks. *Neural. Parallel & Scientific Computations, 12*(1), 1–20.

Astel, A., Astel, K., & Biziuk, M. (2008). PCA and multidimensional visualization techniques united to aid in the bioindication of elements from transplanted Sphagnum palustre moss exposed in the Gdansk City area. *Environmental Science and Pollution Research International, 15*(1), 41–50. doi:10.1065/espr2007.05.422 PMID:18306887

Asuncion, A., & Newman, D. J. (2007). UCI Machine Learning Repository Irvine, CA: University of California, School of Information and Computer Science Blum, A. L., & Langley, P. (1997). Selection of relevant features and examples in machine learning. *Artificial Intelligence, 97*(1–2), 245–271.

Asuncion, A., & Newman, D. J. (2010). *UCI machine learning repository*. Irvine, CA: University of California, School of Information and Computer Science.

Atanasov, K. T. (1986). Intuitionistic Fuzzy Sets. *Fuzzy Sets and Systems, 20*(1), 87–96. doi:10.1016/S0165-0114(86)80034-3

Atkins, B., & Huang, W. (n. d.). A study of social Engineering in Online Frauds. *Open Journal of Social Sciences, 1*, 23–32.

Atramentov, A. (2003). *Multi-relational decision tree algorithm - implementation and experiments*. Ames, Iowa: Iowa State University.

Ayara, M., Timmis, J., de Lemos, R., & Forrest, S. (2005). Immunising Automated Teller Machines. In C. Jacob, M. Pilat, P. J. Bentley, & J. I. Timmis (Eds.), Artificial Immune Systems (pp. 404-417). doi:10.1007/11536444_31

Aydin, I., Karakose, M., & Akin, E. (2009). The prediction algorithm based on fuzzy logic using time series data mining method. *Proceedings of World Academy of Science: Engineering & Technology.*

Bai, L., Gao, B., Tian, S., Cheng, Y., Chen, Y., Tian, G. Y., & Woo, W. L. (2013). A comparative study of principal component analysis and independent component analysis in eddy current pulsed thermography data processing. *The Review of Scientific Instruments*, *84*(10), 104901. doi:10.1063/1.4823521 PMID:24182145

Baloach, Q. B., Khan, M. I., & Alam, A. (2008). Online Banking Services: A Comparative Study of Islamic and Conventional Banks of Pakistan. *Journal of Managerial Sciences*, *IV*, 67–95.

Banstola, A. (2007). Prospects and Challenges of E-banking in Nepal. *The Journal of Nepalese Business Studies*, *IV*, 96–104.

Bargh, J. A. & Mckenna, K. Y. A. (2004). *The internet and social life.*

Bari, P. & Chawan, P. M. (2013). Web Usage Mining. *Journal of Engineering, Computers & Applied Sciences (JEC&AS)*, 2.

Barricelli, N. A. (1954). Esempinumerici di processi di evoluzione. *Methodos*, 45–68

Barth, A., Jackson, C., & Mitchell, J. C. (2008). Robust defenses for cross-site request forgery. Proceedings of the 15th ACM conference on Computer and communications security (pp. 75-88). New York.

Benenson, R., Petti, S., Fraichard, T., & Parent, M. (2006). *Integrating perception and planning for autonomous navigation of urban vehicles.* Paper presented at the Intelligent Robots and Systems, 2006 IEEE/RSJ International Conference. doi:10.1109/IROS.2006.281806

Berendt, B., Mobasher, B. & Spiliopoulou, M. (2002). Web Usage Mining for E-Business Application. *ECML/PKDD-2002 Tutorial.*

Bhasin, D. M. L. 2006. Data Mining: A Competitive Tool in the Banking and Retail Industries. *Banking and Finance*, 7.

Binitha, S., & Sathya, S. (2012) A Survey of Bio-inspired Optimization Algorithms, *International Journal of Soft Computing and Engineering (IJSCE)*, 2(2), 137-151

Blockeel, H. (1998). *Top-Down Induction of First Order Logical Decision Trees.*

Blockeel, H., Raedt, L.D. (1998). TILDE-RT: Top-down induction of First-order logical decision trees. *Artificial Intelligence, 1-2*(101). Bongard Dataset.

Bongard, M. M. (1968). *The Recognition Problem.* DTIC Document.

Bornea, M. A., Deligiannakis, A., Kotidis, Y., & Vassalos, V. (2011). Semi-Streamed Index Join for near-real time execution of ETL transformations. *IEEE 27th International Conference on Data Engineering (ICDE'11)* (pp. 159–170). doi: doi:10.1109/ICDE.2011.5767906

Bradford, J. P., Clayton, K., Ron, K., Cliff, B., & Carla, E. B. (1998). Pruning Decision Trees with Misclassification Costs. Machine Learning ECML-98. *Lecture Notes in Computer Science*, *1398*, 131–136. doi:10.1007/BFb0026682

Brank, J., Grobelnik, M., Milic-Frayling, N., & Mladenic, D. (2002). Interaction of Feature selection Methods and Linear Classification Models. *Proceedings of the ICML-02 Workshop on Text Learning.*

Bredel, M., Bredel, C., Juric, D., Harsh, G. R., Vogel, H., & Recht, L. D. et al. (2005). Functional Network Analysis Reveals Extended Gliomagenesis Pathway Maps and Three Novel MYC-Interacting Genes in Human Gliomas. *Cancer Research, 65*(19), 8679–8689. doi:10.1158/0008-5472.CAN-05-1204 PMID:16204036

Breiman, L. (1994). Bagging predictors [Technical Report 421]. *University of California at Berkeley.*

Breiman, L. (2001). Random forests. *Machine Learning, 45*(1), 5–32. doi:10.1023/A:1010933404324

Breunig, M. M., Kriegel, H. P., Ng, R. T., & Sander, J. (2000). LOF: Identifying density-based local outliers. *Proc. of the 2000 ACM SIGMOD International Conference on Management of Data* (pp. 93-104). Dallas. doi:10.1145/342009.335388

Brighton, H., & Mellish, C. (2002). Advances in Instance Selection for Instance-Based Learning Algorithms. *Data Mining and Knowledge Discovery, 6*(2), 153–172. doi:10.1023/A:1014043630878

Brill, F. Z., Brown, D. E., & Martin, W. N. (1990). *Genetic algorithms for feature selection for counter propagation networks.* Technical Report. No.IPC-TR-90-004. Charlottesville, VA: University of Virginia, Institute of Parallel Computation

Brotherton, T. W., & Simpson, P. K. (1995). Dynamic feature set training of neural nets for classification. In McDonnell, J.R., Reynolds, R.G., & Fogel, D.B. (Eds.), Evolutionary Programming IV. 83-94. Cambridge, MA: MIT Press

Brownlee, J. (2005). Clonal Selection Theory and CLONALG: The Clonal Selection Classification Algorithm (CSCA). Technical Report 2-02, CISCP, Swinburne University of Technology.

Brunswick, S. (2009). eCommerce fraud – time to act? *Card Technology Today, 21*(1), 12–13. doi:10.1016/S0965-2590(09)70019-2

Buddhinath, G. & Derry, D. (n. d.). A Simple Enhancement to One Rule Classification. *Department of Computer Science & Software Engineering University of Melbourne.*

Bui, & Hieu, T. (2013). *Road area detection based on texture orientations estimation and vanishing point detection.* Paper presented at the SICE Annual Conference. Nagoya, Japan.

Bullock, A. D., Hassell, A., Markham, W. A., Wall, D. W., & Whitehouse, A. B. (2009). How ratings vary by staff group in multi-source feedback assessment of junior doctors. *Medical Education, 43*(6), 516–520. doi:10.1111/j.1365-2923.2009.03333.x PMID:19493174

Burgos-Artizzu, X. P., Ribeiro, A., Guijarro, M., & Pajares, G. (2011). Real-time image processing for crop/weed discrimination in maize fields. *Computers and Electronics in Agriculture, 75*(2), 337–346. doi:10.1016/j.compag.2010.12.011

Bursa, M. (2013). *Ant-inspired Metaheuristics for Biomedical Data Mining* [PhD thesis]. Czech Technical University in Prague.

Busby, M., Burke, F., Matthews, R., Cyrta, J., & Mullins, A. (2012). The development of a concise questionnaire designed to measure perceived outcomes on the issues of greatest importance to patients. *British Dental Journal, 212*(8), E11–E11. doi:10.1038/sj.bdj.2012.315 PMID:22516922

Campbell, J., Ramsay, J., & Green, J. (2001). Age, gender, socioeconomic, and ethnic differences in patients' assessments of primary health care. *Quality in Health Care, 10*(2), 90–95. doi:10.1136/qhc.10.2.90 PMID:11389317

Cantú-Paz, E., & Kamath, C. (2001). On the Use of Evolutionary Algorithms in Data Mining. In H. A. Abbass, R. A. Sarker, & C. S. Newton (Eds.), Data Mining: A Heuristic Approach. Hershey: Idea Group Publishing.

Carl_Mays_II. (2008). *Don't Leave Money on the Table - Use a Claim Scrubber.* Retrieved from http://EzineArticles.com/?expert=Carl_Mays_II

Carroll, S. (2010). *From Eternity to Here: The Quest for the Ultimate Theory of Time*. USA: Dutton.

Castro, L. N. d. (2003). Artificial immune systems as a novel soft computing paradigm. *Soft Computing*, 7(8), 526-544.

Castro, L. N. d., & Timmis, J. (2002c). Artificial immune system: a new computational intelligence approach, 380. London: Springer-Verlag.

Castro, L. N. d., & Zuben, F. J. V. (2000). Artificial Immune Systems: Part II - A Survey of Applications [Technical Report - RT DCA 02/00]. Retrieved from ftp://ftp.dca.fee.unicamp.br/pub/docs/vonzuben/lnunes/rtdca0200.pdf

Castro, L. N. d., & Zuben, F. J. V. (2002). aiNet: An Artificial Immune Network for Data Analysis. In H. Abbass, R. Sarker, & C. Newton (Eds.), Data Mining: A Heuristic Approach, Idea Group Publishing. doi:, 231-260. doi:10.4018/978-1-930708-25-9.ch012

Castro, P. A. D., & Zuben, F. J. V. (2008). MOBAIS: A Bayesian Artificial Immune System for Multi-Objective Optimization. *Proceedings of the 7th International Conference*, 48-59.

Castro, L. N. d., & Timmis, J. (2002a). An Artificial Immune Network for Multimodal Function Optimisation.*Proceedings of IEEE World Congress on Evolutionary Computation*, 669-674.

Castro, L. N. d., & Zuben, J. (2000). The Clonal Selection Algorithm with Engineering Applications.*Workshop Proceedings of GECCO, Workshop on Artificial Immune Systems and Their Applications*, 36-37. Las Vegas.

Castro, P. A. D., & Zuben, F. J. V. (2009). BAIS: A Bayesian Artificial Immune System for the Effective Handling of Building Blocks. *Information Sciences*, 179(10), 1426–1440. doi:10.1016/j.ins.2008.11.040

Chakrabarti, B., Kumar, S., Singh, R., & Dimitrova, N. (2012). Genetic diversity and admixture patterns in Indian populations. *Gene*, 508(2), 250–255. doi:10.1016/j.gene.2012.07.047 PMID:22892377

Chakrabarti, T., Saha, S., & Sinha, D. (2013). A Cellular Automata Based DNA Pattern Classifier. *Biometrics and Bioinformatics*, 5(9), 1.

Chakraborty, A., & Singh, A. (2009). A partition-based approach to support streaming updates over persistent data in an active datawarehouse.*IPDPS '09: Proceedings of the 2009 IEEE International Symposium on Parallel & Distributed Processing* (pp. 1–11). Washington, DC, USA: IEEE Computer Society. doi: doi:10.1109/IPDPS.2009.5161064

Chamundeswari, G., Pardasaradhi Varma, G., & Satyanarayana, C. (2012). An experimental analysis of k-means using Matlab. *International Journal of Engineering Research & Technology*, 1(5), 1–5.

Chang, J. T., & Nevins, J. R. (2006). GATHER: A Systems Approach to Interpreting Genomic Signatures. *Bioinformatics (Oxford, England)*, 22(23), 2926–2933. doi:10.1093/bioinformatics/btl483 PMID:17000751

Chaniara, J. M., & Sherasiya, F. (2014). Survey on ameliorate data extraction in web mining by clustering the web log data. *Development*, 1(12).

Chelouah, R., & Siarry, P. (2000). Tabu Search applied to global optimization. *European Journal of Operational Research*, 123(2), 256–270. doi:10.1016/S0377-2217(99)00255-6

Chen, H., Yin, L., & Ma, L. (2014). *Research on road information extraction from high resolution imagery based on global precedence*. Paper presented at the Earth Observation and Remote Sensing Applications (EORSA), 3rd International Workshop. doi:10.1109/EORSA.2014.6927868

Chen, H., Liu, H., Han, J., Yin, X., & He, J. (2009). Exploring optimization of semantic relationship graph for multi-relational Bayesian classification. *Decision Support Systems*, 48(1), 112–121. doi:10.1016/j.dss.2009.07.004

Cheung, D. W., Zhou, B., Kao, B., Lu, H., Lam, T. W., & Ting, H. F. (1999, November). Requirement-based data cube schema design. In *Proceedings of the eighth international conference on Information and knowledge management* (pp. 162-169). New York, USA: ACM.

Chiku, T., & Miura, J. (2012). *On-line road boundary estimation by switching multiple road models using visual features from a stereo camera*. Paper presented at the Intelligent Robots and Systems (IROS), IEEE/RSJ International Conference. doi:10.1109/IROS.2012.6385746

Chun, S. J., Chung, C. W., Lee, J. H., & Lee, S. L. (2001, September). Dynamic update cube for range-sum queries. *Proceedings of 27th VLDB conference* (pp. 521-530).

ClusterMaker. (n. d.). Retrieved from http://www.cgl.ucsf.edu/cytoscape/cluster/clusterMaker.html

Console, R., Murru, M., & Catalli, F. (2006). Physical and stochastic models of earthquake clustering. *Tectonophysics*, *417*(1-2), 141–153. doi:10.1016/j.tecto.2005.05.052

Contandriopoulos, D., Champagne, F., & Denis, J.-L. (2014). The Multiple Causal Pathways Between Performance Measures' Use and Effects. *Medical Care Research and Review*, *71*(1), 3–20. doi:10.1177/1077558713496320 PMID:23877955

Coombs, D., Murphy, K., Lacaze, A., & Legowik, S. (2002, August 6). Driving Autonomously Off-road up to 35 km/h. Proceedings of the IEEE Intelligent Vehicles Symposium 2000, pp. (186–191). Dearborn, MI, USA.

Corban, G. R., Rachit, V., & Bader, J. S. (2010). NeMo: Network Module identification in Cytoscape. *BMC Bioinformatics*, *11*(Suppl 1), S61. doi:10.1186/1471-2105-11-S1-S61 PMID:20122237

Cordill, C., & Grift, T. E. (2011). Design and testing of an intra-row mechanical weeding machine for corn. *Biosystems Engineering*, *110*(3), 247–252. doi:10.1016/j.biosystemseng.2011.07.007

Cover, T. M., & Thomas, J. A. (2006). *Elements of information theory* (2nd ed.). Hoboken, N.J.: Wiley-Interscience.

Crane, C., Armstrong, D., Arroyo, A., Baker, A., Dankel, D., & Garcia, G. et al. (2007). Team gator nation's autonomous vehicle development for the 2007 DARPA Urban challenge. *Journal of Aerospace Computing, Information, and Communication*, *4*(12), 1059–1085. doi:10.2514/1.33342

Crisman, J. D., & Thorpe, C. E. (1991). *Unscarf-a color vision system for the detection of unstructured roads*. Paper presented at the Robotics and Automation, 1991 IEEE International Conference. doi:10.1109/ROBOT.1991.132000

Croker, J. E., Swancutt, D. R., Roberts, M. J., Abel, G. A., Roland, M., & Campbell, J. L. (2013). Factors affecting patients' trust and confidence in GPs: Evidence from the English national GP patient survey. *BMJ Open*, *3*(5), e002762. doi:10.1136/bmjopen-2013-002762 PMID:23793686

Cutello, V., Nicosia, G., & Pavone, M. (2004). Exploring the capability of immune algorithms: A characterization of hypermutation operators. *Proceedings of the Third International Conference on Artificial Immune System (ICARIS'04)*, 263-276. doi:10.1007/978-3-540-30220-9_22

Dasgupta, D., & Gonzalez, F. (2003). Artificial immune system (AIS) research in the last five years. *Proceedings of the Congress on Evolutionary Computation* (pp. 123 – 130). doi:10.1109/CEC.2003.1299565

Dash, M., & Liu, H. (1997). Feature selection for classification. *Intelligent Data Analysis*, *1*(1-4), 131–156. doi:10.1016/S1088-467X(97)00008-5

Dashore, P., & Jain, S. K. (2009). Fuzzy Rule Based System and Metagraph for Risk Management in Electronic Banking Activities. *IACSIT International Journal of Engineering and Technology*, *1*(1), 5. doi:10.7763/IJET.2009.V1.18

De Raedt, L. (2008). *Logical and relational learning*. Springer. doi:10.1007/978-3-540-68856-3

Dehaspe, L., & Toivonen, H. (1999). Discovery of frequent DATALOG patterns. *Data Mining and Knowledge Discovery*, *3*(1), 7–36. doi:10.1023/A:1009863704807

Desai, A. B., & Deshmukh, D. R. (2013). Data mining techniques for Fraud Detection. *International Journal of Computer Science and Information Technologies*, *3*, 1–4.

Dietterich, T. G. (1997). Machine Learning Research: *Four Current Directions. AI Magazine*, *18*(4), 97–136.

Dipiti, D. P., V. M. Wadhai, & J. A. Gokhale. (2010). Evaluation of Decision Tree Pruning Algorithms for Complexity and Classification Accuracy. International Journal of Computer Applications (0975 – 8887), 11(2), 23- 29.

Djamour, Y., Vernant, P., Nankali, H. R., & Tavakoli, F. (2011). NW Iran-eastern Turkey present-day kinematics: Results from the Iranian permanent GPS network. *Earth and Planetary Science Letters*, *307*(1-2), 27–34. doi:10.1016/j.epsl.2011.04.029

Dologlou, E. (2008). Possible relationship between seismic electric signals (SES) lead time and earthquake stress drop. *Proceedings of the Japan Academy. Series B, Physical and Biological Sciences*, *84*(4), 117–122. doi:10.2183/pjab.84.117 PMID:18941291

Doraisami, S., & Golzari, S. (2008). *A Study on Feature Selection and Classification Techniques for Automatic Genre Classification of Traditional Malay Music*. Content-Based Retrieval, Categorization and Similarity.

Drever, F., & Whitehead, M. (1994). Mortality in regions and local authority districts in the 1990s: Exploring the relationship with deprivation. *Population Trends*, (82): 19–26. PMID:8745102

Dubosis, D., & Prade, H. (1980). *Fuzzy sets and systems: Theory and applications*. New York: Academic Press.

Dubosis, D., & Prade, H. (1987). Twofold fuzzy sets and rough sets-some issues in knowledge representation. *Fuzzy Sets and Systems*, *23*(1), 3–18. doi:10.1016/0165-0114(87)90096-0

Dzwinel, W., Yuen, D. A., Boryczko, K., Ben-Zion, Y., Yoshioka, S., & Ito, T. (2003). Cluster analysis, data-mining, multidimensional visualization of earthquakes over space, time and feature space. *Earth and Planetary Science Letters*, 1–11.

Dzwinel, W., Yuen, D. A., Boryczko, K., Ben-Zion, Y., Yoshioka, S., & Ito, T. (2005). Nonlinear multidimensional scaling and visualization of earthquake clusters over space, time and feature space. *Nonlinear Processes in Geophysics*, *12*(1), 117–128. doi:10.5194/npg-12-117-2005

Earl, B. H., Janet, M., & Philip, J. S. (1966). *Experiments in Induction*. New York: Academic Press.

Ebner, M., & Zell, A. (1999). Evolving a task specific image operator. In R. Poli et al. (Ed.), *Evolutionary Image Analysis, Signal Processing and Telecommunications* (pp. 74-89). Berlin: Springer-Verlag.

Eibe, F. (2000). *Pruning Decision Trees and Lists* [Thesis].

Elmi, A., Ganjpour Sales, J., Tabrizi, A., Soleimanpour, J., & Mohseni, M. A. (2013). Orthopedic injuries following the East Azerbaijan earthquake. *Trauma Mon*, *18*(1), 3–7. doi:10.5812/traumamon.8322 PMID:24350141

El-Wahed, W. F., Zaki, E. M., & El-Refaey, A. M. (2010). Reference Point Based Multi-Objective Optimization Using Hybrid Artificial Immune System. *Universal Journal of Computer Science and Engineering Technology*, *1*, 24–30.

Ennis, W. J. (2010). Disaster management, triage-based wound care, and patient safety: Reflections on practice following an earthquake. *Ostomy/Wound Management*, *56*(11), 61–69. PMID:21131698

Esakkiraj, S., & Chidambaram, S. (2013). A Predictive Approach for Fraud Detection Using Hidden Markov Model. [IJERT]. *International Journal of Engineering Research & Technology*, *2*, 1–7.

Esposito, F., Maerba, D., Semeraro, G., & Kay, J. (1997). A Comparative Analysis of Methods for Pruning Decision Trees. *IEEE Transactions on Pattern Analysis and Machine Intelligence*, *19*(5), 476–491.

Fayaad, U. M. (1996). Advances in knowledge discovery and data mining. In U. M. Fayaad, G. Piatetsky-Shapiro, P. Smyth, & R. Uthurusamy (Eds.), *American Association for Artificial Intelligence* (pp. 1–57). California: *(AAAI) press*.

Fayyad, U. (1996). *Knowledge discovery and data mining: Towards a unifying framework*. Proceedings of 2nd ACM international conference on knowledge discovery and data mining (KDD)

Fayyad, U., Piatetsky-Shapiro, G., Smyth, P., & Uthurusamy, R. (1996). *Advances in knowledge discovery and data mining*. Menlo Park, CA: AAAI Press/The MIT Press.

Ferri, F., Pudil, P., Hatef, M., & Kittler, J. (1994). Comparative Study of Techniques for Large-Scale Feature Selection. In E.S. Gelsema, & L.N. Kanal (Eds.), Pattern Recognition in Practice IV, Multiple Paradigms, Comparative Studies and Hybrid Systems (pp. 403–413).

Flach, P., & Lachiche, N. (1999). 1BC: A first-order Bayesian classifier. In *Inductive Logic Programming* (pp. 92–103). Springer. doi:10.1007/3-540-48751-4_10

Fong, S., Deb, S., Yang, X-S, & Zhuang, Yan. (2014, June). Towards Enhancement of Performance of K-means Clustering Using Nature-Inspired Optimization Algorithms, *The Scientific World Journal*, Article no. 564829.

Fong, S., Zhuang, Y., Tang, R., Yang, X.-S., & Deb, S. (2013). Selecting Optimal Feature Set in High-Dimensional Data by Swarm Search. *Journal of Applied Mathematics*, *590614*, 18. doi: doi:10.1155/2013/590614

Forbes, S. A., Tang, G., Bindal, N., Bamford, S., Dawson, E., & Cole, C. et al. (2010). COSMIC (the Catalogue of Somatic Mutations in Cancer): A resource to investigate acquired mutations in human cancer. *Nucleic Acids Research*, *38*(Database issue), D652–D657. PMID:19906727

Forrest, S., Perelson, A., Allen, L., & Cherukuri, R. (1994). Self-nonself discrimination in a computer. *Proceedings of IEEE Computer Society Symposium on Research in Security and Privacy* (pp. 202-212). doi:10.1109/RISP.1994.296580

Forrest, S., & Hofmeyer, S. (2000). Immunology as information processing. In L. Segel & I. Cohen (Eds.), *Design Principles for Immune System and Other Distributed Autonomous Systems*. Oxford University Press, *361*.

Fraley, C. (1999). Algorithms for model-based Gaussian hierarchical clustering. *SIAM Journal on Scientific Computing*, *20*(1), 270–281. doi:10.1137/S1064827596311451

Fraley, C., & Raftery, A. (1998). How Many Clusters? Which Clustering Method? Answers Via Model-Based Cluster Analysis. *The Computer Journal*, *41*(8), 578–588. doi:10.1093/comjnl/41.8.578

Freitas, A. A. (2002). *Data mining and knowledge discovery with evolutionary algorithms*. New York: Springer-Vlag Berlin Heidelberg. doi:10.1007/978-3-662-04923-5

Fu, X., Li, S., Fairbank, M., Wunsch, D. C., & Alonso, E. (2014). Training recurrent neural networks with the levenberg-marquardt algorithm for optimal control of a grid-connected converter. *IEEE Trans Neural Netw Learn Syst*. doi: 10.1109/TNNLS.2014.2361267

Gao, Y., Song, Y., & Yang, Z. (2012). *A real-time drivable road detection algorithm in urban traffic environment Computer Vision and Graphics* (pp. 387–396). Springer.

Garg, A., & Singh, S. (2013). A Review on Web Application Security Vulnerabilities. *International Journal of Advanced Research in Computer Science and Software Engineering*, *3*, 222–226.

Geffner, S., Agrawal, D., El Abbadi, A., & Smith, T. (1999, March). Relative prefix sums: An efficient approach for querying dynamic OLAP data cubes. *Proceedings of 15th International Conference on* (pp. 328-335). IEEE.

Gheitanchi, M. R., Mirzaei, N., & Bayramnejad, E. (2004). Pattern of seismicity in Northwest Iran, revealed from local seismic network. *Geoscience*, *11*, 104–111.

Ghionna, L., & Greco, G. (2011). Boosting tuple propagation in multi-relational classification. Proceedings of the *15th Symposium on International Database Engineering & Applications.* Lisboa, Portugal. doi:10.1145/2076623.2076637

Ghosh, S., Maiti, N. S. & Chaudhuri, P. P. (2012) *Theory and Application of Restricted Five Neighborhood Cellular Automata (R5NCA) for Protein Structure Prediction.*

Glass Identification Dataset. Retrieved from http//archive.ics.uci.edu/ml/datasets/Glass+Identification

Goethals, B., & Le, W. (2008, April 24-26). Mining association rules of simple conjunctive queries. *Proceedings of the SIAM International Conference on Data Mining (SDM).*

Goethals, B., Le Page, W., & Mampaey, M. (2010). *Mining interesting sets and rules in relational databases.* ACM.

Goguen, J. A. (1967). L–fuzzy sets. *Journal of Mathematical Analysis and Applications*, *18*(1), 145–174. doi:10.1016/0022-247X(67)90189-8

Golab, L., Johnson, T., Seidel, J. S., & Shkapenyuk, V. (2009). *Stream warehousing with DataDepot. SIGMOD '09: Proceedings of the 35th SIGMOD International Conference on Management of Data* (pp. 847–854). Providence, Rhode Island, USA: ACM. doi:http://doi.acm.org/10.1145/1559845.1559934 doi:10.1145/1559845.1559934

Goldberg, D. E. (1989). *Genetic Algorithms in Search Opimization and Machine Learning.* Reading, MA: Addison-Wesley.

Goodsell, D. S., & Olson, A. J. (1990). Automated Docking of Substrates to Proteins by Simulated Annealing. Proteins. *Structure, Function, and Bioinformatics*, *8*(3), 195–202. doi:10.1002/prot.340080302 PMID:2281083

Gorea, D. A. (2009, January). *Interoperability and Integration of Processes of Knowledge Discovery in Databases* [PhD thesis]. University Alexandru Ioan Cuza Iasi.

Grol, R., Wensing, M., Mainz, J., Ferreira, P., Hearnshaw, H., & Hjortdahl, P. et al. (1999). Patients' priorities with respect to general practice care: An international comparison. *Family Practice*, *16*(1), 4–11. doi:10.1093/fampra/16.1.4 PMID:10321388

Grossmann, W., Hudec, M., & Kurzawa, R. (2004). Web usage mining in e-commerce. *International Journal of Electronic Business*, *2*(5), 480–493. doi:10.1504/IJEB.2004.005881

Grubbs, F. E. (1969). Procedures for Detecting Outlying Observations in Samples. *Technometrics*, *11*(1), 1–21. doi:10.1080/00401706.1969.10490657

Guo, H., & Viktor, H. L. (2008). Multirelational classification: A multiple view approach. *Knowledge and Information Systems*, *17*(3), 287–312. doi:10.1007/s10115-008-0127-5

Gupta, N., Saikia, A., & Sanghi, D. D. (2007). *WEB APPLICATION FIREWALL.* Kanpur: Indian Instituite of Technology.

Guyon, I., & Elisseeff, A. (2003, March). An Introduction to Variable and Feature Selection JMLR Special Issue on Variable and Feature Selection. Kernel Machines Section, 1157-1182.

Guyon, I. (2003). An introduction to variable and feature selection. *Journal of Machine Learning Research*, *3*, 1157–1182.

Hall, M., Frank, E., Holmes, G., Pfahringer, B., Reutemann, P., & Witten, I. H. (1997). The WEKA data mining software: an update. In SIGKDD Explorer Newsletter (2009), 10-18.

Hallgren, P. A., Mauritzson, D. T., & Sabelfeld, A. (2013). A Lightweight Approach to Web Application Integrity. Proceedings of ACM PLAS'13. Seattle, WA, USA: ACM.

Hall, M. A., & Holmes, G. (2003). Benchmarking attribute selection techniques for discrete class data mining. *IEEE Transactions on Knowledge and Data Engineering, 15*(6), 1437–1447. doi:10.1109/TKDE.2003.1245283

Hall, M. A., & Smith, L. A. (1998). Practical feature subset selection for machine learning.*Proceedings of the 21st Australian Computer Science Conference (pp.*181–191).

Handl, J., & Meyer, B. (2002). Improved ant-based clustering and sorting in a document retrieval interface. *Proceedings of the Seventh International Conference on Parallel Problem Solving from Nature (PPSN VII)*, (pp. 913-923). Springer-Verlag, Berlin, Germany. doi:10.1007/3-540-45712-7_88

Harmer, P. K., Williams, P. D., Gunsch, G. H., & Lamont, G. B. (2002). An artificial immune system architecture for computer security applications. *IEEE Transactions on Evolutionary Computation, 6*(3), 252–280. doi:10.1109/TEVC.2002.1011540

Harrison, S. (2012). *Annual Fraud Indicator*. National Fraud Authority.

Hart, E., & Timmis, J. (2008). Application area of AIS: The Past, The Present and the Future. Applied Soft Computing, 8(1).

Hatamlou, A. (2013, February). Black hole: A new heuristic optimization approach for data clustering. *Information Sciences, 222*(10), 175–184. doi:10.1016/j.ins.2012.08.023

Hawwash, B. & Nasraoui, O. (2010). Mining and tracking evolving web user trends from large web server logs.

Hayes-Roth, F. (1985). Rule-based systems. *Communications of the ACM, 28*(9), 921–932. doi:10.1145/4284.4286

Hessami, K., Pantosti, D., Tabassi, H., Shabanian, E., Abbassi, M. R., Feghhi, K., & Solaymani, S. (2003). Paleoearthquakes and slip rates of the North Tabriz fault, NW Iran: Preliminary results. *Annals of Geophysics, 46*(5), 903–915.

Hinde, S. (2005). Identity theft & fraud. *Computer theft & fraud.*

Hoehle, H., Scornavacca, E., & Huff, S. (2012). Three Decades of Research on Consumer Adoption and Utilization of Electronic Banking Channels: A Literature Analysis. *Decision Support Systems, 54*(1), 122–132. doi:10.1016/j.dss.2012.04.010

Holder, L. B., & Cook, D. J. (2005). Graph-based data mining.

Holder, L. B., Cook, D. J., & Djoko, S. (1994). Substucture discovery in the SUBDUE System Symposium conducted at the meeting of the KDD Workshop

Holte, R. (1993). Very Simple Classification Rules Perform Well on Most Commonly Used Datasets. *Machine Learning, 11*(1), 63–90. doi:10.1023/A:1022631118932

Huang, Y.-W., Huang, S.-K., Lin, T.-P., & Tsai, C.-H. (2003). Proceedings of Web Application Security Assessment by Fault Injection and Behavior Monitoring. WWW 2003. Budapest, Hungary: ACM.

Huang, D. W., Sherman, B. T., & Lempicki, R. A. (2009). Bioinformatics enrichment tools: Paths toward the comprehensive functional analysis of large gene lists. *Nucleic Acids Research, 37*(1), 1–13. doi:10.1093/nar/gkn923 PMID:19033363

Huang, D. W., Sherman, B. T., & Lempicki, R. A. (2009). Systematic and integrative analysis of large gene lists using DAVID Bioinformatics Resources. *Nature Protocols, 4*(1), 44–57. doi:10.1038/nprot.2008.211 PMID:19131956

Hu, H., Yan, X., Huang, Y., Han, J., & Zhou, X. J. (2005). Mining coherent dense subgraphs across massive biological networks for functional discovery. *Bioinformatics (Oxford, England)*, *21*(Suppl 1), i213–i221. doi:10.1093/bioinformatics/bti1049 PMID:15961460

Hunt, J. E., & Cook, D. E. (1996). Learning using an artificial immune system. *Journal of Network and Computer Applications*, *19*(2), 189–212. doi:10.1006/jnca.1996.0014

Hussain, T., Asghar, D. S., & Fong, S. (2010a). A Hierarchical Cluster Based Preprocessing Methodology for Web Usage Mining. Proceedings of *6th International Conference on Advanced Information Management and Service (IMS)*. Seoul, South Korea.

Hussain, T., Asghar, D. S., & Masood, D. N. (2010b). Hierarchical Sessionization at Preprocessing Level of WUM Based on Swarm Intelligence. *Proceedings of 2010 6th International Conference on Emerging Technologies (ICET)*. Islamabad.

Hussain, T., Asghar, D. S., & Masood, D. N. (2010c). *Web Usage Mining: A Survey on Preprocessing of Web Log File. Information and Emerging Technologies (ICIET), 2010*. Karachi, Pakistan: IEEE.

Hussain, T., & Asghar, S. (2013). Evaluation of similarity measures for categorical data. *The Nucleus: The Scientific Journal of Pakistan Atomic Energy* Commission, *50*, 387–394.

Hussain, T., & Asghar, S. (2013). Web mining: Approaches, applications and business intelligence. *International Journal of Academic Research Part A*, *5*(2), 211–217. doi:10.7813/2075-4124.2013/5-2/A.32

Ilas, C. (2013). *Perception in autonomous ground vehicles.* Paper presented at the Electronics, Computers and Artificial Intelligence (ECAI), 2013 International Conference

Inokuchi, A., Washio, T., & Motoda, H. (2000). An apriori-based algorithm for mining frequent substructures from graph data. In *Principles of Data Mining and Knowledge Discovery* (pp. 13–23). Springer. doi:10.1007/3-540-45372-5_2

Inuzuka, N., & Makino, T. (2009). Implementing Multi-relational Mining with Relational Database Systems. In *Knowledge-Based and Intelligent Information and Engineering Systems* (pp. 672–680). Springer. doi:10.1007/978-3-642-04592-9_83

Ishak, A. J., Mokri, S. S., Mustafa, M. M., & Hussain, A. (2007, December). Weed Detection utilizing Quadratic Polynomial and ROI Techniques.

Ishak, A. J., Mustafa, M. M., Tahir, N. M., & Hussain, A. (2008). Weed Detection System using Support Vector Machine.

Ishtiaq, M., & Ali, K. (2010). *Meaningful Use of EHR, the HITECH Act*. EHR Incentives & the Final Rule.

Ives, Z. G., Florescu, D., Friedman, M., Levy, A., & Weld, D. S. (1999). An adaptive query execution system for data integration. *SIGMOD Rec., 28*(2), 299–310. doi:http://doi.acm.org/10.1145/304181.304209

Jafar, O. A. M., & Sivakumar, R. (2013, March). A Study of Bio-inspired Algorithm to Data Clustering using Different Distance Measures, *International Journal of Computer Applications*, 66(12), 33-44.

Jain, A. K. (2010). Data Clustering: 50 Years Beyond K-means. *Pattern Recognition Letters*, *31*(8), 651–666. doi:10.1016/j.patrec.2009.09.011

Jain, A. K., Murty, M. N., & Flynn, P. J. (1999, September). Data Clustering: A Review. *ACM Computing Surveys*, *31*(3), 265–323. doi:10.1145/331499.331504

Jaiswal, A., & Dubey, G. (2013, May). Identifying Best Association Rules and Their Optimization Using Genetic Algorithm, *International Journal of Emerging Science and Engineering (IJESE)*, 1(7), 91-96.

Janikow, C. Z. (1998). Fuzzy Decision Trees Issues and Methods, IEEE Transaction on Systems. *Man and Cybernetics – Part B Cybernetics, 28*(1), 5–12.

Jassal, R. K., & Sehgal, R. K. (2013). Online Banking Security Flaws: A Study. *International Journal of Advanced Research in Computer Science and Software Engineering, 3,* 1016–1021.

Jen, C., & Jane, Y. H. (2002). Fuzzy Classification Trees for Data analysis. *Fuzzy Sets and Systems, 130*(1), 87–99. doi:10.1016/S0165-0114(01)00212-3

Jenkinson, C., Coulter, A., Bruster, S., Richards, N., & Chandola, T. (2002). Patients' experiences and satisfaction with health care: Results of a questionnaire study of specific aspects of care. *Quality & Safety in Health Care, 11*(4), 335–339. doi:10.1136/qhc.11.4.335 PMID:12468693

Jiang, G. Q., Zhao, C. J., & Si, Y. S. (2010, July). A machine vision based crop rows detection for agricultural robots. In *Wavelet Analysis and Pattern Recognition (ICWAPR), 2010 International Conference on* (pp. 114-118). IEEE. doi:10.1109/ICWAPR.2010.5576422

Jianxi. Zhang, Zhao, P., Shang, L. & Wang, L. (2009). Web usage mining based on fuzzy clustering in identifying target group. *Proceedings of ISECS International Colloquium on Computing, Communication, Control, and Management* (pp. 209-212). IEEE.

Jiawei, H., Micheline, K., & Jian, P. (2006). Data Mining, Southeast Asia Edition Concepts and Techniques Book. Guoxiu, L. (2005). A comparative study of three Decision Tree algorithms ID3, Fuzzy ID3 and Probabilistic Fuzzy ID3 [Thesis].

Jiménez, A., Berzal, F., & Cubero, J.-C. (2012). Using trees to mine multirelational databases. *Data Mining and Knowledge Discovery, 24*(1), 1–39. doi:10.1007/s10618-011-0218-x

Jing-Feng, G., Jing, L., & Wei-Feng, B. (2007, August 24-27). An Efficient Relational Decision Tree Classification Algorithm Proceedings of the Third International Conference on doi: doi:10.1109/icnc.2007.195

Jin, W., Tung, A. K., & Han, J. (2001). Mining top-n local outliers in large databases.*InProc. of the seventh ACM SIG-KDD International Conference on Knowledge Discovery and Data mining* (pp. 293-298). doi:10.1145/502512.502554

Jinwook, S., & Shneiderman, B. (2002). Interactively exploring hierarchical clustering results[gene identification]. *Computer, 35*(7), 80–86. doi:10.1109/MC.2002.1016905

John, G., & Langley, P. (1995). Estimating Continuous Distributions in Bayesian Classifiers. *Proceedings ofEleventh Conference on Uncertainty in Artificial Intelligence (pp- 338-345).*

John, G., & Kohavi, R. (1997). Wrapper for feature subset selection. In *Artificial intelligence* (pp. 273–324). Elsevier Science.

John, G., Kohavi, R., & Pfleger, K. (1994). Irrelevant features and the subset selection problem. *Proceedings of Fifth International Conference on Machine Learning(pp.*121-129). doi:10.1016/B978-1-55860-335-6.50023-4

John, M. (1989). An Empirical Comparison of Pruning Methods for Decision Tree Induction. Kluwer Academic Publishers, Boston. Manufactured in The Netherlands. *Machine Learning, 4*(2), 227–243. doi:10.1023/A:1022604100933

Jones, G., Willett, P., & Glen, R. C. (1995). Molecular Recognition of Receptor Sites using a Genetic algorithm with a Description of Desolvation. *Journal of Molecular Biology, 245*(1), 43–53. doi:10.1016/S0022-2836(95)80037-9 PMID:7823319

Jones, S., & Gupta, O. K. (2006). Web Data Mining: A Case Study. *Communications of the IIMA, 6,* 6.

Joslyn, C., Gillen, D., Burke, J., Critchlow, T., Damante, M., & Fernandes, R. (2008, May). Hybrid Multidimensional Relational and Link Analytical Knowledge Discovery for Law Enforcement. Proceedings of *2008 IEEE Conference* (pp. 161-166). IEEE. doi:10.1109/THS.2008.4534442

Jovanovic, N., Kirda, E., & Kruegel, C. (2006, August 28-September 1). Preventing Cross Site Request Forgery Attacks. *Securecomm and Workshops*. Baltimore, MD.

Jovanovic, N., Kruegel, C. & Kirda, E. (2013). Pixy: A Static Analysis Tool for Detecting Web Application Vulnerabilities.

Julisch, K. (2010). *Risk-Based Payment Fraud Detection*. Zurich.

Kako, M., Arbon, P., & Mitani, S. (2014). Disaster health after the 2011 great East Japan earthquake. *Prehospital and Disaster Medicine*, *29*(1), 54–59. doi:10.1017/S1049023X14000028 PMID:24451332

Kaleem, A., & Ahmad, S. (2008). Bankers' Perceptions of Electronic Banking in Pakistan. *Journal of Internet Banking and Commerce*, *13*, 1–16.

Kaleem, A., & Ahmad, S. (2009). Determinants of SMEs' perceptions of electronic banking in Pakistan. *International Journal of Electronic Finance*, *3*(2), 133–148. doi:10.1504/IJEF.2009.026356

Kanade, P. M., & Hall, L. O. (2003), Fuzzy Ants as a Clustering Concept, In *Proceedings of the 22nd International Conference of the North American Fuzzy Information Processing Society* (NAFIPS03), 227-232.

Karimzadeha, S., Cakirb, Z., Osmanoˇgluc, B., Schmalzled, G., Miyajimaa, M., Amiraslanzadeha, R., & Djamoure, Y. (2013). Interseismic strain accumulation across the North Tabriz fault (NW Iran) deduced from InSAR time series. *Journal of Geodynamics*, *66*, 53–58. doi:10.1016/j.jog.2013.02.003

Kaur, M. & Anupnandy (n. d.). Web Logs Conversion to Improve the Analysis of Web Usage Data for Web Usage mining in E-Learning. *International Journal of Computer Science and its Applications*, 6.

Kelsey, J., & Timmis, J. (2003). Immune inspired somatic contiguous hypermutation for function optimisation. *Proceedings of Genetic and Evolutionary Computation Conference - GECCO* (pp. 207–218).

Kennedy, J., & Eberhart, R. C. (1995). Particle swarm optimization. *Proc. IEEE Int'l. Conf. on Neural Networks, IV*, (pp. 1942-1948). doi:10.1109/ICNN.1995.488968

Khaled, A., Abdul-Kader, H. M., & Ismail, N. A. (2010). Artificial Immune Clonal Selection Algorithm: A Comparative Study of CLONALG, opt-IA and BCA with Numerical Optimization Problems. *International Journal of Computer Science and Network Security*, *10*(4), 24–30.

Khandelwal, S., Shah, P., Bhavsar, K. & Gandhi, D. S. (2013). Frontline Techniques to Prevent Web Application Vulnerability. *International Journal of Advanced Research in Computer Science and Electronics Engineering*, 2.

Khiyal, M. S. H., Khan, A., Bashir, S., Khan, F. H., & Aman, S. (2011). Dynamic Blind Group Digital Signature Scheme in E-Banking. *International Journal of Computer and Electrical Engineering*, *3*, 514–519. doi:10.7763/IJCEE.2011.V3.371

Khochare, N., Chalurkar, S., & Meshram, B.B. (2013). Web Application Vulnerabilities Detection Techniques Survey. *International Journal of Computer Science and Network Security*, 13.

Khosravi, H., & Bina, B. (2010). A survey on statistical relational learning. In *Advances in Artificial Intelligence* (pp. 256–268). Springer. doi:10.1007/978-3-642-13059-5_25

Kiani, S., Azimifar, Z., & Kamgar, S. (2010, May). Wavelet-based crop detection and classification. In *Electrical Engineering (ICEE), 2010 18th Iranian Conference on* (pp. 587-591). IEEE. doi:10.1109/IRANIANCEE.2010.5507003

Kim, J., Greensmith, J., Twycross, J., & Aickelin, U. (2005). Malicious Code Execution Detection and Response Immune System inspired by the Danger Theory.*Proceedings of Adaptive and Resilient Computing Security Workshop (ARCS-05)*.

Kira, K., & Rendell, L. A. (1992). A practical approach to feature selection. In D. Sleeman and P. Edwards (Eds.), *MachineLearning:Proceedings of International Conference (ICML'92)* (pp. 249–256). Morgan Kaufmann.

Kira, K., & Rendell, L. A. (1992). A practical approach to feature selection. *Proceedings of the ninth international workshop on Machine learning*. Aberdeen, Scotland, United Kingdom.

Kirkpatrick, S., Gelatt, C. D., & Jr, M. P. V. (1983). Optimization by Simulated Annealing. *Science*, *220*(4598), 671–680. doi:10.1126/science.220.4598.671 PMID:17813860

Knobbe, A. J. B., Hendrik; Siebes, Arno; Wallen, Daniel M. G. van der. (1999). *Multi-relational data mining*. Proceedings of Benelearn

Knobbe, A. J. H., & Eric, K. Y. (2005). *Numbers in Multi-Relational Data Mining*. Proceedings of the Principles of Data Mining and Knowledge Discovery (PKDD). doi:10.1007/11564126_56

Knorr, E. M., & Ng, R. T. (1998). Algorithms for mining distance-based outliers in large datasets. *Proc. 24th Int. Conf. Very Large Data Bases* (pp. 392–403).

Kohavi, R., & John, G. H. (1997). Wrappers for feature subset selection. *Artificial Intelligence*, *97*(1–2), 273–324. doi:10.1016/S0004-3702(97)00043-X

Komi, P. J., Jackson, M. R., & Parkin, R. M. (2007). Plant Classification Combining Colour and Spectral Cameras for Weed Control Purposes.*2007 IEEE International Symposium on Industrial Electronics*, 2039–2042. doi:10.1109/ISIE.2007.4374921

Kong, H., Audibert, J.-Y., & Ponce, J. (2010). General road detection from a single image. *Image Processing. IEEE Transactions on*, *19*(8), 2211–2220.

Koopman, A., & Siebes, A. (2008). Discovering relational item sets efficiently. *Proceedings of SDM*.

Krogel, M.-A. (2005). *On propositionalization for knowledge discovery in relational databases*. Otto-von-Guericke-Universität Magdeburg, Universitätsbibliothek.

Kudo, M. & Sklansky, J. (1997). A Comparative Evaluation of Medium- and Large-Scale Feature Selectors for Pattern Classifiers. *Proceedings of the First International Workshop on Statistical Techniques in Pattern Recognition (pp.91–96)*. Prague, Czech Republic.

Kudo, M., & Sklansky, J. (1998). Classifier-independent feature selection for two-stage feature selection, Syntactical and Structural Pattern Recognition/Statistical. *Pattern Recognition*, 548–554.

Kumar, N., Gangopadhyay, A., Karabatis, G., Bapna, S., & Chen, Z. (2006). Navigation rules for exploring large multidimensional data cubes.[IJDWM]. *International Journal of Data Warehousing and Mining*, *2*(4), 27–48. doi:10.4018/jdwm.2006100102

Kumar, P., Krishna, R., & De, K. (2005). Fuzzy OLAP cube for qualitative analysis. *Proceedings of 2005 International Conference on Intelligent Sensing and Information Processing* (pp. 290-295). IEEE. doi:10.1109/ICISIP.2005.1529464

Kuramochi, M., & Karypis, G. (2001). Frequent subgraph discovery. Proceedings IEEE International Conference.

Kuramochi, M., & Karypis, G. (2004). An efficient algorithm for discovering frequent subgraphs. Knowledge and Data Engineering. *IEEE Transactions on*, *16*(9), 1038–1051.

Labor Relation Dataset. Retrieved from http//archive.ics.uci.edu/ml/datasets/Labor+Relations

Lachiche, N., & Flach, P. A. (2003). 1BC2: a true first-order Bayesian classifier. In *Inductive Logic Programming* (pp. 133–148). Springer. doi:10.1007/3-540-36468-4_9

Ladha, L., & Deepa, T. (2011). Feature Selection Methods and Algorithms. *International Journal on Computer Science and Engineering, 3*(5), 1787-1797.

Lalonde, J.-F., Vandapel, N., Huber, D. F., & Hebert, M. (2006). Natural terrain classification using three-dimensional ladar data for ground robot mobility. *Journal of Field Robotics, 23*(10), 839–861. doi:10.1002/rob.20134

Langley, P. L., Wayne, I., & Thompson, K. (1992). An Analysis of Bayesian Classifiers. *Proceedings of the Tenth Conference on Artificial Intelligence (pp. 233-228). San Jose, California, USA.*

Lau, H., Bate, I., & Timmis, J. (2009). An Immuno-engineering Approach for Anomaly Detection in Swarm Robotics. *Proceedings of 8th International Conference (pp. 136–150).*

Laura, I., Moria, R., Gesellchen, V., Eyckerman, S., & Cauwer, L. D. (2012). The Sin3a repressor complex is a master regulator of STAT transcriptional activity. *Proceedings of the National Academy of Sciences of the United States of America, 109*(30), 12058–12063. doi:10.1073/pnas.1206458109 PMID:22783022

Lavrac, N., & Dzeroski, S. (1994). *Inductive Logic Programming: Techniques and Applications.* New York: Ellis Horwood.

Lawrence, R. (2005). Early Hash Join: A configurable algorithm for the efficient and early production of join results. *VLDB '05: Proceedings of the 31st International Conference on Very Large Data Bases* (pp. 841–852). Trondheim, Norway: VLDB Endowment.

Lee, C.-I., Tsai, C.-J., Wu, T.-Q., & Yang, W.-P. (2008). An approach to mining the multi-relational imbalanced database. *Expert Systems with Applications, 34*(4), 3021–3032. doi:10.1016/j.eswa.2007.05.048

Lee, K.-W., Tsai, M.-T., & Lanting, M. C. L. (2011). From marketplace to marketspace: Investigating the consumer switch to online banking. *Electronic Commerce Research and Applications, 10*(1), 115–125. doi:10.1016/j.elerap.2010.08.005

Leiva, H. A. (2002). *A multi-relational decision tree learning algorithm.* Iowa State University.

Lei, Y., & Huan, L., (2003). Feature Selection for High-Dimensional Data: A Fast Correlation-Based Filter Solution. *Proceedings of the Twentieth International Conference on Machine Leaning(pp.856-863).*

Leon, F., & Atanasiu, G. M. (2006). *Data mining methods for GIS analysis of seismic vulnerability.Proceedings of the First International Conference on Software and Data Technologies.*

Leonhardi, B., Mitschang, B., Pulido, R., Sieb, C., & Wurst, M. (2010, March). Augmenting olap exploration with dynamic advanced analytics. In *Proceedings of the 13th International Conference on Extending Database Technology* (pp. 687-692).ACM. doi:10.1145/1739041.1739127

Li, D. Y., & Hu, Bao Qing (2007). A kind of dynamic rough sets. *Proceedings of the Fourth International Conference on Fuzzy Systems and Knowledge Discovery (FSKD)* (pp. 79-85). doi:10.1109/FSKD.2007.51

Li, S., Shah, S. A. H., Khan, M. A. U., Khayam, S. A., Sadeghi, A.-R., & Schmitz, R. (2010). Breaking e-Banking CAPT-CHAs. *Proceedings of the 26th Annual computer Security Application Conference.* Austin, Texas. New York: ACM.

Li, X., & Zhang, S. (2010). Application of Web Usage Mining in e-learning Platform. Proceedings of *International conference on E-Business and E-Government.* doi:10.1109/ICEE.2010.353

Liao, S. H., & Wen, C. H. (2007). Artificial neural networks classification and clustering of methodologies and applications – literature analysis from 1995 to 2005. *Expert Systems with Applications*, *32*(1), 1–11. doi:10.1016/j.eswa.2005.11.014

Liao, T. W. (2005). Clustering of time series data—a survey. *Pattern Recognition*, *38*(11), 1857–1874. doi:10.1016/j.patcog.2005.01.025

Lopes, C., & Zaverucha, G. (2009). Htilde: scaling up relational decision trees for very large databases*ACM. Proceedings of the 2009 ACM symposium on Applied Computing.*

Lorigo, L. M., Brooks, R. A. & Grimson, W. E. L. 1997. Visually-guided obstacle avoidance in unstructured environments Proceedings of the *IEEE Conference on Intelligent Robots and Systems.*

Lyratzopoulos, G., Elliott, M., Barbiere, J., Henderson, A., Staetsky, L., & Paddison, C. et al. (2012). Understanding ethnic and other socio-demographic differences in patient experience of primary care: Evidence from the English General Practice Patient Survey. *BMJ Quality & Safety*, *21*(1), 21–29. doi:10.1136/bmjqs-2011-000088 PMID:21900695

Madeo, R. C. B., Lima, C. A. M., & Peres, S. M. (2013). Gesture unit segmentation using support vector machines: segmenting gestures from rest positions. *Proceedings of the 28th Annual ACM Symposium on Applied Computing* (pp.46-52). doi:10.1145/2480362.2480373

Madkour, A., Aref, W. G., & Basalamah, S. (2013, October). Knowledge cubes—A proposal for scalable and semantically-guided management of Big Data. *Proceedings of IEEE International Conference on* (pp. 1-7). IEEE.

Mahalanobis, P. C. (1936). On the generalized distance in statistics. Proc. of the National Institute of Science of India (pp. 49-55).

Mansur, M. O., & Sap, M. N. M. (2005). Outlier detection technique in data mining: a research perspective, *Proceedings of the postgraduate annual research seminar.*

Marcos, E. C., Maria, C. M., & Helosia, A. C. (2012). *Fuzzy DT - A Fuzzy Decision Tree Algorithm Based on C4.5.*

Marcos, E. C., Maria, C. M., & Helosia, A. C. (2010). Evaluation of the pruning impact on Fuzzy C4.5. *Congresso Brasileiro de Sistemas Fuzzy.*, *1*(1), 257–264.

Margaret, D. H. (2006). *Data mining, introductory and Advanced Topics.* Pearson Education.

Marinaki, M., Marinakis, Y., & Zopounidis, C. (2010). Honey Bees Mating Optimization algorithm for financial classification problems. *Applied Soft Computing*, *10*(3), 806–812. doi:10.1016/j.asoc.2009.09.010

Marinakis, Y., Marinaki, M., & Dounias, G. (2008). Particle swarm optimization for pap-smear diagnosis. *Expert Systems with Applications*, *35*(4), 1645–1656. doi:10.1016/j.eswa.2007.08.089

Marroquín, I. D., Brault, J.-J., & Hart, B. S. (2009). A visual data-mining methodology for seismic facies analysis: Part 1-Testing and comparison with other unsupervised clustering methods. *Geophysic*, *74*(1), 1–11. doi:10.1190/1.3046455

Martinez, W. L., & Martinez, A. (2005). Model-based Clustering Toolbox for MATLAB. *Naval Surface Warfare Center.*

Maulik, U. & Sarkar, A., (20013), Searching remote homology with spectral clustering with symmetry in neighborhood cluster kernels, *PLoS ONE, 8(2), e46468.*

Maulik, U., & Sarkar, A. (2010). Gene Microarray Data Analysis Using Parallel Point Symmetry-Based Clustering. In U. Maulik, S. Bandyopadhyay, & J. T. L. Wang (Eds.), *Computational Intelligence and Pattern Analysis in Biological Informatics*. Hoboken, NJ, USA: John Wiley & Sons, Inc. doi:10.1002/9780470872352.ch13

Menezes, G., & Zaverucha, G. (2011). HTILDE-RT: Scaling up relational regression trees for very large datasets.

Messaoud, R. B., Boussaid, O., & Rabaséda, S. (2004, November). A new OLAP aggregation based on the AHC technique. In *Proceedings of the 7th ACM international workshop on Data warehousing and OLAP* (pp. 65-72). New York, USA. ACM. doi:10.1145/1031763.1031777

Meyer, R. (2008). *Detecting Attacks on Web Applications from Log Files. SANS Institute 2008. Mobarek*. D. A. E-banking practices and customer satisfaction- a case study in Botswana.

Miaou, S. P., Lu, A., & Lum, H. S. (1996). Pitfalls of using r-squared to evaluate goodness of fit of accident prediction models. *Transportation Research Record, 1542*, 6–13. doi:10.3141/1542-02

Michie, D., Muggleton, S., Page, D., & Srinivasan, A. (n. d.). East - West Train Dataset.

Midtiby, H. S., Mathiassen, S. K., Andersson, K. J., & Jørgensen, R. N. (2011). Performance evaluation of a crop/weed discriminating microsprayer. *Computers and Electronics in Agriculture, 77*(1), 35–40. doi:10.1016/j.compag.2011.03.006

Mirdula, S., & Manivannan, D. (2013). Security Vulnerabilities in Web Application- An Attack Perspective. *International Journal of Engineering and Technology, 5*.

Mitchell, T. M. (1997). *Machine learning*. Boston: WCB/McGraw-Hill.

Miura, T., & Okada, Y. (2012). *Extraction of frequent association patterns co-occurring across multi-sequence data. Proceedings of the International Multi Conference of Engineers.*

Moghadam, P., & Dong, J. F. (2012). *Road direction detection based on vanishing-point tracking.* Paper presented at the Intelligent Robots and Systems (IROS) 2012 IEEE/RSJ International Conference. doi:10.1109/IROS.2012.6386089

Mohammadpourzarandi, P. D. M. E. & Tamimi, R. (2013). The Application of Web Usage Mining In E-commerce Security. *International Journal of Information Science and Management.*

Mokbel, M. F., Lu, M., & Aref, W. G. (2004). Hash-Merge Join: A Non-blocking Join Algorithm for Producing Fast and Early Join Results. *ICDE '04: Proceedings of the 20th International Conference on Data Engineering* (p. 251). Washington, DC, USA: IEEE Computer Society. doi:10.1109/ICDE.2004.1320002

Monmarche, N., Slimane, M., & Venturini, G. (1999). *Ant Class: discovery of clusters in numeric data by a hybridization of an ant colony with the k means algorithm* [Report No. 213]. Laboratoired Informatique, Universite de Tours.

Montalvo, M., Guerrero, J. M., Romeo, J., Emmi, L., Guijarro, M., & Pajares, G. (2013). Expert Systems with Applications Automatic expert system for weeds / crops identification in images from maize fields. *Expert Systems with Applications, 40*(1), 75–82. doi:10.1016/j.eswa.2012.07.034

Montalvo, M., Pajares, G., Guerrero, J. M., Romeo, J., Guijarro, M., & Ribeiro, A. et al. (2012). Automatic detection of crop rows in maize fields with high weeds pressure. *Expert Systems with Applications, 39*(15), 11889–11897. doi:10.1016/j.eswa.2012.02.117

Moore, T., Clayton, R., & Anderson, R. (2009). The Economics of Online Crime. *The Journal of Economic Perspectives, 23*(3), 3–20. doi:10.1257/jep.23.3.3

Morita, M. E., Sabourin, R., Bortolozzi, F., & Suen, C. Y. (2003). Unsupervised Feature Selection Using Multi-Objective Genetic Algorithm for Handwritten Word Recognition. *Proceedings of the 7th International Conference on Document Analysis and Recognition* (pp.666-670). Edinburgh, Scotland. doi:10.1109/ICDAR.2003.1227746

Motoyama, J.-I., Urazawa, S., Nakano, T., & Inuzuka, N. (2007). A mining algorithm using property items extracted from sampled examples. In *Inductive Logic Programming* (pp. 335–350). Springer. doi:10.1007/978-3-540-73847-3_32

Murray, G. C., Lin, J., & Chowdhury, A. (2006, November 3-9). Identification of User Sessions with Hierarchical Agglomerative Clustering. *Proceedings of ASIS&T annual meeting*. Austin, Texas, USA.

Naeem, M., Asghar, S., Irfan, S. R., & Fong, S. (2010). *Multilevel classification scheme for AGV perception*. Paper presented at the Advanced Information Management and Service (IMS) 2010 6th International Conference on.

Nagelkerderde, N. J. D. (1991). A note on a general definition of the coefficient of determination. *Biometrika, 78*(3), 691–692. doi:10.1093/biomet/78.3.691

Nawrocki, M. (2013). A Survey on Web Usage Mining, Applications and Tools. *American Journal of Computing and Computation, 3*.

Nejati, H., Azimifar, Z., & Zamani, M. (2008). Using Fast Fourier Transform for Weed Detection in corn fields.

Newman, D. J., Hettich, S. C., Blake, L., & Merz, C. J. (1998). *UCI Repository of machine learning databases, University California Irvine*. Department of Information and Computer Science.

Nguyen, L. B., Nguyen, A. V., Ling, S. H., & Nguyen, H. T. (2013). Combining genetic algorithm and Levenberg-Marquardt algorithm in training neural network for hypoglycemia detection using EEG signals. *Conference Proceedings; ... Annual International Conference of the IEEE Engineering in Medicine and Biology Society. IEEE Engineering in Medicine and Biology Society. Conference, 5386-5389*. doi: doi:10.1109/EMBC.2013.6610766 PMID:24110953

Niemi, T., Nummenmaa, J., & Thanisch, P. (2001, November). Constructing OLAP cubes based on queries. In *Proceedings of the 4th ACM international workshop on Data warehousing and OLAP* (pp. 9-15). New York, USA. ACM.

Nijssen, S., & Kok, J. (2001). *Faster association rules for multiple relations*. presented at the meeting of the International Joint Conference on Artificial Intelligence

Nitesh, V. C. (2003). C4.5 and Imbalanced Datasets Investigating the effect of sampling method, probabilistic estimate, and decision tree structure. Workshop on Learning from Imbalanced Datasets II, ICML, Washington DC.

Nitsure, R. R. (2003). E-banking: Challenges and Opportunities. *JSTOR, Economic and Political Weekly, 38*(51/52), 5377-5381.

Novakovic, J. (2010). The Impact of Feature Selection on the Accuracy of Naive Bayes Classifier. Proceedings of *18th Telecommunications forum TELFOR*.

Oliveira, R. L., Lima, B. S. L. P., & Ebecken, N. F. F. (2007). A comparison of bio-inspired metaheuristic approaches in classification tasks. *WIT Transactions on Information and Communication Technologies, 38*, 25–32.

Omran, M., Salman, A., & Engelbrecht, A. P. (2002). Image Classification using Particle Swarm Optimization, In *Proceedings of Conference on Simulated Evolution and Learning, 1*, 370-374.

Orihara, Y., Kamogawa, M., & Nagao, T. (2014). Pre-seismic changes of the level and temperature of confined groundwater related to the 2011 Tohoku Earthquake. *Scientific Reports, 4*, 6907. doi:10.1038/srep06907 PMID:25366123

OWASP. (2013). *The Ten Most Critical web Application security Risks. The Open Web Application Security Project*. OWASP.

P, N. (2001). *The patient centred dental practice*. London: British Dental Association Books.

Paget, F. (2009). Financial Fraud and Internet Banking: Threats and Countermeasures [Report]. McAffee Avert Labs.

Pahl, C. (2003). Data mining for the analysis of content interaction in web-based learning and training systems.

Palod, S. (2004). *Transformation of relational database domain into graphs based domain for graph based data mining*. Arlington: University of Texas at Arlington.

Pal, R. N., & Chakraborty, S. (2001). Fuzzy Rule Extraction from ID3-Type Decision Trees for Real Data. *IEEE Transactions on Systems, Man, and Cybernetics. Part B, Cybernetics, 31*(5), 745–753. doi:10.1109/3477.956036 PMID:18244839

Panakkat, A., & Adeli, H. (2007). Neural Network Models for Earthquake Magnitude Prediction Using Multiple Seismicity Indicators. *International Journal of Neural Systems, 17*(1), 13–33. doi:10.1142/S0129065707000890 PMID:17393560

Panakkat, A., & Adeli, H. (2009). Recurrent neural network for approximate earthquake time and location prediction using multiple seismicity indicators. *Computer-Aided Civil and Infrastructure Engineering, 24*(4), 280–292. doi:10.1111/j.1467-8667.2009.00595.x

Panda, M., & Patra, R. M. (2008). A comparative study of data mining algorithms for network intrusion detection. *Proceedings of 1st International Conference on Emerging Trends in Engineering and Technology*. doi:10.1109/ICETET.2008.80

Parpinelli, R. S., Lopes, H. S., & Freits, A. A. (2002, August). Data Mining with an Ant Colony Optimization Algorithm. *IEEE Transactions on Evolutionary Computation, 6*(4), 321–332. doi:10.1109/TEVC.2002.802452

Paulien Hogeweg. (2010) Multilevel Cellular Automata as a Tool for Studying Bioinformatic Processes. Simulating Complex Systems by Cellular Automata Understanding Complex Systems, 19-28. Springer.

Pawlak, Z. (1981). Information systems: Theoretical foundations. *Information Systems, 6*(3), 205–218. doi:10.1016/0306-4379(81)90023-5

Pawlak, Z. (1982). Rough sets. *International Journal of Computer Information Science, 11*(5), 341–356. doi:10.1007/BF01001956

Pawlak, Z. (1991). *Rough sets: Theoretical Aspects of Reasoning about Data*. The Netherlands: Kluwer Academic Publishers. doi:10.1007/978-94-011-3534-4

Pawlak, Z., & Skowron, A. (2007a). Rudiments of rough sets. *Information Sciences, 177*(1), 3–27. doi:10.1016/j.ins.2006.06.003

Pawlak, Z., & Skowron, A. (2007b). Rough sets: Some extensions. *Information Sciences, 177*(1), 28–40. doi:10.1016/j.ins.2006.06.006

Pawlak, Z., & Skowron, A. (2007c). Rough sets and Boolean reasoning. *Information Sciences, 177*(1), 41–73. doi:10.1016/j.ins.2006.06.007

Peng, Z. (2010). Image-blur-based Robust Weed Recognition. *Tc, 10*, 8.

Peng, C., Yang, J., Zheng, Y., Xu, Z., & Jiang, X. (2014). Early magnitude estimation for the MW 7.9 Wenchuan earthquake using progressively expanded P-wave time window. *Scientific Reports, 4*, 6770. doi:10.1038/srep06770 PMID:25346344

Perou, C., Sørlie, T., Eisen, M. B., van de Rijn, M., Jeffrey, S. S., & Rees, C. A. et al. (2000). Molecular portraits of human breast tumours. *Nature, 406*(6797), 747–752. doi:10.1038/35021093 PMID:10963602

Phua, C., Lee, V., Smith, K. & Gayler, R. (2005). A Comprehensive Survey of Data Mining-based Fraud Detection Research. *Artificial Intelligence Review*, 14.

Piron, A., Leemans, V., Lebeau, F., & Destain, M. (2009). Improving in-row weed detection in multispectral stereoscopic images. Computers and Electronics in Agriculture, 69(1), 73–79.

Pokkuluri, K. S., & Babu, I. R. (2014). Clonal-Based Cellular Automata in Bioinformatics. *Journal of Advance Research in Applied Artificial Intelligence & Neural Network, 1*(1), 1.

Poli, R. (1996). Genetic programming for feature detection and image segmentation. In T. Fogarty (Ed.), Evolutionary Computing, in Lecture Notes in Computer Science, 1143, 110-125. Springer-Verlag. doi:10.1007/BFb0032777

Polyzotis, N., Skiadopoulos, S., Vassiliadis, P., Simitsis, A., & Frantzell, N. (2008). Meshing Streaming Updates with Persistent Data in an Active Data Warehouse. *IEEE Transactions on Knowledge and Data Engineering, 20*(7), 976–991. doi:10.1109/TKDE.2008.27

Polyzotis, N., Skiadopoulos, S., Vassiliadis, P., Simitsis, A., & Frantzell, N. E. (2007). Supporting Streaming Updates in an Active Data Warehouse.*ICDE 2007: Proceedings of the 23rd International Conference on Data Engineering* (pp. 476–485). Istanbul, Turkey. doi:10.1109/ICDE.2007.367893

Pradeep, T., Srinivasu, P., Avadhani, P. S., & Murthy, Y. V. S. (2011). Comparison of variable learning rate and Levenberg-Marquardt back-propagation training algorithms for detecting attacks in Intrusion Detection Systems. *International Journal on Computer Science and Engineering, 3*(11), 3572–3581.

Pradhan, S., Chakravarthy, S., & Telang, A. (2009). Modeling Relational Data as Graphs for Mining*Citeseer. Proceedings of the 15th International Conference on Management of Data.* Mysore, India.

Preethi, G., & Santhi, B. (2011). Study on techniques of earthquake prediction. *International Journal of Computers and Applications, 29*(4), 55–58. doi:10.5120/3549-4867

Press, W. H. (1988). Numerical recipes in C: the art of scientific computing, (2nd Ed). New York.

Provost, F., & Domingos, P. (2002). Tree induction for probability based ranking. In Machine Learning (Vol 52, No 3). (2003). Netherland: Kluwer Academic Publisher.

Pujana, M. A., Han, J. D., Starita, L. M., Stevens, K. N., Tewari, M., & Ahn, J. S. et al. (2007). Network modeling links breast cancer susceptibility and centrosome dysfunction. *Nature Genetics, 39*(11), 1338–1349. doi:10.1038/ng.2007.2 PMID:17922014

Qiang, S., Ren, D., & Pan, S., (2012). Feature Selection Ensemble. *Turing-100, 10, 289–306.*

Qing, J., Liang, X., Bie, R., & Gao, X. (2010). A New Clustering Algorithm Based on Artificial Immune Network and K-means Method. *Proceedings ofSixth International Conference on Natural Computation* (pp. 2826-2830). doi:10.1109/ICNC.2010.5583507

Quinlan, J. R., & Cameron-Jones, R. M. (1993). *FOIL: A midterm Report. Proceedings of the European Conf. Machine Learning.* Vienna, Austria.

Quinlan, J. R. (1986). Induction of Decision Trees. *Machine Learning, 1*(1), 81–106. doi:10.1007/BF00116251

Quinlan, J. R. (1990). Decision Trees and Decision-Making, IEEE Transaction on Systems. *Man and Cybernetics, 20*(2), 339–336. doi:10.1109/21.52545

Quinlan, J. R. (1993). *C4. 5: programs for machine learning* (Vol. 1). Morgan kaufmann.

Quinlan, R. (1992). *C4.5: Programs for Machine Learning.* San Mateo: Morgan Kaufmann.

Raedt, L. D. D., Luc. (1997). Mining association rules in multiple relations.*Proceedings of the Seventh International Workshop on Inductive Logic Programming*

Raffaele, M. (2006) Nature inspired Optimization Algorithms for Classification and Regression Trees [PhD thesis]. Università degli Studi di Napoli Federico II.

Rahman, A., Verma, B., & Stockwell, D. (2012). *An hierarchical approach towards road image segmentation.* Paper presented at the Neural Networks (IJCNN) The 2012 International Joint Conference on. doi:10.1109/IJCNN.2012.6252403

Ramaswamy, S., Rastogi, R., & Shim, K. (2000). Efficient algorithms for mining outliers from large data sets. *Proc. of the 2000* ACM SIGMOD (pp. 427–438). doi:10.1145/342009.335437

Ramos, V., Muge, F., & Pina, P. (2002). Self-Organized Data and Image Retrieval as a Consequence of Inter-Dynamic Synergistic Relationships in Artificial Ant Colonies. *Soft Computing Systems: Design, Management and Applications*, *87*, 500–509.

Raymond, D. & Conti, G. (2013). A Control Measure Framework to Limit Collateral Damage and Propagation of Cyber Weapons.

Reavley, N. (2005). Securing online banking. *Card Technology Today*, *17*(10), 12–13. doi:10.1016/S0965-2590(05)70389-3

Report, S. (2012). *Payment Systems Review.* Islamabad.

Ripley, B. D. (1996). *Pattern Recognition and Neural Networks.* Cambridge, UK: Cambridge University Press. doi:10.1017/CBO9780511812651

Robles, G. C. M. A., & Hernandez-Becerril, R. A. (2012). Seismic alert system based on artificial neural networks. World Academy of Science, Engineering & Technology(66), 813-818.

Rocha, L. M. (2001). TalkMine: A soft computing approach to adaptive knowledge recommendation. In Loia, V. and Sessa, S. (Eds.), Soft Computing Agents: New Trends for Designing Autonomous Systems, Series on Studies in Fuzziness and Soft Computing (pp. 89-116). New York: Springer. doi:10.1007/978-3-7908-1815-4_4

Rokach, L., & Maimon, O. (2005). *Clustering Methods. Data Mining and Knowledge Discovery Handbook* (pp. 321-352).

Rosenblatt, F. (1962). *Principles of Neurodynamics: Perceptrons and the Theory of Brain Mechanisms.* Spartan.

Roy, A., Matos, M., & Marfurt, K. J. (2010). Automatic seismic facies classification with kohonen self organizing maps – a tutorial. *Geohorizons Journal of Society of Petroleum Geophysicists*, 6-14.

RSA Online Fraud Report. ([REMOVED HYPERLINK FIELD]2012). Available: http://www.emc.com/domains/rsa/index.htm

Ruiz, S., Metois, M., Fuenzalida, A., Ruiz, J., Leyton, F., & Grandin, R. et al. (2014). Intense foreshocks and a slow slip event preceded the 2014 Iquique Mw 8.1 earthquake. *Science*, *345*(6201), 1165–1169. doi:10.1126/science.1256074 PMID:25061132

Rusch, J. J. (2003). *Computer and Internet Fraud: A Risk Identification Overview.* Computer Fraud & Security.

Salisbury, C., Wallace, M., & Montgomery, A. A. (2010). Patients' experience and satisfaction in primary care: Secondary analysis using multilevel modelling. *BMJ (Clinical Research Ed.)*, 341. PMID:20940212

Sarawagi, S. (2001). IDIFF: Informative summarization of differences in multidimensional aggregates. *Data Mining and Knowledge Discovery*, *5*(4), 255–276. doi:10.1023/A:1011494927464

Sarawagi, S., Agrawal, R., & Megiddo, N. (1998). *Discovery-driven exploration of OLAP data cubes* (pp. 168–182). Springer Berlin Heidelberg.

Sarkar, A., & Maulik, U. (2009). Parallel Point symmetry Based Clustering for Gene Microarray Data. *Proceedings of Seventh International Conference on Advances in Pattern Recognition-2009 (ICAPR)* (pp. 351-354). Kolkata. IEEE Computer Society, Conference Publishing Services (CPS).

Sarkar, A., & Maulik, U. (2013). Cancer Gene Expression Data Analysis Using Rough Based Symmetrical Clustering, Handbook of Research on Computational Intelligence for Engineering, Science, and Business (pp. 699-715) USA: IGI Global.

Sarma, G. & Singh, P. K. (2010). Internet Banking: Risk Analysis and Applicability of Biometric Technology for Authentication. *International Journal of Pure and Applied Sciences and Technology, 1,* 14.

Sathe, G., & Sarawagi, S. (2001, September). Intelligent rollups in multidimensional OLAP data. *Proceedings of 27th VLDB conference*(pp. 531-540).

Schlimmer, J. C. (1985). Automobile dataset. Retrieved from http://archive.ics.uci.edu/ml/datasets/Automobile

Šeatović, D., Kutterer, H., & Anken, T. (2010, September). Automatic weed detection and treatment in grasslands. Proceedings of ELMAR, 2010 PROCEEDINGS (pp. 65-68). IEEE.

Seid, D. Y., & Mehrotra, S. (2004). *Efficient relationship pattern mining using multi-relational data cubes* [Technical Report UCI-DB 04-05]. Univ. of Calif., Irvine.

Semra, E., & Ersoy, Ö. Z. (2010). Comparison of Id3, Fuzzy Id3 and Probabilistic Id3 Algorithms in the Evaluation of Learning Achievements. *Journal of Computing,* (12), 20-25.

Serfling, M., Schweiger, R., & Ritter, W. (2008). *Road course estimation in a night vision application using a digital map, a camera sensor and a prototypical imaging radar system.* Paper presented at the 2008 Intelligent Vehicles Symposium. doi:10.1109/IVS.2008.4621312

Shah, M., & Clarke, S. (2009). *E-Banking Management: Issues, Solutions, and Strategies.* Hershey, New York: Information Science Reference. doi:10.4018/978-1-60566-252-7

Sharan, U., & Neville, J. (2008). Temporal-relational classifiers for prediction in evolving domains*IEEE.* Proceedings of Eighth IEEE International Conference.

Shariq, S. (2006). *Internet Banking in Pakistan* [Master Thesis]. Lulea University of Technology.

Sharma, R. (2013). A Framework to Compare Web Mining Types. *International Journal of Advanced Research in Computer Science and Software Engineering, 3,* 144–148.

Shashidhara, H., & Aswath, A. (2014). *A Novel Approach to Circular Edge Detection for Iris Image Segmentation.* Paper presented at the 2014 Fifth International Conference. doi:10.1109/ICSIP.2014.56

Shelokar, P. S., Jayaraman, V. K., & Kulkarni, B. D. (2004). An ant colony approach for clustering. *Analytica Chimica Acta, 509*(2), 187–195. doi:10.1016/j.aca.2003.12.032

Shirzadifar, A. M. (2013). Automatic Weed Detection System and Smart Herbicide Sprayer Robot for corn fields, 468–473.

Shukran, M. A. M., Chung, Y. Y., & Yeh, W. C. (2011, August). Artificial Bee Colony based Data Mining Algorithms for Classification Tasks, *Modern Applied Science. Canadian Center of Science and Education, 5*(4), 217–231.

Siddiqi, M. H., Ahmad, I., & Sulaiman, S. B. (2009, March). Edge link detector based weed classifier. Proceedings of *Digital Image Processing, 2009 International Conference on* (pp. 255-259). IEEE. doi:10.1109/ICDIP.2009.64

Siddiqi, M. H., Ahmad, I., & Sulaiman, S. B. (2009b). Weed Recognition Based on Erosion and Dilation Segmentation Algorithm. Proceedings of *2009 International Conference on Education Technology and Computer* (pp. 224–228). doi:10.1109/ICETC.2009.62

Siddiqui, M. H., Ali, S. I., Zaman, S., Javed, M. A., Raheja, R., Shafiq, U. & Masood, R. (2011). Branchless Banking Regulations. State Bank of Pakistan.

Siebes, A., Vreeken, J., & van Leeuwen, M. (2006). Item sets that compress. Symposium conducted at the meeting of the SDM.

Sison, L. G., & Chong, E. K. P. (1994). Fuzzy Modeling by Induction and Pruning of Decision Trees. *Proceedings of IEEE symposium on intelligent control* (pp. 166-171).

Sizmur, S., & Redding, D. (2009). *Core domains for measuring inpatients' experience of care. Europe.* Picker Institute.

Sjöblom, T., Jones, S., Wood, L. D., Parsons, D. W., Lin, J., & Barber, T. D. et al. (2006). The consensus coding sequences of human breast and colorectal cancers. *Science, 314*(5797), 268–274. doi:10.1126/science.1133427 PMID:16959974

Slowinski, R., & Vanderpooten, D. (2000). A generalized definition of rough approximations based on similarity. *IEEE Transactions on Knowledge and Data Engineering, 12*(2), 331–336. doi:10.1109/69.842271

Smith, A. R. III. (1971). Two-dimensional Formal Languages and Pattern Recognition by Cellular Automata. *Proceedings of IEEE Conference Record of 12th Annual Symposium on Switchinh and Automata Theory.* doi:10.1109/SWAT.1971.29

Soliman, O. S., Bahgat, R., & Adly, A. (2012). Associative Classification using a Bio-Inspired Algorithm, In *Proceedings of the Tenth Australasian Data Mining Conference (AusDM 2012)*, Sydney, Australia, 119-125.

Sørlie, T., Perou, C.M., Tibshirani, R., Aas, T., Geisler, S., Johnsen, H., … Børresen-Dale, A.L. (2001). Gene expression patterns of breast carcinomas distinguish tumor subclasses with clinical implications. *Proc Natl Acad Sci U S A., 98(19),* 10869–74.

Sorlie, T., Tibshirani, R., Parker, J., Hastie, T., Marron, J. S., & Nobel, A. et al. (2003). Repeated observation of breast tumor subtypes in independent gene expression data sets. *Proceedings of the National Academy of Sciences of the United States of America, 100*(14), 8418–8423. PMID:12829800

Sotiriou, C., Neo, S.-Y., McShane, L. M., Korn, E. L., Long, P. M., & Jazaeri, A., … Liu, E. T. (2003). Breast cancer classification and prognosis based on gene expression profiles from a population-based study. *Proceedings of the National Academy of Sciences of the United States of America*, 100(18), 10393–10398. doi:10.1073/pnas.1732912100

Sotiriou, C., & Pusztai, L. (2009). Gene-expression signatures in breast cancer. *The New England Journal of Medicine, 360*(8), 790–800. doi:10.1056/NEJMra0801289 PMID:19228622

Sousa, T., Silva, A., & Neves, A. (2004, May). Particle swarm based Data Mining Algorithms for classification tasks. Journal of Parallel Computing, 30(5-6), 767-783.

Spyropoulou, E., & Bie, T. D. (2011). Interesting Multi-relational Patterns. *Proceedings of the 2011 IEEE 11th International Conference on Data Mining.* doi:10.1109/ICDM.2011.82

Srinivasan, A., King, R. D., Muggleton, S., & Sternberg, M. J. E. (1997). The predictive toxicology evaluation challenge. *Proceedings of the International Joint Conference on Artificial Intelligence.*

Statlog Heart Dataset. Retrieved from http//archive.ics.uci.edu/ml/machine-learning-databases/statlog/heart/

Tan, P. N., Steinbach, M., & Kumar, V. (2006). Cluster analysis: basic concepts and algorithms. Introduction to Data Mining (pp. 487-568). Addison-Wesley.

Tang, R., Fong, S., Yang, X.-S., & Deb, S. (2012, December). Nature-Inspired Clustering Algorithms for Web Intelligence Data. *Proceedings of IEEE/WIC/ACM International Conferences on Web Intelligence and Intelligent Agent Technology (WI-IAT)* (pp. 147-153).

Tang, R., Fong, S., Yang, X.-S., & Deb, S. (2012b, August 22-24). Integrating Nature-inspired Optimization Algorithms to K-means Clustering. Proceedings of *IEEE Seventh International Conference on Digital Information Management (ICDIM 2012)* (pp. 116-123). Macau.

Tang, R., Fong, S., Yang, X.-S., & Deb, S. (2012a, August 22-24). Wolf search algorithm with ephemeral memory. *Proceedings of IEEE Seventh International Conference on Digital Information Management (ICDIM 2012)*165-172. Macau. doi:10.1109/ICDIM.2012.6360147

Tanzmeister, G., Friedl, M., Lawitzky, A., Wollherr, D., & Buss, M. (2013). *Road course estimation in unknown, structured environments.* Paper presented at the Intelligent Vehicles Symposium (IV). doi:10.1109/IVS.2013.6629537

Tellaeche, A., BurgosArtizzu, X. P., Pajares, G., & Ribeiro, A. (2007). A Vision-based Classifier in Precision Agriculture Combining Bayes and Support Vector Machines. Proceedings of *2007 IEEE International Symposium on Intelligent Signal Processing*, 1–6. doi:10.1109/WISP.2007.4447561

Tewari, V. K., Kumar, A. A., Nare, B., Prakash, S., & Tyagi, A. (2014a). Microcontroller based roller contact type herbicide applicator for weed control under row crops. *Computers and Electronics in Agriculture, 104*, 40–45. doi:10.1016/j.compag.2014.03.005

The Total Revenue Cycle Solution for Physicians. (2009). *Medisoft*. Retrieved from www.slcsoftware.com

Timmis, J., & Knight, T. (2001). AINE: An Immmunological Approach to Data Mining. *Proceedings of 2013 IEEE 13th International Conference on Data Mining* (pp. 297-304).

Timmis, J., Neal, M., & Hunt, J. (2000). An artificial immune system for data analysis. *Bio Systems, 55*(1-3), 143–150. doi:10.1016/S0303-2647(99)00092-1 PMID:10745118

Tripathy, B. K. (2006). Rough sets on intuitionistic fuzzy approximation spaces. *Proceedings of the 3rd International IEEE Conference on Intelligent Systems (IS06)* (pp.776-779). London: IEEE Xplore. doi:10.1109/IS.2006.348519

Tripathy, B. K., & Acharjya, D. P. (2010). Knowledge mining using ordering rules and rough sets on fuzzy approximation spaces. *International Journal of Advances in Science and Technology, 1*(3), 41–50.

Tripathy, B. K., & Acharjya, D. P. (2011). Association rule granulation using rough sets on intuitionistic fuzzy approximation spaces and granular computing. *Annals Computer Science Series, 9*(1), 125–144.

Tripathy, B. K., Acharjya, D. P., & Cynthya, V. (2011). A framework for intelligent medical diagnosis using rough set with formal concept analysis. *International Journal of Artificial Intelligence & Applications, 2*(2), 45–66. doi:10.5121/ijaia.2011.2204

Tsang, W. W., & Lau, H. Y. (2013). An Artificial Immune System-based Many-Objective Optimization Algorithm with Network Activation Scheme. *Advances in Artificial Life, ECAL, 12*, 872–873.

Umano, M., Okamoto, H., Hatono, I., Tamura, H., Kawachi, F., Umedzu, S., & Kinoshita, J. (1994). Fuzzy Decision Trees by Fuzzy ID3 Algorithm and Its Application to Diagnosis Systems. In *Proceedings of the third IEEE Conference on Fuzzy Systems* (Vol. 3, pp. 2113-2118).Orlando.

Urhan, T., & Franklin, M. J. (2000). XJoin: A reactively-scheduled pipelined join operator. *A Quarterly Bulletin of the Computer Society of the IEEE Technical Committee on Data Engineering, 23*, 2000.

Usman, M., & Pears, R. (2010). Integration of Data Mining and Data Warehousing: a practical methodology. *International Journal of advancements in Computing Technology, 2(3)*, 31-46.

Usman, M., & Pears, R. (2010, November).A methodology for integrating and exploiting data mining techniques in the design of data warehouses. Proceedings of *6th International Conference on* (pp. 361-367). IEEE.

Usman, M., Asghar, S., & Fong, S. (2010). Integrated Performance and Visualization Enhancement of OLAP Using Growing Self Organizing Neural Networks. *Journal of Advances in Information Technology, 1*(1), 26–37. doi:10.4304/jait.1.1.26-37

Usman, M., Pears, R., & Fong, A. C. M. (2013). A data mining approach to knowledge discovery from multidimensional cube structures. *Knowledge-Based Systems, 40*, 36–49. doi:10.1016/j.knosys.2012.11.008

Vafaie, H., & DeJong, K. (1998). Feature space transformation using genetic algorithms. *IEEE Intelligent Systems & their Applications, 13*(2), 57–65. doi:10.1109/5254.671093

van Meer, G.J.L., & van Raaij, F. (2003). A suitable research methodology for analyzing online banking behaviour. *Journal of Internet banking and commerce, 32*.

Velat, S. J., Lee, J., Johnson, N., & Crane III, C.D. (2007). Vision Based Vehicle Localization for Autonomous Navigation. *Computational Intelligence in Robotics and Automation.* Jacksonville, Fl

Vogt, P., Nentwich, F., Jovanovic, N., Kirda, E., Kruege, C. & Vigna, G. (2013). Cross-Site Scripting Prevention with Dynamic Data Tainting and Static Analysis.

Waghule, D. R., & Ochawar, R. S. (2014). *Overview on Edge Detection Methods.* Paper presented at the Electronic Systems, Signal Processing and Computing Technologies (ICESC), 2014 International Conference. doi:10.1109/ICESC.2014.31

Wan, Y., Jia, S., & Wang, D. (2013). *Edge Detection Algorithm Based on Grey System Theory Combined with Directed Graph.* Paper presented at the Image and Graphics (ICIG), 2013 Seventh International Conference. doi:10.1109/ICIG.2013.42

Wang, B., Frémont, V., & Rodríguez, S. A. (2014). *Color-based road detection and its evaluation on the KITTI road benchmark.* Paper presented at the Intelligent Vehicles Symposium Proceedings, 2014 IEEE. doi:10.1109/IVS.2014.6856619

Wang, K., Xu, Y., Yu, P. S., & She, R. (2005). *Building decision trees on records linked through key references.* Proceedings of the SIAM International Conference on Data Mining. doi:10.1137/1.9781611972757.64

Wang, S., & Xu, X. (2010). A novel immune clonal selection optimization algorithm. *Proceedings of International Conference on Computer Application and System Modeling* (ICCASM'10), 391-395.

Wang, W., Feng, J., Lu, H., & Yu, J. X. (2002). Condensed cube: An effective approach to reducing data cube size. *Proceedings of 18th International Conference on* (pp. 155-165). IEEE.

Wang, Y., Ewert, D., Schilberg, D., & Jeschke, S. (2013). *Edge extraction by merging 3D point cloud and 2D image data.* Paper presented at the Emerging Technologies for a Smarter World (CEWIT), 2013 10th International Conference and Expo. doi:10.1007/978-3-319-08816-7_61

Wang, X. Z., Yeung, D. S., & Tsang, E. C. C. (2001). A Comparative Study on Heuristic Algorithms for Generating Fuzzy Decision Trees. *IEEE Transactions on Systems, Man, and Cybernetics. Part B, Cybernetics, 31*(2), 215–226. doi:10.1109/3477.915344 PMID:18244783

Watkins, A., Timmis, J., & Boggess, L. (2004). Artificial Immune Recognition System (AIRS): An Immune-Inspired Supervised Learning Algorithm. *Genetic Programming and Evolvable Machines, 5*(3), 291–317. doi:10.1023/B:GENP.0000030197.83685.94

Weed Science Society of Pakistan. (n. d.). Retrieved from http://en.wikipedia.org/wiki/file:Pakistan_agriculture.png

Weiss, U., Biber, P., Laible, S., Bohlmann, K., & Zell, A. (2010, December). Plant species classification using a 3d lidar sensor and machine learning. Proceedings of *Machine Learning and Applications (ICMLA), 2010 Ninth International Conference on* (pp. 339-345). IEEE.

Whitbrook, A. M., Aickelin, U., & Garibaldi, J. M. (2008). An Idiotypic Immune Network as a Short-Term Learning Architecture for Mobile Robots. *Proceedings of 7th International Conference* (pp. 266–278).

Whitbrook, A. M., Aickelin, U., & Garibaldi, J. M. (2007). Idiotypic Immune Networks in Mobile Robot Control. *IEEE Transactions on Systems, Man, and Cybernetics. Part B, Cybernetics, 37*(6), 1581–1598. doi:10.1109/TSMCB.2007.907334 PMID:18179075

Whitbrook, A. M., Aickelin, U., & Garibaldi, J. M. (2009). The Transfer of Evolved Artificial Immune System Behaviours Between Small and Large Scale Robotic Platforms.*Proceedings of the 9th international conference on artificial evolution (EA'09)*.

Wicklund, E. (2008). Alpha II brings "claims scrubbing" to the medical billing market Healthcare IT News.

William, E. S., Jerrold, H. M., & Luis, G. V. (1999). Choosing Data-Mining Methods for Multiple Classification: Representational and Performance Measurement Implications for Decision Support. *Journal of Management Information Systems, 16*(I), 3.

Wilschut, A. N., & Apers, P. M. G. (1990). Pipelining in query execution.*Proceedings of the International Conference on Databases, Parallel Architectures and Their Applications (PARBASE 1990). Miami Beach, FL, USA* (pp. 562–562). Miami, FL, USA: IEEE Computer Society Press. doi:10.1109/PARBSE.1990.77227

Witten, I. H., Frank, E., & Hall, M. A. (2011). *Data mining practical machine learning tools and techniques*. Burlington: Morgan Kaufmann publisher.

Witten, I. H., & Hall, M. A. (2011). *Data mining: practical machine learning tools and techniques*. Amsterdam, Boston: Morgan Kaufmann.

Woldemariam, K. M., & Yen, G. G. (2010). Vaccine-Enhanced Artificial Immune System for Multimodal Function Optimization. *IEEE Transactions on Systems, Man, and Cybernetics, 40*(1), 218–228. doi:10.1109/TSMCB.2009.2025504 PMID:19635706

Wolfram, S. (1983). Statistical mechanics of cellular automata. *Reviews of Modern Physics, 55*(3), 601–644. doi:10.1103/RevModPhys.55.601

Wolfram, S. (1986). Cryptography with cellular automata. *Lecture Notes in Computer Science, 218*, 429–432. doi:10.1007/3-540-39799-X_32

Wu, E., Diao, Y., & Rizvi, S. (2006). *High-performance complex event processing over streams. Proceedings of the 2006 ACM SIGMOD International Conference on Management of Data, SIGMOD '06* (pp. 407–418). Chicago, IL, USA: ACM. doi:http://doi.acm.org/10.1145/1142473.1142520 doi:10.1145/1142473.1142520

Xanthium strumarium, (1998), (1996), 6–38.

Xiao, D., & Hu, X. (2014). *Road detection based on superpixels and anisotropic heat diffusion*. Paper presented at the Digital Information and Communication Technology and it's Applications (DICTAP), 2014 Fourth International Conference. doi:10.1109/DICTAP.2014.6821724

Xiao, X., & Chou, K.-C. (2011). Using Pseudo Amino Acid Composition to Predict Protein Attributes Via Cellular Automata and Other Approaches. *Current Bioinformatics*, 6(2), 251–260. doi:10.2174/1574893611106020251

Xiao, X., Dow, E. R., Eberhart, R. C., Miled, Z. B., & Oppelt, R. J. (2003). Gene Clustering Using Self-Organizing Maps and Particle Swarm Optimization. *Proceedings of the 17th International Symposium on Parallel and Distributed Processing (PDPS '03).*Washington DC. doi:10.1109/IPDPS.2003.1213290

Xuhua, S., & Feng, Q. (2009). An optimization Algorithm Based on Multi-population Artificial Immune Network. *Proceedings ofFifth International Conference on Natural Computation*, 379-383. doi:10.1109/ICNC.2009.574

Yan, X., & Han, J. (2002). gspan: Graph-based substructure pattern mining. *Proceedings. Of 2002 IEEE International Conference.*

Yang, X.-S. (2010). A New Metaheuristic Bat-Inspired Algorithm. In J. R. Gonzalez, et al (Eds.), Nature Inspired Co-operative Strategies for Optimization, 65-74. doi:10.1007/978-3-642-12538-6_6

Yao, Y. Y. (2000). Information tables with neighborhood semantics. In B. V. Dasarathy (Ed.), Data Mining and Knowledge Discovery: Theory, Tools, and Technology (Vol. 2, pp. 108-116). Bellingham, Washington: Society for Optical Engineering.

Yao, Y. Y., & Sai, Ying. (2001). Mining ordering rules using rough set theory. *Bulletin of International Rough Set Society*, 5, 99–106.

Yap, F. W., Koh, S. P., & Tiong, S. K. (2011). Mathematical Function Optimization using AIS Antibody Remainder method. *International Journal of Machine Learning and Computing*, 1(1), 13-19.

Yin, X. H. Jiawei; Yang, Jiong; Yu, Philip S, (2004). CrossMine: Efficient Classification Across Multiple Database Relations. *Proceedings of the International Conference on Data Engineering.*

Younsi, R., & Wang, W. (2004). A New Artificial Immune System Algorithm for Clustering. *Lecture Notes in Computer Science*, 3177, 58–64. doi:10.1007/978-3-540-28651-6_9

Yousafzai, S. Y., Pallister, J. G., & Foxall, G. R. (2005). Strategies for Building and Communicating Trust in Electronic Banking: A Field Experiment. *Psychology and Marketing*, 22(2), 181–201. doi:10.1002/mar.20054

Yudong, Z., & Lenan, W. (2011). *Bankruptcy Prediction by Genetic Ant Colony Algorithm* (pp. 459–463). Advanced Materials Research.

Zadeh, L. A. (1965). Fuzzy sets. *Information and Control*, 8(3), 338–353. doi:10.1016/S0019-9958(65)90241-X

Zarnani, A., Rahgozar, M., & Lucas, C. (2006). Nature-Inspired Approaches to Mining Trend Patterns in Spatial Databases, *Intelligent Data Engineering and Automated Learning – IDEAL 2006. Lecture Notes in Computer Science*, 4224, 1407–1414. doi:10.1007/11875581_167

Zhang, H., & Su, J. (2004). Naive Bayesian classifiers for ranking. *Proceedings of ECML2004 15th European Conference on Machine Learning.* Pisa, Italy. doi:10.1007/978-3-540-30115-8_46

Zhang, L., Zhou, W.-H., & Liu, J.-L. (2007). *A robust road segmentation method.* Paper presented at the Wavelet Analysis and Pattern Recognition, 2007. ICWAPR'07. International Conference. doi:10.1109/ICWAPR.2007.4420799

Zhang, T., Ramakrishnan, R., & Livny, M. (1996). BIRCH: An Efficient Data Clustering Method for Very Large Databases. *Proc. of the Conference of Management of Data* (ACM SIGMOD '96) (pp. 103-114).

Zhang, J., Xiang, Y., Ding, L., Keen-Circle, K., Borlawsky, T. B., & Ozer, H. G. et al. (2010). Using gene co-expression network analysis to predict biomarkers for chronic lymphocytic leukemia. *BMC Bioinformatics*, *11*(Suppl 9), S5. doi:10.1186/1471-2105-11-S9-S5 PMID:21044363

Zhang, J., Xiang, Y., Jin, R., & Huang, K. (2009) Using Frequent Co-expression Network to Identify Gene Clusters for Breast Cancer Prognosis.*International Joint Conference on Bioinformatics, Systems Biology and Intelligent Computing (IJCBS).Shanghai:IEEE Computer Society.* doi:10.1109/IJCBS.2009.29

Zhang, Q. (2009). Study on Fraud Risk Prevention of Online Banks.*Proceedings of International Conference on Networks security, Wireless Communications and Trusted Computing.* doi:10.1109/NSWCTC.2009.312

Zhang, W., Yen, G. G., & Zhongshi, H. (2014). Constrained Optimization Via Artificial Immune System. *IEEE Transactions on Cybernetics*, *44*(2), 185–198. doi:10.1109/TCYB.2013.2250956 PMID:23757542

Zhu, W., & Wang, F. Y. (2007). On three types of covering rough sets. *IEEE Transactions on Knowledge and Data Engineering*, *19*(8), 1131–1144. doi:10.1109/TKDE.2007.1044

About the Contributors

Muhammad Usman has completed his PhD in Computer & Information Sciences from Auckland University of Technology, New Zealand. He is currently an Assistant Professor of Computer Science in the department of Computing at Shaheed Zulfikar Ali Bhutto Institute of Science and Technology, Islamabad, Pakistan. His research interests include Data Mining, Data Warehousing, OLAP, Business Intelligence, and Knowledge discovery. He is currently researching in the novel methods and techniques for the seamless integration of Data Mining and Data Warehousing technologies. He has published in international journals and conference proceedings, and he has served as reviewer for a number of premier journals and conferences

***

Umair Abdullah, with 13 plus years of teaching experience and 7 years of industry experience, is currently working as Assistant Professor at Foundation University Rawalpindi Campus. This Book Chapter is the gist of his PhD research work, which was funded by Higher Education Commission of Pakistan and was carried out at a healthcare IT company. His research interests include Data Mining, Rule Based Expert Systems, and Machine Learning.

Debi Prasanna Acharjya received his PhD in computer science from Berhampur University, India. He has been awarded with Gold Medal in M. Sc. from NIT, Rourkela. Currently he is working as a Professor in the School of Computing Science and Engineering, VIT University, Vellore, India. He has authored many national and international journal papers, and has five books to his credit. In addition to this, he has also edited three books. Also, he has published many chapters in different books published by International publishers. He is reviewer of many international journals such as Fuzzy Sets and Systems, Knowledge Based Systems, and Applied Journal of Soft Computing. Dr. Acharjya is actively associated with many professional bodies like CSI, ISTE, IMS, AMTI, ISIAM, OITS, IACSIT, CSTA, IEEE and IAENG. He was founder secretary of OITS Rourkela chapter. His current research interests include rough sets, formal concept analysis, knowledge representation, data mining, granular computing, and business intelligence.

Waseem Ahmad holds a PhD degree in the field of Artificial Immune System, taking inspiration from metaphors and processes of the natural immune system to create algorithms that solve complex computational problems. Dr. Ahmad has completed his PhD from AUT University in 2012. He also holds a M.Sc. in Intelligent System Engineering from Birmingham University, UK. Currently he is Program Coordinator in Computing Department at International College of Auckland, New Zealand.

Aftab Ahmed is one of the most senior IT academicians in Pakistan. He has over 30 years of teaching experience in well reputed national and international universities. Currently, he is chairman of National Computing Education Accreditation Council (NCEAC) – the apex body of accrediting computing programs in Pakistani universities. He is also serving as Director of Foundation University Rawalpindi Campus, which has an emerging Software Engineering & IT department. His research interests include Software Architecture, Software Design Patterns, and Quality Metrics etc. He is senior member of ACM and IEEE Computer Society.

Muhammad Rizwan Aqeel is a research student at UIIT Rawalpindi Pakistan, under supervision of Dr. Sohail Asgher. His area of interests are robotics, machine vision, and Autonomous Ground vehicles.

Sohail Asghar is working as Chief Technologist at COMSATS Institute of Information Technology Islamabad. In 2011 he joined as a Director of the University Institute of Information Technology, PMAS-Arid Agriculture University, Rawalpindi. Previously, Dr. Sohail was an Associate Professor of Computer Science, Faculty of Computing, MA Jinnah University, Islamabad, Pakistan. He is also one of the founding members of the Center of Research in Data Engineering (CORDE) Research Group in the Faculty. Prior to this position, Sohail also worked as an Assistant Professor of Computer Sciences and Head of R&D section in the Department of Computer Sciences at Shaheed Zulfikar Ali Bhutto Institute of Science and Technology, Islamabad, Pakistan. He has as well worked as Research Associate and Assistant Lecturer in Clayton School of Information Technology, Faculty of Information Technology at Monash University, Melbourne, Australia. In 1994, he graduated with honors in Computer Science from the University of Wales, United Kingdom. From 1994 to 2002, he worked as a Senior Software Engineer in a software company in Islamabad. He then received his PhD from Faculty of Information Technology at Monash University, Melbourne Australia in 2006. Dr. Sohail has taught and researched in Data Mining (including structural Learning, Classification, and Privacy Preservation in Data Ming, Text and Web Mining), Decision Support Systems and Information Technology areas, and he has published extensively (More than 100 publications) in international journals as well as conference proceedings. He has supervised more than thirty students on their Ph.D. dissertations and M.S. theses. He has supervised numerous undergraduate development projects including projects of two students who received ICT R&D Outstanding Undergraduate Award. He has also consulted widely on information Technology matters, especially in the framework of Data Mining. In 2004 he acquired the Australian Post Graduate Award for Industry. Dr. Sohail is a member of the Australian Computer Society (ACS), IEEE, and he also serves as Higher Education Commission Approved Supervisor. Dr. Sohail is in the Editorial Team of well reputed Scientific Journals. He has also served as Program Committee member of numerous International Conferences and regularly speaks at international conferences.

Simon Fong graduated from La Trobe University, Australia, with 1st Class Honours BEng. Computer Systems degree and a PhD. Computer Science degree in 1993 and 1998 respectively. Simon is now working as an Associate Professor at the Computer and Information Science Department of the University of Macau. He is also one of the founding members of the Data Analytics and Collaborative Computing Research Group in the Faculty of Science and Technology. Before joining the University of Macau, he worked as an Assistant Professor in the School of Computer Engineering, Nanyang Technological University, Singapore. Prior to his academic career, Simon took up various managerial and technical posts, such as systems engineer, IT consultant and e-commerce director in Melbourne, Hong

Kong and Singapore. Some companies that he worked before include Hong Kong Telecom, Singapore Network Services, AES Pro-Data and United Oversea Bank, Singapore. Dr. Fong has published over 230 international conference and peer-reviewed journal papers, mostly in the areas of Data-mining and Metaheuristics.

Ali Gazala holds a PhD degree in the field of data analysis and machine learning. He has completed his PhD from Auckland University of Technology AUT in 2015. Dr. Ali also holds a M.Sc. in data mining from Malaysia University of Science and Technology MUST, Malaysia. He has number of publications in the field of data mining and machine learning.

Saira Gillani received her MS degree in Computer Science from M.A. Jinnah University, Islamabad, Pakistan. She is PhD student at Corvinus University of Budapest, Hungary. She is a member of the Corvinno research group. Her current research activities include Text Mining, Ontology, and Ontology Enrichment.

Xueyuan Gong has a B. Sc. Degree in Computer Technology and Application from Macau University of Science and Technology, Macau, and a M. Sc. Degree in Computer Engineering from University of Macau, Macau. Now, he is a PHD student in University of Macau, Macau. His research interests include pattern matching in time series, pattern discovery in time series, data streams, swarm intelligence, clustering, etc. Till now, he has several EI-indexed papers published.

Dong Han received the B.S. degree in electronic information science and technology from Beijing Information Science & Technology University (BISTU), China. He is currently pursuing his master degree in E-commerce technology in University of Macau, Macau S.A.R. His current research focuses on the massive data analysis and outlier selection as well as Bio-inspired optimization. In his free time, he enjoys writing micro-blog.

Tasawar Hussain received his MS(CS) degree from the Department of Computer Sciences, Mohammad Ali Jinnah University, Islamabad, Pakistan in 2010. Previously, he obtained the M.Sc. degree in Mathematics from Peshawar University, Peshawar, Pakistan in 1995. Currently, Mr. Hussain is a PhD (CS) scholar at Muhammad Ali Jinnah University, Islamabad, Pakistan. His research activities are in the areas of data mining, web mining, semantic web mining, and constraint base mining.

Mohsin Iqbal is currently doing Master in Computer Science from the University Institute of Information Technology, PMAS Arid Agriculture University, Pakistan. His research interests include data mining and machine learning. He is researching in exploring efficient feature selection methods and classifiers to enhance the prediction accuracy classification algorithms.

Noreen Jamil received her PhD degree in Computer Science from The University of Auckland, New Zealand. The title of her PhD thesis was "Constraint Solving Strategies for Constraint Based User Interface Layout". In her PhD research she has designed a number of novel algorithms to solve linear constraints for solving constraint based graphical user interface layouts efficiently. She has published more than 14 papers in well-reputed conferences and journals. She has received best paper award of the IEEE-ICDIM 2013 for "Speeding up SOR Solvers for Constraint-based GUIs with Warm Start Strategies". She has also received best student paper award of the University of Auckland in 2013. She has presented her work at national and international conferences. Noreen has more than 5 years research and teaching experience at university level. In addition, she has expertise in a variety of programming tools like Java and Matlab. Before her PhD she has received her Master degree in Mathematics with distinction from The University of Balochistan, Pakistan.

JinYan Li is a PhD student in the Department of Computer and Information Science, Faculty of Science and Technology, University of Macau. His research interests are data mining, sentiment analysis, and swarm intelligence.

Kalyan Mahata has completed his M. E. in Computer Science and Engineering with specialization in Embedded Systems. He is presently an Assistant Professor in IT Department, Government College of Engineering and Leather Technology, Kolkata since 2006. He has published 8 publications including 7 conference papers and 1 book chapter. His research interests include cellular automata, networking, and bioinformatics.

Muhammad Asif Naeem is presently a Senior Lecturer in School of Computer and Mathematical Sciences, Auckland University of Technology, Auckland, New Zealand. He received his PhD degree in Computer Science from The University of Auckland, New Zealand. He has been awarded a best PhD thesis award from The University of Auckland. Before that Asif has done his Master's degree in Computer Science with distinction. He has about twelve years research, industrial and teaching experience. He has published over 30 research papers in high repute journals, conferences, and workshops including IEEE, ACM, and VLDB. He has been reviewing for well-known journals and conferences in his area and has also been serving as a workshop chair in IEEE- ICDIM 2015. He has been invited to be a keynote speaker in IEEE-ICDIM 2013. He is organising an IEEE workshop IWDM since 2013. He also involves in doing his research with one of the biggest New Zealand local companies, Mitre 10. His research interests are Data Stream Processing, Real-time Data Warehousing, Big Data Management, Knowledge Engineering, and Continuous Queries.

Ajit Narayanan is Professor in the School of Computer and Mathematical Sciences, Auckland University of Technology, New Zealand. He has over 100 journal and international conference publications in the areas of computational statistics, bioinformatics, machine learning, artificial intelligence and nature-inspired computing. He is statistical consultant on a number of healthcare related projects, with a special interest in analysing patient satisfaction and colleague feedback data as well as identifying potential biomarkers in gene expression data. He has a BSc (Hons) from the University of Aston and a PhD from the University of Exeter.

Tayyeba Naseer in 2011 joined PMAS-Arid Agriculture University, Rawalpindi as a student of Master of Science in Computer Science MSCS program. She received her MSCS degree University Institute of Information Technology PMAS-Arid Agriculture University, Rawalpindi 2015. She completed her MS Thesis research in the supervision of Dr. Sohail on the topic of *"An Empirical Comparison of pruning method for C4.5 and Fuzzy C4.5"*. Her area of interest in research are Data mining, Machine Learning, Document Image Processing, Simulation & Modeling, Decision Making, Feature Extraction, Robotic, Evolutionary Approaches and Pattern Recognition. She received her Bachelor of Science in Computer

Science BSCS degree in 2009 from University of Central Punjab Lahore Pakistan. She works with the spirit of diligence and dedication and is always ready to take initiative to do the best. Ms. Naseer is sweet natured and intelligent person who has the knack to handle a difficult situation with a smile.

Saeid Pashazadeh is Assistant Professor of Software Engineering at Faculty of Electrical and Computer Engineering in University of Tabriz in Iran. He received his B.Sc. in Computer Engineering from Sharif Technical University of Iran in 1995. He obtained M.Sc. and Ph.D. in Computer Engineering from Iran University of Science and Technology in 1998 and 2010 respectively. He was Lecturer in Faculty of Electrical Engineering in Sahand University of Technology in Iran from 1999 until 2004. His main interests are modeling and formal verification of distributed systems, computer security and wireless sensor/actor networks. He is member of IEEE and senior member of IACSIT and member of editorial board of journal of electrical engineering at University of Tabriz in Iran.

Saif Ur Rehman received the B.Sc and MCS degrees from Gomal University, DIKhan, Pakistan, in 2003 and 2005, respectively and the MS degree from SZABIST, Islamabad campus, Islamabad, Pakistan. He is a PhD (CS) scholar in Abasyn University, Islamabad campus, Islamabad, Pakistan.He has been with the World Bank, USAID, DFID projects in ERRA and NDMA, PM Secretariat Islamabad, Pakistan from 2007 to 2011. His main areas of research interest are Data Mining, Graph Mining, Social Network Analysis. He has good excellent Computer Programming Skills in various programming languages including Java, .Net languages, Oracle etc. At present he is working as Assistant Professor in University Institute of Information Technology, PMAS Arid University, Rawalpindi, Pakistan.

Anasua Sarkar completed her PhD work on Bioinformatics in Jadavpur University, Kolkata, India in 2014. She was also awarded EMMA-EPU fellowship in 2011 to pursue her research work at LaBRI, University Bordeaux, France. She is presently an Assistant Professor in IT Department, Government College of Engineering and Leather Technology, Kolkata since 2007. She has published 10 original research papers in peer-reviewed journals. She also co-authored 8 book chapters and 15 conference papers. She is also a reviewer in the journals Parallel and Distributed Computing (JPDC), Elsevier, and IEEE SMCC-C. She is also a Student member, ISCB, 2010-2011, SMIEEE since 2014, and a member of CSTA, ACM Chapter, ACM IGUCCS and IAENG. She has worked with INRIA MAGNOME group for 18 months in France for the expansion of Genolevures database for inclusion of PISO and ARAD species. Her research interests include Proteomics, Phylogenetics, Computational Biology, Pattern Recognition, Data Mining, Bioinformatics, Embedded, and Parallel Systems.

Negar Sadat Soleimani Zakeri received her B.Sc. degree in Computer Software Engineering, in 2009. She has been a M.Sc. student in Computer Engineering - Artificial Intelligence at University of Tabriz, Tabriz, Iran, since 2011. Now, she is a PhD student in Computer Engineering - Artificial Intelligence at University of Tabriz, Tabriz, Iran. Her research interests include artificial intelligence, artificial neural network, image processing, and seismic feature extraction.

Athanasios V. Vasilakos (M'00–SM'11) is currently a Professor with the Kuwait University. He served or is serving as an Editor or/and Guest Editor for many technical journals, such as the IEEE transactions on network and service management; IEEE transactions on cloud computing, IEEE transactions on information forensics and security, IEEE transactions on nano-bio-science, IEEE transactions on cybernetics; IEEE transactions on information technology in biomedicine; ACM transactions on autonomous and adaptive systems; and the IEEE journal on selected areas in communications. He is also general chair of the European Alliances for Innovation.

Kahif Zafar is working as an Associate Professor in the Computer Science department at National University of Computer and Emerging Sciences, Lahore. Prior to this he was with the Islamabad campus of the same university. Before joining FAST-NU, he worked at GIK Institute of Engineering Sciences and Technology Topi, as Research Associate/Lecturer in the Faculty of Computer Science and Engineering. Zafar has a total of 15 plus years of experience both in industry and academia.

Noureen Zafar has been awarded with "Vice Chancellor Talent Scholarship" in three consecutive semesters. She has also been awarded with a Laptop on the basis of merit by Chief Minister of Punjab. Ms. Zafar has a thorough knowledge of Artificial Intelligence, Web Designing, Dot Net, and Databases.

Index

IRMA

INTERNATIONAL

Information Resources Management Association

Become an IRMA Member

Members of the **Information Resources Management Association (IRMA)** understand the importance of community within their field of study. The Information Resources Management Association is an ideal venue through which professionals, students, and academicians can convene and share the latest industry innovations and scholarly research that is changing the field of information science and technology. Become a member today and enjoy the benefits of membership as well as the opportunity to collaborate and network with fellow experts in the field.

IRMA Membership Benefits:

- **One FREE Journal Subscription**

- **30% Off Additional Journal Subscriptions**

- **20% Off Book Purchases**

- Updates on the latest events and research on Information Resources Management through the IRMA-L listserv.

- Updates on new open access and downloadable content added to Research IRM.

- A copy of the Information Technology Management Newsletter twice a year.

- A certificate of membership.

IRMA Membership $195

Scan code to visit irma-international.org and begin by selecting your free journal subscription.

Membership is good for one full year.